The Rules of the Game

*To those who sailed in the
10th Mine-Countermeasures Squadron
between 1979 and 1994*

The Rules of the Game

Jutland and British
Naval Command

ANDREW GORDON

Naval Institute Press
Annapolis, Maryland

This edition has been brought to publication with the generous assistance of
VADM John M. Richardson, USN, Commander, Submarine Force, and
VADM Peter H. Daly, USN (Ret.), CEO, U.S. Naval Institute, in the interest of
helping put this book in the hands of current and future naval professionals.

Naval Institute Press
291 Wood Road
Annapolis, MD 21402

By the same author
British Seapower and Procurement Between the Wars

First published in 1996 by John Murray (Publishers) Ltd,
50 Albemarle Street, London W1X 4BD
Reprinted 1999
First Naval Institute Press paperback edition published 2000
Reissued in paperback 2012
ISBN: 978-1-59114-336-9

The moral right of the author has been asserted

Library of Congress Catalog Card Number 00a-104385

∞ This paper meets the requirements of ANSI/NISO z39.48-1992
(Permanence of Paper).
Printed in the United States of America.

20 19 18 17 16 15 14 13 12   9 8 7 6 5 4 3 2 1
First printing

Contents

Illustrations

The author and publisher wish to acknowledge the following for permission to reproduce photographs: Plates 1, 19, 20, 39 and 40, Hulton Getty Collection; 2, 3, 4 and 13, *Illustrated London News*; 5, 6, 7, 8, 9, 15, 16, 17 and 18, from Evan-Thomas's album, courtesy of Cdr Martin Bourdillon; 10, 11, 12, 26 and 37, National Maritime Museum; 14, from Reginald Bacon's *A Naval Scrap Book*, Vol.1; 21, 22, 23, 24, 25, 28, 29, 30, 31, 32, 33, 34, 35, 36 and 38, Imperial War Museum.

Acknowledgements

I owe a very big debt of thanks to brothers Mervyn and Martin Bourdillon for allowing me full access to the private papers and photograph albums of Sir Hugh Evan-Thomas, and for other kindnesses.

I am indebted to Her Majesty the Queen for allowing me access to papers in the Royal Archives; to Sir Michael Culme-Seymour and Commander Michael Saunders-Watson for access to their family archive at Rockingham Castle, and to Roberta Gill, the part-time archivist there; to the Hon. Anthony Colville; to the Lord Tryon; to the trustees and the Department of Documents of the Imperial War Museum (particularly to Roderick Suddaby) and to the Sound Records; to the trustees and the Manuscripts Department of the National Maritime Museum; to the Keeper of Manuscripts of the British Library, and the staff at the Reading Room; to the British Newspaper Library; to the trustees and the Manuscripts Division of the National Library of Scotland; to the Keeper of Public Records and the staff of the Public Record Office; to the Scottish Records Office; to the Bundesarchiv in Freiburg, Germany; to the Master and Fellows of Churchill College, Cambridge, and to the Churchill Archives Centre; to the Royal Naval Museum; to the library of the RUSI; to the Royal Geographical Society; to the Board of General Purposes, and Librarian, of the United Grand Lodge of England; and to Dunfermline and Fulham public libraries.

For the photographs other than those owned by Evan-Thomas's family, I am grateful to the Photographic Department of the Imperial War Museum (and especially to Paul Kemp), to the Picture Library of the National Maritime Museum, to the Hulton Getty Collection, and to the Illustrated London News Group.

I have been fortunate to have met a number of Jutland survivors, and thank them for the patience with which they answered my questions. I have also made use of papers (mostly letters and diaries) and interviews deposited in museums and public archives by a further seventy Jutland veterans (or their families) and I must thank all those copyright-holders who have granted me permission to quote extracts. I apologize to the few copyright-holders whom I have not been able to trace or contact. In connection with primary accounts of Jutland I owe a debt also to Robert Church, who did much spadework for a book on Jutland some years ago, and who donated the fruits of his research to the Imperial War Museum.

I am indebted to many friends and colleagues who rummaged through their actual and mental attics for half-remembered information and sources, and/or read draft chapters. Among them are: D. K. Brown, Mary Cross, Evan Davies, Mike Duffy, John Ferris, Jock Gardner, William Glover, James Goldrick, Eric Grove, Richard Hough, Stephen Howarth, Barrie Kent, Andrew Lambert, Nicholas Lambert, Rupert Nichol, Antony Preston, Nicholas Rodger, Jon Sumida, Kay Tapply and Jim Tritten. I hope they (and anyone I may have omitted inadvertently) will remain friends after they have seen the end product.

Serving and retired officers from four navies kindly gave their time to discuss issues arising in the book. Other people helped in practical ways. A very big gold star goes to Gaby Timko for visiting on my behalf the Bundesarchiv, and I am grateful to Isabel Schaechterle for help in translating the German naval war-diaries thus obtained. By involving me in the 75th Anniversary Jutland Diving Expedition, in 1991, Alex Laird and Gerald Moor got me (literally) closer to the event and the veterans than I could otherwise have hoped.

My British publishers, John Murray, have been everything an author could wish a publisher to be. Particular thanks go to Grant McIntyre, Gail Pirkis and Howard Davies. I must thank Andrew Lownie for introducing me to them in the first place. Without them, this book would never have seen the light of day in its present form.

Foreword

by Admiral Sir John Woodward

This book has prompted me to think about several fairly fundamental things concerning preparedness for war. Andrew Gordon's ostensible purpose is with command-and-control aspects of the Battle of Jutland, and these he analyses in considerable detail. I can claim no expertise on the First World War, but I can say that his account seems to me convincing from the professional viewpoint, and feels right in service-cultural terms.

However, the book's main import is the way Gordon demonstrates that, to understand the command-and-control dynamics of Jutland, we have to dig quite a long way back into the Navy's peacetime past. The keynote of battle-doctrine in Victorian times stemmed from the imperative to try to *regulate* everything – even the nature of combat, which, of course, cannot be done. Gordon persuasively argues that a defining moment for the Royal Navy's battle-worthiness was the curtailment (after a disastrous collision) in 1893 of the one really promising attempt to return the Fleet's tactical doctrine to Nelsonic fundamentals. The result was that the Navy had to rediscover, from the bitter experiences of 1914–16, much about warfare which it should never have forgotten in the first place.

The "issues of eternal relevance to the fighting services" (mentioned on the flyleaf) concern not just the realism of the peacetime training of future senior officers, but also the process of selecting those officers – of achieving the necessary balance between (as Gordon puts it) 'regulators' and 'rat-catchers' which any fighting service needs. Each group tends to promote its own. Continuous war will produce a predominance of rat-catchers, as classically demonstrated by the Navy of the French Revolutionary and Napoleonic wars; continuous peace will produce a predominance of regulators, as evidenced by the pre-1914 Navy.

In setting about the writing of my own book a few years ago, Patrick Robinson, who did all the hard work, quite early on remarked: "I thought Admirals sort of fell out of trees – I am just beginning to realize there is a process which serves them up." This book tells us a great deal more about the failings of that process in the long Victorian peace and points out the dangers of allowing ourselves to be overtaken by similar failings today.

It is difficult – but not necessarily impossible – in peacetime, when the stresses and unpredictabilities of war are hard to imagine (and still harder to simulate), to identify those who would be good at it. The Victorian and Edwardian naval establishment did not recognize the need. We must do so, however problematical the task of identification. The real danger occurs when peace changes to war because the consequences of having people in (for them) the wrong jobs can be serious. Our strategic dominance enabled us to win the First World War at sea in spite of having got it substantially wrong at the outset, but that dominance was surely historically unique. And anyway, the human, military and political costs of getting the thing wrong, and learning again from fresh experience, would be unacceptable in the modern world, as well as avoidable (if we can learn from history).

History, Andrew Gordon maintains, offers us not so much 'lessons' but rather 'approximate precedents'. The story he unravels of the pre-1914 Navy represents, in my view, an approximate precedent which today's service (and, indeed, any service in peacetime) should consider carefully. In 1982 most of the characters depicted in this book were still discernible in the Royal Navy, and all had roles to play. For the future the vital thing is to have them in the right places at the critical time – that is, at the beginning of a conflict. A great deal easier said than done.

Sandy Woodward

Introduction

In the late afternoon of the 31st of May 1916, fishermen and villagers on the sandy west coast of Denmark, and even farmers thirty miles inland, stopped in their daily work and turned their heads towards the sea as they heard the rumble of distant gunfire. At first, perhaps, it could have been summer thunder. It went on intermittently for most of the evening and broke out again for a while in the darkest hours of the night. For the Danes, as neutrals, the war had so far meant shortages and rationing and the black market. They had little love for Germany, having lost the duchies of Schleswig and Holstein to Bismarck in the brief war of 1864, but they had less wish to get involved in the holocaust of violence which had gripped the Continent now for nearly two years, and so far they had been spared sight and sound of battle.

But there was no mistaking this. During the night the westerly breeze brought the faint pungent scent of cordite to those still watching and waiting and wondering in the Jutland peninsula. Their ancestors might have imagined Norse sea gods locked in titanic combat. The truth was scarcely less awesome. Seventy miles out to sea 250 warships of the two most powerful fleets in the world were engaged in a fight which might have reshaped the political map of Europe, and the world beyond, for ever. Twenty-five ships went to the bottom and nine thousand men died. In a day or two the wreckage and the bodies started coming ashore, and continued to do so for more than a year.[1] The dead were carefully interred in small neat cemeteries and remote parish churchyards up and down the coast. A few items of flotsam, the odd brass fitting dragged up over the years in fishermen's nets, ended up as curios on mantelpieces or in local museums.

1

Whether the 'Battle of Jutland' was really a battle or just the mother and father of skirmishes, depends on whose gun-turret you peer out of. The German *Hochseeflotte* (High Seas Fleet) blundered into the stronger British Grand Fleet while chasing what was assumed to be an isolated part of that fleet. The Germans had always dreaded a full-scale fleet encounter, and, faced now with this nightmare prospect, Vice-Admiral Reinhard Scheer turned his battle-line around with great skill (and under a hail of shellfire) and melted into the dusk leaving the Royal Navy, by default, the uncontested masters of the North Sea. His 22 battleships failed to score any gunnery hits at all on Admiral Sir John Jellicoe's main battle-line,[2] and thus in purely battle-fleet terms Jutland was one of the cheapest strategical victories in history. Yet for the British the encounter was a heart-breaking disappointment and a source of prolonged acrimony.

It was, as Jellicoe said, "unpalatable", because, while the Germans escaped wholesale destruction, the British battlecruisers – the advanced force of the Grand Fleet, under Vice-Admiral Sir David Beatty – suffered losses out of all proportion to any subsequent gain, in the process of decoying Scheer into Jellicoe's trap. It was to be of little consolation that Jutland persuaded Germany's naval leaders that such an encounter must never be risked again, and assisted their conversion to unrestricted U-boat warfare: if the main fleet engagement had proceeded as morale and mathematics had promised, even the loss of three battlecruisers and their 3,300 men would have appeared justifiable in the grim profit and loss columns of sacrifice.

Beatty's achievement in drawing the High Seas Fleet into the killing ground in front of Jellicoe's 240 heavy guns, in spite of devastating setbacks, was a tribute to his leadership, single-mindedness and stamina, but to have the enemy escape at the last moment, like Houdini, was, in Beatty's own words, "gall and wormwood".[3]

It might be thought that Jutland has already been well enough raked over. And furthermore,

> it is too easy to criticize leaders when sitting in comfort with all the facts available and explanatory diagrams at hand for reference. One is apt to forget the real conditions which existed at the time, when all that could be seen were the dim outlines of a few ships, vanishing before it was possible to distinguish friend or foe.[4]

However, "all the facts" are by no means available, many of the diagrams are far from "explanatory", and Beatty's problems cannot all be attributed to the bad visibility or even to the Germans. And while the tactical management of the four fast battleships of the 5th Battle

Squadron (5th BS), temporarily attached to the Battle Cruiser Fleet (BCF), has attracted criticism from many historians – usually to air their opinions in the post-war 'Beatty *versus* Jellicoe' controversy – the inter-action between the BCF and the 5th BS, and between their respective leaders, Beatty and Rear-Admiral Hugh Evan-Thomas, has never been considered in depth. Their failures to act in unison may be said to represent the fault-line between two incompatible styles of tactical leadership.

*

This book started by accident, in argument with a retired naval officer. I had no primary source knowledge of events and would probably have 'stood from under' had I foreseen the consequences, but I suggested that, on meeting the German battle-fleet, the 5th BS should either have reversed course sooner than it did, or it should have turned away *together* (that is, simultaneously), rather than *in-succession* (which took three vital minutes longer for the last ship). There was nothing original in this, I got it either from Donald Macintyre's *Jutland*[5] or from Geoffrey Bennett's *The Battle of Jutland*,[6] and it seemed an unlikely bone of conten-tion; but I was surprised by the response. I was told that I should watch out or Beatty's ghost would rise up and strike me dead. The book took up much of my spare time for the next seven years.

At first my task appeared obvious and narrow: a navigational analysis of the relative movements of British capital ships in the 'battlecruiser phase' of Jutland. But two seemingly incidental aspects of this subject – the personalities of the admirals involved, and the BCF's and Grand Fleet's respective battle-orders – hinted at fundamentally different atti-tudes towards authority, and led me into the much larger fields of the leadership mores of the late Victorian Navy and of the early career con-ditioning of the future admirals of the Grand Fleet – particularly of Evan-Thomas, who may be taken as broadly representative of the 'Jellicoe group' and of whom (unlike Beatty) comparatively little has hitherto been known.

The result of this historically-backwards linkage is the juxtaposition of the two distinct themes, operational and cultural, of this book. Each could be the subject of study on its own; but the value of the whole is, I believe, more than the sum of the separate parts, and the strength of the link will, I hope, become apparent. For the third strand of the tale, the coloured threads of personal experience, no explanation is necessary.

*

While I hope to make coherent sense of the Battle of Jutland as a whole, my purpose is to focus on certain aspects which may have bearing on issues of fleet command-and-control, and to concentrate on the exploits of certain capital-ship squadrons, and upon episodes which remain in dispute or where I myself dispute the accepted view. In the latter case, it is not sufficient merely to present a 'counter-received' narrative, without explanation. If I did so, I would run the gauntlet of conventionally informed readers unaware of the reasons for my assertions. Thus, it is necessary to indicate what the accepted view is, and what is wrong with it.

This occasional descent into abstrusions ('how many admirals can dance on the head of a belaying-pin') may bemuse readers who want to know about battles between ships, rather than *post-mortem* rows between senior officers and squabbles between historians; but as the historiographical arguments about Jutland stem, more often than not, from the conflict of style[7] (and conflict of conceits) among the major players, they could be said to form an integral part of the tale.

PART I

Background to Battle

1

A Ship which can do Everything

"The battlecruiser should be superseded by the fast battleship."

The 29,000-ton battleship commissioned into the Royal Navy on August the 19th, 1915, in Clydebank, was named after an admiral with no major sea battles to his credit. Charles Middleton's part in Britannia's ascendancy was more fundamental: Controller of the Navy from 1778 to 1790, and First Lord of the Admiralty at the time of Trafalgar, Lord Barham (as he became in 1805) equalled Samuel Pepys as one of the most efficient naval administrators Britain has ever had, and supplied to the fighting admirals the incomparable military machine which carried the RN through the French Revolutionary and Napoleonic wars.

Captain Arthur Craig, "a very efficient gunnery type", gave an elegant speech in which he informed his crew that their new ship's name was pronounced *Barram* as in 'barrel', and not *Bah'ram*, with a long first 'a'. This, he said, was in accordance with the usage of Barham's descendants (of whom the Earl of Gainsborough was head), or was it from the village of Barham in Kent? One or the other. Anyway, anyone overheard referring to "HMS *Bah'ram*" would have his leave stopped. A senior officer's little joke.

After the formalities, the guests and dignitaries went on a tour of the ship. This involved admiring the eight enormous guns and clambering up and down companionways in slow time, the ladies nervously clutching their skirts. Eventually, in the wardroom lobby, they came to the lift, which connected the upper deck with the central engine-room. It was novel for a ship to have an elevator, and some of the visitors professed an interest in the geared turbines which gave *Barham* her vaunted 25 knots. This had been anticipated. The executive-officer (second-in-command), Commander Henry Brownrigg, courteously ushered them into the lift, closed the cage door and pressed the button. They descended five feet and stuck. Electricians were sent for "at the rush", while the commander, clutching his sword, lay down on the Corticine and made polite small talk with the explorers whose heads were now just above deck-level. The midshipmen present savoured the scene for re-enactment in the gunroom later, and dared not look each other in the eye.

That, at least, is how Rear-Admiral Royer Dick (midshipman 1914–16) remembered the commissioning of the third of five *Queen Elizabeth* class battleships,[1] the one destined to be flagship of the class at Jutland.

In retrospect *Queen Elizabeth*, *Warspite*, *Barham*, *Valiant* and *Malaya* seem even more of a milestone than can have been apparent when they first joined the Fleet. For several years they were the largest, fastest and most powerful battleships in the world. They did sterling service in both World Wars, and *Warspite* became the most battle-honoured capital ship of all time.[2] But even in 1915, when the Navy had grown accustomed to a heady succession of bigger and better 'dreadnoughts' taking to the water, it was obvious that these were more than just the usual incremental improvement on their predecessors, and Winston Churchill, the young First Lord of the Admiralty at the time of their conception, claims much (and deserves some) of the credit for them.

They were the first dreadnoughts to carry 15-inch calibre guns, whose shells weighed 1,920 lbs, as against the 1,400 lbs of the $13\frac{1}{2}$-inch projectile or 850 of the 12-inch. Moreover, they were designed around these guns, and their orders placed with the shipyards, before any such weapons existed. Not until hurried prototype guns had been built and tested, while the ships were growing on the stocks, did Churchill know his time-saving gamble had paid off. The 15-inch breech-loading rifle (two specimens of which are impressively mounted in front of the Imperial War Museum) was a huge success. The *Queen Elizabeth*'s guns, and their layout in tiered twin turrets fore and aft, were to influence the five *Royal Sovereigns*, Germany's *Bayern* class, *Renown* and *Repulse*, *Hood* and *Vanguard*, and even *Bismarck* and *Tirpitz*.

They were the first capital ships to be oil-fired, an innovation which ended the "scurrying, miserable, back-broken, black-faced"[3] nightmare of coaling ship and brought great benefits in efficiency, endurance and cleanliness. But here was another gamble, for whereas South Wales was made of coal, Britain had no indigenous sources of oil, and an oil-fired Fleet might be cut off from overseas fuel supplies in time of war. That risk, with all its political and military implications, was lightly shouldered, and Churchill extracted £2.2m. from Parliament to buy a controlling interest in the Anglo-Persian Oil Company: a transaction second only to Disraeli's purchase of the Suez Canal shares in strategic ramifications for Britain and the Middle East.

They had a top speed which, although not as high as intended (more on this later), was unprecedented for battleships and earned them a place in the Royal Navy's front line for thirty years. These revolutionary attributes were expressed in a balanced and reassuringly familiar silhouette – a sublime version of the classic *King Edward VII* class of 'predreadnoughts' of 1902.

> Looking back over the tale of our capital ships we can see at long intervals a few which stand out by virtue of their fine appearance and exceptional military qualities. To them the *Queen Elizabeth* must be added and given pride of place as the most perfect example of the naval constructor's art as yet put afloat.[4]

*

To understand these ships' significance, and the proprietorial rivalry which they aroused, we have to consider the composition and organization of the Fleet in 1915.

The modern capital ships of the British Navy were divided into two distinct 'dreadnought' types with distinct design characteristics and distinct military functions: the battleship and the battlecruiser. The latter's origins were doctrinally precarious. Both types were products of Admiral Sir John ('Jacky') Fisher's epoch-making design revolution of 1906–8, but apart from sharing the common features of heavy guns, turbine propulsion and sheer size, they should not be confused and were by no means interchangeable.

At the turn of the century the standard 'battleship' was a 15,000-ton armoured platform for four 12-inch and various lesser guns, propelled at around 18 knots by triple-expansion engines. Its future was in doubt. Effective battle-ranges were about 2,000 yards, at which short distance even the thickest practicable armour-belt could be perforated by heavy shells fired by the new rifled breech-loaders and striking at near muzzle-velocities. Heavy armour would be mere deadweight burden: all future capital ships, it seemed, would be "eggshells armed with hammers" (to borrow a later description of battlecruisers) whether they had armour or not.

Jacky Fisher had long been obsessed with the concept of a very fast, heavily gunned capital ship – perhaps as a legacy of his service, in the 1860s, as a young gunnery lieutenant in Britain's first 'ironclad', HMS *Warrior* (now preserved in Portsmouth). With armour now of doubtful utility, Fisher became a passionate advocate of a new type of ship, which need not be burdened with thousands of tons of armour, but which would have great speed (to dictate the terms of combat) and great fire-power (to overwhelm any opponent quickly). More specifically, it would be able to deal with the new French armoured-cruisers which were posing a potential threat to British trade routes. When Fisher succeeded to the post of First Sea Lord in 1904, the time looked right for his fast super-cruiser to usurp the battleship.

But technology advances on a broad front, albeit erratically, and the pendulum had, to some extent, swung back. The coming-of-age of the torpedo made it necessary for large warships to exploit the long-range potential of their heavy guns in order to engage beyond the reach of the enemy's flotilla craft; and through improvements in range-finders, and the drive of gunnery reformers such as Percy Scott, Lord Charles Beresford and Fisher himself with his 'Fishpond' of disciples, a succes-sion of technical problems were surmounted and battle-ranges sud-denly stretched out to 8,000 yards – ranges at which large shells, impacting now at oblique angles of descent and with velocities partially spent, could be defeated by hardened armour-plate. The armoured capital ship was back in business. And the new idea that a ship's guns should all be controlled by one centrally placed observer, who would watch their shell-splashes and coordinate corrections in elevation and bearing, favoured a single-calibre armament. Fisher was still loath to be diverted from his super-cruiser concept, but bowed to the 'battleship' lobby and authorized the famous *Dreadnought* in 1905.

By any standards other than Fisher's, the 17,500-ton *Dreadnought* was a bold enough leap in design. As well as having ten guns of 12-inch calibre, she was big enough to carry reasonable armour protection against her own size of main-armament – a rough-and-ready rule of thumb for a balanced warship design. And her turbine-driven 21 knots were a critical tactical advantage over the 18 knots of existing battle-ships. Turbines were a great improvement on reciprocating machinery, for while pistons waste their momentum and start again at the end of each stroke (at the cost of much vibration and wear), turbines keep spinning in a constant direction with enhanced efficiency and service-life. No ship of such size had yet been given turbines, and Fisher's commitment of *Dreadnought* to this power-source was as great a gamble as the guns of the *Queen Elizabeth* class seven years later, and as great a success.

Radical as *Dreadnought* appeared to be, to her putative sponsor she remained a compromise. Fisher still wanted his high-speed predator, arguing a role in imperial defence. The first 'battlecruisers', *Invincible*,

Indomitable and *Inflexible*, were completed in 1908–9. Because they were intended never to encounter accurate heavy shellfire, much of the tonnage taken up by armour in a battleship could be made available for extra propulsive machinery, and so they were able to combine the fire-power of the dreadnought battleship with the 25 knots of the light-cruiser. Then a civilian inventor, Mr Arthur Pollen, entered the debate in a roundabout way with a design for a gunnery fire-control system which promised extraordinary accuracy at extreme ranges.

Pollen had, by chance, become fascinated with the problems of prediction inherent in naval gunnery at long ranges, and had thought the matter through with a professionalism unapproached by naval officers. He perceived the stumbling-block to be the rate of change of range, itself an ever-changing average of the movements of both the firing ship and the target. And while naval officers were still struggling with trigonometry, Pollen devised an analogue computer which could produce constantly updated solutions using differential calculus. Like any computer, a fire-control predictor is hostage to the accuracy of the 'input' data, and until the invention of radar this depended on optical range-finders, their operators, and the men spotting and correcting the fall of shot. But Pollen's inventions at least made optimum use of the obtainable range data, and, for testimonial purposes, it is sufficient to say that the 16-inch guns of the US Navy's *Iowa* class battleships still depend, in the last decade of the twentieth century, on derivatives of the system offered to the Admiralty by Pollen in the first.

How profoundly Fisher understood Pollen's system is uncertain. But he grasped its potential sufficiently to see that a fast ship so equipped (conceptualized by him as HMS *Unapproachable*) would have an extreme-range killing zone which even enemy battleships would be unable to cross to reach their own effective ranges. *Unapproachable*'s speed would enable her to dictate the range and enjoy relative immunity, while her superior gunnery did the business. Here was a rationale for not buying back into the protection offered (once more) by heavy armour-plate.

But what of Arthur Pollen's fire-control computer? The dismal story of how a gunnery-officer, Captain Frederick Dreyer, peddling his own inferior, but attractively cheaper, trigonometrical system, was allowed to nobble the trials and acquisition processes, and how, in consequence, the Admiralty failed to make use of Pollen's brilliant work until after the 1914–18 war, has been exhaustively told by the inventor's son, Anthony Pollen, and by Professor Jon Sumida.[5] The consequence, simply put, was that while the British made early and energetic progress along the path towards the automation of target prediction, setting out on this necessary journey was a different thing from arrival; and British fire-control at the time of Jutland fell between two stools. In taking observed and estimated data, and adding both manual delays and mechanical errors, Dreyer's system deprived the guns of the responsiveness of direct observation, and yet failed to produce accurate results in conditions of fast-changing rates of change of range and bearing. Some gunnery-officers at Jutland would find themselves cutting it out of the 'loop' altogether, in sheer frustration, and dealing directly with the turrets.

Fisher, "a simple and guileful man",[6] did not disseminate the mental acrobatics behind his cherished battlecruisers. Few officers had access to the jealously obfuscated fire-control debate, and fewer properly understood it; and while some senior commanders afloat were slightly puzzled about what these ships were for, and found themselves defining operational roles more or less on the hoof, their bold simplicity found many admirers.

It was obvious, for example, that an *Invincible* could catch and overpower any conventional armoured-cruiser – as she was to demonstrate at the battles of the Falklands (in 1914) and Dogger Bank (in 1915) – and yet use her 25 knots to avoid engagement with battleships. But from 1912, when there were enough battlecruisers to form a squadron, a new role evolved for them in which they would carry out the traditional cruiser function of pushing home a reconnaissance ahead of the battle-fleet. Here they represented an enormous jump in scouting power which the enemy's ordinary cruisers could not hope to parry. Having discovered and, by means of wireless-telegraphy, reported the enemy's battle-fleet, they were to use their 4 or 5 knots speed margin to keep out of effective range of its heavy guns while drawing it into the embrace of their own battle-fleet. So far, so good.

Logically, however, *Invincible*'s suitability for this fleet-scouting role became compromised as soon as the other side possessed similarly armed scouts. This need not have been so had she possessed (as originally intended) a fire-control system which enabled her to hit while still beyond the effective range of the enemy's heavy guns; but as related, this was not the case.

The young German navy, acutely conscious of Britannia's daunting shadow, was conditioned to expect an enemy superior in numbers and firepower and built greater defensive strength into its ships as a matter of habit. But the *Kriegsmarine*'s first battlecruisers, *Von der Tann*, *Moltke* and *Göben* – they were all named after Prussian soldiers – were also designed in the knowledge that they were likely to clash with *Invincibles* and thus be the targets of large-calibre gunfire, and so were better armoured than their British exemplars – almost, in fact, to British battleship standards. The Royal Navy, in its turn, was slow to think through the implications of Germany's commencement of battle-cruisers, and protection levels in *Invincible*'s successors were improved only by small doses. "Their speed is their protection", was Fisher's unrelenting slogan: a dictum now as flawed as the refusal of combat with a nominal equal was unthinkable.

This divergence of the use to which battlecruisers would be put, from the assumptions of their design theory, was widened by the certainty that they would be enlisted as a fast wing of the battle-fleet after they had done their scouting job in a fleet-to-fleet encounter. Indeed, this operational role (an acquired immune-deficiency syndrome) was institutionalized by Rear-Admiral Beatty soon after he took command of the squadron in 1913.[7] Thus, on two counts, the original expectation that their speed would enable them to avoid heavy enemy shellfire was quietly pushed aside and forgotten, and these two potentially self-destructive battlecruiser functions were explicitly laid down in the Grand Fleet Battle Orders in force on the 31st of May 1916.[8]

It would have been looked on askance for battlecruiser officers to ponder the contradictions built into their magnificent ships (anyone doing so "would have injured his professional prospects"[9]). But the fact that it would take 3,300 deaths at Jutland to prompt the admission that they "are unequal to the duties assigned to them, as their protection is insufficient to enable them to encounter the capital ships of the enemy without incurring undue risks of destruction",[10] was a costly rediscovery of the designer's terms of reference, and a testimony to the lack of analysis behind 'the fleet that Jack built'. In the meantime the Royal Navy's attitude towards its battlecruisers contained "an important element of confusion"[11] and laid a lethal trap in the path of these favoured products of Fisher's thematic imagination. The three *Invincibles* were quickly followed by three larger *Indefatigables* and three enormous *Lions*; but the matter of armour-plate was not substantially put right until *Tiger* (1914), the tenth and last mainstream battlecruiser, or even, it could be argued, the *Queen Elizabeth* class of fast battleships.

Herein is the significance of these remarkable, even extravagant, ships: they broke the mould of Fisher's dreadnought-revolution arche-types, being thoroughbred battleships with sufficient speed to toll the bell for the battlecruiser concept. With their commencement, the building of battlecruisers "fell into abeyance".[12] There was in fact initial uncertainty as to their correct designation: their eight-gun main arma-ment had hitherto been a hallmark of battlecruisers, and some expected that they would be so classified on account of their speed, as happened to the elaborately armoured but very fast *Hood* five years later. (As late as 1920, *The Wonder Book of the Navy for Boys and Girls* advised that "they may be described either as battleships or as battlecruisers.") It is axiomatic among naval architects that hybrid designs are rarely successful. But if the *QEs* were hybrids, by discarding the handicaps of both types – the slowness of battleships and the fragility of battlecruisers – and keeping only their strengths, they were to rank among the most successful warships of the twentieth century. The real hybrids, in the context of a fleet action, were of course the battlecruisers. Churchill later explained that *Queen Elizabeth*'s design found favour in the light of the weaknesses inherent in the battlecruiser:

> If it is worthwhile to spend more than the price of your best battleship upon a fast, heavily gunned vessel, it is better at the same time to give it the heaviest armour as well. You then have a ship which can do everything . . . the battlecruiser, in other words, should be superseded by the fast battleship, i.e. fast strongest ship, in spite of her cost.[13]

The idea of a cross between a battleship and a battlecruiser in fact pre-dated not just Churchill's First Lordship, but even the launching of *Dreadnought*.

At the turn of 1905–6 an Admiralty committee considered whether the two projected all-big-gun types (battleships and super-cruisers) should be continued, or whether a single high-value type which combined (or 'fused') the virtues of both should be commenced. The committee was nervous about promoting quality over numbers to such a degree, and concluded that a more expensive type should wait until a substantial inventory of 'dreadnought' battleships had been amassed, whereupon it might be introduced as a fast manoeuvring vanguard to the battle-fleet.[14] It would be unrealistic to connect the *QEs* directly with the 'Fusion Committee', for six years was an aeon in Edwardian naval politics; but clearly the numerical conditions laid down by the committee had been amply attained by 1911, for the new class was preceded into service by no fewer than 22 dreadnought battleships.

It should have followed that the *Queen Elizabeths* usurped the battlecruisers as the fast division of the battle-fleet in a major action – or, to put it another way, relieved them of the dangerous role which had been foisted upon them by the too obvious virtue of their armament and speed. And early in 1914 the Admiralty, in effect, reached just such a decision. The battlecruiser squadron was to be disbanded in May 1915, at the end of the tenure of the incumbent senior officer, and, along with battlecruisers withdrawn from abroad, the ships would be distributed in pairs to four squadrons of the most modern light-cruisers.[15] This return to basic reconnaissance functions was not to be, for war intervened. The incumbent (Beatty) remained in command, the one battlecruiser squadron grew to three, and they were collectively ennobled into their own prestigious 'fleet' within a fleet.

*

One may add that the naming of the new battleships was a saga in itself. Churchill had hardly entered the First Lord's office when he over-stepped his prerogatives: he wanted to call one of the battleships of the previous, 1911, programme HMS *Oliver Cromwell*, an idea which George V understandably vetoed, sugaring the pill by suggesting *Marlborough* in honour of Winston's ancestor. Now, for his new fast battleships the bumptious First Lord put forward *Richard I, Henry V, Queen Elizabeth* and, again, *Oliver Cromwell*. "This was remarkably obtuse of [him], but ships' names seemed to find him at his most obstinate."[16] "There must be some mistake," wrote the King's Private Secretary. Only *Queen Elizabeth* survived.

An extraneous factor militating against new names was the planned 1913 *Signal Book*. It was originally intended that some 150 familiar but currently fallow names would be included, with their three-letter groups, to allow for future use. There was little room for expansion. The *Signal Book* would thus have enshrined a corpus of traditional names from which new warships would be christened (not a bad idea, today's naval critics might think). In the end it was decided that unoc-cupied names would be left out, new names being entered in manu-script against vacant groups as the ships came into service.[17] This was too late for *Richard I* and *Henry V*, which became *Warspite* (an estab-lished battleship name) and *Barham* (recently a cruiser). After another fuss *Oliver Cromwell* became the seventh HMS *Valiant*.[18] *Malaya* was added to the foursome when the Federated Malay States volunteered to pay for her.

That was not quite the end of the story, for there was a sixth *Queen Elizabeth* class unit ordered in 1914, to be built on *Warspite*'s vacated slipway in Devonport. In the meantime Churchill had a third clash with the King, over the 1913 battleships: he wanted to call one of them *Pitt*, which His Majesty (an ex-naval officer) vetoed for scatological reasons, "unworthy of the royal mind" in Churchill's view, connected with rhyming slang. These ships, slower versions of the *QEs* and historically outshone by them, received traditional 'R' names (*Revenge, Ramillies, Resolution, Royal Sovereign* and *Royal Oak*).

The 1914 *QE* was designated *Agincourt*. Churchill liked anniversaries. He had taken over the Admiralty on October 25th, 1911, the 496th anniversary of Henry V's historic victory, and the new ship would have been launched in the battle's half-millennial year. She was cancelled a few days after war broke out, in the belief that hostilities would be over before she could be completed.[19] ('HMS *Agincourt*' tenaciously found her way into the Grand Fleet a month later in the surreal shape of a battleship with fourteen 12-inch guns, built first for Brazil and then for Turkey, and commandeered from Armstrong's fitting-out yard on the Tyne.[20])

2

The Grand Fleet

"Let us hope our destiny is the destruction in a fair fight of the High Seas Fleet."

The Grand Fleet in 1915 was organized and disposed in a manner which directly reflected the distinction between battleships and battlecruisers. The two types were separated into the Battle Fleet (BF) and the Battle Cruiser Fleet (BCF) and based 200 miles apart. Defined military function, geographical necessity, and the personalities of the respective senior officers all combined to institutionalize this demarcation.

Admiral Sir John Jellicoe, the Commander-in-Chief, "a small alert-looking man with a large nose and a rather yellow complexion",[1] had a record as distinguished as could be expected of any officer of a generation denied action experience at sea. He was a high-flyer in professional examinations, and a hero (ashore) of the Egyptian war of 1882. A succession of what could be called 'flag-track' posts took him to the Mediterranean, where he survived the loss through collision of HMS *Victoria*, and thence to China, where his leadership of the Naval Brigade during the Boxer Rebellion gained him the Companion of the Bath from the King, the Order of the Red Eagle from the Kaiser, and a bullet which he carried around in his lung for the rest of his life. After convalescing he became closely involved in the technical and personnel reforms of the pre-war decade. A gunnery specialist, he was very much a man of the new big-gun navy and a protégé of Fisher, whom he ably supported as Director of Naval Ordnance and then Controller of the Navy during the latter's radical first stint as First Sea Lord from 1904 to 1910.

John Jellicoe was a manager rather than a heroic leader and has been described as "the Uncle Arthur of admirals . . . a man of whom it could be difficult to make a hostile or unfriendly comment".[2] A private man, "unimpressive in appearance and short in stature", he was shy of publicity and is alleged to have had no personal ambition. For such an undemonstrative officer, he could engender extraordinary loyalty in anyone who had contact with him and "he possessed the unreserved confidence and trust of the fleet".[3] An American admiral who worked with him at the Admiralty in 1917 remembered him as

> quiet, soft spoken, and unostentatiously dignified; there was nothing of the blustering seadog about the Admiral, but he was all courtesy, all brain, and, of all the men I have ever met, there have been none more approachable.[4]

Jellicoe's strongest leadership gift was his rapport with the ratings of the battle-fleet, with whom his total lack of pretension and phenomenal memory for names struck a rare chord and who "just about worshipped" him.[5] An electrician in the Grand Fleet flagship, HMS *Iron Duke*, recalled that

> Sir John was a very gentle man. Although he was the top man he treated everyone the same. There was never the attitude of 'I'm an officer, you are lower-deck'. If he came around where you were working he wanted to know what you were doing; he was always interested. He would always say 'Carry on. At ease', but you always sensed that he knew more about the job than you did yourself.
> He could be described as a spartan man. His quarters had no frills. His state room in the after end of the ship was almost bare. He had had some partitions taken down and an enormous table fitted with holes in the middle where he could get up through. On it he had a model of every naval ship in Europe, and he would spend hours working out all his various moves, one in particular called the Grid Iron. I made some ship models for his operations table, and he just said 'Thanks, Joe'.[6]

His influence on his officers was equally magnetic, but his relationship with his immediate juniors was less simple. His flag-captain, Frederick Dreyer (fire-control rival of Arthur Pollen), later revealed that his apparent mildness was deceptive: "He had *enormous* self-control. When angry he became silent. Whenever that was with me I wilted on the stalk and would have preferred a couple of dozen."[7] Jellicoe's "mind was a well-ordered filing system of detail".[8] He trusted his own judgement, partly because he had little faith in that of some of his subordinates, and generally speaking both opinions were justified. One result was that he suffered from that malady endemic in British admirals, a disinclination to delegate, and he was burning himself out with overwork. Another was that he sought a clinical solution to every problem and tried to conduct the Grand Fleet through a plethora of standing orders and formulae, drawn up to cater for "every possible contingency".[9]

Since the outbreak of war the battle-fleet had comprised 24 dreadnought battleships, divided into three 8-ship squadrons, numbered the 1st, 2nd and 4th, and attended by dozens of lesser warships. Their 50,000 men – professionals and volunteers – longed for the chance to catch the upstart German fleet in daylight and open water, and to teach the Huns ('baby-killers', since the shelling of Scarborough and the sinking of *Lusitania*) a salutary lesson. It was an article of faith that one day it would happen, and not one man-jack of them doubted the outcome for a moment: "ship for ship and man for man we are fully capable of wiping the floor with them."[10]

The origins of the German High Seas Fleet were complex. The desire to create a focus of pan-nationalist sentiment in the newly unified Germany (a role for which the mainly Prussian army was not naturally suited), and Kaiser Wilhelm II's envy of the British Navy, were major ingredients. Its official nascent role, as defined by the Navy Law of 1888, was very much that of the strategical underdog: it was to be a sallying-fleet (*Ausfallsflotte*) which would venture out unpredictably to do what damage it could to a superior blockading fleet and then dash back to harbour before the enemy could concentrate his forces. The Navy Law of 1897, and that of 1900 (which followed Alfred Tirpitz's appointment as Secretary of State of the Imperial Marine Office), provided for a greatly expanded fleet and ennobled its *raison d'être* to that of a risk-fleet (*Risikoflotte*). The aim was to build "a battle-fleet of such a strength that even for the most powerful naval adversary a war would involve such risks as to make that Power's own supremacy doubtful"[11] – in other words a fleet which would deter England from obstructing Germany's aims, such as belated colonial acquisitions, and threaten losses to the Royal Navy (regardless of who won) which would beggar Pax Britannica and leave the British Empire a hostage to third-party predators.

The logic was persuasive enough to prompt both the reaffirmation of the Anglo-Japanese Alliance in 1905, and Fisher's ruthless concentration of strength in home waters. And in fact, after 'pre-dreadnought' battleships and armoured-cruisers were rendered obsolete by Fisher's design revolution of 1906–8, Tirpitz's *Luxusflotte*, as Churchill caustically called it, came closer to achieving parity than its architect can have dared hope, but could not quite pace the British in the ensuing building-race. So in 1914 the risk-fleet logic presumably still held.

But what was the High Seas Fleet to do if, when push came to shove, Britain declared war (as she did on August the 4th in support of Belgium) in spite of its menacing existence? What was the deterrent to do after it had failed to deter? It was a question which would exercise nuclear theorists half a century later. Was it to come out and be sunk (probably) – at whatever cost to the British fleet – as it had implicitly been promising since 1900? Or was it to rot in harbour and concede, in effect, that its bluff had been called?

Up to a certain rank its bullish and rigorously trained (although mainly conscript) personnel believed that their destiny was to meet the Grand Fleet in one Wagnerian battle, and routinely drank to "*Der Tag*" – a piece of braggadocio which went beyond risk-fleet theory in actually presuming victory. But senior officers – not least the Kaiser, whose special conceit the Navy was – recognized that such a clash would be tantamount to suicide, and feared that, in the words of Admiral Hugo von Pohl (German C-in-C 1915–16), "nothing could turn out better for the English, and nothing could so damage our [reputation], as that our fleet should be the loser in a serious engagement."[12] They therefore opted for the less confrontational desideratum of trapping and defeating isolated parts of the Grand Fleet while avoiding a full fleet-to-fleet encounter. Until British superiority had been suitably eroded, this return to the *Ausfallsflotte* concept was the middle path between the unattractive extremes of pointless sacrifice and demoralizing inactivity, but it was a difficult one to follow – especially as the British adopted an unexpected policy of distant (as opposed to close) blockade – and for most of 1915 von Pohl placed more faith in the U-boat campaign against commerce.[13]

"Meanwhile," as an uncomplicated young officer in the Grand Fleet wrote to his parents, "we wait and prepare, and prepare to make ourselves fit to fulfil our destiny. Let us hope that destiny is the destruction in a fair fight of the High Seas Fleet."[14] But while Jellicoe shared the universal British wish for the day of reckoning, from his perspective (as from that of his opposite across the North Sea) things were not so simple.

He had under his overall command Britain's entire front-line fleet strength: a responsibility borne by no British admiral in wartime since Howard of Effingham in 1588, and one which he carried heavily. With absentees for refit and repair, and depending on what German ships were included in the calculation, the Grand Fleet's margin of strength in dreadnought battleships over the German High Seas Fleet allowed neither carelessness nor complacency. And if, by putting to sea at all, the Germans ran the greater military risk, the strategic stakes for Britain were astronomical, for Tirpitz's *Risikoflotte* theory continued to work its mischief after the outbreak of the war it had failed to prevent, and the buck stopped with John Jellicoe. Britain's survival and the Empire's security rested ultimately on the Grand Fleet, and the potential world-wide consequences of a major disaster in the North Sea caused him to hedge about with provisos and conditions his longing to catch the High Seas Fleet. Churchill, who did Jellicoe few favours in his history of the Great War, was correct as well as clever in saying that he was "the only man on either side who could lose the war in an afternoon"; and Jellicoe would have felt some sympathy for Admiral Lord Torrington's comment on the invasion scare of 1690: "I knew that whilst we had a fleet in being, they would not dare to make the attempt."

Jellicoe was partly assuming responsibility for strategic priorities which rightfully belonged to his political masters, but in view of the burden which he took onto his solitary shoulders with so little (as he saw it) cerebral assistance, it is hardly surprising that he inclined towards caution.

One anxiety was that the enemy might, while feigning flight, make devastating use of submarines and free-floating mines: weapons whose tactical limitations had not been established in the early years of the war. In a much-quoted memorandum to the Admiralty on 30 October 1914 he actually warned: "If the enemy battle-fleet were to turn away from an advancing Fleet, I should assume that the intention was to lead us over mines and submarines, and should decline to be so drawn."[15] Perhaps rather carelessly, the Admiralty under Churchill and Fisher (back again as First Sea Lord) approved his thinking (and he took the precaution of lodging their reply with his bank). But there were several things wrong with it.

It assumed that an encounter would take place on ground preselected by the enemy, and that surface ships could easily operate, and communicate, with submarines. The plausibility of the Germans risking a disastrous fleet engagement in open waters for the sake of so uncertain a ploy as a U-boat ambush was not subjected to analysis, and the likelihood that they might simply be running away was obscured. Its most insidious aspect was the failure to appreciate the singularity of opportunity in war: if the first clash with the High Seas Fleet did not exactly match staff-requirements (it seemed to say), well never mind, there'll be another soon.

But in fairness to Jellicoe and his contemporaries, the destruction of the German fleet, however eagerly anticipated by the rank and file of the Royal Navy, was not a strategic necessity.

'There is no doubt, Sir,' [said Fisher] 'that we are God's chosen people.'

'A comforting thought,' said His Majesty. 'On what is it based?'

'With the great harbour of Scapa Flow in the North and the narrow Straits of Dover in the South, there is no doubt, Sir, that we are God's chosen people.'[16]

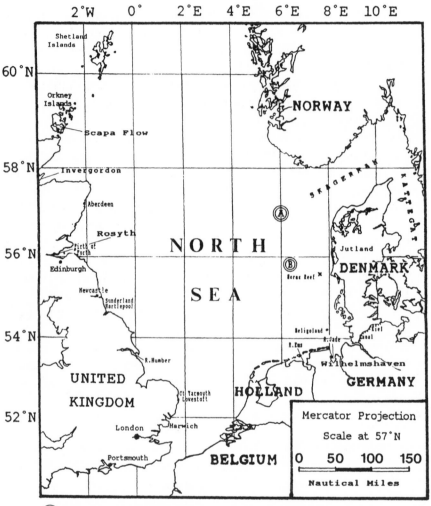

ⓐ Meeting of battle-fleets, 31st May 1916
ⓑ Last 'night action', a.m., 1st June 1916

With its exits from the North Sea barred to the south by the Dover barrage and to the north by the menacing presence of the Grand Fleet, the High Seas Fleet was unable to interfere with Britain's Atlantic trade, her cross-Channel traffic (essential to the Army in France), or her colonial empire. Britain therefore already enjoyed most of the fruits of a victorious fleet action without actually having to fight one: the superior power of her fleet-in-being (in the Admiralty's words) "pervades all the waters of the world".[17]

So, a full fleet action would be pressed only in circumstances acceptable to Jellicoe. In such circumstances, the wholesale destruction of the German fleet would undoubtedly ensue. Otherwise, it was not, in his opinion, "wise to risk unduly the heavy ships of the Grand Fleet in an attempt to hasten the end of the High Seas Fleet".[18] In the meantime, it was of paramount importance that the battle-fleet's numerical superiority should not be eroded by attrition while the big show-down was awaited; and the safest harbour that could be found for a force which, with its attendant cruisers and destroyers, numbered around 100 warships was Scapa Flow in the Orkneys.

The Admiralty had had a file on Scapa for a hundred years. In 1812 the Lords Commissioners were favoured with the opinion of one of their maritime surveyors that the Flow

> is admirably well suited for a Northern Roadstead for a Fleet of Line-of-Battle-Ships; and is doubtless the finest natural Roadstead in Britain and Ireland except Spithead, if all the Qualities which constitute a good roadstead be properly considered . . . Nature seems to have given every degree of Shelter to Scapa Flow that could possibly be expected in a Roadstead of such extent.
>
> If we had a strong Fleet there in War time, it would prevent the enemy from going North-about Britain to Ireland or elsewhere should he ever attempt it. Our Fleet there would also intercept and prevent all the Enemy's Trade North-about Britain . . .
>
> Our Neglect of [the Orkneys] hitherto appears to consist in our not availing ourselves of the Use that Nature seems to have intended them for.[19]

The author of this unsolicited petition overlooked the problems of supplying and maintaining a fleet in such a location, and one can understand why a century passed before Their Lordships so availed themselves.

Then, in the early 1900s, the decision to impose upon the enemy in a future European war a distant blockade (in place of the traditional close blockade) brought Scapa Flow into its own; and although about as far from home comforts as it is possible to get in the United Kingdom, the location suited Jellicoe's purposes well. He was "carried away by a passion for secrecy"[20] and its remoteness obscured, with nature's own censorship, the movements of his fleet, while its expanses provided sheltered ranges for gunnery and torpedo practice beyond the reach of German submarines. In May 1916 an observer in a visiting ship found that it was

> an ideal base from this point of view, and they are all keyed up to concert pitch and wonderfully efficient . . . up here, the Flow, even after 22 months, is always full of ships, exercising gunnery and torpedoes, from the new *Revenge* down to the latest destroyer. Ceaseless activity predominates with but one end – *Der Tag*.[21]

The inaccessibility of the place from Whitehall, Parliament and the national press no doubt commended it further to 'Silent Jack' Jellicoe, although its legendary tedium was hardly to the tastes of his sailors: "Dear Mum, I cannot tell you where I am. I don't know where I am. But where I am there is miles and miles of bugger all. Love Ted."[22]

Scapa Flow had a certain primeval beauty. In summer months, with its profusion of terns, kittiwakes, guillemots, razor-bills and skuas, it was a paradise for bird-watchers, who comprised a statistically invisible percentage of the Fleet. In winter its displays of aurora borealis could be breath-taking; but it was bitterly cold and mostly pitch dark, and days could be spent "hanging on to our anchors with steam up and the wind blowing Force 12".[23]

> It is blowing hard. Everything – sea, sky, land and ships – is a dull dark grey and that only from 10 to 3. The rest of the 24 hours it is black. But yesterday the sun came out for a very short time and shone on the dark brown patches of heather in places which made a wonderfully pretty sight.[24]

Recreational facilities were primitive and depended upon what had been extemporized by the labour and ingenuity of the battle-squadrons: "Imagine the Klondike in the earliest days, and you have it." There was a football pitch on the only level piece of ground, and "a miserable canteen that sold tea and biscuits – what the hell good was that for thirsty young sailors?" – on the island of Flotta. There was in fact a 'wet' canteen at Lyness on Hoy, but it consisted of "a hut, a trestle table, and two or three large beer barrels", and going ashore was "scarcely worth the trouble". Some didn't bother for months on end.

For officers there was a golf-course of sorts on Flotta, each hole of which was landscaped and maintained by a battleship. And some captains and admirals found therapy in digging unlikely patches of vegetable garden, while others therapeutically watched their cox'ns do the digging for them. But officers were hardly better off than the lower-deck, a factor which maintained *esprit de corps* in the face of unrelenting boredom.

They made their own amusements. "Calm-natured men took life philosophically and passed their time reading anything that came to hand, even the ship's notices; restless ones paced any small space of deck available." They tried their hand with home-made lobster-pots, catapulted seagulls, learned languages, took music lessons, played ragtime, staged amateur dramatics, and got morose. Gambling was illegal "and therefore flourished",[25] and ship's dances became ominously popular (considering the absence of females). But their "principal occupation [was just] looking at the other ships";[26] and while the Army was coming to terms with 'shell-shock', the Navy was discovering 'Orkneyitis': a mild form of dementia which could strike in unpredictable guises.

A fleet based in the far north could not hope to intercept or deter hit-and-run raids on English coastal towns by German battlecruisers, and after the bombardment of Scarborough, Whitby and Hartlepool on the 16th of December 1914 the mayors of those towns "demanded coastal artillery and dreadnoughts anchored off their beaches. The Indian Government telegraphed that Madras must be protected."[27] Instead, the battlecruisers were brought together from various deployments, formed into the Battle Cruiser Fleet (BCF) and based on the new dockyard of Rosyth in the Firth of Forth, 200 miles south of Scapa.

Even the Forth was not ideal, being still too far north and chronically beset by fog: the Humber would have been best, but its entrance was highly susceptible to mining and its shallowness would have tidelocked deep-draught ships – a gift to German planners. Of strategic necessity, therefore, the BCF's 10 battlecruisers and satellite cruisers and destroyers, led by Acting Vice-Admiral Sir David Beatty in HMS *Lion*, found themselves far apart from the main fleet and within a stone's throw of Edinburgh with its social diversions, theatres and moving pictures, trains and telephones, visiting celebrities and the press. Unlike the rest of the Grand Fleet, the BCF was kept in the public eye. Why suffer the ordeal of a notoriously awful train journey and sea-crossing to Orkney to visit the fleet if the most glamorous part of it was so easily accessible? Anyway, Jellicoe was ill at ease with the press and discouraged visits to his battle-fleet from outsiders.

Beatty was Drake to Jellicoe's Howard. A scion of hard-hunting, hard-playing Irish landowning gentry, his charisma and panache have been unequalled by any other naval officer this century.

> He had a love of doing everything at high pressure and high speed. This was not a pose: it was entirely characteristic whether at sea or in the hunting field. Things that happened slowly or even normally irked him. I could not imagine David Beatty dry-fly fishing.[28]

He had first earned fame, and acquired a taste for independence, in command of a river gunboat in support of Kitchener's Nile army in the late 1890s. After the 'Omdurman' campaign, which gained him a DSO (almost a VC, it was rumoured), Beatty won further distinction in the Boxer wars which left him with two fingers paralysed from a bullet wound in his left arm. He reached captain's rank at the age of 29 (the average being 42[29]), and his naval future seemed assured. But he would accept the proffered glittering prizes only on his own terms. Both his career and his social life were conducted with a reckless indifference to convention.

Marrying a fabulously rich American divorcee, the daughter of Marshall Field, the Chicago chain-store millionaire, was a risk he shrugged off:

> Society still tended to frown upon divorce and to refuse to receive a divorced woman, and as half the policy of England was settled at dinner parties and social gatherings it could be inconvenient, to say the least, [to be] barred from such meetings.[30]

The Beattys' subsequent acceptance at Court, after he had petulantly threatened to leave the Navy,[31] was something which might well have been denied another officer. Ethel, "beautiful, opulent, ambitious and unhinged by her hereditary fortune", was to grow increasingly neurotic and demanding at the time when his burdens were at their greatest. He would not be exaggerating when, in later years, he said: "I have paid terribly for my millions."[32] But his acquired wealth underwrote his professional carelessness, for unlike the majority of officers he was in no way in thrall to the Navy for his financial security, and more than once he thought of leaving the service for a life of leisure because his wife made heavy weather of his absences at sea. The fact that he could buck the system with impunity was resented by the average career naval officer, and the Beattys invited some of the resentment – as with their flaunting of Ethel's steam-yacht, and her throw-away remark in 1905, when David got into trouble for racking the engines of his armoured-cruiser (HMS *Suffolk*), that she would buy the Admiralty another one.

In 1910, at 38 years of age, David Beatty became Britain's youngest rear-admiral since 1797 (when Horatio Nelson beat him by a few months). Then he jeopardized his career by turning down the plum appointment of second-in-command of the Atlantic Fleet: according to rumour, because he didn't wish to miss the start of the grouse shooting season. His real reason – that he had no wish to be anybody else's direct junior – merely exchanges flippancy for breath-taking arrogance. Either way, ordinary mortals did not get second chances from the Admiralty, and Beatty languished on half-pay. In the normal way of things, that should have been that.

Churchill's rescuing his career will be touched on in a future chapter. Suffice it to say that, as First Lord of the Admiralty, Winston first employed him as his naval secretary, and then gave him command of the Battle Cruiser Squadron – the most highly prized rear-admiral's appointment in the world.

Beatty had arrived. Young, dynamic, arrogant, charming and photogenic, his affectations of uniform – jacket with six buttons (as prescribed for petty-officers) instead of the regulation eight; cap with extra-wide brim, worn at a slant – became as well known as Montgomery's battledress and beret twenty-five years later, or Nelson's eye-shade and armless sleeve[33] (a comparison he would not have sought to suppress).

Beatty's personal attitude towards the popular press was ambivalent. As a junior officer he had become a household name through newspaper coverage of his exploits; and on his appointment to the battlecruisers, in 1912, another session of adulation commenced ("And what would not the battlecruisers do under such a leader?"[34]). He was 'good copy', and he must have been aware of how much his professional and social stock had risen as a consequence of it. In private letters he affected to deplore the eulogies of, for example, the naval journalist Filson Young: he acidly supposed that Young was trying to 'make' him, and hoped that his efforts would not be misconstrued in the service ('misconstrue' is a word he used repeatedly in regard to his public relations). He could surely have stopped much of it, had he wished. Yet not only did it go on, he even hoisted "that terrible fellow"[35] into his personal staff when Young turned up aboard *Lion* in RNVR uniform in 1914.

Even in the Navy's extrovert days, before the triple traumas of Jutland, the RAF, and the Invergordon Mutiny, service opinion was not charitable towards officers who played to the gallery: heroes with two arms were expected to be self-effacing. Whether or not Beatty sought his press exposure – and there is little evidence that he actively did so – he was aware that he was treading a thin line in the eyes of his profession. But to a public disconcerted by stalemate in France and hungry for heroes, he was a gift. Here was the sort of talismanic leader they could adopt as their own, and *Lion*, the greatest warship in the world when Beatty's flag first climbed her foremast, became the most publicized ship of the 1914–18 war.

Beatty strove to cultivate a "band of brothers on the Nelson model"[36] among his subordinates, who were devoted to their dashing

leader and among whose number were to be found some of the Royal
Navy's most conspicuous.

Osmond Brock, Rear-Admiral 1st BCS ('The Splendid Cats': *Lion*'s
sisters *Princess Royal* and *Queen Mary*, and half-sister *Tiger*), was "brilliantly clever . . . his knowledge ranged from art to nuclear theory".[37] "a
great reader and thinker, [he] could never remember the names of staff
officers".[38] "Where Beatty was valiant, Brock was quiet; where one
struck sparks, the other could blow up the fire; where one was instinc-
tively right, the other could discover why."[39] Beatty kept Brock with him
as chief of staff when he succeeded Jellicoe in command of the Grand
Fleet six months after Jutland. Brock was a future admiral of the fleet.

William Pakenham, RA 2nd BCS (*Australia, Indefatigable, New
Zealand*), was one of the great 'originals' of the Navy, of whom many
stories have survived. His personal turn-out was legendary. As an
observer in Admiral Togo's flagship at the Battle of Tsushima in 1905,
he strolled up and down the after bridge armed with notebook and telescope until his tropical whites got splattered with blood from a Russian
hit on a nearby gun battery, whereupon he went off to change into a
fresh outfit, and then resumed his beat. His hosts declared him the
bravest man on either side and gave him the Order of the Rising Sun.
'Old Packs' habitually slept fully dressed, to be ready for action at all
times. He would succeed Beatty in command of the BCF.

The Hon. Horace Hood, RA 3rd BCS (the oldest battlecruisers:
Invincible, Indomitable, Inflexible), belonged to one of England's most
famous naval families. He had commanded a river gunboat alongside
Beatty in the Nile campaign, been present at Omdurman, and won the
DSO in hand-to-hand combat with dervishes in 1904. The Honourable
'Orace was "an officer of exceptional merit", blessed with every ingredi-
ent of leadership, whose "intense sense of duty and moral courage" was
belied by "shyness and child-like simplicity of manner".[40]

Ernle Chatfield, captain of *Lion*, had been an acknowledged gunnery
expert since his admission to the 'Fishpond' in 1900. He first attracted
Their Lordships' notice as a lieutenant by taking a destroyer up the
Thames at 20 knots for a cricket match at Greenwich, and was very
proud of having bowled out a middle-aged W. G. Grace.[41] He would
continue as Beatty's flag-captain when the latter became C-in-C Grand
Fleet. Chatfield was a future admiral of the fleet who, as an effective
First Sea Lord, would oversee the Navy's rearmament in the 1930s.[42]

Walter Cowan, captain of *Princess Royal*, had been a close friend of
Beatty's from both midshipman and Nile-gunboat days. He was a fero-
cious midget who loved war so much that he spent his leave periods in
the trenches in France and wept when the Armistice was announced.

There was trouble in almost every ship he commanded. He became the scourge of the Bolsheviks in the Baltic in 1919, and ended his naval career as admiral of the fleet. Cowan came out of retirement in 1940 to join an Indian armoured regiment in North Africa. Captured by the Italians when he personally attacked a tank, and then released on humanitarian grounds, he joined the Commandos, aged 72.

Not apparent to the public gaze were unNelsonic flaws in, and exclusions from, Beatty's band of brothers. The worst flaw (discussed in Chapter 6) lay in his retention of his particular flag-lieutenant. The exclusions tended to be close subordinates whose appointments had not had his blessing and who had failed to win him over, such as Rear-Admiral Archibald Moore (2nd BCS before Pakenham), Commodore William Goodenough (2nd Light-Cruiser Squadron), and Captain Henry Pelly of *Tiger*. But "as the war dragged on, there was an increasing tendency [for press and public] to make the most of any gleam of talent and turn geese into swans".[43] The BCF's leaders were neither geese nor swans, but as a group they seemed to personify the unabashed *élan*, the easy excellence, admired by the English of that era; and the battlecruisers, long, lean and fast, had already clashed with the enemy several times in the first six months of the war. Heligoland Bight, Scarborough (a near miss), the Falklands and Dogger Bank had all put them into the headlines in connection with the Germans fleeing or sinking, and among their personnel an astronomical élitism developed.

The more pensive among observers were aware that "we have a long while to wait before we attain the superhuman hardiness and war-worthiness of our forefathers off Brest";[44] but the self-assured bravado of BCF personnel was no mere affectation. At the hard-steaming action of Dogger Bank in January 1915, the 'black-gang', slaving with shovels and coal-trolleys in one of *Lion*'s boiler-rooms, sang so loudly that the petty-officer in charge was unable to make his orders heard and applied to have singing banned at action-stations. And their disdain was not confined to the Germans. They "regarded the Grand Fleet's battle-squadrons, which had not yet fired a shot in anger against the High Seas Fleet's major warships, with something approaching contempt".[45] They fancied an affinity with the men who were fighting so hard in the trenches and thought of themselves, not without justification, as 'in the front line': the boring and colourless battle-fleet being hopelessly out of touch 'in the rear' – an invidious metaphor which Jutland would greatly promote.[46] The BCF remained an integral part of the Grand Fleet throughout the war, yet it seems natural to think of it as a separate entity and to use the term 'Grand Fleet' as synonymous with 'battle-fleet' – as Beatty himself did as a matter of habit.

This battlecruiser cult was not lost on the men of the battle-fleet, stuck in the Siberia of Scapa Flow with never a sight of the enemy[47] and little to do but work at their endless gunnery practice, coal ship, and read yesterday's newspapers. In truth the BCF was doing much to keep up the Royal Navy's corporate image at a time when the Army's toils in the mud and the blood were daily headline news; and many battleship men would have given their back teeth for a transfer to the BCF,[48] for the better chances of action and to escape from Scapa. But inevitably Beatty's facility with the press was looked on askance as 'not quite the thing', and the substance of the battlecruisers' glamorous reputation was jealously questioned.

Rumours went the rounds that *Invincible*'s and *Inflexible*'s shooting at the Battle of the Falklands, when they took several hours to sink the armoured-cruisers *Scharnhorst* and *Gneisenau*, had been so wild that the Admiralty had to send an ammunition ship to meet them at Ascension in case they were embarrassed by a German merchant raider on the way home. And how come the enemy had not been handled more decisively after Scarborough and at Dogger Bank? Ships from the Forth, visiting Scapa for gunnery drills, found that "the Battle Cruisers' name up here is mud, owing to the inefficiency of their gunnery and the general casualness and lack of concentration with which they appear to treat the war."[49] An officer posted to *Invincible* reported back to *Barham*'s first-lieutenant that "he was shocked by the standard of efficiency he encountered."[50]

The Navy was always a highly competitive service. A hundred years ago an admiral wrote that rivalry between ships and fleets "is a moral force of the highest value and works almost entirely for good".[51] More recently a historian has said:

> Ships' companies always suffer from mild paranoia, if allowed the chance to do so, become easily convinced that they have a 'green rub' in the matter of leave, mail, seatime, whereas other ships are unfairly blessed with the life of Riley.[52]

The BCF's quality of life in the Firth of Forth would scarcely have met Riley's desiderata – at least, not if he had been a rating. As at Scapa, the routine too often consisted of "coaling, sleeping, sleeping, eating, sleeping, reading mails, writing same, arguing about the War, eating, sleeping and then to sea".[53] Leave was no more frequently awarded than in the battle-fleet and was usually occasioned only by long refit or repair. Thanks to the indulgence of local farmers and landowners, organized recreation was much better provided for, with, for example, several football pitches "twenty-five minutes easy marching from the landing steps"; there was a canteen at Rosyth, courtesy of William McEwan Ltd, where sailors could buy a pint of beer for 3*d.* and escape the confines of their ships for an hour or so, and a YMCA hostel sponsored by Lady Beatty. But unsupervised visits ashore were virtually unobtainable, and the pleasures of civilization – constantly evidenced by Edinburgh and Leith, by trains and ferries, and by the casual comings and goings of officers – were inaccessible to the lower-deck.

For officers it was very different. They could, if they wished, take advantage of the concessionary membership available at fourteen civilian sporting clubs of one sort or another,[54] play rugby or hockey on the pitches reserved for them at Dundas Castle (one of which had a tree in the middle), or run with the RN Bassett Hounds. But on most days in harbour they could get ashore and just do as they pleased. They could "lunch in Edinburgh, go to the cinema or walk down Princes Street looking at the shop windows".[55] While the fleet was at four hours' notice for steam, as it was for most of the war, the usual routine was: work on board until lunch-time and then catch the picket-boat to Rosyth or to Hawes Pier at South Queensferry, returning to the ship by early evening.

A recall system had been perfected. The main Edinburgh cinemas had a message which could be flashed onto their screens. And one junior officer who puzzled over how the hall porter of the Caledonian Hotel knew when the fleet was going to sea before anyone else, could have found the answer in Battle Cruiser Fleet Standing Orders. Every afternoon a petty-officer was stationed in the Edinburgh telephone exchange. In event of emergency, he would be phoned by *Lion* (shore-linked through her mooring buoy) and told to pass on to three specified golf clubs, two gentlemen's clubs, one lawn-tennis club and the North British and Caledonian Hotels the following message:

'Please inform the nearest Naval Officer (without informing any civilian) that the boat leaves Hawes Pier at —'. The officer thus informed [had to] make it his duty to inform all other officers at that place.

The list of venues presumably reflected an official perception of officers' leisure interests. Those whose pursuits took them elsewhere were expected to make their own arrangements to keep in touch.

By 1916 the battlecruiser squadrons had been in the Forth long enough for officers to complain of its boredom. You couldn't do much in Edinburgh in the normal afternoon leave period, they said – a 'drip' which would have cut no ice in Scapa. One officer found "upsetting and disturbing [the reminders of] civilization in the form of shops, tram cars, luncheon-parties, cinematographs and people engaged in ordinary life", whereas he claimed to be quite happy at sea.[56] Others confined themselves to cycle rides or scrambles in the countryside easily accessible from North and South Queensferry, during which their contact with normal human beings would be limited. "Sometimes, for an hour or two one gets away with a pipe into some pretty nook, to lie on the grass and bask in the sun, and the war might be over or never begun."[57]

With the right social ju-ju, one could fish the loch at Dundas Castle, or picnic in the grounds of Dalmeny House. And the Marquess of Linlithgow (whose father had sold the land at Rosyth to the Admiralty in 1903, and whose great-uncle, Admiral Sir James Hope, had befriended Acting-Lieutenant Fisher in China in 1860[58]), opened the extensive grounds of Hopetoun House, two miles west of South Queensferry, to senior officers.

> In return we cut their trees down with perhaps better intention than wood-manship, trimmed their hedges and cleared their garden ditches. The jealousy which the Commodores and some others displayed in keeping each his own axe, saw and clippers away from the rest was worthy of any gardener . . . Seriously, it is not easy to say what the recreation and distraction meant to many of us.[59]

Beatty himself used to march at breakneck pace up hill and down dale, regaling his breathless acolyte-of-the-day with lurid details of his Egyptian campaign.[60] One midshipman discovered the solitary vice of jay-walking across the Forth Bridge, 170 feet above the sea, a stunt forbidden by both naval and railway regulations, for the thrill of pressing himself against the side and feeling the girders sway as trains thundered past.[61]

But many older officers had followed Beatty's example and installed their wives in nearby accommodation ashore: a facility which, as the vice-admiral distantly recognized, further widened the quality-of-life gulf between officers and ratings. And the amenities of Scotland's capital city were hardly forsaken. Beatty himself had assignations with another officer's wife in the North British Hotel; and Rear-Admiral Pakenham, asked by an elderly lady at a civic reception if he was married, replied politely: "No Madam, but I keep a loose woman in Edinburgh."[62]

Possibly Old Packs was lying (no one ever met his vaunted woman). But there is a significant point in all this. Some of the most highly trained and successful military forces – Nelson's fleet, Montgomery's 8th Army, Wingate's Chindits – were worked up to excellence in remote environments, undistracted by the comforts of normal life. This should not be taken too far (witness the Harwich destroyer force under

Commodore Tyrwhitt, or Fighter Command in the Battle of Britain); but the 'Zulu warrior' syndrome, for what it is worth, was more nearly attained in the monastic and classless rigours of Scapa Flow, where "one had an acute sense of detachment from everything but the sea and the Navy",[63] than in the Firth of Forth. A new arrival at Rosyth happily reasoned that "if the night previous to action, you had a good dinner and attended the theatre, why should you not fight as well as a miserable individual who has not been ashore for a month?"[64] But in time the same man-about-town came round to thinking that

> the proximity of Edinburgh to the BCF, the officers of which go there every day, is in many ways a bad thing. There is amongst them a natural tendency to live rather for the afternoons, when one can go ashore, instead of the fore-noons when the turrets go round.[65]

Tensions were no doubt screwed tighter in the Battle Fleet by the thankless months of waiting and training, and by the unacclaimed forays into the North Sea's empty horizons. But the Forth's plausibility as a cushy billet compounded jealousies, and it is hardly surprising that the BF was "inclined to look on the BCs as a gay set of dogs who frequent Princes Street".[66] Old hands from Jellicoe's battle-squadrons still tend to be dismissive of the much vaunted battlecruisers: the more polite ones describe Beatty as "a Prince Rupert"[67] – a term which approximates to 'cowboy' in modern parlance – for whom they "had no use".[68] The analogy with King Charles I's dashing nephew bears some examination: Rupert stood

> in a class by himself. Young, impulsive, brave and very sure of himself, he was inclined to treat with contempt Charles's older advisers and commanders. He antagonized the first two Royalist commanders-in-chief by insisting on complete independence as a general of the horse.[69]

Other epithets, used by Battle Fleet veterans to describe Beatty, have included "big-head", "bombastic bugger", and "bloody Errol Flynn"[70] – malice born of envy and frustration, with an element of truth.

Tribal antagonisms sometimes have trivial beginnings, and a silly incident in August 1914 may have helped to start the battlecruisers off on the wrong foot with the Battle Fleet. After the action of Heligoland Bight, when Beatty took the 1st BCS far into German waters in support of a foray by the Harwich destroyers, and three enemy cruisers were sunk, the 'Splendid Cats' returned to Scapa to a triumphal welcome. The Battle Fleet cleared lower decks and cheered them through to their anchorage. But *Lion*'s anchor stuck in her hawse-pipe, she overshot her bearings and had to do another circuit. "This encore invited more

cheers, most of the men thinking it had been done for their benefit",
and Beatty feared that the manoeuvre would be misconstrued,[71] as it no
doubt was.

It is impossible to reckon accurately the scale of the ill-feeling
between the two forces, or to place it in perspective. The point where
such a thing exceeds healthy competition defies definition – and probably before Jutland it never really crossed the boundary. But it is unsurprising that it was later to infect all ranks for the virus reached the
top at an early stage.

About the only things Jellicoe and Beatty had in common were
scars from Chinese bullet wounds, and the unshakeable loyalty of their
respective followers. Yet in spite of their differences in age (56 and 45)
and temperament, and the infrequency of their meetings, they got
on serviceably well, as their considerable correspondence shows.
However, Jellicoe became irritated by his junior's tendency to get
above himself, and suspicious of his use of private political and social
channels – for example to Churchill, whose naval secretary he had
been, or to Fisher through the medium of the journalist Filson Young
– and although they were men of such different styles, the C-in-C
could expect things to be done in a manner which suited him. Beatty
was not the only unruly subordinate whose independence Jellicoe
found disconcerting (Vice-Admiral Sir Doveton Sturdee was another)
and his recurring irritation was always mixed with high professional
respect. But it was a subtle note of discord in the orchestration of the
Grand Fleet's efforts, and it is difficult not to feel that Jellicoe was
usually in the right.

Into this state of affairs steamed the *Queen Elizabeth* class battleships.

The idea that these ships might work with the battlecruisers already
had a certain history. Jacky Fisher began it in November 1914 with a
typically wild forecast that the new class would do 28 knots – the same
as the fastest and newest battlecruisers.[72] Thus misinformed, Jellicoe
apparently accepted that the two types should operate together.[73]
Churchill compounded the issue by promising *Queen Elizabeth* to Beatty
to quiet the latter's complaints about the sending away of *Princess Royal*
to the West Indies to hunt for Vice-Admiral Graf von Spee. (*Invincible*
and *Inflexible*, sent to the Falklands for the same purpose, had yet to
come under Beatty's command.) "I hope it will be possible", the First
Lord wrote, on the last day of November, "to strengthen your squadron
in the near future by the return of the straying cat and the addition of a
still more formidable feline animal, to wit: the *Queen Elizabeth*."[74] This
was music to Beatty's ears. He knew all about the new battleship, having
been at the Admiralty when her design was finalized. "I shall be sur-

rounded with queens, princesses & cats," he gloated to his wife, "but it is good news and <u>private</u>, as the *Q.E.* is the <u>finest</u> fighting unit in the world."[75]

Jellicoe crystallized his junior's expectations by mooting the plan that if indeed the *QEs* proved capable of 28 knots they should be attached to the 1st BCS, consisting of the newest, fastest battlecruisers of the *Lion* class; whereas if they could do only 26 they should reinforce the older, slower units of the 2nd BCS, which was due to become part of the new, combined Battle Cruiser Fleet under Beatty's command.[76] That battleships designed for 25 knots might in fact do 26 was plausible, in the light of some previous classes exceeding their designed speeds; 28 knots would have been an engineering miracle, as Jellicoe probably knew all along.

In the event, the name-ship of the class was rushed out to the Dardanelles as soon as complete. But enough information must have trickled home by February 1915 for Fisher to modify his prognosis to 26 knots "on a pinch".[77] This was still good enough for Jellicoe to promise *Queen Elizabeth* (on her return) and *Warspite* to the BCF.[78] But within a fortnight of the latter ship's arrival in Scapa Flow from the builders in mid-April 1915, the C-in-C had learned enough of her in-service performance to tell Beatty the bad news: "*Warspite* is only good for about $23\frac{1}{2}$ knots – no use to you";[79] and to turn his mind to a special role for the class with his battle-fleet.

The five new battleships would secure beyond doubt the numerical superiority of the BF over the High Seas Fleet, even if *Der Tag* came at the least opportune moment, and Jellicoe need no longer lose sleep when one or two of his dreadnoughts were away for refit or repair, were having their guns relined, their bottoms scraped or their boiler tubes replaced. He now envisaged for the *Queen Elizabeths* almost a free-lance role at one extremity (preferably the head) of the battle-line, in which they could use their speed on an *ad hoc* basis to 'turn the enemy line'.

This was a departure from the C-in-C's normally inflexible battle-line doctrine.[80] In the early years of the century a similar role had been ear-marked for the armoured-cruisers soon made obsolete by the 'dread-nought' developments, and there was a more venerable historical precedent of which Jellicoe was probably unaware (having little interest in history): the 1778 Instructions laid down that "upon meeting an enemy of inferior force, ships over and above the number of them are to quit the line and rake the enemy's van and rear."[81] It came very close to the fleet-action role Beatty had defined for his battlecruisers after taking command of *Lion* in 1913: "to form a fast division of the Battle

Fleet in a general action".[82] The Grand Fleet would thus have, in effect, two fast divisions in a fleet action.

It was with this object in mind that the *Queen Elizabeths* were formed into their own exclusive battle-squadron, named the 5th after a pre-dreadnought squadron of that title was disbanded; and Rear-Admiral Hugh Evan-Thomas hoisted his flag in *Barham*, fresh from her work-up period, in Liverpool on October the 1st, 1915.

3

The Fifth Battle Squadron

"We regarded ourselves as the goods."

"Evan-Thomas has left to go and hoist his flag in *Barham*," Sir Stanley Colville, the admiral in command of the Orkneys, told King George V. "By Jove What a splendid command he has got, wish I were him."[1]

It was indeed a spectacular appointment for so junior a flag-officer, and might well have gone to a vice-admiral. Whether in Hugh Evan-Thomas the 5th BS had the officer most able to carry the torch of Howe and Kempenfelt is a moot point. The amiable and mild-mannered son of a Welsh landowner, he was descended on his mother's side from the Richard Pearson who is remembered by the Americans for surrendering HMS *Serapis* to John Paul Jones after a bloody fight at Flamborough Head in 1779, and who was honoured by George III for keeping Jones's squadron busy while the convoy he was escorting dispersed safely. His paternal forebears had owned Llwynmadoc, near Beulah in Brecknockshire (now part of Powys), for some two hundred years, and his family had more recently acquired, through marriage and death respectively, Gnoll, near Neath in Glamorgan, and Pencerrig, near Builth Wells. All three were comfortable estates, but their ownership may not have been accompanied by commensurate capital, and the Thomases were a big family – Hugh was one of seven or eight (no one seems to be sure now). Notwithstanding the custom for the captaincy of Dartmouth, which he held from 1910 to 1912, to go to an officer with private means, his nephew's remark that he "was almost entirely dependent on his naval pay" may be taken as more or less true.

His background therefore, privileged though it was, fell far short of qualifying him for membership of that select naval aristocracy which could take good appointments more or less for granted; and in other respects he does not seem an obvious first in a short-list of possible candidates: his undoubted efficiency, integrity and seamanship alone being insufficient to lift him head and shoulders above half a dozen contemporaries and seniors among whom such qualities were routine. From his previous job as second-in-command of the 1st Battle Squadron, leading that squadron's second division of 12-inch gunned dreadnoughts, the post of Senior Officer (SO) 5BS could fairly be described as two steps up the ladder.

Rear-Admiral Evan-Thomas's career had been distinguished but not exceptional, and had been interrupted with about equal frequency by royal service and poor health. A succession of unlikely events, starting when he was a cadet in HMS *Britannia*, had brought him a lifelong association with the future King George V. By the age of 30 he had found his *métier* in signals, and he carried out the duties of flag-lieutenant in the Mediterranean Fleet for three and a half years with such competence that he was subsequently appointed to serve on a committee to revise the *Signal Book*, and went on to command the Signal School in Portsmouth. By the time he had reached captain's rank, therefore, he was one of the Royal Navy's high priests of signalling, with all the punctilious, pedantic regard for procedures endemic in that abstruse craft.

His nephew, Vice-Admiral Sir Geoffrey Barnard, remembered him as

> the most lovable, fine, straightforward and utterly honest character I have ever met . . . He was universally liked and admired by the officers and men of every ship or squadron he commanded. He was adored by his nephews and nieces, because of his sense of humour and fun, and his interest in the simple things of country life like flowers, bird-watching, fishing etc.[2]

His wartime letters to his wife Hilda were (as is so often the case) burned by her after his death, but other letters to his family[3] – to his niece: "My dear little person . . . Here ends my twaddle, Your affectionate old Uncle" – bear out Admiral Barnard's testimony and stand in contrast to Beatty's posturing and manipulations, in letters to wife or mistress, half aimed at the London dinner-party circuit and punctuated with craven appeals for admiration. The comparison is not entirely apt. Possibly the letters which Lady Evan-Thomas destroyed were diatribes of discontent; but it is unlikely, and those that survive betray not a hint of complaint, in spite of all the vicissitudes of war, not a breath of exasperation towards higher authority. Devious or selfish thoughts found no place in Hugh Evan-Thomas's life; he was a stolidly decent chap whose professional and personal relationships were uncomplicated.

When a Fortnum & Mason hamper turned up early in 1916, his inability to thank his benefactor, because he didn't know who had sent it, clouded his private correspondence over a period of weeks.

By most historians he has been praised faintly. Professor Marder recycles Barnard's description of him as "a lovable, straightforward, unassuming man", and adds vaguely that his "professional attainments were highly regarded".[4] Temple Patterson names him as a member of a group of Jellicoe's subordinates who "do not seem to have been men of outstanding initiative [and] had perhaps been over-schooled in the tradition of 'orders are orders' and 'theirs not to reason why'".[5] Roskill describes him as "not a particularly imaginative leader".[6] It should be said in fairness to Evan-Thomas that the lessons of the First World War brought a change in the criteria by which senior naval officers were measured, and that this change in the rules of the game (explored later on in this book) has disfavoured the historical reputations of some of those who were flag-officers in 1914. But the consensus among commentators is marked.

A contemporary "summed [him] up very well as 'a painstaking, loyal, able officer, a careful if rather slow mind and no great imagination'".[7] A midshipman in that first commission of *Barham*'s remembered him as "an affable old buffer" (he was 53; the midshipman was reminiscing at 91), but hastily added that the gunroom was deeply loyal to him and "admired him very much".[8] With the sublime gulf in rank and the avuncular invitations to breakfast, a 'snotty's' impression of his admiral is likely to fall within a limited band of comment, but a different form of words would have been produced to describe Fisher, Beatty, Tyrwhitt, Cunningham or Vian.

Why then, Hugh Evan-Thomas? The appointment was evidently within the Commander-in-Chief's patronage,[9] and a partial explanation may be found in the fact that Jellicoe and Evan-Thomas had been "associated" (in the former's words) "from our earliest days in the Navy".[10] This may be taken to mean from 1883, when they were on coincidental courses at Greenwich and played football together; and a photograph exists, from around that time, of the two of them seated boatered and blazered in the sternsheets of a pulling boat at Henley.[11] Ten years later, Evan-Thomas was flag-lieutenant to the C-in-C Mediterranean, when Jellicoe was flag-commander, in a commission which (as will be seen later) was of crucial importance, not just to the key personnel in that 'flag' team, but also to the battle-training of the Royal Navy. Jellicoe was a man who collected lifelong devotees throughout his naval career – "to serve under him, to live with him and to feel his confidence was a delight," wrote one[12] – and Marder echoes Geoffrey Barnard's remark that the rear-admiral "was a great personal friend and admirer of Jellicoe, with whom he had much in common".[13]

In a service so closely knit and interbred, and whose ships had been routinely manned by a system of nepotism and personal following until almost within (then) living memory, it is possible to detect favouritism of one form or another virtually anywhere and make something of it, if one wishes. Suffice it to say that Jellicoe surrounded himself with his own retainers (who included his brother-in-law and various former shipmates), to the extent that in some cases his

> kindness of heart and loyalty to old friends tended to blind him to [their] limitations – Burney [Sir Cecil, VA1BS and second-in-command Grand Fleet], for example – or to stand by them even when he was aware of their deficiencies, as in the case of Warrender [Sir George, VA2BS until December 1915].[14]

Constitutionally, senior appointments were the prerogative of the First Lord of the Admiralty, but Jellicoe's power of patronage in respect of Evan-Thomas was probably favoured by two changes of wind early in 1915. The perceived failure of Rear-Admiral Archibald Moore, the Admiralty-choice as commander of the 2nd BCS, at the Battle of Dogger Bank in January, helped to discredit the Admiralty's habit of foisting its own junior flag-officer nominees on the senior commanders at sea: by late May, at any rate, Beatty was definitely free to make his own choice (Horace Hood) for rear-admiral of the 3rd BCS.[15] And the stormy departure from the Admiralty of the dynamic and autocratic duo, Churchill and Fisher, after the Dardanelles fiasco, must have assisted the seawards devolution of powers of appointment.

Evan-Thomas was not the only beneficiary of Jellicoe's patronage in the new battle-squadron, for the command of *Warspite* went to Edward Phillpotts, who had been Jellicoe's naval assistant when JJ was Second Sea Lord (1912–14) and would follow him back to the Admiralty in the same capacity when he became First Sea Lord at the end of 1916. (And it may be mentioned that, coincidentally or not, Hugh's nephew, Charles Evan-Thomas, was serving as a midshipman in Jellicoe's flagship, *Iron Duke*.[16])

In the new SO5BS, the C-in-C therefore had a conventionally sound disciple of cast-iron loyalty. Had those been the sole criteria, the appointment would have been unremarkable. But if the *Queen Elizabeths* were to be the Grand Fleet's trump card, to turn the tide of battle with licence and daring at the decisive moment, perhaps a more driven man, less of a *gentle*-man, would have been appropriate: not necessarily an outright firebrand but an officer of independent outlook, alert for the moment when, in Nelson's famous phrase before Trafalgar, "something must be left to chance".

There were at least two vice-admirals who might well have been given the 5th Battle Squadron: Sir Doveton Sturdee and Sir Lewis Bayly, both of whom had had experience of battlecruisers which could have been helpful if the battleships were ever to operate with the BCF.

Sturdee, irascible commander of the 4th BS, was a serious student of naval history and was notorious for straining at the leash of battle-line doctrine. He has been called "a pompous man who would never listen to anyone else's opinion",[17] but he had a proven record as the decisive-but-careful victor of the Falklands battle (he was rare among winners of battles in having excelled in junior officer examinations[18]), and was surely one of the few Grand Fleet admirals eager to recognize tactical openings and able to make use of them. However, with his vaunted expertise, he was a thorn in the Commander-in-Chief's side to the point where, according to one historian, the two men "detested each other".[19] 'Detest' seems a bit strong for Jellicoe, but he certainly felt threatened by Sturdee's independence of mind and feared his subversive influence on other senior officers.

Bayly was a "hard tough independent man [with] a reputation for being a great tactician",[20] who had commanded the battlecruisers before Beatty. He had temporarily "lost Their Lordships' confidence" when a pre-dreadnought under his command was torpedoed in the Channel on New Year's Day 1915, but Jellicoe knew him to be a "really useful officer" of high potential and "unbounded energy".[21] In 1917–18 Bayly was to play a famous and crucial role in the defeat of the U-boat, in command of Anglo-American forces as C-in-C Western Approaches.

It is not known if either Sturdee or Bayly was short-listed for the 5th BS, but at about the time Evan-Thomas was chosen, Jellicoe described Bayly as "occasionally a little mad" and Sturdee "full of fads".[22] And when the idea of replacing Vice-Admiral Burney as second in overall command came up (as it did from time to time) a few weeks before Jutland, he disqualified them separately but on strikingly similar grounds:

> I don't think Bayly would do. He proposes such impossible things that I doubt his judgement now . . . In regard to Sturdee, I should never feel safe with him in command of the most important squadron and leading the van. I am sorry to say that I do not trust his judgement in tactical questions. *I feel very strongly about this.*[23]

Beatty was at least partly justified in his malicious remark, a year after Jutland, that "Jellicoe is absolutely incapable of selecting good men because he dislikes men of character who have independent views of their own."[24] And from the tactical schizophrenia of Grand Fleet Battle Orders it is apparent that Jellicoe was as much concerned with the need for caution on the part of the Senior Officer, 'Fast Squadron', lest he get cut off from the main body of the Battle Fleet, as with his readiness to make impromptu use of his speed margin. "In all cases", a keynote paragraph in GFBOs warned,

> the ruling principle is that the fleet as a whole keeps together; attempted attacks by a division or a squadron on a portion of the enemy's line being avoided as liable to lead to the isolation of the ships which attempt the movement.

In a sense, therefore, the Commander-in-Chief could not really decide whether the 5th BS's high speed was a net asset or a potential liability, and it is reasonable to suggest that this ambivalence was reflected in his choice for its flag-officer. Indeed, more than a year after Jutland, Captain Herbert Richmond, an intellectual and radical among senior officers, probed Evan-Thomas's attitude to independent squadronal action and found he viewed the subject "with alarm" and considered "that any separation is dangerous". Partly, this was acknowledging a real state of affairs: that due to the lack of tactical doctrine and training, (in Richmond's words) "we can't trust divisional leaders to handle their divisions and not get lost";[25] but there is a chicken-and-egg issue here, and it is sobering to reflect that when Evan-Thomas expressed these views he had commanded the Battle Fleet's fast division for nearly two years.

Both the vice-admirals discussed above were positive, self-assured and dynamic: qualities which Jellicoe never learnt to harness in his juniors, still less enjoy. They were liable, in his mind, to act as loose cannon on the Battle Fleet's neat and orderly deck. There was not the slightest suspicion of unorthodoxy about Hugh Evan-Thomas. That, as much as anything, was the factor which commended him.

It may be added that Beatty would hardly have welcomed the appointment of either Sturdee or Bayly to the 5th Battle Squadron, for quite apart from VABCF's jealousy of the former's famous battlecruiser victory, both were confirmed vice-admirals and thus senior to him. Whilst this circumstance might have offered Jellicoe the chance of a shrewd piece of pre-emptive management, such machinations were alien to him.

*

Barham slipped from the Cunard Buoy in the Mersey as soon as Evan-Thomas was on board, on the 1st of October 1915, and headed north to take *Queen Elizabeth*, home from the Aegean, and *Warspite* under her wing. But when her anchor splashed into the chilly waters of Scapa Flow the following afternoon the ripples were felt in the Firth of Forth. David Beatty, proprietorial hopes raised over the winter of 1914–15 and then dashed, still coveted the *Queen Elizabeths* and would do so until he hoisted his admiral's flag over the name-ship of the class in January 1917. And even while the new squadron knuckled down to the relentless Scapa routine of gunnery practice between PZs (fleet manoeuvres) and futile "dithers round the Dogger" in search of Germans, events began combining with VABCF to extract it from Jellicoe's orbit.

Three separate issues came to bear on the deployment of the 5th BS:
• the growing strength of Hipper's 1st Scouting Group as against the BCF;
• the gunnery inefficiency of the BCF;
• pressure to redistribute the Grand Fleet to prevent German coastal raids.

In February 1916, when Evan-Thomas had done much to bring forward the fighting efficiency of the three ships currently under his command, Jellicoe was subjected to an obviously coordinated volley of petitions from BCF flag-officers.

First, Rear-Admiral Brock of the 1st BCS submitted a paper on February the 18th, the day *Malaya* joined her sisters in Scapa, about the alleged relative strength of Rear-Admiral Franz Hipper's battlecruiser force – pending completion of the 15-inch gunned *Renown* and *Repulse* (the 'hush-hush ships') – and the unlikelihood that it would stray far from the support of the High Seas Fleet, after its narrow escape in the pursuit action of Dogger Bank:

> The BCF will have to be extremely careful not to be drawn on top of the enemy's battle-fleet, and must be prepared to withdraw at any moment unless our battle-fleet is near. [He suggested the substitution] of two *Queen Elizabeths* for the three *Invincibles*. [The former] are better protected, more heavily armed and the difference in speed is not great.

This would involve breaking up the 5th BS, but Brock argued that with his remaining three *QEs* and the three *Invincibles*, Jellicoe could have a fast squadron at each end of his battle-line.[26] The next day Rear-Admiral Pakenham (2nd BCS) submitted a similar paper on the 'Reinforcement of Battle Cruiser Fleet', with the difference that he claimed one more *QE* than Brock:

> As the prime need of the Battle Cruiser Fleet is an addition of fighting strength, it is deemed that at least three of the *Queen Elizabeths* should be at once transferred from the main fleet to the Battle Cruiser Fleet, and that the others should follow when the *Royal Sovereigns* have come into service.[27]

On the 21st, Beatty wrote to Jellicoe endorsing his juniors' opinions, except that he claimed all five. "I respectfully suggest that the Fifth Battle Squadron should be based on Rosyth . . . giving us a definite superiority over anything less than the High Seas Fleet."[28]

Jellicoe disagreed. Beatty, he replied on the 24th, was labouring under

> a misapprehension of the speed of the Fifth Battle Squadron. The ships composing this squadron have not carried out any measured mile trials, but I have formed the opinion that their maximum speed does not greatly exceed $23\frac{1}{2}$ knots. It is certainly less than 24 knots . . . Under these conditions I am very doubtful whether the Fifth Battle Squadron would, as suggested by you, afford any material support to the battlecruisers in an offensive operation.

He then asserted – overlooking the fact that Hipper would be as much constrained as Beatty by the speed of his slowest ships – that with the new *Lützow* and *Hindenburg* the high speed of the 1st Scouting Group would prevent the BCF from bringing it to action and "the Fifth Battle Squadron would be of no assistance".[29]

Beatty was undeterred. Even if the *QEs* could only do $23\frac{1}{2}$ knots, he wrote on March 3rd (the day *Valiant* completed the squadron), "their value would be enormous". And he suggested that if their fuel was reduced by 1,000 tons, their lesser draught would "enable them to acquire the speed for which they were designed, i.e. 25 knots – equal to the 3rd Battle Cruiser Squadron [the *Invincibles*]". He then presented an argument which has direct bearing on the opening moves of the battle-cruiser phase of Jutland: the 5th BS

> would in all cases be able to keep with us until the moment when we sight the enemy. If we are then East of the enemy [blocking their retreat], the 5th Battle Squadron would be invaluable. Taking the worst case, we may be West of them and may have a long chase at full speed. After chasing for three hours, i.e. a distance of at least 75 miles, the 5th Battle Squadron with their $23\frac{1}{2}$ knots would then be at most $4\frac{1}{2}$ miles astern of the 3rd Battle Cruiser Squadron. I can imagine no better or more valuable support.

The flaw in this 'worst case' reasoning is that it would only be valid if the 5th BS was in close company with the BCF at the moment of sighting, or at least stationed on a bearing at right angles to the subsequent line of advance. The significance of this will become clear in Chapter 6. Suffice it to say here that Beatty was not describing the worst case at all, although it would lie in his power on *Der Tag* to ensure that he was. Another feature of this letter was that the idea of swapping the *QEs* for the 3rd BCS had quietly disappeared: Beatty wanted them all. He ended by hoping Jellicoe would "favourably consider the strategic rearrangement I have submitted to you", and adding that he had "ventured" to send the Admiralty a duplicate of his letter.[30]

Jellicoe was furious. He sharply reprimanded his subordinate (who "abjectly apologized"[31]) for sending copies of their private correspondence over his head to Whitehall,[32] and hurriedly wrote to the First Sea Lord, Sir Henry Jackson, countering the vice-admiral's arguments. Beatty, he said,

> has returned to the charge about the Fifth Battle Squadron but I am sure it would be wrong to send them to him. It would for one thing lead to his getting far afield from me, which is wrong, and in thick weather might be almost disastrous.[33]

His rebuttal to the Admiralty, on March the 10th, was more thorough:

> It is necessary to consider the conditions under which the Battle Cruiser Fleet and First Scouting Group may meet again.
>
> These conditions appear to be those of a raid on our patrols, a bombardment of our coastal towns, or a trap designed to draw the Battle Cruiser Fleet into a position in which it could be intercepted by the German Battlefleet.
>
> For the first two the Fifth Battle Squadron would arrive too late to take part in the engagement, whilst under the last condition the Fifth Battle Squadron would not save the Battle Cruiser Fleet, but would hamper [it] by its lack of speed.
>
> If the High Seas Fleet is in support [of the 1st SG], it would be wrong for our Battle Cruiser Fleet to become seriously engaged either with or without the support of the Fifth Battle Squadron. The Vice-Admiral must keep in touch, but fall back on the main [British] Battlefleet.
>
> The whole truth of the matter seems to me to be that the Fifth Battle Squadron has not the speed necessary to work with the Battle Cruiser Fleet, and the omission of 1,000 tons of oil would, I imagine, certainly not raise the speed by even half a knot.[34]

In this the C-in-C was avoiding the question of whether the BCF could still be expected to defeat the enhanced 1st SG if they were met beyond the support of the German battle-fleet. But, aside from this, his arguments are sound and he was surely right, and Beatty wrong, in the matter of the pay-off between oil fuel and speed: a reduction of fuel by 1,000 tons would have lessened the 32-foot draught of the *QEs* by only ten inches, and would have made no discernible difference to their speed.

Henry Jackson was a man of impassive features who rarely said anything that was not absolutely necessary.[35] His paperwork, however, was "admirable",[36] and by letter of the 7th (presumably in response to an anxious telephone call from *Iron Duke*) he assured Jellicoe that "I see what you mean about the Fifth Battle Squadron and Beatty, and probably you are right."[37] But fears were growing in Whitehall of a recommencement of raids on the East Coast by German battlecruisers under the regime of their new C-in-C, Vice-Admiral Reinhard Scheer, and Jellicoe was urged to bring the whole battle-fleet down to Rosyth.[38] This he resisted, on grounds of practicalities.

For a start, only the battlecruisers could hope to intercept their opposites, and they were in the Forth already. Secondly, there was insufficient room upstream of the Forth Bridge for the Grand Fleet, and a large enough area to seaward of the narrows had yet to be made safe from submarine attack (such was the U-boat phobia that a periscope had even been reported west of the bridge). Thirdly, the efficiency of the Grand Fleet demanded the safe playground of Scapa Flow. Fourthly (he argued), the time taken by a huge fleet to navigate the long meandering exit from the Forth would diminish Rosyth's apparent geographical advantages over Scapa. And finally, there was still the fog. (Beatty himself described "the horrid Forth" as "a great ditch full of thick fog which makes everything so cold . . . there is no joy in life under these conditions".[39])

Underlying these contentions was a nagging concern about the BCF's gunnery. The Forth had few of the facilities for practice available in Scapa and the BCF's shooting could hardly be of a high standard. This, indeed, was one of Jellicoe's more powerful answers to those who wanted the Grand Fleet based on Rosyth. It was not merely idle Battle Fleet gossip that deprecated the battlecruisers' marksmanship: the Grand Fleet's senior officers were seriously worried and even Beatty acknowledged the problem – at least *before* Jutland.[40] The lack of U-boat-secure gunnery ranges was the fault of nobody in the BCF, deriving from the immutable facts of geography and the impracticability of stretching boom defences across the outer Forth estuary. But Beatty and his flag-captain, Ernle Chatfield (who had begun making excuses as early as the Heligoland Bight post-mortem), were extremely touchy in the years after Jutland about the battlecruisers' gunnery,[41] and made much, instead, of the deficiencies of British armour-piercing shells. They were right, inasmuch as there were design deficiencies compounded by proof-testing loopholes of almost criminal scale, but this was partly a diversion; the best shells in the world are of little use if they miss. And even a group of junior officers from the BCF's light-cruisers, putting the world to rights in *Southampton*'s wardroom one night in March 1916, "collectively and separately came to the conclusion that the Battle Cruisers' shooting was rotten".[42]

In the meantime, denied access to full-calibre firings, the BCF's gunnery mandarins – Chatfield himself, former commander of HMS

Excellent (the RN's gunnery school), and Commander Sidney Bailey, the fleet gunnery-officer – sought to compensate by drilling the battlecruisers for maximum rate-of-fire, through the medium of ammunition-handling practices and competitive turret drills. Indeed rate-of-fire seems to have become something of a panacea to Chatfield, and this extract from a letter of his after the Dogger Bank battle would have caused Jellicoe serious misgivings had he been privy to it: "Whoever gets the biggest volume of fire, short or hitting, will gain the ascendancy and keep it as the other fellow can't see to reply."[43] (One is reminded of the saying that 'fanaticism' consists of redoubling your efforts when you have forgotten your aim!)

There were consequences to this resort-through-default to high rates-of-fire in the battlecruisers. Every impediment to the movement of cordite between magazines and guns which could be unshipped or clipped back out of the way, was so treated. Ironically, *Lion's* chief gunner, Warrant-Officer Alexander Grant, braved Chatfield's displeasure by refusing to condone these loose practices,[44] and *Lion* had had certain safety modifications made while she was repairing after her near-loss at Dogger Bank, but in other battlecruisers the result was a directness of access to magazines which "would have been viewed with terror by an eighteenth-century sailor".[45] On top of this, over-eager ammunition-handlers stacked 'ready-use' charges in magazine passages and in exposed positions behind the secondary guns. The extent to which slack flash-proof discipline alone was responsible for the battlecruiser losses at Jutland has been debated ever since: other factors were the easy penetration of gun-turret armour, the volatility of the cordite charges, and the exposed condition of their ignitors;[46] but it was certainly one ingredient in a deadly cocktail of defects.

The only proper corrective to the gunnery inefficiency of the BCF – at least as far as marksmanship was concerned – was to send its squadrons one at a time to the Orkneys for periods of intensive training. But thus seriously reduced, the BCF could only be sure of besting the German 1st Scouting Group if reinforced. And, as Beatty believed,[47] the obvious force to do that was the 5th BS, although Jellicoe briefly toyed with the unlikely idea of palming him off with a miscellany of older, slower dreadnoughts.[48]

This, then, was the state of play when two dramatic events at the end of April 1916 greatly weakened Sir John's grip on the disputed squadron.

First, on the 22nd, the battlecruisers *Australia* and *New Zealand* illustrated his worry about fog by colliding in it, on a sweep towards the Danish coast. Zigzagging by flag signal, in line abreast at 19 knots, the

BCF entered a sudden fog-bank which made the flagship invisible. What should the individual ships do? *Australia* zagged by the clock while *New Zealand* held her course. The enquiry found BCF Signal Orders to be ambiguous, and Beatty himself shouldered the blame[49] – an object lesson, perhaps, that relying on initiative can be dangerous. *New Zealand* could be fixed at Rosyth in a few days, and thus became the first ship to enter the new No. 2 Dock (curiously, in March the pre-dreadnought *Zealandia*, originally named *New Zealand*, had been the first to enter No. 1 Dock).[50] But *Australia* had to go down to Devonport for repairs and would be absent for several weeks, diminishing Beatty's margin of strength over Franz Hipper.

Then, on the 25th, Hipper's battlecruisers bombarded the East Anglian towns of Lowestoft and Great Yarmouth. Two hundred houses were demolished. The Grand Fleet's lunge southwards to cut the enemy off from his home base was hopelessly late, and press and Parliament demanded to know where the Navy had been. One of the objects of the raid had been to force "dispersion on the British Fleet in response to clamour from East Coast towns";[51] and as early as December 1914, after the shelling of Scarborough, Jellicoe had fulminated that "it would be the faultiest possible strategy to base our fleet with the idea of preventing a bombardment."[52] But sure enough Balfour, First Lord of the Admiralty, promised the mayor of Lowestoft a fleet redisposition which would prevent or deter another such outrage.

These matters were worked through at a meeting at Rosyth on May the 12th between the First Sea Lord (Jackson), Jellicoe and Beatty. Here it was proposed to develop the Firth of Forth into an alternative base for the Grand Fleet, in spite of its detailed disadvantages. In the meantime, a start must be made in rectifying the BCF's gunnery and it was agreed that the 3rd BCS (*Invincible*, *Indomitable* and *Inflexible* under Rear-Admiral Hood) would shortly be sent to Scapa for ten days' main-armament target practice. In Hood's absence, and with *Australia* out of action, the BCF would be four ships short at a time when Hipper's force was thought to have been augmented by the new *Hindenburg* as well as the *Lützow*, both of which were credited with 15-inch guns (the former with 17-inch, by Jacky Fisher[53]). So Jellicoe reluctantly agreed that when Hood brought his three prototype battlecruisers north to Scapa, Evan-Thomas would take his five fast battleships south to Rosyth, *Queen Elizabeth* would go into dock for a refit and the other four would temporarily reinforce the BCF. On Friday the 2nd of June a Grand Fleet concentration would take place off the Skagerrak (the strait between Denmark and Norway), while light-cruisers penetrated the Kattegat (between Denmark and Sweden) in the hope of drawing out the

German fleet. At the rendezvous of the BCF with the BF, Hood's squadron and Evan-Thomas's would exchange places once more.

Jellicoe had had misgivings about the battlecruisers' being given the title 'Battle Cruiser Fleet' when the three squadrons were brought together under Beatty's command early in 1915. It had been the then First Sea Lord's idea, not his.[54] Battlecruisers were Jacky Fisher's brain-children; Heligoland Bight and the Falklands (both examples of their correct usage) had dramatically vindicated their concept and he was blind to their limitations. The contrast between 'Battle Cruiser Fleet' and Hipper's less grandiloquent 'First Scouting Group' is obvious, the German term accurately reflecting the battlecruisers' function in rela-tion to the battle-fleet. The danger was that the 'fleet' handle would encourage Beatty to regard his command as an independent and élite alternative to the Grand Fleet rather than an integral, if specialized, part of it. And if he were too headstrong, he might give the High Seas Fleet its dreamed-of opportunity to corner and destroy a significant portion of the Grand Fleet and thus diminish Jellicoe's overall numer-ical advantage.

Even Beatty's own junior flag-officers were allegedly "terrified lest David's Fleet should catch the German Fleet and that Jellicoe should not come up in time".[55] Now, the addition of the 5th BS would augment the BCF's military status to well above that of Beatty's normal full quiver of battlecruisers, and the C-in-C's fears that he might try to win the war on his own redoubled: "The stronger I make Beatty, the greater is the temptation for him to get involved in an independent action."[56] Jellicoe was not alone. Horace Hood, when he heard that the powerful 5th BS was to act as locum tenens while his own squadron was away, was also uneasy: "This is a great mistake. If David Beatty has these ships with him, nothing will stop him from taking on the whole German fleet if he gets the chance."[57] They were doing him an injustice (although not by much), for events both at Jutland and after he became C-in-C were to show that Beatty was a more artful, less quixotic tactician than his Jack-the-lad persona led associates to believe. But if the image he projected was part caricature of the real man, the fault was his own.

*

The five battleships of the 5th BS duly left Scapa Flow on the afternoon of Sunday the 21st of May for foggy overnight passage to the Forth. The last several days had not been eventful. Sir Roger Casement had been charged with high treason, but the Easter troubles in Ireland were already fading from the headlines. In Berlin the Kaiser's Foreign Secretary informed the man from the *Chicago Daily News* that Germany had given up waging submarine war against commerce. In Paris two diplomats, Sir Mark Sykes and M. Georges Picot, signed a secret agreement to divide the Middle East into British and French spheres of influence after the war. On the Western Front, compared with the remnants of the 'Old Contemptibles' in Flanders to the north, or the French army haemorrhaging in front of Verdun to the south, Kitchener's volunteer divisions gathering in the quiet valley of the Somme seemed to have been bypassed by the war. There was even some faint pie-in-the-sky talk of the prospects of peace.

However, as a perceptive junior officer feared, the British people had "not yet shouldered the weight of the war, they have only been having the harness put on as yet, if only they knew it";[58] and even now the gears of state control were crunching their way uncertainly towards total mobilization. The bill for universal conscription was about to receive royal assent; and on the night before the squadron's departure from Scapa, clocks were put forward by one hour, to reduce the lighting costs of war-production shiftwork. The civilian world made the switch to British Summer Time smoothly enough, apart from the odd hitch over morning service in remote country parishes, but the Grand Fleet would still be at sixes and sevens ten days later: telegrams and signals remained on Greenwich Mean Time, as did warships in Scapa Flow (but not the Orkney population); elsewhere ships were supposed to observe BST in harbour and revert to GMT at sea – or was it the other way round?[59] And whose damn fool idea was it anyway? No doubt many hours were whiled away in wardrooms and messdecks in Scapa arguing the pros and cons of light-saving-time, but the *Queen Elizabeths* had better things to talk about. They were going south.

Nobody had told them how long for, but "the move was a very welcome one as it [would enable] us to go ashore in civilized surroundings",[60] and a vista of possibilities opened up. Admiral Dick remembered the mixed feelings in *Barham* at the move:

> We were longing to get down to Rosyth, both professionally and socially. We were always very envious of the battlecruisers based on Rosyth, where you could get ashore and go to the movies. When the ships were in harbour you could have some sort of social life, none of that up in Scapa Flow, and we were delighted when we went down. But I think we would always have been Jellicoe men. Evan-Thomas himself was very much a Jellicoe man. Our loyalties were to Jellicoe rather than to Beatty [who was] a show-off, a showman, though undoubtedly a good fighting man.

Of all the Battle Fleet, the men of the 5th BS were the least disposed to be impressed by the battlecruisers' public image.

They were the show-offs, had all the glamour – not very deserved glamour. We were rather jealous . . . You have to remember that their reputation for gunnery was very very shaky indeed.

We regarded ourselves as being the goods. We were *very* proud of the 5th BS which we regarded as undoubtedly the finest of the lot, rightly or wrongly – I think rightly. I would say undoubtedly there was a feeling of jealousy between the 5th BS and the Battlecruiser Fleet. We always felt that we were the real cavalry.[61]

An off-watch sub-lieutenant in *Warspite* graphically recalled being woken at first light on Monday the 22nd and sent forward to 'the eyes of the ship' to watch the fog-buoy trailing astern of the flagship while ghostly shadows loomed and receded in the white-out and banshee sirens wailed.[62] At 11.30 a.m. the five *Queen Elizabeths* passed under the Forth Bridge, the imposing gateway to the *Lion*'s lair. They were the largest ships to have done so and the event was memorable in itself:

We actually cleared the bridge by some 12 feet at midspan; but on approaching, it appeared, right up to the last moment, that we must inevitably hit it. Hardened seafarers on the upper deck could be seen starting to turn up their collars or even disappear under cover to dodge the falling topmast! Then at the last moment the mast seemed to oblige by dipping clear. This phenomenon never ceased to fascinate.[63]

Once through the bridge, *Barham* led her squadron in stately procession past the battlecruisers, with her ship's company fallen in and a Royal Marine band playing (which "galled them not a little"[64]), and anchored further upstream. That afternoon Hood's 3rd BCS slipped and proceeded north to Scapa, while '*Big Lizzie*' placed herself in the charge of tugs and was chivvied into Rosyth dockyard. The next day the 5th BS flagship shifted to *Invincible*'s buoy among the Splendid Cats.

4

The Grass Was Never Greener

"The ship was buzzing with rumours that the Huns were out."

It was not the first time the battlecruiser heroes had seen a *QE* at close quarters, for *Warspite* had visited the Forth in September 1915 (and run aground while being led in via the small-ship channel, in fog, by BCF destroyers). But off-duty men from both groups probably whiled away the unaccustomed long evenings by taking away whalers and pulling boats to inspect their new neighbours,[1] exchange banter with men idling on deck and perhaps (if the 'crushers' were not looking) be the targets of cordially lobbed potatoes.

Most of *Queen Elizabeth*'s men went home on leave, leaving a maintenance crew on board. The ratings of the rest of the 5th BS settled into the battlecruisers' recreational routine, making use of the football pitches and the large canteen in Rosyth. "We were issued with one or two beer tickets [each for half a pint[2]] so we didn't get drunk on that."[3] To the battleships' officers, after Scapa, Rosyth seemed like the Garden of Eden, with the chance to renew acquaintance with officer-like outdoor pursuits and with easy access to a well-appointed major city. Some were content merely to ramble in the rich spring foliage of Hopetoun and Dalmeny woods.

> It was lovely! Of course we haven't seen a tree for practically five months [but] never have I known the budding leaves and the grass look so green . . . The great question is how long are we going to stay here? Nobody seems to know.[4]

Other remissioned exiles found their way to North Queensferry or Turnhouse golf-courses, the Limekilns Hotel near Rosyth, the Drumsheugh Public Baths ("By Jove! They're simply topping"), Ferguson & Forrester's restaurant in Princes Street, and a variety of

Edinburgh theatres and picture-houses. The big attraction in town was Mary Pickford, starring in *Madame Butterfly* at the Palladium. The less refined may have opted for the double-bill of *The Devil's Bondman* and *The Woman Who Dared* at the West End Cinema; but *The Floating Mine* at the Tollcross, and *The Second in Command* at the Haymarket, were probably shunned – likewise the band of the Grenadier Guards at the Usher Hall.

Even on early-closing day, Edinburgh seemed attractive to Sub-Lieutenant Ashworth, as his diary entry for Tuesday the 23rd records:

> Did spotting table as GCT [gunnery control-tower] ratekeeper this morning & made a frightful balls. Gardener & I got ashore by 1.15 boat and got up to E. about 3.0 . . . All shops were closed, so we just strolled around a bit and then had tea.

The next day *Warspite*'s padre took him fishing on the trout loch at Dundas Castle, by permission of Mr (later Sir John) Stewart-Clark. They did some damage with a March Brown and a Teal & Red, and were then given tea "by the butler, in the 3rd reception room (I should think, judging by the size of the place)". By the time they returned to *Warspite* they had a new shipmate: Midshipman Richard Fairthorne, transferred from the old armoured-cruiser *Leviathan*. Seventy-five years later he recalled standing at Hawes Pier with his sea-chest, waiting for the picket-boat. He took in the scene: the famous railway bridge towering massively overhead, the legendary battlecruisers lying in the fairway, and his destination, the most powerful battleships in the world, anchored beyond. He could hardly believe his luck.

Compared with *Leviathan*, or even with the coal-burning dreadnoughts to which other *Leviathan* snotties had been sent, *Warspite* was "a different world! Much more civilized altogether, oh yes!" – and he found a friendly ship awaiting him.[5] Soon Fairthorne, too, was exploring Edinburgh. Sauntering down Princes Street, he was surprised to bump into Captain Marcus Hill, his old CO. They spoke for about a minute before parting, never to meet again. "Some people thought he was mad," he mused without elaboration, in 1991.

For many junior officers there were opportunities, quite impossible in Scapa, for schoolboy-type outings with family or friends. Fairthorne proudly showed his new ship to cousins who had to sit down before they were half-way through. Doting parents took groups out to nearby hotels for high tea, to play tennis and meet each others' sisters. Ashworth's mother brought his bicycle (for which he had been "offered a pew in *Tiger*'s bike-shed") up to Edinburgh by train – which seems to

confirm that no warning had been given about the temporary nature of
the squadron's visit, for the good lady could surely have been spared
this chore.

Among slightly more senior officers, there were many hurriedly
snatched marital reunions and at least one marriage. Rear-Admiral
Hugh Evan-Thomas got his wife up to Edinburgh for a few days, and
Surgeon-Lieutenant Duncan Lorimer RNVR of *Malaya* did likewise.
Lieutenant James Young RNR, also of *Malaya*, managed to arrange
a room for his wife in the Hawes Inn at South Queensferry, and im-
patiently awaited her arrival. *Barham's* gunnery-officer, Lieutenant-
Commander Francis Tower, had a five-day rush to organize his
wedding, which took place in St Giles's, in Edinburgh, on Saturday
the 27th.[6] The battleship hoisted the customary wedding-garland at
the main truck, and sent him off on a few days' local honeymoon
leave.[7]

There were also, needless to say, exchanges of hospitality between
the two groups of capital ships: a rare chance to renew old friendships
and catch up on gossip. On Wednesday the 24th, for example,
Commander Roynon-Jones, *Tiger's* navigator, "dined in *Warspite* with
Hodgson. McLeod there too. Billiards after." The next night it was
Tiger's turn: "Lots of guests, Seymour and Graham-Watson were
mine."[8]

*

Interaction between Beatty and Evan-Thomas appears, by contrast, to
have been non-existent.

Evan-Thomas was by age, temperament and background a root and
branch Jellicoe man and by no stretch of the imagination a potential
member of the Beatty club. His Victorian code of honour – his sense of
what was and wasn't 'the done thing' – itself precluded a hail-fellow
friendship with his fast and flashy (and considerably younger) superior.
Vice-Admiral Sir Geoffrey Barnard later wrote:

> My uncle was a career naval officer of limited means, utterly devoted to his
> wife and with rather strict moral principles about any questions of divorce or
> extra-matrimonial entanglements. It is evident that <u>he could have had
> nothing in common personally with Beatty</u>, with his riches, his wife's yacht
> etc etc., and I am sure that he did not <u>like</u> him personally because of his flair
> for publicity and dress and also because he was 'Winston Churchill's pet'.[9]

But the fact that the two admirals were chalk and cheese should have
been irrelevant. Duty and loyalty were watchwords to Evan-Thomas,
and Beatty must take the blame for the apparent, if scarcely believable,

fact that he neither interviewed him, in those eight days before sailing, nor sent over a copy of BCF Standing Orders (although *Barham* must have been supplied with those administrative memoranda which related to harbour routines, leave, dress, football pitches, shore canteens etc.). Whether this means that RA5BS was discouraged from reporting in person to VABCF on arrival, is unclear (Beatty may have been ashore, at Aberdour House or elsewhere, for much of the time), but it seems there was no meeting worth the name between the two admirals.

If Beatty had run his 'fleet' strictly by the book – that is to say, Jellicoe's book – this omission might not have mattered much. But he did not. He had institutionalized, in the BCF, an approach to action-leadership which was less formal and less signals-dependent, and which expected more of his juniors' awareness and initiative. It was perfectly within his prerogatives to promulgate his own standing orders to define and regulate the specialized role of his command, as a supplement to those governing the Grand Fleet as a whole. But Beatty's BCF *Orders* had the characteristics of *instructions*, the semantic distinction of which held an old, but at the time buried, significance in British naval ethos.[10] Furthermore, his action-doctrine pre-dated both the Grand Fleet and Jellicoe's command-in-chief by sixteen months (having been developed under the more indulgent regime of Sir George Callaghan, the last C-in-C Home Fleets). With the onset of war he was all the more determined that the battlecruisers should continue to be "imbued with the ideas & principles which have governed our training in the past",[11] and thus, for better or for worse, Jellicoe's GFBOs had an uphill task to attain the authority, over this portion of the Grand Fleet, to which seniority entitled them.

Of the transposition of Hood's squadron and Evan-Thomas's, Captain Geoffrey Bennett offers these confusing remarks:

> That this might have repercussions on the Grand Fleet's tactics, if it should be ordered to sea to counter an enemy sortie, was understood by Jellicoe and Beatty. Hood's ships were no substitute for Evan-Thomas's: they could only be used as a spearhead for Jellicoe's cruisers. The British battle-fleet would, therefore, be without the fast van squadron with which the Commander-in-Chief envisaged achieving a concentration of fire on part of the enemy line. On the other hand, if the heavy guns and armour of the 5BS were to be an adjunct to the BCF, Beatty would have to allow for its slightly lower speed. For these reasons neither Admiral issued any instructions for using the temporarily attached squadrons with their own fleets; Beatty intended that, at the first opportunity, Evan-Thomas should rejoin Jellicoe, who he knew would send Hood to the BCF.[12]

Firstly, there was no question of "*if* it should be ordered to sea". The planned sweep towards the Norwegian coast had been in the programme since the transfer of squadrons was first agreed, and, once at sea, it was known that the 5th BS and 3rd BCS would have to occupy their respective temporary billets until the BCF could rendezvous with the Battle Fleet – upon which they would swap places again.

Secondly, the BCF was much more likely to meet the enemy while separated from the Battle Fleet (for that was its job) than the Battle Fleet was to meet the enemy in the absence of the BCF. Only if Jellicoe came upon a High Seas Fleet which Beatty had failed to find first, would the battle-line have to be deployed with Hood still standing in for Evan-Thomas. But if the BCF encountered enemy forces in its more southerly sweep before joining up with Jellicoe, action would necessarily commence while Evan-Thomas was still standing in for Hood.

And thirdly, Beatty had argued strongly for the transfer of the *Queen Elizabeths* on positive operational grounds. Nobody had forced these ships on him. The idea that VABCF, having made all that fuss, really regarded the 5th BS as a net handicap, is too big to be infiltrated in an off-hand manner.

Whatever reasons of circumstance or prejudice lay behind Beatty's neglect of RA5BS, he appears at least to have assumed that the German 1st Scouting Group would not be encountered before Evan-Thomas and Hood had re-exchanged places. Not only does such an assumption make a nonsense of the 5th BS's transference to Rosyth – for if the BCF was not going to meet the enemy while the 3rd BCS was absent, then the battleships might just as well have stayed in Scapa Flow – it was also, of course, a shockingly unprofessional gamble.

In other instances Beatty seems to have been commendably aware of the importance of 'community of thought' between senior officers. Referring to his old friend Commodore Reginald Tyrwhitt of the Harwich destroyer force, in a letter to Jellicoe only a few weeks before Jutland, he said: "I have had many operations with [the] Commodore and have seen him once, for five minutes! Surely this is not wise or practical. One hour's conversation is worth a volume of correspondence."[13] Why this timeless desideratum should not have extended to Hugh Evan-Thomas is unclear.[14] An hour's conversation might have saved a thousand lives.

Many notorious military blunders have been set up by poor personal relationships (if not wilful taciturnity) between key participants, the need for whose informal collaboration seems, in retrospect, to have been blindingly obvious. "It is instructive to mark how the squabbles of historic admirals with their Admiralties and with their captains have played into the hands of the enemy."[15] Furthermore, if he was as well read in naval history as his biographers make out, Beatty must have been aware that the failure of a supporting force adequately to back up the van has been a recurring theme: Beachy Head (1690), Santa Marta (1702), Toulon (1744), and Ushant I (1778), Chesapeake Bay (1781), and no doubt many other disappointing engagements, were object lessons in this respect, and, between them, yielded a dozen courts-martial, two death sentences, and the loss of the American colonies.

In the recriminations which followed Jutland, Beatty was to declare that he and Evan-Thomas could not have been expected to understand each other, as the rear-admiral had never "trained with me at sea", and that only if they had been together "constantly, as I had asked" could they have co-operated properly.[16] In similar vein, both W. S. Chalmers, Beatty's junior navigator and biographer, and Ralph Seymour, his flag-lieutenant, later laboured the *apartness* of the BCF from the rest of the Grand Fleet: the informality, the tactical experiment, the exposition of principles over procedures. Indeed, Seymour (who will be dealt with in due course) makes the 'wide' allegation that "progress in these matters was so marked that the arrival of a new cruiser heralded the certainty of a weak spot in the advanced forces until she had worked for quite two or three months at sea."[17]

In this he was over-egging the 'reform-and-enquiry' pudding (in reality "the real arduous headwork was shirked"[18]). But there is, here, the genesis of an excuse for the neglect of Evan-Thomas before Jutland: that Beatty's methods differed so radically from those of Jellicoe that it would be futile to try to implant them into the skull of a battle-fleet rear-admiral in the ten days before the scheduled Skagerrak sweep. Beatty had omitted to mention any such factor as a reason for not mixing a Battle Fleet squadron with his BCF; and the matter must be placed in perspective: when four US battleships joined the Grand Fleet in December 1917, they had

> to stow [their American] signal flags and books, and learn the British signal language. This they did so well that four days after their arrival they went out and maneuvred successfully with the Grand Fleet.[19]

The adjustment to be made by the 5th Battle Squadron to the BCF's *modus operandi* was trivial by comparison, but for how long Evan-Thomas would have had to swing around a buoy a few hundred yards from *Lion* before Beatty bothered to talk to him, is unknown.

It is difficult not to conclude, from a distance of eighty years, that it was somehow more important to extract the 5th BS from the Battle Fleet (perhaps to set a precedent for future redeployment) than it was to induct it into the BCF front-line.

Nevertheless, "when time permits, a subordinate's duty is to take all such measures as may be possible to enable him to know his chief's mind";[20] and if Evan-Thomas felt that VABCF's indifference might compromise his ability to handle his squadron to his senior's satisfaction, he could perfectly easily have jumped in his barge and banged on Beatty's door. And if Beatty was unavailable he could have gone to chew the fat with Osmond Brock (RA1BCS) in *Princess Royal* or William Pakenham (RA2BCS) in *New Zealand*, or invited them to *Barham*. Brock was in fact an old shipmate of Evan-Thomas's, as were all three light-cruiser senior officers and Captain Henry Pelly of *Tiger*. It is unclear whether the deck-logs of the ships concerned should have recorded the informal comings and goings of senior officers, but there is none mentioned in any of them.

*

On Friday the 26th of May, Major Claude Wallace, a civil engineer and West African explorer by trade but now a staff-officer with the British 32nd Division in the Somme valley, packed his bag and hitched a lift to the railhead. Wallace was a man with a strange mission: he believed his presence to be essential to the sea battle which was about to take place. Night after night in his trench dug-out he had dreamt of a great naval engagement. The dreams remained consistent but grew in detail. Early in May he persuaded his superior, Major-General William Ryecroft, to write to Admiral Jellicoe and ask if he might visit the Fleet.

Jellicoe wired back his consent, but left the timing open. Ryecroft probably thought Wallace could do with some leave, and wanted him to get it over with, for there was work to be done before the big offensive for which the French were pestering. But

> for some indefinable reason I did not want to go: something held me back, although I was longing for a spell out of the trenches. I told the General that, unless he insisted, I should prefer not to go on leave just then . . .
>
> During the following days I was practically obsessed by this feeling of witnessing a naval battle, until the very course of the action and the movements of the units of the fleets were added to the general impression. Then, on the 25th of May, on a sudden impulse, I went to Ryecroft, asking him if I might take my leave at once.

On Saturday the 27th he reported to the Admiralty, where he refused to be palmed off with somewhere convenient, like Portsmouth, Dover or Harwich. On Sunday he received instructions to join the battleship *St Vincent* in Scapa Flow, headed for King's Cross and found his seat on the infamous 'Jellicoe Special'.[21]

*

There is said to have been an increase in tension in naval circles in the early months of 1916: a sense of calm before the storm.[22] The German Commander-in-Chief, Admiral Hugo von Pohl (an advocate of U-boat warfare against commerce), was known to have been superseded, for reasons of illness, by Vice-Admiral Reinhard Scheer, who was thought likely to use the High Seas Fleet more offensively than his predecessor; and with the Army deadlocked on the Western Front, it was possible that the German high command might cast about for other ways to take the initiative and vary the daily diet of depressing news from the trenches. To what extent this is hindsight, is difficult to say; but there were other, more tangible, signs of possible change.

The British, by virtue of the Admiralty's 'Room 40', were far ahead of the Germans in signals intelligence. This was substantially, but by no means entirely, a matter of luck. Accounts vary, but there appear to have been two gifts which fell into the Admiralty's lap early in the war. In August 1914 the Russians salvaged a Signal Book from the wreck of the German cruiser *Magdeburg*, and passed it on. Then, in November, a sinking German destroyer was alleged to have jettisoned a cipher book (or, alternatively, a grid-map of the North Sea) which was subsequently dragged up in the nets of a Harwich trawler.[23] At any rate, the Admiralty quickly established a network of coastal listening and direction-finding stations, and Room 40 was gleaning so much from German transmissions that the British were obsessively careful over their own use of wireless, with dummy signals to disguise decreases in routine harbour traffic,[24] and a regime of strict silence for ships at sea.

Now, as May progressed, signal decryptions (or 'Japanese telegrams', as they were none-too-subtly called) confirmed the withdrawal of U-boats from the Western Approaches: a movement consonant both with the German claim to have ceased attacks on merchant shipping, and with the possibility of imminent fleet operations in the North Sea. And Scheer was indeed planning an exploit – within the 'Guiding Principle' that the "existing proportion of strength ruled out the High Seas Fleet seeking decisive battle with the Grand Fleet".[25]

A new bombardment of Sunderland by Hipper's 1st Scouting Group would draw Beatty into a High Seas Fleet trap in the Dogger Bank area, while Zeppelins, acting as airborne cruisers, watched out for Jellicoe to make sure the scheme did not backfire. Originally scheduled for the 17th of May, owing to repairs to the battlecruiser *Seydlitz* (damaged by a mine during the Lowestoft and Yarmouth raid), this plan was postponed, first to the 23rd, then to the 29th,[26] while U-boats laid mines off British bases and slid into ambush positions. Finally, it was abandoned, because the weather was deemed unsuitable for Zeppelin reconnaissance; and instead – so as not to waste all the preparations – a less adventurous foray northwards up the Danish coast towards the Skagerrak was arranged for the 31st, the last day before the U-boats' endurance limits would compel their withdrawal.

The High Seas Fleet's order, on the morning of May the 30th, to prepare for sea, was within two hours deciphered by Room 40 and reported to the Operations Division of the Admiralty. Its essentials were in Admiral Sir John Jellicoe's hand by 2.20 p.m. (GMT). If Scheer was really coming out, the possibility presented itself of a fleet action; a possibility which would rise to near-certainty if Jellicoe could interpose the Grand Fleet between the High Seas Fleet and its base at Wilhelmshaven in the Jade estuary.

The south-east corner of the North Sea, the Heligoland Bight, had been mined in places by both the British and the Germans. There were two safe routes through it and two round it. Of the former, one was known only to the British, who had left a gap in their minelaying; and the other was a swept path known only to the Germans (but, being unmarked at its seaward end, could only be used as an exit). Therefore if Scheer wished to quit the open sea in a hurry, he would more or less have to return to the Jade by one of the two coastal swept channels. The 'Frisian' route, which would take him home eastwards past the mouth of the Ems, would be the most convenient if his sortie had been a south-westerly one, towards the Thames estuary or against the British Army's cross-Channel traffic. Otherwise the 'Danish' route, which stretched southwards from the Horns Reef, down the coasts of Denmark and Schleswig, would probably offer him sanctuary soonest. *In extremis*, if he feared his homeward path was blocked, he might even circumnavigate Denmark, regaining the Jade via the Baltic and the Kiel Canal, although badly damaged ships might have problems both with the length of the journey and with the shallow waters of the Sound.

Jellicoe had pondered the possibilities a hundred times over. The Horns Reef seemed to hold the key: 400 miles from Scapa Flow and almost level with the Firth of Forth. If the Grand Fleet were reported *en route* by U-boats, it would not matter where it went, for the enemy would be safely back in harbour by the time it got there. So he would have to wait until dark before putting to sea, and then make progress east and south as fast as his destroyers' consumption of fuel (leaving enough for several hours of action at full speed) permitted. There was one particular problem which nagged at Sir John's mind.

However often he walked his dividers across the chart, if he departed Scapa at nightfall he would not arrive in the vicinity of the Horns Reef until late afternoon the next day. Only the previous month he had warned the First Sea Lord that it was

> very improbable that any action [near the Horns Reef] could commence before 5 p.m., and my opinion is that this would be a most unsuitable time at which to commence an action, particularly in that vicinity. It would be much too late for any decision to be arrived at.[27]

He would have to cross that bridge if and when he came to it.

Now, at 5.28 p.m., the Admiralty told him to raise steam – an order which he immediately passed on to his two detached subordinates, Sir David Beatty at Rosyth, and Vice-Admiral Sir Martyn Jerram with the 2nd BS, lying at Invergordon in the Cromarty Firth. Another signal from the Admiralty to Jellicoe and Beatty, at 5.55, explained that the German fleet was due to sail tomorrow and proceed to sea via the Horns Reef channel.[28]

*

Tuesday the 30th of May started as a routine day in the life of a fleet in harbour. *Queen Elizabeth*'s men returned from leave, and were set to cleaning their ship and preparing her for undocking. Nine boys in *Barham* were vaccinated.[29] One of their shipmates, an able-seaman, was sent to the RN Hospital in Queensferry with syphilis.[30] He was accompanied by a boy from *Warspite* with gonorrhoea, and a midshipman from *Princess Royal* with German measles. The last-mentioned (later, Admiral Sir Conolly Abel Smith) was to curse his luck for the rest of his life.[31] In the afternoon the usual recreational and marching parties were landed, while off-duty officers were free to please themselves.

Few will have bothered to go up to Edinburgh on this early-closing day, but it was a glorious afternoon and other attractions pulled. A sizeable group of officers from the 3rd LCS landed at Charlestown, opposite the light-cruiser anchorage above Rosyth, and made the four-mile country ramble to Dunfermline, where they had tea in the park and listened to the band. The sunshine extracted Commander the Hon. Barry Bingham (who, tomorrow, would win the VC) from the destroyer *Nestor*, to play golf. *Warspite*'s Assistant-Clerk Gilbert Bickmore took a messmate ashore to meet his mother and sister, play tennis and have tea at the Limekilns Hotel. Two midshipmen in *Queen Mary* missed what was, happily unbeknown to them, their last chance to set foot on terra firma, having had their leave stopped for boat-work misdemeanors: Mark Austen had "smashed up" the '*Mary's*' gangway, while Percy Baldwin had passed *Lion* with someone smoking in his sternsheets.[32]

Malaya's Surgeon-Lieutenant Lorimer saw his wife off home at Dalmeny Station and then went for "a good hard tramp" in Dalmeny and Hopetoun woods.

For those within sight, the big ships denoted the recall by striking their ensigns from the peak and rehoisting them at the main truck; Rosyth's base-ship, *Columbine*, by hoisting a three-foot black ball. Men from *Warspite*'s quarterdeck division, ashore at Rosyth playing a late football match (married men *v.* single), abandoned their game and returned to the ship.[33] While Bickmore, accompanied by mother, sister and gunroom-pal, was waiting at Rosyth landing-steps for the liberty boat to come in,

> the flagships of the fleet hoisted the signal preparatory for leaving harbour with urgency. I said nothing to my mother. But when we got onboard, the ship was buzzing with rumours that 'the Huns were out'.[34]

One man who had gone up to town was Father Tom Bradley, *Tiger*'s Roman Catholic chaplain, who had been making arrangements for the marriage of *Queen Mary*'s Major Gerald Rooney RM. Returning to catch the picket-boat at Hawes Pier, the diligent 'sky-pilot' bumped into the groom-to-be and they discussed the progress of the wedding plans.

> This was the last I saw of him. Going off in the picket-boat we noticed that the ships were firing up and when we got on board we heard that we were probably going to sea . . . The 5th BS also got up steam. This meant we were either going out on serious business or on a general practice with the Grand Fleet.[35]

Barham's gunnery-officer's honeymoon was abruptly curtailed.

The 'Dunfermline' party returned to catch the 7 o'clock boat, and found the light-cruisers hectic with activity. In *Southampton*, Lieutenant Stephen King-Hall was seized with an unreasoning compulsion to retrieve his shipmate, Sub-Lieutenant Francis Haworth-Booth, from a nearby hospital ship. He sent word by late steam-boat, as a consequence of which young H-B "practically broke out" and brought himself, minus tonsils, back to the '*Suzie*' – whose scandalized surgeon ordered him to bed. When King-Hall went to see him, the fugitive hoarsely pressed for news of the Huns, and K-H had sheepishly to confess "that as far as I knew they were not out at all".[36]

At 8.37 (BST) Jellicoe gave Beatty his orders:

> URGENT, PRIORITY. AVAILABLE VESSELS, BATTLE CRUISER FLEET, FIFTH BATTLE SQUADRON, PROCEED TO APPROXIMATE POSITION LAT 56°40′N LONG 5°0′E [240 miles from Scotland, 100 from Denmark]. DESIRABLE TO ECONOMIZE T.B.D.S' [destroyers'] FUEL. PRESUME YOU WILL BE THERE ABOUT 2.0

P.M. TOMORROW. I SHALL BE ABOUT [70 miles NNW] BY 2.0 P.M. UNLESS DELAYED BY FOG. I WILL STEER FOR HORN REEF FROM [that position]. IF NO NEWS BY 2.0 P.M., STAND TOWARDS ME TO GET IN VISUAL TOUCH.

This meant that the Grand Fleet would not operate in full cruising array until sometime around 3.30 p.m. GMT on the 31st. Before then, the BCF (with the 5th BS) would be separated from the main body. Thereafter, Beatty would assume his appointed position 15 miles in advance of the battle-fleet.

*

In Scapa Flow, as cable parties were closing up and shortening in, as boats were being hoisted, and upper decks secured for sea, the sun set in a blaze of "red and orange which seemed a foreboding of something dreadful about to happen".[37] A last picket-boat collected a travel-weary army officer from the depot ship, *Imperieuse*, and delivered him to the battleship *St Vincent*.

"It is a very curious thing", said his host, Captain William Wordsworth Fisher (whose imposing stature earned him the sobriquet 'The Great Agrippa'), "that you should turn up just a few minutes before the Fleet was due to weigh anchor to go to sea." After some small talk the major broached the subject of his dreams. "'Oh no, my dear Wallace,' retorted Fisher, laughing as if I had cracked a fine joke, 'I'm afraid there is nothing like that going to happen. I only wish it would.'"

*

Whether Beatty, as *Lion*'s slip-rope was rove and her bridles cast off, and as 'darken ship' routine was being enforced, had any misgivings that nothing had been done to brief RA5BS on the BCF's ways, now that serious blood was in the air, will never be known. Later Jellicoe was to tell the Admiralty that he had

> felt no anxiety in regard to the advanced position of the force under Sir David Beatty, supported as it was by four ships of the Fifth Battle Squadron as this force was far superior in gun power to the First Scouting Group and the speed of the slowest ships was such as to enable it to keep out of range of superior enemy forces.[38]

But, by that time, words were being chosen carefully.

There was a last-minute flap in *Barham*, where everyone seemed to be "looking for a Mr Wilson, an overseer or charge-hand fitter, to enable him to catch the last picket-boat for shore".[39] He couldn't be found, and so he sailed with the ship and learned the true meaning of overtime in the first-aid party the next day.

Barham slipped from her buoy at 10.08 p.m., *Lion* at 10.54.[40] Their respective consorts slipped or weighed, and fell in astern. *Queen Mary*, her cables twisted, had trouble unmooring,[41] and *Tiger* had to wait for her. In *Queen Mary* Midshipman Archie Dickson fretted that his middle-watch (midnight to 4.0 a.m.) would be five hours long because of reverting to GMT after leaving harbour: a "beastly nuisance"[42] (in fact *QM*'s routines remained on BST). In *Warspite* Midshipman Fairthorne, fresh from an old cruiser with reciprocating engines, savoured the novelty of getting under way in a turbine-driven ship: "no vibration; just a gentle hiss, and we're moving!" Destroyers uncoiled themselves from their tightly packed trots in Port Edgar, opposite Rosyth. Slowly, squadron by squadron, flotilla by flotilla, Beatty's warships slipped or weighed in the gathering twilight and turned seawards into the full strength of the spring flood.

Barham passed under the Forth Bridge at 10.30. Her midshipman-of-the-watch "could hear much of what was going on, [and overheard] that reports had been received that there was a possibility of an air raid by Zeppelins on Edinburgh".[43] On at least one previous occasion the battlecruisers had cleared out in case the Forth Bridge was brought down, trapping them upstream (a product, surely, of ignorance of how difficult lattice bridges are to destroy by bombing). As *Malaya* slid under the bridge, Surgeon-Lieutenant Lorimer and Lieutenant Young, chatting on the upper deck, wondered if the foremast was going to scrape it. Young had just pointed out a lighted window at the Hawes Inn, at South Queensferry, which he believed was his wife's: he had not seen her since 1914, and she was due to check in about now. Within twenty-four hours Lorimer would be trying to identify his remains in the charnel-house of the starboard 6-inch battery.[44]

They proceeded at 12 knots to the 'outer gate' of boom defences, between Inchcolm and Oxcars, where they increased to 18 for the long pilotage past Inchkeith and May Island.

> From the bridge of each mass of towering shadows the [dimmed] stern light of the next ahead could be discerned through binoculars, and on these pin-points they steered. What the flagship steered by, only the little knot of figures on her forebridge knew, the admiral and flag-captain, the navigator and officer-of-the-watch moving mysteriously around the glow-worm arc of light from the binnacle and chart-table. One by one the long black shapes slid through the outer defences, ebon shadows in a world of shades. The escorting destroyers came pelting up astern, heralded by the rush and rattle of spray-thrashed steel, funnels glowing and the roar of their fans from the

engine-room exhausts. Night, and the mystery of darkness, enfolded them. The battlecruisers were unleashed.[45]

At Inchkeith special-sea-dutymen were fallen out and the fleet went to defence watches. In big ships this was no great hardship, involving a three-watch system with the armament partially manned. There was no moon. Summer lightning flickered like distant gunfire on the horizon astern, lending weight to the buzz in *Barham* about a Zeppelin raid on Edinburgh.[46] That this theory was still current on the 5th BS flagship's bridge, two hours after sailing, supports Marder's belief that Beatty had not troubled to apprise Evan-Thomas of the details of the operation. In *Southampton* the word was that they were going out in support of "an air raid [by seaplanes, against Zeppelin sheds] or perhaps a mine-laying expedition in the Bight".[47]

They reached the North Sea soon after midnight, when the low black lump of May Island slipped by to starboard. Here, where Lord Howard left off pursuit of the Armada and consigned the Spanish to "the winds of Hell and the wrath of God", Sir David Beatty's 52 ships (6 battlecruisers, 4 battleships, 14 light-cruisers, 27 destroyers, 1 seaplane-carrier) took up night-steaming formation, with the "heavy metal"[48] grouped together, the light-cruisers on short rein ahead, and the flotillas close astern. Beatty led to sea that night a combined force which, on its own, could have seen off almost any other navy in the world, and outmanoeuvred all of them. Not since Nelson had so young an admiral commanded so élite an array of offensive power. Nearly 2,700 of its 18,000 men would never see land again.

The Grand Fleet had sailed from Scapa Flow, Cromarty and the Firth of Forth, "four and a half hours *before* the first units of the High Seas Fleet left the Jade".[49]

5

Another Wild Goose Chase

"We have tried to do this so often."

In the early-morning twilight of the 31st of May, off the mouth of the Forth, *U-32* was almost run down by the light-cruiser *Phaeton* and fired two torpedoes at *Galatea*. In the course of this sudden encounter Lieutenant von Spiegel also became aware of two capital ships and a number of destroyers.

His subsequent wireless report was received in Wilhelmshaven but did not interrupt the business (which involved much W/T chatter) of the High Seas Fleet's putting to sea. Had he seen more, the foray might have been abandoned, or, at the very least, Hipper's battlecruisers would have been held back on a shorter leash from Scheer's battle-fleet. As it was, to cancel or curtail on the strength of *U-32*'s information would have been inconsistent with the German fleet's abiding objective of trapping and destroying isolated British forces, and the reported ships may have been on coastal passage anyway. An hour later Scheer received another signal, from *U-66*'s Lieutenant von Bothmer, who had spotted Jerram's lone battle-squadron 130 miles to the north, apparently steaming north-east. It was beyond the German naval staff to divine a British master-plan from these two reports. They were interesting, but little more.

On the cliff-top at Hunstanton in Norfolk the duty-watchmen in one of the Admiralty's eight coastal listening posts were having a frustrating night. There was much enemy traffic, loud but not clear, and they could make little of it. When war broke out Wireless-telegraphist J. Ruberry was a Post Office W/T operator in Cornwall and was twice deemed medically unfit for the Army. The gift of a white feather from a girl in the street moved him to try the Navy, and now here he was, doing what he was best at, in a sailor-suit. He would sometimes find himself listening to the faint test-transmissions of Zeppelins, as they left their moorings in Germany, and 'accompanying' them across the North Sea until they were blaring so loudly he had to take off his headphones. The 'SSD' (*sehr sehr dringend*/very very urgent) report he now found himself picking up from a U-boat (it is not clear which) was mostly jammed out with interference and he could catch only coded fragments, which were passed to the Admiralty. Thereafter, "owing to the din, which sounded as though a German band was in full blast",[1] the rest of the long midnight-to-8.0 a.m. watch was spent with his headphones on the table.

*

Half an hour before sunrise, when flag signals became discernible to chief-yeomen, Beatty's ships opened out into cruising formation, with

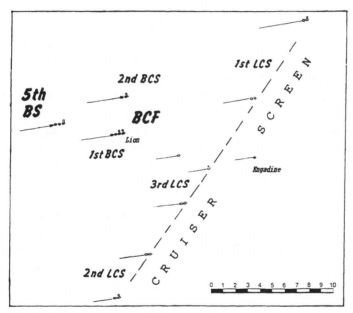

Beatty's eastwards cruising formation

the 1st BCS in line astern of *Lion*, the 2nd BCS two miles broad on her port bow, and the 5th BS five miles fine on her port quarter. Each group was attended by its own destroyers. The three light-cruiser squadrons formed an advanced reconnaissance line, several miles ahead of the heavy ships, with their front tilted slightly to the south of east (as if towards the Horns Reef).

One of the lessons Beatty professed to have learnt from the Dogger Bank battle was "the necessity of CONCENTRATION!!! If we had been spread it was quite possible that the slower ships would have never got up at all."[2] As we have seen in Chapter 3, when he was pestering Jellicoe for the *Queen Elizabeths* back in March, he depicted the benefits they might bring to a BCF encounter with Hipper, declaring that after three hours of pursuit the battleships would only have fallen astern of the battlecruisers by $4\frac{1}{2}$ miles. As already mentioned, this calculation depended on the 5th BS's being in close company with the BCF at the moment of sighting, or at least stationed on a bearing at right angles to the subsequent line of advance. With the disposition adopted on the morning of Jutland the battleships would start the south-south-easterly pursuit already 5 miles astern and would have been lagging by $9\frac{1}{2}$ rather than $4\frac{1}{2}$ miles at the end of Beatty's hypothetical pursuit.

He knew perfectly well, from the Admiralty's signal of 5.55 p.m. yesterday, if not from common sense, that the most likely direction of any pursuit of the enemy was to the SSE – towards the Horns Reef – and appears to have disposed both his cruiser screen and his slowest ship, the 21-knot seaplane-carrier *Engadine*, accordingly. At the start of an engagement *Engadine*, sea-state permitting, would stop and hoist out one or more seaplanes, a process which would take at least 20 minutes while the rest of Beatty's command would be speeding into action. In order to limit her separation from her admiral her cruising station was no less than 12 miles to the SSE: *Lion*'s probable direction of attack.

Either Beatty's reasoning with Jellicoe was valid, or his disposition of the 5th BS was competent. He cannot have it both ways. The prizes available in this matter are mutually exclusive. The argument in the above-quoted letter was opportunistic, no doubt, but essentially sound; and his positioning of the 5th BS was correspondingly unsound. The SSE'ly direction of the nearest German bolt-hole should have told him where to place his slower battle-squadron in relation to the BCF: either in the same direction from *Lion* as *Engadine*, or at least at right angles to it. Stationed (say) 3 miles to the SSE of *Lion*, the 5th BS might still have been in close company with the slowest battlecruisers, *Indefatigable* and *New Zealand*, at the end of Beatty's rhetorical three-hour chase. Stationed no better than at right angles – WSW or ENE – the outcome rosily promised to Jellicoe might still have obtained. In either case, in the real world of the afternoon of May the 31st, he might have put some of Hipper's battlecruisers under the North Sea instead of losing two of his own. With his battleships placed where they were, the vice-admiral would either go into action without their support, or he would have to hang around for them to catch up while the enemy got away.

So why did he not dispose his heavy forces in concentration? After Jutland, and even more so after the war, when the matter was a bone of contention, the 'Beatty faction' concocted excuses which will be touched on in the next chapter. Perhaps the prospect of Evan-Thomas's enemy reports being received in *Iron Duke* and the Admiralty before the battlecruisers had sent any themselves, was unthinkable to the BCF. But the heart of the matter seems to be that (as suggested in the last chapter and in spite of the information so recently conveyed by the Admiralty) Beatty had a mind-set about not meeting the enemy. One of the items of homespun wisdom to be found in BCFOs is the warning that "War is a perpetual conflict with the unexpected." An out-and-out professional would have disposed his battleships solely for action, however remote its likelihood.

*

Shortly before dawn, as they took up cruising formation, Beatty's squadrons began zigzagging: each heavy group turning in unison every 10 minutes, 2 points on either side of the mean line of advance, orchestrated from the centre by flag signals. That an admiral should attempt to control by flags the movements of a squadron 5 miles distant is a source of amazement to today's signallers. There was much tradition connected with flags – indeed, a ship's efficiency was partly measured by its smartness in handling, and responding to, flag signals – and the brightest and keenest boy-ratings had long been channelled into the signalling branch, for which they had to get 95% in their exams. Initially, they were treated as "the lowest form of life, next to a jelly-fish"; but as they gained in experience they became heavily relied upon by the 'command team'.

> You can expect a stoker to do something stupid or you might expect a seaman. But a signalman, never. And remember, you're always under the eyes of the officers: you're on the bridge, they're the bridge. When a signal was hoisted you knew exactly what you were supposed to do. And of course you had to tell the officers. 'Course, they had no idea at all . . . you used to be instructing them, and telling them what speed to do and all the lot, you know.
>
> Oh! it used to be very amusing. I mean to say, all the blah-blah, and after a four-hour watch telling him what to do, perhaps he'd turn round and you'd be in the rattle for something.[3]

The unfaltering speed with which yeomen-of-signals could juggle multiple hoists, in the gale of wind which was usually blowing across a flag-deck at sea, would embarrass their modern descendants; and there were definite advantages in flags: they were external and (in theory) visible to all simultaneously, which are good things for orders relating to seamanship evolutions to be. And the Size 1 flags issued to capital ships were big: the rectangular ones 11 feet by 9; the triangular, 15 feet by 11. But there were still practical limits, imposed by distance, visibility, funnel smoke and wind direction, to what could be expected of them; and from dawn on the 31st Beatty had detailed *Tiger*, rear ship of the 1st Battle Cruiser Squadron and nearest to *Barham*, to repeat VABCF's flag signals by searchlight to Evan-Thomas. This arrangement, together with the 5-mile distance, concealed a flaw which did not become apparent until it really mattered.

*

The morning was warm, with light airs from the SSW and a flat-calm sea, albeit with "a haze on the eastern horizon".[4] In addition to the brush with *U-32*, there was an imagined submarine sighting, at 8.23 a.m., which caused Beatty's force to dog-leg evasively to the north for some 20 minutes,[5] but no other incident of note. Divisions and prayers were held in all units, followed in many cases by physical drill and the exercise of 'general quarters', 'action-stations' or 'control' (which all meant much the same thing for the gunnery organization). Thereafter hands were "employed as required" – a phrase which usually covers cleaning, painting and routine maintenance duties.

The last day of the month was pay-day in the BCF (the 5th BS would have to wait till tomorrow), and off-duty men were mustered, cap in hand, to receive their money. In *Lion*, one stoker – who probably ran his mess's illegal 'Crown and Anchor' board, and now collected his gambling debts – stuffed a wad of banknotes into his sock: a circumstance which would become of acute interest to him when he lost his leg a few hours later.[6] Next, they queued up for their daily rum ration. In *Barham*, eight of the nine boys who had been vaccinated the day before complained of sore arms – some of them probably skiving – and were put to bed in the sick-bay. Boy (1st Class) Henry Hawkins toughed it out and thereby saved his life.[7]

*

Given that they enjoyed identical weather conditions, the logged noon positions of the heavy ships under Beatty's command provide a cameo insight into the comparative operational standards of the BCF and the battle-fleet. Today, they would have found themselves in sight of the Ekofisk oil and gas platforms, but in 1916 they had to use the sun or make do with dead-reckoning (DR). This daily ritual should have been a matter of pride among navigating officers; and three of Evan-Thomas's ships – *Barham*, *Valiant* and *Malaya* – logged a full 'observed position', indicating that they had also taken an earlier sun-sight (longitude at noon has to be extrapolated from an existing position line). But of the four battlecruisers which were to survive the day, only *New Zealand* had previously bothered about the sun, for only she was able to log an 'observed' longitude. *Princess Royal*, at least (like *Warspite*), observed a latitude at noon; but *Lion* and *Tiger* left their sextants in their boxes and made do with DR.

If all the noon positions (both DR and Obs.) are plotted on the chart, *Lion*'s DR position is the most south-westerly, being about 9 miles from group-centre. This appears to be the wrong way round, in view of the fact that, when Jellicoe and Beatty finally made contact amid shot and shell at around 6.0 p.m., the BCF was found to be several miles further *west* than the C-in-C had expected. But in fact there can be no connection, for the coordinates transmitted by Beatty a few minutes before 4.0 p.m. were demonstrably accurate,[8] indicating that the error crept in between then and 6.0 p.m. We do not know whether *Lion* called in, by searchlight, individual ships' positions, although we do know that she gave out a noon position (averaged or not) for adoption as a common benchmark.[9] This is an unsatisfactory little vignette, leaving questions unanswered, if not actually inviting the wrong moral for navigators.

*

Far to the north, the battle-fleet had a similarly uneventful morning and observed similar sea routines. Initially, Jellicoe's force comprised the 16 dreadnoughts of the 1st and 4th BSs, deployed in 'divisional' cruising formation of four columns of four ships each, steaming ESE at 15 knots. This speed would enable destroyers to inspect the occasional merchant ship or fishing boat without having to waste precious fuel by steaming hard to catch up again, but it was still roughly compatible with the scheduled rendezvous with Beatty. At around 11.30 a.m. Jerram's 2nd BS joined on a converging course from starboard and manoeuvred slickly into place to form the port divisions of what now became a six-column formation of 24 battleships.

In *St Vincent* Major Wallace attended morning prayers, and found himself moved by the sight of "about a thousand bare-headed sailors standing erect in dead silence on the quarterdeck". Then, Captain Fisher called the assembled company around a 12-inch gun-turret on whose side had been painted a map of the North Sea, and described what he knew of the movements of the fleet.

'We have tried to do this so often [he said], but without bringing the Germans to book; but today it is a little different. We have a staff officer who has come direct from the trenches. Please God, may the shells follow him here: he may bring us luck.'

His words sent a cold shiver down my spine, for they were almost exactly the words which had been heard by me in just such a scene as this in my premonition of the battle. This made me even more certain that what I had been dreaming about for months was about to come true.

Wallace was then given a detailed tour of *St Vincent* and had "the mysteries and complexities of a British dreadnought" revealed to him. He was a stranger to naval ways but, for reasons already given, his interest and observations were unusually acute. The fire-control organization was explained: how the guns would be controlled from the foretop; and, if that position was knocked out, from the maintop; and, only as a last resort by each turret's own range-finders and spotting-officers. He climbed with some difficulty up to the foretop, 80 feet above the upper deck, his clumsy army boots gaining precarious purchase on the 2-inch rungs on the foremast. The ascent was worth it, for the sight of the battle-fleet, steaming placidly in six divisions, "was magnificent and thrillingly inspiring". He noted the positions of the flagships, and the hazy conditions, and reckoned visibility at 4 or 5 miles[10] (although landsmen commonly underestimate distances at sea).

*

Shortly before noon a scene of tragi-farce was acted out in the Admiralty. Captain Thomas Jackson, Director of Operations, "made one of his very rare visits" to Room 40. Jackson (no relation of the First Sea Lord) disliked the miscellany of gifted amateurs who comprised the Room's crew, and resented the notion that such people could contribute anything of use to naval affairs. He had entered Room 40 only twice previously,

> once to complain that he had cut his hand on one of the red boxes in which the decodes were circulated, and once, when a change in key had caused a temporary stoppage in the flow of decodes, to express his pleasure that he would not be further bothered with such damned nonsense![11]

Now this ridiculous angry blustering officer (the species survives) curtly demanded to know where direction-finding placed Admiral Scheer's call-sign 'DK', and was told, correctly, that it was in Wilhelmshaven.

In asking the question, he was making a mistake which anyone in Room 40 could have corrected. DK was Scheer's *harbour* call-sign: when he put to sea it was transferred to a permanent base-ship, and he used another. But "without further ado and without asking for an explanation or comment, the insufferable Jackson turned on his heel and left the room"; and, about the time the Horns Reef lightship was pitching gently in the wash of Hipper's battlecruisers, he reported to Rear-Admiral Henry Oliver, the Chief of War Staff, that the German fleet was still in the Jade. Acting upon this intelligence, Oliver despatched the following signal to Jellicoe and Beatty at 12.30:

NO DEFINITE NEWS OF THE ENEMY. THEY MADE ALL PREPARATIONS FOR SAILING EARLY THIS MORNING. IT WAS THOUGHT FLEET HAD SAILED BUT DIRECTIONALS PLACE THE FLAGSHIP IN THE JADE AT 11.10 A.M. GMT. APPARENTLY THEY HAVE BEEN UNABLE TO CARRY OUT AIR RECONNAISSANCE WHICH HAS DELAYED THEM.

The consequences of this misinformation (analysed in a later chapter) were by no means as drastic as often alleged: the two British groups had an R/V to keep (although both were slipping behind schedule). However, if the Grand Fleet was to find itself loitering off the Skagerrak while enemy movements clarified, Jellicoe's concern about his destroyers' limited range (typically 41% greater at 15 knots than at 20[12]) would naturally become accentuated. At 1.55 p.m. he semaphored for each battleship to report the rate at which she would be able, if necessary, to oil a destroyer alongside (replies varied from 20 tons per hour, to 150). And although Beatty, for his part, continued on his way at 19 knots, the Admiralty's signal can only have vindicated his casual assumption that there were no Germans in the offing, and contributed to the atmosphere of lassitude which prevailed in the BCF. Steam remained at half an hour's notice for full speed.

*

Nothing much was happening after lunch. "We did not appear to be expecting Huns, as we cruised along to the eastwards at no great speed."[13] In both the BCF and the 5th BS, Wednesday afternoon was a 'make and mend': a half holiday for off-watch personnel, who settled themselves on mess tables and lockers, or basked in the sun on the upper deck. In *Malaya* Seaman Gaskin lounged on the roof of one of the forward turrets.[14] In *Tiger* Midshipman John Ouvry had a "nice little sleep on the quarterdeck",[15] while the padre repaired to his cabin and turned in. Officers dozed in wardroom armchairs. Beatty read a book, while a small cloud of zzzs hung in the haze above his ships. To Midshipman Roger Frampton of *Barham*'s afternoon watch, "it looked very much as though this was to be another wild goose chase"; and, indeed, many were expecting to receive "the customary signal 'Return to Base'".[16]

There remained one or two people moved by an uncanny sense of impending drama. In *Lion*, Lieutenant Atwell Lake actually went to his cabin to "put on a boiled shirt [because he] wanted to be dressed for the occasion".[17] In *Queen Mary*, the gunnery-officer, Commander Llewellyn Llewellyn, sent for the four gunner's-mates and asked them to double-check their respective turrets, adding, "I believe they are out and we have got a grand time ahead of us." They exchanged indulgent heard-it-all-before smiles between themselves and went off to do as bid. Petty-Officer Ernest Francis went over 'X' turret as with a fine tooth-comb, found (as expected) everything in order, and reported back. He then sloped off to the diving store and made himself comfortable amongst the rubber suits and coils of flexible air-pipe.[18]

Beatty's force was now approaching, slightly late, the 'waypoint' where it would turn north towards his rendezvous with Jellicoe. At 1.30 p.m. he made restationing signals which swivelled his outlying groups clockwise somewhat. The 5th BS moved from 5 miles WNW of *Lion* to the same distance NNW; the 2nd BCS, likewise, shifted right (from *Lion*'s viewpoint), while maintaining its 2 miles' distance.

As far as the *Queen Elizabeths* were concerned, the purpose of this adjustment was to ease their resumption of their customary station in the van of the battle-fleet. Rear-Admiral Chalmers, who was *Lion*'s assistant navigator in 1916 and thus probably helped Commander Arthur Strutt draw up the formation, admits that this was the case: in fact in his view *Barham*'s 5 miles were something of a concession, since Evan-Thomas's designated BF cruising station was 10 miles astern of the BCF.[19] The redisposition ordered by VABCF (or at least issued in his name) for the northward leg was therefore a peacetime one, a parade-ground exercise, rather than a wartime measure. It suggests that VABCF and his staff were rather bored and were, as a consequence, planning too far ahead. Of course the 'Tom Jackson' signal, which had been received only three-quarters of an hour earlier, can be cited in Beatty's defence; but this restationing was merely an adjustment of the formation established at dawn, when he had no such excuse.

At first sight Beatty's redisposition of his cruiser screen at 1.30 p.m., for the short dog-leg northwards to meet Jellicoe, appears to be a similar product of the 'no-Germans-at-sea' syndrome: for instead of being redeployed as a shield across the (soon-to-be) north front of the BCF, the cruiser-line, too, was canted round clockwise from *Lion*, as if Beatty was about to turn SSE towards the Horns Reef. Altogether it looks as if Beatty's overriding desideratum was that he should be able to swing his forces smartly into station ahead of Jellicoe: capital ships, cruisers and uncle Tom Cobbley already deployed for the Grand Fleet's stately parade south-south-eastwards. But in the case of the cruisers he had no choice, for the relative-velocity problem of redisposing the screen to present a 'north' front was insurmountable: some ships (notably Commodore William Goodenough's 2nd LCS) would have had no hope of attaining their new stations before Jellicoe's screen hove into sight ahead, the BCF turned round, and the whole performance would have to be done again.

Therefore, for the trip northwards of perhaps an hour and a half, there was little choice but to leave the cruisers spread out astern of the northbound capital ships in a manner which would, for the time being, deprive them – except for those at the extremities of the line – of any reconnaissance value.

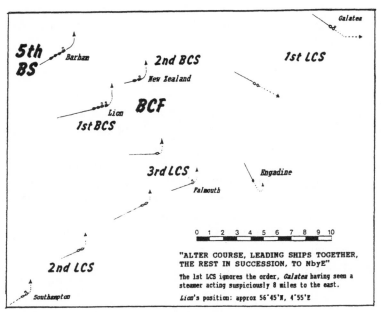

0 1 2 3 4 5 6 7 8 9 10

"ALTER COURSE, LEADING SHIPS TOGETHER, THE REST IN SUCCESSION, TO NbyE"

The 1st LCS ignores the order, *Galatea* having seen a steamer acting suspiciously 8 miles to the east.

Lion's position: approx 56°45'N, 4°55'E

Beatty's 'waypoint' turn at 2.15 p.m.

However, even this modest redisposition of cruisers presented those ships with speed, time and distance problems of varying magnitude. The southernmost units had merely to slow down and move north to intercept their new stations (which were invisibly attached to *Lion* and moving eastwards at 19 knots). But the northernmost ones, those of Commodore Edwyn Alexander-Sinclair's 1st LCS, had some serious work to do. For example, while *Galatea*'s new position appears to be only about 8 miles south of her old, even if the cruiser increases to 26 knots, she has effectively 21 miles to travel on a course of SEbyE – a journey which will take the best part of an hour on the present base-course.

*

Some 50 miles to the east of the BCF, Hipper's 1st and 2nd Scouting Groups (comprising, respectively, battlecruisers and light-cruisers), with their escorting destroyers, were steaming northwards. Shortly before 4.0 p.m. (Central European Summer Time) the cruiser *Elbing* spotted a steamer to the west, and two destroyers were detached to investigate. *B-109* and *B-110* closed the Danish *N. J. Fjord*, and ordered her to stop. Boats were lowered, one from each destroyer, and began to make their way over to the neutral merchant ship, to check her papers, verify her cargo, and so on. They were half-way across when they were suddenly recalled, and considerable agitation could be seen on the destroyers' bridges.[20]

*

Galatea was still steaming SE to gain her new station when, a few minutes after 2.0 p.m. (GMT), Chief-Yeoman Wiseman spotted smoke on the horizon to the east. Its source was identified as a small steamer, a common enough item in the North Sea, but she was blowing off steam, which a ship on passage would only do if she had had to stop. Presently an explanation became apparent, and at 10 minutes past the hour *Galatea*'s starboard bridge-wing signal-lamp blinked westwards, over her right shoulder as it were, towards *Inconstant*, for relay across the 18 miles to *Lion*: "TWO-FUNNELLED SHIP HAS STOPPED STEAMER BEARING ESE, 8 MILES, AM CLOSING."

Meanwhile *Lion* had returned her zigzagging consorts to base-course in line-ahead, in preparation for the big turn; and at 2.15, whether Beatty had received *Galatea*'s information or not, he made "ALTER COURSE, LEADING SHIPS TOGETHER, THE REST IN SUCCESSION, TO N BY E." In *Galatea*, Commodore Alexander-Sinclair, a "dour red-haired Scot with a scrub-hammock face",[21] ignored the order and pressed on eastwards, with his three consorts strung out astern (which, with his message of 2.10, he had given himself Beatty's permission to do unless overruled). A couple of minutes later "ENEMY IN SIGHT" was hoisted to *Galatea*'s masthead and her forward 6-inch gun went off with a clap of thunder, shattering the afternoon's tranquillity. On the bridge, an enemy report was stuffed into a small brass container and dropped on a piece of string down the voice-pipe to her W/T office. It read: "URGENT. TWO

CRUISERS, PROBABLY HOSTILE, IN SIGHT BEARING ESE, COURSE UNKNOWN. MY POSITION LAT 56° 48′N, LONG 5° 21′E." It was encoded, and transmitted at 2.20. Nominally addressed to SOBCF, it was intended for a wider audience (Beatty did not need to know *Galatea*'s position) and was caught by every alert afternoon-watchman telegraphist in the Fleet and beyond.

PART II

Chasing Hipper & Evading Scheer

6

Failure to Concentrate

"The damned 5th Battle Squadron is going to take the bread out of our mouths."

Upon receipt of Alexander-Sinclair's 'enemy in sight' signal of 2.20 p.m., both of his cruiser colleagues, Rear-Admiral Trevylyan Napier (3rd Light-Cruiser Squadron) and Commodore William Goodenough (2nd LCS), turned their ships eastwards in support without waiting for orders. Napier, in the centre of the line, notified *Lion* by searchlight that he was doing so. Some historians have criticized this abandonment of station by Beatty's entire 12-ship cruiser-screen on the hindsight grounds that had Napier remained in station to the southeast of *Lion*, he would have been well placed in an hour's time to give VABCF earlier warning of the German battlecruisers; but it was encouraged by BCFOs – until the local strength of the enemy had been established – and whatever later inconvenience may be traceable to it, its 'big issue' simplicity is beyond reproach. For Goodenough, at the distant SW end of the line and with the furthest to go, it made little difference in the 12 minutes before the BCF turned SSE and interposed itself between him and the two other cruiser groups.

Beatty, still steaming north, warned the destroyer flotillas to redeploy around their respective big-ship squadrons in preparation for a course of SSE ($144\frac{1}{4}°$ true), and then made a general signal by flags at 2.32 ordering his forces to turn in-succession in that direction. The signal was: *nine pendant* (= ALTER COURSE, LEADING SHIPS TOGETHER, THE REST IN SUCCESSION) *above* (= TO STARBOARD) *flags DH* (= ONTO A NEW COURSE OF SSE). Without waiting for acknowledgements from senior officers – as BCFOs warned he might not – VABCF hauled the signal down (making it executive), and the 1st BCS wheeled round astern of *Lion*. The 2nd BCS, 3 miles to the ENE, conformed. While turning,

Beatty ordered steam for full speed and an immediate increase to 22 knots, which set the BCF's stokers to forcing the draught in their furnaces and raking forward the coal heaped up in reserve at the back of the grates.

Five miles to the NNW, *Barham*'s yeoman saw the flag-hoist but was unable to read it. However, a recommencement of the zigzagging routine (two points either side of the base course), which had lapsed with the turn to the north, was expected, and *Barham*'s officer-of-the-watch, Lieutenant Alfred Phillips, assumed that this was it. Her hoist for "ALTER COURSE TOGETHER 2 POINTS TO PORT" (*numeral 2 above blue pendant*) was probably already bent on the halyard in anticipation, and it now shot up to the yardarm and down again and the four battleships turned simultaneously onto a course of NbyW ($335\frac{3}{4}°$) – almost exactly the opposite course to that adopted by Beatty.

With the 'waypoint' turn to the north at 2.15 *Tiger* had become the furthest battlecruiser from the 5th BS, and she not unnaturally supposed that her signal-relaying-by-searchlight duty had ended. *Lion* however, what with the excitement of the enemy sightings and the destroyers racing to new screen positions, did not grasp this and for several fateful minutes nobody thought to repeat the turn-SSE signal to RA5BS in *Barham*.

So, while Beatty powered off to the SSE behind a great pall of coal smoke, Evan-Thomas's squadron put itself onto a reciprocal course with every second adding 20 yards to its distance from the battlecruisers it was supposed to support. Up till now the confusion could be put down to Beatty's stationing the 5th BS so far away and to Murphy's Law. But this is where we enter the opaque waters of Jutland controversy, for the 5th BS persisted with its west-of-north course for several fateful minutes, long after it should have been clear that the BCF's turn was much more drastic than a mere zigzag restart, in fact until *Lion* – almost out of sight in the afternoon haze – woke up to the fact that the 5th BS was not following and at last repeated by searchlight the order to turn SSE. One belief is that *Tiger* asked *Lion* by W/T whether her repeating duty was still in force.[1] Meanwhile on *Barham*'s bridge, both Captain Arthur Craig and, according to some, Wilfrid Egerton, RA5BS's flag-commander, "endeavoured to persuade our admiral to turn and follow Beatty";[2] but Evan-Thomas made a stand on waiting for a clear order.

It is not certain that general manoeuvring signals automatically applied to the 5th BS. They did not apply to *cruiser* squadrons unless they were specifically flashed,[3] but there was no guideline, if such were needed, for the case of a semi-detached *battle-squadron*. The regime by which *Lion* had been zigzagging *Barham* with flags and searchlight repeats before 2.15 p.m. is not absolutely clear: probably the searchlight repeats were in respect of the 5-mile distance between the two flagships, but it is just possible that *Lion*'s signals staff were treating the 5th BS as a cruiser-squadron for the purposes of signalling procedures. There is, though, no evidence that the flagship of the Grand Fleet's proudest battle-squadron understood this to be the case, and its senior officer never produced this argument in his defence.

The question of the precise sequence and spacing of events is one which raises hackles to this day. This writer has seen a resourceful 'analysis' which claims to prove that Evan-Thomas turned SSE only $1\frac{1}{2}$ minutes after Beatty. After three-quarters of a century, nobody's knowledge of the signalling practices of 1916 is complete, and expertise can be recruited to support any desired conclusion with arguments so loaded with assumptions as to be unacceptable as building-blocks of evidence. Furthermore, creative reconstructions are inappropriate while there remain anomalies in the documentary evidence.

For example, the sequence of signals for the 5th BS listed in the Admiralty's *Official Despatches* –

1. turn *in-succession* NbyE at 2.17;
2. turn *together* NbyW at 2.32;
3. turn *in-succession* SSE at 2.40

– is nonsensical (see diagram overleaf). Only a formation in line-ahead can be turned in-succession. The turn-together listed at (2) above changed the formation from line-ahead into a 2-point line-of-bearing on *Barham*'s port quarter: a disposition from which the third listed turn is, strictly speaking, impossible.

So what really happened? Perhaps, before turning SSE, Evan-Thomas brought his ships back into column (as Beatty had at 2.09, before the waypoint turn) with an unrecorded turn-together 2 points to starboard. Perhaps the line-of-bearing was shallow enough ($22\frac{1}{2}°$) for his captains to fudge the turn-in-succession to SSE, although 15° is held to be the limit of looseness within which a 'loose line' (which this wasn't) can be turned in-succession; and one cannot imagine Evan-Thomas, an officer with "a highly deserved reputation as a ship and squadron handler"[4] and a one-time CO of the Portsmouth Signal School, authorizing such a shoddy manoeuvre. The quickest orderly solution – given the line-of-bearing – would have been for *Barham* to turn her consorts *together* to the SSE and then redeploy them at leisure into column if this was felt necessary; yet nowhere is this suggested in official accounts. Even Captain Harper, Director of Navigation and

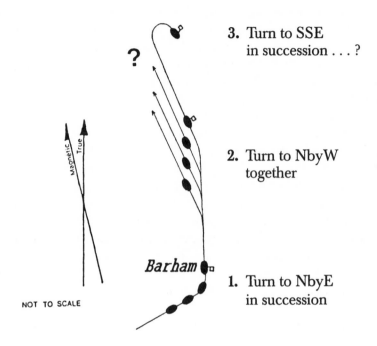

3. Turn to SSE
in succession . . . ?

2. Turn to NbyW
together

1. Turn to NbyE
in succession

controversial Jutland author, and Sir Julian Corbett, the official historian, recycle without comment the mismatch of manoeuvring signals.
Professor Marder avoids mention in his narrative of the brief NbyW
course, although it appears in his charts. Perhaps these authorities are
wise to hurry past, for we can never resolve the issue. But the existence
of a flaw in the record is certain, and the matter is raised here to demonstrate that indicators which point to the general sequence of events are
safer than detailed speculation.

Unlike Evan-Thomas's report of proceedings (ROP), which gives no
hint of his delay in following Beatty, Captain Craig's says somewhat
pointedly that "The Battle Cruiser Squadron turned rather before the
5th Battle Squadron and were out of sight for some time." The 'out of
sight' is an exaggeration, but we are reminded of his spurned advice that
Barham should turn SSE without further delay. Whatever the delay
between *Lion*'s turning and *Barham*'s following,

a. sufficient time must have elapsed before Craig's suggestion to
allow that the squadron's junior captain was not trying to teach his
admiral to suck eggs – there must have been delay enough to provoke a
presumably reasonable man into speaking out;

b. the stop-watch of delay should not start until *Princess Royal* was
seen to be following *Lion* round; and,

c. although it is possible that the searchlight-repeat came through the moment RA5BS finished voicing his refusal, it seems reasonable to concede sufficient lapse of time after Evan-Thomas's reply for his stance to be perceived to have had some influence on proceedings, otherwise nobody would have remembered it.

These considerations support a more-than-token delay. Furthermore, if *Tiger* really did make the W/T enquiry about the searchlight-repeating duty, the message had to be composed, sent down the tube to her wireless office, encoded, transmitted, received in *Lion*, decoded, and delivered by hand to the flagship's bridge; all of which requires some minutes even for organizations slicker than the BCF could boast in May 1916. (It has to be said that Morse-key W/T is an unlikely way of asking a simple question of a ship in close company – much quicker to haul out of line and semaphore – and no such enquiry is mentioned either in the *Official Despatches* signals list or in Captain Pelly's report.)

Evan-Thomas's delay in turning to the SSE and his consequent distance astern of Beatty have been assessed by various sources as follows:

Source	*Barham*'s delay in minutes	Resultant distance from *Lion*
ODs (Craig's report)	–	out of sight
Frampton[5]	9	9 miles
Admiralty Narrative	6[6]	over 9 miles
Corbett (text)	a few	over 10 miles[7]
Corbett (maps)	8 (by interpolation)	10 miles
Harper *Truth*	some	over 10 miles
Godfrey RNC lectures	8	an extra 5 miles
Chalmers	6	nearly 10 miles
Bennett	7	10 miles
Marder	6 or 7	nearly 10 miles
Campbell	8	about 10 miles
Average	$7\frac{1}{3}$	10 miles

Even allowing for the probability that some of these sources are recycling the opinions of others, there is a remarkable degree of consensus. Decision by committee is as bad a way of writing history as it is of composing music or designing aircraft, but it is at least possible to check if these proportions of time and distance are compatible by plotting the relative-movement costs:

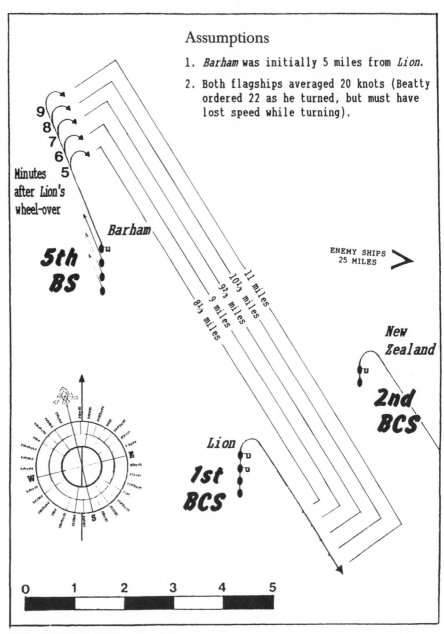

Assumptions

1. *Barham* was initially 5 miles from *Lion*.

2. Both flagships averaged 20 knots (Beatty ordered 22 as he turned, but must have lost speed while turning).

Minutes after *Lion's* wheel-over

9
8
7
6
5

5th BS

Barham

ENEMY SHIPS 25 MILES >

11 miles
10⅓ miles
9⅔ miles
9 miles
8⅓ miles

New Zealand

2nd BCS

Lion

1st BCS

E
W
S

0   1   2   3   4   5

When did *Barham* turn?

This shows that each minute of delay in *Barham*'s wheel-over to the SSE added two-thirds of a mile to her 5-mile separating from *Lion*, and therefore the 7-ish minutes and 10 miles averaged by the sources listed above are plausible. And if one figure is wrong, both are wrong, which is half as likely. The point is that anyone wishing to reduce *Barham*'s delay has to explain why the subsequent separation has been so unanimously overstated and then justify a lesser one; and in any case the equation contains an enormous margin for reduction before there ceases to have been a problem between *Barham* and *Lion*.

Whatever his exact distance astern of Beatty, by dint of cutting corners on his elusive leader, RA5BS managed to bring it down somewhat over the next hour or so; but the fact remains that had flag-officers been acting in harmony, he would have started only 5 miles astern of *Lion* and by cutting (smaller) corners could have reduced this to 4 or less by the time the battlecruiser action was joined. As Churchill was to say in *World Crisis*, the result of Evan-Thomas's delay in turning "was inexorably to keep him and his tremendous guns out of the action for the most critical and most fatal half-hour".

∗

The blame-game did not take long to start, after Jutland; and even Beatty's post-battle ROP, when his avowed regard for Evan-Thomas was at its most generous, describes the 5th BS's eventual joining the action as "unfortunately at very long range", which is a curious comment for this most unself-critical of admirals to make about a force under his own tactical control, and can only be taken as containing a reproach.

The issues are byzantine in their complexity (some of the obfuscation having been deliberately injected by the protagonists after the war), but they may be grouped under three general headings:

1. Evan-Thomas's slow response to the developments at around 2.32 p.m.

2. *Lion*'s signalling inefficiency.

3. Beatty's stationing of the 5th BS in relation to the BCF.

Before proceeding, it should be mentioned that in HM ships afternoon tea was, and is, normally available from 3.30 p.m. ('seven-bells tea', it used to be called, from the bells rung half-hourly throughout a watch). It was timed to straddle the change of watch at 4.0, to benefit both those going on watch and those whom they would relieve; but on an uneventful afternoon at sea it would be a welcome event for everyone. This was the first time they had gone to sea after the confusing clock-change, and although by now (the afternoon of the 31st of May) all the battlecruisers which were to survive the day, except for *Lion*, and all the battleships except for *Malaya*, had switched their bridge logs back to GMT, as will become evident in the next chapter, most of them (including *Barham*) were running their internal routines on the new BST. It is therefore likely that members of the 'flag' teams left their respective bridges after witnessing the 2.15 (3.15 BST) 'waypoint' turn to the north, intending to get tea comfortably out of the way before the junction with the Battle Fleet and the various demands which that event would place upon them. The deciphering of Com1LCS's enemy report of 2.20 may therefore have caused the hasty locating and recalling of officers who had only just gone below. The ladders up to *Lion*'s bridge totalled 80 steps (Lewis Bayly pushed the elderly Queen Alexandra up them in 1912 and they counted them).[8]

Evan-Thomas's slow response

As far as Evan-Thomas knew there was no self-triggering arrangement which would throw the BCF from its normal cruising mode into pursuit mode without specific orders from the senior flagship. These circumstances – a surprise sighting calling for a knee-jerk pursuit – were characteristic of the BCF's function and were unlikely to be met by the Battle Fleet. As discussed in Chapter 4, Evan-Thomas had not been favoured with a copy of BCFOs. Had he been, he would have found informative Beatty's 'Instructions for Concentrating Battle Cruisers when Spread, and Forming Order of Battle', for while these injunctions were framed with individual battlecruisers, rather than a squadron of battleships, in mind, the impression they impart of the thrust of BCF lore is unmistakable:

> A sudden alteration of course by the ship sighting the enemy is seen by those on either side of her far more rapidly than any signal could be sent, and, being an almost certain indication of an enemy having been sighted it should be acted upon immediately.
>
> All ships that *may* be required to support must proceed to do so until they know definitely that they will not be required.
>
> The immediate sequel to concentrating is forming Order of Battle and engaging the enemy. In future this will be done so far as possible without signal, and each Captain is to use his discretion in handling his ship as he considers that the Admiral would wish . . .
>
> Each detached ship should, at her discretion, close and engage the enemy without waiting for further orders . . .
>
> Ships must never suppose that the absence of a signal implies that any given action is not sanctioned by the Flagship; on the contrary it usually denotes that the Admiral relies on each ship to take whatever action may be necessary without waiting to be told . . .

The sole object of these instructions is to enable ships to understand beforehand the principles of rapid co-operation, so that the enemy may be brought to action at the earliest possible moment without any ship needing or wishing to wait for detailed orders from the Admiral.[9]

To point out again that Evan-Thomas's ignorance of BCFOs was not mainly his fault is to emphasize again the divergence between the tactical regimes of the Battle Fleet and the BCF, and more specifically, between the habits of thought expected of their respective junior flag-officers. But if one ferrets around in the "70 closely printed pages" of GFBOs, one finds, amongst the "mass of detail which should have been common knowledge",[10] 'initiative' injunctions which, while designed to preserve the unity of a deployed battle-line, are at least partly transferable in sense to *Barham*'s dilemma at 2.32:

The Fleet is to be guided generally by the movements of the division led by the Commander-in-Chief, which should be considered as the rallying point. The movements of the Commander-in-Chief must therefore be very carefully watched and his wishes if possible anticipated. Signals may either be indistinguishable or they may take too long to get through to a large fleet. This does not mean that they will not be made, but the movement signalled may be commenced before the executive is given . . . In the event of a movement of the Commander-in-Chief's division carried out without signal or before a signal has got through to all ships in the line, the other divisions should conform.[11]

Jellicoe's post-war opinion that Evan-Thomas's "actions were perfectly correct", and that his squadron's delay was "entirely due to the neglect of the Vice-Admiral Commanding the battlecruisers",[12] is therefore questionable in the light of his own standing orders – which legitimize Captain Craig's and Commander Egerton's insubordinate desire to follow Beatty without further ado. To Sir Charles Madden (Jellicoe's chief of staff) also, the question of initiative was not an issue, the delay being due to the battlecruisers' funnel smoke and to "the fact that the flag signals could not be read in *Barham*, and that they were not repeated by searchlight or W/T guardship".[13] But Evan-Thomas and others knew that this was too selective and too simplistic an explanation, and found it necessary to produce more complicated alibis.

For example:

1. After the war he argued that his very distance and bearing from Beatty led him to believe that VABCF was relying on him to carry on northwards to prevent the enemy's escape in that direction or to catch him in a crossfire.[14] Marder is quite impressed with this riposte, and at

first sight it looks good; though as Evan-Thomas had had seven years to brood about it, well it might. It has three faults:

a. It requires *Barham* to have read the 'SSE' signal, or at least to have understood *Lion*'s movements. Yet RA5BS's basic alibi was that the "intense smoke made by the battlecruisers' bringing forward their fires [made it] impossible to see what *Lion* was doing".[15] It also requires those on *Barham*'s bridge to have felt certain that they knew what Beatty wanted them to do, whereas Captain Craig's and Commander Egerton's suggestion, and Evan-Thomas's alleged response, rule out certainty.

b. Instead of continuing on its NbyE course, the 5th BS, as we have seen, actually turned 2 points further away onto a course of NbyW. Now, either *Barham* had received *Galatea*'s W/T report of hostile cruisers "bearing ESE, course unknown", or she hadn't. RA5BS's ROP, his post-war statements, and the midshipman-of-the-watch, all say she had;[16] in which case a new course at an angle of 11 points ($123\frac{3}{4}°$) from the enemy's reported location – *course unknown* – was of no imaginable use. Professor Marder for some reason says she hadn't, in which case Evan-Thomas possessed no information about the enemy. Either way, the 2-point NbyW turn cannot possibly have been an interception ploy (and would probably not have been a turn-*together* if, somehow, it had been).

c. Had Beatty intended the 5th BS to carry on northwards, he would have exempted its destroyer screen (the 1st DF) from the warning order to destroyer flotillas to redeploy round their respective heavy groups for a course of SSE. Marder alleges that this signal was not listed in *Barham*'s signal log as having been received, but the rest of the squadron copied it and *Fearless*, 1st DF leader, is said to have listed it as relayed by *Barham* (nearly all signal logs were destroyed long ago).[17]

2. Admiral Chalmers, *Lion*'s assistant navigator in 1916 and later Beatty's biographer, points to a signal at 2.25 from Beatty to Evan-Thomas to "look out for advanced cruisers of Grand Fleet" and suggests that this probably resulted in "all eyes on the bridge of the *Barham* being turned northward".[18] Marder echoes this speculation. This too has flaws, however.

a. Jellicoe – assuming he was on schedule, which he wasn't – was still 70 miles away and visual contact with his scouts could not be expected for an hour and a half. In fairness, though, the likelihood that Evan-Thomas had not been apprised of the agenda should be borne in mind.

b. A more substantial problem is presented in the *Handbook of Signalling*:

No man can be regarded as an efficient signalman unless he is able to keep a good look-out in every direction; everything in sight should be observed by signalmen and any occurrence of importance or interest brought to the notice of those concerned.[19]

Indeed, the warning signal to destroyers to re-form for a course of SSE should certainly have kept the battleship's duty-telescope focused on *Lion* – assuming, of course, the signal was reported to the bridge.

In fact, the attention of those on *Barham*'s bridge was distracted, for a few minutes after the mistaken 2-point turn to port, by the 5th BS's station-keeping. At 2.35 *Barham* semaphored to her three sisters: "LENGTH OF LINE IS 12 CABLES INSTEAD OF 9. TAKE UP APPOINTED STATION." This activity involved monitoring the range of the rear ship with a sextant or a station-keeping range-finder (too far for a distance-meter), hoisting the semaphore flag, working the mechanical sema-phore and reading back the acknowledgement. As we have seen, the squadron was on a $22\frac{1}{2}°$ line-of-bearing on *Barham*'s port quarter (the opposite side to the BCF); the appropriate semaphore position was on the port wing of the bridge,[20] and the business may have engaged the attention of the officer-of-the-watch, up to two signalmen and perhaps, for educational purposes, the midshipman. But any lapse of attention towards *Lion* was of short duration, for Craig and Egerton (who, with Evan-Thomas, may have arrived on the bridge in the meantime) would not have urged the rear-admiral to follow VABCF if they had not been aware of *Lion*'s behaviour.

To me the greatest problem presented by this sorry episode is the time which ensued (while the 5th BS persisted with its NbyW course) after it must have become apparent from the BCF's radical behaviour that the illegible signal had not, after all, been a general order to recom-mence zigzagging. During these minutes *Barham* can hardly have con-tinued to imagine that she was either obeying orders or conforming to the senior ship's movements, and RA5BS should immediately have turned his squadron together back to starboard, at the very least to the previous course of NbyE (the last known to have been ordered), pending clarification. If he had done so, the belated alleged turn-in-suc-cession would make more sense, for reasons already explained. Possibly he did, but (as remarked above) no known log, report or track chart sug-gests it, and Evan-Thomas would surely not have kept such prompt corrective action secret.

It is also arguable – and Craig and Egerton may have had this in mind – that the stationing regime of 5 miles NNW of *Lion* was independent of any given course, and remained in force until cancelled or super-seded, regardless of *Lion*'s antics. The duty to keep station falls entirely on the consorts of the flagship (or nominated 'guide'), however unreasonable her behaviour appears to be – unless she has obviously been disabled. *Barham* should therefore have striven to remain in station by copying *Lion*'s major course and speed changes without delay. This is the fail-safe solution, for if Beatty had not meant the 5th BS to follow, Evan-Thomas would in the meantime at least have remained in the visual range necessary for *Lion* to convey other instructions; whereas by persisting northwards as he did – by letting go the 5-mile station ordered at 1.30 p.m. – he would have been beyond recall by visual means in a few more minutes.

At this distance in time these factors are difficult to weigh one against another. It may be asserted, in the light of influences which will be explored in a later section of this book, that Evan-Thomas was a stickler for correct signalling procedures and trained his team to recognize only clear statements which arrived in proper executive-order format. A presumption of by-the-book signalling practices, compounded either by dullness of mind or by incomplete attention, certainly seems to have been present on *Barham*'s compass-platform.

No doubt there were distractions. There was the station-keeping problem astern; and perhaps captain, admiral, staff-commander and flag-lieutenant (all of them or some of them) arrived out of breath, each demanding to know what the hell was going on. Lieutenant Phillips would have had to put them in the picture, with interruptions, and probably chose his words carefully with regard to the 2-point turn to NbyW. One may speculate that Evan-Thomas took some minutes to get his bearings and clarify in his mind the sequence of events. In the meantime he was not sure that Philips had done the wrong thing and so persisted with the zig, by way of taking refuge in a familiar pattern of behaviour, while making a public stand on the worthy principle of waiting for orders. This would explain but not excuse. At any rate, far from being, as Marder judges, the product of positive thinking, the delay in following the senior flag-officer was almost certainly the result of doubt and dither. The contrast to Collingwood's first response to an array of flag-hoists in *Victory*'s rigging at the opening of Trafalgar – "I wish Nelson would stop signalling. We know well enough what to do" – could hardly be greater.

Lion's signalling efficiency

However, the onus would not have devolved onto Evan-Thomas's initiative if *Lion*'s signalling had been conducted professionally and in accordance with Grand Fleet Battle Orders. To order Evan-Thomas to close the flagship was the easiest thing in the world and had been provided for in signal orders for two hundred years. A *Lion* of 1776, for example, would have hoisted a blue and white flag at her foretop-masthead and fired a gun, the process being repeated if necessary by her consort nearest to *Barham*. It was even simpler in 1916. The letters 'EJ' flashed by searchlight would have done the deed in seconds – unless, of course, the right people failed to think of it.

This is where Beatty's flag-lieutenant, Lieutenant-Commander Ralph Seymour, enters the spotlight. The flag-lieutenant was the admiral's public mouthpiece: in harbour he was his social secretary, at sea he was his signals adviser and oversaw the fleet's (or squadron's) signalling efficiency. Historians such as Roskill, Marder and Hough are scathing about Seymour, with justification. The sorry catalogue of errors for which he has been held wholly or partially responsible accounts for a reckonable proportion of the Royal Navy's disappointments in 1914–16.

A less indulgent flag-officer would have had Seymour transferred after either of two separate incidents more than a year before Jutland:

1. On December 16th, 1914, after Scarborough had been bombarded, Beatty was well placed to trap Hipper's retreating battlecruisers when a badly addressed signal from *Lion* caused Commodore William Goodenough, in the light-cruiser *Southampton*, to break off a skirmish with German light forces, thus severing the only point of contact with the enemy.

What happened was this. Two of Goodenough's cruisers, *Southampton* and *Birmingham*, were exchanging fire with a German light-cruiser and destroyers. His other two ships, *Nottingham* and *Falmouth*, were nearby but not actively involved. All four were absent from their normal screening positions ahead of the 1st BCS, and Beatty wished the unengaged ships to return to station. Seymour's searchlight order to *Nottingham* appeared to be addressed to the whole squadron rather than to the two ships intended, and in this form *Nottingham* relayed it to Goodenough in *Southampton*.

Bill (or 'Barge') Goodenough has been universally admired for his performance at Jutland, to the point where he is almost beyond historical criticism. However, he was by no means the free-thinking radical which, for example, his father James had been, and was representative of the sort of street-wise no-nonsense seaman typically produced by the Edwardian Navy: "He was a rascal! What 'e didn't know about the sailor-fish didn't matter."[21] However, his understanding of action-priorities – and of working with Beatty – was less complete, in December 1914, and on this day of 'Scarborough' his learning experience was steep and painful. He did what he understood he had been told, and broke off the engagement.

In the recriminations which followed, Beatty wanted him sacked; but Jellicoe (an old friend and patron) intervened, to the future benefit of the BCF. No doubt Goodenough should have found the enemy of a more compelling interest than *Lion*'s signals, and there are various 'tally-ho' clauses in BCFOs which could be cited against him. But the viciousness with which Beatty laid the whole blame on the commodore, in sympathy-seeking correspondence with all and sundry, seems almost to have been founded on the premiss that wrongly addressed signals from flagships are to be expected and it is the duty of subordinates to allow for them. This is taking the 'initiative' ethic to the threshold of abdication.

2. In the BCF's pursuit of the 1st SG at Dogger Bank a few weeks later there was more of the same.[22] After *Lion* and the German quasi-battlecruiser *Blücher* had both been crippled, an ambiguous signal from the former caused *Tiger*, *Princess Royal* and *New Zealand* to break off pursuit of Hipper's other ships and gang up on the doomed *Blücher* – which could have been dealt with by the lagging *Indomitable* and destroyers.

Lion, engines stopped, had fallen astern of the action, her sister 'cats' racing past her. They were temporarily steering NE, 90° to the south-easterly-flying enemy, in fact towards the helpless *Blücher*, because of an anti-U-boat manoeuvre ordered (but not explained) by Beatty who thought he had seen a periscope.[23] He now wanted to make sure they resumed the pursuit of Hipper, and Nelson's "Engage the enemy more closely" was searched for in the signal book, in vain. "Attack the rear of the enemy" was the best Seymour could offer. *Lion* had no electrical power to her searchlights, and her W/T aerials and most of her halyards had been carried away by shell-splinters. But two halyards remained, one of which was still carrying "COURSE NE" in belated reference to the evasive alteration a few minutes earlier. The stirring new signal was duly hoisted on the other halyard, only to be hauled down simultaneously with the "Course NE" hoist, appearing to make a combined executive order to "ATTACK THE REAR OF THE ENEMY, BEARING NORTH-EAST". Up till then the battlecruisers' primary quarry had been obvious to a man of the meanest intelligence. But now all was doubt.

To Rear-Admiral Archibald Moore in *New Zealand* the unexpected order pointed to *Blücher* and appeared to shed light on the unexplained change of course. Under his leadership the battlecruisers surrounded their lone victim like baying hounds. At this juncture Hipper could have responded like the French admiral being pursued off Cape Ortegal in 1805: when his slowest ship fell astern he turned back with his other three in support and lost them all to Sir Richard Strachan. But he had more sense; and Beatty's real trade, *Seydlitz*, *Moltke* and *Derfflinger*, escaped.

Beatty was beside himself with rage. Moore, whom he disliked and whose appointment to the 2nd BCS he had resented from the start,[24] was replaced by William Pakenham and sent to a backwater command in the Canary Islands. Henry Pelly, the captain of *Tiger*, the leading ship after *Lion* was knocked out, was grudgingly given the benefit of the doubt, although Fisher, the First Sea Lord, thought he should have refused to turn back and follow Moore ("any fool can obey orders"). Another spate of hard-luck letters issued from Beatty: "there was never a more disappointing day . . . it was terrible . . . a very severe shock . . . the blackest week in my life . . . it nearly broke my heart."[25] What he overlooked or suppressed, was an item in BCFOs in the light of which his subordinates look slightly less poltroonish:

> When fighting a retarding action with the rear ships of an enemy's fleet, it is possible that some of them may be already damaged and reduced in speed. Fire will be concentrated on these.[26]

Seymour's apparent signal harmonized with this misconceived instruction, and the bare fact of the matter is that, as at Scarborough, it was the signal itself that was the root cause of the débâcle.

In the first place, it was a piece of amateur dramatics and unnecessary (as Seymour almost admitted in the following topsy-turvy explanation to a Greenwich staff course in 1919: "The *Lion* disabled, the command devolved upon another who, misinterpreting signals which were made from a disabled ship, instead of being guided by tactical principles, lost touch"[27]). Secondly, the principle that two flag-hoists, if hauled down together, are associated, was elementary signals toilet-training. Goodenough's acid comment (still stung, no doubt, by memory of his Scarborough reprimand) sums up the episode: "I would suggest that the fewer signals made in action the better."[28] And as historian James Goldrick has remarked, if *all* the flagship's halyards had been shot down, the Battle of the Dogger Bank might have ended differently.

Seymour wouldn't have lasted a week with Fisher, Jellicoe or Cunningham (or Evan-Thomas, for that matter) and it is astonishing that a man with Beatty's responsibilities should have sheltered such a liability. Much has been made of the fact that he was not a properly trained signals-officer, having done the standard (or 'short') signals course but not the 'long course' which would have qualified him for an 'S' after his name in the *Navy List*. This argument is, to some extent, a case of the 'signals school' grinding the axe of the Signal School. The 'long course' was a recent innovation, and was still optional. Since flag-lieutenants had become a fixture in flagships in the early nineteenth century, three or four generations of them had done the job, usually with a high standard of competence, without any formal baptism as specialists. Seymour would no doubt have benefited from the class-room conditioning of the long course, and it might have made all the difference; but, on the other hand, it might not. The unreal world of peacetime laboratory conditions, which the 'S's tried to project into warfare at sea, had its own dangerous pitfalls; and the only certain point about Seymour is that, in the distractions and alarms of battle, he was not very good at it. The question of how he had got the job in the first place is one which will be explored in a later chapter. But why did Beatty keep him on after the signalling gaffes became apparent?

A shipmate wrote that Seymour "had a cheerful disposition well suited to Beatty's temperament" and the admiral developed "a great affection for him and referred to him as 'my little round flag-lieu-tenant'".[29] James Goldrick believes simply that "Seymour was a pleas-ant face to have around" and that Beatty, although arrogant and ambitious, "was rarely one for the knife in the back of a subordinate".[30] Roskill, also, comments on the admiral's loyalty to his immediate team, "carried to excess" in his flag-lieutenant's case. After Scarborough Beatty made the following pious declaration to Jellicoe, with Goodenough's alleged misdemeanour in mind:

> The issues are too important for us to be allowed to indulge in the luxury of mistakes. We cannot afford to make any. And I am of the opinion that when men fail under the test of war to carry out the most elementary duties of their work they should not be given opportunities of making others which will have more disastrous results. If you take this view I would earnestly submit that an officer should be appointed in his place who we *know absolutely* would not fail . . .[31]

Beatty could have arranged a destroyer command for his friend without loss of face to either, or at least sent him away to get fully educated in the business of signalling. He did neither.

Instead, he kept Seymour with him throughout the war, both in the BCF and later (to the dismay of the 'S' lobby) in the Grand Fleet flag-ship; and even took him to the Admiralty as an *ex officio* man-Friday when he became First Sea Lord. In the early 1920s, when informed analyses of Jutland were tarnishing his glory, the admiral unendearingly came round to blaming his flag-lieutenant – "he lost three battles for me"[32] – and (as will be related) played a role in Seymour's extraordinary illness and death. But during the war, when it really mattered, his per-sistent blind-spot in respect of his protégé was another striking case of double standards, comparable to his lack of interest in 'community of thought' with Evan-Thomas. In Hough's words its cost to the Navy was "immeasurable".[33]

It is permissible to judge that the misunderstanding over the 5th BS's turn to the SSE was another Seymour-assisted fiasco. Jellicoe certainly held this to be the case. After the war he wrote that Beatty's

> signal officer throughout disobeyed my Battle Instructions that when in the presence of the enemy all signals were to be made by flags, searchlight and wireless. Had these instructions been carried out I think Hipper would have been annihilated.[34]

And Madden consoled Evan-Thomas with:

> I think that I am correct in stating that had the GF Signal Procedure been practised at PZ's by the BCF as was done in the Battle Fleet, the signal in question would, as a matter of routine, have been passed to *Barham* by searchlight and W/T guardship.[35]

In broader terms the episode, like Scarborough and Dogger Bank, speaks poorly of the standard of signalling discipline tolerated in the BCF. But considered in the light of BCFOs, were Seymour's failings really so heinous? The argument that Beatty's tactical fundamentalism was intended to liberate his command from the priesthood of signals officers will be discussed later. Here, however, it only returns us to his failure to brief RA5BS in Rosyth.

The stationing of the 5th BS

Beatty's stationing of the 5th BS, so far from *Lion* and in the worst possible direction for the pursuit of the enemy, has been discussed in the last chapter. As stated there, it was a peacetime disposition, designed to smooth the restationing of Beatty's forces on their junction with the battle-fleet, rather than one ordered with the prospect seriously in mind of meeting Hipper's battlecruisers. It has also been asserted that a true professional would have held the possibility of action in mind at all times. In view of events at least partly attributable to his unfortunate stationing of the battleships, it is no surprise that Beatty and his partisans retrospectively contrived other reasons for it.

At an acrimonious meeting at the Admiralty, on the 26th of June, Beatty cast aspersions on Evan-Thomas's shiphandling. Present were Sir Henry Jackson (First Sea Lord), Jellicoe, Commodore Allan Everett (naval secretary to the First Lord) and Beatty. According to Beatty's own notes, he restated his demand that the 5th BS should be attached to him in future, to which Sir Henry remarked that "the next time I had them with me he hoped that 'I would keep them in line with me.'" At this VABCF brazenly declared that if they had worked together before, he would have put them at 2 miles, but "as this was the first time we had ever been at sea together, it was considered advisable to give them more sea room. Squadrons of the heaviest ships moving at 25 knots require room unless they have been previously manoeuvred together."[36] This is fairly outrageous: it does nothing to justify the direction in which the battleships were stationed; there was little anyone in the BCF could have taught Evan-Thomas about 'fleetwork'; and although the 5th BS had probably had little practice in manoeuvring at '25 knots', full-speed would only arise in the presence of the enemy, when safety factors would be disregarded.

After the war, in private memoranda and marginalia unlikely to meet Jellicoe's eyes in his lifetime, Beatty sought to infiltrate the idea that Sir John had tied his hands with respect to the *Queen Elizabeths*, for fear of his endangering them:

> The C-in-C was obsessed with the idea that the ships of the 5th BS were not as fast as anticipated and that the German Battleships were faster than antici-pated. He was very reluctant to allow them (5th BS) to take the place of the 3rd BCS when they went North for practices at Scapa and only consented to agree to my urgent request on the strict understanding and definite instruction that they were only to be used as a Supporting Force to avoid the possibility of their being engaged by a superior force when their lack of speed would prevent them from making good their retreat. Consequently they were disposed as they were, 5 miles away from anticipated position of sighting enemy.[37]

In this Beatty was exploiting and twisting Jellicoe's well-documented misgivings about the real speed performance of the 5th BS. In fact Jellicoe deplored Beatty's stationing of the *Queen Elizabeths* and rightly complained that had the 3rd BCS been present instead of the *QEs*, as was usually the case, VABCF would not have so dispersed his forces.[38]

Beatty was correctly representing Jellicoe in asserting that he had rejected the 5th BS as a supporting force in a Beatty–Scheer encounter: the C-in-C indeed worried about such a meeting but knew that a Beatty–Hipper encounter was more likely and would almost certainly come first. That was the whole point. In the words of Jellicoe's chief of staff:

> The C-in-C gave the 5th BS to VABCF so that in Hood's absence he should be so superior to von Hipper that the result of a meeting should not be in doubt. This needed keeping the 5th BS close in hand on account of its lower speed.[39]

The 5th BS would not have been loaned to Beatty if an out-of-the-blue meeting with Scheer's battle-fleet had been considered the most likely hypothesis. Also, it may be mentioned that had Beatty himself genuinely considered such an encounter probable, stationing *Engadine* as he did, 12 miles to the SSE, would have been tantamount to throwing the converted cross-Channel ferry away.

Chalmers, Beatty's first biographer, attempted a further justification of the stationing of the battleships which hardly seems compatible but can be rejected on substantially the same grounds:

> If Beatty had placed the Fifth Battle Squadron any closer, they would have become part of his own fleet. Hipper, on finding himself confronted with such a superior force, would certainly have refused action, and there might not have been a battle at all.[40]

The detailed rightness or wrongness of this bland assertion depends on matters of opinion and to argue it either way would be a waste of time. It makes a nonsense of why Beatty had been given the *Queen Elizabeths*, and if it has any validity, he had failed to think of it when he pestered Jellicoe for the battleships back in March. One finds oneself repeating that nobody had forced the 5th BS on him; and, far from worrying about frightening the Germans away, his claim to the squadron had been based on alarmism about the BCF's possible inferiority over the (reputedly) enhanced 1st SG.

*

Finally, there is a complaint raised by Jellicoe in 'A Criticism of Errors made in Jutland Battle' written in 1932, when he was 72 years old. Jellicoe, who did not spare himself in this document, pointed out that, contrary to Beatty's claim in his despatches that upon receipt of *Galatea's* 2.20 message he "immediately" altered course to the SSE (Jellicoe actually wrote 'ESE' in error), he did not in fact do so until 2.32. In the intervening time he could "have concentrated his force".[41] The listed timings of signals indeed suggest that 5 minutes (a reasonable enough time) elapsed between *Galatea's* signal and the *Lion's* warning order to destroyers, and then a further 7 before the general order to "turn SSE". In other words at least 7 minutes passed between Beatty's deciding to try to cut the enemy ships off from their line of retreat and his taking action on that decision. If he had turned at once, leaving the destroyers to sort themselves out, he would have gained 2 miles (4,000 yards). More pertinent, perhaps, is the comment that he might have accompanied the warning order to destroyers with a searchlight order to Evan-Thomas to close, a precaution which would have formally broken the 5-mile stationing regime, would have reduced the 5th BS's separation from *Lion*, and would have pointed *Barham*'s attention in the right direction. It makes much sense, and there is a case to answer.

However, it was not in Beatty's nature to dither, and the accuracy of official timings cannot be taken for granted (see Appendix I), useful though they may be to prove this or that in retrospect. It may be that *Galatea*'s enemy report did not reach his hand until some minutes after receipt in *Lion*, and that the destroyer warning more closely preceded the general "turn SSE" order. Beatty should be given some benefit of the doubt. Besides, if he was unable to see his stationing priorities clearly in the quiet calm of the admiral's chart-house as *Lion* wended her way down the Forth on Tuesday night, or as he lunched with his staff before he sent his restationing signal at 1.30, it is unrealistic to expect clarity to strike when enemy reports were coming in, *Lion*'s command team was closing up and demanding to know what was happening, and the adrenalin was beginning to flow.

*

It is one thing to think through the arguments on both sides of the issue, it is quite another to apportion blame. Beatty, Seymour and Evan-Thomas (and possibly *Barham*'s officer-of-the-watch) could each have prevented the thing going awry, and each was remiss in the manner in which he failed to do so.

Evan-Thomas's later explanations of what went wrong had some of the characteristics of Vice-Admiral Richard Lestock's sophistic defence for trailing astern of Admiral Thomas Matthews at the Battle of Toulon in 1744. Lestock's rear division was several miles astern of station – out of supporting distance of the main fleet. Matthews ordered him into station, and to help him get there signalled the fleet to slow down. The signal was a general one, and so Lestock also obeyed it. His defence (which his court-martial chose to accept) was that the 'slow down' signal overrode the 'station' signal.

Where Beatty was in error in matters which could be covered by the term 'staff work', Captain Rudolf Bentinck, his chief of staff, and the Hon. Reginald Plunkett, his flag-commander, must share the liability; for he had a rare understanding, when it suited him, of the role of staff-officers and often paid attention to their opinions.

*

Sir David therefore charged off to the SSE to sort out *Galatea*'s enemy light-cruisers – or rather to block their line of retreat – with his heavy support trailing far behind. Had only light-cruisers been in the offing, the 5th BS's absence wouldn't have mattered two pins. But as *Barham* belatedly put her helm over, 30 miles to the east *Galatea*'s Morse-key was tapping out "URGENT. HAVE SIGHTED LARGE AMOUNT OF SMOKE AS THOUGH FROM A FLEET BEARING ENE." Beatty now came round to a north-easterly course to give Alexander-Sinclair direct support, and within the hour five large sleek pale-grey shapes were looming dimly in the haze to the north-eastwards of *Lion*. The die was cast. Beatty later defended himself by asking rhetorically if six British battlecruisers should wait for support before tackling five German. Of course not, had that equation been the whole story; but until Hipper's force was sighted and counted, it was believed that the 1st Scouting Group had been joined by the new *Hindenburg* and would thus number six in total and possibly include two battlecruisers with 15-inch guns. If such odds were unexceptionable to VABCF, why had he made such a fuss about needing the *Queen Elizabeths* in the first place? Having hustled for the 5th BS, and won, VABCF was about to engage the 1st Scouting Group no better off than if the battleships had stayed in Scapa, and it was substantially his own fault. Nelson, with whom he was wont to identify, would have deplored the loss of opportunity to field crushingly superior force.

But even now, it is unlikely that anyone in the BCF who was aware of the *Queen Elizabeths'* distance astern, was much bothered. Indeed, Walter Cowan, the captain of *Princess Royal*, was seized with the fear that "that damned 5th Battle Squadron is going to take the bread out of our mouths";[42] and Roskill considers it "reasonable to extend Cowan's thinking to the admiral whom he so dearly admired".[43]

"Damn those heavies, they'll have the laugh of us today," Lord Cardigan had fumed on the slopes of Balaclava, as he watched James Scarlett's Heavy Brigade pitch into a mass of Russian cavalry in the valley below. The battlecruisers were certainly not going to be upstaged.[44]

7

The Battlecruiser Duel

"Something wrong with our bloody ships."

The sounding by buglers, and relaying by call-boys, of 'ACTION STA-
TIONS' (the term 'general quarters', historically accompanied by a
drumbeat to the rhythm of *Heart of Oak*, was falling into disuse) seems
to have printed itself indelibly on many men's memories and provides a
freeze-frame of daily life at sea in British warships. In those ships whose
routines were running on GMT the enemy-sighting caught off-watch
personnel still recovering from their midday meal, and many of them in
the land of nod.

Galatea, the ship which first sighted the enemy, was the first to go to
action-stations. Her signals-officer was

> on the quarterdeck, basking in the sun. I had heard that we were going to
> action-stations for drill purposes sometime during the afternoon, so [when
> the bugle sounded] I strolled forward to my station: a little home-made
> Wireless Office on the foc'sle, where I coded and decoded signals in action.
> Just as I went up the ladder to the foc'sle I was deafened by the [forward] 6-
> inch gun firing, and was almost blown down the ladder again by the blast. I
> nipped in to my little W/T rabbit-hutch quicker than it takes to tell, and as I
> entered there rattled down the communication tube from the upper bridge,
> the first enemy report of the Battle of Jutland.[1]

As other light-cruisers arrived in headlong support, and the first
German shells began crashing into the sea around them, the reaction of
one officer, accustomed to towing targets for the Grand Fleet, was
"Hey, watch out! You're going to hit us!"

In *Southampton*, near the other end of the cruiser screen, Lieutenant
Stephen King-Hall was

dozing in the smoking room after lunch when the secretary put his head in, and said: '*Galatea*, at the northern end of the line has sighted and is chasing two hostile cruisers.' This was at 2.23 and woke us all up with a jump.

I quickly went to my cabin and made certain preparations which I always did when there was a chance of something happening. These preparations consisted in putting on as many clothes as possible, collecting my camera, notebook and pencils, chocolate, and other aids to comfort in case of a prolonged stay at action-stations.[2]

In those ships whose routines were running on British Summer Time the Germans interrupted afternoon tea.

A signal delivered to *Malaya*'s bridge visibly excited the small knot of officers on the compass-platform. The midshipman-of-the-watch,

being, like all snotties, very curious, eventually mustered enough courage to ask the officer-of-the-watch what it was about, only to be snubbed for my pains. A few minutes later, however, the captain sent me down to the engineer-commander with a copy of the signal (which naturally I read). It was from *Galatea*, reporting two enemy ships in sight. I duly returned to the bridge after telling the engineer-commander that the captain wanted steam for full speed as soon as possible.

By this time I was beginning to feel slightly excited, but a few minutes later the hands were piped to tea, and my excitement cooled; only, however, nearly to consume me again, when, on receipt of another signal, I was told to call all officers in their cabins, and to order the bugler to sound off 'Action'.[3]

Sleeping in the gunroom armchair, Sub-Lieutenant Clifford Caslon was

awoken by some excited conversation on the part of the midshipmen, one of whom had just come down from the bridge, and said there was a 'buzz' that a German destroyer had been sighted by 'someone, somewhere' – it didn't sound very promising. The steward was laying the table for tea, but we never sat down to it, as just at 3.30 the bugles sounded for 'action' and we all ran to our stations.[4]

New Zealand's wardroom received the news "with cold suspicion, and although one or two officers came on deck to have a look around, the general attitude was one of scepticism".[5] Her 'young gentlemen', on the other hand, were taking no chances:

the snottie-of-the-watch dashed in to inform us that the *Galatea* had sighted enemy ships and that we should be going to 'Action Stations' in ten minutes time. Not knowing what this might lead to, we made the most of that ten minutes stowing away as much food as possible.[6]

In *Barham*, Midshipman Royer Dick, rushing off to his 'action' post down in the (range-)transmitting station, cast a wistful glance at tea, laid out immaculately on the gunroom table, and wondered when they would get the chance to eat it.[7] When he next saw the gunroom it was an utter shambles.

In *Warspite* 'ACTION STATIONS' was in fact a mistake by Commander Humphrey Walwyn, the executive-officer. He had got a message from Captain Edward Phillpotts "to get the hands up at once", and at the same time he was shown *Galatea*'s report of an enemy cruiser. So he

> sounded off 'action' and passed the word round to everybody to get cleared away as fast as possible. Message from the Captain to ask why I had sounded 'action' and that he wanted me.
>
> Went up to fore-bridge and got rather 'bitten', as apparently he only meant get the hands shaken up and get some tea etc. early. Anyway, I explained that we were well on the way [to] clearing away and should like to get everything ready and get tea after if there was time.

To this the captain agreed, and so most Warspites missed their tea.[8]

Bugle calls for practice-purposes were prefixed and suffixed with 'G' notes, denoting 'for exercise'. People were unaccustomed to hearing 'action-stations' without the Gs and in many cases it took some moments for the penny to drop. In theory it should have made little difference to the speed of response; but most ships had already practised 'action' that morning (some had done gunnery 'control' in the afternoon, in spite of the make-and-mend) and tea is, after all, tea. *Warspite*'s Assistant-Clerk Bickmore

> had just sat down in the Gunroom when the bugle for Action Stations sounded outside in the flat. For a minute I did not realize that the call had not been followed by the one G which [would have] meant it was for exercise only; in fact it was the real thing. Grabbing as much portable food as I could, I dashed back to my turret and as soon as I got there we heard that the enemy was in sight. The Battle of Jutland had begun.[9]

If the impression has been imparted that midshipmen were pre-occupied with food, this is correct; but others too were inconvenienced. In *Malaya*'s No. 19 Mess

> we had a two-badge [= long service] able-seaman called Stevens, the senior bugler of the ship. At first we thought it was just a practice when we heard the first sound from on deck, but suddenly Stevo jumped up and grabbed his bugle, saying 'There's no bloody G!', and sounded full blast on the messdeck. That was the end of our tea.[10]

An engineer lieutenant in *Tiger*

> was slightly indignant [at] having to go to Action Stations at that time of day, thinking that it could only be 'exercise action' and not the real thing . . . I

thought I had misheard the call on the bugle but I soon found out I was wrong . . . So my proposed cup of tea went west.[11]

And his messmate, the padre, was only wakened from the sleep of the just by the increased vibration of the propeller shafts beneath him. The wardroom was like the *Mary Celeste*: "All the cups and plates were on the table but the room was empty. They had evidently been called away in the middle of tea, and suddenly."[12]

The most dilatory respondent to 'action-stations' was probably Midshipman Anthony Combe of *Lion*. There is a certain rough irony in that many years later this man had his leg bitten off by a lion (having unwisely shot it with too light a rifle). He had just been stood down from control practice at the foretop range-finder and was in the gunroom,

having a boiled egg and bread and butter, and enjoying my food immensely when 'control' again sounded off. Why they sounded off control 5 minutes after they had been at control for an hour, I couldn't make out at the time, but I wasn't going to leave my boiled egg or my tea until my hunger had been appeased. At 3.55 I thought I might as well stroll up and see what was doing and upon coming on to the bridge, I enquired why they had sounded off again. The chief yeoman of signals told me that there were some hostile cruisers on the horizon. This sounded rather exciting, so I thought, and proceeded immediately to the foretop which is my station during action.

Upon arriving up there I found the gunnery lieutenant-commander and Lieutenant Lake [he of the boiled shirt!] and the fleet paymaster and two seamen, one who works the 'time of flight' card and the other who takes down on some paper spotting corrections and so forth. I was cursed for being so late but I was in high spirits so I didn't mind and took my seat by the voice-pipe which I look after. I can remember feeling very excited and pleased with life at the prospect of there being an action with the Huns.[13]

*

By now in every unit under Beatty's command, patrols were going through the ship systematically wetting the decks, laying flat tables and stools, lighting action-candles, and closing steel doors with all eight clips instead of the usual two. Medical parties were at sick-bays and casualty distribution centres, laying out their surgical implements and medical bags, their stretchers, dressings, morphia and syringes. Fire-and-repair parties were sorting their splinter mats, boxes of sand, softwood wedges, mallets, shoring-up timbers, spare electrical gear, etc. On the upper deck, swivel-mounted fittings and guard-rail stanchions in the way of gunnery arcs were struck flat; hoses were faked out, turned half-on and left running; extra chain-stoppers were fitted to the cables to prevent the anchors being let go by action-damage. The glass wind-screens on the bridge were unshipped and stowed. Union Flags were hoisted at the main,[14] and numerous White Ensigns at yardarms and gaffs. *Malaya* broke out the ensign of the Federated Malay States, which, in action, made her look like "an enraged P. & O." (due to its similarity to the house flag of that shipping company). *Barham's* mainmast was still sporting the gunnery-officer's wedding garland.

On his way from *Barham's* bridge, where he had been standing the afternoon watch, to his action billet in 'X' turret (the Royal Marines' turret), Midshipman Frampton passed his turret officer, Captain Clutterbuck RM, "hurriedly engaged in removing some tins of petrol from his private skiff, which he kept on board and in which he used to go pigeon-shooting at Scapa, and throwing them over the side". Presently Clutterbuck joined Frampton and Lieutenant Ryan RM in X turret's 'silent cabinet' –

> a small compartment (not at all silent) at the rear of the turret and almost immediately below the Officer of the Turret who stood on a platform and could see through a slit in the roof. I was supplied with a stop-watch, marked off showing the time-of-flight at different ranges so that when a gun fired, I started the watch and when the shell was due at its destination, shouted 'Splash'. The idea was, of course, to enable the officer of the turret to dis-tinguish which of the many splashes round our target were ours. It was a rather rough and ready system, and obviously more important when in local control, but it did give the turret officer an idea as to how our shooting was going.[15]

New Zealand's action-stations check-off list included some unortho-dox procedures which were a legacy of her pre-war visit to the domin-ion whose name she bore and which had paid for her (or rather, which would be paying for her until 1958). There was a special steering-wheel which had to be shipped in the conning-tower, built from different kinds of indigenous New Zealand wood and inscribed with the Maori war-cry "*Ake, Ake, Ake, Kia Kaha!*" (Fight on, fight on, fight on, for ever!). And, on the bridge, Captain John Green was faced with one of those little dilemmas for which captains drew command-pay. There were two symbolic tribal garments which had been presented to the ship by a Maori chieftain, after a suitable war-dance, with the warranty that the great grey canoe would come to no harm in battle as long as her captain was wearing them. The items were a greenstone pendant known as a *tiki*, and a sort of rush-mat apron, called a *piu piu*, to be worn round the waist. Green's predecessor, Lionel Halsey, had donned them as prescribed at the Battle of Dogger Bank, from which the ship duly emerged unscathed. Green now put the *tiki* round his neck but was too stout to wear the *piu piu* without discomfort, so he just kept it close at hand, "ready to put on should things become too hot".[16]

Engadine, the ugly duckling of the BCF, was going through her own particular processes. At 2.37 *Falmouth* (Rear-Admiral Napier's 3rd LCS flagship), charging off to support *Galatea*, flashed her a brief explanation about the enemy sightings, and told her to close the BCF, which was by now heading towards the seaplane-carrier anyway. This gave a few minutes' warning of what followed: a flashed order from *Lion* to "SEND UP SEAPLANES TO SCOUT NNE, [adding] AM SENDING TWO DESTROYERS TO YOU." *Engadine*'s stern was now a scene of frenzied activity. The awkward hangar-doors were opened; a Short seaplane was extracted, its wings were unfolded, its engine was cranked, and it was hoisted out and dunked in the sea. By 3.08 (said to be a record) it was airborne. Its pilot, Flight-Lieutenant Frederick Rutland ('of Jutland') had three weeks earlier submitted a paper urging the construction of aircraft-carriers with 600-foot flight-decks and 35 knots' speed. He was more or less describing the future light-battlecruiser conversions *Glorious*, *Courageous* and *Furious*; but this afternoon *Engadine* was the best the Royal Navy could manage. The larger seaplane-carrier *Campania* (which at least had a flying-off deck) had somehow got left behind in Scapa Flow.[17]

In *Warspite* Commander Walwyn did a quick below-decks tour of the ship, "saw all doors and everything closed", and reported to Captain Phillpotts that the ship was 'closed up'. On his way down from the bridge he went to his sea-cabin and collected his Gieves inflatable waist-coat, and then went to his post in B turret (from whence he could most easily take over command in event of the captain's death). As the turret trained massively round from side to side he studied those parts of the upper deck which were visible through the sighting-hood, and spotted two omissions in the clearing-away procedure: the port-side sounding boom (a long pole used to work the Kelvin depth-machine) was still rigged, and the jackstaff was still standing proudly in the bows. He wondered ruefully if the latter, a brand-new replacement of one recently lost in heavy weather, would get blown away by *Warspite*'s own gun-blast. Too late now. Anyway,

> everybody in the turret was in very good spirits, and I asked [Midshipman Geoffrey] Grenfell if he had any cotton-wool. He said he hadn't and passed me [instead] a lump of cotton-waste, enough to stop the ears of a donkey, which I chucked back at him and almost at once got the order to 'stand by'.[18]

Astern, in *Malaya*'s B turret, the men were "greatly cheered" by the news that the light-cruisers were in action. They assured the turret officer that no chance would be missed to ease off a round at the Huns, and at once began to make little preparations, taking off superfluous clothing and so forth. They made all sorts of weird and wonderful jokes as to what would happen to any German ship unfortunate enough to come within range.[19]

*

While the light-cruisers of the German 2nd Scouting Group were sparring with Alexander-Sinclair's squadron (and being buzzed by a lone float-plane), Rear-Admiral Franz Hipper, with *Lützow*, *Derfflinger*, *Seydlitz*, *Moltke* and *Von der Tann*, was pressing westwards to lend decisive support. In the spotting-top of *Derfflinger*, the gunnery-officer, Lieutenant-Commander Georg von Hase, watched the 2nd SG suddenly turn about and steam hard for the protection of the battlecruisers. The view ahead blew clear of smoke, and there, starkly silhouetted against the bright south-western horizon, were Beatty's famous battlecruisers. Magnified and foreshortened fifteen times by his Zeiss gunnery-control periscope, they appeared as

> black monsters; six tall, broad-beamed giants steaming in two columns. They were still a long way off, but they showed up clearly on the horizon, and even at this great distance they looked powerful, massive . . . I could now recognize them as the six most modern enemy battlecruisers . . . It was a stimulating, majestic spectacle as the dark-grey giants approached like fate itself.

Upon sighting the German battlecruisers, Beatty told the 2nd BCS to fall into line, and came up to 25 knots. *New Zealand* and *Indefatigable* swung to starboard and took station astern of *Tiger*. To von Hase, the two groups "closed on one another, like a herd of prehistoric monsters, with slow movements, spectre-like, irresistible".[20]

Hipper's response was to reduce speed for a few minutes, gather his dependants around him, and reverse course by wheeling his squadron (16 points to starboard) round to the SSE – towards the Horns Reef channel, or, rather, the High Seas Fleet which had only recently emerged from it. Beatty without hesitation followed suit to try to cut him off, and there now commenced what was to prove a dramatic and bloody race to the south.

Lieutenant His Serene Highness Prince George of Battenberg, at his observation slit in *New Zealand*'s A turret, sought permission from the bridge to go to his cabin to fetch his cine-camera (one of only two present at Jutland), and was curtly refused.[21] Down in the transmitting station, Midshipman Eady heard the order "All guns load!" being passed with great glee, by the marine bandsmen who operated the telephones in the four turrets. At this moment somebody rang up from a remote action station asking if we had packed up yet as he wanted to get his tea.

Ranges now began to come through to us from the range-finders in the turrets and the foretop. The action, in so far as I and my assistant snotty were concerned, had begun. Facing us were six range-transmitters, worked [remotely] by the men at each range-finder. As these flicked round altering the ranges it was our job to mark them down on a large moving roll of paper spread out on the table in front of us. This was called the Plotting Table and each range-transmitter was shown by a different coloured pencil. Two snotties and two ABs as voice-pipe men completed the Plotting Table's crew. Making marks in coloured pencils on a piece of paper seemed a funny way of fighting a naval action, but by plotting the ranges we were able to determine at what rate the enemy was opening or closing on us.

Several miles astern, and unable to see any ships except *Malaya*, the small group in *Warspite*'s torpedo control-tower (at the after end of the superstructure), were beside themselves to know what was going on; so the torpedo-lieutenant put a trunk call through to the gunnery-lieutenant in the foretop. Their chat was interrupted by the booming of gunfire, and word was passed that the battlecruisers were in action.

Hipper's pale-grey ships blended well against the lowering overcast to the east, and the British, overestimating the range, waited too long before opening fire. It was the Germans who broke the tension, at 3.45 GMT, at about 18,500 yards and closing fast. "Then began an ear-splitting, stupefying, din."[22] Far astern, in *Malaya*'s starboard 6-inch gun control-tower Sub-Lieutenant Caslon watched through the slit in the armour as the battlecruisers "formed a single line, at the same time altering course to the SE and increasing to full speed. A few minutes afterwards they opened fire – it was the most glorious sight and I was tremendously thrilled."

*

Derfflinger's gunnery-officer felt afterwards that his ship had been slow to find the range. He put this down to the men at the range-finders being "completely overwhelmed by the first view of the enemy monsters. Each one saw the enemy ship magnified 23 times in his instrument." Apology was hardly necessary, for the Germans did much better than the British; indeed everything seemed to start wrong for the BCF.

In von Hase's own words "the English battlecruisers had a decidedly unfavourable tactical position". He alluded to three of the handicaps under which they were labouring.[23]

1. "The visibility facing east was inferior to that facing west." Certainly, in report after British report, memoir after memoir, the prejudicial visibility conditions are underscored by witnesses. It was, in Stephen King-Hall's words, "extremely difficult for our BCs to see the German BCs [for the latter] were against a very dark background, while we were silhouetted against the western sky".[24]

2. Whereas the Germans' gun-smoke ("clouds as high as houses") was quickly "driven by wind and way over the ship", the westerly breeze was "blowing the smoke from the English guns between them and us. As a result of this their view was often hampered."

3. At the same time, British smoke hardly inconvenienced the Germans, for their precise stereoscopic range-finders could produce a result "from the smallest speck of [a] masthead". That the 'coincidence' range-finders of the British ships were more robust and less stressful to the operator, was a factor which would yield benefits only after a time.

Whether these problems might have been ameliorated by tactical skill on the part of Beatty, is doubtful. The BCF did, however, allow the enemy to cross the 'danger zone' in which the 13.5-inch guns of *Lion* and the 1st BCS held a theoretical long-range advantage, and soon found itself under accurate and rapid 11-inch and 12-inch shellfire at medium ranges of between 15,000 and 11,000 yards.

To British and Germans alike, incoming shells "appeared just like big bluebottles flying straight towards you, each time going to hit you in the eye; then they would fall and the shell would either burst or else ricochet off the water and lollop away above and beyond you, turning over and over in the air."[25] They would arrive with a noise like an express train, and throw up waterspouts, "twice as high as the masts",[26] which would then "cascade, drenching water on decks and superstructures".[27] "Occasionally, above the noise of battle, we heard the ominous hum of shell fragments and caught a glimpse of polished steel as it flashed past the bridge."[28] Only a few could see out, and those on the wrong side of the ship passed the time in various ways. Some tried to elicit information from voice-pipes or telephones; others busied themselves sighting non-existent periscopes. Marines in *New Zealand*'s starboard 4-inch battery squatted on the deck and played cards.[29] Below decks, other men, labouring in the stokeholds, tending machinery or just waiting – "remote watchkeepers entombed deep in the hull who were required to stay lonely and brooding with only fear and imagination for company"[30] – could only vaguely divine what was going on from sounds and seismic shocks.

The Germans scored quickly: as many as fifteen times in the first twelve minutes, and were hit only four times in return.[31]

The fire of the English battlecruisers [did not cause] our battlecruisers [critical] damage. The fall-of-shot was rarely in proximity to our own ships [and] it is not possible to judge very accurately the spread of the shot.[32]

Owing to the BCF's 6 to 5 numerical advantage, *Princess Royal* was told by signal to join *Lion* in shooting at Hipper's flagship, *Lützow*, leaving the rearmost four ships to pair off against the remaining Germans. *Princess Royal* duly complied, but for a while *Queen Mary* shot at her own numerical opposite, *Seydlitz*, leaving the German no. 2, *Derfflinger*, free to conduct undisturbed target practice against *Princess Royal*, which was hit twice. One 12-inch shell pierced side-armour and burst in a coal-bunker, the second burst against armour below the bridge, dislocating power to range-finding and fire-control gear.[33] *Moltke* is said to have hit *Tiger* nine times with 11-inch shells, putting both Q and X (the midships and aftermost) turrets temporarily out of action – a phenomenal piece of shooting by any standard. Thick brown smoke from burning cordite filled *Tiger*'s engine-room and, for a time, electric torches had to be used to monitor dials and gauges. Meanwhile, *Queen Mary* hit *Seydlitz* twice, causing considerable damage; and *Lion* hit *Lützow*, also twice, but received three 12-inch hits herself. The last of these, at 4.00, was very nearly the end of Sir David Beatty's flagship.

It penetrated the roof of Q turret and burst inside, removing most of the roof and setting alight the wreckage of the gun-house. After an interval this fire spread down to the working chamber where it ignited cordite charges, burning to death most of the men stationed there and causing a spectacular venting of flame through the roofless turret. Fortunately by this time the magazine doors, below, had been closed (traditionally, by the dying order of Major Francis Harvey RM), and the magazine itself flooded.[34] Had these actions not been taken, the whole ship would have blown up. As it was, more than eighty officers and men were killed, and *Lion*'s offensive power was reduced by a quarter.

About the time of this hit, there drifted across the centre of the arena a bizarre vision of beauty, quickly passed and left astern, a Masefieldian reproach at the bleak industrialized mayhem around it:

a silent ship with a pyramid of white canvas, serene, quiet and peaceful . . . a large barque lying almost becalmed, but moving gently through the water, rippling with the light breeze, her canvas only half filled.[35]

*

Two groups on the British side were still struggling to get into action. The destroyers of the 13th and 9th/10th flotillas were steaming hard up the BCF's engaged side to gain bearing on the enemy: to be able to parry Hipper's destroyers in the no man's land between the fleets, and, if the opportunity arose, to attack with torpedoes the 1st SG itself. The oil-fuel smoke which they produced at 34 knots compounded the battlecruisers' ranging and spotting difficulties. And, far astern, the 5th BS was trying to close the range and make up their lost ground.

The enemy battlecruisers were barely in sight.

> They were steaming the same way as we were and going very hard. A mass of black smoke, and I could only see their masts and the tops of their funnels above the horizon and [their] stern-waves showing up white and very high.[36]

Less than a year ago Jellicoe had welcomed Evan-Thomas to the command of the *Queen Elizabeths* with the words: "Please don't be too modest. I know full well that you will be on the spot at the right moment and that I can depend on your squadron for anything that it is asked to do."[37]

Right now it was perfectly obvious that he was not on the spot at the right moment, and whoever's fault it was, his mortification at finding himself in the position of letting down John Jellicoe can be imagined. It would get much worse before it got better. In the meantime there was nothing RA5BS could do except use his interior-lines advantage of position to cut the corners[38] and wait while the range on the hindmost German battlecruiser crept down at an achingly slow 200 yards a minute.

Then, a couple of minutes after the gutting of *Lion*'s Q turret, disaster struck the rearmost British battlecruiser – the one nearest to the 5th BS, but whose opponent, *Von der Tann*, was still just out of reach. Sub-Lieutenant Caslon, in *Malaya*'s starboard 6-inch gun-control, was "watching, absolutely fascinated", with Midshipman Tillstone, when

> suddenly he said 'Look at that!' I thought for an instant that the last ship in the line had fired all her guns at once, as there was a much bigger flame, but the flame grew and grew till it was about three hundred feet high, and the whole ship was hidden in a dense cloud of yellow brown smoke. This cloud hung in the air for some minutes, and when it finally dispersed there was no sign of the ship. Although I did not know the order of the battlecruiser line, I had a feeling at the time that it was *Indefatigable* in which I had a very great friend, and I learnt afterwards that it was so.

Indefatigable had failed to follow *New Zealand* in a shallow turn to port, perhaps through damage to her steering-gear (some accounts say she was sinking by the stern), and, when she was about 600 yards on *NZ*'s starboard quarter, took a salvo on her forecastle. "There was then an appreciable interval, said to be about thirty seconds", at the end of which she "blew up completely".[39] Two ratings from her foretop survived out of her company of 1,019.

Professor Marder scorns the idea that Evan-Thomas's distance astern may have cost *Indefatigable*, and there is an obvious wisdom-after-the-event about the assertion. But it is undeniable that the separation of Beatty's forces made it impossible for the 5th BS to give the BCF active support when it mattered. And Marder's dismissive "it would appear that *nothing* could have saved [*Indefatigable*] unless [she] had refused to fight"[40] ignores both the fact that she must have been spared if her opponent had been forced to shift fire to *Barham* earlier, and the fact that three battlecruisers as poorly armoured as she survived Jutland in good shape.

Beatty now sought to open the range by leading his ships round more towards the south. Hipper followed, and, in doing so, lost bearing on the British. This allowed RA5BS to cut the corner again and at last he was able to open fire, first on the light-cruisers of the 2nd SG and then, at about 4.08, when he was some 6 miles astern of Beatty, at *Von der Tann*, fine on his port bow.

According to Evan-Thomas's and Captain Craig's reports, the initial gun-range was 19,000 yards. This is generally accepted, and all historians agree that *Barham*'s fire was accurate. But these ranges raise problems, and there is conflicting testimony. If Evan-Thomas opened fire at 19,000 yards, he had forsaken more than 4,000 yards of his 15-inch guns' reach, for perhaps 15 minutes. The visibility was not yet so bad that *Barham* couldn't see the enemy until 19,000 yards, and other evidence deserves consideration.

Commander Walwyn, in *Warspite*'s B turret, remembered opening fire (a minute or two after *Barham*) at 23,000 yards, and added the persuasive detail that, although their first shots fell short, his two guns "were constantly bumping [elevation] stops and layers reported they could not follow"[41] – a state of affairs which speaks of maximum elevation. And in *Malaya*, Sub-Lieutenant Caslon, who was given a running commentary by voice-pipe, understood his ship to have opened at 23,800. This last range was virtually impossible, although the extra 800 yards roughly suits *Malaya*'s station astern of *Warspite*.

These conflicting gun-ranges are not necessarily irreconcilable, for the guns were in director-control, and *Barham* may – just may – have been firing at the end of her outward roll, and *Warspite* and *Malaya* at the end of their inward. The sea-state was slight, but three or four degrees would make the difference. In its own right it hardly matters; however, the issue – if there be an issue – has ramifications for whether the 5th BS's track lay *inside* or *outside* the BCF's, on this long curve round to the south. The 'interior-lines' advantage which Evan-Thomas

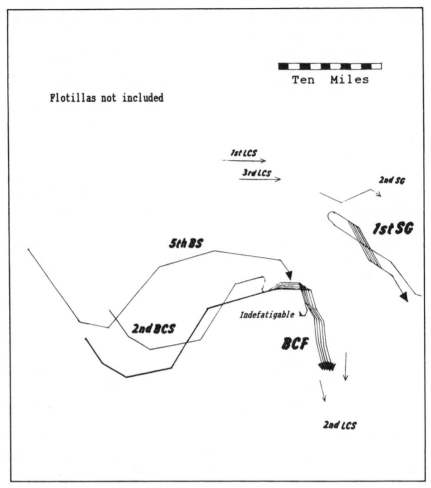

Plot of the action from 2.45 to 4.15 p.m.

claimed to have taken of Beatty's course alterations is consistent with the longer range from Hipper. Most maps and sketches – Harper's, [42] the German Official History's, Corbett's, Marder's, Campbell's[43] – put Evan-Thomas outside (i.e. to the east and closer to Hipper) until he crossed Beatty's wake at around 4.22. Roskill's sketch has it the other way round: inside, until he later crossed to the east.[44] To whom should one listen?

Why not Leading-Signalman Farmer (or Falmer) of *Indefatigable*? Clinging to wreckage and praying for rescue, he watched the *Queen Elizabeths* forging past and felt the concussion of German shells aimed at them *but falling short.*[45]

The range at which the 5th BS opened fire certainly impressed von Hase:

> Behind the battlecruiser line appeared four big ships. We soon identified these as the *Queen Elizabeth* class. There had been much talk in our fleet of these ships. They were ships of the line with the colossal armament of eight 15-inch guns, 28,000 tons displacement and a speed of twenty-five knots. Their speed, therefore, was scarcely inferior to ours but they fired a shell more than twice as heavy as ours. They engaged us at portentous ranges.[46]

And their shooting, in contrast to that of the BCF, "produced an excellent impression. The salvoes arrived absolutely dense (with no spread). The fall, in both elevation and direction, covered almost the same spot."[47]

The last *QE* to get into action was, of course, *Malaya*, the rearmost unit. The men in her torpedo control-tower (who, initially, could only listen to the action unfolding ahead)

> heard the other ships of our own squadron open fire, one after the other ahead of us, each salvo helped on its way by a cheer. We were so interested in what was going on that when *Malaya* herself opened fire the blast from X turret's guns, which were only a few feet away from us, sat us down with a 'whump', and the range-taker came down from his seat with a crash.[48]

Soon the 5th BS – more intensively trained in gunnery than the BCF, and equipped with 15-foot, instead of 9-foot, range-finders – were subjecting Hipper's rear ships to "a regular hail of 15-inch projectiles";[49] and *New Zealand* had to shift fire away from *Von der Tann* to *Moltke* because the battleships' shell-splashes were obscuring the former target.[50] Evan-Thomas now issued a fire-distribution signal which pitted *Barham* and *Valiant* against *Moltke*, and *Warspite* and *Malaya* against *Von der Tann*; and as the range fell slowly over the next 20 minutes, although target visibility was sometimes intermittent, both German ships sustained damage.

A 15-inch hit from *Barham* on *Von der Tann* was followed by two 13.5-inch hits from *Tiger*, and Hipper's tail-end Charlie shipped hundreds of tons of water aft. Her forward turret was put out of action permanently, her after one for several hours. She shifted out of line to port where smoke from her consorts' funnels, augmented by that from a fire on board (courtesy of *Tiger*), afforded some sanctuary. *Moltke* was considerably knocked about by four 15-inch shells and one 13.5-inch, and had to counter-flood to correct a list to starboard. On both ships, heavy torpedo nets fell loose from their deck-level stowages, trailed in the sea and threatened to snag the propellers. Of the 5th BS, only *Barham* was hit (twice) in this phase of the fight, her gunroom and part of the admiral's accommodation being demolished, allegedly by *Lützow*.

Meanwhile, the vicious fight between the battlecruisers had continued, in this three-cornered engagement, and still the Germans gave better than they got. Several 12-inch hits (from *Lützow* or *Derfflinger*) were received by *Lion* and *Princess Royal*, and 11-inch by *Tiger*. It has been estimated by John Campbell that in the first hour after opening fire, the BCF received 44 hits from the 1st SG, while the latter received only 11 in return, plus 6 from the 5th BS.[51] To the Germans, it was the fast battle-squadron pressing hard from astern, with its long reach, enormous punch, and thick skin, which posed the mortal danger; yet, although his ships were now weaving to confound British gunnery, a notable feature of the run to the south is Hipper's potentially suicidal speed restraint.

He had steamed at 21 knots from the first few minutes of action until 4.12, when – presumably becoming aware of the new threat to his rearmost ships – he increased to 23, which was still some 3 knots short of the 1st Scouting Group's theoretical maximum. Later on in the day he tried to order 26 knots, which was by then beyond the reach of the partially flooded *Von der Tann*, *Seydlitz* and *Derfflinger*.[52] His initial holding back, however, appears to have been voluntary; it allowed Beatty to draw forward of his beam, and Evan-Thomas to gain ground from astern. What was he doing? It has been suggested that he was trying to limit vibration in his spotting-tops.

It is true that, as a generality, vibration increases with speed; but for the German battlecruisers' foremasts to have had a resonance problem with high revolutions would have amounted to a serious military handicap, which a dockyard could probably have cured by adding or removing weight. The same battlecruisers had had no speed inhibition at Dogger Bank, and the key to the matter was probably more tactical than technical. From the start, Hipper's "intention was clear: he meant to engage the enemy battlecruisers and draw them on to our main fleet"[53] in a manner which caught them between two fires. He knew from Scheer's W/T signals that the High Seas Fleet's intervention was imminent, and he just had to hang on until his commander-in-chief hove into sight.

The BCF was officially under a speed regime of 25 knots for the run to the south, and although it appears to have exceeded this slightly towards 4.30, it cannot have done more than 26, which, with *New Zealand* in company, was its absolute 'formated' maximum. In no group were slower units left to straggle, as both Hipper and Beatty had allowed at Dogger Bank.

The exact speed of the *Queen Elizabeths* has become a connoisseur's item. They were commonly regarded as 25-knot ships – "we claimed it,

but I don't think we ever did it".[54] They entered the action under a signalled regime of $24\frac{1}{2}$ knots, but this was too ambitious, for at 4.18
RA5BS modified it to 24. Campbell believes a clue lies in their turbine
nozzles. *Valiant*, through some error, had been commissioned with
nozzles which limited her maximum output to 71,000 horsepower, as
against the 76/77,000 of her three sisters. Wartime speed-trial data is
scarce,[55] but it is known that, under load conditions similar to those at
Jutland, 71,000hp produced 23.9 knots. Campbell reduces this by a
tenth of a knot to declare that "*Barham*'s average speed during this
period can be taken as 23.8kn."[56] However, a formation of ships must
have in hand a 'stationing margin', above the signalled speed, to enable
subordinate ships to maintain and adjust their station.

The best speed of a formated squadron was considered to be "1 knot
less than the maximum, thus allowing a reserve of 1 knot for the
remaining ships to maintain station with".[57] With newish sister-ships
that knot might be reduced *in extremis*, but scarcely to less than half a
knot. According to the Ministry of Defence's Chief Naval Architect, if
a ship of the description of a *Queen Elizabeth* did 23.9 knots at 71,000hp,
she would do only 0.35kn. more at 76,000.[58] Thus, even if everyone had
the same turbine nozzles, a stationing margin greater than *Valiant*'s
handicap would have to be subtracted from 24.25 knots. This means
that, if *Barham*, the squadron flagship, was informally pacing *Valiant* –
thus absorbing the 'nozzle' anomaly in the stationing margin –
Campbell may be approximately right about its speed, but for the
wrong reasons. If not, the 5th BS was slower than he calculates.

British station-keeping discipline was more strict than that of the
Germans, who seem to have enjoyed considerable freedom of movement in detail. The BCF conformed to the Grand Fleet standard 'close
order' of $2\frac{1}{2}$ cables (500 yards) between ships, with $3\frac{1}{2}$ between
squadrons. As the distance was measured from bridge to bridge
(pelorus to pelorus, strictly speaking), rather than between the stern of
one ship and the bow of the next, and as these ships were each over a
cable long, this left little more than a ship's length of water between
them. The stationing regime was a product of the battle-fleet's imperative to concentrate its gunpower into a compact line only six miles (!)
long. What is surprising is that the BCF conformed to battle-fleet practice in the matter of $2\frac{1}{2}$ cables, when it was arguably unnecessary for it
to do so, and when Evan-Thomas allowed his squadron three (and, for
a time, $3\frac{1}{2}$) cables' separation.

"Anyone who had any idea of what fleetwork was would readily
recognize that the strain and risk of moving these monsters about was
considerable";[59] and Evan-Thomas was right to reject $2\frac{1}{2}$ cables, for a

post-Jutland enquiry under Beatty's staff-commander, Reginald Plunkett, found that

> increased distance up to four cables between ships would be an advantage under many conditions, and would give more freedom for altering course to avoid torpedoes and gunfire, and also under bad conditions of [funnel] smoke.[60]

In fact it is unlikely that the official distances were kept throughout the fast and furious 'battlecruiser phase'. Photographs of the BCF,[61] and German eyewitness impressions of the 5th BS, both indicate larger gaps (and it is convenient to use 4 cables as a working separation – because that places ships one minute apart at 24 knots).

The ultimate refinement had been introduced by Jellicoe at the beginning of the war. He ruled that, instead of allowing the helmsman to exercise his skill in following the next ahead, the officer-of-the-watch of a ship in column must order an exact gyro-compass course, which would have to be modified by a couple of degrees every couple of minutes.[62] This vesting of responsibility for the minutiae of helming in officers-of-the-watch has continued ever since and, at the time, must have been as galling to experienced helmsmen as it was irksome to the officers. It stemmed from the 'non-helm-free' nature of gunnery fire-control. By ordering a series of brief courses (= a very shallow zigzag), it was hoped to reduce the constant small meanderings of steering by eye. It probably made little difference, for yaw was still present. But, in action, the constant need to act as the quartermaster's brain can only have distracted the officer-of-the-watch from bigger issues.

Not having to station-keep, *Lion*, by comparison, had it easy; but the buffeting of the wind at $25\frac{1}{2}$ knots and the cacophony of her own gunfire made conversation difficult on the compass-platform, and at about 4.20 an error – not the only one at Jutland – occurred in her helm-orders. A small alteration of course was misunderstood, and the flagship veered out of line to starboard, engulfed in the smoke of her various fires. To the enemy she fell out of view, and it was some minutes before she could regain her place. In the meantime further tragedy took place.

Derfflinger's gunnery-officer, re-engaging after a short interval the second British battlecruiser,

> was under the impression that it was the same ship I had engaged before, the *Princess Royal*. Actually, however, it was the *Queen Mary*, the third ship of the enemy line. This was due to the fact that . . . Admiral Beatty's flagship, the *Lion*, was obliged to fall out of the enemy line for a time, and, owing to heavy smoke, could not be seen by us . . .[63]

(Von Hase attributed *Lion*'s temporary retirement to the brilliance of *Lützow*'s gunnery, believing that the British flagship's conning-tower had been put out of action and Beatty had had to transfer to *Princess Royal* – though how he accomplished this at 25 knots was unexplained.) *Queen Mary* therefore came under fire from the 12-inch guns of *Derfflinger* as well as the 11-inch guns of *Seydlitz* (her numerical opposite), and almost immediately switched fire to the more dangerous *Derfflinger* and subjected her to a succession of full broadsides.

> I could see the shells coming and I had to admit that the enemy were shooting superbly. As a rule all eight shots fell together. But they were almost always over or short – only twice did the *Derfflinger* come under this infernal hail, and each time only one heavy shell hit her.

However, von Hase and *Seydlitz*'s Lieutenant-Commander Förster ("our crack gunnery expert") had a clearer target and spaced their salvoes to avoid confusing each other's fall-of-shot. Equally important, for four minutes from 4.22 *Derfflinger* steered such a straight course that the relative bearing of the target altered by only 1°. A witness in *Tiger* described what then happened. The enemy

> had been poking about for the range for some minutes without effect, when suddenly a most remarkable thing happened. Every shell that the Germans threw seemed suddenly to strike the battlecruiser at once. It was as if a whirlwind was smashing a forest down.[64]

One of these hits "caused a disastrous magazine explosion forward, blowing the ship in two".[65] Astern, in *Tiger*'s conning-tower, the torpedo officer was watching *Queen Mary*, and had the impression that her armour was keeping the shells out, but "then the ship seemed to open out like a puff ball, or one of those toadstool things when one squeezes it. There was another dull red glow somewhere forward, and the whole ship seemed to collapse inwards."[66]

Lieutenant-Commander Edward Roynon-Jones, *Tiger*'s navigator and OOW, also had his eyes on his next-head:

> My impression at the time was that a full salvo fell on her centre turret which blew up and this detonated every other explosive in the ship. There were definitely two explosions with only a fraction of a second between them but the second one with its flame and smoke was much greater than the first. Of course the two explosions blended into one in less than no time . . . an enormous height of dull red flame [was] followed by a great mass of black smoke amongst which was wreckage thrown in all directions. The blast was tremendous.[67]

In *Queen Mary*'s X turret, a great shock bulged the floor upwards and knocked one of the 13.5-inch guns off its trunnions, crushing two men who had slipped into the gun-well. Power and communications went dead. The order to evacuate was given and a number of men scrambled out of the door in the rear of the turret onto the canting deck, in some cases to tumble and slide down to port. Petty-Officer Francis was one of the last out, and the ship was by then listing so steeply that he could never have reached the starboard guard-rail (cleared away, flat on the deck) had not two able-seamen, Long and Lane, stretched themselves downhill towards him, one hanging onto the other's legs. In this way he gained the scupper, the side, the bilge-keel, and finally, after some token hesitation, the sea beneath huge spinning propellers. The officer-of-the-turret, Lieutenant Victor Ewart, was last seen going back for someone unaccounted for.[68]

Tiger, close astern but to port of station, avoided the wreck narrowly but without difficulty on the downwind side. She was for many seconds enveloped in dense smoke, which was sucked down her engine-room fans causing stokers to don their gas-masks and fear for their own ship. A rain of debris fell on her decks. In the shock of the moment trivial but graphic details were remembered by Tigers and New Zealanders as they rushed past their pole-axed half-sister: the blizzard of paperwork venting out of her quarterdeck hatch; the sharp hiss of her gun barrels meeting cold North Sea. Within two minutes nothing was left of her but "a great mushroom-shaped cloud of smoke about 600 to 800 feet high".

It is no coincidence that *Queen Mary* was both "our wonderful crack gunnery ship",[69] and the only battlecruiser partially equipped with Pollen's fire-control apparatus. Sinking her was the *Kriegsmarine*'s greatest single achievement of the 1914–18 war: in purely military value she was worth two *Indefatigables*. More than $1\frac{1}{4}$ thousand men died, including a Lieutenant-Commander Shimomura Chusuke, one of three Japanese naval observers in the Grand Fleet.[70] There were fourteen survivors. The disaster took place 24 minutes after *Indefatigable*. Eyewitness estimates naturally disagree with each other, but this is one Jutland statistic about which the evidence is strong, for the wrecks lie in shallow water 24 minutes apart at $25\frac{1}{2}$ knots.[71]

On *Lion*'s compass-platform Beatty and Captain Chatfield had both turned round in time to witness the appalling spectacle. And even as *Tiger* leapt forward "from the dark abyss"[72] the admiral made that most square-jawed of remarks: "There seems to be something wrong with our bloody ships today." The legend, promoted by Churchill, that he added "Steer two points nearer the enemy" is not supported by the evidence. In fact, he altered 2 points away. Hipper, meanwhile, altered away by 5 points over a period of a few minutes.[73] He was under fire from two directions and threat of torpedo attack by destroyers, and far from seeking to capitalize on his dramatic success, he turned away more to the south-east and pointed his stern at Evan-Thomas. His job was almost done, and his battered but successful ships had acquitted themselves better than they could have dared hope. The range opened, and, while a vicious destroyer free-for-all continued unabated, *Derfflinger*'s heavy guns did not fire at all between 4.36 and 4.45.[74]

*

Vice-Admiral Reinhard Scheer was taking in the sunshine on *Friedrich der Grosse*'s quarterdeck when his flag-lieutenant, Ernst von Weizsäcker, broke the news that Hipper, fifty miles to the NNW, had encountered British light forces, and his immediate reaction was one of irritation.[75] However, subsequent reports that Hipper was engaged with Beatty had a galvanizing effect. The purpose of the originally planned foray against the English East Coast had been to trap the Battle Cruiser Fleet, and now here it was on the doorstep, and Hipper was even now drawing it towards the guns of the High Seas Fleet in the prescribed manner. At first, the plan was to get to the west of Beatty's expected line of advance, to block his retreat; but excitement became tinged with alarm when the British 2nd Battle Squadron (the 5th, really) was reported as joining in, and the commander-in-chief turned his cumbersome fleet onto a direct course towards Hipper, informing his junior of his position, course and speed (a transmission which the Admiralty's direction-finding stations duly plotted).

Scheer had with him 22 battleships, preceded proudly by the light-cruiser *Rostock*. The fleet's bulk and core comprised 16 stoutly built 11-inch and 12-inch gunned dreadnoughts. They were of much the same size and speed as their British equivalents, but (like Hipper's battle-cruisers) represented a more defensively biased mix of protection and gunpower. The fleet's Achilles' heel was the squadron of six slow pre-dreadnoughts which took up the rear and which were unkindly known as the '*Funf Minuten Shiffe*', because that is how long they were expected to last when the Grand Fleet found them. Scheer should have left them behind in the Jade (or, more usefully, the Baltic), but had yielded to pressure from their officers to take them along for the jaunt.

After Dogger Bank, his less popular but clearer-thinking predecessor, Hugo von Pohl, had ruled that "the loss of the *Blücher* has brought the proof that the older ships cannot be taken into a battle".[76] What *Blücher* had been to the 1st Scouting Group, the *Deutschlands* were to Scheer's battle-fleet. The German C-in-C made four seriously incompetent, and easily avoidable, decisions at Jutland, any one of which might have led to the loss of his fleet. It is a measure of British cack-handedness that he was to get away with all of them. This was the first.

Early in the war (until April 1915), when the Grand Fleet's numerical margin over the High Seas Fleet was low, Jellicoe also had taken with him to sea a squadron of slow pre-dreadnoughts, the *King Edward VII* class. The difference was that the British were the hunters and the Germans the hunted: in pursuit, the *KEs* could safely have been left astern, and in no circumstance would their presence have cost Jellicoe his fleet. For Scheer, in May 1916, by contrast, the *Deutschlands* could not imaginably tip the scales in a fleet encounter, and would only be a liability to themselves and to the mobility of the High Seas Fleet.

With these antiques in company, the formated top speed of the German battle-fleet was no more than 17 knots; and with poor quality coal and reciprocating machinery of doubtful reliability, even that could not be demanded of the pre-dreadnoughts for very long. This afternoon, however, it looked as if the Germans were destined to be the pursuers, and the *Deutschlands* could be allowed to drop astern. Orders were given to raise steam for full speed. This was a slow, laborious procedure, involving (as with the BCF earlier) 'bringing forward' the coal heaped in the back of the furnaces, and increasing the forced draughts. A side-effect was the dense pall of black smoke first seen by Goodenough at about 4.35.

*

Commodore William Goodenough's automatic response to Alexander-Sinclair's first enemy report – to turn his light-cruisers eastwards in support of his distant colleague – and Beatty's turn to the SSE at 2.32, had caused the paths of their groups to converge, and the BCF had, in effect, picked up the 2nd LCS as a close escort. Thereafter Goodenough found himself steaming flat out to overtake and draw ahead of the battlecruisers.

> There was only one decision necessary in the run to the south. Should we support the destroyer attack on the enemy battlecruisers made by Captain [Commander] Bingham, or, finding that we were by now favourably placed for observation, keep that position? Knowing that we were the only light-cruisers so placed, I chose the latter.

By the time of *Queen Mary*'s loss he had worked his cruisers into positions about 2 miles ahead of *Lion* (two on either bow, with *Southampton* one of the easterly pair), and was almost immediately afterwards "rewarded [by the sight of] first smoke, then masts, then ships".[77]

Goodenough's first W/T signal was sent at 4.30: "URGENT ONE

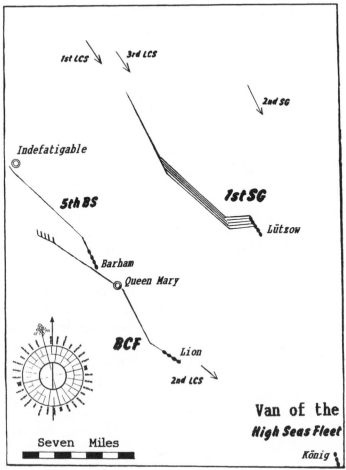

Plot of the action from 4.15 to 4.40 p.m.

ENEMY CRUISER BEARING SE STEERING NE" (plus own lat. & long.). It was addressed to both Jellicoe and Beatty, and referred to *Rostock*, stationed about 2 miles ahead of Scheer's battle-fleet. A few minutes later the serried masts and funnels of the High Seas Fleet became apparent beneath the smoke and against a backdrop of lowering grey overcast, and enough was clear for Goodenough to flash to Beatty "BATTLESHIPS IN SIGHT". At 4.37 he was on the air again to his seniors with "URGENT PRIORITY. HAVE SIGHTED ENEMY BATTLEFLEET BEARING APPROXIMATELY SE. COURSE OF ENEMY N" (plus own lat. & long.). By the time this was decoded, VABCF, who, on receipt of the first message, had turned to port to follow *Southampton*, could see for himself.

Much has been made – no doubt to rub in the matter of Captain Jackson's intelligence fiasco – of the unexpected nature of Scheer's intervention: "a startling development", "scarcely credible", etc. A critical British observer might well have been pondering the meaning of Hipper's earlier speed restraint, which had not been apparent at Dogger Bank and which was only explicable in terms of a mechanical handicap or the forthcoming intervention of the High Seas Fleet. It may be noted that Commander Walwyn, of *Warspite*, "realized we were steering south and it crossed my mind whether we should meet the HSF". And Rear-Admiral Pakenham (2nd BCS, *New Zealand*) wrote in his report of the action:

> In the Battle Cruiser Fleet it had been constantly assumed that the German battlecruisers would never be found far from adequate support [presumably following their salutary experience at Dogger Bank], and thus no surprise was felt when their battle-fleet was sighted.

Nevertheless, the Wagnerian drama of this moment for those on *Lion*'s bridge has to be appreciated. For nearly two years the High Seas Fleet had been the monster these officers had talked about, day after day and month after month; whose methods, qualities and tactics had been the subject of endless speculation, and whose downfall had been planned and rehearsed. Not one of them, since the outbreak of war, had actually seen it. But now, here it was, like some legendary creature from the underworld caught in the broad light of day, charging at 10 yards a second. Add to this the sombre slate-grey backdrop, and the black funnel smoke belching forth as thousands of German stokers laboured like demons to feed their furnaces, and David Beatty could perhaps be forgiven for being momentarily spellbound.

However, "this was the supreme moment of his career, and [a] split-second decision was required of him."[78] Only one man could slay this dragon, and that was Sir John Jellicoe. The intervention of the German battle-fleet radically changed the military dynamics of the afternoon. Suddenly Beatty's failure to defeat Hipper, even the loss of his two battlecruisers, counted for little: in the context of a prospective battle-fleet encounter, the first half of his task – to locate the enemy battle-fleet – was already done. Now his was "the responsibility of bringing about a fleet action in conditions favourable to the Commander-in-Chief",[79] and he could not hope to succeed if the BCF was caught and overwhelmed. At 4.40 the compass-pendant above numerals 1 and 6 rose to *Lion*'s masthead and descended: "ALTER COURSE IN SUCCESSION 16 POINTS TO STARBOARD." The flagship's helm was put over and her three surviving consorts followed her round to starboard until they had steadied onto 308°, the reciprocal of their previous course.

*

To declare, as I have just done, that a given event at Jutland took place at a particular minute of clock time is historiographically insupportable. (The issue of time-keeping is discussed in Appendix I.) However, a trawling of the mass of primary-source testimony for relative timings, combined with information calculable from the positions of the wrecks, enables us to construct a relative timetable of key events, in minutes, as follows:

Indefatigable's loss	0
Queen Mary's loss	24
Lion's wheel-over	38

The coherence of the narrative requires that this calibration be anchored to real clock-time. My assertions that *QM* blew up at 4.26, and that *Lion* began her turn at 4.40 are connected to the premiss that *Indefatigable* blew up at 4.02. And, while they carry the warning that they may not be right, if any one item is more than a minute or two out, the others require corresponding adjustment.

*

Even as *Lion* was straining to regain speed lost while turning, Scheer's leading battleships – those of the élite 3rd Squadron under Rear-Admiral Paul Behncke in *König* – rippled with flame, and presently their 12-inch shells arrived among the rearmost battlecruisers, with an express-train howl and pursued by the deep rumble of gunfire. Instead of Hipper being bombarded from astern by the Grand Fleet's fast battle-squadron, it was now Beatty's turn to be the target of the High Seas Fleet's equivalents (if not quite the equals) of the *Queen Elizabeths*; and Behncke's ships were now piling on the speed, and drawing ahead of the rest of the German fleet. But they were firing at ranges of around 20,000 yards, close to their limits, and their shooting was more optimistic than effective. By luck or judgement Beatty had dodged out of the trap contrived by Hipper and Scheer. His turn at around 4.40 was timed perfectly.

Having turned, the BCF trained its guns round to starboard and ranged again on Hipper's harassed battlecruisers, as if ignoring the German battle-fleet. 'A arcs' – the fields of fire on each side of a ship within which all her heavy guns could bear at one target – were closed towards the High Seas Fleet; every battlecruiser except for *New Zealand* was probably masked by the one(s) astern, and *NZ*'s older Mk X 12-inch guns lacked the range to reach either Behncke or Hipper. To her navigator, the HSF was "an imposing sight, ship after ship melting away into the haze, all showing up white, lit by the sun".[80] Midshipman William May, down in the starboard 4-inch gun control, was less easily impressed. Offered a peek by his officer-in-charge, he could just about make out a distant line of masts, funnels and superstructures, flickering with orange.

"Is that all?"

"Why, you ungrateful little scoundrel!"[81]

On *Lion*'s bridge it was time to take stock, gather the BCF's light forces safely together and report this dramatic development to the Commander-in-Chief, Grand Fleet.

*

For different reasons neither Goodenough nor Evan-Thomas reacted to Beatty's signal to reverse course.

Goodenough had had no end of grief from Beatty for obeying his recall at Scarborough, and he wasn't going to make that mistake again. But more importantly, he had a reconnaissance task to perform for John Jellicoe. And so he stood on to the south, into the killing ground fully on the beam of the High Seas Fleet, to perform a classic piece of cruiser work, comparable to Henry Trollope's service to Duncan before Camperdown, or Henry Blackwood's to Nelson before Trafalgar.

In *Southampton*'s torpedo control-tower (a thinly armoured hutch abaft the fourth funnel) Lieutenant Stephen King-Hall studied the High Seas Fleet: 16 dreadnoughts, led by the 4 *Königs*, with 6 pre-dreadnoughts in the rear. They were old friends, in a manner of speaking, for he was a veteran of the fleet visit to Kiel in July 1914. On that occasion he had considered that

> the Germans present a somewhat more pleasing picture to the eye than the British Dreadnoughts. They look more yacht-like, and the silvery grey paint they use is very becoming. On the other hand our ships possessed a savage grimness which was totally lacking in the Germans.

Now, once again, he "could see them plainly", though whether he revised his earlier aesthetic opinion – and, indeed, whether he identified *Southampton*'s erstwhile 'chummy ships', *Hannover* and *Schleswig-Holstein* – he did not say.[82]

Through the bridge voice-pipe King-Hall could hear the impassive, distant voice of Petty-Officer Barnes intoning the range-finder readings: "'Range, one three five double-ho! Range, one three two double-ho!'", and so on.[83] Astonishingly, as the 2nd LCS pressed closer and closer, the German battle-line forbore to fire at it although the little squadron was within easy reach (even of secondary armament) and the leading German battleships were plugging away at Beatty, who was barely a viable target. The reason, Goodenough discovered after the war, when he met a warrant-officer from the spotting-top of one of the German ships, was that while his four cruisers were closing more or less head-on, their nationality was unclear: they could have been Hipper's 2nd SG fleeing to gain the protection of the battle-fleet.

Finally, Goodenough's XO, Commander Edward Rushton, "efficient and cool, said 'If you're going to make that signal, you'd better make it now, Sir. You may never make another.' "[84] A signal duly rattled down the voice-pipe, and at 4.48 the W/T office tapped out:

URGENT. PRIORITY. COURSE OF ENEMY'S BATTLEFLEET N SINGLE LINE AHEAD. COMPOSITION OF VAN KAISER CLASS. BEARING OF CENTRE E. DESTROYERS ON BOTH WINGS AND AHEAD. ENEMY'S BATTLECRUISERS JOINING BATTLEFLEET FROM NORTHWARD. [plus lat. & long.]

It was only now, when *Southampton* and her consorts at last turned away and presented their four-funnel silhouettes at a distance of around 12,500 yards, that the German gunners who had been tracking them let fly.

While Goodenough was ignoring Beatty's recall and pressing on towards the enemy battle-fleet, Evan-Thomas, 8 miles astern of VABCF, also continued southwards. He was heavily engaged with the German battlecruisers and was under threat of torpedo attack by destroyers. Historians are confused about Beatty's signals to him at this juncture and, rather than admit that they don't really know what happened, tend to lapse from clear speech into mumbling. By and large it seems customary to assume that Beatty's 'reverse course' signal at 4.40 was addressed *inter alia* to the 5th BS. This can be dismissed on three counts.

1. It presupposes that Beatty was happy about the distance separating his two heavy groups and would rather preserve it than take the opportunity to reduce it. The *Queen Elizabeths* were 8 miles astern. Had they turned round at the same time as the BCF, they would have been 8 miles ahead (steaming northwards) and Beatty could scarcely have caught up before dark unless they slowed down. This is an important consideration. Evan-Thomas's ships were doing essential work punishing and distracting Hipper's still-southbound battlecruisers, and forcing them to keep their distance. If both British groups had reversed course simultaneously, the 1st SG would have been out of range of the 5th BS in a couple of minutes and free to give its full attention once more to the

bloodied BCF. Beatty could have meant Evan-Thomas to turn at 4.40 only if he wanted him to clear off the battlefield. Such an intention, less than 15 minutes after the loss of *Queen Mary*, can be ruled out.

2. At 8 nautical miles, *Lion* was as far from *Barham* as is the Tower of London from the Public Record Office at Kew (or Manhattan Bridge from Yankee Stadium). Her height from waterline to masthead could have been hidden by a matchstick held horizontally at arm's length; and even Beatty's hapless flag-lieutenant cannot have supposed that *Barham* would be able to read a flag-hoist at that distance, especially after the fiasco at 2.32 when the two ships were considerably closer. Nor can Seymour have forgotten the other part of that lesson: that flag signals to distant addressees have to be duplicated by searchlight (in accordance with Grand Fleet Signal Orders).

3. Beatty was to turn a further 4 points (45°) to starboard at 4.44 with the specific intention of passing on Evan-Thomas's exposed side (see the next chapter). Had he meant *Barham* to obey the 4.40 signal, instead of deciding which side to pass her, he would have had searchlight repeats hammered from his bridge-wing until Evan-Thomas woke up and complied.

Common sense therefore says that Beatty was content for the battleships to close the Battle Cruiser Fleet by continuing southwards for the time being, and that the 4.40 signal was not meant for them. There is therefore a small injustice to be put right for the record: Marder attributes the lack of a searchlight repeat to *Barham* at 4.40 as "another instance of Seymour's unreliability".[85] This is unfair. Ralph Seymour's inimitable contribution to the 'turn to the north' was yet to come.

8

Standing into Danger

"An absolute cloud of shells landed under the next ahead's stern as she turned 16 points."

Beatty completed his turn and steadied on a north-westerly course to find *Barham* still some 7 miles off but now approaching rapidly from a relative bearing of about green 20° (i.e. 20° on *Lion*'s starboard bow), just showing her port bow but almost head-on. In *Lion*'s foretop Midshipman Combe watched "the 5th Battle Squadron steaming towards us at full speed, shells falling all around them, and I must say it was a grand sight seeing these fine big dreadnoughts firing their 15-inch guns as hard as they could."[1] But what were they going to do now? Had both admirals stood on, their squadrons would have passed very close green-to-green. Then one of Beatty's staff asked him on which side he wanted the battleships to pass, and he replied, "Our disengaged side" (i.e. his own port side). This decision required the BCF to alter to starboard, and *Lion* accordingly turned 4 points (45°) in that direction on to 347° (N mag.) at 4.44-ish, when *Barham* was still some 5½ miles away.

Beatty's reasons are unknown. It may have been pride and convention which prevented him from allowing a junior squadron to pass between him and the enemy. A seaman's instinctive response to an emerging navigational situation may also have influenced his decision (and prompted the question). Where the Rule of the Road applies, altering to port to avoid other shipping is highly irregular, and only done under peculiar circumstances. The normal rules did not apply during fleet manoeuvres, and were certainly superfluous now; but the fact remains that this alteration has the appearance of a rule-of-the-road manoeuvre. The situation was now, at 4.46, as follows:

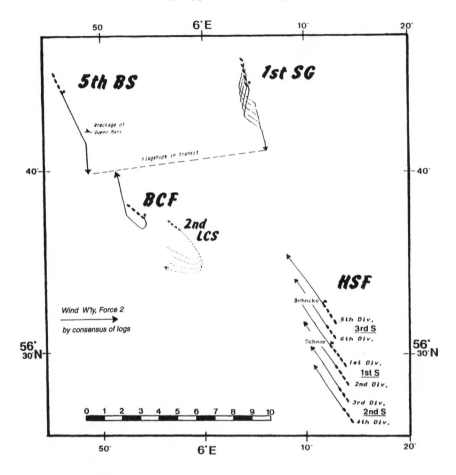

The BCF's turn to the North 4.40–4.51 p.m.

Whether Evan-Thomas saw *Lion*'s aspect change, realized that he was the cause of it and sought to give his senior officer searoom, or whether he was merely avoiding a torpedo threat from German destroyers, he also altered to starboard, at 4.47, onto a course of about 177° (SbyW). The two groups were now set to pass red-to-red, less than 2 miles apart, in a very few minutes.

Chalmers applauds Beatty's passing on Evan-Thomas's engaged side as "typical of his audacity" and supports his enthusiasm with some muddled tactical reasoning.[2] Beatty's decision was no doubt the product of traditional warrior qualities – courage, aggression, bravado, etc. – but in my view he should have allowed Evan-Thomas to pass between the

BCF and the enemy, if necessary altering slightly to port to make his intention clear, for the following reasons:

1. It would not have caused Hipper to transfer his main attention from the well-armoured battleships back to the damaged and diminished BCF.

2. It would have won a brief period of relative calm during which Beatty and his staff could concentrate on their all-important command, control and communications functions (C3, to use modern parlance), undistracted either by Hipper's incoming shells or by *Lion*'s own gunfire.[3]

3. It would have enabled Beatty to continue, without detour, in the direction in which he really wished to go.

4. It would have avoided a manoeuvring problem concerning the battleships' approaching turn, which a very sharp staff-officer might have foreseen: Evan-Thomas could not be expected to know that Beatty intended, as soon as the 5th BS had passed, to alter back to port, across the 5th BS's wake, to regain his NW'ly course, and for this reason wished the 5th BS to turn round to *starboard*. A 16-point turn to *port* would have swung the battleships round towards the advancing High Seas Fleet and would have caused them to describe more than a half-circle in total if they were to follow the BCF across their own wake. Assuming that RA5BS's tactical purpose was still to close his elusive senior, as it had been for the last two hours, the BCF's passing to starboard (green-to-green) would have made it obvious to him which way to turn. Seymour need only have flashed the instruction "PROLONG THE LINE", or just "JOIN ME", and Evan-Thomas could have judged his own turn to starboard and fallen into line astern, as Beatty now intended (see diagram overleaf (a)). To have flashed "PROLONG THE LINE" or "JOIN ME" while passing to port would have invited Evan-Thomas to turn the wrong way (see (b)). To have flashed something like "PROLONG THE LINE, TURN TO STARBOARD" while passing to port would have made no sense to the recipient (see (c)). So, short of flashing *Barham* an elaborate explanation, *Lion* would now have no option but to take executive control of Evan-Thomas's squadron and turn it to starboard with a formal tactical *order* by flag signal (see (d)) – and this at a time when the hapless Seymour's signalling load was at its heaviest.

It was not like Beatty to ponder such details in cold logic, and the tempo of events cannot have helped. Given his overall tactical achievement that afternoon it seems impertinent to begrudge him his own idiosyncratic decision in this detailed matter. But these several objections to passing red-to-red are relevant and rational, and

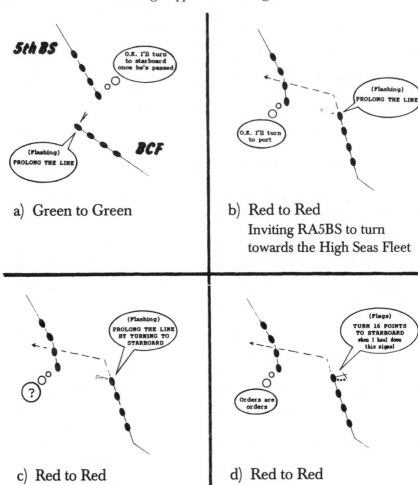

a) Green to Green

b) Red to Red
Inviting RA5BS to turn
towards the High Seas Fleet

c) Red to Red
Incomprehensible
to RA5BS

d) Red to Red
As happened

a flag-officer of Jellicoe's mental precision would probably have been swayed by them to allow the 5th BS to pass green-to-green. The signal made necessary by Beatty's refusal to do so was to become a fiercely disputed bone of contention between Beatty and the 'Jellicoe school'.

*

Meanwhile, as the 5th BS and the BCF advanced towards each other, the former, in the words of an observer in *Warspite*,

> passed a large amount of wreckage with one of our destroyers standing by. I could see people clinging to it, and I distinctly remember one poor

fellow, half undressed, sitting on some wreckage in an attitude which struck me at the time as being very conventional for a shipwrecked mariner, meaning that he appeared exactly like the pictures one sees of 'a castaway'.

It was blithely assumed to be "Hunnish wreckage".[4] It was of course *Queen Mary*'s. And, as in the case of *Indefatigable*, a survivor, Midshipman John Lloyd-Owen, watched the *Queen Elizabeths* steam by

in perfect order at about 25 knots firing continuously. The enemy's shells were falling a good deal short of this squadron [and] one of them apparently exploded in the water close to me causing me to lose consciousness.[5]

Amidst these 'shorts' the destroyer *Laurel*'s seaboat picked up a dozen men, including Lloyd-Owen who 'came to' on her forecastle at 9.30. She later complained about "the huge wash made by the big ships while they passed her".[6]

*

Some minutes – probably three – before the flagships passed each other, *Lion* hoisted a flag signal ordering Evan-Thomas to "ALTER COURSE IN SUCCESSION 16 POINTS TO STARBOARD". This was the order which was necessary to bring the 5th BS into line astern of *New Zealand*, allowing for the battlecruisers' alteration to port (back to NW), as soon as the battleships were out of the way. The success of the manoeuvre depended on the order's being executed by *Lion*, and implemented by *Barham*, at about the time the flagships were abeam. Unfortunately there occurred a communication hitch between the two flagships which, like the one at 2.35, was to have serious tactical consequences.

From the *Official Despatches*, published during Beatty's First Sea Lordship, the belief gained acceptance, and has never seriously been questioned, that Beatty executed (i.e. hauled down) the signal at 4.48[7] and Evan-Thomas obeyed it at 4.57.[8] The 1924 *Admiralty Narrative* (very much a 'Beatty' publication) appeared to support this. If 9 minutes did indeed elapse between order and action, then, with the 5th BS advancing by $3\frac{1}{2}$ miles and the van of the High Seas Fleet advancing obliquely by 3 miles, the range between the two would have closed by some 10,000 yards while Evan-Thomas presumably dithered. This is spatially impossible, for it would have placed *Barham* only about 12,000 yards (*Malaya* 11,000) from Scheer's van at the end of the turn, instead of around 18,000. Most historians have recycled the 4.48, though some have balked at the 4.57.

To start with, the manner in which this signal, as with other flag signals, is listed in the *Official Despatches* is open to interpretation:

Time of Despatch	From	To	System	Message	Time of Origin
4.48 p.m.	SO BCF	5th BS	Flags	Alter course in succession 16 points to starboard.	–

This format, with columns for 'time of origin' (TOO) and 'time of despatch' (TOD), is tailored to W/T signals: flag signals do not properly fit. The TOO is the time at which the signal is ordered to be made. The communications officers and chief-yeomen with whom I have discussed this agree that, given the unsuitability of the format, it is sensible to regard the TOD of a flag signal as its executive motion or hauling-down. This view is also Professor Marder's.[9] For the TOD to refer to a flag signal's hoisting would be virtually meaningless, for a manoeuvring signal is not effective until executed and may be left at the masthead for several minutes or even cancelled and not executed at all. But the *Official Despatches* are inconsistent on this matter, as the following extract (which has no other relevance here) demonstrates:

4.30	SO 5BS	5th BS	Flags	Alter course together, 4 points to port.	–
4.31	SO 5BS	5th BS	Flags	Negative alter course 4 points to port.	–

Since this was to have been a turn-together, the manoeuvre cannot possibly have been aborted (unactioned) after the 4.30 signal was made executive, and can only have been negated in the normal way – by hoisting the negative pendant on another halyard and hauling them both down together. The attachment of a 'time of despatch' to the 4.30 message therefore defies comprehension and leaves wide open the question of what is meant by TODs for other flag signals.

There is in fact an impressive array of evidence and circumstantial factors which point to *Lion*'s '4.48' signal's having been *hoisted*, rather than *hauled down*, at 4.48:

1. Evan-Thomas, with his penchant for obedience, could not imaginably have waited the 9 minutes implicit in Beatty's chronology, or even 30 seconds, before carrying out an order which he had understood and which he could perfectly easily have obeyed (if, indeed, these conditions applied).

2. He asserted, both in his report-of-proceedings[10] – when the future allegation of '4.48' and its implications were unknown to him – and in a post-war complaint about the Admiralty's draft *Narrative*, that the signal was still flying when the flagships passed.[11] As we shall see, this is supported by evidence from his flag-lieutenant.

3. The rear-admiral further alleged that *Barham* was unable to read the signal until the flagships were passing.[12] This is lent credibility by three considerations: (a) with several other flag-hoists running up and down *Lion*'s halyards, the signal may not have occupied the optimum position; (b) the layout of *Lion*'s forward superstructure and masting made her signals (in Jellicoe's words) "difficult to distinguish";[13] (c) *Lion*'s relative wind was blowing the flags more or less end-on, away from *Barham*. An order by flag signal to a *specific* addressee should not be hauled down by the sender until the addressee has acknowledged it, and indicated his ability to obey, by hoisting a repeat 'close-up' to his masthead. (If for some reason he is not ready to obey, he leaves his repeat 'at the dip' until he is.) If *Barham* hadn't read this signal, she cannot have acknowledged it, either close-up or at-the-dip; and it would have been pointless for *Lion* to make it executive.

4. *Lion*'s assistant navigator, who "was on the bridge throughout the action" (although that included the chart-house) states that the signal was hoisted at 4.48.[14]

5. *Lion*'s captain, Ernle Chatfield, says[15] that the BCF

passed close to the Fifth Battle Squadron, who were also ordered to alter course. Unfortunately the signal could not be made in time to prevent the Fifth Battle Squadron from unduly closing the German Battle Fleet, and they came under a very heavy fire and some ships suffered severe damage.

We shall return to the wording of this. Suffice it to say here that it precludes the signal's execution at 4.48.

6. The business at 4.44 about whether Beatty wanted the 5th BS to pass green-to-green or red-to-red at least indicates that he intended to place the *Queen Elizabeths* astern rather than ahead of the battlecruisers. The optimum time for *Barham*'s turn to have commenced was 4.51, if the 5th BS was to be in a position to extend the BCF's line astern after regaining speed lost while turning. For the squadron to have actioned the turn at 4.48 would have caused it to turn, speed reduced, into line partly ahead of the BCF but with an increasing overlap as the faster battlecruisers overhauled it. For a while the entire main-armament of the 5th BS would have been masked by the BCF, the latter's searoom towards the west would have been crowded, and it would have taken

many minutes for the two groups to draw clear of each other. Beatty cannot have intended this.

*

As 3 minutes is a reasonable time to expect to have a signal flying, we are justified in concluding that the signal was *hoisted* at 4.48, and that it was still flying when *Lion* passed *Barham* at 4.51-ish (by which time *Barham* had understood and acknowledged it, and it should have been hauled down). However – here we come to the crux of the matter – *Barham* went on for about another 3 minutes before turning, at an opportunity cost of 4,000 yards' range on the High Seas Fleet. There can be little doubt that Evan-Thomas turned *Barham* later than Beatty can have intended when he originated the signal. According to the *Official Despatches*, the 5th Battle Squadron turned at:

4.57	Beatty's report (p. 134)
4.53	Evan-Thomas's report (p. 193)
4.53	*Barham*'s report (p. 199)
4.57	*Valiant*'s report (p. 206)
4.55	*Warspite*'s report (p. 202)
4.57	*Malaya*'s report (p. 217)

The average of these six offerings is 4.55 (although it is not clear whether the last three refer to the time of *Barham*'s turn or of their own subsequential turns: if to their own turns, we must subtract 1, 2 and 3 minutes respectively, and the average time for the flagship's wheel-over becomes 4.54).

Of more value is the fact that the two 5th BS primary sources (*Valiant*'s report and Evan-Thomas's entry in the C-in-C's 1916 *Narrative*) to state the time-lapse between Beatty's fouling the line of fire with Hipper and the 16-point turn to starboard, plus an observer in *Princess Royal*,[16] all give it as 3 minutes, placing the turn at 4.54 in the time-calibration adopted in the last chapter (the clock-time also arrived at by Campbell).

It seems clear, therefore, that *Lion*'s '4.48' signal
1. was not hauled down at 4.48,
2. should have been hauled down at 4.51, and
3. was not obeyed by *Barham* until 4.54.
<u>So why the delay? – or rather, *where* the delay?</u>
There are two possibilities:
a. *Lion* hauled the signal down at 4.51, whereupon there ensued a 3-minute delay, for some reason internal to the 5th BS, before *Barham* put her wheel over.

b. *Lion* left it flying until 4.54.

With reference to the first of these propositions, it is just within the bounds of possibility that, set on a turn in-succession as ordered, Evan-Thomas had to wait for a couple of minutes on account of bad station-keeping. Unlike a turn-together, a turn-in-succession to starboard would have invited collision if ships 2 or 3 had been seriously out of station to port, or 2, 3 or 4 out of station to starboard. This can be illustrated by the photograph of the 5th BS in line ahead (taken on another occasion) which appears as Plate 27.

There is a simple procedure for a ship to follow if she finds herself out of line with a turn-in-succession commencing: she takes a bearing of the leading ship at the moment of the latter's wheel-over, and steers for that spot. The most inconvenient ship to be out of station is no. 2, because she has the least time to regain the line before turning, and *Valiant* might have been out of station deliberately, to ameliorate her small speed handicap by keeping out of *Barham*'s backwash. Indeed *Valiant* had already been reprimanded by RA5BS for being out of station to starboard at 4.29.[17] But common seamanship should have warned captains not to be out of line by more than one point of bearing "lest [as BCFOs put it] they hamper the squadron when turning in succession"; and even if *Barham*'s consorts had somehow failed to read *Lion*'s signal, both the BCF's charge past in the opposite direction and *Barham*'s repeat-hoist must have alerted them to expect a turn and get back into line. Placed in perspective the idea of the 5th BS being committed to the guns of the High Seas Fleet by bad station-keeping does not cut much ice.

With regard to the second possibility – that *Lion* caused the delay – in his post-Jutland amendments to Battle Cruiser Orders, Beatty warned his juniors not to rely on the flagship as an infallible source of tactical orders:

> It has been proved again and again that nothing is more fatal than 'waiting for orders'. The Senior Officers may be closely engaged, their signal apparatus may be destroyed, or for many other reasons they may be unable to issue orders by signal. It therefore becomes the duty of subordinate leaders to anticipate the executive orders and act in the spirit of the Commander-in-Chief's requirements.[18]

Although this appears in a section aimed at cruiser commanders, it is difficult to think of any incident other than the 5th BS's turn at 4.50 which could have provoked it. At 2.35 *Lion* was both unengaged and undamaged. At around 4.50, on the other hand, all hell was breaking loose:

• *Lion* was shifting fire from the cruiser *Wiesbaden* to Hipper's *Lützow*, and was being shot at by the latter;

- although she hadn't been hit for some 25 minutes, *Lion* had sustained nine 12-inch hits; Q turret had been gutted and was still burning, there had been a serious hit at the base of the bridge, and about now (according to *Princess Royal*, who had the best view), a fire flared up aft;
- the rear ships of the BCF were still being ranged at by the pursuing German battle-fleet;
- Hipper began his own 180° turn to the north and was now joining the pursuers;
- Goodenough's 2nd LCS had been slow to comply with Beatty's 'turn to the north' signal and was in danger of being sunk by the HSF;
- several destroyers were too busy skirmishing (and one of them torpedoing *Seydlitz*) to notice their recall;
- although *Lion*'s W/T gear had been damaged, Beatty had to get a report of the German battle-fleet through to Jellicoe, via *Princess Royal*, without delay;
- as well as semaphoring *Princess Royal* to pass a report to Jellicoe and to recall the unobservant destroyers, in the 9 or 10 minutes from 4.43 *Lion*'s signals staff handled a total of six separate flag-hoists:

1. a destroyer recall;

2. a general signal announcing the enemy battle-fleet;

3. a signal telling the light-cruiser *Fearless* (leader of the 1st DF) to pick up survivors from *Queen Mary*;

4. The 5th BS's order to turn;

5. a destroyer stationing signal;

6. a speed signal.

These were in fact the most hectic moments of the entire war for the BCF and by far the most demanding for *Lion*'s unsound signals organization. With such distractions it would be unsurprising if Ralph Seymour overlooked the 5th BS's 'execute' for 3 minutes. Chatfield's account, already quoted – "unfortunately the signal could not be made in time to prevent the 5th BS from unduly closing the German battle-fleet" – not only makes a cause-and-effect connection between the execution of the signal and *Barham*'s late turn, but actually hints that something went wrong on *Lion*'s flag-deck. What almost certainly happened is that priorities were lost sight of amongst the toiling signalmen and the heaps of bunting; and of all eight outgoing signals this was, unfortunately, the only one whose exact timing was critical.

Evidence from *Barham* points to a problem of this sort. As already mentioned, in 1923, when the blame-game was in progress, Evan-Thomas wrote to the Admiralty's Director of Training and Staff Duties in protest against the wording of the *Admiralty Narrative*; he complained about the insinuation that he delayed turning of his own volition: "The signal was not hauled down until some time after *Lion* had passed; so it should be stated."[19] And hearsay evidence from his flag-lieutenant agrees. The Hon. C. A. Colville[20] was killed in 1945, when his son Anthony was a small boy. But Anthony clearly recalls his mother's rendition of his father's account of the delay: *Lion*'s signal was seen and understood by *Barham*'s officers, who then waited and waited on tenterhooks for the haul-down, knowing very well that they were thundering straight towards the High Seas Fleet.[21]

It may be pertinent, here, to introduce a disclaimer in *Lion*'s 'Fair Signal Log' which could have bearing on this matter. Beatty's flagship was unable to comply with Jellicoe's after-battle order that "the strictest precautions [are] to be taken that all signal logs in use prior to and during the action are placed immediately in safe custody under lock and key".[22] The log-book produced by *Lion* had the relevant half-page blank, with the following explanation:

> 4.55: – most of the records of the outgoing visual signals were lost and destroyed in the action. The records had been sent down to the port Signal Station to be logged, but, on account of bursting shells and smoke and fire, they got lost or destroyed. This log was preserved with difficulty, not before a hose had been turned on it.[23]

To doubt this stirring scenario is a bit like questioning a lady's age; and it may have been intended to deter, through sanction of poor taste, critical interest in *Lion*'s signalling.

It appears to mean that the Rough Log (i.e. the scruffy original notes) of visual signals was destroyed in the port signal station at 4.55, having been sent down earlier. In this case the primary record of signals made at around this time would have been safe on the bridge in a different notebook. It might, on the other hand, mean that the Rough Log was taken down from the bridge at 4.55 to meet its end subsequently, in the port signal station. If so, this was a most unsuitable moment to send a man away on a routine administrative errand which should have been left to a hiatus in the action.

And what of these "bursting shells and smoke and fire"?

The port and starboard 'war signal stations' were beneath the upper deck, with uptake tubes (wide enough for an agile signalman to slide down, although that was not what they were for) through which the outer flag halyards passed. Their purpose was to provide sheltered emergency positions for the handling of flag signals and to spare some of the signalmen in the event of the flag-deck's being hit. The 'stations' themselves were usually no more than partitioned-off sections of whichever messdeck happened to be directly below the outer ends of the foremost yardarm, with voice-pipes from the bridge and duplicate flag-lockers.[24] According to Campbell there had been a 12-inch hit from *Lützow* an hour earlier near the forward funnel which caused a fierce and prolonged fire (whether this was the 'explosion' which collapsed Chalmers's chart-table is unclear: Chalmers appears to place that surprise in the run-to-the-north period). Campbell gives no other evidence of bursting shells in the base-of-the-bridge area at around this time (although he details three hits well aft); so, if he is correct, there was, or had recently been, a well-established fire in the close vicinity of the port signal station. Better to have taken the signal log elsewhere, even back up to the bridge.

Is it an unacceptable slur on David Beatty to suggest, in the absence of proof, that the loss of the primary record of *Lion's* outgoing flag signals might have been assisted? His willingness to paper over Seymour's signalling errors has already been mentioned – indeed (as we shall see) he was highly sensitive about anything which might reflect badly on his team's performance, even to the point of falsifying the documentation. The truth about the Rough Signal Log's fate will probably never be known. The possible convenience of its demise, accidental or not, is obvious. Either way, we are justified in concluding that Beatty or Seymour omitted to have the '4.48' signal executed until 4.54 and that Evan-Thomas waited for the proper executive order, as he had done at 2.35, before turning his squadron. During the delay the 5th BS stood on into grave danger.

As discussed in detail in Appendix III, the time-calibration of events put forward in the last chapter may now be extended to read:

Indefatigable's loss	0	(4.02 p.m.)
Queen Mary's loss	24	(4.26)
Lion's wheel-over	38	(4.40)
Barham passes *QM's* wreckage	41$\frac{1}{2}$	(4.43$\frac{1}{2}$)
Flagships pass	49	(4.51)
Barham's wheel-over	52	(4.54)

A plot of the action can be seen opposite.

*

While Evan-Thomas waited for *Lion* to haul down the signal to turn, Scheer's vanguard division was advancing at a combined closing speed of 40 knots, and gained 4,000 yards. As a consequence, the *Queen Elizabeths*

1. missed the chance to fall into line astern of the BCF and operate thereafter with the battlecruisers as a united force;

2. were within range of the enemy fleet by the time they turned, and became the targets of heavy shellfire while they were turning;

3. continued to be the targets of concentrated and potentially fatal shellfire for a protracted period after their turn.

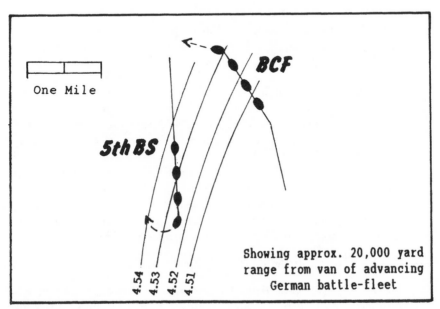

Barham's belated turn at 4.54 p.m.

Item 2 above is disputed by N. J. M. Campbell, widely accepted as the authority on technical matters at Jutland, who declares that "contrary to the usual accounts, none of the 3rd Squadron was firing at the 5th BS, while they were making their turn".[25] Campbell's revisionist assertion will be dealt with presently, but first let Bernard Brodie, in his classic *A Guide to Naval Strategy*, explain why Campbell's being wrong would mean that Evan-Thomas's ships had got themselves into a notorious position of helplessness.

If an admiral, having been outmanoeuvred by the enemy fleet, has his

leading ship turn abruptly in [a] new direction with the remaining ships turning in succession on the same hub until the process of changing the direction of the line is complete, the enemy has the advantage of concentrating all his fire on the ships which are making the turn. Moreover, the enemy will have got the exact range of the knuckle of the turn and will pound each vessel mercilessly as it comes up unavoidably into that position.[26]

Professor Marder dismisses considerations of this sort on the grounds that they were out of date by 1916. His objection is flippant.[27] A committee formed after Jutland under Reginald Plunkett, Beatty's staff-commander, to consider 'Points of interest gathered from all ships of the BCF and 5th BS', reported that "many officers noted the efficiency with which the enemy concentrated a rapid fire from more than two ships on a particular ship or turning point of our line";[28] Jellicoe – the RN's senior gunnery specialist – criticized the *QEs'* turn-in-succession for this reason;[29] and among the Admiralty War Staff's remarks on Beatty's reports is the following (comments in square brackets added by me):

> At 4.38 p.m., enemy battle-fleet were sighted and course was altered [by the BCF] 16 points in succession. From track charts the enemy Battle Cruisers appear to have stood on to the southward till 4.52 p.m., which must have given them a rare opportunity of concentrating on our ships at the turn, but no mention is made of exceptionally heavy fire at this period [Hipper had his hands full of 5th BS at this time]; enemy responded to our movements late by also turning 16 points (presumably together [wrong!] as the leading ship is stated to have been *Von der Tann* [wrong!], whereas it had previously been the *Lützow*). No mention is made in the reports as to our fire at this moment of their turning, which would seem to corroborate that their turn was made together.

The War Staff then considered the 5th BS's turn:

> At about 4.45 p.m. the 5th Battle Squadron joined from the northward and were directed to turn by Compass Pendant so as to form astern of the Battlecruisers. *Princess Royal's* report says – 'They were then heavily engaged by enemy battlecruisers and a division of battle-fleet'. *Lion's* report does not mention the joining up of the 5th Battle Squadron, but it would appear to have been better to have turned them by Blue Pendant [i.e. together] instead of turning in succession under heavy fire.[30]

Vice-Admiral Henry Oliver, Chief of the War Staff, almost certainly composed this himself, for his disinclination to delegate even tasks as mundane as typing was notorious. For reasons not given, but probably at Beatty's behest, he subsequently deleted the last two lines and initialled the deletion, although its sense remains clearly conveyed by the preceding remarks about the battlecruisers.

This merely demonstrates that, notwithstanding Marder's opinion, the idea of concentrating fire upon the hub of an enemy's turn-in-succession was very real to the naval officers of 1916. It is the eyewitness accounts of the enemy's fire during the 5th BS's turn at 4.54 that are persuasive. Taking evidence from the four ships in their correct sequence:

1. According to Midshipman Frampton, in *Barham's* X turret:

By this time, the head of the German line was within range and when we turned, they naturally concentrated on the turn. An officer in the *Southampton*, who had a good view of this movement, wrote afterwards 'The 5th Battle Squadron were a brave sight. They were receiving the concentrated fire of some 12 German ships but it did not seem to worry them although I saw several shells hit the *Warspite*. The enemy fire did not impress me favourably.'

In view of the time it takes to turn a squadron of ships right round, there is little doubt that Beatty should have ordered the ships to turn together rather than in succession.

The *Barham* was straddled and received two hits from heavy shells but no very serious damage was done. When the turn was complete . . .'[31]

2. Midshipman Haldane of *Valiant*, having described the BCF's passing, in an account written for Captain Woollcombe and unlikely to include conscious invention, went on to say:

We (the 5th Battle Squadron) then followed round by turning 16 points to starboard, being under heavy fire all the time. The *Barham* appeared to be hit once or twice . . .[32]

3. Captain R. A. Poland, Royal Marines, in charge of *Warspite*'s Y turret[33] recounted, in a letter after the battle, how

as we turned we got our first hit (the only one I actually saw). It got us very low down right aft and threw up a big cloud of grey smoke and shook the ship all over.[34]

Poland is unlikely to have been mistaken about the turn, for this was one of only two occasions when he had to train his turret right round from one side to the other.

4. The Midshipman stationed in *Malaya*'s torpedo control-tower corroborates Poland's story. By the time of the turn:

we were under a very hot fire, and were zigzagging slightly to avoid it. I was very impressed by the absolute cloud of shells which landed under the next ahead's stern as she turned 16 points, and I remember thinking what a mess her quarterdeck would have been in if she had been going a few knots slower.[35]

5. Even down in *Malaya*'s main W/T office

we could feel that we were altering course, turning about a full 180°. While this turn was in the course of being carried out and shortly after, we received our punishment from the enemy. They had concentrated on us the very rear ship of the line and at the turn, and here we received several 12-inch shells.[36]

6. The officer in charge of *Malaya*'s B turret, Lieutenant (later Admiral Sir Patrick) Brind, brings us to the most convincing piece of

evidence, one which is hardly susceptible to exaggeration. After passing the northbound BCF,

> we continued on our course on towards the enemy battle-fleet for what seemed an eternity, but which in reality was only about 5 minutes. Then we turned 16 points to starboard in succession. I must admit to a feeling of relief when I realized that we were to turn round, although I did not like it being done in succession. When it was time for *Malaya* to turn, the turning point was a very 'hot corner', as the enemy had of course concentrated on that point. The shells were pouring in very fast, and it is doubtful whether we, the last ship of the line, could have got through without a very severe hammering if the Captain had not used his initiative and turned the ship early.[37]

7. Sub-Lieutenant Caslon, positioned as he was in *Malaya*'s starboard 6-inch gun control-tower, was equally well placed to observe the squadron's starboard turn:

> [It] was an unpleasant affair, as we turned in succession and the Germans naturally concentrated their gunfire on the turning point. Moreover we were the last in the line. *Barham*, *Warspite* and *Malaya* were all hit during the turn and I think we should have suffered considerably if it had not been for the fact that the captain turned the ship slightly inside the wake of the other ships. As it was we were hit twice, both times on the armour, with no damage. The whole ship seemed to jar – one might compare the sensation to the feeling in one's arm if one takes a sledge-hammer and brings it down as hard as possible on an anvil.[38]

8. *Malaya*'s captain, the Hon. Algernon Boyle, in his report (of which "the times and principal items can be considered reliable") says simply:

> 4.57: Altered course 16 points (in succession) to starboard and followed our Battle Cruisers. Enemy's Battle Fleet opened fire on the turn, so *Malaya* turned short.[39]

What exactly did this early turn of *Malaya*'s amount to? It is likely that Boyle turned (say) 20 seconds early, with less than standard rudder, crossed close astern of *Warspite* as the latter was emerging from her turn, overshot the line to port and remained for a while in loose station on *Warspite*'s port quarter.[40]

Campbell admits that Boyle's short-cut took place, and even says it was "wisely" done[41] – without suggesting what possible use it could have been other than as a means of evading shellfire. If *Malaya* was not under bombardment, Boyle's behaviour is inexplicable. The only purpose of turning early was to throw German gunlayers off his ship. The other disadvantages of the squadron's late turn-in-succession – the waste of time and the gift of ground to Scheer – were not remediable by

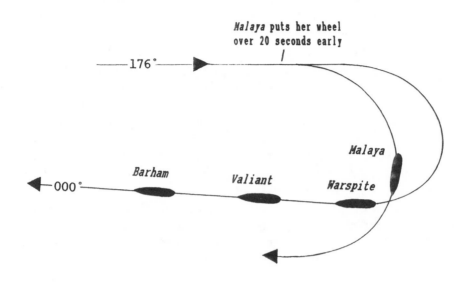

Boyle's cutting the corner because *Malaya* would remain tail-end Charlie after the turn.

However, we have Campbell's word that the HSF wasn't shooting at the *QEs* as they turned. In fact, he has nobody at all shooting at them for the 4 minutes between their being 'wooded' from Hipper, by Beatty's passing between, at about 4.51, and 4.55, when he has the battlecruiser *Derfflinger* reopening at *Barham*, scoring a hit at 4.58, and persisting until 5.19 (in prompt disobedience of Hipper's order to his ships at 4.57 to shoot at Beatty's group 'from the right, ship against ship'). He then has *Von der Tann*, Hipper's tail-end supernumerary *vis-à-vis* the BCF, gamely starting up "with her one remaining heavy gun on the *Malaya* at 5.00";[42] while, of the High Seas Fleet, the battleship *Grosser Kurfürst* opened at *Valiant* at 5.00, followed by *Markgraf* at *Malaya* or *Warspite* at an unspecified time, and *Kronprinz* and *König* at *Malaya* at 5.08 and 5.10 respectively.[43]

If *Malaya* was not under shellfire during the turn, then Boyle was mad and the witnesses quoted above (not an exhaustive list) were hallucinating. If, on the other hand, Boyle was forced to break ranks through pressure of shellfire, then the squadron had been mishandled, for, with presence of mind, the danger could have been avoided. The issue is as important for Hugh Evan-Thomas as it is for Algernon Boyle.

It is possible that some German timings, upon which Campbell may have relied, are fast. Their official Plan no. IV has Beatty completing his turn to the north at 4.48[44] – 6 minutes later than in British records – and some of their war-diaries are similarly ahead. If we imagine, for a moment, that certain other timings were also 6 minutes fast, we can have Hipper ordering his 1st Scouting Group to concentrate on Beatty's ships at the moment Beatty began masking the 5th BS (minute 51-ish); we can also have *Grosser Kurfürst* opening at *Valiant* at around 4.54 – as *Barham* began the turn. This is worth bearing in mind. But the eye-witnesses (and the fact of *Malaya*'s short-cut) are backed by much stronger evidence, which, with my supporting argument, is to be found in Appendix IV. Suffice it to say here that telling anomalies in Campbell's own assertions, an analysis of the plot, sheer common sense, the German Official History, and the 3rd Squadron's *Kriegstagebücher*, all indicate (or allow) that, as they turned, Evan-Thomas's ships – especially the rearmost two – came under bombardment from Behncke's 3rd Squadron of Scheer's High Seas Fleet.

*

Between 4.54 and 4.59 the 5th BS trundled round a 180° arc at 2 cables' radius from a fixed spot in the ocean. During these 5 minutes, this semi-circle boasted an aggregate of 8 *ship-minutes* (including 3 *two-ship-minutes* and 2 *three-ship-moments*); and from the German line of sight there were 6 *two-ship* overlaps. Up to three of the most prized targets afloat were to be found in a stationary area only a few acres in size. If several of Scheer's battleships had been shooting simultaneously, as I believe is the case, the business would by no means have been problem-free for the Germans. Their spotting-officers would tend to focus on 'short' splashes, whether their own or not, and compensate erroneously (*Prinzregent Luitpold*'s war-diary says that "splashes were mainly short, hits could not be observed";[45] and *Southampton*, at around this time, watched shells falling up to 3,000 yards beyond the *Queen Elizabeths*). But their fire-controllers needed to allow only for their own movements, which were known quantities: there was no 'target course and speed' to be estimated. Gunnery-officers, like farmers, are always whingeing. The basic fire-control computation was as simple as that for a shore bombardment.[46]

If one of the 5th BS had been disabled at the turn or at any stage during the subsequent 'run to the north' she would have shared the fate of the crippled destroyers *Nestor* and *Nomad*, which had no choice but to wait for the High Seas Fleet to steamroll over them, or of *Blücher* at Dogger Bank, or of *Bismarck* in 1941. If she were abandoned by her sisters, the damage to the morale of the Grand Fleet would have been serious. If Evan-Thomas had turned his other ships back to help, they too would have been lost, however good a 'show' they might have put up. Scheer would have achieved his dream of isolating and defeating a proportion of the Grand Fleet – and its most prestigious and powerful squadron to boot. Goodenough would no doubt have added some of his cruisers to the altar. This may be hypothetical, but it was only one unlucky shell, on a day of unlucky shells, from reality. The hammering suffered by the 5th BS during the run to the north will be related in Chapter 20; suffice it to say here that the consequences to the British ships of damage to propulsive machinery or steering-gear were obvious to friend and foe alike. Had the engagement gone on for long enough, a *Queen Elizabeth* must have fallen victim to the High Seas Fleet sooner or later.

As it happens the *QEs* were very lucky, in the sense that none of them actually fell into the arms of their pursuers; but the damage they sustained, the 250 men killed, maimed and burned, and the risk of very much worse, were pointless and avoidable. The extra 4,000 yards which would have been retained by a timely turn-in-succession or a belated turn-together would have kept the High Seas Fleet just out of range, and enabled the 5th BS and BCF to operate as a single, tight, tactical force. There was no useful military purpose in four isolated battleships getting caught in a fire-fight with the German battle-fleet. It was an 'own goal' for the Royal Navy.

If Scheer had grown uneasy about Beatty's northerly course, and extricated his fleet before meeting the British battle-fleet (as Lütyens wanted to do after his success against *Hood* twenty-five years later), the day's work would have looked bleak indeed for the Rosyth force. The tactical handling of Beatty's heavy groups would have come in for searching scrutiny in the subsequent recriminations – not least from Jellicoe whose fears about VABCF would have appeared abundantly vindicated. If, in addition to *Indefatigable* and *Queen Mary*, *Malaya* or *Warspite* had been lost before Scheer abandoned the chase, senior heads must have rolled. As it was, Beatty and Evan-Thomas were spared the sort of investigation which follows a perceived fiasco.

In his ROP Evan-Thomas infiltrated the idea that he didn't know the High Seas Fleet was there until after he had turned:

> During this turn, it appears that the *Malaya*, the last ship of the line, sighted the enemy's battle-fleet; it was sighted by *Barham* approximately SSE a few minutes after she had steadied on her Northerly course.

This is both debatable and tendentious. Other witnesses are divided on the issue, but a majority suggests a clear sequence of events:

1. saw the HSF;

2. turned.

From *Barham's* captain (who was presumably standing beside Evan-Thomas[47]), for example, we have:

> the 1st and 2nd Battle Cruiser Squadrons [the BCF] turned in succession 16 points, and it was seen that the enemy Battle Cruisers had turned also, and that some of the Germans' 3rd Squadron were coming up astern of them. [VABCF] ordered the 5th Battle Squadron to turn 16 points in succession to starboard.[48]

From a *Warspite* midshipman:

> The battlecruisers then turned and steamed [northwards]. We then engaged the leading ships of the High Seas Fleet, one of the *Kaisers*, and got some good hits on her. We then turned and followed astern of the battlecruisers.[49]

From *Malaya's* captain:

> Shortly after our Battle Cruisers passed, observed enemy's Battle Fleet on port bow in three or four columns heading straight for us. (Aloft reported three columns, the fourth column seen from below may have been cruisers in the haze: very hard to distinguish.) 4.57 Altered course 16 points (in succession) to starboard.[50]

And, from the officer in charge of *Malaya's* B turret:

> I saw the enemy battlecruisers turn 16 points together, and looked to the southward of them to see if I could discover the reason for this manoeuvre. I saw, just discernible in the mist, a warship of sorts [*Rostock*], coming from the SE. I pointed this out to the Commander, but he did not know what to make of it. We were not kept long in suspense as to what this new ship was, for very shortly after sighting her, I saw following her a long line of others, which were soon recognized as German Dreadnought Battleships of the *König* and *Kaiser* classes . . . Now matters took a quite different complexion. We were closing the High Seas Fleet at a relative rate of about 40 knots . . .[51]

It is impossible to state the moment when RA5BS personally saw the High Seas Fleet, but *Barham* is said to have received Goodenough's 4.38 sighting report within 2 minutes of its being sent.[52] Evan-Thomas must have realized that Beatty would hardly reverse course without good reason, he must have seen the shells dropping around *Tiger* and *New Zealand* as the BCF approached, and he must have been aware of Goodenough's 2nd LCS (now only about $2\frac{1}{2}$ or 3 miles to the south) weaving northwards at full speed through a forest of splashes. And Beatty, who finalized his own ROP after receiving Evan-Thomas's, took care to say:

> The 5th Battle Squadron were now closing on an opposite course and engaging the enemy Battle Cruisers with all guns. The position of the enemy Battle Fleet was communicated to them, and I ordered them to alter course 16 points.

This 'communication' was less personalized than the above implies: it was merely the general flag-hoist at 4.45, one of the several which were challenging Seymour at around this time, saying "HAVE SIGHTED ENEMY BATTLEFLEET BEARING SE". But there is no reason to suppose *Barham*'s yeomen failed to read it, since they read the fateful turning signal, and Lieutenant Colville's handed-down description of the nail-biting wait for the haul-down conveys an acute awareness on *Barham*'s bridge of the relentless approach of Scheer's battle-fleet – indeed that they were looking both ways with mounting alarm.

It is implicit in his BCFOs amendment and in the 1924 *Admiralty Narrative* what conclusion Beatty would have us reach on the question of who was to blame: Evan-Thomas had an opportunity to make his own skilled contribution to the performance of British arms at around 4.50, and he blew it.

This, as we know, is far from the whole story. If Beatty had refrained from signalling, RA5BS would probably have turned himself on his own authority at the right time – after all, he had been directing his squadron perfectly well on his own for the last two hours, and striving to catch up. (The likelihood of his turning the wrong way would have been a minor thing.) But *Lion*'s act of hoisting a manoeuvring signal to RA5BS amounted to a resumption of executive responsibility for the 5th BS, in effect: "If you had any plans, forget them, because I'm taking direct control again." Thus, in a sense, usurped, Evan-Thomas was left hanging about while Seymour forgot to haul the signal down. It would have taken a more independent man than he to initiate his own manoeuvre after *Lion* had intervened. Roger Keyes's opinion, that "Beatty had every right to suppose that the 5th Battle Squadron would conform to his movements", and that "it is incredible that Beatty should be blamed",[53] is both simplistic and partisan.

However, contrary to what might be inferred from many British secondary accounts, Jutland is not a 'zero-sum game' of credit and blame between the Jellicoe-ites on the one hand and the Beatty-ites on the other; and even if the spanner in the works bore the indelible stamp of D. Beatty & R. Seymour, the ultimate responsibility for the 5th BS rested with its appointed senior officer. There would have been no procedural problem in Evan-Thomas's pre-empting or amending Beatty's order to turn. His captains may have witnessed the signal to RA5BS, but it was not addressed to them. Beatty was not the squadron's appointed flag-officer: he could not give orders to Craig, Woollcombe, Phillpotts or Boyle over Evan-Thomas's head. It would even have been navigationally unsound for Beatty to exercise direct executive responsibility for a squadron which was not actually formated on him. He would be in no position to assess whether it was safe to perform a certain manoeuvre: some of its units might be out of station, or there might be some hazard which he couldn't see. Evan-Thomas was not there merely to be an automatic boost-transmitter for Beatty's signals.

*

Inevitably, when discussing RA5BS's options at 4.50, the term 'obedience' is produced by his apologists, partly as a shield against accusation of lack of initiative: they make their stand on his punctilious obedience both at 2.35 and at 4.50 as if he had no responsible alternative.

It need hardly be stated that a military organization depends on the probability that seniors will be obeyed: the idea is virtually tautological. "Obedience to commands is the very foundation of discipline,"[54] and the concept of 'military initiative' is – at least at subordinate level – partly oxymoronic (and certainly more so than that hackneyed butt of jokes, military intelligence). But what if the delay in *Lion*'s executing the signal had been extended indefinitely, with Scheer bearing down on the 5th BS at a combined closing speed of more than 20 yards a second? For how many more minutes does the 'obedience' school consider Evan-Thomas should have continued rushing headlong to oblivion? Common sense says that Britain's finest battle-squadron should not have found itself, in effect, 'not under command' at this critical juncture, and that, when Beatty passed on his opposite course, an admiral worthy of 120,000 tons of capital ships should have manoeuvred them of his own accord.

There are issues here, concerning tensions endemic in any authoritarian hierarchy. Most people today would regard as unremarkable the proposition that 'orders' and 'national interest' are not necessarily synonymous. But this may be a cynicism which has been hammered home by the wholesale blunders and horrors of this century. Many of the more ghastly and idiotic aspects of the Great War were made possible by the coincidence of mass-production and the social religion of deference. This is not to say that the nineteenth century was without its military fiascos: it produced some crackers; but they were usually remote and picturesque by twentieth-century standards, and became in some cases a perverse source of regimental pride. It was the holocaust of the trenches, notably the battles of Ypres and the Somme, shortly before and after Jutland respectively, and, for the Royal Navy,

Jutland itself, which toppled the military establishment off its pedestal of sanctity.

By the time the next war came round, British attitudes towards authority contained an element of scepticism, not to say ribaldry. No doubt, since before the Roman legions, 'other-ranks' have always had a sense of senior-officer absurdity as part of their barrack-room culture – 'Big fingers, little maps: lots of death for the chaps' – but to society as a whole it was novel (and even healthy, like an antibiotic breeding from decay, for it secured the pre-eminence of civil authority over military, in war as in peace). No schoolchild has been taught about the 1914–18 war in a manner which accepts the infallibility of 'the top brass' as an article of faith; and the generations who grew up with Nuremberg's rejection of obedience as a defence for war crimes, with the satire of *Catch 22*, *Dr Strangelove*, *MASH* and *Oh! What a Lovely War*, with thermonuclear weapons and Vietnam, are no more disposed to accept it.

The senior officers of the 1910s were, by contrast, products of the privileged Victorian squirearchy, of the structural certainties of a secure patrician society, and, in their formative years, of the Fleet which had dozed unchallenged in the long calm lee of Trafalgar. They would have regarded an interpretative view of 'duty' as disruptive and potentially subversive – partly through a vague but instinctive class nervousness that any concession might release some kind of genie of degeneracy or social upheaval. There are major culture-gap difficulties in trying to evaluate the behavioural dilemmas of military leaders who learnt their trade a hundred years ago.

In the late Victorian Navy it was a well-suppressed secret – or, at best, a museum oddity, stuffed and mounted – that the professional conflict between obedience and initiative was at least two centuries old. And when spectacular tragedy dragged the debate into the public domain in the 1890s, the genie was adroitly shoved back in the bottle by a supremely efficient fraternity of officers who enjoyed the mellow sunlight of royal approval and included many of the future seagoing admirals of the dreadnought era – conspicuous among them Commander John Jellicoe and Lieutenant Hugh Evan-Thomas. It is to this momentous story, which may be considered the underlying explanation for some of the problems of Jutland, that we shall now turn, leaving the 5th Battle Squadron in suspended animation at its misjudged turning-point.

PART III

The Underlying Reason Why

9

The Long Calm Lee of Trafalgar

"The canker of a long peace is a bad preparation for war."

A distinction between 'centralized' and 'spontaneous' approaches to battle, in English naval operations, may first be discerned (or imagined) in the command attitudes of Lord Howard of Effingham and his subordinate, Sir Francis Drake, during the Armada campaign in 1588. But as far as the professionalized Royal Navy was concerned, it was during the second and third Dutch Wars of the late seventeenth century that a doctrinal conflict between "two schools of tactical opinion" first emerged.

> There was the school represented by the Duke of York [the future James II] and [Admiral Sir William] Penn, which inclined to formality; and by pedantic insistence on well-meant principles tended inevitably to confuse the means with the end. On the other hand we have the school of Monck [Duke of Albemarle] and [Prince] Rupert, which was inclined anarchically to submit all rules to the solvent of hard fighting, and to take tactical risks and unfetter individual initiative to almost any extent rather than miss a chance of overpowering the enemy by a sudden well-timed blow.
>
> It was the school of Penn and the Duke of York that triumphed at the close of these great naval wars, [and] the attempt of Monck and Rupert to preserve individual initiative and freedom to seize opportunities was discarded. Knowing as we do the extent to which the principles of the Duke of York's school hampered the development of fleet tactics till men like Hawke and Nelson broke them down, we cannot but sympathize with their opponents.[1]

This hampering of tactics may be seen in the Earl of Torrington's irresolute conduct of his fleet at Beachy Head in 1690, Edward Russell's at Barfleur in 1692, and Sir George Rooke's at Verez Malaga in 1704. Its legacy was still sufficiently potent in 1781 to taint the methods of Hyde

155

Parker at Dogger Bank, and Thomas Graves at Chesapeake Bay; but by that time it had become more the exception than the rule.

Following the exhibition of Captain Robert Jenkins's ear (severed by a Spanish sword) in the House of Commons in 1739, the Royal Navy was at war for fifty of the next seventy-five years. The interludes of half-pay were insufficient to break career-continuity for three successive generations of sea officers, and Britain's fleets came to be dominated by seasoned practitioners who understood profoundly the capabilities of their ships, their weapons, and each other.

The graph by no means showed a constant incline,[2] but, roughly speaking, starting with George Anson and Sir Edward Hawke (and ignoring the sometimes conspicuous lapses) a culture developed of community of thought between supremely self-confident officers. When Commodore Horatio Nelson took HMS *Captain* out of the line to cut off an enemy movement at the second Battle of Cape St Vincent, in 1797, in anticipation of the wishes of Admiral Sir John Jervis, he ushered in the high noon of British naval competence. Writing of that battle, a Spanish tactician pondered the manner in which the Royal Navy stood apart from its Continental opponents. He overstated his case, but his idealized view casts a deep shadow of indictment over Sir John Jellicoe's fleet of 1916:

> An Englishman enters a naval action with the firm conviction that his duty is to hurt his enemies and help his friends without looking out for directions in the midst of the fight; and while he thus clears his mind of all subsidiary distractions, he rests in confidence on the certainty that his comrades, actuated by the same principles as himself, will be bound by the sacred and priceless law of mutual support. Accordingly, both he and all his fellows fix their minds on acting with zeal and judgement on the spur of the moment, and with the certainty that they will not be deserted. Experience shows, on the contrary, that a Frenchman or a Spaniard, working under a system which leans to formality and strict order being maintained in battle, has no feeling for mutual support, and goes into action with hesitation, preoccupied with the anxiety of seeing the commander-in-chief's signals, for such and such manoeuvres . . . Thus they can never make up their minds to seize any favourable opportunity that may present itself. They are fettered by the strict rule to keep station.[3]

At this time the French Navy's signalling ideas were more advanced, and tactical writings more sophisticated, than those of the British. The contrast between the two navies' emergent tactical doctrines appears to echo, in microcosm, that between British empiricism and Continental rationalism in the eighteenth century (though it is unlikely that the King's sea officers saw the matter in such grandiose terms); and, despite the increasing yield of their own robust methods, the British feared the vaguely imagined advantages of tactical control with which theorizing might endow the French Navy. In particular, was signalling the thumb-joint of articulation which could lift a fleet up the evolutionary ladder? The grandee quoted above clearly did not think so – indeed he came close to drawing the opposite conclusion – but for some years British backwardness in signalling had worried prominent seamen like Lord Howe and Richard Kempenfelt. Admirals had always sought more efficient means of communicating with their ships, and since Tudor times piecemeal advances had accreted in successive *Fighting Instructions* and their amendments. But during the American and French revolutionary wars the Royal Navy's quest for signalling fluency began to assume Grail-like qualities, although it was not unattended by scepticism: "Now my dear Kempy, do, for God's sake, oblige me by throwing your signals overboard, and make that which we all understand – 'BRING THE ENEMY TO CLOSE ACTION'!"[4]

Howe drew up a *Numerary Code* which "separated the *Instructions* from their flags, tabulated the latter into a logical sequence, and related them to numbered messages in the *Signal Book*". When combined with Kempenfelt's *Primer of Speech for Fighting Ships*, "it was adapted throughout the Navy as *The Signal Book for Ships of War* in 1790", and led to the first official signal manual in 1799.

> This was a considerable advance; but although with a three-flag hoist the sender could transmit nearly 1,000 messages, and with a four-flag hoist nearly 10,000, he could still only refer to what was in the *Signal Book*: if the words he wanted were not there, the possible number was purely academic.[5]

It was thus still impossible to send complex messages, and the *Signal Book* did not allow admirals to suppose that they could orchestrate the detailed movements of their subordinates in battle. If those subordinates were to be trusted to extemporize, objectives, priorities and methods would still have to be thrashed out in advance; and, as verbal ship-to-ship dialogue was usually impracticable, there was nothing for it but for captains to meet frequently in the flagship. This procedure was not popular. In rough seas it could mean upset boats and drownings. Even in calm weather, boats' crews would have to lie off from the flagship, resting on their oars, perhaps in freezing conditions and wet clothing, for an hour or more while they waited for their captains. But it meant that senior officers met and talked and listened. And it gave us the timeless, evocative image of Lord Nelson's 'brothers' around the table in *Victory's* great cabin: the low beams, the yellow lamplight, the weather-lined faces of old friends and shipmates, and all eyes fixed enthralled on the slight, animated figure of the admiral as he laid out his plan (as Collingwood put it) for "something which the world may talk of hereafter". The scene is redolent of daring and destiny, with iconographic nuances of the Last Supper, and is, perhaps, to some degree the product of legend. But in no broad sense is it a lie.

Horatio Nelson was no more and no less than the apogee of a generation of officers who, through years of remorseless war at sea, had acquired a near perfect understanding of their trade – and had been fired with zeal by "the great and good Earl of St Vincent" (Nelson's words). The Arthurian 'Band of Brothers' theme, which Nelson borrowed from Shakespeare's *Henry V*, referred originally to the 'crocodiles' of the Nile campaign, and gives a misleadingly select impression of the men who ultimately enjoyed his confidence. In 1805 Lord Barham "handed [him] a Navy List and invited him to choose his own officers. Nelson handed it back. 'Choose yourself, my Lord. The same spirit actuates the whole profession. You cannot choose wrong.'"[6] But he, above all, made clear, through meeting and talking and infusing, what he expected of his juniors in terms of their own pro-active contributions to a major action. Such was his charisma, so valued his esteem, that to a man they applauded his demands and strove to vindicate his trust to the limits of their considerable abilities.

The shortcomings of inter-ship communications, particularly during action, therefore actually militated towards the famous 'community of thought' of the Nelson fleet. When improvements in signalling promised greater control from the centre, the perceived need for prior consultation waned. The waning process took time, and there were broader cultural factors at work; but those improvements in signalling were under way before Nelson was dead.

Captain Home Popham, on picket-duty off Copenhagen in 1800, found that he frequently wished "to make communications of very essential moment far beyond the capacity of the established signals".[7] Popham was "a damned cunning fellow" and he re-thought the business of flag signals from linguistic principles. The key to it, he realized, was letters and words, and not numbers. He composed a *Marine Vocabulary* divided into sections relating to certain subjects and consisting of commonly used phrases. To this he added a dictionary of 1,000 words. From the various flags in use, he selected 24 and attached a letter to each; in hoists of three, there would be over 13,000 combinations, with the first (or 'superior') letter indicating in which section of the lexicon the message was to be found. If the whole message was not provided for, a superior pendant (= pennant) would refer the recipient to the dictionary. If the word was not in the dictionary, another pendant indicated that the ensuing flags were to be read as individual letters. If hoists of four flags were used, the possibilities were 330,000. There was no end to it, and it "enabled the Admiral, *for the first time*, to say exactly what he liked by signal".

Popham stressed that his system was meant to complement, rather than replace, the *Signal Book*, and a pendant (the telegraph flag) was provided to indicate when his system was being used. In the private-enterprise way in which such things happened, the diffusion of the *Marine Vocabulary* in the seagoing Fleet was erratic and for some years it remained the case that only the standard (Howe–Kempenfelt) *Signal Book* was in use throughout the service. But in September 1805 Nelson called at the Admiralty to secure several copies of Popham's latest edition before leaving for Spanish waters, and its value was soon demonstrated by Captain Henry Blackwood of *Euryalus*, who, while watching Cadiz, found himself able to converse, through relaying frigates, with Nelson fifty miles away. Nevertheless it was still thought of as a novelty and made no difference to the way Nelson planned to lead the fleet in the forthcoming battle: his famous *Memorandum* of October the 9th expected little of signalling ("shot will carry away the masts and yards of friends as well as foes"), and as much as ever of the initiative of his juniors.

Shortly before noon on October the 21st, as *Victory*, gundecks cleared away for action, crept down upon the enemy, Nelson turned to Popham's vocabulary for entertainment: "I will now amuse the fleet with a signal." His first idea was to say: 'NELSON CONFIDES THAT EVERY MAN WILL DO HIS DUTY', and he told Lieutenant John Pasco to be quick, "for I have one more signal to make which is for close action". Pasco explained that there were no single groups for 'Nelson' or 'confides', and rather than spell them out letter for letter it would be quicker to find alternatives.[8] How about 'ENGLAND EXPECTS'? "That will do, Pasco, make it directly." Rear-Admiral Collingwood in *Royal Sovereign*, was irritated to see festoons of flag-hoists[9] ascending *Victory*'s rigging: "I wish Nelson would stop signalling: we know well enough what to do." When the signal was translated he repented – "Great man!"

Never before had such a message been broadcast to a fleet at such a moment. Until now the means had not existed. The sheer sleight of hand was at least as remarkable as the signal itself (which got a mixed reception in a number of ships). Nelson then got on with the serious business of the day and told Pasco to hoist numbers 8 and 63 from the official *Signal Book*: 'PREPARE TO ANCHOR AT CLOSE OF DAY'; and, a little later, number 16: 'ENGAGE THE ENEMY MORE CLOSELY'. No further tactical signal was made by *Victory* until the battle was won.

In the generations following Trafalgar, the attention of popular
mythology was captured by the aura which Nelson cast over his fleet
and over his countrymen. Thus was obscured the fact that his most
essential contribution to British naval mastery was as a trainer of
Collingwoods, Blackwoods and Hardys: his greatest gift of leadership
was to raise his juniors above the need of supervision. His extraordinary magnetism certainly assisted him in this task, but as the medium
rather than the message. The Victorians confused the two and missed
the point. As we shall see, there were cultural reasons why they should
be resistant to the real secret of Nelson's greatness, even had they
analysed it: by their authoritarian lights it was subversive. The
retrogression started in the year after Napoleon's final defeat and four
years before Queen Victoria was born, with the issue of a new official
Signal Book.

In 1816, while weather-beaten squadrons were paying off and some
of Nelson's surviving 'brothers' were being rowed ashore for the last
time, the Lords Commissioners of the Admiralty "thought fit to adopt
for the use of His Majesty's Fleet"[10] Rear-Admiral Sir Home Popham's
system of signals. It was to form "the basis of all subsequent systems in
which the flag is the principal medium".[11]

No doubt, at the time, the apparent obviation of hazardous and time-
consuming boat transfers was welcome – how could it be otherwise? –
but terse, formal and public exchanges by flag-hoist could never really
substitute for the meeting of minds brought about by the discussion,
argument and persuasion of those Nelsonic gatherings in the flagship.
For the time being, and for the foreseeable future, it scarcely mattered.
So complete had been the success of the 'Nelson' generation that the
era of fleet actions appeared to be over for ever. In the long calm lee of
Trafalgar the Royal Navy found itself with very different tasks to get on
with, tasks which came to characterize the Victorian era.

*

British explorers, missionaries, settlers, farmers, planters, engineers,
miners and 'box wallahs' found their way to every habitable and hitherto non-Europeanized corner of the globe, to be followed (more often
than preceded) by the Union Jack, the garrison regiments and the civil
servants. Gradually, bit by bit, an enormous sprawling maritime empire
took shape, often with grudging initial support, or none at all, from
Whitehall.[12] By the time Britain was in the full grip of the industrial
revolution she found herself with the most extensive resources and distribution system in history – accrued behind the benevolent and usually
passive shield of the Royal Navy. Trade meant ships. Merchant ships

doubled and redoubled in number, and demanded safe access to the myriad ports and estuaries now opening up.

Although the captains of HM ships

had been under explicit instructions since about 1760 to make observations of foreign shores and harbours, [as late as 1830] 'there was scarcely what could be termed a correct chart of any portion of the globe in existence'.[13]

There now blossomed the age of "great surveys and great surveyors, recollected with awe and admiration by hydrographic professionals ever since".[14] Demand was part of it; in due course technology would be part of it (steam power enabled "surveyors to run direct lines of soundings in weather impossible for sailing craft"); but the most important factor was the leadership of the most famous marine surveyor in history, the driven and perfectionist Captain Francis Beaufort. The inventor of the Wind Scale was Hydrographer of the Navy from 1829 until 1855, and under his paternal supervision a dedicated clutch of officers in an assortment of vessels systematically plotted the hazards of pilotage for the benefit of all seafarers. One of his trusted team was Commander Robert Fitzroy, whose command of *Beagle* is best remembered for the contemplations of the naturalist Charles Darwin, but whose survey of the south and west shores of South America was, in its own right, a "monumental achievement".[15]

In many parts of the world it was dangerous work. Death at the hands of unfriendly natives, from tropical fever, or from the capsizing of small boats, was a constant risk. It was not unknown for surveying ships to disappear with all hands.[16] Nevertheless, with a small budget and minimal staff at the Admiralty, Beaufort published nearly 1,500 charts which were so accurate that many "are still used today by countries all over the world, often amended and updated – but not always so".[17]

While the world's coastlines were being charted, the only major regions which remained to be explored and claimed (aside from the great continental interiors) lay around the North and South Poles. In 1818, Parliament offered rewards for the discovery of the supposed North-West Passage, and the first to respond was Commander William Parry, who preceded Beaufort as Hydrographer of the Navy.[18] Sporadically, for almost a hundred years, the Admiralty was entwined with polar exploration in unofficial partnership with the Royal Society and the Royal Geographical Society. As an expedition leader, Parry was followed by George Lyon, John Ross, James Ross, John Franklin, Frederick Beechey, Erasmus Ommanney, Robert McClure, Edward Belcher, Francis McClintock, George Nares and Robert Falcon Scott. All were naval officers and nearly every one was knighted (in Scott's case, his widow was entitled). It is difficult to be precise about their motivation. They assumed the roles of surveyors, meteorologists, biologists, naturalists, hydrographers, astronomers and physicists (it was vital to study the Earth's magnetic field near the poles, they said); but above all they wanted to be first.

One of the longest, most altruistic and thankless campaigns in military history was the Royal Navy's dogged crusade to deny the use of the sea to slave transporters.

> When John Wesley said of the African Slave trade that it was the sum of all human villainies he certainly did not exaggerate, and it is useless to try to gloss over the part that Great Britain took in its hellish traffic for over two hundred years. We need not charge ourselves with undue hypocrisy, however, if we sugar the pill of shame with some other historical records . . . It is true to say that we were the first to heed the voice of conscience and renounce for all time the abominable if lucrative practice; and when the chance to suppress it came, we alone were whole-hearted in our endeavours.[19]

In fact the Act of Abolition in 1807 was the product of a fluke of politics which brought about Lord Grenville's brief coalition administration of 1806–7,[20] and whole-hearted endeavours had to wait until the end of the Napoleonic and American wars. Thereafter, however, "the war against slavery ran quietly on for sixty years, making no headlines but creating substantial gaps in the Navy List".[21]

Much of the relentless patrol work was done by open boats, which, under the command of sub-lieutenants or midshipmen, might be sent away from their parent ships for up to six weeks. In the words of one "incredulous" observer: "to use ships' boats for open sea work as if they were ships is a practice surely never heard of in any other Navy, one that must be experienced to be realized."[22] Crews in East African waters learned not to approach an Arab dhow from the lee side, in case the great lateen sail was dropped on top of them and they were leapt upon and massacred while they struggled beneath it.[23] Death in some disease-ridden East or West African swamp was not an uncommon fate for Jack Tar. Forays ashore to punish slaving warlords in the Persian Gulf or China Sea brought a steady trickle of casualties.

> The rest of the civilized world applauded the British Government's noble aims and the Royal Navy's devotion to the nastiest of duties, but offered neither to share the work, nor contribute to the cost, nor allow the squadrons the facilities they needed.[24]

The labyrinthine legal difficulties, especially where 'flags of convenience' were involved, can be glimpsed in the 684-page reference-book *The Slave Trade, Instructions to Naval Officers*, which the Admiralty printed in 1844. The moral issues could be equally daunting: slave-ships would start throwing their human cargo overboard to confront the pursuing warship with the dilemma of whether to stop and save the wretched swimmers, or to press on with the chase. Captains had to deal with such problems as they arose, and only a robust common sense would see them through. As late as 1888, the sloop *Penguin* captured fifteen slave dhows in eight months, and found herself "cruising about with thirty-four native children on board".[25]

> It was regarded as a tremendous victory when President Lincoln of the United States agreed to allow patrolling British warships to stop and search his country's merchantmen. When finally won [the war against slavery] rated no victory parade, general celebration or distribution of honours. The spoils were no more than a sentence in the history books to say that civilization was largely indebted to the British Admiralty and British Fleet for the abolition of the slave trade in African negroes.[26]

To attach a Gilbert-and-Sullivan image of genial and fusty ineffectiveness to the Victorian Navy is easily done – the Victorians started it – but in important ways it is misconceived. Great Britain's giant status, the principle of free trade, and the policing of the world's sea lanes, were all underpinned by a naval supremacy which international consensus held to be beyond plausible challenge.

> The prestige of the Royal Navy was tremendous and the rumble of chain cable through the hawse-pipe as a cruiser or gunboat wearing the White Ensign came to anchor was, time and time again, enough to bring quiet to a troubled spot.[27]

The *Who's Who* entry of one Rear-Admiral Leicester Chantry Keppel, a contemporary of Jacky Fisher, illustrates the opportunities for action, adventure and sudden death available to personnel on remote stations, far away from the main fleets, in the middle years of Victoria's epic reign.

> 2nd *s.* of late Rev. Canon the Hon. Thomas Robert Keppel. Served as midshipman of H.M.S. *Bellerophon*, 1854; was actively engaged in embarking the army at Varna and landing at Old Fort; served at Eupatoria in defence of that town; at bombardment of Sevastopol, 1854, and bombardment of Fort Constantine at 600 yards; served in H.M.S. *Magicienne*, at bombardment in destruction of Friederichsham, 1855; in charge of boat under fire against Viborg, and lifted two infernal machines [mines] when under fire and cleared passage; in charge of mortar vessel at bombardment of Seveaborg, 1855; was engaged with Russian artillery at Ravenoari in Finland, 1855; engaged in suppression of Slave Trade on East Coast of Africa and captured several slave dhows under fire, 1861; served in expedition up Zambesi with Dr

Livingstone; in command of gunboats *Janus* and *Insolent* at Chefoo, 1867–69; kept Neinfe Rebels in check; obtained redress for outrages on British subjects at Jamone, Formosa, 1868 (received thanks of Commander-in-Chief and Her Majesty's Minister); punished piratical natives for attack on Sharp Peak River Min, Chefoo, and attacked Pington and subdued natives at Foochowfoo (received official thanks, 1869); West Coast of Africa – served in Niger Expedition when several piratical villages were destroyed, and severe punishment inflicted on river pirates, 1877 (despatches); as Commander in H.M.S. *Avou* up Congo, commanded expedition for punishment of pirates, who had attacked and pillaged American vessel *Joseph Nickeroon* (received approval of Lord Derby, also approval from their Lordships for skill and gallantry with which the operations were conducted, as well as approval of the Secretary of State for Foreign Affairs); commanded H.M. ships *Constance* and *Cleopatra* in China and Japan; Flag-Capt. to Commander-in-Chief at Nore . . .

The details of this much-skirmished officer's later career become vague, suggesting that some recurring illness, or alcoholism, may have precluded further promotion; but greater (and less deserved) honours might have come his way had he had the good fortune to serve in safe, glamorous flagships rather than remote, treacherous backwaters.

By the close of the Victorian age Britain's officer classes were increasingly the inheritors, rather than the winners, of empire. They "had no doubts". Theirs was the Earth (or, at least, a quarter of it) and they "behaved with the careless and humorous arrogance of supremacy". At the time of one of the Armenian massacres in Turkey:

William Pakenham went ashore from his ship to restore order in a particularly violent village near the southern coast. He was accompanied only by a midshipman and a Turkish interpreter, both very frightened, and he was dressed in every refinement of British naval elegance, his buttons blinding, his beard impeccable, his high white collar stiffly starched. The village toughs suspended their atrocities to gather round this incongruous visitor from the sea, fingering their weapons and cursing, and presently Pakenham called for silence. 'Let us begin,' he said to his interpreter. 'Tell these ugly bastards that I am not going to tolerate any more of their bestial habits.' Thus spoke the voice of late Victorian England.[28]

Retrospective lampooning of this most successful agency of this (by its own lights) most successful society, tends to boil down to 'hindsight' comparison of the RN's nineteenth-century capabilities with its twentieth-century challenges. The Fleet performed very well the multifarious world-wide tasks demanded of it by its paymasters, and that is the criterion by which it must be judged.

Less competent societies marvelled at evidence of a discipline not less rigid because it was remote, not less firm because it was slow to act, as they marvelled at the latest news of bigger guns, longer ranges and faster, heavier ironclads.[29]

*

In some respects, however, the outward impression of blasé serenity was more a matter of form than of substance. In spite, or because, of Britain's Olympian industrial lead, the Fleet was subjected to a stream of piecemeal advances in metallurgy, ordnance and engineering, which it neither welcomed nor knew how to synthesize into an operational doctrine – a task made harder by the absence, between 1860 and 1895, of homogeneous squadrons of major warships. The Crimean War produced no fleet challenge, and the naval actions of the American Civil War of 1861–5, the Austro-Italian War of 1866, the Russo-Turkish War of 1877–8 and the Chile-Peruvian War of 1879–81 provided more red herrings for debate than clear pointers to the way ahead for a global seapower. The years of economizing in the late 1870s, the 'Dark Age' of the Victorian Navy, were made easier for the Treasury by the lack of clear direction in future technology and ship design.[30]

The slow death of masts, yards and sails seems, in retrospect, to be the classic anachronism of the times. In fact the Admiralty, given its matchless reputation as an opponent of innovation, was not slow to adopt steam as an auxiliary form of propulsion[31] – especially after the show-piece tug-of-war in 1845 between *Alecto* and *Rattler* settled the conflict between paddle-wheels and screws in favour of the latter. Progressive officers, such as Captain Astley Cooper Key in the mid-1860s and Commander John Fisher in 1871,[32] argued that masts and sails could have no place in the battleship of the future. Dispensing with sails, however, proved a protracted business.

The curtailment of cruising radii imposed by the constant need to re-coal was unwelcome to admirals accustomed to almost limitless endurance, and, as late as the first years of the twentieth century, there was no way of patrolling the Pacific other than by sail. Primitive engines were too prone to breakdown to commit a ship's propulsion to machinery alone. Vessels without acres of canvas to steady them in rough weather were highly seasickening. Funnels, furthermore, "meant filth". In the 1840s, a First Naval Lord (usage remained ambiguous until 1904 when the old term 'Sea Lord' was readopted) "complained that since the introduction of steamers he had never seen a clean deck or a captain who, when calling on him, did not look like a sweep".[33] And machinery had socially undesirable ramifications. Wardrooms began to be infiltrated by men with discordant accents and gauche manners from the industrial Midlands, Tyneside or Glasgow – men who lived on their pay – and for several decades, steam engines,

> the engineers who operated them, and the coal they consumed – the disgusting mineral that tarnished brasswork, fouled decks and gangways and smutted pure white canvas – were regarded with almost equal loathing. Whenever possible, the hated funnels were telescoped almost out of sight, propellers hoisted in and boilers allowed to cool off.[34]

For half a century the two forms of propulsion co-existed while engines gained in power, economy and reliability; and sails became less and less compatible with efficiency. A steam warship had less need of high freeboard amidships, for example, and the trend towards heavy trainable gun-mountings on the upper deck not only required low centres of gravity but was literally obstructed by the rigging needed to support heavy masts.

In 1875 Captain Philip Colomb demonstrated mathematically that more coal was burnt transporting masts and spars around than was saved by their occasional use; and in 1882 Captain Penrose Fitzgerald – one of the most capable seamen in the service, and the author of *Hints on Boat Sailing* – goaded the Royal United Service Institution (RUSI) with the view that

> Sending steamers which sail badly to make long passages under sail is a waste of time, and both officers and men know this and it disgusts them. The men read now much more than they used to, and they know perfectly well that a high state of efficiency in 'shifting topsails' will be of no use to them in wartime, nor enable them to fight their ship any better than if they had never seen a topsail yard in their lives.[35]

'Rough Fitzgerald's' remarks were all the more pointed in that he had just commanded HMS *Inconstant* on a round-the-world cruise, almost entirely under sail, for the benefit of Midshipmen Prince Albert Victor and Prince George.

It was the proliferation of twin-engines which really put paid to sails, for twin-screws created so much drag in the 'trail' mode that sailing wasn't worth the bother. HMS *Alexandra*, one of the last great fully-rigged ironclads, had a small auxiliary engine to keep the shafts turning while under sail and she could still barely make six knots (compared with *Victory's* twelve, with the right wind). And the odds on a twin-screwed ship suffering total propulsion breakdown are the square root of those in the case of a single-engined vessel. The decision to banish sails from battleships was finally taken in 1887,[36] thirty-three years after

Jacky Fisher joined the service, fifteen years after John Jellicoe. But cruisers and sloops on remote stations kept them for years longer, and "how hard the mast and sail died and how absurd were the arguments raised for their retention!"[37]

There was the question of physical fitness, for example: what would happen to the bodily and moral fibre of British tars if they were no longer exercised in the gymnasium of masts and sails? As late as 1890 Admiral the Earl of Clanwilliam feared the worst:

> The idea of keeping up the physique of the men with a leaping bar and a mattress instead of masts and sails is absurd. A doctor just returned from an iron-clad in the Mediterranean told me there was a marked difference in the physique of the iron-clad men – they had nothing to do from morning till night, everything was done for them by machinery, even to hoisting up the small boats with the steam winch.[38]

Even Reginald Bacon, a young and technically progressive officer, regarded drills aloft as "tremendous aids" to discipline.[39]

The swan-song call on the masts-and-sails bugle was sounded in the RUSI in 1892 by two officers whom we shall meet again. Captain Charles Johnstone presented a paper (which drew support from Admiral Stephen Luce of the US Navy) on the value of *Masts and Sails as a Means of Training*, and in the ensuing discussion Captain William Dyke Acland declared:

> I am certain that the only way of training officers and men to be sailors is in masted ships, making them work the ships under sails, working the masts and yards, and entirely depending upon masts and sails. I cannot understand, in a mastless ship, what the officer of the watch has to do.[40]

That these views were sincerely held is beyond doubt, but it comes as a shock to realize that they could receive applause in the leading public forum of military debate only twenty years before the keels of the *Queen Elizabeths* were laid down. Such were the material changes with which officers who rose to high command in those days had to contend.

The quaint emphasis on the ram and the lack of interest in long-range gunnery also require explanation. The two issues were closely linked. The Admiralty had been partly led up the garden path of ever bigger and slower-firing guns by armament firms competing to amaze the public. But while the cumbersome muzzle-loaders and breech-loaders in service in, say, the mid-1880s had the latent capacity to project their shells to considerable distances, the extreme range for battle-practice was about 1,200 yards – much the same as at Trafalgar. Why was this so?

Short range lay deep in the English naval psyche. Sir Walter Ralegh's standing orders of 1617 (paragraph 26) laid down that "The gunners shall not shoot any great ordnance at other distance than point-blank." More than 150 years later, the *Fighting Instructions* of 1775 (paragraph 20) directed that "Every commander is to take care that his guns are not fired till he is sure he can reach the enemy upon a point blank." Then the new 'carronade', an easily handled, large-calibre, low-velocity 'smasher', sealed England's reputation for invincibility at short range (the Americans built ships which could fight outside the carronade's reach in the war of 1812, but the British have a way of sublimating embarrassments). And of course Nelson famously said that "No captain can do very wrong if he places his ship alongside that of an enemy."

A wish to engage at a distance implied a shyness of close quarters; and gallant Victorians, like Admiral Sir John Commerell VC, "would have scorned [to do so] unless obliged".[41] But there were also persuasive practical reasons why there was little point in thinking in terms of long ranges. Accurate range-finding was still beyond technical reach.[42] And the elevation of the gun could not be usefully calibrated, even had ranges been available, while the chemical composition of the powder remained erratic. None of this mattered at point-blank, the attraction of which was that the shell – by definition flying on a flat trajectory – would hit as long as the gun was pointing at the target. It was hard enough to let the gun off at the moment in the ship's roll and pitch when the shell would proceed horizontally, without having to elevate precisely for range as well.

Furthermore, until the Armstrong wire-wound breech-loading 12-inch of 1894, the Navy's heavy ordnance failed to shake off a reputation for exploding. Although in reality the incidence of burst guns was very small, it was sufficient to engender acute nervousness among those who had to work them. Sailors were superstitious; and it was not unknown for the petty-officer who was supposed to pull the lanyard to faint with fear and for ratings to report sick to avoid being present. For their part, officers hated gunnery practice for, like funnels, gunfire meant dirt, and that cost them money. While the Admiralty provided for three coats of paint a year,[43] a ship might need as many as eight, and the balance had to come from her officers' pockets. One commander complained that repainting after target practice cost him £100[44] (more than a quarter of his annual pay). There is testimony that practice ammunition was sometimes thrown overboard,[45] and Admiral Sir Percy Scott tells of "one case where the powder was sold and paint bought with the proceeds". The doctrine of ramming had much to commend it.

It was also a product of the tactical constraints of heavy guns. With fighting ranges of only three or four tactical diameters (= turning circle widths) and reloading cycles of three or four minutes, ramming seemed the only plausible way of remaining in control of an encounter between salvoes. And if the enemy were closing you to ram, you would be lucky to get off more than one round between his coming into range and the collision, and the gunnery-officer's acute state of excitement (and lack of practice) would probably cause that to miss. Ramming became the main weapon.

'Ironclads' were built with ram-like prows as soon as it was appreciated that an iron ship might do fatal damage to a wooden one by deliberate collision. The first was the French *Couronne*, a cousin of the more famous *Gloire*, laid down in 1858. The British quickly followed suit in *Resistance* and *Defence*, cousins of *Warrior*. But the vogue for the ram really began in 1866, when the Austrian flagship *Ferdinand Max* rammed and sank the *Re d'Italia* at the Battle of Lissa, and thereafter appeared to be vindicated by spectacular accidental collisions, such as those which sank *Vanguard* in 1875, *Grosser Kurfürst* in 1878, and even *Victoria* in 1893. It seemed a promising method of getting decisive quantities of water into an enemy ship (something which shells on a flat trajectory were unlikely to do).

Unwelcome theorists pointed out that at Lissa the Italian's steering-gear had been disabled, and argued that it should normally be very difficult to ram an unwilling victim: all he has to do is get inside your turning circle and stay there, laughing, while colandering you with his quick-firers. In 1894 the historian William Laird Clowes went further. He identified 74 attempted rammings in the minor wars around the world between 1861 and 1879, and presented the RUSI with a startling analysis of the results. His figures showed that in the few cases where contact was made, the rammer usually somehow came off worse than the rammee; and that, with plenty of searoom and both ships under control, it was safer to be the intended victim.[46] Clowes was demonstrating what a naval staff might have worked out fifteen years earlier, had a naval staff existed; but, by the time he addressed the issue, the ram debate was more or less at its last gasp.

These considerations go a long way to explain why less interest was taken in main-armament gunnery practice than in "the landing party, and the Thursday drill in small arms and company manoeuvre"[47] – skills which were much more likely to be of practical use to the Queen's sailors in the age of Empire. Indeed, most of the Victorian Navy's forty VCs were won in the naval brigades which "played a vital part in many military expeditions, often marching far inland",[48] and of which the

Royal Tournament's famous Field Gun Competition remains a legacy to this day.

While the industrial revolution was elbowing its way on board, the Navy was receiving the benefit of organizational and administrative modernizations. The Victorian age saw the irresistible rise of accountancy management in all fields of official activity. It started roughly contemporaneously with the elevation of 'pursers' into 'paymasters', paid by salary in place of profit and percentage, and it spread outwards from the Admiralty until the ways of measuring efficiency – and even the understood meaning of naval discipline – had insidiously changed.

In the 1840s "immense books of forms began coming aboard". Those with numbers prefixed by 'S' were for use in ships, 'D' meant dockyards, 'M' medical. By 1851, one captain was driven to anonymous pamphleteering against their proliferation:

> If a bag of biscuits is found to be mouldy, the Captain has to receive long written reports thereon. He must then issue warrants to the different officers, the wording of which fills sheets of foolscap, desiring them to survey the mouldy biscuit and report at length in writing. If the smallest thing requires repair, similar forms have to be gone through. If an extra bucket of lime were required to wash the holds, on which the health of all on board might depend, the number of documents, vouchers and letters that must be written to procure the said bucket of lime at Government expense would drive the pursers and clerks mad . . . [the] correspondence might go on for years.[49]

When Captain Fitzgerald mislaid a corkscrew, the administrative repercussions took four years to run their course.[50] The Admiralty clerks argued, with unimpeachable logic, that paperwork was a deterrent to frivolous requisitioning. But form-filling was just one symptom of a general trend.

In the late 1850s the first uniform regulations abolished the old slop-chest system and formalized the characteristic clothing which sailors had been wearing since Anson's days. The result was "a dramatic improvement in personal cleanliness".[51] At first, the rules were not greatly particular about detail, and sailors "decorated their jumpers with coloured silks, and some wonderful results were obtained".[52] But in the 1880s (when public schools were also adopting uniforms), with the deforestation of ironclads and the descent of sailors to deck-level, regulations about dress were tightened up[53] – at the cost "of some discontent among men who were now required to alter garments that they had been allowed to wear in [previous] ships and on other stations".[54]

Meanwhile the milestone Naval Discipline Act (NDA) of 1864 brought regulation to captains' traditional prerogatives of punishment, and in its wake "extensive bureaucratic machinery was mobilized to maintain strict scrutiny and control".[55] The NDA and its associated corpus of standing orders in *Queen's Regulations & Admiralty Instructions* were effective because they were consistent and (by the standards of the day) moderate; and they reduced the incidence of 'trouble' by defining clearly what seniors may expect of juniors and vice versa. In all aspects of shipboard life, "guides, tables, reports, logs, books, inspection provisions and other methods of supervision were developed, mostly in the 1860s, to ensure compliance and uniformity".[56] But with the defining of boundaries and performance criteria, the broader conceptual sense of duty was all but eclipsed by the narrow hierarchical sense.

Even the simple deferential act of saluting was only standardized in 1889 to appease the Germanic compulsion for uniformity. Hitherto, salutes had been rendered anyhow: "Some actually took off their caps, others took the brim between finger and thumb, while some touched the peak."[57] Then the newly crowned Kaiser Wilhelm II came over, preening himself as an honorary admiral in the British Navy, and complained that no two officers saluted him in the same way. So the matter was put right.

These things were trifles compared to what was happening in the backwaters of Portsmouth Harbour where the gunnery training ship *Excellent* was colonizing a 40-acre island created by convict labour out of harbour dredging-spoil. The whole process took some forty years, but the first part of 'Mud Island' (later Whale Island) to be drained and levelled provided the Navy's first parade-ground and the gunnery instructors never looked back. Had *Victory's* men of 1805 been witnessed on parade they would have presented an anthropologically strange spectacle. The sources of their discipline were the Darwinistic hazards of balancing barefoot and bow-legged high up a heaving mast, xenophobic élitism and total group-loyalty. It owed nothing to the contrived, cosmetic regimentation of square-bashing. But

> now the successful firing of a gun seemed to depend upon the dressing by the right, the stamping of feet, the swinging of arms, the shouting of commands, and all that had previously been thought of as Army stuff.[58]

Uniformity distinguishes men by rank rather than character; and "as ships became divided [in departure from central batteries] and gun positions more isolated, did we take enough trouble", William Goodenough wondered later,

> to teach the mass of men a feeling of individual responsibility? – or did we fall into the easier custom of considering it necessary to have a commissioned officer in every isolated position and creating more and more petty officers and leading seamen, so that each small compartment had its leading hand?

The known opinion is that we erred in over-inspection and did not, when the chance was first made, pay sufficient attention to individual responsibility.[59]

Another new plant for the standardization of naval personnel lay moored in the River Dart in Devon. Since 1863, naval cadets had been channelled through a dedicated two-year apprenticeship on board two hulks, *Britannia* and *Hindustan*, before being distributed around the Fleet. It is difficult to argue that this was not an advance on the previous practice of sending them straight to sea to learn their trade haphazardly from scratch, hostages to whatever interest, or lack of it, their captains chose to take in them. But the new system

> was based on forcing cadets into a pre-conceived and rigid mould by the application of harsh, even inhuman discipline. Obedience to orders was the hallowed principle of the system, and woe betide any boy who was deemed to have transgressed that tenet. Any signs of originality or independence were severely frowned on – if not actively suppressed; while intellectual accomplishments always came a bad second to athletics.[60]

This narrow formal schooling caused Commodore James Goodenough (killed by poison arrows in the South Pacific in 1875) misgivings as early as 1871. He deplored "the loss of individuality, which is inevitable when all young gentlemen are passed through the same course from the age of twelve years", and argued that they should receive the mind-broadening benefits of a public-school type education before embarking on their professional training.[61] One can easily see why Goodenough's modernist views fell on deaf ears; it would be three-quarters of a century before they were adopted. The pros and cons, for the Navy, of having its 'young gentlemen' culturally assimilated and possessed of advanced boat-handling skills at such an early age are difficult to evaluate. Either way, by the late 1890s almost every officer of promise below the rank of captain, and certainly all the future flag-officers of Jutland, were products of the Dartmouth battery farm; and, what with the meagre food, the bullying and the public canings, many would have echoed the bleak comment that "there is no period of my life that I look back upon with less pleasure than I do the time I spent in the *Britannia*."[62]

That these and many similar developments brought 'improvements' to mass-management, which could be measured, tabulated and reported upon with satisfaction, is beyond doubt. In characteristic matters of form and process – rank structure, discipline, specializations, routines, dress, ceremonial – the Royal Navy of today was recognizably hammered out on the Victorian anvils of accountability and standardization. By them the life of a bluejacket was turned into a decent career:

a nice girl might now love a sailor without distressing her mother too much. But as early as 1877 a rating could complain of the new fashion

> of trying to make the lower-deck *uniform*, and [that] this is often done at the expense of comfort. What advantage accrues to the service by having all the mess-traps of a uniform pattern? Why should each man's ditty-bag be required to be of the same size and pattern? Why is it essential that hats should be stowed in a particular way?[63]

And in the long view, the extent to which the encroachment of accountancy management may have occasioned loss – perhaps avoidable loss – in matters which were not so susceptible to measurement is, itself, not susceptible to measurement. In 1894 the *Saturday Review*, a civilian journal with obvious 'insider' knowledge, denounced what it called "the over-regulation of the Navy". In words which ring bells a century later, it blamed the proliferation of petty rules and regulations at least in part on the need "to quiet someone who is asking questions in the House of Commons":

> To tell an officer what to do and leave him to decide how to do it by the light of proper professional knowledge, which is the way to form self-reliant men with alert brains, is not the object of a modern Government Office. On the contrary, the aim is apparently to have an instruction for everything, so that the Office may have something to appeal to for the purpose of showing that it is not to blame. Of course these things are subject to continual modifications and amendment of modifications, till it has become a commonplace that no officer can know all the printed instructions by which he is supposed to act. All this, we allow, is merely the canker of a long peace, but it is a bad preparation for war, which of all human conditions must call for self-reliance.[64]

Questions in the House of Commons are easily (and only) satisfied by 'accountancy' answers. An enquiry which cannot be so answered carries with it the whiff of administrative laxity and concomitant political embarrassment. Unfortunately, whether the permeation of the Victorian Navy with the petty habits of accountancy management was caused by Parliament with the Admiralty's complicity, or vice versa, there was no counterbalancing study of the nature and practice of naval warfare; and an inordinate amount of time was devoted to activities of little or no military application.

As long as ironclads retained their masts and sails, competitive drills aloft continued to be the yardstick of comparison and were performed with great verve. The most highly skilled ratings – the 'upper yardmen' – would be humoured with a considerable degree of licence by officers whose reputations depended on them.[65] At the descent of a flag or the firing of a gun, every ship in the fleet would hurl herself into some labour-intensive, acrobatic routine. Some captains kept printed ledgers of seamanship drills, laid out like sportsmen's game-books with columns for Date, Evolution, Ships taking part, Time and Remarks. One of these testifies to the efficiency of the fully rigged *Sultan* when Captain HRH Prince Alfred, Duke of Edinburgh, was in command in 1876:[66]

Down Royal Yards	22 secs
Down Topgallant & Royal Yards	34 secs
Down Topgallant Yards & Masts	2 mins 23 secs

Fifteen years later the *St James's Gazette* remarked on the spirit which had "prevailed in the Navy in recent years" as

> a spirit of swagger; and its signs are a love of ostentation and of theatrical showing off, a mania for doing everything at a great pace in order to break the record and get one's name mentioned as a smart officer, a passion for doing all work with a margin for safety cut to the quick.[67]

The Mediterranean Fleet's 'Monday evolutions' in Grand Harbour, Malta, were a byword for swagger, and Maltese people would crowd the battlements of Valletta to watch.[68] Competition between ships was so frenetic that it was difficult for officers to prevent the taking of short-cuts. A gun might be loaded surreptitiously in the night,[69] running-rigging loosened, or boats' falls unbent to the last couple of turns in (perhaps wrong) anticipation of a particular evolution; and fatal accidents were common. One Mediterranean ship in the 1890s killed a man a month.[70] Queen Victoria's sailors considered themselves the world's smartest, and they didn't care who knew. Sometimes two rival crews – such as those of *Colossus* and *Alexandra* in the late 1880s[71] – had to be prevented from going ashore at the same time "for fear of battle, murder and sudden death".[72]

As masts and yards were at last phased out from ironclads in the 1880s, the focus of seamanship drills shifted on to sailing regattas, pulling round the fleet, cable-work, clearing for action, spreading awnings, or rigging anti-torpedo nets. But the traditions of hemp and canvas were to the Victorian Navy what horsemanship was to the cavalry in the 1920s, and they were relinquished with equal reluctance.[73] Even in the 1890s, "many of the customs of the sailing era were somewhat ostentatiously carried on, [and] 75% of the questions asked in the [sub-lieutenant's] examination in Seamanship were upon the details of a moribund art."[74]

Equally pervasive, and militarily sterile, was the obsession with glitter and cleanliness. This had taken root in the 1830s and '40s and was looked upon askance by old 'Nelson' hands, such as Admiral Sir William Parker.[75] By the 1880s it had assumed pathogenic proportions and, if anything, grew as manpower was released by mechanization.

> Snow-white decks, the spotless enamel, the gleaming brass tompions plugging the gun muzzles, were accepted as the hallmarks of naval quality; the punctilious perfection of time-honoured ceremonial as the evidence of efficiency.[76]

Ships' companies were roused before dawn to 'holystone' the decks on hands and knees with blocks of sandstone. Executive-officers and first-lieutenants routinely forked out for lacquer and metal polish if they wanted their careers to shine; and even midshipmen would dip into their monthly £2 13s. to buy brass fittings and gold leaf for the boats in their charge. When the Duke of Edinburgh was C-in-C Mediterranean, the officers of his flagship, *Alexandra*, were said to have spent £2,000 on her decoration.

Most of the Royal Navy's legendary late Victorian tyrants and cranks were cleanliness fundamentalists. Whole chapters, even books, have been written about them.[77] One of the best known, Sir Algernon ('Pompo') Heneage, has become a historical tourist attraction, although he was by no means the worst martinet (that palm probably goes to George Cherry, whose tyranny in command of *Argonaut* in 1900–4 prompted his survivors to have the Cherry Medal struck in their honour[78]).

Pompo had an enormous sense of his own person. He broke two eggs over his flowing blond hair every morning. He would remove his uniform coat before saying his prayers, allegedly because the idea of a captain RN kneeling before higher authority on his own ship was an absurdity. He once tried to court-martial a carpenter for entering his cabin without permission: a bad sea was flooding the compartment through the open scuttles, and the trespasser merely went in to close them. Commander Francis Bridgeman (a future First Sea Lord) was driven to locking himself in his own cabin by Heneage's tantrums, and refused to come out until the surgeon wryly diagnosed "a slight rupture" and obtained his ticket home.[79] As an admiral, Pompo took 240 dress shirts out to the Pacific and sent batches home to be laundered in London and returned in airtight crates, and his flag-captain, James Hammett, carefully copied him. He was the originator of the white kid-gloves routine during ship inspections: his cox'n would follow him around with a dozen clean pairs on a silver tray while he groped around behind pipes etc., the accumulation of soiled gloves auguring the career prospects of the executive-officer. He once spent minutes peering down a seamen's lavatory bowl, disputing the unhappy XO's assertion that a small visible mark was a flaw in the glaze rather than dirt.

We must be wary of 'culture-gap' differentials in judging even the most authoritarian of Victorian officers, and make allowance for a less self-analytical age. For all his affectations and petty tyrannies, Heneage was no weakling. When one of *Thunderer's* guns burst, killing the turret crew during fleet gunnery practice in 1879, he was one of two captains who rendered medical assistance and then readdressed their own ships to the target, loading full charges to forestall any nonsense about jinxed guns (the other was George Tryon, whom we shall meet again).[80] And in the mid-1880s he "brought the Channel Squadron under full sail to a running moor in Vigo harbour in half a gale of wind, [and] the Spaniards who observed this feat never stopped talking about it".[81] Nevertheless the wholesale neglect of genuine warrior aptitudes (the "sheer monkey-wit, rat-catching instinct for war", in Walter Cowan's incisive phrase) in favour of narrow seamanship, housekeeping and show-piece talents, in the criteria by which efficiency was measured, penetrated every corner of the Fleet.

> There are, of course, good arguments for 'bull': that it ensures a level of orderliness, cleanliness, discipline, personal pride, obedience and morale which, so it seems, could not be reached by any other means.
>
> However the case against is also strong. It is time-wasting, excruciatingly boring for those with more than the most mediocre intellect, and a poor substitute for thought. Since it aims to govern behaviour by a set of rules and defines rigid programmes for different occasions, it cannot meet the unanticipated event.[82]

Well might a restless 30-year-old commander named John Fisher complain of

> getting horribly tired of being a sort of upper housemaid, devoting severe thought to the cleaning of paintwork and, by way of relief to the mind, investigating the correctness of midshipmen's watch bills or (still more interesting) following the trail of a missing bucket.[83]

This state of affairs was all the more insidious in the light of a promotion system by which officers became admirals without undergoing any assessment of their capacity for high command. In 1874 the First Lord of the Admiralty, the obese and ineffectual Mr George Ward-Hunt, cancelled a scheme of selective compulsory retirement introduced by his predecessor. His reasoning was that after an officer had been selected from the lieutenants', and subsequently from the commanders', list, he must be one who would make a good flag-officer. [He therefore] stopped selection after officers had arrived at the rank of captain, which made it certain you could never have young flag-officers, or if a few were rather young from having been made captains early, there was no guarantee they would be efficient officers after being on the captains' list 16 to 19 years.[84]

At the risk of labouring the point, this meant that once a commander had out-performed his peers in competitive drills, out-painted and out-polished them, and thus obtained his captaincy, his promotion to rear-admiral and thence up the flag-list was purely a matter of dead men's (or superannuated men's) shoes. No matter that Nelson's ships were known for their untidiness, or that his seamanship left something to be desired,[85] his professional legatees were guaranteed to be above reproach in these respects.

*

Psychologists have a ready supply of jargon-projectiles – of which 'anally retentive' is pre-eminently pleasing – to sling at conformist personalities and vocations. In respect of military career hierarchies they appear to be on firmish ground. Professor Norman Dixon, in his illuminating *On the Psychology of Military Incompetence*, discerns two distinct officer types which broadly equate with what are sometimes called 'left-side' and 'right-side' brain talents. He calls them 'authoritarians' and 'autocrats', placing a sharper distinction on these terms than their common usage conveys.

According to him, the *authoritarian* officer joins the armed forces to make a virtue out of various personality disorders which make him particularly adaptable to military life. These problems can, allegedly, range from childhood scatology, through parental neglect, sexual repression and virility self-doubts, to a need for the peer-group approval and promotion with which the peacetime armed services reward conformity. He draws self-esteem from the status imparted by his rank and uniform. He defers naturally to seniority and obeys orders to the letter, loves order and ceremony, is meticulous in attention to detail and is often paranoid about cleanliness. He is strong in sequential reasoning processes, suppresses his imagination, rejects information which conflicts with his (and his seniors') preconceptions, and is fearful of using his initiative. He is often prudish, idealizes women (a state of mind assisted by unfamiliarity), shuns publicity and seeks safety in secrecy. He keeps an unblotted copybook and thus gains unhindered advancement in peacetime. But he is easily disorientated by the crises and dilemmas of war, and responds inappropriately or not at all.

The *autocratic* officer is approximately the obverse of the above. He tends to think laterally, rather than serially, and his convictions often follow his instincts. He uses his initiative as a matter of habit. He is receptive to the possibility that his juniors might be right or his seniors wrong, and takes his career into his hands when he believes the latter to be the case. His attitude to hierarchy and military 'bull' is casual or even overtly ironical; and he tends to be individualistic, or negligent, about dress. His peacetime career ascent is often difficult because he lacks the docility convenient to his immediate seniors and he is typically considered disruptive. In wartime it falls to him to clear up the mess pioneered by the authoritarian who gained preferment over him in the years of peace.

Dixon produces much anecdotal and entertaining evidence, mainly from the generous historical kitbag of the British Army, to illustrate the two contrasting officer-types. Unsurprisingly, in view of the very nature of military organizations, authoritarians are easier to find than autocrats. For example, he names as archetypical authoritarians Lord Cardigan, who always (in the words of another historian)

> demanded more glitter, more polish, pipeclay, smarter drill, greater perfection in turnout. A superb horseman and utterly unmoved by the heaviest cannon and musket fire, he led the brigade wherever ordered, with the greatest dash and elan. If not ordered nothing would move him . . .[86]

and Douglas Haig, whose tramline thought processes carried half a generation of young men to their deaths and who was strangely obsessed with personal hygiene.

Like the 'laws' of Northcote Parkinson, Norman Dixon's analysis resides, perhaps, in the margins between scholarship and mischief; but the manner in which late Victorian naval officers fit his authoritarian *v.* autocrat model is, in some cases, striking – although the exercise requires at least two overriders.

Firstly, while Dixon naturally focuses on extremes, most people seem to draw characteristics from both sides of the Dixonian spectrum. Secondly, 'incompetence', in the detailed practical sense, finds fewer pegs in the Navy than in Dixon's principal theme-park. The sea-service was professionalized two centuries earlier than the Army, and the necessities and hazards of daily shipboard life demanded a higher degree of basic vocational competence. It was impossible for a ship's officer not to know where his men's latrines were (for crude example), and a total incompetent would probably have fallen overboard long before he was put in charge of anything important. Captain Johnstone was not wrong when he suggested to the RUSI that, owing to the demands of working masts and sails, "the Navy contains a far smaller proportion of inefficients than the other Services".[87]

On the other hand, Dixon's broader thesis – that peacetime military hierarchies naturally attract, beget and reward authoritarian officers[88] – has much relevance to the condition of the Victorian Royal Navy. Indeed it takes only a few moments' thought to wonder how it could be otherwise.

However, organic imperatives were not the only source of authoritarianism in the late nineteenth-century armed forces. They were also subjected to a cultural climate more unremittingly authoritarian than at any other time in British history, for the Victorians sought to structure and codify as many fields of behaviour as possible in order to regulate their world, disarm the unpredictable and perpetuate the *status quo*.

> Behind the calls to honour, duty and glory lay the Victorians' firm belief in obedience – absolute obedience to God, the Queen, and one's superiors, in the family as much as in the army. It was a time of pervasive authoritarianism . . . Unquestioning submission to orders was taught to schoolboys as soon as they reached the age of awareness; they recited *The Death of Nelson*, *Drake's Drum*, *The Boy Stood on the Burning Deck*, *The Wreck of the Hesperus*, and *The Charge of the Light Brigade*. Every story of Victorian children had a point, a moral, usually one of dutifulness . . . By the time a youth of good family had reached manhood, he had heard more than a thousand sermons.[89]

At the heart of this duty-and-obedience culture lay the Victorian revival of chivalry.

When chivalry's original heyday was, and what it amounted to, nobody really knows (the legend of King Arthur is rooted in the Celtic mists of the Dark Ages, but he is invariably accoutred in the style of many centuries later). "We can only look back upon it as a beautiful and fantastic piece of frostwork, which has dissolved in the beams of the sun."[90] Its enduring historical utility was as a means of legitimizing power and privilege: at best it was a codification of honour to bind the lesser ranks of the nobility to the service of kings and princes, and it was never very chivalrous, except to the most highly born, and often not even to them. It was certainly floundering by the time longbows and gunpowder enabled men to kill each other remotely.

But then, in 1485, the year in which Henry Tudor usurped the throne at Bosworth, William Caxton printed Sir Thomas Malory's *Morte d'Arthur*, and the new King sought to portray himself as a returned Arthur (for whom he named his first-born son). Chivalry's half-mythologized values thereafter became woven into the fabrics of

English literature and English self-perception. They defined Elizabeth's courtier-warriors, infused the works of Shakespeare, resurfaced uncertainly in the Civil War, were invoked on behalf of radicalism by William Blake, and inspired Nelson.

The full-scale revival of chivalry (or the advent of *neo*-chivalry) really got under way in the early nineteenth century, and has been explored by Mark Girouard in *The Return to Camelot*. The pump was primed among the privileged by "fear of democracy, of disaffection in the lower classes, and of the effects of the French Revolution".[91] The impetus came from the 'Waverley novels' of Sir Walter Scott – romanticist of yesterday's lost causes and pied-piper of tomorrow's – from the epic poems of Lord Byron, and from Kenelm Digby's ethereal and bewitching *Broadstone of Honour* (1822), which became almost a manual for the English gentleman. Chivalry placed 'character' far above 'intellect'. It espoused the virtues of duty, honour, service, self-control, fellowship, courtesy, modesty and, above all, obeying the rules. It caught on.

The Arthurian idiom was fostered by the Prince Consort, and was not unconnected with Alfred Tennyson's laureateship. It was balm to the insecurities of the burgeoning *arriviste* middle classes, and a gift to the Victorian social establishment. It favoured the *status quo* by promoting the conscientious performance of obligation (English *noblesse oblige* was meant to mesmerize other nations and races as well as the British lower classes), and was tinged with benevolent feudalism.[92] The surcoat of chivalry, with its connotations of high ideals and pure motives, was obligatory cladding for whatever political beliefs Victorians chose to hold.[93] And this was the golden age of Round Tables, Ancient Orders of various species, and Freemasonry – societies which combined philanthropy and self-improvement with their own codes of conduct and feudalistic rituals. Freemasonry accompanies the story told in the next few chapters as a recurring biographical characteristic of the naval officers involved. It "distinctly enjoins us to respect all social distinctions, so that while some must rule, others must obey and cheerfully accept their inferior positions";[94] the moral disciplines which it notionally demands, closely mirror the chivalric virtues listed above; and, like British royalty (which heads it), Freemasonry is steeped in the symbolism of chivalry.[95]

Chivalry's prime constituency was young men. Like the adventure of empire, it placed a premium on the idealism and vigour of youth; and its knightly, crusading derivation easily fired the imaginations of middle-class boys whose reading material it saturated. Public schools and, later, boys' brigades espoused it with enthusiasm, the more so after there emerged a sublime refinement, tailor-made for the moral development of young men. The term 'muscular Christianity' caused a stir when first used by Thomas Hughes (of *Tom Brown's Schooldays*) and Charles Kingsley (of *Westward Ho!*) in the 1860s. Chivalry, they said, aimed at "producing whole men, and consecrating their masculinity to God in all activities of normal life, including the battlefield".

> The doctrine that a Christian should dedicate his body, mind and will to the service of God was, as Hughes and Kingsley pointed out, by no means new. But the way in which they wrote and talked about it made it clear that emotionally they found physical prowess gloriously exciting; that they preferred a strong man to a clever one, and that they regarded a clever man with instinctive suspicion, unless he could prove himself by following hounds, swinging dumb-bells or taking cold baths.[96]

Chivalry was uncerebral, extrovert and physically healthy; and, insofar as it channelled energies and curtailed behavioural choices, it was a priceless aid to social discipline. It supplied the beacon by which three generations of Englishmen were kept more or less on the straight and narrow, and the faint glow of its embers may still be discerned today. In a cruder society and a more strident age it might have acquired politically sinister dimensions. In Victorian England its most pernicious effect was the confusion of warfare with ritualized team games.

The concept of Playing the Game, in life as in sport, appeared in print at least as early as 1849.[97] After the 1864 Royal Commission on Public Schools commended the character-forming properties of football and cricket,[98] its rise and rise was assured. Cricket, in particular, was believed to impart "the true principles of chivalrous honour".[99] Later, popular writers such as Rudyard Kipling, Henry Newbolt and Robert Baden-Powell (all Masons, incidentally, as was Sir Walter Scott), to whom the "mixture of sport and public service seemed to epitomize the ideal of the English gentleman",[100] took up the refrain.

Newbolt, "whose belief in the public school as well as in the imperial ideal verged on the mystical",[101] is credited with the sublime definition of the link between the playing-field and the battlefield, with his poem *Vitae Lampada* in 1897. Today it is embarrassing. At the time, it articulated the sporting and patriotic ideals of the age:

> The sand of the desert is sodden red,
> Red with the wreck of a square which broke;
> The gatling's jammed and the colonel dead,
> And the regiment blind with dust and smoke.
> The river of death has brimmed his banks
> And England's far and Honour a name,
> But the voice of a schoolboy rallies the ranks:
> 'Play up! Play up! And play the game!'

A generation later an unconventional soldier, Major-General J. F. C. Fuller, pondered the harm which the cult of regulated sports had done to Britain's warrior classes:

> All our hunting and polo and cricket and football had in no way helped to sharpen our animal instincts. All were but matters of routine – sports and games based on rules. What is there more conventional than fox-hunting or cricket? They are but pleasant forms of drill which restrict the cunning in man . . . A retrospect into history will show that the most efficient armies were those in which the sporting instinct was non-existent.[102]

The tendency of the late Victorians to ritualize and regulate, and thereby 'tokenize', warfare was perhaps a natural one for the world's foremost territorial freeholder. The more rules, the fewer nasty surprises – as long as everyone else observes the same conventions. For the British Army the consequences should have been unmistakably apparent in the almost self-inflicted surprises of the Boer War: Lord Roberts, when he took command, found it necessary to sack 5 generals, 6 brigadiers and nearly 20 colonels.

> Let us admit it fairly,
>   as a business people should.
> We have had no end of a lesson:
>   it will do us no end of good.[103]

*

The Royal Navy was subjected to no comparable test of its habits and attitudes before 1914, and it would be a calumny against the senior service to suggest that it would have fared as badly if it had been. But the Navy was at least as susceptible as the Army to the ambient values already touched upon, and above all to the assumption that seniority must know best – in fact must know everything. In this it was in some degree a victim of its own success. From Nelson's trio of crushing victories, the Victorians chose to extract the myth of the central genius directing his lovingly obedient fleet with brilliance and precision. His famous invocation of DUTY suited them very well – how they would have dealt with 'ENGLAND EXPECTS EVERY OFFICER TO ACT ON INITIATIVE' (which more aptly defines his doctrine) one can only speculate – and his statue, raised 145 feet above Trafalgar Square in 1843 and later placed under the guard of Sir Edwin Landseer's huge bronze lions, was conceived as a monument to genius and authority, rather than to the culture of insubordination.

It was forgotten that at Trafalgar no tactical instruction emanated from the flagship after the fighting started; or that the battle would have ended much as it did if Nelson had been killed with the first shot, because his subordinates understood exactly his purposes and how each could best contribute to their realization. Now it was assumed that any admiral, who quite likely owed his rank to his sometime management of paintwork and obsolete seamanship acrobatics, would supply his subordinates with detailed and brilliant orders which need only be obeyed to the letter to bring about a new Trafalgar. It was a far cry from the day when Pierre de Villeneuve could remark ruefully, "In the British fleet off Cadiz, every captain was a Nelson." The enabling key was the *Signal Book* which, to an extent unimagined by Sir Home Popham, had become the supreme agent of centralization.

For many years the *Signal Book*'s potential for the manoeuvring of fleets had largely lain fallow. Sir Charles ('Black Charlie') Napier had tested it with the Channel Squadron in the late 1840s, and formed the veiw that, while it might be of use for training purposes, it was not to be relied upon in battle.[104] The catalysts for change were the departure from the Fleet of Nelson's last subordinates and the arrival of steam propulsion.

One of the redeeming features of mechanization appeared to be the opportunity it afforded for the precise tabulation of manoeuvring data. In 1854 a hydrographer, Captain Alexander Becher, published the first 'Distance Off' tables for fleetwork, which enabled ships to keep precise station for distance by monitoring the sextant angle between the guide's masthead and her waterline – a procedure which requires the guide to be more or less upright (and thus not under sail) and which is still practised today. That was just the beginning. It was quickly appreciated that for each ship or class of sister-ships a given number of turns of the screw per minute would produce a precisely predictable speed, that the slight variations caused by the state of the ship's bottom could themselves be tabulated according to rules-of-thumb based on the months which had elapsed since the last dry-docking, that rates of acceleration and deceleration could be ascertained and thereafter relied upon, that a certain rudder angle would unfailingly produce a certain turning-circle, with its own unvarying loss of speed according to the size of the turn, etc. In the new seamanship of iron and steam, mathematics were subverting the art of centuries and a vista of possibilities opened up for tightly choreographed geometrical evolutions – far beyond what had been possible with sailing fleets. The 'science' of Steam Tactics was the result, and every movement, every change of course, speed or formation, could be ordered and executed by flag signal.

The early parameters of steam-tactics were explored in the Mediterranean by Vice-Admiral Sir William Fanshawe Martin, Commander-in-Chief from 1860 to 1863. The son of Admiral Sir

Thomas Byam Martin, who had learnt his trade as a midshipman under William Bligh and served as a lieutenant in *Victory* under Nelson in 1804, Sir William was a keen disciplinarian and is said to have been the original 'Pincher Martin', so-called because he would have men pinched (= arrested) for minor offences.[105] When Martin arrived in the Mediterranean he found the fleet in a state of unrest, "but by tact, by care, by unremitting attention and by judicious severity he brought [it] into admirable order".[106] He was an enthusiast for Monday seamanship evolutions, and (according to legend) would hoist "BURY YOUR DEAD" as a matter of routine upon their completion. He was also an enthusiast for squadron manoeuvres, and, while Superintendent of Portsmouth Dockyard in 1858, had produced a booklet (whose sophistication is belied by its title) called *Observations on Steam Tactics and Rowing Boat Evolutions*.

The ideas in this slim but seminal volume he put to the test in the Mediterranean, and, in the later testimony of his flag-captain, established the principles which formed the basis of the Royal Navy's future accomplishments in 'fleetwork'.[107]

That flag-captain was Geoffrey Phipps Hornby, whose father, Admiral Sir Phipps Hornby, had also served in *Victory* in 1804. (Martin's flag-lieutenant, as a matter of interest, was Pownoll Pellew, grandson of the first Lord Exmouth.) Captain Phipps Hornby – he used 'Phipps' as part of his surname after the death of his elder brother – was to become the Victorian Navy's most celebrated practitioner of steam-tactics. Now, while serving Martin, he enthused to his father:

> it is no use fancying that steam-ships can only form as sailing ships used to do; [for] by adhering to those ideas instead of following the new system, which [has] been shown to be possible under most circumstances, we are throwing away the advantages that steam has given us.[108]

After the Mediterranean, Hornby came home to command *Edgar* as flag-captain to Rear-Admiral Sir Sydney Dacres in the Channel Squadron, and endeared himself for ever to his profession by becoming the last man to sail a ship-of-the-line out of Portsmouth unassisted by machinery.

It was in command of *Edgar* that he met Commander Philip Colomb, with whom he was to be linked as a co-father of modern steam-tactics. As a mere lieutenant, Colomb had established a name as a pioneer of night-time signalling, and was now attached to *Edgar* to experiment with flashing lights and Morse code. The outcome of his demonstrations was the acceptance into service of Colomb's Flashing Signals; but he also worked on manoeuvring with Hornby and Dacres, for by 1865 he had drawn up a geometrical system of fleet evolutions and he later named 1864 as a 'breakthrough' year in steam-tactics. In 1868 he was put onto a two-man committee to expand and revise the *Signal Book* – the other member (and to some extent a sleeping partner) being a Commander Brent. What with his seminal work on collision avoidance[109] and the Rule of the Road, Colomb was rapidly becoming an Expert.

By this time he and Phipps Hornby had (for the time being) gone separate ways, the latter having reached flag-rank. But further progress in steam-tactics took place in the Channel Squadron between 1868 and 1870, under Sir Thomas Symonds (whose flag-captain was James Goodenough), and, as Colomb had been Symonds's flag-lieutenant in the Devonport guard-ship *Indus* in 1862–3, it may be supposed that the admiral was susceptible to Colomb's ideas. At any rate, years later, Colomb acknowledged Symonds as a pioneer in the same way that Hornby honoured Pincher Martin.

The main manoeuvring problem which was surmounted in the 1860s was as follows. When a fleet was ordered to change formation, each ship was free to seek her new station by whatever combination of course and speed her officer-of-the-watch chose – with the result that her movements were unpredictable to her neighbours, who were trying to solve their own re-stationing problems with their own course and speed solutions. In a large fleet this gave rise to danger (and endemic fear) of collision.[110] However, it was realized that if speed changes were disallowed and only helm were used, the movements of all ships must conform to fairly predictable dynamic patterns, and the diffidence which officers felt about reflex-responding to manoeuvring signals would be much alleviated. At first (probably under Martin and/or Dacres) this system was called Rectangular Movements; but when lines-of-bearing and triangular formations were added to the repertoire (probably by Colomb and Symonds) its name was changed to Equal Speed Manoeuvres.

Equal Speed simply means that, even when changing station, all ships maintain the same speed as the 'guide' of the fleet.[111] It governs manoeuvres through certain "kinematical laws",[112] and its application guarantees safety as long as "those laws are not violated". There are some evolutions for which equal-speed cannot be used: for example, if any formation other than a single line-ahead alters course while preserving *relative* bearings, the pivotal ships have to slow down and the outer ones speed up. But overall, equal-speed opened the door to the complex and rapid fleetwork for which the main squadrons of the late Victorian Royal Navy became famous.

Philip Colomb became the foremost prophet of the opportunities for geometrical precision which the industrial age offered to the move-ment of ships and fleets. In the early 1870s he was employed at the Admiralty composing what became the 1874 *Manual of Fleet Evolutions* (sometimes called the *Manoeuvring Book*), whose 300 pages "read like a glossary of ballet evolutions; elaborate, complex, spectacular and pro-hibitive of all initiative".[113] This publication secured his reputation as the authority on steam-tactics.

By academics, Colomb is celebrated for other labours. In 1886 he became a 'yellow admiral' – that is, he was promoted to rear-admiral the day before he retired – and, once off the Active List, followed his schol-arly leanings by teaching at the Royal Naval College, helping to found the Navy Records Society, and publishing serious works of seapower analysis and history. He was, for example, the author of *Memoirs of Admiral Sir Astley Cooper Key*, of *Essays on Naval Defence* and of *Naval Warfare: Its Ruling Principle and Practice Historically Treated* – a book "whose very great merit is somewhat obscured by what many would think its needless length".[114]

In *The Education of a Navy*, Professor Donald Schurman rejects Colomb's belittling by the self-proclaimed real salts of the Navy.[115] In connection with his work as a historian, he is right to do so: Philip Colomb was one of the few lanterns in the pre-dawn twilight of higher defence studies (his emphasis on maritime communications has weath-ered its first century very well), and the belittling was partly an attempt to discredit the messenger to avoid bothering with the message. But in the context of Colomb's vaunted expertise in fleet manoeuvring, the charge of 'armchair-expert' is both relevant and supportable, for his naval service had provided scant opportunity to practise the subject of which he was the notional expert,[116] "and thus his views did not always, among naval men, meet with that ready acceptance which many believed they were entitled to".[117] He also became "an untiring corres-pondent of *The Times*, [with] an opinion to express on every naval subject of the day"[118] – an unattractive trait in a shore-loafer, and one which caused him to be dubbed 'Columbus', and (by Jacky Fisher) 'Colomb-Inches' or 'Colomb-and-a-half'. His saving virtue, perhaps, was his friendship with Sir Geoffrey Phipps Hornby, whom he had served as flag-captain in Hornby's final, elder-statesman post of C-in-C Portsmouth.

Colomb was not a participant in Phipps Hornby's epic reign in the Mediterranean in 1877–80, chiefly marked by the 'Eastern Question' crisis of Russia's war against Turkey, which saw Hornby taking his fleet through the Dardanelles to Constantinople ('We don't want to fight / But by Jingo, if we do . . .') and which was resolved *pro tem* at the

Congress of Berlin. Less well-known to the public, but remembered with reverence for many years by the service, was Hornby's supreme mastery of steam-tactics. This quintessentially Victorian patriarch – he "entered public service", he liked to say, "in the same year as the Queen" – combined personal geniality with professional severity, and the "terror of his name" had set the Mediterranean captains to reading up the *Manoeuvring Book* weeks before his arrival in Malta. Jacky Fisher claimed to be distraught at having to leave the station (to be flag-captain to Cooper Key in North America) at this juncture, and told Sir Geoffrey that he had set his heart

> on remaining a few months at least under your Flag in the certainty of learning a good deal, more especially in the way of Fleet manoeuvring. No one in the Mediterranean had the faintest notion of it as far as I could make out . . . you may possibly be agreeably surprised. But I venture to warn you that one of the captains can't see an armchair 5 yards off and another has an inverted cranium which frequently causes him to understand signals upside down.[119]

Hornby started beguilingly enough, as if dealing with idiots. Soon after reaching Malta he issued a memorandum entitled *Notes on Fleet Manoeuvring*. There were two signal codes, he explained patiently: the *General Signal Book*, which

> is an adaptation of the old *Signal Book* – chiefly the work of Sir Home Popham, Sir Thomas Hardy and other officers of their time – to the requirements of steam fleets; [and the *Manual of Evolutions*, which] is written for experiment and criticism.
>
> Our principal instrument is the *Signal Book*, and we must study it as we would any other book if we wish to master its contents.[120]

He then set out to put his fleet through a remorseless regime of manoeuvring drill, beginning on its first day out from Malta, ably assisted by Rear-Admiral Sir John Commerell. To Fisher, who returned to the Mediterranean for a while in 1879 and was a guest in the flagship, HMS *Alexandra*, he was "astounding":

> He would tell you what you were going to do wrong before you did it; and you couldn't say you weren't going to do it because you had put your helm over and the ship had begun to move the wrong way . . .[121]

The manoeuvring procedure depended on the eyesight and knowledge of the yeoman, the correct stationing of the ship, and the prompt response of the officer-of-the-watch:

> The yeoman would stand on the fore-bridge, his telescope glued to his eye, and his whole frame quivering with excitement, like a pointer about to flush a covey of partridges. Up would go a hoist of flags in the flagship. As each flag

was hoisted clear of the deck, although to the normal eye only a loose bundle of bunting was apparent, the yeoman spotted what it was and shouted it down to the signalmen on the bridge. There would be a rush towards the flag-locker and rolled up flags would be hauled out of their pigeon holes, bent together and hoisted, with a frantic effort to get them to the masthead before the flagship mastheaded her signal. The yeoman would report the meaning of the signal to the captain, the navigator and the officer-of-the-watch. Down would come the signal on board the flagship, and at the same time down would come the signal on board the repeating ship.

'Signal's down Sir,' would shout the yeoman, repeating the significance of the signal, over would go the wheel and the ships, all over 10,000 tons and spaced at intervals of 300 yards, would swing together into the new formation.[122]

Often it did not go this smoothly. It might be difficult to make out the colours and patterns of the flags if they were 'up sun', or hanging limply because the flagship was steaming downwind. They might wrap themselves around the halyard while being hoisted, stand out in the breeze 'end on' to the addressee, or be obscured by smoke. And it bothered a few that in battle there would be shell splinters and machine-gun bullets to slice through halyards, mow down signalmen, and perhaps even kill the admiral. But no matter; one can readily understand how the new steam-tacticians were seen as representing the Royal Navy's triumphant assimilation of the industrial revolution. They could now relinquish gracefully the old ways of thinking about warfare – principles as well as practices – and if they discarded too much, if they were seduced by their own mastery of new methods into supposing that more had changed than was really the case, one can understand that too. The eclipse of empiricism by rationalism was near-total.

In 1878, while Hornby was busy in the Mediterranean, a committee met in Devonport, under Rear-Admiral Charles Hope, to revise the *Signal Book* in the light of the success of the *Manual of Evolutions*. For Captain Colomb, to have his manoeuvring system spliced into the Navy's *General Signal Book* was the highest accolade, although the committee by no means ran smoothly: according to Colomb's own later testimony, he met obstructionism (as he saw it) from a fellow committee member, Captain George Tryon, and had to rescue the committee (with Hope's complicity) by marginalizing Tryon's casual ideas and doing all the work himself.[123]

With these accumulative processes, by the 1880s

fourteen thousand variations of signals were considered the minimum requirement of a fleet, [and the *Signal Books*] were huge volumes containing voluminous instructions for every conceivable description of formation and manoeuvre, most of which required long hoists of many coloured flags.[124]

The C-in-C Channel in 1888–90, Admiral Sir John Baird, made so many signals of six or seven hoists that his second-in-command's flag-lieutenant, Edward Inglefield, was driven to invent a simple snatch-clip for flags, which reduced the amount of urgent fumbling required of (perhaps numb-fingered) yeomen and which is in universal use today.[125] Captains and admirals were sometimes "so obstructed by the signalmen bustling about with their bunting and halyards in the confined space of the bridge, that it was even difficult to see what other ships of the squadron were doing".[126] Worst of all, the *Signal Book* was "so bewilderingly ingenious that no one completely understood it, and to acquire a working knowledge took years of training".[127]

Fleetwork had become more than a means of training officers in shiphandling, of sharpening (and sometimes scaring them out of) their wits: it had become their ultimate attainment. Colomb's *Manual of Fleet Evolutions* actually declared that "To work a fleet at speed, in the closest order, is now admitted as the chief aim of the naval tactician"[128] – there was nothing about the enemy, or what to do in action if signalling should fail. Practised as an end in themselves, steam-tactics had the effect of ritualizing the Navy's concept of battle in the way that ballroom dances were intended to ritualize courtship: to regulate the naturally erratic. As time went by even Phipps Hornby began to have misgivings about the system's practicability in war conditions.

In January 1886 the Admiralty called into being a new committee on signals, to meet in Devonport under Admiral Sir William Dowell[129] (C-in-C Plymouth) and Captain Harry Rawson (Captain of the Devonport Steam Reserve). A memo by Sir Geoffrey, who had retired a few weeks before, explained the concerns about the *Signal Book* which had prompted this step. For instance, when it had last been revised, ships commonly had three masts and sometimes five, whereas now, with the retreat of sails, ironclads were coming into service with two, or in some cases, just one. Where were all the flags to be hung? He mentioned a report by Captain John Fisher (his chief of staff in the Evolutionary Squadron during the brief 1885 Russian scare) who had found that

> some 18 or 19 flags might be necessary for some very elementary formations, and I think he gave a case where nearly 40 would be necessary. Methods which require the use of so many flags must be abandoned.

And he foresaw a pitfall of timeless pertinence: "it is certain that in wartime we shall not have the super-abundant staffs of trained signalmen that we luxuriate in during peace."[130] The committee's terms of reference were thus to simplify, abbreviate and, where possible, de-skill the business of fleet signalling. Sorry to relate, its results were otherwise.

After only a few days Admiral Dowell requested Captain Colomb's attendance, for they were "desirous of questioning him on certain points". Colomb was only in Portsmouth, having stayed on as flag-captain to Sir George Willes (Hornby's successor as C-in-C), but there seems to have been a difficulty: he would be unavailable until March because of prior engagements. May saw him ordered to Devonport; and, thus helped or hindered, the committee "revised the private signals, the *General Signal Book*, the *Manual of Naval Manoeuvres* and the *Night and Fog Signal Book* [another Colomb creation], and considered the question of signalling between the Army and Navy". After many months, it circulated the draft of a new *Signal Book* comprising two volumes and over 500 pages.

It is true that some signals could be made with fewer flags by the new book than formerly, and that the number of general flag signals was reduced by recourse to the new three-arm semaphore; but the manoeuvring flag signals were (in the admission of the interim report) "greatly increased". A dismayed Phipps Hornby warned Sir William that its "very size has already struck terror into the minds of some officers. You will make its acceptance far easier if you will give your reasons for the changes."[131] Privately Hornby considered that the 'committee' approach had allowed basic principles to be lost sight of, and in 1891 he replied ruefully to a junior officer (Allan Everett), who had written to him questioning the *Signal Book*, that "our predecessors seemed to be clearer headed than some of us are."[132]

Dowell had the new draft book, once printed, tested in two ways. He equipped six small Reserve Fleet gunboats with reduced-size flags and semaphores and sent them out to manoeuvre around St Austell Bay, communicating; and he sought an early opinion from the commodore of the Training Squadron, Albert Markham. Markham was a firm friend of Colomb, having been helped by him over a little legal difficulty after a collision in 1885, and initiated by him into Freemasonry in Portsmouth in 1886. These things may be irrelevant. But he judged the revised book to be a welcome improvement, praised the resolution of certain anomalies which were a feature of its predecessor, and submitted 59 manuscript pages of alterations and additions (some of which the committee accepted). He also, to his credit, forwarded the verdicts of his two immediate subordinates, who were outspoken in condemning the new tome.

Captain Gerard Noel deplored its need for "a greater number of flags and pendants, all of which – in action – will have to be handy for use", and urged that "every endeavour should be made to reduce this number". Captain Charles Johnstone found the increase in flags "objectionable". In his view the new book was

> more bulky and complicated and I think these disadvantages are not compensated for by general increased utility . . . [It] seems to me to demand a more highly trained and intelligent class of signalman than we have at present, and it is the possibility of the system having to be worked in the absence of such men (owing to the signal staff having been disabled in action or otherwise) which makes me attach great importance to simplicity.[133]

These profanities struck at the very heart of the committee's labours. No amount of tinkering could have appeased them, and presumably for this reason they were ignored. In October 1889 the Admiralty declared its satisfaction at the "manner in which the Committee have performed this important work";[134] and the new *General Signal Book*, riddled with printing errors, was issued to the Fleet.

*

Whatever the Royal Navy was good at, it was best at it in the Mediterranean Fleet (or 'Squadron' as it was properly called), the importance of which, *circa* 1890, as a formative influence on those officers to whom would fall the task of taking the Grand Fleet to war twenty-five years later, can hardly be exaggerated. The Mediterranean served as a maritime adventure playground to which the British had, to all intents and purposes, monopoly rights. The fleet's cruises were built round political and social programmes, punctuated with sessions of impeccable parade-ground manoeuvres; and there were usually ships showing the flag independently around the Levant (defined as east of Cape Matapan), an occupation which many today would equate with a once-in-a-lifetime package-holiday.[135] Wherever they went, it seems, there were opportunities for adventure or recreation ashore, and usually a ready supply of wildlife to kill ("Shooting in the neighbourhood of the anchorage was often exceedingly risky, there being so many guns in action"[136]).

The centre of the fleet's world was Malta, whose economy substantially depended on the Army garrison and the Navy. London shipping companies, department stores and banks had agencies and branches in Valletta; pay stretched further than in England; and, aside from the midsummer heat and the unsolved mystery of 'Malta fever' (brucellosis), the island offered an agreeable way of life which combined the familiar with the exotic. Malta "was very popular with the fleet";[137] and nobody flipping through photograph albums can doubt the fun they had.

There were dinner parties, fancy-dress balls, visits to the Opera House,[138] picnics in St Paul's Bay, sailing regattas, tennis parties, golf tournaments, cricket matches and, of course, for a certain financial outlay, there was polo. The polo teams read like a preview of flag-officers and courtiers of 1914: Rosslyn Wemyss, Hedworth Lambton, Stanley Colville, Colin Keppel, Bryan Godfrey-Faussett, Lewis Bayly, Edwyn Alexander(-Sinclair), Christopher Cradock, Mark Kerr, George Aston, Hugh Evan-Thomas and young David Beatty. Afloat, for their less fortunate part, the lower-deck had pulling regattas, Monday evolutions and the four Bs: Blanco, Bluebell (a brand of metal polish), Bugles and Bullshit. Ashore, there were the three Ps: Pubs, Priests and (expatriate English) Prostitutes.[139] Here the Royal Navy was culturally self-sufficient; a world in itself. England was a distant concept, a source of letters from the family, a home to idealize and to anticipate with no great urgency.

It was here, in spacious idyllic exile, that the service's daunting clannishness was nurtured and perpetuated, its chauvinism and its complacency. And it was here that the ritual military 'bull' was most highly developed, with the all-pervading drive for order and cleanliness, the labour-intensive competitive drills against the stop-watch and, at sea, the robotic genuflexions to the *Signal Book*. The Mediterranean Fleet was the greatest display team in the world, and for this reason it was here that any drive to informalize tactical attitudes, to wean the fleet off the *Signal Book* and back to Nelsonic principles, would be made or broken.

10

Sir George Tryon's Action Principles

"Schemes of exceptional unorthodoxy indicate the genius of one man.
You do not associate them with a Government department."
Leslie Gardiner, *British Admiralty*, p. 22

Only a formidable officer could hope to shift the weight of inertia and vested interests, and Vice-Admiral Sir George Tryon, a friend and former disciple of Sir Geoffrey Phipps Hornby, was the man most likely to succeed.

> He was quite the beau ideal of a sea-dog, vast of physique and burly, with no poor landsman's reservations about deportment and language, and with a highly vocal contempt for everything not marked down on his own mental chart.[1]

The world first heard about George Tryon in connection with the 1888 Annual Manoeuvres, which were followed as avidly by the newspapers as any Test Match and made him a national celebrity. He was a master at public relations, and he

> set an example to other admirals by taking the correspondents who were with the fleet entirely into his confidence and concealing nothing from them. And this frankness he never had cause to regret.[2]

He commanded the inferior 'enemy' forces (B Fleet) and began the Manoeuvres blockaded in anchorages on the west coast of Ireland. After he had worn out his gaolers in A Fleet – Vice-Admiral Sir John Baird (C-in-C Channel), Rear-Admiral Charles Rowley and Commodore Albert Markham[3] – with several days of false starts, he escaped in the night and proceeded to run amok up and down Britain's coasts like a mob-handed John Paul Jones. Tryon attacked the west coast while Commodore Robert FitzRoy (whose father, as a matter of interest, had been Charles Darwin's host in *Beagle* in 1831–6) took his

193

2nd Division round the north of Scotland to attend to the east coast; and they rather too easily persuaded the mayors of numerous towns and cities to surrender, pay pretend ransoms and get invited to dinner. It was a good game. On August the 9th, he cabled Phipps Hornby: "HAVE TAKEN LIVERPOOL. AM ANCHORED OFF LANDING STAGE WITH SIX IRONCLADS THREE TORPEDO BOATS FIVE CRUISERS. FITZROY HAS MADE FIREWORKS ON EAST COAST."[4]

> It was true that several of his subordinates got rather out of hand, that crack Atlantic liners were 'sunk' by 13-knot cruisers, that large towns were 'wiped out' by lightly armed torpedo-boats without warning. But to Tryon this was war, not a polite exercise.[5]

His detractors said he had cheated; but the public was thrilled and alarmed, and glad he was British and not French. The subsequent 'Report of the Three Admirals' (Sir William Dowell, Sir Richard Vesey Hamilton, Sir Frederick Richards),[6] reinforced by the agitation of naval lobbyists such as Philip Colomb, Lord Brassey and Captain Lord Charles Beresford MP, brought about the passage of the 1889 Naval Defence Act, which institutionalized the 'two-power standard' – the principle that the RN should be at least equal to the two largest foreign navies combined.

George Tryon was more than just brawn and bluff. A junior officer wrote: "The best expression that can be used of him was that he was big: big in figure, big in ideas, his generosity equal to his ideas, massive, constructive, and a man of the world and of a big world."[7] But there was another way of looking at him. After his untimely death a society journal remarked:

> Much has been said about George Tryon's charm of manner, and the rest of it, but in truth he was, at any rate when officially engaged, a very brusque and dictatorial man. Unfortunately he was a 'viewy' man too, a man of theories . . .[8]

This is closely borne out by a letter which his 'Australia Station' flag-captain, Francis Clayton, had written home in 1885:

> I hardly know whether I like the admiral or not, he is an odd fellow, very brusque in his manner but I think good at heart. He is the most tiresome man to talk to on service matters. You go to his office, he is always smoking a very big cigar which fills his mouth well up. He talks first of one matter, then of another, so that it is all but impossible to follow him, everything jumbled up and then when you ask some question to clear matters up a little, he said 'I have just told you that'. Fortunately he puts things into writing.[9]

Tryon had started his naval career with two advantages. First, he had been educated at Eton until he was 16 and thus joined the Navy three years older and more worldly-wise than his peers, who had not even been through *Britannia* (which did not yet exist as a cadet school). As a consequence he was unusually at ease, for a naval officer, among statesmen and intellectuals. Secondly, he had powerful political 'interest' in an era when this was still useful for career preferment.[10] He also possessed a rare perception of the wider ramifications of defence.

As Secretary of the Admiralty in 1882–4 (the last naval officer to hold the post), he set up the Foreign Intelligence Committee which was to mature into the Naval Intelligence Department of legend under Captain Reginald ('Blinker') Hall in 1914–18. As Admiral Commanding the Reserve Fleet, he recognized the potential of the Royal Naval Reserve[11] at a time when the fashionable view was that warships were becoming too technical for part-timers. And he launched a campaign for the Government insurance of merchant shipping in time of war: an innovation which would prevent insurance rates from acting as an inhibitor of British trade.[12] This project was frustrated, for the time being, by vested interests in the City and had to be pushed through in haste in 1914. But Tryon's chief ambition "was to break up the traditionalism that had paralysed initiative in the Navy for half a century".[13]

His mission stemmed from his belief that the Victorian Navy had forgotten the 'fog of battle'. He identified the root of the problem as the "thoroughly dangerous cult" of signalling.[14] If the few men in the flagship capable of handling flag signals were mown down by splinters, or their halyards shot away, what then would happen to the fleet's tactical cohesion? And even if everything worked,

> the speed at which modern battleships travel, and the extreme rapidity with which a sudden alteration of course or formation on the part of either combatant would change the whole tactical aspect of an encounter, seemed to point to the probability that, however smartly signals might be made, understood and answered, it would be impossible for an Admiral to take advantage quickly enough of opportunities which would be likely to offer themselves in the course of a battle.[15]

Tryon realized

> that decentralization was essential in a fleet. An Admiral must make his general plans clear to all his Captains and must trust chiefly to their loyalty and initiative in carrying out those plans during the course of an action.[16]

This in itself, even in the Victorian age, was not new. Rumblings against the *Signal Book* had been emanating from 'salt-horses' for many years, and Tryon was only one of the rumblers.

As long ago as the Crimean War, 'Black Charlie' Napier (then C-in-C Baltic) "wanted to use the new-found independence of steam to simplify the tactical niceties" and would have no truck with the growing fashion for formalizing steam-tactics.[17] And in 1871 Commander John Fisher sent to Captain James Goodenough (who, in turn, passed to the Admiralty) a discussion-paper which declared that in close action

> the *Signal Book* will be practically useless. In fact the use of signals at such a time would be fraught with danger. They would fetter the action and diminish the responsibility of the Captains.[18]

Jacky Fisher had been a friend and collaborator of George Tryon since they served together in *Warrior* in 1863, and remained so until death intervened. Especially at this stage of his career, Fisher often made use of the ideas of other forward thinkers, and in the paper quoted above he may well have been amplifying Tryon's views, for they used each other as sounding-boards. (For example, in 1883, when Fisher was CO of *Excellent*, he mentioned to Hornby that Tryon had "spent an hour with me . . . but I hadn't an opportunity of saying a word to him!"[19] One may doubt that Fisher was mute for sixty minutes, but equally they were probably not discussing gunnery.)

Also, in 1880 another of Tryon's friends, Captain Edmund Fremantle, won the RUSI gold medal with an essay on naval tactics which attacked the *Signal Book* as a hindrance to fluid movement in battle.

We have already seen that Tryon had clashed with Colomb on Rear-Admiral Hope's signals committee in 1878; and Colomb would later brandish, as evidence of his opponent's degenerate ideas, extracts from memoranda which Sir George had written in 1881.[20] Tryon had therefore been restive about the role of the *Signal Book*, and about the eclipse of Nelsonic action-principles, for some considerable time, but it was probably not until the spring of 1891 that he applied his mind to the question of the antidote, for then two things happened. It was made known that in September he would accede to the Navy's senior sea-going command, that of the Mediterranean Fleet; and he was consulted over a theological argument in the Mediterranean about an ambiguity in the new (1889) *Signal Book*.

The moot point was whether the flagship should always be the 'guide' of the fleet, irrespective of where she might be in the formation, or whether the leading ship should be the guide, irrespective of who that ship happened to be. The question arose because it was (and is) notoriously difficult to keep station on a ship astern of you. Tryon's response was that, regardless of her position, the flagship must always be guide: for if she were not, the admiral would have to communicate his every tactical wish by flags for implementation by the ship which was guide, and "with mast shot away, his own flag flying and other signals, fog, smoke and darkness and many other conditions" signalling was liable to fail. On the other hand if the flagship was understood to be guide, as long as she was afloat and manoeuvrable, the fleet could take its cue from her movements even if her signals were illegible or non-existent:

> Suppose [the admiral] desires to avail himself of an opportunity that presents itself suddenly and is only available for a brief time, he should be able without signal to manoeuvre as necessary, confident that the rest of the fleet would conform itself to his movements. The principle involved in this consideration is or should be the base of all manoeuvring systems; the admiral's hands should be absolutely untrammelled, and all should feel it is their first duty to stick to their chief and to follow his movements whatever they are.

He then made his first documented reference to the signal which was to become indelibly connected with his name. He drew attention to the cryptic group 'TA' in the *Signal Book*. This meant (to quote the 1889 book):

> Observe very attentively the Admiral's motions as he will probably alter his course, make or shorten sail, increase or decrease speed, &c, with or without signals, as may be most convenient.[21]

(The obsolescent phrase "make or shorten sail" was dropped from the next, 1898, revision of the *Signal Book*.) And he pointed out that if the flagship were invariably the guide in action, the meaning of TA would apply all the time without its having to be displayed by the admiral and seen by the rest of the fleet.[22]

It is evident that he lost the 'guide' argument – probably because his view was not conducive to the precise station-keeping of parade-ground steam-tactics. But having been prompted into ordering his thoughts thus far, Tryon prepared for his command-in-chief of the Mediterranean by thinking the thing through from first principles. In modern jargon, he perceived the problem as a conflict between *process* and *product*, although he characterized it as one between a seaman officer's *primary* and *secondary* educations. By *primary* education, he meant the officer-of-the-watch skills of shiphandling and fleetwork, the training of "eye and judgment to a correct and rapid appreciation of speed, distance, turning power, etc.",[23] which were already over-provided for in the elaborate set-piece manoeuvres, ordered in detail and executed by flag-hoist, which were routine events in the major fleets. By *secondary* education, he meant the trainee flag-officer skills of interpretation and initiative which had been commonplace at the time of Nelson but which had been progressively squeezed out by the Victorian Fleet's exclusive reiteration of its primary educational syllabus.

He made it his objective to address the Navy's future leaders to their proper secondary education, a process which would marginalize (Trafalgarize, one might say) the use of the *Signal Book* in future fleet actions. And while certain other officers were advising the Admiralty that the 1889 book was already fit for revision, Tryon intended to bypass it altogether.

As he propounded his ideas, he gathered enemies. He met resistance from those he had vaulted in the seniority stakes and who considered that the glittering prizes had come to him too easily. He encountered, as would Fisher, Beatty and Mountbatten in their time, the Navy's peculiar distrust (part jealousy) of officers suspected of self-promotion. Whether he was breaking or rediscovering faith with the glorious past depended on where one stood. Tryon was heeding, consciously or otherwise, Nelson's warning that "nothing is sure in a sea fight, beyond all others; shot will carry away the masts and yards of friends as well as foes";[24] and he was echoing St Vincent's rejection of tactical frippery[25] and his assertion that "the great talent is to take prompt advantage of disorder in the fleet of the enemy, by shifts of wind, accidents, and their deficiency in practical seamanship." But the *Signal Book* had come to be considered by many to be sacred – the repository of a hundred years of accumulated wisdom, the Royal Navy's Ark of the Covenant. Conservatives and authoritarians condemned his agenda as heretical and foolhardy.

The most entrenched opposition came from Rear-Admiral Colomb who, in his own words, contended "heartily against [Tryon's] views on fleet manoeuvring".[26] As we have seen, his reputation as the leading theoretician on steam-tactics stemmed from the *Manual of Fleet Evolutions* which he had composed at his desk in Whitehall in 1870–4 and thereafter dilated upon in the RUSI. We have established that friction between the two men dated from as far back as 1878 when both sat on Hope's committee to revise the *Signal Book* in the light of Colomb's *Manual*: Tryon had been included "to look after the practical aspects of manoeuvring and steam-tactics",[27] a role which in itself must have been a thorn in the flesh of Colomb's vanity. Colomb's resentment of his junior position on this committee is evident from his manuscript note inside the cover of the 1878 *General Signal Book* now in the National Maritime Museum: he tartly makes clear that he was the only member who knew anything about signals, since "neither Admiral Hope, nor Capt Tryon, nor Lord Walter Kerr had ever been called into counsel on the subject before", whereas he had made a special study of it for the last thirteen years; and he paints a picture of frequent rows between Hope and Tryon, in which he had to act as mediator. As we have seen, he claimed (elsewhere) to have salvaged the committee by completing its work single-handedly.

Then, for a few months in 1880 Colomb, Tryon and Kerr coincided as battleship captains in the Mediterranean, and the then C-in-C, Sir Beauchamp Seymour (later Lord Alcester), formed them into a local three-man signals committee which was chaired by Tryon in *Monarch*, and whose meetings, according to Colomb, were characterized by animated debate.[28]

Now Colomb was threatened, as never before, by Tryon's proposition that the battle-worthiness of the Royal Navy was actually being jeopardized by the system of which he was the renowned architect, and he took the very idea of unsignalled manoeuvres as a personal affront. The debate which Tryon stirred up around the *Signal Books* had some of the hallmarks of a user *v.* supplier controversy.

*

In September 1891 Vice-Admiral Sir George Tryon took passage out to Malta in the new battleship *Nile* and hoisted his flag over Admiralty House (now the Museum of Fine Arts) in succession to Admiral Sir Anthony Hoskins, who went home to be First Sea Lord. His great opportunity had come, and not since Phipps Hornby had an admiral's arrival been so feared. Both the Mediterranean Fleet and the naval world in England awaited developments with interest and foreboding. There were plenty of experts, the authoritarian and the hidebound, the jealous and the faint-hearted, ready with "Told you so!" if he should fail.

Within a few days the new C-in-C had issued three Mediterranean Fleet temporary memoranda (TMs), A, B and C, setting out his plan for tactical reform. Building on the text of the 'TA' signal already referred to, he called it 'manoeuvring with and without signals', and, as TM/A revealed, it was startlingly simple – although to suggest that no great brain-power was required to understand it, is not to say that it was the product of no great brain. When he wished the fleet to go into 'initiative' mode, Tryon would hoist the flags for TA to his masthead. In plain language this meant that the fleet might now be manoeuvred without signals, or with as few and as brief as humanly possible; and if he *did* signal a manoeuvre in advance, he was unlikely to wait for the usual acknowledgements and repeats.

TMs/B and C merely dealt with speed differentials when wheeling in formation, and with the management of scouts and look-out vessels. The essence of the scheme was in TM/A, which gave guidelines by which ships could keep approximate station without becoming slaves to station-keeping,[29] and listed eight one-flag signals for simple formation changes which the dimmest watch-keeping officer could learn by heart:

Flag 1	Ships are to form in wake of the flagship, or other ship denoted, and will continue to manoeuvre in his wake till otherwise ordered.
Flag 2	Ships are to form in the wake of divisional leaders, and will continue to manoeuvre by divisions till otherwise ordered.
Flag 3	Ships are to form in wake of sub-divisional leaders, and will continue to manoeuvre by sub-divisions till otherwise ordered.
Pendant 5	In the next movement, and without further signal, divisional leaders are to alter course with the flagship and follow his motion, preserving their distances apart. Divisions will form on their leaders. The Fleet will manoeuvre by divisions until further notice.
Pendant 6	In the next movement, and without further signal, sub-divisional leaders are to alter course with the flagship and follow his motion, preserving their distance apart. Sub-divisions will form on their leaders. The Fleet will manoeuvre by sub-divisions until further notice.
Blue Pendant –	*at masthead.* All ships will turn together with the flagship (or appointed guide) when he turns. He will haul it down when his turn is complete.
Blue Pendant –	*in an inferior position.* Ships of division or sub-division specified are to turn in the direction the guide is turning or steering, and maintain their positions relative to each other.
Flag V	The re-form flag. Ships will re-form in line ahead.[30]

On October the 15th Vice-Admiral Sir George Tryon shifted his flag from shore to HMS *Victoria*, an odd-looking 10,000-ton battleship with two monstrous $16\frac{1}{4}$-inch guns of uncertain reputation, and took the 1st Division of the fleet to the Aegean to put 'TA' to its first test. His flag-captain was the Hon. Maurice Bourke, "one of the most charming and beloved of men, [whose name] was almost a synonym for good luck. Everything had gone well with him."[31] His flag-lieutenant was Lord Gillford, son and heir of his friend and long-ago shipmate, the Earl of Clanwilliam. His master-of-the-fleet was a Staff-Commander Thomas Hawkins-Smith, a man of great experience of fleetwork (in the 1890s, 'staff-commander' was still a rank, rather than a post, being a remnant of the old navigation branch). And among *Victoria*'s watch-keeping lieutenants was a 29-year-old Hugh Evan-Thomas, whose efficiency had won the esteem and patronage of Tryon's predecessor.

The first gingerly attempts at TA were encouraging. Within days amended versions of the temporary memoranda were circulated. A track chart drawn up by Lord Gillford showed what it could do. The 1st Division, manoeuvring in sub-divisions, was put through a sophisticated series of 13 turns and formation changes. To achieve this by the *Signal Book* would have taken considerably longer, and would have required the timely display of 202 flags – 35 by the flagship, 93 by repeating ships, and 74 by answering addressees. An error or delay with any one of these could have caused the fleet difficulties in the presence of an enemy ('For the loss of a nail', etc.). Under TA it was done with the flagship using just 10 flags,[32] or, if you discount the original 'TA' warning, just 8.

Tryon attached (in his own words) "great value to free criticism [of TA] by officers who have studied the question involved", and at the beginning of November he received from his subordinate, Rear-Admiral Lord Walter Kerr, whose 2nd Division had joined the 1st for a few days, the first critical reactions of a fellow flag-officer. Kerr "was not a man to initiate change, but when he recognized its necessity, he at once adopted it and gave it his firm support."[33] This was evidently such an occasion:

> I have long been of the opinion that, when closing an enemy, the carrying out of the formal movements in the *Manoeuvring Signal Books* would not be practicable, and that some more rapid method of altering direction or formation must be adopted. The 'T.A. System' seems to supply this want. The movements are carried out at equal speed, and the ships can be turned in succession, or together, or worked in a single line, divisions or sub-divisions, without signal or by the display of a single flag, which may be acted on without the delay of waiting for an answer.
>
> I foresee no difficulty, in a squadron that has been practised in squadron manoeuvring, in working the 'T.A. System' satisfactorily. It is simple. The few flags that are used convey their meaning at a glance and no reference to the *Signal Books* is necessary.[34]

Near the end of November Tryon sent to the Admiralty his report on *A System of Fleet Manoeuvres With and Without Signals* for circulation among flag-officers on other stations. It consisted of the three updated TMs already mentioned, accompanied by a lengthy covering memorandum (reproduced in full in Appendix V). Sir George was explaining himself to the senior naval world and trying to stimulate debate.

A month later he penned a less formal account of his crusade to Sir Geoffrey Phipps Hornby, who had written to know from the horse's mouth what was going on. It is a marvellous cascading letter which conveys well both his conviction that the theorists were undermining the Royal Navy's fitness for battle and his clear vision of the remedy. If it can be lumped together with his temporary memoranda and their covering explanation to the Admiralty, it represents as important a tactical testament as the 'Nelson Memorandum' in October 1805 – arguably more important, since Nelson was mostly articulating an existing state of doctrine. Insofar as Tryon's scrawl can be deciphered, this is what he said:

H.M.S. *Victoria*
Dec. 23 1891

My dear Admiral,

Thank you for your letter. I will not if I can help it in this my reply refer to others or to the opinions of brother officers and yet to touch on the subject of your letter if I am not to allude to others it puts me in the confessional and condemns me to speak of my own views – I am so full of the subject that I cannot hope to express myself on a sheet of paper.

What I have so far been driving at most is this – I long have been convinced that it is not possible to maintain a large staff of signalmen such as is required to work the present system of signalling, on exposed positions & there is no possibility of giving them protection & even if there was many complications are sure to arise in action from flags being kept at the dip or not dipped or from some non-compliance with the present elaborate system of signalling – while a single bullet may cut a halliard and make a signal executive at the wrong moment.

For a large fleet on an average it takes over 3 minutes before an evolutionary signal is repeated, taken in & the fleet is ready to execute it – this is of no matter when it is immaterial whether a signal is hauled down now or presently, but what does it mean when you are manoeuvring on another gentleman who is quite as anxious to get an advantage of you as you are of him? 3 minutes means 1,000 yards at 10 knots and 2,000 at 20 knots and a great alteration in bearing.

If ever an advantage in manoeuvring is lost what right have we to suppose that the opportunity will recur to us, surely it is probable by the doctrine of chance that the other chap will have the next turn, vide *Alabama* & *Kearsage*. Such a delay as 3 minutes or even of 1 minute is unindurable unless forced on us by some imperative condition . . . it ought not to be forced on us to suit *Signal Books*.

I regard the mass of these books as barrack-yard, goose-step, parade-drill books, most necessary and important as preliminaries leading up to other things – they teach principles necessary in manoeuvring, how ships can in very close order be safely manoeuvred, they inspire confidence to those not accustomed to ride fresh horses in company. Once outside the barrack-yard we come face to face with an opponent whose views may or may not be the same as our own custom; we should be in a position to take initiative and to force his hands, & the admiral who has his fleet best in hand & most mobile will have a great pull. In action the drill book should be put to one side & sat on. The compass only in use for navigation purposes.

I find I can alter the course of the fleet in any direction at a moment's notice – can throw it in any direction, with divisions in subdivision or in a single column by the use of single flags – I have tried it with only one squadron of the fleet but I have made the leaders of divisions manoeuvre the fleet at will – Bourke handling *Victoria* like a private ship. One forenoon as an example we used 8 flags; if we had used *Signal Books* we should have used over 200 & owing to the delays could not have done so much by one third in the same time.

I don't say it is perfect, nothing is, but I am convinced it is a step in the right direction. I don't think men should be set to construct *Signal Books* or to formulate systems of manoeuvre without they are acquainted with what is wanted. We want *Signal Books* to give us what we want, we do not want to be dragooned by *Signal Books*.

If a fleet comes out and relies on *Signal Books* & signals to manoeuvre with the view to obtain an advantage, he will not be in it with a fleet trained to action principles with very few signals & those single flags.

With all the best wishes for you . . . Believe me you are missed.[35]

Early in 1892 Sir George began to get replies from fellow admirals to his 'report' of November '91. Some answers were much longer in coming, for flag-officers on minor stations only rarely had enough ships together for worthwhile experiment, but (after he pestered the Admiralty) he received a total of six, in addition to that from his own second-in-command.

From Bermuda, Vice-Admiral Sir George Watson, C-in-C North America and West Indies, forwarded only a technical suggestion from his flag-lieutenant, Ernest Troubridge,[36] although the brief endorsing remarks imply that Watson's flag-captain, Charles Drury, at least, understood the general drift and thought it good.

A year later Watson's successor, Vice-Admiral Sir John Hopkins, hastened to add his say and was much more fulsome: TA was

excellent; and it has the effect of considerably enlarging an officer's capacity for acting promptly in squadron tactics . . . On the whole the system worked admirably, and was very intelligently rendered by the squadron.[37]

Meanwhile, from Simons Bay, Vice-Admiral Henry Nicholson, C-in-C Cape of Good Hope, regretted that "the dispersed state of the few vessels" under his command made it impossible for him to test the TA system for himself, but he hailed Tryon's initiative in raising questions about the Navy's dependence on the *Signal Book*:

I have always considered the present manoeuvres too complicated for use in the immediate presence of an enemy, and that a too theoretical Commander-in-Chief, taking the opposite view and attempting at the critical moment to work a fleet by them, on some system developed in the lecture hall of the United Services Institution, would run great risk; and therefore I am pleased to think that so distinguished an officer as Sir George Tryon has approached the question of 'Simplicity of Manoeuvres in the Presence of an Enemy' . . .[38]

From the East Indies Station, Rear-Admiral William Kennedy reported:

> The system seems to be very simple so far as I could judge with so few ships, no mistakes were made, and the officers commanding thoroughly appreciated the idea which would be invaluable in time of war.[39]

And from the China Station, Vice-Admiral Edmund Fremantle (who, twelve years earlier, had won an essay-prize for denouncing the *Signal Book*) wrote:

> I am entirely in agreement with Sir George Tryon when he speaks of 'the importance of exercising a fleet from the point where the drill books leave off', in fact the *Signal Book* is now as I pointed out that it was in 1880: a drill book having little connection with action requirements.[40]

The reply of the C-in-C Channel, Vice-Admiral Sir Michael Culme-Seymour, is by far the most interesting to this study, for it was he who would take over the Mediterranean after Tryon's sudden, tragic death, and it would fall largely to him to determine whether 'Manoeuvring With and Without Signals' survived its creator. Culme-Seymour's own attempts at TA proved no more than "fairly satisfactory". He and Tryon had been having a career needle-match for some time, and his verdict on the TA system was distinctly competitive. He dealt with Tryon's two main claims for TA: that it reduced the time an admiral would have to wait before commencing a manoeuvre; and that it reduced the number of flags which would have to be used.

In answering the first point, which he judged "not so important as claimed", Sir Michael took a deliberate snipe at the efficiency of Sir George's fleet:

> It appears to take from 2min 30sec to 3min 50sec in the Mediterranean Squadron 'before a general signal is repeated and answered under circumstances of every advantage'. My attention having been called to this, I had the time taken on the last two occasions I have exercised the Channel Squadron at manoeuvres, and the time from the signal leaving the deck until repeated and hauled down averaged on the first occasion 40.5secs, and on the last 43secs. Many of these signals were repeated by all ships in single line ahead and abreast, and some were signals that had never been made in the squadron before.

His remedy for slow signalling was a counsel of perfection which, even a century later, could send a shiver down the spine of the averagely indolent watch-keeper (and raise a cheer from any harassed yeoman):

My experience shews me that the delay in answering manoeuvring signals is not due to the signalmen, but to the officers. Many officers never trouble their heads about signals until they are at sea on the bridge of a ship, and [when the] signal goes up they keep the answering pendant at the dip until they perfectly comprehend the signal; hence the delay. Officers should study the *Signal Books* and make themselves perfectly acquainted with them in harbour, and have them at their fingers' ends. There will then be no delay. I have insisted that there should be no delay in this squadron, and the result is, I think, satisfactory.

He then turned to the reduction of flags; and this, he agreed, "will be of the greatest advantage if this system can be carried out in a satisfactory manner" (although he wanted to add a second flag, to indicate port or starboard, to the blue pendant denoting a turn together). The faintly patronizing tone of his conclusion was probably inspired by private 'upmanship' (and may have been received in that spirit in Malta):

As invited, I have freely criticized this system. I cordially recognize it as the first, and most important, move in the right direction, and I fully anticipate that when Admiral Sir George Tryon has had more practice with this system, aided by the experience of other officers who have tried it, a result will be arrived at of great benefit to the service.[41]

*

TA became the main feature of the Mediterranean Fleet's sea training throughout 1892, although

for a time even George Tryon was unable to convince some of the captains of the Mediterranean Fleet that the system of signals on which they had been brought up, and which had been practised for decades, was other than the best.[42]

He would call them to *Victoria* after a day's exercises and patiently explain what he had meant and what had gone wrong, inviting comment and criticism; and in Malta he would meet them every so often

on the Corradino, the naval parade ground, and there he would draw from their ideas and, I believe, for I speak only from hearsay, pounce on those who could not express their views with strength and break a lance with those who could[43]

– and woe betide the author of a foolish suggestion, or the officer with no ideas at all.

They could not for ever resist his enthusiasm, and partly by intimidation, partly by instilling in them some of his own abundant self-confidence, he had the whole fleet carrying out the free and easy T.A. system of evolutions during the summer Manoeuvres of 1892 with some show of confidence, although numerous mistakes were made.[44]

By the end of the year there was little Tryon could not have done with his fleet, had it come to war with, say, France or Russia. He was guided by the precept that emancipation from the *Signal Book* was the "only possible method of keeping his squadron in hand" once battle had begun, "and those who practised [TA] under his guidance came to a similar conclusion".[45] Or rather, some of them did.

He was fortunate to have had as second-in-command an officer of the calibre of Lord Walter Kerr, who had served with him on the acrimonious 1878 (Hope–Colomb) *Signal Book* committee. A little story which Tryon related to Hornby indicates Kerr's receptiveness to reform. It was common during 'steam tactics' for an admiral to station himself on his flagship's after bridge, so he could observe his squadron (which was usually astern of him), while the flag-captain, on the forward bridge, concentrated on handling the ship. One day after experimenting with TA, Lord Walter asked Tryon

> to approve a demand for a few planks. What for?
> 'Oh, I find with these manoeuvres I no longer can stay aft. I must be close to the wheel, & the [wheel-]house there won't hold me.'
> He and the Capt. & the young fellows with him are a good bit bitten by them.[46]

Sadly Rear-Admiral Kerr's stint in the Mediterranean ended in March '92, and his place was taken by a man of very different kidney.

Two of Tryon's most senior captains quickly became converts to TA. Rough Fitzgerald, captain of *Collingwood* and the leading progressive in the steam *v.* sail argument, thrived on TA, and was later to write a biography of Tryon which partly took the form of a polemic against Sir George's critics. Regrettably, he also left Tryon's fleet, in January '93.

The hatchet-faced Gerard Noel, of HMS *Nile*, whose discordant views on the new *Signal Book* had been water off the Dowell committee's back, was a blunt and difficult man who infrequently agreed with anyone. He was famous for insisting on sailing HMS *Temeraire*, the last fully masted battleship in the Mediterranean, up to the anchorage in Suda Bay in Crete against a headwind in 1891: he tacked her thirteen times while the rest of the fleet watched, mesmerized. His no-nonsense methods may be gauged from his leadership of the Allied Intervention in Crete in 1898 (by which time he was a rear-admiral). Foreseeing that English law would be unlikely to hang insurrectionists, he used French procedures to his full satisfaction. It comes as something of a fright to find letters addressing him as "Dear Old Skips".

There was another side to 'Sharky' Noel (a great-grandson of Lord Barham). He had presented papers to the Institute of Naval Architects, corresponded with the great American historian Captain Alfred Mahan,[47] and published an impressive 100-page essay on naval tactics.[48] He was, above all, "a born tactician with nerves of steel"[49] and he wasn't in the least fazed by manoeuvring without signals – indeed, like Fitzgerald (with whom he was at loggerheads on other matters[50]), he became one of Tryon's staunchest defenders; and the C-in-C, for his part, formed "the highest opinion" of the captain of the ship whose usual station was next astern of *Victoria*. Sir George would point to *Nile* from his stern gallery and say, "Oh I wish they were all like that!"[51] Noel's XO, as a matter of interest, was the behemoth Reginald Prothero ('Prothero the Bad'): they were "both grim, taciturn and gruff"[52] and rarely on cordial terms – or so it seemed to their ship's company.

And after Tryon's death, John Brackenbury of *Edinburgh* was to write privately of "that great system of tactics [Sir George] was working out ... without signal or warning he used to manoeuvre this squadron with the most marvellous rapidity and skill"[53] (although by then Brackenbury was finding discretion to be the better part of conviction). Many others in the Mediterranean Fleet merely went along with TA as best they could. They were in the presence of a formidable and gifted leader, and if they were ordered to act without orders, well, that was an order.

Tryon's offhand confession that manoeuvring without signals "places a somewhat increased responsibility on leaders of columns, but no more than was the case during the old wars"[54] scarcely hints at how the system traumatized some of his more hidebound captains. TA could be described as a surface-ship version of the modern submariners' 'Perisher Course' – a mild version, certainly, but one for which the students had not volunteered, and their ability to cope with it varied greatly. Officers who had spent their careers in the regulated, apron-stringed discipline of the main fleets, and who owed their promotions to an impressive grasp of their profession's primary skills, could draw upon no experience to help them. No longer were chief-yeomen, armed with The Book, able to tell officers-of-the-watch what they were supposed to do: they would have to decide for themselves, and fast! No longer did arrays of bunting blossoming above HMS *Victoria* signify detailed tactical spoon-feeding: now – as likely as not – they meant a blistering reprimand for any hapless ship slow on the uptake.

A few senior officers, who did not relish the new informality or who had misgivings about its safety, remained hostile. One such was Arthur

K. Wilson VC ('Old Ard Art' in later years), captain of *Victoria*'s sister-ship *Sans Pareil*.

Wilson was a disciplinarian with an irreproachable record for personal courage. At the Second Battle of El Teb, in 1884, he rallied soldiers of the 65th Yorks & Lancs who were breaking under a Mahdist attack,[55] and fought dervishes with his sword until it snapped and then with his fists. It was nothing, he said; he was only there "as a loafer, just to see the fight", and the sword broke having a "cool prod at an Arab".[56] His diary covered his return home with: "Docked ship, received VC." He also received a new sword, subscribed to by the staff of the Torpedo School, HMS *Vernon*, of which he had recently been commander. (At first he refused the sword, pointing out that to accept would be a breach of *Queen's Regulations* "which I am sure the officers of the Torpedo School would be the last to wish me to commit".) Wilson had impeccable ideas about conduct[57] and he considered the TA system "dangerously unorthodox". It is extremely likely that his young XO and close personal friend, John Jellicoe, shared his views. Walter Kerr's successor, Albert Hastings Markham, who had been the captain of *Vernon* when they gave Wilson his new sword, certainly did.

For a man with so little aptitude for the stresses of high command, Rear-Admiral Markham had had a most distinguished early career and, in that sense, he caricatured the condition of the Victorian Navy's officer corps.

He belonged to the junior branch of a notable family in which strands of piety and naval service were intertwined, though his father had left the Navy "because of ill-health, with the rank of lieutenant, and [subsequently] lived on his inadequate capital".[58]

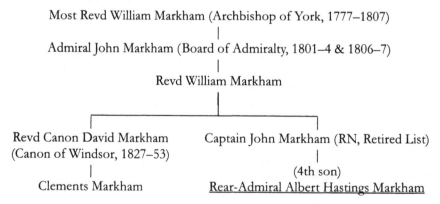

Most Revd William Markham (Archbishop of York, 1777–1807)
|
Admiral John Markham (Board of Admiralty, 1801–4 & 1806–7)
|
Revd William Markham
|
Revd Canon David Markham   Captain John Markham (RN, Retired List)
(Canon of Windsor, 1827–53) |
| (4th son)
Clements Markham   Rear-Admiral Albert Hastings Markham

Albert was thus brought up in straitened circumstances, in which the Royal Navy and the Church were the presumed career options. At the age of 13 he was sent to London to lodge with his aunt (Canon

David Markham's widow), while he sought entry into the former institution.

There he came under the thrall of his older cousin Clements, who had found a midshipman's life disagreeable and had left the service to devote his time to exploration and the Royal Geographical Society. Unlike Clements, Albert lacked the private means to evade the Navy, but whenever circumstances permitted, the Markham cousins became inseparable, and often formed a travelling, touring trio after Clements married. Meanwhile Albert got on with his chosen vocation with neither relish nor compromise.

As a midshipman he attacked Arab pirates from an open boat and captured, for trial and execution, wanted murderers. As a lieutenant he so rigorously suppressed the illegal 'labour' traffic in the South Seas that islands whose banana harvests depended upon it complained to the Admiralty. His moment of greatest personal achievement came as a 34-year-old commander on Captain George Nares's Arctic expedition of 1875–6.

The project was a heroic, hopeless attempt on the North Pole, sponsored jointly by the Royal Geographical Society, of which Clements Markham was now secretary, and by the Admiralty. The expedition "epitomized both the best features of British exploration and the worst".[59] It nearly became a classic British disaster from a failure to learn the dietary lessons of previous expeditions, and from the early escape or death, due to incompetence, of the dogs which were to have pulled the sledges. Undaunted, Albert Markham gave it his best shot; and his men stolidly hauled their heavy loads northwards and progressively fell victim to scurvy. They were away for ten weeks. Their provisions were medieval, and although there was ample lime juice onboard the ships, the labour and fuel involved in thawing it out every day had persuaded Markham to leave it behind. When they got to within 400 miles of the Pole (a record which stood for twenty years) he planted the flag in the snow, sang *The Union Jack of Old England*, and started the long stumbling journey back. They endured appalling privations, were reduced to crawling on hands and knees, and were lucky only one of their number died.

It was the stuff of ripping yarns. What country would not have rewarded such men? There was a Parliamentary enquiry into the scurvy problem,[60] but George Nares (author of the monumental classic *Seamanship*) was knighted, and Markham presented with a gold watch by the RGS and promoted to captain. The expedition left two dangerous legacies for future British polar endeavour: a distrust of dogs; and a romanticization of the camaraderie, as Clements Markham saw it, of muscle-power.[61]

Fortune remained a fickle friend to Albert Markham. In July 1885, while he was in command of *Vernon*, he took the torpedo-tender *Hecla* to sea for trials and rammed and sank a passenger-steamer, the SS *Cheerful*, in fog off Land's End. Eleven civilians drowned, and two more died after their rescue by *Hecla*. The warship had "a rent in her bow 10 feet long above and below the waterline" and limped into Plymouth with her forward compartment filled with water.[62] Captain Markham and his officer-of-the-watch were tried by a court-martial under the presidency of Pompo Heneage, second-in-command Channel Fleet. Captain Philip Colomb stepped in to act as prisoner's friend. It emerged that the ships had been on roughly opposite courses, set to pass green-to-green, and that *Cheerful* had made a too-late attempt to cross *Hecla*'s bows. There were questions (or should have been) about the alertness of the sub-lieutenant who had just taken over *Hecla*'s morning watch, about his response to *Cheerful*'s sudden appearance and erratic behaviour, and even about his qualifications; but verdicts of 'not guilty' were returned.[63]

By middle age, Markham had become an anxious, scholarly recluse whose real interests were not so much the Navy as exploration, natural history and archaeology – in short, trying to emulate his more famous cousin. He spent much time immersed in writing and reading, and would issue little homilies of a Baden-Powell nature to junior officers on the supposed perils and temptations of youth.

> He was often moody, irritable and defensive, resenting his naval career the more because his sense of duty, as well as his need of the pay, demanded that his loyalty to the service should be uncompromising. This moral dutifulness, supported by his strong, almost puritanical religious convictions, led to conflicts which made him a difficult fellow officer in the wardroom. He neither smoked nor drank, and was always ready to express his disapproval of those indulgences. Later, when he reached senior rank, he was often a domineering commander, and once lectured his officers: 'A gentleman may be forgiven an occasional cigar, cigarettes are only for effeminate weaklings, but the low, filthy, and nauseous black pipe can only be compared with gin and other disreputable liquors which ruin mind and body.'[64]

This description is foreshortened by modern perspective, and emphasizes the negative.

In reality 'Old Marco' was liked and admired: for his polar achievements he was a minor celebrity, and in his commitment to unyielding moral standards he epitomized the desiderata of the times. He stuck to the rules, men knew where they stood with him (which was not always the case with George Tryon), and he was untiringly interested in his subordinates. For the education of his flagship's company he would publish his own sort of Baedeker's Guide to places of historical interest which *Trafalgar* was programmed to visit. His standing orders specified that "when men are being mustered, their Christian names are *always* to be called"[65] – an injunction which was partly a patrician relic of the Old Navy – and in later life he was known for his consideration towards newly married junior officers. John Jellicoe, whose brother Edmund was a midshipman in *Trafalgar*, said: "I always felt that I had in him a true friend and his friendship was indeed worth having."[66] To expect his juniors to perceive that his anxious finicky ways might be symptoms of wider limitations of high command is to expect too much: it was not their place to do so and many of them were not that dissimilar.

Rear-Admiral Markham is justly named by Professor Dixon as an authoritarian. His moralizing and his unbending views on duty and hierarchy also make him archetypical of the earnest Victorian minor gentry who were drawn to Freemasonry. As already mentioned, he was introduced to the Craft by Colomb in 1886, the year after the *Hecla–Cheerful* collision, and he took it, like everything else, very seriously. He had not been in the Mediterranean long before his masonic ultimate superior, the Prince of Wales, appointed him District Grand Master of Malta, along with an impressive clutch of other masonic dignifications.[67] At sea, his mastery of his surroundings was less sure. He had been one of the blockading officers of whom George Tryon had made fools in the Manoeuvres of 1888, and now, as second-in-command of the Mediterranean Squadron, he was so apprehensive at the prospect of leading his division in the manoeuvres of a 'Tryonized' fleet that he tried every means of delaying his participation.

Markham's last employment before succeeding Kerr as rear-admiral in the Mediterranean had been as flag-captain to Jacky Fisher, when the latter was Superintendent of Portsmouth Dockyard, in the harbour HQ ship *Asia*. In terms of personalities, a more striking example of 'chalk and cheese' could hardly be found. But as mentioned above, Markham had been captain of Fisher's special baby, HMS *Vernon*, coincident with Fisher's command of the nearby gunnery school *Excellent* in 1883–6, and Fisher no doubt saw him as a steady if somewhat pedestrian yeoman in the technological crusade. For all radical Jack's autocracy, he liked controllable, docile juniors, and Markham's narrow ideas of leadership – routines, standing orders, ceremonial, brasswork, temperance – were just the thing for a sedentary public-eye command. He would have given no cause for complaint, and Fisher's testimonial may have had something to do with his next appointment. If so, it was a role which Fisher must have come bitterly to regret.

From having a keen and capable second-in-command, Tryon now had an awkward and unsure one; and personal relations between the two were known to be "unfortunate".[68] A historian's comment on an authoritarian and disastrous Boer War general is applicable to Rear-Admiral Markham: "he found himself promoted beyond his abilities, and became hesitant, confused, and demoralized."[69]

One can readily understand the stresses which manoeuvring without signals placed upon captains and divisional leaders, especially in the early days. The C-in-C was enjoined by *Queen's Regulations* "to ascertain [their] skill, capacity and intelligence"; but they had not bargained for this. They had been brought up to regard independent thinking, at least within signalling reach of a superior, as "a form of mutiny",[70] and many were content to find refuge in that philosophy. Now Tryon was opening the door to the anxieties which the routines of military life were meant to keep at bay. Back in 1885 Captain Clayton had described him as "a queer fellow who I have not yet fathomed so one has to be very careful in all you do. He likes to be mischievous, I think, and catch you unprepared so I must take care that he does not succeed with me."[71] And Sir Geoffrey Phipps Hornby was to make a telling observation in 1893 when he said that "the good-natured banter which I remember in the Mediterranean seems to have been missing of late."[72] Whether TA was actually dangerous is a moot point.

It could be argued that it required officers to commit their ships to group movements in which neither the intended outcome nor the responses of other units were obvious in advance, and thus nullified some of the safety introduced by equal-speed. But it also gave them the widest possible remit to decide for themselves what actions were appropriate, and if years of geometrical set-piece evolutions, prescribed and executed by formula, had had the insidious effect of shifting a captain's responsibility for his ship onto the admiral's shoulders – of increasing the former's habitual dependence on higher authority, as Professor Dixon would say – then a forcible return to fundamentals was all the more timely.

Far from seeing individual responsibility as a source of danger, Tryon saw it as an agent of safety. Early in his regime he issued a memorandum which began with a misquotation of England's greatest soldier:[73]

It may frequently happen that an order may be given to an officer which, from circumstances not known to the person who gave it at the time he issued it, would be impossible to execute, or the difficulty or risk of the execution of it would be so great as to amount to a moral responsibility.

Wellington's General Order of 11th November 1803

1. While an order should be implicitly obeyed, still circumstances may change and conditions may widely vary from those known or even from those that presented themselves at the time orders were issued. In such cases the officer receiving orders, guided by the object that he knows his chief had in view, must act on his own responsibility.

2. (a) Orders directing the movement of ships, either collectively or singly, are invariably accompanied, as a matter of course, with the paramount understood condition – 'With due regard to the safety of HM Ship'.

(b) When the literal obedience to any order, however given, would entail a collision with a friend, or endanger a ship by running on shore, or in any other way, paramount orders direct that the danger is to be avoided, while the object of the order should be attained if possible.

3. An admiral leading a fleet relies with confidence that while the order of the fleet is maintained, each ship will be handled and piloted with all the care and attention that is exercised in the guidance of the leading ship.

4. Risks that are not only justifiable, but are demanded during war, are not justifiable during peace.

*

This, then, was how Tryon set about resurrecting the officer corps' secondary educational syllabus. But its primary education was not entirely deserted, for while he saw the *Signal Book* as "not at all for use in the presence of an enemy", he still valued it as the essential school-book of shiphandling. And his other forte (other than 'TA') was his mastery of steam-tactics which dug deep into the *Manual of Evolutions*; indeed only an admiral whose command of the *Signal Book* and the *Manual* was second to none could have had the credibility to introduce signal-free manoeuvring. So, as one of his captains later said,

> Tryon often gave us [signalled] manoeuvres that looked dangerous, and so they would have been unless faithfully carried out according to order. I have myself led a sub-division round 32 points [= full circle] according to order & thought when I started there must be an accident, but found myself exactly astern of the division following me, where he wanted me to be.[74]

These two opposite but complementary aspects of his regime – the informal TA revolution and the formal set-piece manoeuvres by signal – later became merged and confused in popular mythology.

Those few who got close to him, such as the initially terrified staff intelligence officer Captain (later General Sir George) Aston, Royal Marines, discovered that while Tryon "may have posed a bit, not out of any smallness of nature, but for the good of the service", he was actually (as is often the case with ogres) quite soft-centred.[75] Once, when about to interview a midshipman, who had done something reprehensible, he asked his flag-lieutenant, "Am I looking cross enough?" He was, evidently, for Gillford returned after an interval to find the youth in tears, being consoled on the Commander-in-Chief's shoulder. There is another tale of him, in shabby civilian clothes, being mistaken by a boat's crew for a Maltese boatman and called an "old bastard", and no retribution descending upon the midshipman in charge;[76] and another, of his forbidding the over-zealous CO of a survey vessel to send his boats out before 9 o'clock in the morning.

But these were not the widely recognized images of George Tryon. "He was the most formidable figure in the Royal Navy, with an equal capacity for instilling fear, loyalty and confidence in those serving under him";[77] and an irony of his labours is that this man who sought to reduce centralization and to devolve responsibility – to debunk the paralysing myth of the senior admiral's infallibility – was regarded by his subordinates with "a professional confidence almost equal to that given to the Deity".[78] His force of personality thus combined with his legendary grasp of manoeuvres to make his task harder, and ultimately it helped to kill him.

11

Meanwhile, by Royal Appointment

"The young Duke does not forget old friends."

In March 1892, when Tryon had been in command of the Mediterranean Fleet for just six months, Lieutenant Hugh Evan-Thomas was summoned home from *Victoria* to be first-lieutenant and XO of *Osborne*, the junior of the two royal yachts[1] and the one generally used by the Prince of Wales and his family. He took passage home from Malta in the troopship *Hymalaya* and reported on board his new ship, a classically beautiful schooner-rigged paddle-steamer of 1,850 tons, at South Railway Jetty in Portsmouth on April the 12th.

An appointment to a royal yacht was a seal of approval for a junior officer of unexceptional social background, and was alleged to carry with it, in Bacon's faintly caustic words, "special promotion for a sub-lieutenant and lieutenant".[2] William Goodenough recalled his posting at about this time to the senior yacht, *Victoria and Albert*, in the following words:

> I had just time to buy the gold-laced trousers and laced mess waistcoat that traditions enjoined to the Sub-Lieutenant, and we joined – Victor Stanley, Michael Seymour and myself. It was, of course, an appointment of patronage. I, for instance, went as my father's son [he might have added that Queen Victoria was his mother's godmother]. There was some tradition that the Commander and Lieutenants were appointed to give an early promotion to some who had done good service, but to whom it was not easy to give recognition in other ways. I don't know how far this was observed in reality.[3]

At a time when overseas appointments commonly lasted for three, four or even five years, Evan-Thomas had been in the Mediterranean for only two; and the full explanation for his appointment, at this

215

curious juncture, to the "courtly dawdling billet"[4] of a royal yacht is a story which might have been written by Edgar Wallace or C. S. Forester, with hindrance from W. S. Gilbert. It takes us back to Evan-Thomas's earliest days in the Navy.

*

Albert Edward, Prince of Wales (later King Edward VII), looked back on his repressive schooling under the supervision of his father, the humourless paragon Prince Albert, with such distaste[5] that he and his Danish wife Alexandra indulged their own two sons, Albert Victor (known as 'Eddy' by everyone except the Queen) and George, with a certain educational neglect during their early childhood. It couldn't last. In 1871, when the boys were 7 and nearly 6 years old respectively, Victoria tumbled to what was, or rather was not, happening. There was no time to lose. A tutor must be appointed without delay to subject the little princes to a regime as unrelentingly Teutonic as that which had extracted such poor results from their father. She knew just the man.

John Neale Dalton had been appointed curate to Canon George Prothero in the parish of Whippingham on the Isle of Wight at the age of 30 in 1869. Within the parish lay Osborne, the Queen's summer retreat and museum to Prince Albert, and Her Majesty was a seasonal attender at Whippingham Church. From time to time the young curate was allowed to deliver the sermon, and she liked the cut of his jib. In 1871 John Dalton became tutor and almost constant companion to Eddy and George, and took up residence in the cloisters of Windsor Castle. In entering the exclusive world of royal clergy he was following in the footsteps of Canon David Markham, of the Christian-socialist writer Charles Kingsley, and of Randall Davidson, who was to be Archbishop of Canterbury from 1903 to 1928. He took to the life of courtier in holy orders with selfless dedication; and

> for the greater part of [the next] fourteen years, the two young princes – shy and intellectually backward, isolated from their peers – were nurtured and trained and, to a limited extent, educated by the former curate, who made their upbringing his life's work. Dalton's regime, based on a meticulously strict routine and an obsessive concern with every error or transgression, would not commend itself to a modern educationalist. Queen Victoria, however, strongly approved.[6]

As the bringer-up of the two princes, it may fairly be said that Dalton won one and lost one. The difficulty was with the elder, Eddy, who was backward, lazy and obtuse. A battle of wills, of a sort no doubt familiar to teachers of 'problem' children, developed between the tutor and the

second in line to the throne. Little George, by contrast, was cooperative, dutiful and easy to teach – and Dalton thoroughly "instilled into
[him] the unwavering sense of duty which thereafter became the main-
spring of his character".[7] It has been suggested that they may in fact
have been only half-brothers, George's natural father being the Russian
Grand Duke Nicholas. This disgraceful idea grates with everything
believed about his saintly mother, Alexandra, but is circumstantially
possible, for in September 1864, when George was conceived, the
Waleses were at Elsinore in Denmark meeting Nicholas, who was
getting engaged to Alexandra's sister Dagmar (who actually married the
Grand Duke Alexander after Nicholas's sudden death).[8] To have been
fathered by Nicholas would have made George a double first-cousin of
the future Czar Nicholas II, of whom he appeared to be an identical
twin: their mothers being sisters and their natural fathers brothers.

Be that as it may. The point is that the two young princes were very
dissimilar (one royal biographer describes them as "diametric opposites"[9]), and it would have mattered less had they been the other way
round, with Eddy the obedient learner and George the delinquent, for
it was the former who was being groomed for kingship. At times his
tutor and his parents – not to mention his grandmother – despaired of
the task.

> Plans to send Eddy to public school – an unprecedented step for royalty –
> were dropped when Dalton persuaded the Queen that this would separate
> the prince from the supposedly benign influence of his younger brother, and
> that the 'evil associations' of school life presented risks too serious to take.[10]

Prince George was expected to join the Navy. How much say he had in
the matter is unclear: if he was possessed by a wish to emulate Uncle
Alfred, Captain HRH the Duke of Edinburgh, his biographers have
missed it; but he was ever amenable to guidance. The solution was
adopted of placing both boys in the cadet training ship *Britannia* at
Dartmouth, where they could be kept together and closely supervised
in a disciplined environment.

They arrived in September 1877, the year in which Grandmama
became Empress of India, accompanied by Mr Dalton with whom they
shared a cabin. Dalton probably appreciated *Britannia* rather more than
his charges. Acting *in loco parentis* for the Prince of Wales, he enjoyed
considerable prestige, and he took with gusto to the job of naval chaplain. He "possessed a resonant voice and much enjoyed listening to
it",[11] and his published volume of *Sermons to Naval Cadets* would cast a
gloom over anyone's day in the British Library, with its reiteration of the
wholesome virtues to be cultivated by young men ("resist the foul fiend

bent on your destruction and he will flee from you!" etc.). He was also of course spared, and may have been incompletely aware of, the surreptitious bullying which the gullible and immature princes suffered at the hands of older cadets who relished the chance to push royalty around. "There was much to be said in favour of punching a royal nose."[12]

Eddy and George – whose disparity in height earned them the nicknames of 'Herring' and 'Sprat' – were unaccustomed to the robust society of other boys, but learnt to bear the bruises with outward cheerfulness. The few genuine friendships which he formed in *Britannia* lasted George for the rest of his life. One of the senior cadets in particular, a 15-year-old named Hugh Thomas, took a kindly interest in the princes in their first term and exemplified Dalton's stringent moral desiderata. For reasons which have been lost to history, the royal pair nicknamed him 'Old Voice' (possibly because Dalton had advised them to listen to an older voice), and in the short time before he left *Britannia*, in December 1877, he made a deep and lasting impression on Dalton and the princes.

On Christmas Eve, both boys sent him cards from Sandringham. George's contained a note:

My Dear Thomas,
 I wish you a very merry Christmas and so does Mr Dalton. We are very busy this morning getting all our presents ready so good bye ever yours truly,
Sprat, George[13]

Thomas was shortly to sail from Portsmouth to join his first ship in the Mediterranean, but Dalton was anxious that the friendship should continue. He wrote from Sandringham on January the 11th:

My Dear Thomas,
 . . . both princes, I am bound to say, have frequently been full of thoughts of you, and I had hoped very much it might have been possible to arrange for you to have paid them a short visit here in the holidays . . . Neither I nor they are at all likely to forget you or the good influence you had over them during their first term on board *Britannia*. I hope that opportunities may occur for their seeing a good deal more of you. I think they will like to send you a letter every now and then, and I am sure they will be very pleased if you will write them from time to time about yourself.[14]

At the end of the month both princes wrote again. Thomas's first step into the big world of the seagoing Fleet was an experience they seemed to share vicariously. George's letter also mentions a passing encounter at a London railway station and shows an incomprehension of the diffidence a normal mortal might feel about hailing royal friends in public:

My Dear Thomas,

I hope you will like your new ship that you are going in with Edward Martin and [Herbert] Lyon in the Mediterranean and I hope you will often write to me when you are in her and tell me about all you do and see. Please remember me very kindly to Martin and Lyon. We miss you here very much but [Frederick] Pasco is very kind to us and there are several fellows we know very well now. Today and yesterday we have had a very good game of football and enjoyed it very much. We saw you at Paddington. Why did you not come and speak to us? Please send me one of your photographs before you start as you have one of mine. I shall think of you on Sunday, starting.

Yours Affectionately, George. [15]

Eddy also wanted a photograph:

My Dear Thomas,

I write to you a few lines to say goodbye before you go to sea, and I hope you will have a good voyage . . .

If you have a photograph of you to spare please let me have one to put in my book here. We often think of you and miss you. Gymnastics are compulsory for all cadets this term so I hope I shall soon be able to do what I saw you and the others doing last term.[16]

In February 1878 Thomas took passage to the Mediterranean, where Sir Geoffrey Phipps Hornby's virtuoso stint as C-in-C was in progress, and joined the barque-rigged battery-ship *Swiftsure*. Around this time his father, Charles Evan Thomas, incorporated 'Evan' (his own father's first name) into the family surname. He got good reports at sea. This being the heyday of demon drink in the Victorian Navy, it was mandatory for captains to mention an officer's sobriety – "if deserving of it" – when writing 'flimsies'. Hence the refrain in 1878's big box-office hit, *HMS Pinafore*: 'We're sober men and true / And attentive to our duty.' And hence the wording of *Swiftsure*'s CO's testimony that Midshipman Evan-Thomas had "conducted himself with sobriety zeal & attention & to my satisfaction".[17] Captain Nowell Salmon VC refrained from mentioning an escapade of Evan-Thomas's which had involved his ship in a minor international incident.

The details are sparse. In July 1878 the fleet was in the Gulf of Saros on the north-west coast of Gallipoli, exerting by its presence a check on the Russo-Turkish War. On the 20th, Evan-Thomas and a lieutenant (also from *Swiftsure*) were arrested by Cossacks while walking ashore. They "received very rude treatment" from their captors, and were taken some distance to be paraded before a colonel. This officer ordered their release, gave them dinner and had them escorted back to the coast.[18] There appears to have been a separate occurrence (probably not involving Evan-Thomas) a few days earlier, in which one of *Swiftsure*'s boats had been fired upon by soldiers. The Treaty of Berlin had been signed only the week before and the Russians were no doubt smarting from its terms. Hornby sent his flag-captain, Robert FitzRoy, to obtain satisfaction, and the local general duly tendered his regrets: the boat's flag was not recognized in the dark, he said, and the two officers had been in civilian clothes.[19] Midshipman Evan-Thomas may not have endorsed *The Times*'s statesmanlike view that "the matter is thought to have no importance."[20]

In August *Swiftsure* started for home, and he moved across to the barque-rigged turret-ship *Monarch*, whose captain, Algernon Lyons ("a kindly individual [with] a furious temper"[21]), was a first cousin once removed. Cousin Algernon allowed him merely the standard "has conducted himself with sobriety, and entirely to my satisfaction"; but his successor, George Tryon, gave him ". . . with sobriety & in accordance with the *Queen's Regulations & Admiralty Instructions*. A very promising young officer in every respect." He was in *Monarch* on that day, already referred to, when one of *Thunderer*'s guns burst and Tryon sent *Monarch*'s doctors over and then carried on with his own gunnery.

As Dalton hoped, the princes' separation from their friend by no means led to their forgetting him, although they never got the hang of his new double-barrelled name (George disliked composite names[22]). In October 1878 Eddy wrote:

> Dear Thomas,
>   I am sorry that I did not write to you before but I often think about you and how kind you were to me and George when we joined the ship this time last year.[23]

In 1879, the year of Isandhlwana, Rorke's Drift and Ulundi, of Little Bob's march on Kabul, and the Tay Bridge disaster, the princes' time in *Britannia* came to an end and the question loomed again of what to do with them. They were now 15 and 14, and again it was suggested that the older boy be sent to a boarding school. Again the Reverend Dalton insisted that the backward Eddy should not be removed from the companionship of his brother (or himself), and the idea evolved that they would all be placed in a seagoing training-ship and sent on a series of educational cruises. When the Admiralty produced *Bacchante*, a fully rigged corvette with muzzle-loading guns, Dalton queried her stability. Her captain was "ordered to cruise in search of a storm to see if she will capsize", and when she did not, Their Lordships stood their ground.[24] Now the stability of her officers came under the myopic minister's scrutiny. Queen Victoria had warned that the princes must avoid the company of people who were "fashionable and fast"[25] (a dig at the Prince of Wales's 'Marlborough House set') and now Dalton, in consultation with naval officers of his acquaintance, went through the lists of lieutenants, sub-lieutenants, midshipmen and cadets in order to secure that the princes should be accompanied only by shipmates of irreproachable character.[26]

One by one *Bacchante*'s billets were filled by officers who passed his litmus test. She was commanded by Captain Lord Charles Scott, a son of the 5th, and brother of the 6th, Duke of Buccleuch. (*Bacchante* joke: "Your captain's name is Lord Charles Scott ain't it?" "No it ain't, it's the Lord God Almighty."[27]) The first-lieutenant was the Hon. Assheton Curzon-Howe, whose family had long-established royal connections and who had recently served the Duke of Edinburgh in *Sultan*. Among the midshipmen were: the captain's nephew, the Hon. John Scott (future 7th Duke of Buccleuch and the son of the Queen's Mistress of the Robes); Lord Francis Osborne (son of the 9th Duke of Leeds); Arthur Limpus (future naval adviser to Turkey); Rosslyn Wemyss (future First Sea Lord); and Hugh Evan-Thomas, who was extracted from Captain Tryon's battleship *Monarch* and placed in *Bacchante*'s starboard watch where he could look after Cadet HRH Prince Albert Victor (Eddy).

HMS *Bacchante* undertook three separate cruises. The first two, to the Mediterranean and the West Indies, and to Spain and Ireland, occupied most of the first year and were preparations for the big one: a 'round-the-world cruise' of nearly two years' duration. For this expedition, she left South Railway Jetty ('Heartbreak Pier') amid tearful royal farewells, in September 1880, accompanied by three other corvettes and the frigate *Inconstant*, which flew the flag of Rear-Admiral the Earl of Clanwilliam. *Inconstant*, too, had some notable officers.

Her captain was the Penrose 'Rough' Fitzgerald who thought masts and sails a waste of space and freely sowed his seditious views among his juniors[28] (he also predicted that the Americans would be the first to reach the moon[29]); the flag-lieutenant was Alfred Winsloe, who had served Phipps Hornby in the same capacity and who, a dozen years later, was to side with Fitzgerald in the main controversy of this story; and the gunnery-officer was the young radical Percy Scott, who whiled away the time inventing an electrical range-telegraph, which the Admiralty ignored. The watch-keeping lieutenants included William May who had been George Nares's navigator in the Arctic in '75 and who would be a contender for First Sea Lord in the pre-1914 era; and His Serene Highness Prince Louis of Battenberg, who was First Sea Lord from 1912 to 1914, and who had become seized with the virtues of a sea voyage after getting Lillie Langtry, the Prince of Wales's favourite, pregnant. And one of the midshipmen was Mark Kerr, future naval adviser to Greece.

One must admire Albert Edward's enlightened common sense in sending his two sheltered sons – the monarchy's future – away on such a long and adventurous, possibly even hazardous, odyssey, much of the time beyond easy recall: the more so since the training ship *Atalanta* had disappeared without trace in the West Indies only that April. Unfortunately, the stricture that the princes should be treated "just like ordinary midshipmen"[30] was defeated by the Reverend Dalton's obsessive guardianship. No doubt he was haunted by fear of returning to Windsor with two overgrown louts at the end of the trip, but he made it his business to ensure that poor Eddy and George formed no potentially corrupting friendships, and were exposed "to no influence other than his own".[31] What vices they were in danger of learning from their fellow cadets and midshipmen, apart from high spirits and mischief, it is hard to imagine, but perhaps these were threatening enough to the dour and anxious sky-pilot; and he

> dealt as he wished with anybody who had the temerity to befriend his charges. When the senior midshipman showed signs of familiarity, Dalton engineered the removal of the unfortunate young man from the ship. Others, taking note, kept their distance. Not surprisingly, cadets regarded Dalton as a martinet and a kill-joy, and he was seen by officers as 'an incubus' of rows in the wardroom.
>
> Dalton's embargo on close social contacts did not extend to one midshipman, Hugh Evan-Thomas; under seventeen at the beginning of the first cruise, [he] became an accepted member of the royal group.[32]

Bacchante, with her escorts, her slightly wrong-headed prince and his brother, their near-paranoid tutor, and Hugh Evan-Thomas, wafted round the planet. Almost the entire voyage was done under sail and was on that account condemned by *Inconstant*'s captain as a waste of time for the hundreds of officers and men involved, for it neither "trained nor exercised them in subjects which would be useful to the country in wartime".[33]

The World Cruise was not literally a circumnavigation, for when they were in the Falklands, about to round Cape Horn, they were diverted to South Africa by the outbreak of the first Boer War. They extemporized a Naval Brigade as they crossed the South Atlantic, while Queen Victoria panicked about the princes serving at the front (the Prince Imperial of France had been slain by Zulus only the year before).[34] In the event they were not needed; and, instead, the young princes visited Cetshwayo in his farm compound, and goggled at the number and size of his wives. After an interlude for social junketing the squadron departed Cape Town and set course across the Indian Ocean.

The Young Gentlemen did rifle drill, cutlass drill and ropework, and played 'prisoner's base' around the upper deck in the dogwatches. They fished over the stern, somehow caught an albatross, and read improving works of literature (though presumably not *The Ancient Mariner*). Sometimes the little squadron furled its sails and did sessions of steam tactics; but Lord Clanwilliam's dislike of mechanical propulsion brought days of unrelieved boredom. On one occasion, when the sails were idly slatting and his lordship was below, Fitzgerald arranged for *Bacchante* to raise steam and take his own ship in tow. "The admiral noticed through the open port that we were slipping at some speed through the glassy water. He sent for the captain and then the murder was out."[35]

There was at least one crisis of real danger. On May the 12th, 1881, the squadron was scattered by a storm not far from Western Australia. *Bacchante*'s rudder was all but wrenched off and she broached to. Lord Charles Scott forced her bows back downwind by dint of

> ordering the whole of the watch-on-deck to climb into the weather fore rigging and spread themselves out from the top to the bottom of the shrouds, and the pressure of the wind on their bodies gradually forced the ship's head to leeward. This was an old-world method which had not been used for many years. A terrible disaster had been narrowly averted.[36]

Bacchante limped into Albany, to the immense relief of Clanwilliam who had searched for her and feared her lost.

In June 1881 John Scott was promoted to sub-lieutenant and made his way home from Melbourne. The role of senior midshipman, vacated twice, thus devolved onto Evan-Thomas, and he now became their royal highnesses' unrivalled companion on adventures ashore. In Australia they went riding, tried on Ned Kelly's armour, and were taken down a gold-mine; in Fiji they watched torchlit native dances; in China they went up the Wusung River in a houseboat for a week's shooting. In Japan they were visited by the Mikado ("the ugliest little man I have ever seen," in one sailor's opinion, "but a king every inch"[37]), and stayed with the British Consul,

> where we had a musical entertainment and went out one day with a mounted paperchase and another day with the hounds – and we went back to the ship having enjoyed ourselves about as much as it is possible to do.[38]

On the way home across the Indian Ocean, in the spring of 1882, *Bacchante* parted company with her consorts, went north through the Suez Canal and took the princes, by way of Crete, to visit their Danish Uncle William, the elected King (George I) of Greece, and Aunt Olga.

It was now Evan-Thomas's turn to become a sub-lieutenant (with a first class pass), and at Corfu orders arrived for him and another promotee to return home. On the 6th of June his gunroom messmates rowed them across to the Brindisi steamer, and waved their hats as she left harbour.[39]

For Evan-Thomas and the princes the *Bacchante* cruises had been an experience which few adolescents before or since have been able to match. For Dalton, they were the high adventure of his life. He had been treated as surrogate royalty at every port of call, and in later years his house in Windsor was

> cluttered with naval mementoes: model ships and sailing prints and pictures of ruddy-faced matelots. A sailor-servant on the *Bacchante* became his personal retainer in St George's Chapel for the next half-century. Time and again, in later life, Dalton would hark back to the *Bacchante* and its supposed pleasures.[40]

The middle-aged cleric acquired a more important legacy of the *Bacchante* experience. Evan-Thomas had shown him letters from his older sister 'Kitty', and these prompted him to request an introduction to the authoress. This was arranged on *Bacchante*'s return to Portsmouth in August, and within three days Dalton, undeterred at being twice her age, proposed to Catherine Alicia Evan-Thomas. It has recently been construed that he was transferring "a fancy" from Hugh to Kitty. It is, of course, possible that the repressed and high-minded parson idealized certain of life's values to the point of confusion, but the author of the allegation supplies no reason for it (other than that it suits his theme).[41] For Miss Evan-Thomas, he was not a bad catch, by Victorian criteria, one supposes. In due course he would become Chaplain-in-Ordinary and Deputy Clerk of the Closet to Queen Victoria and then to King Edward VII, Honorary Chaplain to Prince George when the latter was Duke of York and Prince of Wales, Canon of Windsor, and ultimately Sir John Dalton. But there was to be no wedding for a while, for the problem of Prince Albert Victor, now 18 years old, required his undivided attention.

Notwithstanding Dalton's best endeavours, and perhaps to some extent because of them, Eddy had remained "lethargic, dissipated, impervious to education and manifestly unsuited to the high position for which he was destined".[42] Outshone by his younger brother in everything practical or academic – no great feat on George's part – and consigned to the status of dunce by Queen Victoria, his father and his tutor, he remained a hopelessly low achiever. Only Motherdear, from whom he inherited partial deafness, appears to have made allowances and discerned in him artistic leanings ('artistic', in upper-class English families, is often a euphemism for autistic). And through the Danish Alexandra he also inherited a loathing of everything German. She had been alienated in her first year of marriage by the royal family's unconcealed support for Prussia in its war against her country in 1864,[43] and thereafter had had to live with the German accents and German culture prevalent in palace circles. Her delinquent son now refocused the resentment, amplified by his own hostilities, at Grandmama.

The time had come to split the boys up. Young George must be allowed to make his own way in the Navy. But what to do about Eddy? At length it was resolved that after another year of hard cramming from Dalton he should be sent to Cambridge, where the atmosphere of enquiry and the company of men of letters might stimulate him and broaden his mind (which it did, although not in the manner hoped).

Bacchante having decommissioned, her company dispersed. Sub-Lieutenant Evan-Thomas went to the Royal Naval College, Greenwich, where he remained for seven months on his lieutenant's courses, injured a leg playing football, and became friends with Lieutenant John Jellicoe. The photo of the two of them relaxing in a boat at Henley dates from these days. He then did his sub-lieutenant's (= introductory) gunnery course at *Excellent*, at the end of which Captain John Fisher wrote him an illegible testimonial.

It is impossible to know how actively Evan-Thomas's friendship with the princes was maintained in the years following the world cruise; the opportunities for meeting were only spasmodic and the initiative, by protocol, was not his to take. But there remained a direct link with Eddy and the Waleses through Dalton, his future brother-in-law; and the following letter from George, written from up the St Lawrence River in HMS *Canada* in September 1883, indicates that Hugh was still very much in royal orbit and, more specifically, that he had kept the 19-year-old Eddy company at Sandringham for a while in the summer of that year:

My Dear Old Thomas,

I was very sorry that you hurt your leg at the college. But hope it is alright now. I hope you spent a pleasant ten days with my brother at Sandringham. You must write and tell me what you have been doing with yourself since you went to college. Dalton came out here a week ago and is looking very well. He is going with us tomorrow to Niagara where I hope we shall spend a very pleasant week. He returns to England on the 29th. I suppose you will go and see him at Cambridge after his return. Dear Old Wemyss got his first in seamanship yesterday which I am very glad of . . . I think the last time I saw you was onboard the *Osborne* at Cowes. I shall be very glad to see you again in England in about June or July next, now goodbye. I remain . . . [44]

By the time Evan-Thomas received this, Eddy was ensconced in Trinity College, Cambridge, where Dalton was yielding his charge to the tutorship of his handsome and cultured room-mate James Stephen, a cousin of Virginia Woolf who had extensive avant-garde contacts in art and literature. "There is no doubt that of all those whom the Prince and Princess of Wales could have chosen as their eldest son's tutor, Jim Stephen was the worst possible choice."[45] The 'Eddy' problem, more or less under control until now, was about to go into a spin.

*

Evan-Thomas visited Eddy at Cambridge just before Christmas 1883 while on leave after finishing at *Excellent.* He had already met, at Sandringham in August, some of the "more-or-less epicene *literati*"[46] with whom Eddy was to associate in Cambridge; but the proper young naval officer was closely linked with Dalton, and Eddy would have kept on something approaching his best behaviour. Hugh's chief concerns at the time were his promotion to lieutenant and his next appointment, and he had the unusual advantage of having three princes helping him. Prince George wrote on the 4th of January from Sandringham:

> My Dear Old Thomas,
>   Let me write you a few lines to congratulate you very heartily on your pro-
> motion to Lt. I hope you will have every success. My father has been doing
> his best to get it for you for some time & it was not until two days ago that he
> got a letter from Lord Alcester [a Naval Lord] saying that you were pro-
> moted. Dalton is coming here tomorrow & I know he will be delighted to
> hear it . . . I shall never forget the nice time we had together on board the
> "Bacchante". I Remain, Your Old Messmate,
>
> > George[47]

A week later Eddy wrote:

> My Dear Old Voice,
>   . . . I was glad I was of some use to you in mentioning to Lord Alcester that
> you preferred going to the *Sultan.* If he had not mentioned your name I should
> have known nothing about it, except what you told me at Cambridge.[48]

Evan-Thomas apparently saw *Sultan* as no more than a short-term stepping-stone, for only a few weeks later John Dalton accosted the Queen's private secretary over his suitability for the royal yacht *Victoria and Albert.* His testimonial contains several factual distortions:

> He was senior naval cadet on board HMS *Britannia* when the two princes first
> went to Dartmouth in 1877; and on account of the admirable and sens-
> ible way in which he then discharged his duties as head boy there, he was

afterwards selected when the *Bacchante* was commissioned to go as senior midshipman of her gunroom.

For five years he was thus the older companion of the two princes and they are I think under a deep obligation to him for the influence he uniformly exerted by his manly character and thorough trustworthiness not only over them but also over all the other youngsters in the mess. He was always cheerful, smart at his duty & in every aspect a sterling example of all that a young naval officer should be.

He was one of the two officers who were taken prisoner by the Russians at Gallipoli during the late Turkish war when you may remember they in one of the *Swiftsure*'s boats were under fire . . . He happens to be the nephew of Admiral Lyons, who is now in command in the Pacific . . .[49]

The Prince of Wales wrote to assure Dalton that he considered young Evan-Thomas to have very good claims to a spell in the royal yacht, and pressed the First Naval Lord, Sir Astley Cooper Key, formally to submit the sub-lieutenant's name. He was subsequently very much annoyed to learn that Key had evidently let him down, and that the admiral's own son had won the coveted appointment.[50]

Sultan was a barque-rigged ram-bowed successor to *Warrior.* In the Russian war scare of 1885 she joined an assortment of misfits, known as the Special Service (or 'Evolutionary') Squadron, under the venerated Phipps Hornby, who interrupted his 'sunset' command of Portsmouth to return to sea. Evan-Thomas served in *Sultan* for thirty-one months, under three captains. The last, Richard King, commended him as "a thorough seaman and a most efficient officer in every way. Active and zealous." But then, in the summer of 1886, when he was expecting to be appointed flag-lieutenant to his cousin, Rear-Admiral Sir Algernon Lyons, on the North America and West Indies Station, he fell ill. The nature of the illness is not clear. But Captain King wrote to Lyons to say that he was "very sorry to hear about young Evan-Thomas. He was without exception the best lieutenant in *Sultan* . . . The doctors had a very extensive overhaul and swear there is no actual organic mischief yet."[51]

For six months he went on 'half-pay'.[52]

*

John Neale Dalton married Catherine Alicia Evan-Thomas on the 16th of January 1886. Even in his procreation, he was moved by an urge to honour the royal family: he wanted two sons, to be named after the princes. When Kitty produced a son, at the Evan-Thomas home in Glamorgan in August 1887, he was christened Edward Hugh (after his two godfathers) John Neale Dalton. The boy was known as Hugh, and

Queen Victoria – shrewd judge of character – disliked him at first sight. Hugh Dalton in turn took against his privileged, servile upbringing, "under the shadow" of Windsor Castle, took up with socialism at Cambridge and became Chancellor of the Exchequer in Clement Attlee's 1945 Labour Government.

In 1891, when John Dalton learned that his second child was a daughter, "he turned on his heels in disgust and left the room".[53] The hapless girl was named Alexandra Mary, after the Princess of Wales and Mary ('May') of Teck, but had to endure the nickname 'Georgie'.

*

Meanwhile, one of young Hugh Dalton's godfathers was kicking over the traces in no uncertain fashion. Much relating to Prince Albert Victor in the Royal Archives appears to have been embargoed or destroyed. In consequence it is open season for Eddy, even if historians are largely confined to the rough ground of rumour and theory. It seems beyond question, however, that James Stephen, Eddy's (probably homosexual) Cambridge tutor, found him a willing explorer of the permissive Bohemian world which now opened before him. The contrast to Dalton's constant harping on about obedience and duty, and his repressive "passion for tidyness and order",[54] could hardly have been more refreshing. Eddy discovered a taste for "every form of dissipation and amusement",[55] and before long he was rumoured to be sexually indiscriminate. He is even alleged to have conceived a child with a Catholic shop-girl and artist's model named Annie Crook, and to have married her in a clandestine ceremony[56] – an unthinkable procedure for the future defender of the Protestant faith. It is said that he began to be shadowed by Inspector Frederick Abberline of the Metropolitan Police: an 'unofficial bodyguard', he was told.[57]

An attempt was made in 1885 to reclaim him by initiating him ("in the most impressive manner"[58]) into the Royal Alpha Lodge and by gazetting him into the 10th Hussars, a society regiment in which his dissipations would be less conspicuous.[59] General Lord Wolseley tried to be positive. "Some of our very best & ablest men have mentally matured with extreme slowness," he ruminated vaguely. But the prince could muster little interest in this pretend military life (which must have seemed alien to a youth trained as a sailor); Bohemia continued to pull, and before long the Prince of Wales accepted that the Army was "simply a waste of time".[60]

Inevitably the subject of marriage reared its head. A suitable wife, it was to be hoped, would both steady young Eddy and ensure the succession. Annie Crook – if she existed – disappeared (according to some, into a mental hospital); and the serial killings in Whitechapel in 1888 have been sensationally, and not very plausibly, linked with efforts to conceal the alleged union. Eddy now suffered a bout of false starts in his matrimonial endeavours, and sought consolation by implicating himself in the Cleveland Street 'telegraph boys' scandal of 1889. He was sent on a heavily supervised six-month trip to India.

These were difficult times for the monarchy. The 1880s had seen a resurgence of republicanism; and there had been socialist riots in Trafalgar Square. The Prince of Wales himself did not help by getting involved in two scandals, the 'baccarat' and 'Lady Brooke' affairs, over, respectively, cheating at cards and adultery; but clearly his son and heir was presenting the Crown with a hideous problem. When he returned in 1890, Eddy was created Duke of Clarence and Avondale, and took up more or less where he had left off. He frequented the transvestite Hundred Guineas Club, where he disported in drag under the pseudonym of 'Victoria'; and there was open speculation in Court circles about his forthcoming certification. In November 1891 he is said to have tried, with some measure of success, to burn down Sandringham.

A month later the world learnt of his betrothal to Princess May of Teck (who, despite her name, was a niece of the Duke of Cambridge and as English as royalty got in those days). It was not his idea. It had been mooted by his father's private secretary, Sir Francis Knollys, and initially the scheme had looked pretty thin. Sir Henry Ponsonby, the Queen's private secretary, wrote glumly: "I am told he don't care for Princess May of Teck and she appears to be too proud to take the trouble of running after him, for which I rather admire her."[61] The marriage was not to be.

In the early hours of January the 14th, 1892, six weeks after his engagement, the Duke of Clarence died. His father, the Prince of Wales, reported to the Queen that "a sharp attack of influenza had developed into pneumonia of his left lung", and Victoria brooded blackly about how his death had occurred on the anniversary of Prince Albert's, which came round on the 14th of every month. Eddy's death, no less than his life, has attracted speculation.

According to a theory based on a doctor's prescription, he had incurable gonorrhoea contracted over ten years earlier in the West Indies during the *Bacchante* cruise.[62] This is unlikely, in view of his social backwardness in 1880 and John Dalton's manic supervision. Another theory has him murdered by poisoning. A third has his death faked so he could be shunted aside in favour of his brother, and compelled to live in seclusion until his real death forty-one years later.[63] (The inference that his mother, brother and fiancée, among many others,[64] collaborated to invent a long and distressing death scene is obnoxious.) When all is said and done, maybe dying was Eddy's way of registering dissent.

On Wednesday, the 20th of January, Prince Albert Victor's coffin, draped with the Union Flag and topped with his busby and sword, was borne to the Memorial Chapel at Windsor by officers of the 10th Hussars (from whom he had never formally resigned). The royal houses of Europe were represented. Never had he had so much attention or been so eulogized. (Two weeks later James Stephen died from self-starvation in a Northampton lunatic asylum.)

Prince George, on whose worthy if reluctant shoulders now fell the mantle of direct succession to the throne (as it would on his own second son's), was distraught and disorientated. A new life of training for kingship lay before him, and his naval career would have to end – though not quite yet. As a first step, he was sent to the South of France to regain his bearings away from the damp gloom of the Norfolk winter. As a second step, he was made Duke of York in the Queen's Birthday Honours List on May the 24th. For the third step the Prince of Wales looked to the Navy.

George had recently been promoted commander at the early age of 26. Harold Nicolson's assertion that he was not favoured with acceler-ated promotion[65] is mistaken. An officer was usually eligible for his commander's 'brass hat' after twelve years as a lieutenant, including four years wearing the $2\frac{1}{2}$ rings of a lieutenant of more than eight years' seniority (the American title of lieutenant-commander was not formally adopted until 1914). A random check of fifteen new commanders in 1891 and '92 finds that their average lieutenancy was fourteen years and none was less than twelve. Prince George, on the other hand, got his brass hat after less than six (a feat which even Beatty couldn't quite match), and skipped his half-ring altogether. The next youngest new commander in 1891 was John Jellicoe, who was 32. The prince (or Duke of York, as he was now normally called) had previously commanded a gunboat, HMS *Thrush*, and before that, a tiny torpedo-boat; and he now believed he would be given command of the royal yacht *Osborne*,[66] which was due shortly to emerge from a major refit. It was in the light of this expectation that in March '92 he arranged for *Osborne*'s first-lieutenancy to be offered to Hugh Evan-Thomas: as he said to Dalton, "I don't know of any man who would suit better & then he knows all of us."[67]

*

Five years previously, at the age of 24 and after his six months' sick leave, Evan-Thomas had belatedly taken up his appointment as flag-lieutenant to Sir Algernon Lyons, Commander-in-Chief North America & West Indies, in *Bellerophon* under Captain Bouverie Clark.

> I am sorry to hear that poor old Thomas is not well yet [George had told Dalton], but spending the winter at Bermuda will no doubt do him a lot of good; it will be very nice being flag-lieutenant too, as he won't have so much night work & he will live on shore.[68]

The fully rigged '*Old Billy*' was one of the Navy's smartest and best-loved flagships, and while Evan-Thomas's flimsies from sea make it impossible to assert that this plum appointment was unmerited, there is a definite sense of its having been kept open for him. It has already been mentioned that Sir Algernon was a close relation; to this it may be added that Lady Lyons's family lived near Hugh's birthplace in Glamorgan. But if the job was won through 'interest' – the naval Taffia, one might call it – little surprise would have been evinced at the time and nor should it be in retrospect; that was the way the Navy worked: "the main qualification for appointment as flag-lieutenant was that of being a relation either of the Admiral or some friend of his."[69] Hugh Evan-Thomas served his kinsman as 'flags' in *Bellerophon* for nine months, in Lyons's formal assessment "with sobriety and in every respect to my satisfaction. He is a very zealous and intelligent officer, keenly interested in his profession."

There now appears another health-related gap in his records, this time of ten months. At the end of it, in August 1888 (while the famous Baird–Tryon Manoeuvres were going on) he was sent to the boys' sail-training ship *St Vincent*, whose captain he impressed with his "great zeal and attention". While he was on leave from *St Vincent*, in December '88, he canvassed for his father (Conservative) in the Glamorgan County Council elections. He went into a pub in Neath, stood unwittingly under the mistletoe and was grappled by a buxom lass in full festive spirit: "the delight of the spectators was unbounded."[70] In the spring of 1889 he went successively to *Excellent* (under Captain Compton Domvile) and *Vernon* (Arthur Wilson) for short courses in gunnery and torpedoes. Prince George was a fellow course member, and in Portsmouth they held a *Bacchante* reunion dinner, to which Dalton was summoned. "I don't know if Eddy will be able to come," George regretted, "– I am rather afraid not, his time is so fully occupied."[71]

For the 1889 Manoeuvres Evan-Thomas was appointed to the newly completed *Camperdown* under his old friend Richard King, and in December he returned to her when she was sent out to the Mediterranean to act as temporary flagship to Vice-Admiral Sir Anthony Hiley Hoskins ('Sir Hanthony Sir Iley Sir Oskins', to the lower-deck). She was standing in for *Victoria*, whose completion had been delayed by her troublesome $16\frac{1}{4}$-inch guns. When the laggard arrived in Malta in May 1890, the two battleships swapped crews, and *Camperdown* returned home to be flagship of the Channel Fleet until she was ousted by *Royal Sovereign* two years later.

Evan-Thomas was an ordinary watch-keeper in *Camperdown–Victoria*, but he gained the trust and interest of Hoskins, who "had a reputation, quite wrongly, of being unsympathetic and inhuman".[72] Mark Kerr, the flag-lieutenant, testifies to the admiral's surreptitious kindnesses: the lending of books on history and biography; and the leaving of the bridge during steam-tactics pleading paperwork, thus allowing 'flags' to finish manoeuvring the fleet on his own. Sir Anthony's confidence in Evan-Thomas was such that, after *Victoria* ran aground in February '91 in the Gulf of Corinth, he sent him to Patras to arrange contracts with civilian lighterage and salvage firms, and to be at the end of the telegraph from the Admiralty.[73]

During these months E-T kept in touch with Prince George, both directly and through his brother-in-law. In August '91 he congratulated him on his promotion to commander, and in his reply George referred to the arrival in *Victoria* of Captain Maurice Bourke, who had commanded *Surprise*, the C-in-C's yacht, during Uncle Alfred's tenure of the Mediterranean:

> Very many thanks for your kind letter of congratulations for my promotion . . . I am pleased your ship is so comfortable & you are all so happy. Now you have got Bourke as your captain you ought to be still more comfortable, he is hard to beat!
>
> I certainly agree with you that you ought to have my sister's [presumably Princess Victoria's] photograph in your mess as you have all the others . . . Dalton has asked me to be godfather to his little girl, I saw him in London the other day . . .[74]

By the time this letter arrived, *Victoria* also had a new admiral in the formidable shape of Vice-Admiral Sir George Tryon. A month later, in England, Prince Eddy got engaged to May; not long after that he was dead.

HMS *Victoria* was at Malta on January the 14th when the Admiralty telegram arrived at 1.00 p.m. announcing the death of the Duke of Clarence. It befell Evan-Thomas, as the officer of the afternoon watch,[75] to give effect to its directions that "COLOURS ARE TO BE HOISTED HALF MAST UNTIL FUNERAL WHICH DATE WILL BE FURTHER COMMUNICATED. FLAGSHIPS HOIST ROYAL STANDARD HALF MAST. COMMUNICATE FOREIGN WARSHIPS PRESENT."[76] What was he thinking and feeling as he did so? No one else in the fleet can have been affected so personally.[77]

He had looked after Eddy in *Britannia* and *Bacchante*; together they had kept long night watches, weathered hurricanes in the South Seas, and met the Emperor of Japan; they had kept each other company at Sandringham, perhaps more than once, and in Cambridge. Even if their active friendship had petered out in recent years, no other 'outsider' had shared as much of Eddy's protracted adolescence, and Hugh must have known that all had been far from well with his engaging, if incorrigibly louche, royal chum. He will certainly have known at least as much as his sister, Mrs Dalton, which was presumably a great deal. His sorrow and confusion will scarcely have abated six days later when, to mark Eddy's interment, all ships fired 30 minute-gun salutes in stately succession and reverse order of seniority – a procedure which wreathed Grand Harbour in drifting smoke all afternoon. He probably felt, in an unpretentious way, a desire to be of use to the bereaved; to offer support to Prince George and to rally round his brother-in-law. To be there. A few weeks later he was called home to the royal yacht *Osborne*.

*

So, just as the needs of royalty had removed Hugh Evan-Thomas from Captain Tryon's Mediterranean battleship in 1879, they now extracted him from Vice-Admiral Tryon's Mediterranean flagship in 1892. Had the normal cycle of appointments left him in *Victoria* he would probably have fallen under Sir George's spell, as did all (except the least able or most conservative) eventually. His mind would have been stimulated and sharpened, and he might have been drowned.

The Duke of York's plan to join him in *Osborne* went awry. The royal yacht would hardly have stretched the prince as a commanding officer, and might have given rise to role-confusion. But more importantly, the ship was not nearly ready for sea, and even as Evan-Thomas arrived home, George had pangs of guilt that he had called for him on false pretences. He confessed to Dalton from the South of France:

> [Captain Bourke] speaks in the very highest terms of Thomas & regrets extremely he having left them. And now we have just heard that the *Osborne* cannot be ready until the end of August owing to the boilers not being delivered in time and therefore poor Thomas will have nothing to do all this time which is most unfortunate, but when we come home we will see if something can't be arranged for him. Better not say anything about it to him yet.[78]

George was angling for a bigger fish to fry, and at the beginning of June the First Naval Lord, Sir Anthony Hoskins, interviewed

Evan-Thomas, whom, of course, he knew well from the Mediterranean, about his role.[79] George, meanwhile, revealed all to Dalton:

> I have a secret to tell you, and a proposition to make to you. I hope you will keep the first and accept the second. The secret is that I am going to have command of a ship for the Manoeuvres, called the *Melampus*. Old Thomas is going to be my first lieutenant, Anson navigator, Cust and Godfrey-Faussett the other 2 lieuts, & Dyer paymaster. The proposition is that I want you to come with me as my guest. You always promised you would come one day & perhaps this will be the last ship I will ever serve in, & she is over 2,000 tons & goes 18 knots & is a very fine ship for a commander.[80]

This last remark was no exaggeration. *Melampus* was a major warship with a complement of 270 and should have been a captain's command, whereas George should still have been a lieutenant(-commander). Naturally he sought the support of officers he knew and trusted. On the 25th of June, the *Globe* reported that "The Duke of York is gathering several of his old shipmates around him in *Melampus*." The choice of Evan-Thomas (who assumed the rightful duties of a commander) as first-lieutenant attracted special comment:

> Although the Duke of York is a very young commander, and has been appointed to the command of a large cruiser, the Admiralty can scarcely be said to have pandered HRH with a 'nursing' first-lieutenant. In the old days, grey-haired lieutenants were usually put under young captains promoted by interest. Mr Evan-Thomas, who has been selected as senior lieutenant of the *Melampus*, is less than two years older than the Duke of York [$2\frac{1}{2}$ years, actually] and previously served with him in the *Britannia* and *Bacchante*, and the remainder of the executive officers are, of course, still younger.[81]

Like Hugh Evan-Thomas, *Melampus's* other seaman lieutenants were ex-shipmates of Prince George. As the *Globe* observed, "The young duke does not forget old friends, and this is one of the many pleasing traits in his character."[82] The wardroom was a hatchery of courtiers.

Charles Anson had served in the C-in-C Mediterranean's yacht, HMS *Surprise*, when Prince Alfred (the Duke of Edinburgh) was C-in-C and George himself was serving in the flagship, *Alexandra*. Sir Charles Cust and Bryan Godfrey-Faussett had been messmates of the two princes (and of Evan-Thomas) in *Britannia* and again of George in *Alexandra*; and Cust had served in *Osborne* before her refit.

In appointing Godfrey-Faussett ('Gusset'), George was fulfilling a pledge. They had met in Halifax, Nova Scotia, in 1890. The prince had adopted Bryan as his ADC during visits to Quebec and Montreal, and several times said that when he got his next ship he would take Ernest Troubridge (evidently supplanted by Evan-Thomas) as first-lieutenant and Bryan as a watch-keeper. Godfrey-Faussett had set some store by this promise, for it would "give me a chance of getting ahead in the service"; and news of Prince Eddy's death was thus an especially "dreadful calamity . . . Prince George being now in the direct line of succession to the throne will never go to sea again I suppose, so I shall not go with him in his next ship as per arrangement." Now he was looking forward to spending the summer ashore, when a telegram arrived as he was shaving on the 25th of June, appointing him to *Melampus*: "I have no idea what sort of ship [she] is, except that she is brand new," he told his diary, "– or who my shipmates are likely to be." Later, he bought a paper at Oxford railway station, and "saw to my huge joy that the *Melampus* is to be commanded by Prince George, Duke of York. What good fortune. I am glad. So that explains his vague message to me the other day about meeting again soon!"[83]

A fifth lieutenant, Arthur Leveson, joined the team. Assistant Paymaster Harry Dyer had served with George in *Thrush* (as had the chief-engineer), and was now on loan from Uncle Alfred, Duke of Edinburgh and currently C-in-C Plymouth.

Melampus was commissioned at the end of June 1892. "Evan-Thomas has done wonderfully well, getting the ship into such perfect order in such a short time," Godfrey-Faussett wrote on July the 2nd. The Prince of Wales (an honorary admiral of the fleet) came and drank champagne to her success. They did their full speed trial – 19 knots – on the 4th, and went to the west of Ireland for a few days' shakedown. In the event the Manoeuvres were a miserable, "unhappy episode".[84] The weather was dismal,

> and as usual [George] was extremely sea sick; night after night he had to remain on deck and for six days he never took off his clothes. 'The flagship', he wrote in his diary for July 27, 'made any number of mistakes . . . I hope I shall never be in any other manoeuvres . . . Hate the whole thing.'[85]

There were the usual small incidental seamanlike rewards ("All the ships are keeping station beautifully . . . a very fine sight"[86]); and there was the odd day snatched at anchor to clean ship, dry clothing and sleep. On a couple of evenings the captain was able to lose himself in his stamp collection while his officers played poker and bashed the keys of the wardroom piano; but day after day of rough seas took their toll and it became little more than a trial of endurance. On August the 10th, "I am overtired, feel quite done-up"; and on the 18th, "Thomas has worked very hard."[87]

The Manoeuvres were followed by Cowes Week and then by a final inspection of the ship by Admiral Lord Clanwilliam, C-in-C

Portsmouth, and the Prince of Wales. *Melampus* cleared this daunting hurdle with ease, and George, who had lost no time in moving ashore – almost certainly to stay at Government House with his uncle Arthur, Duke of Connaught, Army C-in-C Southern Command – wrote a note to thank his XO:

> Both my father & the Admiral were extremely pleased with the ship & every-thing they saw onboard. As for myself, I am delighted & I must say you and the men must have worked devilish hard to get her to look what she does . . . Give the usual leave today till tomorrow morning. Look after Mr Dalton and bring him to dinner tonight. Probably I shall not come on board tomorrow forenoon, not unless you want me.[88]

Two months later George returned from a trip to Heidelberg to receive the Admiralty's formal report on the inspection. He hastened to thank his old shipmate again and enclosed a copy:[89]

> 1. . . . . [the ship] was throughout very clean . . . in a highly creditable condition, and officers and men appeared to have taken much pride in the ship.
> 2. My Lords desire that a similar expression of their approval may be com-municated to Lieutenant H. Evan-Thomas, your late senior executive-officer in *Melampus*.

By this time *Melampus*'s company had gone their separate ways. Her seaman officers' links with George lasted for life. Arthur Leveson would become First and Principal ADC to King George in 1927. Charles Anson (of whom the Queen's Press Secretary, at time of writing, is a namesake and distant relation) would command *Osborne* in 1901–4. And Charlie Cust accepted the prince's invitation to become his equerry; "I wish I was in his shoes," Bryan G-F told his diary.

Godfrey-Faussett himself went out to the Pacific to be flag-lieu-tenant to Rear-Admiral Henry Stephenson (equerry to the Prince of Wales, 1878–93). He "undoubtedly owed the appointment to the good offices of Prince George",[90] whose additional equerry he became in 1901 and remained for thirty-five years. Suitably for a courtier, he married Eugénie Dudley Ward whose uncle, the 2nd Viscount Esher, was a member of Queen Victoria's private circle. Bryan later took pains to smooth the acceptance at Court of Captain David Beatty and his divorcée wife[91] – to be repaid with Beatty's affair with Eugénie. The Godfrey-Faussetts' son David, as a matter of interest, was the Swordfish pilot credited with spiking *Bismarck*'s rudders in 1941.

Evan-Thomas resumed his duties on board *Osborne*, under the command of Captain Archibald Berkeley Milne ('Arky-Barky' or 'The Great Arch Bark'), an urbane and handsome dandy with a distinctly carnivorous charm. *Osborne* was rightfully a commander's command.

Jacky Fisher's amiable Bird's Eye look-alike brother, Commander F. W. Fisher (already known as 'Uncle Bill' for his impressive train of nieces, some of them genuine), had been offered her in late 1891, but preferred not to have his sea career tainted by suspicion of royal interest.[92] Hence Captain Milne in command of *Osborne* in 1892. He by no means shared Bill Fisher's reservations about royal yachts: rather he made of them a deliberate career specialization which would launch him into flag-rank through the post of Rear-Admiral Commanding. His meagre subsequent sea service as a flag-officer would be interrupted by Ruritanian posts such as groom-in-waiting to King Edward VII or extra-equerry to King George V, and his career progress was thought, through absence of other plausible explanation, to be "largely due to Court influence".[93]

The son of an admiral of the fleet, Arky-Barky was a society swell and lifelong bachelor whose hobbies were collecting rare orchids and cultivating royal ladies.[94] He had distinguished himself as ADC to Lord Chelmsford in the Zulu War of 1879 and had the good fortune to be with the general ten miles away from the main camp at Isandhlwana on the calamitous 22nd of January – indeed his telescope was brought to bear from the top of a tree to try to ascertain what was going on. As a naval officer, he modelled himself on Pompo Heneage,[95] and assumed "an air of effortless superiority that was to prove ill-founded".[96] Royal yachts were the innermost temple of formality, ceremonial and cleanliness; nowhere in the Navy afloat was further from the mentality and practices of war, and in these sterilized conditions, Milne thrived. Once, when he "suffered the ignominy of having his sleeve brushed by a passing seaman, he took out his handkerchief, flicked the pollution from his sleeve, and threw the contaminated fabric over the side".[97] He expected his officers to be thorough gentlemen, to be clean and well-dressed and to have good manners – criteria which (in one historian's ingenuous view) symptomize his confusion "of service priorities".[98]

For the rest of 1892 *Osborne* remained exactly where Evan-Thomas had found her, with her boilers in pieces; and her main function – from the terse evidence of her log – seems to have been to send daily working parties over to *Victoria and Albert*. Her XO had spare time on his hands; and his game-book reveals that over the next three months he killed a variety of wildlife in Glamorgan, Brecon and Hampshire.[99] No doubt he paid visits to the Daltons (and perhaps others) at Windsor, and he certainly spent some time seeing a Miss Hilda Barnard, the pretty, if rather solemn, daughter of a Bedfordshire banker.

By the end of the year *Osborne*'s new boilers were installed, and a change of tempo took place. There was much painting and cleaning, and loading of stores, and the working parties were needed on board, George wrote from Sandringham at the beginning of January:

> My Dear Thomas,
>   I am delighted to hear that the old *Osborne* is ready for sea, they have certainly been a long time over her. Dalton is coming here this evening, I shall be glad to see him again, we will talk over the *Melampus* days. How I should have enjoyed them if only we had not been on those beastly manoeuvres . . . [100]

Something was about to happen. And, sure enough, on the 9th of February 1893 *Osborne* sailed from Portsmouth, turning her bowsprit west to Plymouth and then south towards Spain. At Gibraltar they unshipped her rudder, looked at it, and put it back. She sailed on at 12 knots to Genoa, and there, on the 5th of March, embarked Prince George, his mother Alexandra (Princess of Wales), and his unmarried sisters the Princesses Victoria and Maud, plus attendants of the Royal Household.

With this stately company aboard, the little steamer paddled her leisurely way to Spezia, Leghorn, Elba, Naples, Salerno, Messina, Catania, Corfu and Corinth, and then round Cape Matapan to Piraeus (they were four months too early for the Corinth Canal). On most days, their royal highnesses went ashore sightseeing; occasionally they were 'at home' to august kinsmen such as the King of Greece, or the Duke and Duchess of Sparta, whose children rampaged screaming about the yacht.

The family atmosphere of a small ship, the excited talk of the day's adventures, the sparkling blue sea, dazzling white awnings, cool evening breezes, immaculate uniforms – the elegance, the privilege – all spring easily to mind. How one may envy Hugh Evan-Thomas his part in such a heady experience, in the self-assured high noon of Empire and the evening of European royal houses. "There have been a good number of picnics and excursions to which most of us have always been asked," he told his father from Athens.[101] Notwithstanding the fact that the two young princesses appear to have shared some of their late brother's social shortcomings[102] (and had been nicknamed 'The Hags' by Palace staff), the 30-year-old executive-officer's position could have been mishandled by a less unassuming and level-headed man, for although he was present by virtue of his friendship with the Duke of York and was so nearly a member of the family circle, he was there to serve and to work. And he must have worked hard throughout this odyssey with the exquisite Berkeley Milne and his carefully tended herbaceous border of royalty.

He bore the direct responsibility, day in day out, for every aspect of the ship's management and efficiency. Not for one moment could he relax his attention to detail in matters of safety, smartness, routines, the conduct of personnel, the planning of supply and replenishment, or his own ever-tactful response to any whim of the "pathologically unpunctual" Princess of Wales[103] and her gormless daughters. A fluffed ceremonial salute, a splash of paint on the deck, a badly cheesed rope, a sailor clumsy in his boatwork or incorrectly dressed or the worse for cheap retsina, an irritable comment overheard, a problem with the hot water supply – a hundred little dramas would reflect on his diligence and test his temper. And the several members of the Household borne to attend to intimate domestic matters may not always have seemed a net asset, with their own demands and their own prickly hierarchy. In addition to all that, the small officer-complement of *Osborne* did not permit his exemption from sea watches, and when the ship was on passage his initials often appear beside the morning watch and one of the evening dog watches – indeed the sanctuary of the bridge may have seemed a welcome refuge.[104]

Prince George was a man preoccupied. "It had now become vital" for him to beget heirs.[105] Queen Victoria, his father had warned him, was "in a terrible fuss about his marrying" and it was her "most cherished desire that he should become engaged to Princess May of Teck".[106] He knew this already: at the end of the *Melampus* manoeuvres he had dropped in on Osborne House and the Queen had bent his ear about the blessings of matrimony and had made her agenda clear. The union, indeed, was widely predicted – although some, like the grand old Duke of Cambridge who had perversely married for love, found the idea repugnant. The family reminded themselves of the fortuitous precedent of George's aunt Dagmar and the Russian throne (mention of Henry VIII and Catherine of Aragon was less welcome).

"Nervous and bewildered",[107] George increasingly felt himself destined for his brother's intended wife, as well as his crown; and now, spurred by his beloved Aunt Olga, Queen of Greece, he left *Osborne* at Piraeus and returned home alone to England. He was on a mission of duty, but one which presaged over forty years of exemplary marriage.

To Evan-Thomas's relief (for Athens was "getting hot and smelly"), *Osborne* left Piraeus at the end of April, and headed south and west to Malta, where she arrived on the 4th of May, to be greeted by news of the Duke of York's engagement to May of Teck. On the morning of the 5th, the Governor of Malta and the Commander-in-Chief Mediterranean paid official visits to the Princess of Wales on board the yacht, and they no doubt conveyed to the mother of the groom-to-be the felicitations of all under their respective commands. Later, Sir George Tryon escorted Alexandra and her daughters on a tour of the island.[108] Privately, he may have regarded their visitation as a mixed blessing.

He had already had a heavy burden of formal duties that spring: he had attended Queen Victoria during her visit to Florence; he had entertained Prince and Princess Ferdinand of Bulgaria; and he had hosted the First Lord of the Admiralty, Earl Spencer, on an inspection of fleet and dockyard.[109] He was also busy planning the fleet's summer cruise programme, and was, as always, prolific with ideas and schemes of naval defence. Colonel Sir George Sydenham Clarke, recently secretary to a Cabinet committee on colonial defence, was a frequent guest of Tryon's at Admiralty House in early 1893, and

> on many nights he used to give me lessons on naval matters. With a large unlighted cigar in his mouth, he would address me impressively to a late hour, generally ending by saying 'Next time you must do the talking!' That time never came.
>
> ...Among the many distinguished naval officers I have known, I rate none more highly than Sir G. Tryon. He had a powerful intellect, a wide grasp of affairs, and imagination of the right kind.[110]

Manoeuvring without signals remained high on his agenda. The experimental stage was past. This year he expected his officers to cope easily with TA, and he was still evangelizing. In March, for example, he had written to a fellow admiral:

> When manoeuvring on an opponent, and having got into a good position, you can only maintain it by taking your orders as it were from him, and by turning as he turns. There is no time for a signal, or you lose your position. If signal masts and yards are shot away, or signal halyards gone, you can still manoeuvre a fleet. Those without some such system cannot.
>
> The system does not pretend to secure barrack-yard precision: that is not possible in action, and not even necessary, but it is surprising how nearly it is attained. I am convinced it will be impossible to work the signal-books in action, but it may be possible to work single flags, and the fewer the better.[111]

And on the 6th of May – even while *Osborne* and the royal party were in Malta – he addressed a new memo on the subject to Whitehall:

> Having received from the Lords Commissioners of the Admiralty reports from many officers on the TA system of manoeuvring a fleet, and while a very general opinion has been expressed that it is a step in advance and in the right direction, some suggestions and observations of undoubted weight have been made with a view to improve the method adopted . . .

He appealed for constructive suggestions but urged that the system's simplicity must not be corrupted by the accretion of piecemeal additions. Ease of operation was crucial: "Signals should be so few and simple that it would rarely be necessary to refer to a book . . . If the wording of the instructions are not clear they should be made clear, if there is any difficulty it must be removed." The memo was copied at the Admiralty and sent out to flag-officers on the 10th of June.[112]

Sir George was also plotting a renewed assault on the *Signal Book*, and, in the month of *Osborne*'s visit, circulated a memorandum to his captains calling for their criticisms and recommendations. One reply which has survived (at least in draft form) is that of Gerard Noel, in whose predictable opinion the *Book* was clogged with hundreds of unnecessary words and required "very extensive and careful revision or reconstruction".[113]

Evan-Thomas will certainly have taken the chance to drop in on his old friends in *Victoria*, which had just recommissioned after a short refit. He was no doubt surprised and pleased to find that Arthur Leveson, his *Melampus* shipmate, was now the flagship's gunnery-officer, and that John Jellicoe, his friend of ten years' standing, was now her XO. The position of 'the commander' in *Victoria* had fallen vacant at the end of the old commission, and Tryon and Captain Bourke had invited Jellicoe to transfer from Arthur Wilson's *Sans Pareil*. This was a great compliment to so junior a commander, and it could not imaginably have been refused; but Wilson (not Tryon's most committed disciple at the best of times) took the poaching of his young friend badly, railed against admirals who behaved like that, and swore never to do so himself.[114] Some of *Victoria*'s people, Evan-Thomas would never see again.

Osborne quit Malta on May the 7th, and proceeded up the Adriatic to Venice, whence the royal party made its way home by railway. Evan-Thomas's pride in a difficult job well done must have been mixed with considerable, if well-concealed, relief as he saluted the three princesses ashore for the last time. Thus unburdened and a 'private ship' once more, *Osborne* made her own way home. When the wind was on the quarter, after turning Cape St Vincent, they hoisted the foresail to gain half a knot, and secured to South Railway Jetty on the 3rd of June. Evan-Thomas had not disappointed Captain Milne. He had been "a zealous and hardworking officer and in every way to my satisfaction", and needless to say he had conducted himself with sobriety.

After de-storing ship, Evan-Thomas went up to London on leave and checked into the Naval and Military Club in Piccadilly. This served him as a base: probably to visit the Daltons in Windsor; presumably to make up for lost time in respect of Miss Barnard; and perhaps to be at hand for the Duke of York in the days before his wedding, which was set for July the 6th. He had not been at the 'In and Out' for long when suddenly, around noon on June the 23rd, a shocking message was splashed across newsvendors' placards all over central London: "*HMS VICTORIA SUNK. COLLISION WITH IRONCLAD.*"[115] The known facts, received by the Admiralty at midnight via the Foreign Office and the British Consul in Tripoli, were "meagre but appalling": following a collision, the Mediterranean Fleet flagship had foundered with the loss of Vice-Admiral Sir George Tryon, twenty-one other named officers and an unspecified number of men.

> In the three Service clubs, according to *The Times*, 'the disaster cast a heavy gloom, and the anxious, sorrowful features of the naval men as they commented on the all-absorbing topic afforded striking testimony of the anguish of soul amongst them.[116]

No one can have been more anguished than Hugh Evan-Thomas, who had lost many recent shipmates. He can have had no inkling of how profoundly, and how soon, his career would be changed by the disaster.

12

Nemesis

"Now we are going to see something interesting!"

Vice-Admiral Sir George Tryon and most of the Mediterranean Fleet left Valletta on the 27th of May 1893, for the summer Manoeuvres. Before departing, John Jellicoe,the flagship's new XO, did two things which can be stated with certainty. He bought out of his own pocket a stock of paint for HMS *Victoria*; and he drank some goat's milk (probably in his tea or coffee[1]), for that was later identified as the cause of the 'Malta fever' which had long been endemic in the fleet and with which he soon became ill.

The fleet proceeded by way of Nauplia (where it stayed for three days), Marmaris (eight days), and Acre (two days), to Beirut (four days).[2] It was joined *en route* by a detached squadron which had been cruising the Levant and practising TA under the direction of Captain Gerard Noel,[3] and, somewhat later than scheduled, by Rear-Admiral Albert Markham, who had been detained in Greece by real or psychosomatic indisposition. Owing to *Trafalgar*'s being in refit, he was flying his flag in *Camperdown*, and he now took his rightful place at the head of the 2nd Division.

We have already come across *Camperdown*'s captain, Charles Johnstone. Biographically, he remains difficult to pigeon-hole. He was an outspoken critic of the complexity of the draft (1889) *Signal Book*, yet one of the flat-earthers of the masts and sails debate. He had made his reputation in command of the sloop *Dryad* in 1883 during an international crisis in Madagascar, in which he behaved with both tenacity and restraint in the face of outrageous provocation from a French admiral (who died soon after "in circumstances which pointed to insanity").[4] But he was by no means universally admired: there were those – as we shall see – who rated him an "ass", and a "blunderer". And with Markham (a fellow "chucklehead") he was to play a key role in the tragedy now about to take place.

On the evening of the 21st of June, with the full fleet of eleven iron-clads (eight battleships and three large cruisers) lying at anchor off Beirut, the commander-in-chief gave one of his many dinner parties. Tryon had a 'thing' about the carrying of passengers, and had recently issued a memorandum forbidding it.[5] He attributed to the presence of passengers a number of recent accidents to HM ships, and, while his reasoning was evidently pragmatic, it is not difficult to read an element of superstition in the force with which he stated it. However, he had allowed an exception – no doubt with pleasure – for the 79-year-old Admiral Sir George Wellesley, who was taking passage in *Edinburgh* as a guest of Captain John Brackenbury (his flag-lieutenant in the Channel Fleet of the early seventies); and over dinner, in the affable company of present and past comrades, Tryon confessed to "how proud and happy he felt in commanding such a fleet of efficient vessels".[6]

The next morning they weighed and proceeded northwards up the Lebanese coast towards their next stop at Tripoli. On that hot windless midsummer day Commander Jellicoe was confined to his bunk with a high temperature and dosed with quinine. As the first-lieutenant, Edward Inglefield (inventor of the Inglefield clip), had been left behind in hospital in Malta, Jellicoe's duties were taken over by the torpedo officer, Lieutenant Herbert Heath, and the first-lieutenant's by the gunnery-officer, Arthur Leveson. No one, either at the enquiry or since, has suggested that the absence from duty of two of the flagship's most experienced seaman officers may have contributed to the ensuing disaster: *Victoria* was a taut ship.

By early afternoon the fleet was steaming at 8 knots in two columns, the 1st Division to starboard and the 2nd to port, 6 cables (1,200 yards) apart. They had turned the corner at the south-western end of the bay, onto a course of east by north, and had passed their prospective anchorage. Before turning into the bay on their final approach they would have to double back, presumably maintaining their compass bearings from each other if the customary anchorage formation – with the flagship's division closest inshore – was to be attained. They would also have to close the distance between them from 6 cables to the standard anchoring separation of two. Whatever plan Tryon had thought up to bring about the intended result, he kept it, as usual, to himself; but, beyond reasonable doubt, he had in mind the procedure shown here, which required an initial separation of 10 cables (= one nautical mile). By wheeling the divisions 180° at 'A' he would bring the fleet into anchoring formation, and by turning all ships *together* 90° at 'B' (as his head-mark came onto the desired bearing) he would place it neatly on its final approach course.[7]

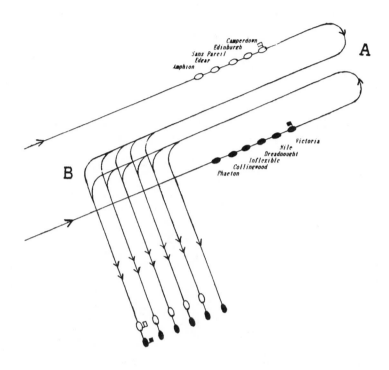

A   1st Division. turn in succession. 16 points to port.
      2nd Division. turn in succession. 16 points to starboard.

B   All ships turn together 8 points to port.

A perfectly safe plan
(If columns had started 10 cables apart)

As was his custom, the commander-in-chief summoned Staff-Commander Hawkins-Smith, and his flag-lieutenant, Lord Gillford, to his lavishly appointed cabin in *Victoria*'s stern to receive his instructions. When he mentioned curtly that he was going to make both flagships lead their columns in simultaneous 180° inward turns, they were at once struck by the discrepancy between the combined turning diameters – roughly $7\frac{1}{2}$ cables without allowing for any separation after the turn – and the columns' current 6 cables apart. Had they been *10* cables apart, it would have been perfect; but this was all wrong. Both officers gingerly raised the subject of the divisions' separation, and after some inattention (the doctor was examining an ulcer on his leg) Sir George confirmed that 6 cables was the distance he wanted, and actually wrote it down on a slip of paper which he gave to Gillford. They withdrew and went up to the bridge where, presently, he joined them. Their bafflement was still tinged with anxiety, but he "was not a person who was agreeable on being asked questions or cross-examined",[8] and their efforts to bring the matter again to his attention went little further than dropping clumsy hints and talking loudly about the distance between *Victoria* and Markham's flagship *Camperdown*. They made no impression on the C-in-C, and so assumed he had chosen his distance for an express purpose which had eluded their pedestrian minds.

The columns could have been turned *outwards* with just one signal; but, owing to a peculiarity of the *Signal Book*, inward turns needed a signal to each division. The two orders were hoisted in *Victoria*.

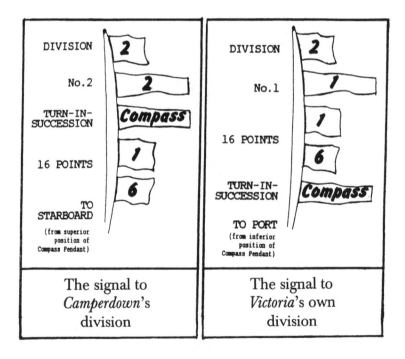

DIVISION **2**	DIVISION **2**
No.2 **2**	No.1 **1**
TURN-IN-SUCCESSION *Compass*	**1**
	16 POINTS
16 POINTS **1**	**6**
6	TURN-IN-SUCCESSION *Compass*
TO STARBOARD	TO PORT
(from superior position of Compass Pendant)	(from inferior position of Compass Pendant)
The signal to *Camperdown*'s division	The signal to *Victoria*'s own division

Suddenly the atmosphere on every bridge of the fleet was electric. With the columns 6 cables apart, if the signals were taken literally and executed at the same time, there could only be one logical outcome: a collision. Captains Gerard Noel and Arthur Moore, of *Nile* and *Dreadnought*, the battleships next astern of *Victoria*, reminded themselves of their handier turning-circles and prepared to turn, if need be, inside *Victoria*'s wake.[9] "Now we are going to see something interesting!" Moore said to his officer-of-the-watch.[10] Captain 'Abe' Jenkins[11] of *Collingwood* supposed that the signalled direction of the turn was a mistake and *Victoria* would actually turn outwards. Arthur Wilson of *Sans Pareil* could only imagine that "an arrangement had been made for one division to circle round the other".[12]

At the head of the port-hand column, Albert Markham was alarmed and bewildered, and hesitated to hoist his repeat close up to his masthead – an action which would have indicated that he understood the signal and was ready to comply. His customary incomprehension of what the C-in-C intended was fighting with his fear of a public rebuke, and in rising panic he looked around to see how other ships were responding. But when Tryon semaphored a peremptory "WHAT ARE YOU WAITING FOR?" he hauled close-up and obeyed the 'execute' which followed instantaneously. He was embarrassed now, as well as confused, and, like *Victoria*'s officers, hoped that the maestro had something up his sleeve. Unfortunately, however, as Phipps Hornby later lamented, "though bodily [Tryon] was present on the afternoon of June 22 last, the guiding brain that made him so dear to us was absent."[13] One historian, Captain Geoffrey Bennett, believes, from the evidence of garbled letters written near the end, that Sir George was suffering from a progressive mental disorder (his letters always seemed slightly garbled).

When the ships were more or less bows-on to each other, with *Victoria* slightly more advanced in her turn than *Camperdown*, their officers acknowledged reality by ordering their engines astern. Had *Victoria* rung on 'full ahead' and *Camperdown* reversed her helm, actions arguably contrary to human nature in such a situation, it seems possible that even at this late stage they might have missed. But as it was, Johnstone's ship embedded her ram into *Victoria*'s starboard side, pushing the flagship bodily to port, and then removed the plug from the hole by backing away before all of her victim's watertight doors had been closed. The other captains had braced themselves for avoiding action and by dint of much jockeying and asterning the fleet came to a halt in disarray but without further mishap.

The flood of water into the flagship was such that in four minutes her foredeck was submerged and the sea was pouring in through the open casemate doors in the side of the bridge superstructure. Efforts to manoeuvre a heavy canvas collision-mat over the hole in the hull were abruptly curtailed, and most of the crew (some 600 of them) fell in, four deep, on the quarterdeck and silently waited for the order to move. The state of *Victoria* now was as depicted overleaf:

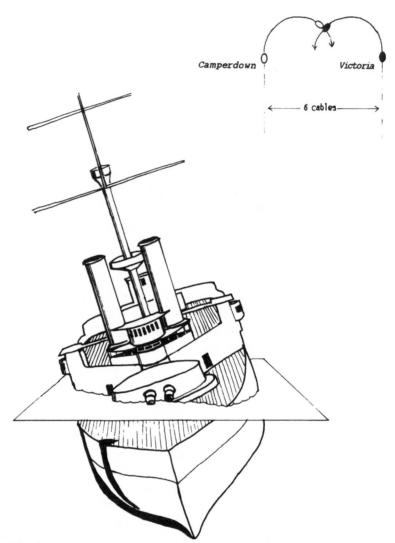

Camperdown

Victoria

←------ 6 cables ------→

The logical outcome, with columns six cables apart

Nobody broke ranks.[14] Then "without any warning she appeared to fall over to starboard, slowly at first but with increasing rapidity".[15] Lieutenant Heath gave the order to jump, and "the disciplined ranks of bluejackets broke up like a flock of roosting birds at a gunshot".[16]

> As she went the boats and weights on the port side fell over to leeward with a terrible crash. The ship then turned keel up, and something after a minute after this she sank out of sight at an angle of about 30 to 40 degrees from the perpendicular.[17]

358 officers and men died.[18] Many of the victims, like the entire engine-room staff and most of the midshipmen, failed to get away from the ship. Some were caught by the still-turning propellers. Some were non-swimmers who had prided themselves on never getting their feet wet. Some were killed by debris rocketing to the surface after the ship had gone. Sir George Tryon joined the tragic and exclusive list of British admirals who have been lost with their flagships in accidental ship-wrecks.[19] John Jellicoe fumbled his way to the upper deck before the ship rolled over, was helped down the port side of the hull by Arthur Leveson, and swam for his life. He would probably have drowned, in his enfeebled state, had not a midshipman – "a very nice fellow indeed"[20] – supported him until they were rescued by a boat from *Nile*. Maurice Bourke viewed his own survival as a mixed blessing:

> Of 650 souls committed to my charge 360 are gone, in a moment, in the twinkling of an eye. It would have been better I think had I not been saved. This is an awful cross to bear . . . And Oh those poor little midshipmen, 8 gone. Why oh why? The loss of Sir George is irreparable. What is this fiend of misfortune which follows my steps whenever I am at sea?[21]

Camperdown was herself in a critical condition; her bows had almost been wrenched off and lapses of training and discipline nearly did for her. It was later established that extreme helm had never been put on; that vital watertight doors had been left open; and that the "d—d fool of a chief engineer" had opened a sluice valve to try to drain a compartment which was open to the sea, thereby letting an extra 500 tons of water into the ship.

> At one time she had her bows awash and her stern right out of the water and had it not been for *Sans Pareil*'s diver who crawled thro a hole in the bows and closed the collision bulkhead doors she would have had to be put on the beach.[22]

13

Court-Martial

"To say, as many did, that inferiors should disobey in the event
of anything very dangerous taking place, would never do."
Queen Victoria's Journal, 21 July 1893, Royal Archives

The British people were appalled by the loss of HMS *Victoria*, her
famous admiral and so many of her crew. The Navy occupied a
unique place in national sentiment; ordinary people could recite the
vital statistics of the latest battleships, children were dressed in sailor
suits, posters of bearded Jack Tars sold cigarettes. "England", a provincial newspaper wrote, "has not been moved as the loss of the *Victoria*
has moved her since Kempenfelt went down with the *Royal George*."[1]
Public interest in the collision, and the issues raised by it, was intense.
The heroism industry sprang into action, led by the *Morning Post*:

> All this week the Angel of Sorrow has hovered over the land and darkened it
> with the shadow of his wings. [But] dull must be the mind and poor the heart
> of him who can read this solemn story of the sea without feeling a thrill
> of pride as well as a pang of grief . . . Sir George Tryon stood waiting for
> the end with folded arms, and a look of solemn peace upon his steadfast
> countenance.[2]

(The papers most given to flights of angels, etc., proved to be those
least inclined to criticize Markham's obedience to the fatal order.) The
City of London hastened to open a fund which, spurred by the
redoubtable Miss Agnes ('Aggie') Weston of the Royal Sailors' Rest,
reached more than £50,000 in three weeks, and, in the end, provided
well enough for bereaved dependants.

Other things were not so amenable to swift solutions. The
Mediterranean Fleet was "bewildered & half crazy at the the awful catastrophe"[3] and was pervaded with a gloom which was to last for many
months.[4] *Dreadnought*'s captain wrote to a friend, early in July:

250

You can well imagine our feelings at this great disaster, truly we have been very low, and I fear that everything will be very flat during the summer – the flagship gone, our Chief gone and some 350 officers and men. Our mails are somewhere and we don't know what people say.[5]

And as the *Saturday Review* put it: "What the country has lost in its own confidence in its warships and in the nerve of the men who have to handle them remains to be seen."[6]

In London the news, unaccompanied as it was by explanatory details, "quite paralysed the Admiralty. There is nothing to be got out of them. No one appears to know what was the cause of the disaster"[7] – or what was to be done now. The First Sea Lord, Sir Anthony Hoskins, was greatly distressed: having flown his flag in *Victoria* less than two years ago, "he had a very great affection for the ship and knew many [of those who had drowned]".[8] For several days "all sorts of wild rumours" chased each other unchecked around town.[9] Tryon was mad, on morphia, or drunk, they said;[10] or showing off to Sir George Wellesley. The best-known, which was soon "all over London", was the story that

at that party which dear Lady Tryon gave [at No. 45 Eaton Place] the very night of the event, two ladies <u>saw</u> Sir George & spoke to him & both went to Lady Tryon and said, 'Why is Sir George here and why won't he speak to me.'[11]

Meanwhile, the naval *cognoscenti* scanned and rescanned the flag-list for a man of sufficient stature to take Tryon's place, although some considered that "not one in his generation could properly black his boots".[12] 'Uncle Bill' Fisher reported to Gerard Noel a rumour that the C-in-C North America & West Indies, Sir John Hopkins, would be transferred to the Mediterranean – "I should think a very good selection, for there are few [vice-admirals] with any experience in handling fleets."[13] In fact, by the time Fisher wrote these words, the choice had already been made and the rumour was wrong.

The First Lord of the Admiralty, the 5th Earl Spencer (the 'Red Earl'), less paralysed than his sailor colleagues, had acted decisively and spurned the inventory of vice-admirals. For seven days the old frigate HMS *President*, a Royal Naval Reserve drill-ship and Admiralty annex moored in the Thames, became the unlikely flagship of the Mediterranean Fleet and her masthead boasted the red-on-white cross of St George of a full admiral.

Admiral Sir Michael Culme-Seymour, 3rd baronet, belonged to the Seymour tribe which provided Queen Victoria with five admirals (cf. the Napier dynasty's seven generals). Sir Michael had commanded the Pacific in 1885–7, and the Channel in 1890–2. He had a reputation as a martinet. An admiral's influence on the tone of his flagship is indirect, but the diary of a petty-officer in his Channel flagship, *Camperdown*, alleges that on a cruise around the UK in 1890 no shore leave was granted for eight weeks, and that forty punishment warrants were read out in two months.[14]

Austere in appearance, Culme-Seymour was slight and wiry and a physical fitness enthusiast. He "feared no man and was as straight as a die";[15] and, because he was rather deaf, he tended to shout. In civilian clothes he might have been mistaken for a hell-fire lay-preacher, and he had the ramrod faith in his convictions to match – plus a certain wry humour. He was not a stranger to the First Lord, which perhaps had something to do with the latter's speed of decision. Spencer's wife and stepmother were both Seymours, the admiral's wife Mary was Spencer's first cousin once removed (the generations had got out of kilter), and her family, the Watsons of Rockingham Castle in Northamptonshire, had had close links for many years with the Spencers of Althorp. But in spite of all this, it must be said that the letters between admiral and politician, while informal and implicitly between equals, convey a mutual diffidence and lack of close familiarity.

Culme-Seymour and Tryon had never been shipmates; but Tryon's birthplace was only eight miles from Rockingham and through Lady Culme-Seymour's family, if not through shared service, he was well enough known to Sir Michael. The two admirals had been sparring for some few years. They had been adjacent commanders-in-chief on the Pacific and Australia stations in the mid-1880s. Culme-Seymour had been senior to Sir George in the flag-list, having been promoted to full admiral in May 1893, but had been eclipsed by him in recent years and, of course, pipped to the ultimate seagoing prize of the Mediterranean. This may have piqued him the more while he was C-in-C Channel since it was understood that, in the event of the two fleets having to combine east of Gibraltar, it was the prerogative of the C-in-C Mediterranean to take overall command. Culme-Seymour's non-committal, sardonic response to Tryon's original TA memorandum has been detailed in Chapter 10. They had been placed in direct rivalry in the 1890 Annual (home waters) Manoeuvres, and the result was more or less a draw.

The Admiralty had planned to use the Manoeuvres – which "generally gave one side or the other a hopeless task"[16] – to make a public relations display about the defence of the United Kingdom. This time Tryon, who had caused such a rumpus in '88, was the defending admiral with much the stronger fleet and could be relied upon to demonstrate, by defeating Culme-Seymour's attacking squadron, how much the Navy had progressed in the last two years. Culme-Seymour, for his part, felt he was being set up for a show-piece trouncing, and was disinclined to play. Noticing that Their Lordships had omitted to put a southern limit on the manoeuvre area, he escaped from his 'home base' in Ireland and took his fleet at a leisurely pace "through an 'ole in the rules"[17] 1,200 miles to a spot near the Canaries. There he coaled his ships at sea[18] and came back just as the end-date of the exercise passed.

He wrote to Sir Geoffrey Phipps Hornby about it, archly, at the end of his three-week vanishing act:

> The war is over & there has been no blood shed. One of Tryon's cruisers had a look at me the night after I left Bantry and since then I have seen nothing whatever of either George Tryon or his ships, and am rather curious to know where he went to look for me.
>
> It has been hottish South and we went down to 32° [latitude]. I don't quite see what has been learned by these manoeuvres – it seemed to me simply a question of coal-endurance. This 20 days at sea has however been a capital thing to shake down the 4 newly commissioned Channel ships . . . We have had lovely weather.[19]

It was splendid, but rather pointless. Culme-Seymour had avoided tactical defeat, but Tryon's powerful squadron (as with the Grand Fleet in 1914–18) had served its main strategic function by merely existing. The Admiralty was furious, but Sir Michael cared not a hoot.

The next year Their Lordships got their own back. Arrangements had been made for Culme-Seymour's 'Northern Fleet' to discharge its surplus coal in Harwich at the end of the '91 Manoeuvres, but the vice-admiral (as he was then) took his reserve ships directly to Sheerness to pay off. The Admiralty peremptorily ordered him to Harwich; and there is a newspaper cutting, savouring the event, preserved like a trophy in his family papers:

> We are very glad that the Admiralty have publicly snubbed the Senior Officer of the Channel Squadron; he is too much given to imagining that the Service was made for his convenience, and far too ready to manipulate it for his own comfort and advantage.[20]

Now, when he had been expecting no further seagoing appointment, bizarre and horrible circumstances made it Sir Michael's duty to pick up Tryon's fallen trident as C-in-C Mediterranean. The Queen summoned him to Windsor Castle on Wednesday the 28th of June.

Culme-Seymour, like Spencer, had family connections with Windsor. His grandfather, Michael Seymour, was captain of *Amethyst* when she captured the frigates *Thétis* and *Niémen* in classic duels in the Bay of Biscay in 1808–9 (and led the boarding of *Thétis*, sword in hand). He was rewarded with the baronetcy and became a royal favourite; and after commanding royal yachts for ten years died in harness as C-in-C South America in 1834.

His father, the Reverend Sir John Culme-Seymour, 2nd Bt., served George IV, William IV and Victoria as chaplain-in-ordinary from 1827 until his death in 1880. In his early years at Windsor he was a subordinate of Canon David Markham. He added his first wife's maiden name of Culme to his surname after her early death in 1840.

His uncle, Admiral Sir Michael Seymour KCB, had occupied the archaic ceremonial post of Vice-Admiral of the United Kingdom and Lieutenant of the Admiralty from 1875 until his death in 1887 (when it was, for the time being, abolished).

And his brother, Colonel John Culme-Seymour, rejoiced in the plumage of Adjutant to the Queen's Royal Body Guard of the Honourable Corps of Gentlemen-at-Arms.

Victoria therefore needed no introduction to Sir Michael – indeed he is said to have been the only man who was allowed to shout in her presence.[21] There was, as a matter of interest, a persistent story in the gutter press that his daughter Mary (also 'May') had secretly married Prince George in 1890 – implying that George's subsequent marriage to May/Mary of Teck was bigamous. This was pure invention, and was formally judged libellous after Mary's right to be Queen was unwisely impugned in 1910.[22] (Mary Culme-Seymour married Commander Trevylyan Napier in 1899.)

To Queen Victoria, who, for obvious reasons, had been closely associated with the lost flagship, the news which arrived from the Eastern Mediterranean on the 23rd was "too dreadful to contemplate",[23] and she cancelled a state ball scheduled for that evening.[24] After dinner on the 24th, according to her journal, she "talked for some time to Sir A. Hoskins about this terrible catastrophe"; and on the 25th her second son, Admiral of the Fleet Prince Alfred, Duke of Edinburgh, came to see her about "this dreadful misfortune".[25] Prince Alfred had only that month yielded the command-in-chief of Plymouth to his successor, Sir Algernon Lyons. He had commanded the Mediterranean in 1886–9, and as an expert in fleet evolutions he had been second only to Sir Geoffrey Phipps Hornby (as Culme-Seymour, with typical directness, told Victoria[26]). He was "deeply attached" to HMS *Victoria*'s captain,[27] who had commanded his official yacht in the Mediterranean; and he was now in a state of distraction on Maurice Bourke's behalf.

Sir Michael's "attendance at Windsor Castle in response to Her Majesty's command", on June 28th, is reported in the *United Service Gazette*, but not in the Queen's private journal. She had public engagements in the late afternoon and evening, and in the morning she sat out

under the trees, writing. Perhaps she interviewed him there; perhaps it
was just a formality (even today, all senior military appointees see the
Queen before assuming their duties). Perhaps he was seen, instead, by
Prince Alfred, with whom he was close friends. At any rate, that day the
new C-in-C Mediterranean somehow acquired as secretary Staff
Paymaster Henry Rickard, who had been Alfred's secretary during his
recent Plymouth command.

Culme-Seymour returned to London to confer, the following day,
with members of the Board of Admiralty. They certainly discussed his
future flag team, for on that day (the 29th), he chose the second
member of his staff. He sent a telegram, presumably by hand, to Hugh
Evan-Thomas at the Naval and Military Club: "WILL YOU COME WITH
ME TO THE MEDITERRANEAN AS FLAG-LIEUTENANT? − SIR A. HOSKINS
RECOMMENDS YOU." The message had been seen by Admiral Lord
Clanwilliam, who had written in the margin, "I hope you will take it."[28]
Clanwilliam had been a gunroom messmate of Culme-Seymour's in
Calcutta, a two-decker 84-gun ship-of-the-line, in 1852–4, and his
current command of Portsmouth had overlapped with Sir Michael's
command of the Channel. He will have remembered young Evan-
Thomas as the princes' companion and exemplar on the *Bacchante* cruise
in 1880–2. More recently, both as C-in-C Portsmouth and as a friend of
the Prince of Wales, Clanwilliam had supervised the manning of
Melampus for the Duke of York in the spring of '92, and had performed
the final 'admiral's inspection' which had earned plaudits for the
cruiser's XO. This sudden volley of praise from three full admirals was
no less of a surprise than the news of the collision six days earlier, and
it placed Lieutenant Evan-Thomas in a dilemma.

It was not the best moment to ask him to turn his mind to a new and
wholly unexpected direction in his professional life. He had found his
niche in royal yachting and would happily have remained there, and he
was up in London now for various, but mostly private, purposes. There
was a bigger problem. 'Flags' was customarily an appointment for a
junior lieutenant. He had already done the job once, at the age of 24,
and now, at 30, had just put on the half-ring of a lieutenant of eight
years' seniority. It was thus by no means clear to him that he should
embark on a long commission as a flag-lieutenant at this stage of his
career. Probably he was also worried about Hilda Barnard: what would
she think? − and, even worse, married flag-lieutenants were unheard of.

It says something for Evan-Thomas that he could go knocking on
the doors of admirals (although there were fewer mechanisms then than
now to keep senior and junior officers remote from one another), but
that is what he did. He hastened, first, to see Clanwilliam, presumably at

his house in Belgrave Square. We can safely assert that it was a fraught meeting, for Clanwilliam was the father of Lord Gillford, Tryon's 'flags', who had narrowly escaped drowning when his legs got caught in *Victoria*'s rigging and who might yet – for all anyone knew – be blamed for the collision. Even three weeks later the earl was (in Queen Victoria's words) "very much affected in talking of the *Victoria*: in fact could hardly get out his words".[29] Nevertheless, as Evan-Thomas reported to his father, the admiral "put the whole case before me and strongly recommended my taking it".[30] The next day Hugh went to the Admiralty, where he sought an interview with his old chief (and Tryon's predecessor in the Mediterranean), Sir Anthony Hoskins.

It was exactly a year since the First Sea Lord had interviewed him about going to *Melampus* as first-lieutenant, for the '92 manoeuvres, while *Osborne* was awaiting her new boilers. Like many Victorian senior officers Hoskins was "stern, strict, and even severe in his Service relations, [but] in his private and personal character, one of the most genial of men".[31] He had a high regard for Evan-Thomas and he took some trouble now to talk through the issues with his young protégé. He probably spoke obliquely of the need to return the Mediterranean Fleet to the safe ground of signal-book manoeuvres – short of being overtly disloyal to the memory of his successor. At any rate, he told him that

> the responsibilities of the Mediterranean have increased [and the job of flag-lieutenant] is now on a different footing. [The Admiralty had therefore] recommended Sir M. Seymour to take the best he can get and pretty senior so Hoskins said he had recommended me. He further said it might do me a great deal of good and can do me no harm.[32]

Reassured and flattered, he accepted Culme-Seymour's invitation – in the circumstances, he could hardly have refused – subject to the Palace's releasing him from *Osborne*. This was quickly obtained, for on the 1st of July Prince George wrote: "My Dear Old Thomas . . . we shall miss you very much, but you have a good billet with a splendid chief."[33] (His place in the yacht was given to Lord Francis Osborne – like 'Noel of *Nile*', an appointer's little joke.)

Some months later Evan-Thomas wrote to thank Sir Anthony for his support, and his patron replied from retirement:

> If I have in any way befriended or assisted you it was because I knew you deserved it and I have been amply repaid by the way in which you worked for the Service and for me. I am sorry that I shall no longer be able to put a spoke in the wheel of yourself and other deserving men. I am afraid Lemnos will be cleared of its partridges if the Fleet visit it so often . . .[34]

If Hoskins and Clanwilliam had commended Hugh to Culme-Seymour as prospective flag-lieutenant, there can be no doubt that the admiral already knew him or knew of him. He was certainly known to his son, for on at least one occasion in September 1892, Lieutenant Michael Culme-Seymour (who was on his gunnery course in *Excellent*) was a guest in *Melampus*'s wardroom to drink whisky and play bezique.[35] And at that time *Victoria and Albert*'s wardroom – Culme-Seymour Jnr's next appointment – included not only Sir Michael's recent Channel flag-lieutenant, Frederick Morgan, but also his Channel flag-commander, Arthur Prothero ('Prothero the Good'), son of the rector of Whippingham in whose employ the curate John Dalton had first attracted the notice of the Queen. Therefore we have the makings of a loose family-ish group whose natural orbit was around royalty and whose members would have migrated easily from one wardroom to another in the course of a convivial evening in Portsmouth. Culme-Seymour was also no doubt amused by the fact that Evan-Thomas's brother-in-law now occupied the position in Windsor which his own father had held. (As a whimsical footnote it may be added that they had both started life with single-barrelled surnames.)

*

On the afternoon of Sunday the 2nd of July, Rear-Admiral Markham's formal despatches arrived at the Admiralty having been brought overland across France by a midshipman. The First Lord and the First Sea Lord, who had been waiting for them, sat down to study them intently, and Spencer boldly decided to release them to the press immediately, in time to be carried in the morning edition of *The Times*.

Meanwhile, in York Terrace on the edge of Regent's Park, Charlotte Noel was writing one of her effusive letters to her husband who, notwithstanding his forbidding countenance, was blessed in his marriage. Mrs Noel's combative heart beat fiercely both for her "beloved" captain and for the memory of their friend George Tryon. It was a match made in heaven (Noel had recently sent her a pair of socks and Mahan's book on seapower: she was to darn one and read the other, and one cannot doubt that she did both), and her letters are a roller-coaster of devotion, loyalty and partisan abuse, seasoned with acute observation and impressive nautical knowledge. She could very well have run her own court-martial and was by no means backward in pronouncing her sentence. Her testimony not only gives a good idea of what Jerry Noel was writing to her, but also, despite its obvious bias, provides a barometer of opinion in London society during these weeks of horror, bewilderment and recrimination.

Now, as the lights burned late in the Admiralty, she wrote:

> How will Culme-Seymour succeed the great man? – it dont seem a popular
> appt. at all. I long to hear if you are to be flagship, or [Edmund Jeffreys's]
> *Hood*, or what will be done about it all. I do wish Captain Bourke had stuck to
> the ship. He will never have much prestige again. Never. Everyone says the
> same.

The next day, Monday the 3rd of July, Miss Evelyn Moore (sister of
Dreadnought's Captain Arthur Moore, and one of the Queen's maids-of-
honour) came to tea and

> we talked our hearts out – we can't believe the C-in-C could have made such
> a mistake. You and *Dreadnought* must have been very near together, if she was
> behind you . . .
> I wonder what the new C-in-C will do – and where he will make his flag-
> ship. He can't be so popular as dear Sir George. One wants to hear of the
> court martial now, where it will be – you can't all be brought home for it –
> However I suppose its all cut and dried by now . . . [36]

Even as she wrote, the 'cutting and drying' were taking place, for that
morning Sir Michael Culme-Seymour and Prince Alfred had gone to
the Admiralty to confer at length with Hoskins and Spencer.[37] This very
senior group (which Clanwilliam may have joined) took the decision
that the mandatory court-martial of *Victoria*'s officers for the loss of
their ship would be held in Malta under Sir Michael's presidency.
Hitherto it had been assumed – and even reported[38] – that the trial
would take place in Portsmouth, and the change of venue caused
dismay in certain papers. The *Manchester City News* supposed that its
purpose was "to maximize the difficulty and expense of the attendance
of the press";[39] and the *St James's Gazette* considered that the reason
given – convenience – was "mere subterfuge".[40] To the *Western Morning
News*, it was

> an indication that the inquiry may be neither thorough nor impartial. The
> officers who form the court will all be more or less interested parties. The
> court can scarcely fail to come to a [verdict] with minds influenced by per-
> sonal knowledge of, and by friendly relations with, the officers who may be to
> blame.[41]

In the House of Commons, the Parliamentary Secretary to the
Admiralty, Sir Ughtred Kay-Shuttleworth, was hectored by
Conservative MPs to bring the court-martial home, beyond the thrall of
directly interested parties.[42] He could only emphasize the dislocation
involved in bringing home so many witnesses, and assure the House
that, "as a matter of course, no officer whose conduct on the occasion

might probably become the subject of investigations, will sit as a member of the court"[43] – a promise to which we shall have cause to return.

In the meantime, with only two days before Sir Michael's departure, the Admiralty appointed a prosecutor, Captain Alfred Leigh Winsloe, who would travel out to Malta with the new C-in-C and his small entourage. Winsloe had been flag-lieutenant to the great Sir Geoffrey Phipps Hornby in the Mediterranean in the late 1870s, was "considered an authority on signals and fleet manoeuvres",[44] and had served on the Dowell committee which produced the 1889 revision of the *Signal Book* (although he had, in the end, fallen out with its chairman).

At 1.00 p.m. on Thursday, July the 6th, the cruiser *Hawke* (Captain Pelham Aldrich, Commander Cecil Burney), like every other warship in Portsmouth, fired a 21-gun salute in honour of the Duke of York's wedding to Princess May. Half an hour later the Cross of St George broke out at her masthead, and at five minutes past two Sir Michael Culme-Seymour stepped on board, accompanied by his secretary and Captain Winsloe. Exactly when Evan-Thomas joined the ship is unrecorded. It is not even clear whether he had been invited to the royal wedding: his name appears on the manuscript draft list, but not on the final printed edition.[45] George had little influence over the choice of guests. It was a State occasion, and room had to be found in the procession, at the service in St James's Palace, and at the subsequent breakfast in Buckingham Palace, for dozens of officials of the royal household, most of the crowned heads of Europe and their attendants, batteries of ambassadors, Privy Councillors, and so on. A number of naval courtiers – including Berkeley Milne and Rear-Admiral John Fullerton, the CO of *Victoria and Albert* – were invited, but Spencer had rather exceeded himself in a bid to navalize the event. He had wanted three admirals of the fleet to serve as 'gentlemen of honour', and Sir Henry Ponsonby, wry as usual, had to put him straight:

> The Queen will not hear of the 3 admirals. This is not a specially naval wedding and beyond the naval guards of honour, no more naval presence is required. So cut out the gentl^mn of honour altogether . . . There are too many naval officers on the list (!)[46]

Perhaps Lieutenant Evan-Thomas fell victim to the Queen's hatchet. She was still bickering about the guest list a week before the Big Day ("the Earl and Countess of Cadogan may be omitted. Why the Lord Mayor?"[47]). But even if he had been invited, by no stretch of the L&SWR timetable could he have attended the 12.30 service – a thorough job, as one would expect – and got down to Portsmouth before the cruiser slipped and proceeded at 4.35.[48]

*

In the summer of 1893, therefore, owing to a long and extraordinary chain of events, Hugh Evan-Thomas found himself heading back to Malta as a key member of the incoming C-in-C's entourage – and no ordinary C-in-C, but one with a mission which would rest heavily on the proficiency and dedication of the flag-lieutenant. He would have been less than human had he not reflected, as the cruiser dipped her elegant bows into the long Biscay swell, that, notwithstanding his personal mis-givings at leaving England, with care and average luck from now on his career worries were over. For the immediate future he would have time to collect his wits, for his signalling competence would not be tested until the legal proceedings in Malta were over; but however developed had been his thinking on tactical doctrine, he was – as we shall see – irretrievably committed now.

As *Hawke* forged southwards the admiral must have spent much time planning the trial with Staff-Paymaster Rickard whose task, as deputy judge-advocate, was to "advise the Court on points of law and in the end sum up both sides, placing the case for prosecution and defence lucidly and impartially".[49] Rickard was well qualified for this role, having recently performed it in the court-martial of Vice-Admiral Fairfax (Culme-Seymour's successor as C-in-C Channel) for the grounding of *Howe* off Ferrol – indeed his experience may have been a marginal factor in the decision to hold the *Victoria* case in Malta. Whether Culme-Seymour discussed the forthcoming trial with Captain Winsloe, the prosecutor designate, in the close society of the cruiser's wardroom (and if so, to what extent) there is no way of knowing. As we have seen, Winsloe had been thrown into this at even shorter notice than Sir Michael or Rickard – indeed, "the only thing I had given me was a copy of *The Times* with the official letters in it so I had to do everything myself"[50] – yet he foresaw considerable scope for prosecutions ahead of him, and he was determined that the public would be properly informed. In spite of all his preparations, he found time to give personal coaching to the Press Association representative, who also travelled out in *Hawke*, on the arcane ways of the Royal Navy; and he arranged that "if he did not understand anything he was to ask me instead of telegraphing home a lot of rot."[51] The line between Malta and London[52] was going to be busy.

They left astern of them a national press in something of an uproar (albeit diverted for a while by Prince George's nuptials). Markham's despatches – "the most painful reading which could possibly meet the eyes of Englishmen"[53] – were being digested. Hitherto it had been hoped against hope by the wider naval community that the accident had been "caused by some sudden defect in the engines or steering gear of one of the colliding vessels",[54] but now it was evident that the commander-in-chief had made a mistake, and *that*, as far as the more conservative papers were concerned, was all there was to it. On the day *Hawke* sailed from Portsmouth a deeply depressed Mrs Noel wrote: "the press and public are all blaming the C-in-C – some reluctantly, others ghoulishly – I will not allow it to be said before me at all . . . (I hear distant guns so I imagine the R. Wedding is over)." Two days later she added:

> Beloved, it has been too horrible here, to have all the wild rejoicings of the Royal Wedding going on while the dreadful sorrow of the *Victoria* was so fresh in all hearts (or ought to have been) . . . the whole nation should be in the deepest gloom & mourning . . .
>
> One woman here the other day said 'He was off his head you know' – I went down her throat pretty smart, I can tell you. How dare they speak of him like that, its too horribly wicked.
>
> Poor Captain Bourke: he must have felt it bitterly. His warm-hearted Irish temperament would intensify everything.
>
> I am <u>longing</u> to know what you all think of Sir M. Culme-Seymour's appt.[55]

Had she diversified her reading she would have found that, as a rule of thumb, those papers fettered least by 'establishment' pretensions and based furthest from the centre of London were turning from shock and patriotism to amazement and derision at the conduct of those officers who had obeyed the fatal order. On July the 6th, for example, the *Truth* observed that

> 'Theirs not to reason why' seems to have been the rule which governed everybody concerned.
>
> Now, is this all right? I am only a civilian, who is not supposed to have the right to form an opinion on such matters, much less to express it; but I decline to recognize that this is a proper state of things. Discipline is one thing, purblind obedience to an order which is obviously an error of judgement, and must lead to inevitable disaster, is another.
>
> Suppose that [Tryon] had been temporarily attacked with mental aberration, and had ordered *Camperdown* to run aground, or to attack a Turkish fort, or to commit any other manifest absurdity. Does the Naval Discipline Act require implicit obedience in that case? It strikes me that what Rear-Admiral Markham wanted on June 22 was Lord Nelson's blind eye.

Two days later, the *Brighton Herald* declared that "Not since the days of the Light Brigade at Balaclava had the lives of hundreds of Britain's defenders been so terribly squandered"; while the *Saturday Review* could hardly find words to say what it is to learn that the loss of this great ship, and of some 350 officers and men, has been caused by the blind obedience of a body of highly trained officers to an order which was actually impossible of execution.

If discipline was shown at its very best during the last moments, it is impossible not to believe that it had also been shown at its worst – that is in the excess which amounts to mere slavish pedantry by the officers around the Admiral in the moments immediately preceding the collision . . . The flag-captain of a squadron of this importance is not a cadet fresh from the *Britannia*, where duty is simply to hear and obey. This is even more the case with Admiral Markham.

The *Evening Telegraph*, the *Scotsman*, the *Northern Echo*, *Vanity Fair*, the *Speaker*, the *Southampton Times*, the *Sussex Daily News* and many others said much the same in their own different ways. The *Devizes Gazette* referred to "criminal stupidity".[56] The *Spectator* embarked on a dissertation on the nature of blundering.[57] The *Morning Post*'s leader impishly suggested that "the case of a superior officer who is clearly not in possession of his senses [may not be] as rare as one is apt to suppose."[58]

This sort of stuff was denounced by *The Times* as "wild" and "subversive".[59] The *Newcastle Leader* called it "claptrap".[60] The *Yorkshire Post* said, "It will be a sorry day for England when the ready response of her soldiers and sailors to the orders of their superior officers habitually gives way to contemplative review of the situation."[61] The *Army & Navy Gazette* consoled its readers with the thought that "The discipline of the *Victoria* will be a glorious memory."[62]

Culme-Seymour's task was not going to be easy. His investigations would have to be sufficiently searching, and their conclusions decisive, to end the sudden unwelcome interest in Royal Navy affairs ("the nauseous torrent of gabble, much of it from the penny-a-liners of American journals"[63]). And with Russia apparently squaring up for another confrontation over the Ottoman Empire, this was no time for the Mediterranean Fleet to be demoralized and disunited.

On arrival in Malta, on July the 13th, the new C-in-C played racquets with John Jellicoe. (The commander's fever had been cured by his ducking and by 'Old Ard Art' Wilson's tender ministrations in *Sans Pareil*.[64]) This friendly game of squash between the president of an imminent court-martial and one of the officers formally accused – a practice which continued almost daily throughout the trial[65] – might be considered improper by a modern naval lawyer. As we have seen, Jellicoe was in his bunk at the time of the collision, and his good name was scarcely in jeopardy (unless damning evidence emerged about *Victoria*'s internal efficiency); but the incident suggests that at least to this limited, and perhaps permissible, extent the court's verdict was anticipated by its presiding officer.

As we have seen, a number of journals were sceptical about the trial's outcome. Two days before it began, the splendidly titled (but brazenly independent) *Admiralty & Horse Guards Gazette* took up the refrain:

> We need scarcely say that we have the fullest confidence in the impartiality and judgement of Sir Michael Culme-Seymour and the other officers who may sit on the court-martial, but we should have preferred it being held at home in order to avoid even the slightest suspicion of a desire to hush up the matter, or stifle the expression of public opinion which is so profoundly and properly interested in the *Victoria* catastrophe.[66]

In theory the court might be just the opener in a series of trials, for the evidence brought to light would determine whether proceedings against anyone else were warranted – Albert Markham and *Camperdown*'s Captain Johnstone being the obvious candidates. This placed Markham in an acutely stressful position, for while "the sword lying across the table might belong to Captain Bourke, it was his own future that was at stake"[67] and he had none of the accused's legal facilities. "He would not be able to hear evidence, to cross-examine, or to call witnesses on his own behalf."[68] His own sword might very well find its way onto the table – and, indeed, it was widely expected to do so. For example, the *Admiralty & Horse Guards Gazette* told its readers:

> there can be little doubt that this will not be the only tribunal in regard to the *Victoria* disaster . . . The fact cannot be overlooked that the *Victoria* was run into and sunk in broad daylight by the *Camperdown*, on board which Rear-Admiral Albert H. Markham had his flag flying . . . We imagine Sir Michael Culme-Seymour will take with him to Malta a warrant from the Admiralty to assemble a court-martial for the trial of Rear-Admiral Markham and Captain Johnstone of *Camperdown*.[69]

Even the *Morning Post* agreed.[70]

As related in Chapter 10, Albert Markham was not entirely a beginner at courts-martial pursuant to his ramming other people's ships, and he had emerged unscathed before. He was also fortified by letters of sympathy from friends and supporters, conspicuous among whom were: his cousin Clements Markham; Admiral Sir Richard Vesey Hamilton, the president of the Royal Naval College; Vice-Admiral Philip Colomb, the doyen of fleet manoeuvrers who had helped Markham after *Hecla*'s collision; Rear-Admiral John Fullerton, the permanent CO of *Victoria and Albert*; Captains William Dyke Acland and John Brackenbury, who had witnessed the disaster from, respectively, *Edgar* and *Edinburgh* and who considered Markham blameless; James

Goodenough's widow, Victoria, and her son, William; and Captain Lord Charles Beresford. The observation can scarcely be avoided that there was a strong Freemasonic strain in these names (a matter which will be considered in due course); and it was only natural, since Markham was District Grand Master, that the Malta Masonic Hall Committee should express its "deep sympathy with the Rt. W[orshipful] Bro. in this hour of anxiety" and fervently hope that the Great Architect would give him strength.[71] Charles Beresford's missives were the giddy mixture of charm and passion which he used to such effect throughout his turbulent career, for example:

> Oh the wild cruelty of this awful matter. We all feel for you and weep with you in your terrible misfortune. I feel as if a great black cloud had settled around me and I can't see my way along.[72]

The challenge facing Markham and Johnstone – to forestall their own trial by persuading the *Victoria* court, from their unrepresented position in the witness-box, that the loss of the Mediterranean Fleet flagship and the deaths of Britain's best-known admiral and 350 sailors had nothing to do with them – must have seemed an unlikely project.

In fact, warrant or not, the new Commander-in-Chief had no intention of trying them. He confided to Hoskins that he hoped "to make one job of this affair",[73] so he could get the fleet back to sea as soon as possible for intensive refresher-training in drills and manoeuvres.[74] It has already been mentioned that Culme-Seymour's father and Markham's uncle had coincided in Windsor as 'royal' clergymen. It is unlikely that the two admirals had met in childhood at Windsor, for Albert Markham went to live with his aunt (in London) only after his Uncle David's death, by which time Culme-Seymour had been in the Navy for five years; but Sir Michael must have known Clements Markham in boyhood,[75] and his own cousin, Rear-Admiral Edward Hobart Seymour, sat with the Markham cousins on the Council of the RGS. He therefore had an implicit bond of shared background with Albert, although he privately regarded him as a nuisance. More to the point, Culme-Seymour, as ever, had his own agenda; and he could certainly do without a protracted series of trials in the sweltering heat of high summer in Malta, with his wretched fleet confined to harbour as if in disgrace.

*

The *Victoria* trial was convened with great speed under the awnings of HMS *Hibernia*, an old wooden ship-of-the-line (base-ship of the Admiral Superintendent of Malta Dockyard), in Valletta Harbour on July the 17th – just four days after *Hawke*'s arrival in Malta.

As predicted, among "the officers who may sit on the court" were friends of Markham, though not as many as originally planned. Amazingly, *Camperdown*'s Captain Charles Johnstone was an appointee – if Johnstone, why not Markham? – until Bourke's counsel got him and *Edgar*'s Captain William Dyke Acland (Markham's XO in *Triumph*, 1879–82) disqualified on the grounds that they had been present at the disaster and would be required as witnesses. (To the *Northern Echo*, "it remains a puzzle why they ever should have been deputed to such an office".[76]) The attempt to enrol Johnstone either confirms that Culme-Seymour had no intention of trying him, or breached Shuttleworth's above-mentioned undertaking to Parliament.

The ineligibility of witnesses disqualified, as members of the court, not just *Camperdown*'s captain but also virtually every senior officer who had prospered under Sir George Tryon's leadership. And the seven men finally selected (in addition to the president) still included *Trafalgar*'s Captain Charles Robinson, who was Markham's normal flag-captain, and who had previously served him both on the staff of *Vernon* and as his XO in the cruiser *Active* (including during the embarrassing 1888 Manoeuvres against Tryon); *Hood*'s Captain Edmund Jeffreys, who had been XO of *Vernon* before commanding the torpedo-tender *Hecla* when she was attached to *Vernon* during Markham's tenure of command; and *Hawke*'s Captain Pelham Aldrich, who had been first-lieutenant of Nares's and Markham's ship *Alert* in the 1875–6 Arctic expedition, and with whom Culme-Seymour had taken passage out to Malta.

Markham was not yet on trial and it would be legal nonsense to infer impropriety in these officers' participation. Nevertheless, he must have been glad to note their presence. Another member of the court was Rear-Admiral Sir Richard Tracey (Superintendent of Malta Dockyard, and one of Evan-Thomas's old captains), who, as will be seen, had his own reason to identify with Markham. The only court member whose service background was likely to incline him towards the late C-in-C was Captain Atwell Lake (Gibraltar Dockyard), who had been Tryon's XO in *Raleigh* in the mid-1870s, his flag-captain on the Australia Station ten years later, and his flag-captain again for the 1890 Manoeuvres (the ones spent looking for Culme-Seymour).

The court's proceedings have been well related by Richard Hough in his celebrated *Admirals in Collision*, and the original transcription may be perused in the Public Record Office.[77] Markham's and Johnstone's performances under cross-examination were not impressive, and the prosecutor was (in his own words) "almost struck dumb" by some of their replies.

Asked why he did not reverse *Camperdown*'s helm when it became obvious that the two ships were collision-bound, Markham replied that that would have been against the Rule of the Road and thus "utterly wrong"; yet it was later extracted from him that the 'rules' did not apply during fleet manoeuvres. Captain Winsloe was obliged by the president to let it go.[78] When Markham claimed to have been encouraged by the fact that ships astern of him had close-upped Tryon's signal (and so presumably thought it safe), Winsloe pointed out that it was less critical to them, for they would simply follow him; yet the matter was not pressed. Again, when Markham's 'flags', Lieutenant Henry Bradshaw, contradicted him by asserting that he had ordered the fatal signal to be acknowledged *before*, rather than *after*, Tryon's "WHAT ARE YOU WAITING FOR?" had been translated to him, the matter was allowed to pass. He was even "not sure" what *Camperdown*'s turning-circle was.

By virtue of the electric telegraph, the British press was able to regale the public with a blow-by-blow narrative; and as the days went by the perception spread that there were issues bearing on the collision which had not been highlighted by the rear-admiral's official despatches. In London, Mrs Noel's spirits discernibly rose:

> We are all furious with Adl Markham, he is mean and shifty. Johnstone's too futile for words – 'I don't know' and 'Can't say' – but he is stupid and so ignorant of fleetwork that one blames the authorities who put him in command of a ship. Adl Markham, on the contrary, don't ring true . . . he comes out shadily, as I thought he would; and dangerous as the evolution was, the blame of the collision rests with the *Camperdown* and the chuckle-heads in charge of her . . .
> Dear Captain Bourke is splendid. Capt Acland <u>most</u> feeble . . .[79]

After the first week Charlotte was beside herself at the growing possibility of a right result, and when she bumped into an ally (plus niece) in Bond Street her welcome was ecstatic:

> Who should I meet but 'Uncle Bill'. I nearly hugged him, it really was an escape for him. But the joy of coming across a real sailor, one of your chums, was quite bewildering. I promptly made Miss Fisher promise to bring him to tea tomorrow.

She was now able to report that people had "left off saying Sir George was off his head, and now they say Markham was off his".[80]

Modern historians have had fun with Albert Markham. According to one, his culpability would have been obvious to "the most junior char-lady at the Admiralty, had she pondered the facts".[81] However, the lesson of the collision is lost if it be supposed that he stepped across a clearly marked threshold of stupidity, with lights flashing and bells ringing (although they should have been flashing and ringing in his head). Had he known there was definitely going to be a collision, even he would have balked at executing the order; and there were several straws available for grasping, as he mastheaded his acknowledgement of the fatal signal:

a. The mistake which *Victoria* appeared to be making was so elementary that perhaps it somehow wasn't a mistake after all – 'What Tryon does must be right.'[82] Think it through again.

b. If Markham was correct in perceiving danger in the manoeuvre, it was likely that Tryon, usually streets ahead of him, was aware of it and had somehow allowed for it.

c. It did not necessarily follow, from the fact that *Victoria* had signals to both divisions flying simultaneously, that she would haul them down together (though as the fleet was approaching shoal-water, there was little time to stagger them). If Markham had this in mind, when they *were* hauled down together he would have only a split second to intervene in *Camperdown*'s helm orders, and he was probably in the wrong place.

d. Even if the two signals, taken together, *were* a mistake, *Victoria* had probably realized it by now and it would be easier for her than for *Camperdown* to do something else, for she would not be disobeying a senior ship's order – though Captain Bourke, with Tryon breathing down his neck, might have seen it differently.

Markham's main 'defence' for obeying the order was that it had suddenly dawned on him that *Victoria*'s port-turning column was going to half-circle round the outside of *Camperdown*'s starboard-turning column. In support of this assertion, he paraded the phrase "preserving the order of the fleet" which formed part of the literal text of the signals to turn 16 points in-succession. He laboured it in his despatches – having (probably) found it after the collision while thumbing miserably through the *Signal Book* in the terrible solitude of his tilted cabin – and grasped it as a possible career-saver. With these six words he hoped to persuade the world that Tryon had intended the two squadrons of the Mediterranean Fleet to retain their *relative* positions: in other words, after the manoeuvre *Camperdown*'s division must still be to port of *Victoria*'s. To achieve this, one of them would have to half-circle outside the other; and, because nothing had been said to *Camperdown* about modified rudder-angle, it was reasonable to suppose that *Victoria* should have done the circling.

This specious idea was the product of wishful construction and/or (like the Rule of the Road and turning-circle issues) ignorance. Markham tried it on at the trial, and, although he was technically only a witness himself, the court took the unusual step of allowing him to invite other witnesses to corroborate his evidence. Three were unwise enough to oblige: Vander-Meulen[83] of *Inflexible*, Acland of *Edgar* and Brackenbury of *Edinburgh*, and under the scrutiny of a genuine expert their good intentions crumbled to nothing. For example:

> PROSECUTOR: Where do you get your authority, from what book, for one column to circle round the other in performing the manoeuvre ordered?
> ACLAND: I have no authority.

Mrs Noel was not alone when she remarked that Markham's "calling such geese to confirm his interpretation of the signal puts him on their level of incompetence".[84]

However, the circling-round theory has proved remarkably resilient, receiving endorsement from two historians who have been gulled (as Markham hoped) by "preserving the order of the fleet". It was first championed, with a rabbit-out-of-hat flourish, by William Laird Clowes in a letter to *The Times* on the 5th of July 1893 – just after the publication of Markham's despatches – and demolished the following day by Lieutenant Mark Kerr (who had served as 'flags' to two admirals and left *Victoria* as recently as March, and who was distantly related to Lord Walter Kerr). Unchastened, Clowes was still enthusing about his insight in 1907.[85] More recently, in 1958 and 1993, Richard Hough has recycled it, suggesting that Tryon meant *Camperdown* to do the circling.[86]

It is time this fallacy was knocked on the head. Markham, Clowes and Hough are misunderstanding – the first-named, wilfully – the function of the phrase "preserving the order of the fleet". It did not mean what it appears to say. It came from the 1889 *Signal Book*'s page of definitions and was merely its belt-and-braces description of a *turn-in-succession*, as distinct from a *turn-together*: the word 'fleet' being a cover-all term for whatever column of ships was the addressee of the signal.[87] It was impossible, in 1893, to signal a turn-in-succession without the words "preserving the order of the fleet" forming part of the definitive text (just as it is impossible to turn a column of ships in-succession without preserving its order). It is not within the power of a divisional leader *per se* to guarantee the order of a whole fleet: here the other division was signalled separately, and could perfectly easily have been told to do something incompatible or have just steamed on and done nothing. The phrase "preserving the order of the fleet", therefore, applied independently (as per signal) to each division and cannot possibly, in either case, have referred to the Mediterranean Fleet as a whole.

This is not a matter of opinion. The ambiguous (to a layman) wording of the signal's definition was idiot-proofed in the next, 1898, edition of the *Signal Book* to read: "to alter course in succession; if addressed to the whole fleet, *preserving the order of the fleet*; if addressed to a column, *preserving the formation of the column*."[88] (Commander Hugh Evan-Thomas was secretary of the Signals Committee which authorized this rewording.)

There are, furthermore, serious practical objections to the Clowes/Hough solution. The first is that it could not have been done without some *ad hoc* arrangement having been made for the intended 'outside' ship to use less than standard helm.[89] The others are best explained by reference to the diagram with which Hough illustrated his solution in the *Weekend Telegraph* in June 1993. His diagram looks like Figure 1.

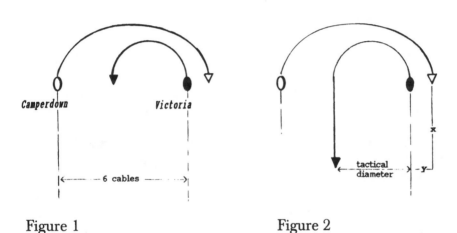

Figure 1   Figure 2

What is wrong with it is that, with both ships starting their turns at the same time, *Victoria* would have been nearly half a mile down her new course by the time *Camperdown* had completed her much wider wheel (as in Figure 2), and no combination of equal-speed manoeuvres[90] could have brought the latter to her anchoring station on the former in the time and searoom available.[91] Furthermore, while the approach to a formation anchorage requires precisely predictable spatial relationships between ships, there would have been two distances (*x* and *y* in Figure 2) impossible to know accurately in advance because they would depend on how closely *Camperdown* had dared to wheel past the counter-wheeling 1st Division.

Tryon would thereby have thrown his fleet into a muddle for which he could have had no planned solution, its details being unforeseeable; *Camperdown* would not have known what her station was supposed to be, and even if she were ordered to catch up with an 'unequal' speed increase (a slovenly expedient), his two divisions would still have been a completely useless distance apart in parallel – $4\frac{1}{2}$ to $5\frac{1}{2}$ cables – which would somehow have to be reduced to two before anchoring. And the wrong division would have been to seaward. At the risk of begging the question of Sir George's mental state,[92] no sane person, let alone a renowned seaman, would deliberately rot up a formation anchorage in this comprehensive manner.

But as things happened, of course, it was rotted up about as completely as it could have been. So what was he trying to do? The court failed to offer an opinion, and the alleged mystery has endured. Any idea that he was meaning to lead his fleet in a scissors-type manoeuvre, *in-succession* at the collision point (as suggested by Robert Massie[93]), can be disregarded. With both divisions *under helm*, judging the gaps would have required clairvoyant gifts of calculation, and these lumbering ironclads were too unforgiving in their steering to correct mistakes easily. It was unheard of then, and has remained so. A team of stunt motor-cyclists would think twice before attempting it. (The nearest manoeuvre to it, the 'gridiron', turns the two divisions onto straight, opposite courses before the intersection, and is not performed in succession.)

As stated in the last chapter, with something close to certainty, the manoeuvre Tryon had in mind was that depicted on page 245. This evolution answers his anchoring plan perfectly, although of course it requires an initial separation of 10 (rather than 6) cables between divisions. Since both Lieutenant Gillford and Staff-Commander Hawkins-Smith had drawn his attention to the fact of 6 cables, it may be surmised that this, in itself, was not his mistake. That leaves two possible errors:

a. he was allowing for the turning diameter of only one ship;

b. he was confusing the 2 cables of searoom which each ship needed for a quarter-circle with the $3\frac{1}{2}$–4 cables needed for a half-circle.

The second of these explanations is strongly supported by both Arthur Wilson[94] and Mark Kerr. The latter wrote in his memoirs:

Half-circles are very seldom executed, while quarter-circle turns are constantly made. When manoeuvring the fleet, one gets accustomed to allowing two cables of searoom [per ship] for a quarter-circle turn, and I felt sure this was the cause of the mistake. The two lines were six cables apart. The harbour was astern of them, and they were to enter it two cables apart. The

Admiral evidently forgot for the moment that the half-circle required more searoom . . .

A year later I met a lieutenant [Charles Collins] who had been in the *Victoria* with me, and was the officer-of-the-watch on the bridge near the Admiral when the fatal collision occurred. I gave him my opinion of the cause of the accident as above, and he replied, 'That was exactly the reason. The Admiral himself told me that that was the mistake he had made. I could not make up my mind what I would do if I was called as a witness, for we had all been told by Captain Maurice Bourke that we were to do everything to preserve Sir George's reputation. I could not make up my mind whether I was to perjure myself or not, but fortunately I was not called to give evidence.'[95]

(Richard Hough well describes Bourke's over-elaborate attempt to avoid interrogation about Tryon's last words. Having thus hinted that he had something sensational to reveal, he let it be extracted from him that the C-in-C had said, "It's all my fault" – a statement which, as Hough points out, is open to various interpretations. As a matter of fact, Lieutenant Collins *was* called to give evidence, but was not asked directly whether Tryon said anything after the impact.)

Tryon had made the same mistake, at the same distance, near the Scilly Isles in the 1890 Manoeuvres (while waiting for Culme-Seymour to turn up): a fact which the prosecutor decided, after careful thought, not to mention.[96] On that occasion *Anson*'s Captain Bouverie Clark (in Johnstone's role) refrained from answering the signal and conferred urgently with Rear-Admiral Sir Richard Tracey (= Markham). Clark tried to persuade Tracey to signal his doubt,

but he wouldn't. At last he said to me – 'Look here, there's no Act of Parliament to make you run into your neighbour, but you've got to obey that signal.' So I said 'All right', and told them to hoist it. Just then Tryon annulled it and semaphored me 'the last evolution could not be performed because you were not in station'.

Clark did not believe the station-keeping charge, and a couple of days later "had it out" with Tryon, in a friendly way over dinner, but remained unconvinced that the admiral really saw the point. "Strange", he mused, in July '93, "that a man like him should have again done such a thing."[97] Equally interesting is the question of what had been in the mind of Sir Richard Tracey (who was on the panel of the *Victoria* court) when he told his flag-captain to comply with the signal – and, indeed, what was going on in Captain Clark's head when he made to obey.

That Tryon miscalculated one way or another is beyond doubt. He was also at fault in a sense indicated by the modern-day *Admiralty Manual of Navigation*, which serves as fair comment on his autocratic command-style. Under 'Manoeuvring a Force', is the following: "one of the best forms of insurance against danger, and an incumbent duty of a senior officer, is to make known his intentions so far as he is able";[98] and under 'Anchoring in Company' is: "the Senior Officer's intentions should be signalled early, so that other ships can appreciate what the Senior Officer is trying to do."[99] It was not Tryon's practice to make known his detailed intentions – the whole point of his methods was to train his immediate juniors to take the unpredictable in their stride – but he could at the least have rehearsed his plan with his staff-commander, Hawkins-Smith, or his 'flags', Lord Gillford. Had he done so, they could surely have discussed the turning-circle problem without insubordination.

On the other hand the *Navigation Manual* – partly the product of an accretion of cautionary tales like that of *Victoria* and *Camperdown* – also admits that "to achieve fighting efficiency it is clearly necessary to practise manoeuvres which could be described as potentially dangerous."[100] This has been recognized at least since 1904[101] and, then as now, the responsibility of officers for the safe navigation of their own ships is legally undiminished by the presence of a senior officer in tactical command.

In fact the Naval Discipline Act (NDA) in force in 1893 proffers the charge and the defence for either argument, and thus appears to snooker itself: any person subject to the Act could be dismissed with disgrace, both for wilfully disobeying a lawful command (Section 17), and for hazarding a ship in Her Majesty's service (Section 29).[102]

The NDA, however, was also the fount of authority for the various standing orders which may have bearing on the case. The best known of these, *Queen's Regulations and Admiralty Instructions* (*QR & AIs*), deal mainly with administrative and ceremonial matters, and shed no light. I have not found a copy of the standing orders of the Mediterranean Station, but clearly Tryon's 'Wellington' memorandum on initiative was one of them. The *Admiralty & Horse Guards Gazette* thought it "so wise, and so brimful of common sense, that [it] should be rescued from the obscurity of the Mediterranean Order Book and embodied in the *Admiralty Instructions*";[103] and it is difficult to see what more explicit action a C-in-C could have taken to elevate the meaning of Section 29 of the Act above that of Section 17.

The court was told that Tryon had reissued the Wellington memorandum shortly before the disaster, and was reminded that the *Signal Book* explicitly affirmed a captain's overriding responsibility for the safety of his ship during fleet manoeuvres.[104] But as with so much else, it let these details go.

Admiral Sir Reginald Bacon's perspective of the collision goes to the heart of the matter. After attributing it, with a seaman's regard for medical terminology, to a "kink" in Tryon's brain, he goes on to say:

> Still more extraordinary was the fact that although the Captain of the *Victoria* and the Admiral second-in-command who flew his flag in *Camperdown*, and the Captain of *Camperdown*, that is three separate officers of rank and experience; although all three knew that if the signal was obeyed then there was bound to be a collision, yet they allowed the helms of their ships to be put over and the collision to occur. Vaguely we may imagine dim reasons that may have obsessed them . . . but no rational explanation can completely account for the universal dementia that paralysed the minds of the principal actors in that tragedy. The one lesson to be learned is the necessity for every officer to cultivate belief in his own judgment, so as not to be afraid of acting correctly when the day of trial comes. <u>This incident has provided the Navy with a lesson of the duty owed by juniors towards senior officers that it is well for officers to ponder over and digest.</u>[105] [underlining added]

Bacon was by no means alone in this view. Several newspapers may be represented here by the *Admiralty & Horse Guards Gazette*'s assertion that "the time must come when, in a disciplined Service, the highest and noblest duty may be to disobey a superior's orders."[106] Given that Tryon was stuck on his mistake and impervious to the unsubtle hints of his immediate staff, it lay within the power of three men, in varying degrees, to prevent the disaster, and all of them – Markham, Bourke and Johnstone – failed to act as circuit-breakers against danger.

Markham's failure lay in his lack of the self-possession to reject out of hand a manoeuvre which was prima facie impossible, and in his taking refuge in the hope that the signal was a riddle to which he alone couldn't see the answer, rather than a straightforward blunder:

> I thought that the Commander-in-Chief would never give orders to perform either an impossible or a dangerous manoeuvre, and that there was something in his mind that I did not quite grasp.[107]

This state of mind – if indeed it really was his state of mind in the moments before the collision – amounts to what psychologists call 'denial' (= 'This isn't really happening!'), and the truth is that Markham "wasn't a strong enough man for such an emergency";[108] although, as the *Saturday Review* archly remarked, "it is, perhaps, difficult for those who have not been broken to military servitude to realize how hard it is for a subordinate to offer even respectful opposition to a resolute and able superior"[109] (and one wonders how many closet-Markhams have evaded detection over the years).

He by no means got it all his own way under cross-examination. He was unable to get expunged from the record a devastating comment by Gerard Noel. Pressed to agree that *Victoria* might, for all Markham knew, have turned outside *Camperdown*, the captain of *Nile* blurted out that *Camperdown* could equally well have turned to port (= outwards).[110] Sharky Noel's hostility was all the more noteworthy in that he had served under Markham in the Training Squadron in 1888, and that Markham had shifted his flag, the day after the collision, from the damaged *Camperdown* to *Nile*. It must be a personal comment on Markham that both his flag-lieutenant and his adoptive flag-captain went on record against him, though (as will be seen) Noel's personal ire was directed at least as much at Captain Johnstone.

In the event, Noel's interjection failed to sway the court. On July the 27th, after hearing evidence for ten days, it placed virtually the entire blame, "with the deepest sorrow and regret", on the ever-broad shoulders of the dead. Its verdict comprised five paragraphs:[111]

1. The collision was due to an order given by Sir George Tryon.

2. Everything possible was done to save the flagship and to save life.

3. No blame was attachable to Captain Bourke or to any other of the survivors of HMS *Victoria* for the loss of that ship; they had behaved splendidly and were accordingly acquitted.

4.

The Court strongly feels that, although it is much to be regretted that Rear-Admiral Albert H. Markham did not carry out his first intention of semaphoring to the Commander-in-Chief his doubt as to the signal, it would be fatal to the best interests of the Service to say he was to blame for carrying out the directions of the Commander-in-Chief present in person.

5. The court was not competent to express an opinion on why HMS *Victoria* capsized.

These, then, were the findings which were telegraphed around the world and which it was the Board of Admiralty's prerogative to ratify, or not.

Captain Bourke was given back his sword.

14

Their Lordships' Predicament

"I never read such rot as Columbus has written. I should not be surprised to hear [of] one of the Mediterranean captains' having punched his head."

Captain Alfred Winsloe was exhausted and somewhat embittered. Prosecutors are there to prosecute, and he felt he had never been let off the leash. The "weak verdict" was the product of the composition of the court, he confided to Sir Geoffrey Phipps Hornby soon after returning to England. There had been "plenty to hang a dozen Markhams if the court wanted to" – and not just Markham: the internal efficiency of *Camperdown* had been lamentable, but "her Captain is an ass and her Commander is rather worse so what can one expect?" The performance of some of the other captains in giving evidence was

> simply pityful; Acland of *Edgar* made one turn hot & cold all over. Brackenbury slapped his chest and struck an attitude, but did not answer one question he was asked.

Winsloe was "quite played out". The least he deserved, in his opinion, after "such a very unpleasant duty" – people in Valletta had crossed the street to avoid him[1] – was command of a second class cruiser[2] (Their Lordships obliged).

Paragraph Four attracted adverse comment at once. What did it mean? "One of two things", in *Vanity Fair*'s analysis:

> either Markham did his duty, or he failed to do it. In the first case, he did nothing that is 'much to be regretted'; in the second, he is to be blamed. The court had clearly said either too much or too little . . . A pitiful compromise.[3]

With reference to the court's 'regrets' about Markham's failure to semaphore, the *Cork Examiner* acidly added that "sentiment or opinion on irrelevant matters is not expected from a high tribunal of this kind."[4] One or two papers spotted the illogicality of commenting on Markham at all, for the court had not been assembled to pass judgement on him. As the *Saturday Review* pointed out, either he should have been placed on trial, or no notice should have been taken of him except as a witness – "it is impossible to understand the rule by which the court was guided."[5] (It may be added that, in presuming to pass judgement on Markham, the captains on the court were arrogating to themselves – with Culme-Seymour's complicity – the authority of rear-admirals, for he could not have been legally tried by officers of inferior rank.)

In fact, as we know, Sir Michael Culme-Seymour was treading a precarious path. To trigger a court-martial of Markham for obeying orders would rattle bones from the Navy's deep past and threaten ramifications for the future definition of discipline: better to keep the genie securely in the bottle. But aside from these issues – and irrespective of whether he was being steered, to some extent, by the First Lord of the Admiralty – he needed the *Victoria* business finished with so he could get his fleet to sea; and his hope was that this mild public admonition of Markham would appease those who blamed the rear-admiral, and defuse the demand for his trial.

Whether he was already aware of the counter-currents surging around his court's verdict – press reactions were wired from London – or whether he merely expected them, he sought reassurance from the First Lord four days after the trial. He commended to Spencer an "excessively good" leading article in the *Spectator*, the drift of which he paraphrased for his chief's benefit as follows:

> If the doctrine that officers were supposed to think for themselves when a manoeuvre was ordered to be performed, instead of obeying it, were once laid down, it would strike a terrible blow at the efficiency of the Service.[6]

Can he really have believed this? Surely, when he imagined himself into Markham's shoes, as he must have done many times during the trial, he thought for himself and averted the collision? Anyway, Spencer agreed, and returned his private and premature opinion that

> we [the Board] shall accept without any difficulty your finding. It deals in common sense with the problem before you: you went most thoroughly into the question & there will be no desire for future CMs or for criticism.
>
> That poor Tryon was to blame, everyone agrees. Some difference of opinion may event as to what individual admirals would have done had they been in Markham's position, but few would desire that the CM or the Admiralty should lay down what might be taken as a doctrine of disobedience to the orders of a C-in-C present in person. Grave mischief might follow such a declaration . . .[7]

*

While most of the national papers and 'establishment' journals – for example, *The Times*, the *Telegraph*, the *Enquirer*, the *Daily Chronicle*, the *Birmingham Post* and the *Army & Navy Gazette* – sonorously welcomed the reaffirmation of the principle of unconditional obedience, many of the provincials and independents, equally predictably, did not.

The *Dundee Courier* thought the implications of the verdict "startling".[8] The *Bristol Mercury* considered that the whole moral of the collision was that "it is *not* 'to the best interest of the Service' to obey a command blindly and without exercise of reason."[9] The *Yorkshire Herald*, the *Scotsman*, the *Glasgow Herald*, the *Manchester Courier*, the *Speaker*, the *Nautical Magazine*, the *Shipping Gazette*, the *Journal of Commerce*, the *Admiralty & Horse Guards Gazette*, and no doubt many others, expressed similar views; and many of them wanted Markham to be placed on trial. Only the *Saturday Review* went so far as to speak of "the moral cowardice" of Tryon's juniors, but it summed up the general consensus among the dissidents when it said: "the court has evaded the real point with a slipperiness (for we cannot say dexterity) not wholly worthy of the candour we expect from officers and gentlemen."[10] (In 1912 some of the same titles lined up for and against Lord Mersey's findings on the *Titanic*.) Captain Reginald Custance, who ferried some of the survivors home in the cruiser *Phaeton*, was probably reflecting a mixture of press and service opinions when he wrote to Noel from Plymouth:

> The general view of the *Victoria* affair at home I find coincides with what I believe is both yours and mine, except that possibly it is more pronounced against the people on board *Camperdown*. The finding does not meet with approval on that ground.[11]

Charlotte Noel reported a rumour in London naval circles that the whole affair "will cause a revolution in one way: that admirals will be selected, and that a man will not get his flag rank *merely* because he is next in turn".[12] (Alas, it proved not to be so.)

Captain Noel now became something of a rallying point for Tryonite discontent. His sister was correct when she wrote: "you, Dear, will miss [Sir George] more than any of his captains, as I think you were always very much drawn to one another."[13] He was depressed that his testimony had not tipped the scales against *Camperdown*, and to some extent blamed his own reticence (as he saw it) for the verdict. His wife hastened to reassure him:

> Beloved, your evidence was not the failure you think. Everyone says you were the only man who gave evidence from *knowledge* and not from 'I think', and the only man who kept his head. However darling you were evidently boiling

over with much more & to those who read between the lines it was evident
you were keeping back a great deal.[14]

Now, he relieved some of his anger by getting himself into a squalid
exchange of letters with Markham.

He started it, two days after the verdict, by attempting to justify
his damaging comment about *Camperdown* during the trial. His sheer
ineptitude hints at why he was not universally liked.

> My firm belief is that if you had been onboard of any ship other than the
> *Camperdown*, the fatal accident would in all probability have been avoided. She
> is notably the worst handled ship in the Fleet, with a captain who has always
> been a blunderer. Had you been quite yourself instead of recovering from a
> long bout of sickness, I quite think that you would have been equal to the
> occasion even in spite of being so badly served . . .
>
> PS I do not know what you will think of this letter: it is intended as an
> explanation not an apology, though I am sorry that my words at the CM were
> misunderstood.[15]

It is unlikely that Noel's contempt for Johnstone stemmed wholly
from the collision. Johnstone had not been among those officers with
whom he either walked or dined in the three weeks preceding the disaster,[16] although they were far from strangers and, superficially at least,
had much in common. They had both served in the Training Squadron
under Markham in 1888, when, it may be recalled, they submitted very
similar criticisms of Dowell's draft *Signal Book*; and they were both RUSI
gold medal essayists.[17] But early remarks by Mrs Noel, written before
details of the accident were known in England, imply that their antipathy was a well-established state of affairs: "Captain Johnstone", she
said on the 27th of June, "ought to be hung"; and, on the 8th of July,
he "ought to be flogged".[18] Now she wrote that

> it was a fatal thing to send such a weaklet out to the Mediterranean –
> Markham must have been possessed when he put his flag in him . . . I wonder
> what Prince Louis [of Battenberg] is doing about his Course Indicator, do tell
> me . . .[19]

Markham, needless to say, was outraged by Noel's letter with its
insults and insinuations, and sent it directly back with a loyal denial of
Johnstone's incompetence[20] – an action which does him credit,
although it may be noted that Winsloe described Johnstone (to Hornby,
above) in terms similar to Noel's.

The rear-admiral received many supportive letters from friends in
England and Malta, including Vice-Admiral Philip Colomb, and
Captains Charles Robinson (a member of the court), William Dyke
Acland (who, a year earlier, had wondered what the officer-of-the-watch

was for, in a ship with no sails), Arthur Moore and Lord Charles Beresford. They variously celebrated the verdict and subtly stoked his discontent over Paragraph Four. Moore privately blamed the Camperdowners "for sinking the *Victoria* when with twin screws it was so easy to avoid coming into collision"[21] (rather than for doing so through blind obedience), but now he wrote to Markham:

> I am so glad to think that the Court recognized the traditions of the service – no doubt they felt bound to make allusion to the semaphore but I do trust you will not feel it personally.[22]

And the *ex-officio* naval 'establishment' closed ranks around Markham and his flag-captain. The padded leather armchairs of clubland shook to the pronouncements of retired military experts. The *United Service Gazette* (a journal which, by its own advertisement, was "by no means disposed to lend itself to ill-considered censures of the authorities") rather too hastily declared that "the verdict has been received with the greatest satisfaction by all sections of the Service" – which was quite untrue (and how would it know, anyway?) – and exulted in the "exhibition of discipline and order that maintained in *Victoria* to the very last", comparing it to the heroic saga of the wreck of the *Birkenhead*.[23]

Two authorities to whom many deferred automatically, for reasons given in Chapter 9, were Admiral of the Fleet Sir Geoffrey Phipps Hornby and Vice-Admiral Philip Colomb. Now several years into retirement, they personified, as practitioner and theorist respectively, the two separate dimensions to the issues surrounding the death of Sir George Tryon: the immediate question of who was at fault in the manoeuvre which caused the ships to collide, and the wider controversy of Tryon's 'secondary educational' agenda. Both came out in public support of the *Camperdown* duo, although privately their perspectives of the business were very different.

*

Phipps Hornby was 'Uncle Geoff' to a whole generation of senior naval officers. They looked back on his tenure of the Mediterranean in the 1870s, with its big 'Russian scare' and its perfection of fleet manoeuvres, as a heyday; and they corresponded with this "naval Gamaliel"[24] freely and informally. Many letters found their way from the Mediterranean to his Hampshire estate in the days after the collision. He hastened to write supportively to Bourke, eliciting the following grateful reply: "When all is dark and black before one, words of encouragement from a man like you and in your great position is indeed oil to a troubled soul."[25] And he wrote to Culme-Seymour that he was "wondrous glad" to hear of his appointment as Tryon's successor,[26] although there is a strong hint elsewhere that he had offered his own services, at the age of 68 (like a new Lord Howe, a century on), and been gently rebuffed by the Admiralty.[27]

Hornby was distressed to find his children set against each other by the *Victoria* business. He had known Hoskins for half a century (since they were midshipmen in *Winchester* in 1842). He had gladly endorsed the careers of Heneage, Culme-Seymour and Colomb. And he had presented Wilson with his VC on behalf of the Queen in 1884. But his mutual admiration with George Tryon went back thirty years, and he felt "very acutely the loss of his old friend".[28] He no doubt recalled with pain a reconnaissance visit he had paid in 1879 to Tripoli Bay – now *Victoria*'s grave – in the despatch vessel *Helicon*, accompanied by Captain Tryon, flag-Commander Atwell Lake and flag-Lieutenant Alfred Winsloe. Tryon had long addressed him as "My Dear Old Chief", and as John Brackenbury told him after the disaster, "You were one of his most intimate friends & he was proud to call himself a pupil of yours."[29] Hornby could only suppose that "Tryon must have been temporarily off his head",[30] or at least ill, on June the 22nd, and privately he was inclined to blame Markham for obeying the impossible order.

There can be no question about this. He was tactless enough to write to Clements Markham and tell him so – provoking by return of post the following blend of *reductio ad absurdum* and umbrage:

> Your view is that the Rear-Admiral ought at once to have assumed that the Commander-in-Chief was incapable and deliberately intended to cause a collision, and to have disobeyed the order . . . It will add to my cousin's most abiding and poignant grief that you should be so uncompromising and so determined to ignore everything that tells in his favour.[31]

Sir Geoffrey received other letters, from officers such as Captain Winsloe, Rear-Admiral Robert FitzRoy (his ex-flag-captain, and Tryon's junior in the 1888 Manoeuvres), and even Admiral Andrei Alexandrovitch Popoff of the Imperial Russian Navy, who held Markham responsible and clearly assumed that he would agree. Even six months after the trial he was berating Captain Lake (a member of the court) for letting Markham off the hook (Lake protested that "Neither he nor his officers were on trial – very probably a good job for them!!!").[32] Hornby considered that if he had made the same dangerous signal, during his command of the Mediterranean, none of his captains would have come near him, except perhaps George Tryon who might have sheered extra-close deliberately.[33]

How, then, can one explain his publication, in association with

Captain Lord Charles Beresford on the 12th of August, of the following pronouncement?

> Admiral Markham might have refused to perform the evolution ordered, and the *Victoria* would have been saved. Admiral Markham, however, would have been tried by court-martial, and no one would have sympathized with him as it would not have been realized that he had averted a catastrophe. Unconditional obedience, no matter at what cost, is, in brief, the only principle on which those in the Service must act.[34]

This is possibly the most dogmatic prostration to the principle of seniority to be found in military annals anywhere. It implies that Hornby deplored the failure of the captains astern of *Victoria* and *Camperdown* to drive their ships, two by two, into the flagship pile-up; and that, if the afternoon of June the 22nd could somehow have been rerun, he would have wanted Markham to ram *Victoria* again. What had gone wrong? Hornby's reputed "scrupulous honesty and dislike of half-truths"[35] seem to have failed him on this occasion. Some of his friends may have recalled that he had received a head injury in 1891, when his horse shied at the sight of a traction engine and his dog-cart overturned.[36] But it appears he had been got at both by Philip Colomb ("Winsloe has been making my hair stand on end"[37]) and by the silver-penned Charles Beresford.

'Charlie B' was a gallant, glamorous officer "of engaging personality though mediocre intellectual attainments".[38] He had become a public hero at the bombardment of Alexandria in 1882, when he had taken the sloop *Condor* in beneath the depression of the Egyptian guns to attack at point-blank range. He was a shameless flatterer. When Sir Geoffrey had his dog-cart accident he hastened to assure the retired admiral "without the slightest doubt of contradiction, that there is no one that would be such a loss to the country as yourself".[39] Beresford had the gift of being all things to all men. He was now in command of the steam reserve at Chatham, but until recently he had commanded the cruiser *Undaunted* in the Mediterranean and had enjoyed Tryon's high esteem. In return, he rated the admiral "the best man we had"[40] and now consoled Lady Tryon with "the whole Navy weeps with you. The State has lost its most brilliant seaman; the Navy its most generous and affectionate friend."[41] Elsewhere, he declared that Markham had been "crucified alive for another man's blunder";[42] and he wrote to assure him that he would have done exactly the same himself.[43] These positions were not literally incompatible – a politician could have occupied both without discomfort – but naval officers' loyalties were normally more linear.

A few days before their joint 'obedience' declaration, Beresford had sent Hornby a powerful, fervent, rambling letter, which praised Tryon to the skies (he knew his man) but whose chief concern was the preservation of authority. The relevant bits may be regrouped as follows:

> No matter what accident has occurred, it would never do to allow for one moment that juniors are to criticize the orders given. Of course there must be exceptions: all the greatest things or nearly all the greatest things in our Service have been done on independent initiative or by not seeing or by disobeying orders; [and] of course we shall all disobey orders. But I do not believe that we can lay down any other public rule than absolute and implicit obedience. I cannot help thinking that in the interests of our great Service the findings of the Court-Martial were as we all shall wish.[44]

So that was it. That phrase again. That hallowed mantra and refuge: "the interests of our great Service". But this time its use was an unabashed *Name of the Rose* attempt to suppress an essential article of the faith, for fear that its admission would prompt a surge of fundamentalism and, no doubt, the overthrow of icons (the *Signal Books*).

A week after the Hornby–Beresford letter, *The Times* carried an anonymous rejoinder – thought to have been written by the septuagenarian Admiral Sir John Hay[45] – asserting that all this braying about obedience was irrelevant and theatrical, for the *Signal Books* had contained for a hundred years a caveat to the effect that

> if obedience to [a] signal would set up risk of collision, then the order is not to be obeyed. The general principle of the article [is] that no inconvenience arising from disobedience to a signal can be so great as that which would arise from 'the hazard of two ships falling on board of one another'.[46]

Hay's memory – assuming it was he – was not quite exact. The time-honoured instruction to which he alluded was that each ship, while manoeuvring in formation,

> is to do whatever may be necessary to avoid [any] danger to which she may be exposed; for it can scarcely happen that as great an inconvenience will arise from a ship being out of station, as may be occasioned by two ships falling on board each other.[47]

Regrettably, this splendid Old Testament simplicity had become corrupted by the 1889 *Signal Book*, which had added words and subtracted meaning until, at first glance, the injunction appeared to refer to the narrow activity of station-keeping rather than to the general business of manoeuvring in company:

> Although it is the duty of every ship to preserve as correctly as possible the station assigned to her, this duty is not to be held as freeing the Captain from

the responsibility of taking such steps as may be necessary to avoid any danger to which she is exposed, when immediate action is imperative and time or circumstances do not admit of the Admiral's permission being obtained.[48]

Nevertheless, it still suffices; and, together with Tryon's Wellington Memorandum and the NDA Section 29, it leaves little room to suppose that Markham, Johnstone or Bourke could have been convicted of disobedience (as postulated by Hornby and Beresford) had they refused to execute the signal. The simple assertion that it was not obviously safe would have been an adequate defence; indeed the verve with which an admiral manoeuvres a fleet must rest in part on a belief that any captain will extricate his ship if he sees the thing going wrong. We may note that *Victoria* is not the only warship whose loss through collision was preceded by a peremptory "WHAT ARE YOU WAITING FOR?";[49] yet the *Manchester Courier* was surely right in suggesting that Tryon, in spite of his overbearing manner (or at least when his temper had cooled), was "the very last man who would have insisted on carrying out a wooden discipline".[50]

At the bottom line, the *Globe*'s perception that "the responsibility for the loss of a ship while in company with a fleet is a very ticklish question"[51] hit the nail on the head with a realism which eluded those naval dogmatists who insisted on dragging the debate out of its proper seamanlike context and inflating a matter of mere 'inconvenience' into an issue of insubordination. If they believed what they publicly said about obedience, they must have viewed the above-mentioned *Signal Book* codicil as subversive, and should have petitioned the Admiralty to have it expunged before some impressionable junior officer read it.

*

In the resigned words of the *Admiralty & Horse Guards Gazette*, "it was hardly to be expected that Vice-Admiral Colomb would permit such an important naval occurrence as the loss of the *Victoria* to pass uncommented on by him";[52] and indeed he did not. Like Phipps Hornby, Colomb-inches publicly held Markham and Johnstone to be blameless, but his posture on the collision was both less ambivalent and more elaborate than Sir Geoffrey's, for, as we saw in Chapter 10, he had a very large axe to grind about Sir George Tryon. He had been offended by the latter's "firm reliance on the inexact",[53] and had "fought relentlessly against [the] TA system";[54] and he now seized upon the accident as the predictable consequence of Tryon's unscientific methods – which "the Admiralty might have taken steps"[55] to ban. It was not *Camperdown* or *Victoria* so much as the Mediterranean Fleet which had taken a wrong turning under Tryon's leadership. (This gambit had the added virtue of dodging the issue of Markham's erroneous, vaunted interpretation of the signal – a matter of which Colomb, as the *Signal Book*'s chief author, must have been keenly aware.)

Colomb admitted that 'TA' was not in operation at the time of the collision[56] – as indeed it could not have been, on the approach to a formation anchorage – but in associating the two issues he did have a point, albeit an oblique one: the ordeal of manoeuvring without signals probably accustomed officers to second-guessing the admiral and to thinking beyond the obvious, and, but for his traumatic experience of TA, Markham might have been quicker to reject an evidently unsafe signal. However, that is as far as the connection goes; and such limited pertinence as Philip Colomb's arguments possessed was squandered by his overweening 'side' and by the tendentious nature of his reasoning.

He wrote three long, self-promotional and, in places, almost impenetrably pontifical letters to *The Times*. The first appeared on July the 31st: "The whole Navy will recognize my unique position in regard to all that relates to fleet manoeuvring," he drooled, by way of introduction. ("What the whole Navy will recognize is that Admiral Colomb has never commanded a fleet at sea," was the *Pall Mall Gazette*'s riposte.) He was much concerned that his readers should be aware of his antecedents, and he called for a return to the choreographical certainties of manoeuvring as he claimed to have pioneered them between 1865 and '78. Essential to this pitch was the premiss that Tryon had been possessed of a foolhardy disdain for the immutable kinetic forces involved in fleetwork and believed that he could make ships behave in defiance of them. This was a fallacy: Sir George had merely taken the 'primary' skills of fleetwork as pre-conditional and moved on to the next grade; even a Mediterranean captain who held him wholly responsible for the collision, rated him a "consummate tactician who prided himself & whose study it was to do things to a yard".[57] Worse than this, Colomb strayed into the margins of personal abuse with a reference to "a second-rate brain" which appeared to compare the dead admiral unfavourably with such an item. The letter was widely condemned as poor taste,[58] and two of Sir George's most forthright champions took off their coats and climbed into the ring.

'One of Sir George Tryon's late Captains' (rumoured to be Custance, but in fact Fitzgerald) wrote to *The Times* that Colomb's letter was "so eminently calculated to mislead 'the lay mind' as to the indirect cause of the disaster that it certainly requires an answer from a practical seaman". He rubbished Colomb's elevation of the theoretical over the practical and pointed out that he

had fallen into the extraordinary error of mistaking the means for the end –
the error of supposing that manoeuvres in peacetime [are] the end of all our
training and not merely the means of preparing officers for handling ships in
the presence of the enemy.[59]

And Gerard Noel took public exception to Colomb's repeated use of
the pejorative phrase 'poor Sir George Tryon':

> In what way is he poor? What naval officer worthy of the name would not
> give anything they possess to be considered so great and rich in accomplish-
> ment as our late beloved Commander-in-Chief?[60]

When the Admiralty directed Culme-Seymour to enquire why Noel had
written to the press, the captain claimed that his letter "had no reference
to the Naval service [and] was purely a personal matter";[61] which was at
least partly true. (He could not have known that Spencer had alluded to
"poor Tryon" in correspondence with Culme-Seymour.)

Predictably, given his precipitate and liverish nature, Noel also wrote
personally to Colomb. His letter has not survived, but Colomb's nine-
page reply has[62] – as, of course, has his second letter to *The Times*, in
retaliation against the published replies to his first.

The methods to which Colomb resorted now reached their nadir. It
is not the tolerant *bonhomie* of a worldly-wise master welcoming errant
pupils back into class which offends the most. Nor his repeated self-
description as "an old fleet manoeuvring hand". Nor his implied claim
to have invented TA himself[63] (although he had "been able to gather
little" about the system, and had probably not deigned to read Tryon's
1891 memorandum). One could even put down to personal opinion his
assessment (in his letter to Noel) of Sir George's intellect as being "not
of a high character". What is most offensive – because it was likely, and
probably intended, to obscure, confuse and render inarticulate with
frustration – was his insistent and unscrupulous misalignment of
symptoms with diagnosis.

He made much, for example, of the careless reference of 'One of Sir
George Tryon's late Captains' to a ship's turning "diameter". The use of
this terminology, Colomb claimed with self-satisfaction, amply proved
his point about the slipshod approach to manoeuvring which Tryon
encouraged in his fleet, because, when a ship turns 180°, she actually
describes an elliptical arc (like a Limerick fish-hook) rather than a true
half-circle, and the chord cannot correctly be called a diameter. This
well-known and unremarkable fact has absolutely nothing to do either
with why *Camperdown* and *Victoria* collided or with TA, and it almost
defies belief that a man of academic standing and presumed integrity
should have invoked such a *non sequitur* to divert the debate onto the

dead ground of his own expertise.[64] His historical admirers may decide for themselves whether he should be excused by plea of stupidity.

To expose his multi-layered fallacies called for a steady, lucid and logical response. Sharky Noel may have deemed the task beyond him. Penrose Fitzgerald did not, and in *The Times* of August the 26th a second letter appeared from One of Sir George Tryon's late Captains. It could not have been bettered:

> So much of a personal nature has entered into this discussion on fleet manoeuvres that it is extremely difficult to confine oneself to that aspect of the subject which alone concerns and interests the general public. Admiral Colomb appears to claim for himself such a special knowledge – I might even say such a monopoly of accurate knowledge – of the manoeuvring powers of steamships that I fear it will be impossible to avoid wounding his feelings if the subject is to be discussed with truth and freedom.
>
> I must again expose my ignorance of his antecedents by submitting to your naval readers that his only claim to our gratitude (so far as this particular subject is concerned) rests upon the fact that he demonstrated, formulated, and tabulated certain physical facts which had already been for many years common knowledge to all experienced captains and pilots . . .
>
> Admiral Colomb takes great exception to our speaking of the diameter of a ship's turning-circle, instead (I presume) of the length of the chord of the parabolic curve which a ship describes in turning 16 points. He treats this descriptive error as fundamental to the discussion, or, at any rate as 'an organic detail'. To my mind it is a mere triviality. If I speak of the diameter of the turning circle, everybody knows what I mean, but if I use the longer but more correct term, nine out of ten men would take some time to gather my meaning. We all know that a ship does not turn in a circle when the helm is put over; but whether it be a parabola, an ellipsis, or a hyperbola, it is sufficient for practical men to know – as they undoubtedly do know – where they will find her at the end of the turn . . .
>
> Admiral Colomb fails entirely to grapple with the only point which is of practical and vital interest to the Navy and the country – that the object of all fleet manoeuvres is to teach officers to work their ships by the eye in the presence of an enemy, whose turning powers they will not know, and whose intentions they will not know until they are actually put into execution. All fleet manoeuvres by signal are the mere goose step, the squad drill, to prepare our battalions for war. We must learn to walk before we can run, but we must learn to run too, if we want to win the race.
>
> The loss of the *Victoria* was a national calamity caused by a temporary aberration in the mind of one man, and not by the 'T.A.' system or a "want of common knowledge" of the manoeuvring powers of their ships by the admirals and captains of the Mediterranean Fleet. That [Tryon] made a mistake and paid the penalty with his life proves nothing save that human nature is not infallible. To assign [*Victoria's*] loss to a wrong cause, as I believe Admiral

Colomb does, would probably lead to a far greater calamity in the loss of our naval supremacy, for it would arrest that development in the practical art of fleet manoeuvring which was so ably carried out by Sir George Tryon, and which we can only hope will still be carried on, upon the same practical lines by those who shall succeed him, and that they will in no case, and for no consideration, allow practice to be swamped by theory . . .

The Navy has made great strides in the practical handling of steamships of all sizes since 1878, and we must in no wise go backwards, or even halt. We can replace an ironclad, but the loss of our position as a leading power would be irreparable, and would carry with it consequences which it is not pleasant to contemplate. The leading idea of Sir George Tryon's life was the maintenance of this supremacy, and he worked at it with a singleness of mind and concentration of energy which excited the admiration of all those who knew him . . . With some little practical experience in handling ships myself, I believe that Sir George Tryon was right . . .[65]

Sad to relate, Colomb responded to this trenchant corrective with a graceless three-column exercise in last-wordism, in *The Times* of September the 7th. Maurice Bourke, convalescing at Battenberg's Rhineland *Schloss*, had "never read such rot as Columbus has written. I should not be surprised to hear [of] one of the Mediterranean captains' having punched his head."[66]

*

By this time even Colomb had perceived "a very strong feeling at present running against me in the service".[67] His unsavoury essays in self-aggrandisement helped opinion in the Fleet to crystallize, more or less, against the court-martial's verdict and against those whom he meant to succour. For example, Robert Noel, XO of the Channel flagship, *Royal Sovereign*, wrote to his brother:

> I have been intending to write and tell you how much I sympathize with the views you have expressed about the late disaster and the way people have spoken and written about the C-in-C. Whatever the papers say, there is a general feeling in naval circles that the blame has been thrown on the wrong shoulders and that . . . the rear-admiral displayed a want of seamanship and resource very lamentable in a flag-officer.[68]

The unwelcome controversy and the hardening of opinion placed The Ruler of the Queen's Navee in an invidious position. Lord Spencer's hope – indeed his promise to Culme-Seymour – had been that the Board of Admiralty would rubber-stamp the verdict when it came to review it in the autumn; but the Board was not the cabal of *éminences grises* which had exiled the judicial processes to Malta, and as the summer wore on he became increasingly aware from the temper of his naval colleagues that it was unlikely to be that simple. Furthermore, while certain disagreeable newspapers were calling for

> an authoritative ruling which will relieve commanders of HM ships of all doubt as to how they ought to act in such an emergency [as threat of collision while manoeuvring, because] the point is of too much importance to be left in any doubt . . . [69]

it was now on record in *Hansard*, in answer to a written Parliamentary Question, that Their Lordships must refrain from commenting on the matter of a captain's responsibility for his ship's safety until they had given "full consideration [to the] minutes of the court-martial" – which both conceded a link between the two issues and promised comment in due course.

This was the product of a sharp manoeuvre on the part of Captain Alfred Winsloe, who had gone directly to the Admiralty on his return from Malta (on or about August the 8th). There, the frustrated prosecutor was well received, and found that "My Lords think the finding a very weak one." He also found them engaged in pass-the-parcel. The 'PQ' had been put down by Tommy Gibson Bowles, an Opposition MP with a lifelong interest in maritime affairs (and an editor of *Vanity Fair*, whose pro-Tryon stance has been quoted). The issue was one which the Parliamentary Secretary, Sir Ughtred Kay-Shuttleworth, had dodged once already;[70] but Bowles had done his homework and appeared to have him cornered,[71] and Winsloe happened upon the Minister "almost in tears" because he could not find a naval lord prepared to draft an answer for him. So,

> I sat down and wrote the answer, which he gave word for word [in the House of Commons on August the 10th], and then I went to Sir A.H. and said 'after that answer you must take notice of what was said as it would never do to allow such rot [as the verdict] to go out as gospel'.[72]

As Winsloe remarked to Hornby, with permissible satisfaction, "I have got My Lordships in a place so that they must say something"; but his *coup* at best presented them with the public searoom to distance themselves from a verdict over which most were already restive.

Sir Anthony Hoskins, the senior sailor, had told Spencer that he was "surprised the CM did not notice" the inefficiency of *Camperdown*,[73] and in an emotional interview with the forlorn Maurice Bourke (his own flag-captain before Tryon's) he "tried to pump [*Victoria*'s CO] about Johnstone & Markham".[74] But Tryon's reforms had been implicitly unflattering of his preceding tenure of the Mediterranean, and he had been friends with the Markham cousins for a very long time (and a fellow Fellow of the RGS for over thirty years). Albert Markham had been his XO in *Sultan* in 1873–4, and when the Arctic Expedition of 1875 was in preparation, it was Hoskins who suggested the stimulating motto for the North Pole sledging party: *I dare do all that may become a man. Who dares do more is none!*[75] Markham clearly expected the First Naval Lord's sympathy,[76] and Sir Anthony had been instrumental in the original decision to hold the court-martial in Malta rather than Portsmouth. However, he was scheduled to retire on the 1st of September and be succeeded by the current Second Naval Lord, the taciturn, impassive Sir Frederick Richards.

'King Dick' was in nobody's pocket, and he had ideas which (the *A & HG Gazette* believed) were "more advanced than those of Sir Anthony".[77] He had recently been C-in-C China, and, interestingly, in January '92 – before the TA Memorandum reached him from the Admiralty – he had sent in a method of manoeuvring without flags, which one of his subordinates had invented and tested with a squadron of gunboats. Captain W. H. Hall had submitted that

> Several times I [have] desired to rapidly alter the course of my division in order to oppose a corresponding alteration of course by the other division and I found the present system of signalling alterations of course by means of flags much too slow . . . however well adapted it may be to directing the movements of a fleet during steam tactics in peace time, [it] proved on the occasion of sham fights to be too slow and uncertain a mode of conveying orders to a squadron opposed to a hostile one approaching at high speed . . . It is a matter of common observation how difficult it is sometimes to 'take in' a signal made by flags . . .

Hall had designed a system of simple shapes, in place of flags, and although Richards was dubious about its practicability, he endorsed his junior's motives by commenting that he had "addressed his attention to an undoubted want".[78] Richards was not one of nature's controversialists, and there is no evidence that he was an active TA partisan; but we do at least know that he was disconcerted by some of the misinformation which, he considered, was being put about after Tryon's death. When he tore a ritual strip off Lieutenant Mark Kerr for writing to the papers (to correct Laird Clowes's 'preserving the order of the fleet' solution), he said, "You had no business to do it, but I'm damned glad you did."[79]

The Controller of the Navy was the volatile Jacky Fisher, a Tryon-admirer of thirty years' standing, who wrote that "If I were Markham, I would never hold my head up again";[80] but he was untypically discreet with his opinion and its proof remained submerged in private papers for decades. His position was an uncomfortable one. As suggested in Chapter 10, he may have played an ill-judged role in Markham's appointment to the Mediterranean – in which case he would have had a harrowing sense of having let down his old comrade-in-arms, George Tryon. His prominence as the Navy's leading technocrat certainly associated him with some of the 'obedience' partisans, such as Lewis Beaumont (his XO in Cooper Key's flagship *Bellerophon* in 1877–8 and now CO of *Excellent*), Arthur Wilson, and (as discussed) Markham himself. Also, although his regard for Colomb, high during the steam *v.* sail debate, had dwindled into derision, Fisher "simply adored" Phipps Hornby,[81] whose flag-captain he had been during the Russian scare of 1885, and was still on serviceable terms with Charles Beresford. Nevertheless, of his private view there is no doubt. He thought the anonymous letter (by Sir John Hay) to *The Times* "excellent" and sent the cutting to Spencer with a note that he was "very strongly of the opinion that the Admiralty should avoid any encouragement of the idea that an Admiral second-in-command is to be an Automaton".[82] And he may have influenced the editorials of certain papers – such as the *Pall Mall Gazette* and the *Review of Reviews* – associated with his long-term journalist accomplice, William Stead.

The Junior Naval Lord was Lord Walter Kerr, Tryon's able and compliant number two in the Mediterranean until superseded by Markham; and the Parliamentary Secretary, Kay-Shuttleworth, had urged the First Lord right from the beginning that Markham should be court-martialled.[83]

This lot would be awkward enough but it was about to get worse, for the knock-on effect of Hoskins's retirement would create a vacancy for a junior naval lord which was due to be filled by Gerard Noel, whose contempt for the *Camperdown* duo was well known. In reviewing the court-martial verdict, Lord Spencer's fellow Board-members would therefore be almost as heavily inclined against Tryon's subordinates as the Malta court had been in their favour. In the last week of August the First Lord announced that Hoskins would be "allowed to retain [his post] for a couple of months longer, as the Board had not concluded its deliberations in regard to the *Victoria* disaster and the circumstances arising therefrom".[84]

The Board of Admiralty convened to consider the matter onboard its yacht, HMS *Enchantress*, in Chatham on 26th of September.[85] Who, if anyone, dominated the discussion is unknown; although in Fisher's words "Lord Spencer was pretty bad in his want of lucid exposition", while Richards (admirable on paper) was verbally "as dumb as Moses".[86] As the First Lord feared, the Board as a whole balked at Paragraph Four. If two senior officers – Markham and Johnstone – who had turned their ship into a predictable danger (the argument probably went) were so easily absolved, any careless or indecisive officer doing the same would only have to allege that he believed himself to have been obeying orders to claim the shelter of the *Victoria* precedent.

However, there were other issues involved now, such as Spencer's political position, and the desirability of supporting the authority of Sir Michael Culme-Seymour. And, while Their Lordships had been adroitly shepherded from one direction by Captain Winsloe, they found themselves barred in the other by Sir Michael: for while it would be unrealistic to expect to obtain a court-martial conviction of Markham and Johnstone when Bourke had been cleared (in effect) of the same offence, to reverse the decision on *Victoria*'s captain would be seen as highly vindictive. And even if Johnstone were summarily removed from the command of his ship (as an alternative to being tried),

> it would be impossible to make the reason for this clear to the public, even if it is made clear to the Navy, and I cannot avoid considering the effect on public opinion, for I have to defend the action of the Board for which I am responsible.[87]

So, with the issues thus "pushed under the wheels of the juggernaut",[88] the Board's formal response to the verdict had to fall short of what some of its members wanted. It took another month to emerge. Spencer thought it over for more than a fortnight, the wording had to be agreed, it had to go to the printers, and finally it had to be presented to Parliament in conjunction with a technical report on *Victoria*'s design. Meanwhile the First Lord prepared Culme-Seymour for what was still likely to prove an embarrassment.

> The discussion upon [the verdict] has taken place. We shall substantially approve the finding. The difficulty has been in regard to the *Camperdown* & the management of that ship and not in regard to those in *Victoria*. But I must not go into detail upon this and within 10 days I hope you will receive the formal Minute . . .

He went on to raise the subject of Sir Michael's recommendation for a KCB.[89]

The C-in-C was less than happy at the prospect of the Admiralty minute, and unmoved by the proffered knighthood (after all, he was already a 'Sir' by heredity):

> Whatever the nature of the minute may be on the *Victoria* CM, we shall receive it in a loyal spirit, but I cannot help regretting it is thought necessary. The whole subject has [been?] dropped and the public have forgotten it, and I fear that bringing the subject up again after 3 months, when everyone thought it was finished, will only raise further discussions and do no good –

besides it looks as if it is always necessary to revise important CMs, and it tends to shake the confidence of the Service in their finality.[90]

As far as KCBs were concerned, he understood that the military division had been created for distinction in battle, and to give one to someone who had not fought a battle would be to drive "a coach and horses" through the regulations.

Culme-Seymour, in turn, braced Markham for the forthcoming minute:

> I am sorry to tell you confidentially that a minute is coming out on the *Victoria* Court. I do not know the exact nature of it but I believe it reflects on the handling of *Camperdown* . . . I did my best to stop anything of the kind & I had thought successfully . . . I am very sorry indeed about the Admiralty minute, but I thought you would like to know before it actually comes to you.[91]

The 'Admiralty Minute' was dated the 28th of October and published in the press on the 2nd of November. It concurred with such criticism of Markham as was contained in the court-martial verdict, but added that "the proper interpretation of the signal" did not justify his belief that the C-in-C would circle outside him, and that this misconception delayed *Camperdown*'s taking proper precautions against a collision. Further, Their Lordships did not accept that the rear-admiral's presence entirely relieved Captain Johnstone of his "distinct and separate responsibility" as captain of his ship, and they noted that he failed to exercise the "promptitude and decision which the occasion demanded" and to "carry out the orders which he received with due rapidity and efficiency".[92]

The *Saturday Review* was

> glad to find the Admiralty confirming the opinion we expressed from the beginning, that the Captain of one of Her Majesty's ships is not bound to be the brainless echo of his immediate superior. What does cause surprise is that no censure is passed on Captain Bourke for conduct similar, at least in kind, to Captain Johnstone's. The doctrine as to the responsibility of officers should be laid down on some consistent, intelligible, principle. This is not done in the Admiralty Minute. It blames Captain Johnstone very severely, and thereby throws over the whole theory of passive obedience, yet it deals very tenderly with Admiral Markham.[93]

The *Admiralty & Horse Guards Gazette* failed to see how Markham and Johnstone could "with self-respect continue to hold their present appointments in view of such a censure" and was surprised that it was not to be followed up "by any action in regard to those officers".[94]

Spencer apologized to Culme-Seymour for the minute:

I sympathize with much that you say about the revival of the *Victoria* discussion. It was inevitable: a strong feeling prevailed about it, especially as to the actions of the *Camperdown*. The Board shared this feeling. We endorsed the general finding but emphasized certain points as to Markham and Johnstone. Had there been no finding dealing with Markham, it would have gone very hardly with him and Johnstone [implying that Paragraph Four of the Verdict had indeed saved them from court-martial].

It seemed clear that while obeying the unfortunate order they might have taken steps which would have avoided collision.

It was impossible to deal differently with the Capt. than with Markham, but Johnstone's ship seemed to have been in a strange condition of discipline, as evidence showed many points of great looseness.[95]

About the KCB, he assured the admiral that the Duke of Cambridge feared the military division would die out if the rules weren't bent, and that the Prince of Wales wanted him to have it (in the event he got the GCB, which was one better).

Culme-Seymour had feared that the Admiralty minute would be worse than it actually was, and the diplomatic manner in which he adjusted to the Board's review of his court's verdict, and handled the disconsolate and prickly rear-admiral – who was fully obtuse enough to seek a court-martial to exonerate himself – was all that the First Lord could have wished.

With regard to the Minute on the *Victoria* CM [Culme-Seymour wrote to Spencer, on the 16th of November], I feel bound to say I don't think, speaking generally, there is anything anyone can quarrel with in it. I had wrongly inferred, I think from a former letter of yours, that it would be very different, but I don't see that there is anything in this that the Service can criticize adversely, indeed, from all I hear it is generally agreed with. The point as to a flag-captain being responsible, although he has practically the charge [of his ship] taken out of his hands, is one that will no doubt be talked about and discussed, but it will be dropped in a few days. Of course Markham will not like the Minute, although he stayed with me after the CM and we are the best of friends. I have [arranged to have] a word with him on the subject.

He is a very sensitive man, and I believe his friends at home have been trying to clear his name and he has been led to believe, or allowed himself to believe, that if any Minute came from the Admiralty it would remove any implied censure of him by the CM. He takes the line that if he had been tried and on his defence he would have been able to prove he *was* justified in the view he took [about Tryon turning outside him]. I am perfectly sure he could not do this, and entirely agree with the Minute.

The Minute went to him officially yesterday and I have written to him privately telling him he could never prove he was justified in the view he took; [and] after all he is only told he committed an error in judgement.

It was well that the Minute came out before Noel joined the Admiralty. He has very strong ideas about Johnstone and would hardly speak to him – indeed I believe he would not speak to him . . . [96]

It is difficult not to view this letter as a matter-of-fact admission that Sir Michael knew very well his enquiry had papered over some of the issues arising from the collision, and that he had – intentionally or incidentally – been sheltering his inadequate junior.

Johnstone now jostled the rear-admiral for the crown of thorns: "I have been accused, judged and condemned absolutely unheard," he complained, accurately;[97] and he received, by way of consolation, Philip Colomb's "sincere sympathy".[98] Markham, meanwhile, received a flurry of sympathy from his geographical friends. Admiral of the Fleet Sir John Commerell FRGS offered moral support.[99] Admiral Sir Richard Vesey Hamilton FRGS, who with young Clements Markham had searched for Sir John Franklin and who was now president of the Royal Naval College (Colomb's strutting-ground), wrote: "If you allow a remonstrance in one case, you open the door to every old woman who doesn't know his work to cavil at the orders of a St Vincent or a Nelson."[100] Captain Lewis Beaumont FRGS, a fellow member of the 1875–6 Arctic expedition and now captain of *Excellent*, wrote: "I cannot tell you how greatly distressed Mary and I have been to think how much you must be pained and deeply hurt at the Admiralty minute."[101] Several correspondents urged Markham neither to resign not to seek redress. The former would be seen as an admission of guilt; and the Admiralty, as Lord Charles Beresford FRGS astutely told him, would never reverse an opinion it had once publicly expressed.[102]

At the beginning of December Sir Michael broke the good news to Lord Spencer: "I am glad to be able to tell you that Markham has taken my advice and will do nothing about the Minute. Tho he does not think so, he has nothing to complain about."[103] After nearly six months the *Victoria* controversy had run out of steam. The commander-in-chief must have heaved a sigh of relief. War clouds had been gathering for some time, and there was talk of a Russian squadron heading for the Mediterranean, where it might, in theory, combine with the French fleet against his own. He had more pressing things to worry about.

15

Counter-Reformation

"You will have to catch a good hold of each [captain] and put them through
the goose-step for a long time before you can trust them."

The Mediterranean Fleet swept out of Grand Harbour on August
15th, 1893, and turned north-eastwards towards the familiar playground of the Ionian islands. Within twenty minutes it was exercising
at steam-tactics, which were on the agenda the next day, the day after,
and the day after that.[1] Admiral Sir Michael Culme-Seymour flew his
flag in Arthur Wilson's *Sans Pareil*. This was a stop-gap measure. He
had known Wilson since they were shipmates in uncle Sir Michael
Seymour's flagship *Calcutta* in the late 1850s, but he considered *Sans
Pareil* unsuitable as a permanent flagship. Her accommodation was
cramped, he complained to Lord Spencer, and her single central mast
inconvenient for flag signals. To Hoskins, who of course had flown his
flag in her sister-ship before Tryon, he had written:

> Though I am afraid it may be treason to say so to you, I am not impressed
> with [her] arrangements in any way for a flagship . . . It has come out in evid-
> ence at the C.M., that all *Victoria*'s signal arrangements were most incon-
> venient and all the officers of the *Victoria* concur . . . I hope you will be able
> to give me *Ramillies* or one of those ships later on . . . [2]

Ramillies, of the new *Royal Sovereign* class, was completing in Portsmouth;
and Their Lordships were soon able to tell him that she would be his.

The *Royal Sovereigns* were the most conspicuous products of the 1889
Naval Defence Act which had been kick-started by Tryon's depreda-
tions in 1888. When they joined the Fleet these handsome and sea-
worthy 14,000-ton vessels were "the finest group of fighting ships
afloat".[3] They were the first 'ironclad' battleships to enjoy the ocean-
going capabilities of cruisers, and the first of the dynasty of capital ships

295

destined to be known to history as 'pre-dreadnoughts'. The key factor which placed them apart from their predecessors was the extra deck of freeboard forward, which was made possible by increased size and by the adoption of barbettes in place of heavy armoured turrets for the main-armament.

Royal Sovereign herself was already in service as flagship of the Channel Squadron. Jacky Fisher, as Superintendent of Portsmouth Dockyard in 1891–2, had originally forecast to Hornby that "We are going to hoist (I hope) Sir George Tryon's flag in the *Royal Sovereign* on Sep. 30, 1892, three years to a day from the time she began to be built";[4] but the Admiralty wanted her available for trials ahead of the rest of the class and nobody was better at hurrying ships than Fisher. She was completed four months early and went to the Channel, and Sir Michael only just missed her, for when he hauled down his flag in *Camperdown* in May 1892, his successor, Vice-Admiral Henry Fairfax, took her as flagship (and *Camperdown* went out to the Mediterranean[5]). Prince George, the day after he commissioned *Melampus* in Portsmouth Harbour, had written in his diary, "*Royal Sovereign* looks beautiful."[6]

"I am very much obliged", Culme-Seymour wrote to Spencer on the 22nd of August from Greece, where he was testing the fleet's manoeuvring mettle and shooting partridges,[7]

> for the arrangements you have made for the *Ramillies* to come out which is very satisfactory & precisely what I should have wished. I am afraid it is doubtful whether I can induce Wilson to remain as flag-captain – the work of getting a new ship into order in addition to the heavy duties of flag-captain, is, he feels, very great & he doubts if he could do it without one or the other suffering, & he will be promoted in '95.[8]

To bring *Ramillies* into commission and then to serve as his flag-captain Sir Michael prevailed upon his familiar Channel Fleet partner, Francis Bridgeman (who, in 1912, would succeed Wilson as First Sea Lord). In the meantime he set to work in *Sans Pareil*.

For the first few months Culme-Seymour led a fleet still tense with unspoken rancour. There was, needless to say, a distinct frostiness between Noel on the one hand and Markham and Johnstone on the other; and the captain of *Nile* also had an aversion to Pelham Aldrich, who had brought Sir Michael out to Malta and who had been a member of the *Victoria* court. Charlotte Noel wrote from Ryde in the Isle of Wight on the 21st of August: "I am so glad you are cruising in comfort again [away from the heat of Malta], tho' it is to be hoped that *Hawke* may be removed from your immediate neighbourhood before very long ..." A week later she said, "Darling I hope you and the R.A. will settle down in time", adding that she could see "*Resolution* and *Ramillies* [on trials] careering about in front of us" and that they looked magnificent.[9]

No admiral could wish to command a traumatized fleet, still over-shadowed by his predecessor; but this was a highly disciplined service and to some extent the closing of ranks in times of trouble was instinctive. Moore had received news of Culme-Seymour's appointment with the comment that "this is as it should be, the one man we hoped for",[10] and later loyally welcomed the court-martial verdict.[11] Even Noel had greeted the new C-in-C with a short and sufficient note saying, "The loss is intense . . . [but] you will find we are all ready for business whatever it may be and only too willing to follow the good lead we don't doubt you will give us."[12] For his part Sir Michael was a conciliator and a healer, with more sense than to compete with Tryon's memory. After the little contretemps over Noel's writing to *The Times*, he assured his fractious subordinate that he was

> much obliged for your letter [of explanation] and quite appreciate the spirit in which it is written. We are many of us apt to be impulsive and I am afraid Admirals are no exception. 'The incident may be considered closed' and I have already almost forgotten it occurred.
>
> George Tryon was brought up 8 miles from my wife – & as she wrote to me, we have lost one of our oldest and staunchest friends.[13]

Another potentially divisive incident which was quickly *de facto* closed was the Admiralty's equivocal statement on the court-martial verdict. To most officers the discussion of issues of obedience and initiative was "quite unknown",[14] and Culme-Seymour was right to assure Spencer that the Minute would have only a short life-span as a topic of debate. He certainly had no intention of fostering it.

In time, the remaining protagonists departed. Gerard Noel went to the Admiralty in November, leaving any remaining Tryonite sentiment leaderless. Charles Johnstone stayed on in *Camperdown* until June '94, but "rightly or wrongly, the disaster proved the end of his active career".[15] Albert Markham likewise served out a few more months, until he was superseded by Rear-Admiral Compton Domvile. After the publication of the Admiralty Minute he had wrapped himself in his work as second-in-command of the fleet, bewildered, defensive and un-exonerated. From time to time he grumbled about the injustice of it all (for example to Hoskins, who patiently replied that he was now powerless to help); but his public dignity in a position which others might have found unsustainable went some small way to restoring his tattered reputation in the fleet. In Jellicoe's words, "his was a fine character and he never showed that better than in the days which brought him so much sadness."[16] No doubt 'There, but for the Grace of God!' lurked at the back of many an officer's mind.

When his stint in the Mediterranean expired he was seen off with cheers, bands playing *Auld Lang Syne,* and an eleven-gun salute. He was never again employed at sea. For a long time he was not employed at all. He busied himself in helping to found the Navy Records Society and the Navy Lodge, and by getting married. When one of *Trafalgar*'s midshipmen, Charles Gervers, had fallen ill, Markham had given up his cabin for him and arranged for his family to visit. Now, at the age of 54, he married the boy's sister Theodora and presently had a daughter who gave him "much solace during his last years"[17] and to whom Prince George was godfather.

Markham visited Malta with his young wife in 1895–6 and retained his leading positions in local Freemasonry until Culme-Seymour left the station. In 1901, after he had been on half-pay for seven years, this officer who, in the Arctic and in *Hecla* and *Camperdown*, had had the misfortune to be associated with 372 accidental deaths, and the fortune to be officially blamed for none of them, was brought out of the wilderness and given the prestigious elder-statesman post of C-in-C The Nore – an appointment which (according to Beatty's flag-captain) was "much criticized" in the service.[18] And finally, in 1904, he was knighted. The hand of his old friend and masonic superior, Albert Edward, who succeeded to the throne as King Edward VII in 1901, may be discerned in these belated and controversial honours.

It is relevant to mention here that a reference-book issued by the Admiralty in 1904 (when Lord Walter Kerr was First Naval Lord), entitled *Remarks on Handling Ships &c.,* includes the pointed statement that

> With regard to the navigation and pilotage of ships in a fleet, it should be borne in mind that officers are at all times responsible for the safety of their own ships. While conforming to the movements of the flagship as closely as possible, they should not blindly follow, for, after all, he is liable to error. By exercising care on their part they may be able to correct in time the consequence of any such error and so save an accident.[19]

Sir Albert Markham worked tirelessly for the Minesweepers Fund in the Great War and died a fortnight before the Armistice. Richard Hough was astonished to learn that Lady Markham was still living when his book *Admirals in Collision* was published in 1959.

By the time Markham hauled down his flag, *Ramillies* had arrived in Malta, gone off for a two-month work-up cruise and then joined the fleet in the Gulf of Patras. And on January the 16th, 1894, the C-in-C had transferred himself, his flag, his secretary, his staff-commander and his flag-lieutenant from Arthur Wilson's ship to Francis Bridgeman's.[20] *Ramillies*'s officers, from captain down, were largely of Sir Michael's choosing.

When he took over the Channel Squadron in 1889 he had made it clear that he wanted none of his predecessor's people to stay on for *Camperdown*'s new commission (and kept Lieutenant Bacon as intelligence officer only "for the not very satisfactory reason that he could not find anyone else"). Nobody would have been surprised had he done the same in the summer of '93. But, instead, he took pains to see that key positions in his designated flagship went to *Victoria* survivors. This was considerate, sensible and shrewd. It smoothed over distressing memories, avoided dislocating the careers of several efficient officers (none of whom had been in *Victoria* for long), and pre-empted the survival of a dissident Tryonite nucleus in the naval wilderness. He had started, on arrival in Malta, by adopting Staff-Commander Hawkins-Smith.

One of the most important appointments was that of executive-officer. Sir Michael may have been acting on the advice of Arthur Wilson in appointing John Jellicoe; but the term 'Nelsonic', over-used by naval biographers, is permissible at least in connection with the extraordinary esteem and affection in which the young commander was already held by everyone who knew him. For example, at the instigation of Sir Geoffrey Phipps Hornby, a private fund was opened after *Victoria*'s sinking "against the loss he sustained in paint". It is hard to imagine such an appeal today, when there are various official and semi-official channels to deal with cases of need and when Englishmen are less demonstrative in their casual friendships. Remarkably, Lord Gillford, a fellow survivor, acted as the fund's treasurer; and among those who subscribed were:

Albert Markham	£2
'Pompo' Heneage	£5
Lord Charles Beresford	£5
Sir Geoffrey Phipps Hornby	£10
Arthur Wilson	£20
Jellicoe's successor as XO in *Sans Pareil*	£5
Jellicoe's predecessor as XO in *Victoria*	1 guinea
Inglefield's predecessor as 1st Lt. in *Victoria*	£5
Hornby's son-in-law, Captain Frederick Egerton	2 guineas

The collection closed at around £75 – a fifth of a commander's annual pay. "This will, at any rate, give him a good start in the *Ramillies*," Gillford noted,[21] presumably so Jellicoe – a man "obsessed by correcti-

tude and exactness, and by a wish always to do the proper thing"[22] –
could buy more paint.

Three other key appointees, the first-lieutenant and the gunnery
and torpedo officers, were also late *Victorians*, being respectively
Lieutenants Edward Inglefield, Arthur Leveson and Herbert Heath. It
was later said that *Ramillies* was "a veritable nursery of flag-officers".[23]
More specifically, she was a nursery of Grand Fleet flag-officers, for,
aside from Jellicoe and Evan-Thomas, Leveson was RA2BS in 1916,
and Heath RA2CS. And during the commission the ship was joined by
Lieutenants Edwyn Alexander-Sinclair (Com1LCS), Lionel Halsey
(Captain-of-the-Fleet) and Osmond Brock (RA1BCS).

Also in the *Ramillies* circle was Lieutenant William Goodenough
(Com2LCS), who came fresh from the royal yacht *Victoria and Albert* to
be first-lieutenant of the C-in-C's yacht, HMS *Surprise*. His late father
and Culme-Seymour had served together (along with young Wilson) in
Calcutta long ago, and now "Sir Michael treated me almost as an extra
Flag-Lieutenant". One of the enduring prizes Goodenough gained
from the commission "was to make the friendship and to obtain the
confidence of John Jellicoe. That in itself was worth far more than three
years."[24] Another officer who came under Jellicoe's spell in Malta was
Frederick Dreyer, his future gunnery collaborator and Grand Fleet flag-
captain. Their meeting, at a rifle competition, greatly impressed
Midshipman Dreyer. They each had a given time to shoot at the target
with a .45 Martini-Henry. Young Dreyer banged away in rapid fire,
gained seven hits and thought he had won; then Jellicoe arrived, carefully fired seven times, and shared the prize.[25]

At the turn of 1894/5, Captain Bridgeman had to be invalided home.
To succeed him as flag-captain,[26] William May moved to *Ramillies* from
his post as Assistant Director of Torpedoes. 'Handsome Willie May' –
also known as 'Christmas May', for claiming Christmas Island for
Britain – had been George Nares's and Albert Markham's navigator in
the Arctic Expedition of 1875–6, and had spent almost four consecu-
tive years in royal yachts in the 1880s. As C-in-C Home Fleet, 1909–11,
May was to play a key part in the training of the dreadnought Navy.
Now, under him, the Mediterranean flagship continued to be "one of
the finest and best disciplined ships in the fleet".[27]

These, then, were the men with whom Sir Michael Culme-Seymour
surrounded himself. In Jellicoe's words, they were "all most delightful
companions and excellent officers".[28] It has been alleged that "affability,
courtesy, generosity, veracity, were the qualifications most pretended to
by the men of arms, in the days of pure uncorrupted chivalry",[29] and
these sunny virtues were nowhere better exemplified in the Victorian

Navy than among Sir Michael Culme-Seymour's juniors in the Mediterranean Fleet. Late Victorian army messes and naval wardrooms were easily possessed by the Arthurian cult of the round table, and some of them

> developed their inherited codes to new heights of demandingness. A number of one-off groups gave dedicated and devoted support to individual heroes. Wolseley had his 'ring' in India; Kitchener had his 'cubs' in Egypt and the Sudan; Milner had his *Kindergarten* [in] the Transvaal;[30]

and, in his less deliberate way, Culme-Seymour – patrician figure, if not actually hero – had his clique in the Mediterranean. A visiting gossip columnist discovered that

> there is a word which seems to have caught on lately in Malta and that word is 'clique' . . . I have heard a good deal lately about 'the clique' sometimes called 'The Set'; they are all very good friends and they seem to have more fun than anybody else and they call each other by each other's Christian names; they are hospitable, friendly, and happy, and a real good set.

It is likely that William Goodenough is reading the above piece to Hugh Evan-Thomas in the photograph of the two favoured lieutenants lounging under the awnings of *Surprise*, for cutting and photo were inserted overlapping each other in Evan-Thomas's album.[31]

How far the 'clique' extended is impossible to say, and too much should not be made of it; but in as much as it represents the loose circle of good friends in and around the flagship, it is a useful term and there are many candidates for associate membership.

Rear-Admirals Richard Tracey and Richard King, both of whom had written highly of Evan-Thomas in *Sultan* ten years before, were successive superintendents of Malta Dockyard. Compton Domvile, as mentioned, succeeded Albert Markham as second-in-command of the fleet. To be his flag-captain in *Trafalgar*, Domvile chose the royal-yachtsman Archibald Berkeley Milne (whose role in the opening moves of the Great War will be mentioned in Chapter 19); and to be flag-lieutenant young Allan Everett (Jellicoe's Captain-of-the-Fleet in 1914–15, before Halsey). Arky-Barky in turn chose, as his XO, Stanley Colville (future son-in-law of Clanwilliam, and uncle of Evan-Thomas's 'flags' at Jutland).

Prince Louis of Battenberg (who would succeed Bridgeman as First Sea Lord in 1913) commanded the cruiser *Cambria* and then *Camperdown*. Henry Jackson (First Sea Lord 1915–16) was XO to John Brackenbury in *Edinburgh*. Cecil Burney (VA1BS in the Grand Fleet) was, as already mentioned, XO of Aldrich's cruiser *Hawke*. Lieutenant

Archibald Moore (sacked as RA2BCS after Dogger Bank) was gunnery-officer of *Anson*, having previously been GO of Culme-Seymour's flagship *Camperdown* in the Channel. Lieutenant Charles Le Mesurier (Commodore, 4th 'John Jellicoe's Own' Light Cruiser Squadron at Jutland) was a watchkeeper in *Collingwood*. Lieutenant Trevylyan Napier (Sir Michael's future son-in-law, and RA3LCS in 1916) was a watchkeeper in Wilson's *Sans Pareil*. And Lieutenant Michael Culme-Seymour (CO of *Centurion* in the Grand Fleet) came fresh from *Victoria and Albert* to be GO of *Howe*.

Efficiently served by these and many other officers, Culme-Seymour rehabilitated the fleet. "It required a man of personality to restore the confidence and the normal life that had received so violent a blow, and Sir Michael restored it to the full."[32] Phipps Hornby had warned him, at the time of his appointment: "You will have to catch a good hold of each [captain] and put them through the goose-step for a long time before you can trust them";[33] and, sure enough, he "devoted his time to putting the fleet through every conceivable manoeuvre in case the nerves of any of the captains or other officers should have suffered after the *Victoria* disaster".[34] "I am not an advocate of squadrons manoeuvring against each other and fighting sham actions," he told Spencer,[35] "but mobilizing ships, getting them together and manoeuvring them is of very great benefit"; and he believed that "the secret of all good manoeuvring is good comradeship"[36] – an echo of Hornby's lament, in the aftermath of the disaster, at the seeming absence of the easy banter which he recalled from his own time as C-in-C. Sir Michael "was a delightful man to serve with, sometimes rather brusque and off-hand, but he never meant anything by it";[37] and by the time he was done, his captains might have echoed the words of General-at-Sea George Monck, 230 years earlier: "We are all together now, and behold each others' faces with comfort."

It would be wrong to imagine that he was the antithesis of his predecessor. They were both consummate masters of steam-tactics;[38] and he fully acknowledged the thrall in which Sir George had held the fleet, and deplored some of the wilder remarks published about him. Reginald Bacon even managed, in different parts of his memoirs, to award them both the exclusive accolade of "*facile princeps* among our admirals",[39] and grouped them with Phipps Hornby and Fisher as the four admirals of the era "who would have made world-wide reputations had our country been involved in a war of magnitude"[40] – an assessment with which one can hardly take issue.

However, Culme-Seymour was a conservative and a consolidator, and his terms of reference had been largely defined for him by the circumstances of his appointment. His manoeuvres came from the *Signal Book* and the *Manual,* and he demanded and received excellence in the conventional 'primary' sense in which performance had come to be measured in the late Victorian Navy. He knew perfectly well what TA was about. He had received his copy of Tryon's circular memorandum in 1891, and (as we saw in Chapter 10) tested the Channel Fleet in manoeuvring without signals. The subject had also been discussed, perhaps more than necessary and tendentiously, at the court-martial. Furthermore, Gerard Noel left him his personal copy of the TA booklet[41] when he (Noel) departed the Mediterranean, in the encouraging manner of a farmer placing a porcelain egg in a hen-house. But Maurice Bourke was hoping and trusting in vain when he wrote to Noel from *Schloss Battenberg*:

> I do hope and trust that everyone will fight hard for T.A. principles, for I am convinced that unless many fight its battles, it will die for years to come. Damn these obstructives [such as] Columbus.[42]

Under Sir Michael's vigorous direction "the command [was] wholly centralized in the Commander-in-Chief, [and] subordinate commanders had little opportunity to exercise initiative";[43] and the tactical orders and responses of the Mediterranean Fleet were regressed until the 'TA experience' had been erased, so to speak, from the corporate record.

The *Camperdown–Victoria* collision was triggered by signals as explicit as any signal-book *aficionado* could wish (in modern jargon it was a C3-assisted disaster). 'TA' was not in use at the time, and, if it somehow had been, Markham would probably have copied *Victoria*'s turn to port with complete safety. Yet the association was easy and, in some quarters, welcome. When news of the catastrophe reached the Pacific Station, for example,

> everyone was convinced that the collision had taken place when [Tryon's] method of manoeuvring with a minimum of flag signalling was being practised, and as often is the case, everyone was wrong.[44]

But the mud stuck easily. And whereas the accident should have driven home with all the force of *Camperdown*'s ram the rightness of Sir George's mission to train subordinate senior officers to exercise their own tactical judgement, to all intents and purposes it had the opposite effect.

TA had been merely the means to an end; and the hidden cost of the *Victoria* affair was that, with Tryon's death and the apparent discrediting of the *means*, the all-important *end* – the return of the Royal Navy to fundamental action-principles – was orphaned and implicitly tabooed. Well might one officer (of no great intellectual pretensions) observe, "Perhaps the *Victoria* disaster in 1893 delayed for some years that progress in tactics that might otherwise have ensued."[45] Tryon became labelled in popular mythology as a hidebound Victorian curiosity (and was briefly portrayed as such by Alec Guinness, in the guise of Admiral Lord Horatio D'Ascoyne, in the film *Kind Hearts and Coronets*). His torch was extinguished as much by the *Victoria* court-martial and the subsequent 'rehabilitation' of the fleet as by the waters of Tripoli Bay, and it remained unlit until David Beatty, in his instinctive, careless way, began to draft Battle Cruiser Memoranda twenty years later. In the meantime the rightful place of a seaman officer's 'secondary' education – the only antidote to the alarms and dislocation of real action – was reoccupied by the perfection of the routines of his primary syllabus.

Percy Scott, the gunnery fanatic, missed the 'Tryon experience', having left the Mediterranean in 1890 and returned in 1896. He hoped to find great improvements. His testimony must, as usual, be adjusted for jaundice, but

> to my surprise everything was just as it had been; no advance had been made in any way, except in housemaiding the ships. The state of the paintwork was the one and only idea. To be the cleanest ship in the fleet was still the objective for everyone; nothing else mattered.[46]

Culme-Seymour was not oblivious to the concerns about the *Signal Book* which had troubled Tryon and even (to some extent) Phipps Hornby. He, too, worried about the opportunities which might be lost in battle while each manoeuvring signal was hoisted at the dip, acknowledged by all addressees at the dip and then at the masthead, hoisted to the masthead, and then executed. But where Tryon resolved to cut out the *Signal Book*, Sir Michael's best solution was to go through the formal rigmarole as fast as possible – as indeed his 1892 response to the TA memorandum had foreshadowed. In May 1895 he issued a booklet entitled *Notes on Manoeuvring*, which was to be read and countersigned by all COs, NOs and OOWs. It started by commending careful study of the *Manoeuvring Book*, which (it incorrectly alleged) "was drawn up by Sir Geoffrey Phipps Hornby", and went on to say:

> I consider quickness in answering signals of very great importance. It might make the whole difference when manoeuvring in the face of an enemy whether signals were answered at once, or the answering pendants kept some time at the dip . . . Even in a large fleet the time for a signal leaving the deck to the time it is hauled down should not average more than from thirty to sixty seconds.[47]

It may be doubted whether such speed was attainable in any other than the most antiseptic conditions,[48] but the admiral must have proffered it in confident knowledge of the efficiency of his flag-lieutenant, and quite possibly Hugh Evan-Thomas drafted the booklet for him.

Placing Culme-Seymour accurately in the '*Signal Book* debate' is problematical. Throughout his $3\frac{1}{2}$-year command of the Mediterranean he and his tireless 'flags' sent copious suggestions, alterations and errata back to the Admiralty. The last of these memoranda contains a passage which might have pointed another man towards Tryonism. The detailed matter under discussion is not of great importance here but, at the risk of descending into abstruse arcana, we have already come across it, early in Chapter 10, when Tryon argued (before going out to the Mediterranean) that the flagship must always be the guide of the fleet, wherever she was in the formation. Culme-Seymour, for his part, could not imagine a case where the flagship would not be the leading ship, and wanted the *Signal Book* to dispense with the terms 'guide' and 'commander' and make do with just 'leader', because in his view three terms were confusing and the first two superfluous.

It may be observed that both admirals were saying that the guide and the flagship were one and the same, but for opposite reasons: Sir George, because the C-in-C needed freedom of spontaneous movement wherever he happened to be in the formation (the fleet's station-keeping being less important); Sir Michael, because the C-in-C would always be in front, so the conflict of roles would never arise – a dogmatism which may have bearing on why his flag-lieutenant refrained from turning the 5th Battle Squadron 16 points *together* in the face of the High Seas Fleet at Jutland twenty years later (a manoeuvre which would have relegated the flagship to the rear of the line).

Tryon's extreme view had not been widely accepted in 1891 and nor was Culme-Seymour's in 1897. Sir John Hopkins (his successor), Lord Walter Kerr (now C-in-C Channel) and even Compton Domvile (now president of the Signals Committee) all disagreed with him, arguing that provision must remain for an admiral to be wherever he liked or wherever fate took him. Indeed it seems obvious that if, in the heat of battle, the admiral-leader turned his fleet *together* by more than 8 points, Sir Michael's system would turn into Sir George's whether he liked it or not. But they were unprepared to dispense with a facility by which a fleet could 'formate' on another ship if ease of station-keeping required[49] (and, today, the *Signal Book* compromises by providing both for a guide and for an 'officer in tactical command').

However, Culme-Seymour, *inter alia*, invoked a general argument of unimpeachable, Tryonic common sense:

> It should always be borne in mind [that] the *Signal Books* should be drawn up not for drilled fleets but for undrilled ones. When a number of ships are commissioned in a hurry in war time and have to go to sea, with many of the captains and officers undrilled in fleet work (possibly the admiral also), it is of utmost importance [that] everything should be perfectly simple and easily understood.[50]

While this 'idiot-proofing' principle is obviously compatible with the desideratum on which he conducted his fleet and on which he had partially rebutted TA in 1892 – that delays in flag-signalling be obviated by officers knowing the *Book* chapter and verse – he was ignoring the matter of battle conditions and was only chipping away at the problem. Tryon's way of idiot-proofing (i.e. de-skilling) fleet tactics – weening his fleet off the *Book* altogether – was both safer and more radical. Presumably Culme-Seymour was aware of the discrepancy, but had set his mind against so controversial a solution as Tryon's, and it is unlikely that many of his subordinates argued the case with him. He was not a man to brook disagreement. At the end of the above memo he declared defiantly, "I have probably more experience in handling a fleet than most men, certainly than any man now on the Active List"; and in 1897 his successor remarked (about the guide-and-flagship issue) that "one rear-admiral who served under his command, now President of the Signal Committee, has evidently changed his opinion, and how many captains might do the same now Sir Michael is not with them?"[51]

*

The Admiralty, meanwhile, found itself embarrassed from time to time by remotely stationed admirals still erectile about Manoeuvring With and Without Signals. They had every right to be so, for Their Lordships had never officially cancelled the TA circular of November 1891.

In February '94 the C-in-C Australia, Rear-Admiral Nathaniel Bowden-Smith (whose son would soon serve Fitzgerald as flag-lieutenant), submitted enthusiastic suggestions about the TA system. And in March the C-in-C North America & West Indies, Sir John Hopkins, supplemented his earlier endorsement with a plan of his own for 15 tactical movements by single flags. Their letters were placed in a file which bears the cover note: "No action seems necessary. There is no proposal to adopt Sir George Tryon's TA system as an addition to the *Signal Books* at the present time."

A year later the Training Squadron's Rear-Admiral Robert Harris ("a very impatient man"[52]) favoured his masters with his opinion that the somewhat elaborate manoeuvring signals as laid down in the *General Signal Book* are most excellent exercise for the officers and signalmen when a fleet is going through its preliminary drills . . . yet in action they would be hopelessly impracticable.

This time the cover note said irritably: "Admiral Harris is probably unaware the question is no longer under discussion, and that T.L.s have no present intention of again discussing it." It was filed away for the future interest of the Signals Committee.

A year later still – 1896 – Vice-Admiral Alexander Buller (whose son would be Fisher's 'flags') had a go at putting the China Squadron through TA, and injudiciously told the Admiralty about it. His letter, too, was consigned to the bureaucratic dustbin.[53]

*

It would be quite misleading to imply that the *Signal Book* and the goose-step quadrille were Culme-Seymour's sole or even major preoccupations. The proceedings and transactions which passed across the desk of the commander-in-chief of a major station were myriad, and many of them had international ramifications. For example, there was a new session of Turkish atrocities in Armenia to be curbed. And the Russian Scare had Sir Michael studying anew the feasibility of taking the fleet through the Dardanelles ("the defences are very different indeed from when Hornby went up," he warned Spencer[54]); and he was much concerned with his inventory of torpedo-boats in case Malta should come under blockade by the French. But it is in the tacit disavowal of his predecessor's action-principles, and in the reversion of energy from the 'secondary' back to the 'primary' professional syllabus, that his tenure of the Mediterranean concerns us. And in these matters his 'flags' was by far his most important assistant. This was the watershed appointment, and the longest, of Evan-Thomas's career. It established his reputation for *Signal Book* fleetwork and familiarized him with all practical aspects of communications; and "it may be" – as his devoted nephew, Vice-Admiral Sir Geoffrey Barnard, later conceded (after serving as one of Cunningham's staff-officers in the Mediterranean in 1940–3) – "that this background of precision in signals caused some of the later troubles at the time of Jutland."[55]

The Mediterranean played its part in the surge of garden-shed invention which possessed the Royal Navy in the 1890s. There was much experiment with semaphores, concertina shapes which expanded and contracted, masthead lights hidden by canvas skirts which rose and fell at the tug of a lanyard, lamps with venetian-blind shutters (still in use), and even pigeons (not still in use). In September '93 Lieutenant Everett,

who at a very junior rank corresponded with retired admirals on sub-
jects relating to signalling and fleetwork, and who was shortly to be
Compton Domvile's 'flags', reported to Philip Colomb from the cruiser
Amphion:

> A few days ago I met Evan-Thomas our new Flag-Lieutenant who I'm happy
> to say is very keen about extending the distance limit of our day signalling.
> Now that cruiser people are beginning to think how the intelligence they
> acquire is to be imparted expeditiously to the main body, this is recognized as
> of due importance.[56]

Helped by Pelham Aldrich,[57] Arthur Wilson and, of course, his
flag-lieutenant, Culme-Seymour "worked out schemes for locating the
enemy by cruiser search, and introduced the masthead semaphore for
long-distant signalling".[58] Meanwhile, Battenberg's prototype 'Course
Indicator'[59] (standard kit a hundred years later) was being tested by
Culme-Seymour's captains; and Prince Louis now tried his hand with
his own masthead signalling device, which worked "on the umbrella
principle" – except that it didn't, really.[60] And Evan-Thomas offered
prizes for pigeon races between Sicily and Malta.[61]

*

Hugh Evan-Thomas's service on Culme-Seymour's staff was not uninterrupted. As we have seen he suffered debilitating illnesses from time
to time, although their exact nature is unclear. A letter home in October
1893 mentions "bad neuralgia",[62] a term which embraces a wide range
of painful nervous disorders. There is testimony of his being barred,
by doctor's orders, from playing polo at about this time;[63] and when
George Aston wrote to him after Jutland, twenty-two years later, he
alluded to "the time at Malta when the future looked so black for you on
the doctors' reports and how well you stuck it out". In the spring of
1894 he was packed off to England. Prince George, Duke of York,
sympathized:

> I am indeed distressed to hear that you have been so seedy & had influenza
> twice & have been obliged to come home on sick leave. What bad luck, do be
> careful now and don't do too much.[64]

At this juncture, at least, his ailments were exaggerated, with Sir
Michael's complicity. His Service Certificate reveals that as far as the
Admiralty was concerned, the admiral had granted him "leave to come
home on urgent private affairs". He was certainly well enough on arrival
to betroth himself to Hilda Barnard ("He did not waste much time over
the business," muttered Prothero the Bad darkly, "I wonder at her

1. Sir William Fanshawe Martin   2. Sir Geoffrey Phipps Hornby

3. Philip Colomb   4. Sir Archibald Berkeley Milne

5. *Bacchante*

6. John Jellicoe and Hugh Evan-Thomas in the sternsheets of a skiff at Henley, *c.* 1885

7. *Melampus*, 1892

8. *Melampus's* officers. Sitting on ladder at left, Revd John Dalton and Bryan Godfrey-Faussett. Seated in front row, from left, Hugh Evan-Thomas, Charles Anson and Prince George. Standing at Anson's right shoulder, Arthur Leveson

9. The Royal Yacht *Osborne* in Venice, May 1893

11. Albert Markham with daughter, c. 1901

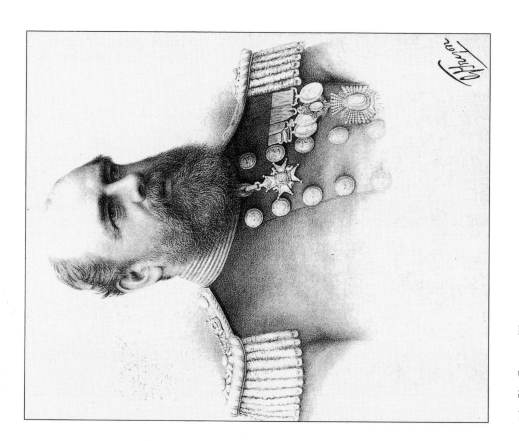

10. Sir George Tryon

12. *Victoria*'s final plunge, June 22nd, 1893. *Nile* stands by

13. Scene from court-martial aboard *Hibernia*, base-ship of Malta dockyard.
Standing, left, Albert Markham on the defensive. Standing, right, Alfred Winsloe
(prosecutor). Seated, right, Sir Michael Culme-Seymour (president).
On the table is a cut-away model of *Victoria*'s bows

14. Sir Michael Culme-Seymour

15. Sir Michael leading the fleet in manoeuvres

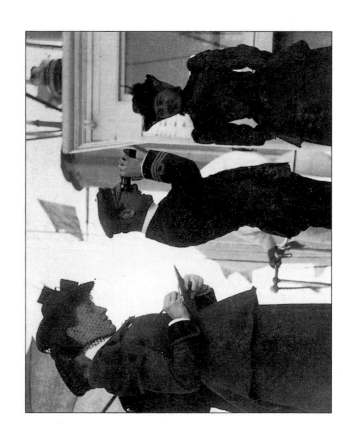

There is a word which seems to have caught on lately in Malta and that word is "clique". That there is some reason for the term goes without saying, for without doubt Malta, like most other places, is not without its "clique". I have heard a good deal lately *about* "*the* clique" sometimes called "The Set"; they are all very good friends, they seem to have more fun than anybody else and call each other by each other's Christian names; they are hospitable, friendly, and happy, and a real good set.

18. Commander Jellicoe reads a signal to the Admiral's daughter

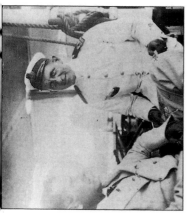

16. Evan-Thomas and William Goodenough relaxing aboard *Surprise* (the C-in-C's yacht), Goodenough evidently reading item at top right

17. Sir Michael Culme-Seymour with his staff (*c.* 1896): Hugh Evan-Thomas, William May and Staff-Paymaster Rickard

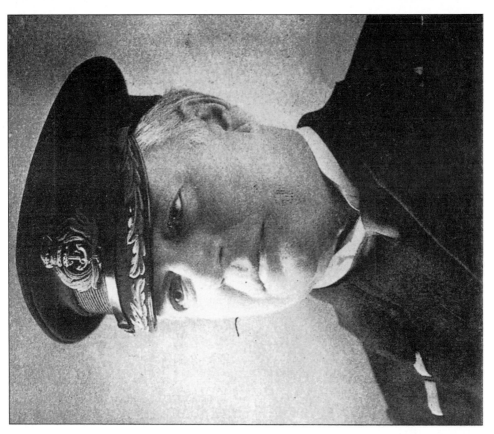

20. Lord Charles Beresford

19. Sir John Fisher

21. *Iron Duke*

22. High Seas Fleet flagship, *Friedrich der Grosse*

23. *Queen Elizabeth*

25. Vice-Admiral Reinhard Scheer

24. Sir John Jellicoe on *Iron Duke's* quarterdeck

26. *Tiger* alongside *Princess Royal* in Rosyth after Jutland

27. The 5th Battle Squadron manoeuvring in heavy weather

28. *Warspite* and *Malaya* at *c.* 2.00 p.m. on May 31st, 1916

30. *Lion*'s Q turret erupting

29. *Indefatigable* sinking, taken from *New Zealand*

31. The same turret after the battle.
Part of the turret-roof may be seen on the deck at right rear

32. A Battle Cruiser Fleet light-cruiser under fire from the High Seas Fleet

33. Sir Robert Arbuthnot's flagship, the armoured-cruiser *Defence*

34. The German battlecruiser *Seydlitz* limping home

35. *Invincible* blowing up

36. *Badger* closes *Invincible's* wreck to rescue survivors. Taken from a battleship of the 1st (*Benbow's*) Division of the 4th Battle Squadron. *Superb* and *Canada*, rearmost ships of the 2nd Division, can be seen in the background

37. Grand Fleet destroyers. The one on the right is *Hydra*

38. Body language. Evan-Thomas and Beatty on *Queen Elizabeth*'s quarterdeck, June 1917. The King has just knighted Sir Hugh with Sir David's sword

39. and 40. Beatty (here in 1923 and 1925) "had in him some elements of a bounder"

Ladyship's allowing it"[65]). The Duke of York's letter of congratulations shows that George had neither met his fiancée nor even heard about her from the Daltons – which suggests that he had been curiously secretive in his courtship:

> My Dear Old Thomas
>
> I have just received your letter in which you tell me you are engaged to be married. My dear fellow I wish you every possible joy and happiness & congratulate you with all my heart. I am sure Miss Hilda Barnard must be everything that is charming since you have chosen her to be your partner in life & I know you have got very good taste.[66]

Meanwhile Lieutenant Arthur Christian feared a cloud on his old shipmate's horizon:

> Is she 'the nicest girl I've ever met in my life'? We'll hope so. Do you remember how you used to come on board the old *Bacchante* and rave after every dance that you went to?
>
> I expect old Culme-Seymour will kick you out of your billet now, no one ever heard of a married flag-lieutenant at Malta.
>
> Chin chin old chap – ask me to the wedding.[67]

Evan-Thomas now embarked on a crash string-pull to secure an appointment to the royal yacht *Victoria and Albert* – exactly ten years after he had last tried (through John Dalton). It is not clear what game he was playing, for the Culme-Seymours knew perfectly well that he meant to get married – Miss Barnard had probably stayed with them in Valletta[68] – and he knew perfectly well that Sir Michael was not going to kick him out. But he wrote to Prince George and he wrote to Sir Anthony Hoskins. George replied:

> My Dear old Thomas,
>
> . . . perhaps you are not aware that every year three lieuts' names are sent by the Admiralty to Admiral Fullerton [permanent CO of *Victoria and Albert*] as candidates for the 'Yacht', they are submitted by him to the Queen who chooses one of them. So until you can assure me that the Admiralty have sent in your name as one of the three, I can do nothing for you. But as soon as you let me know that this has been done, I will do all in my power to get your name selected, I will also speak to my father about you. I am exceedingly sorry that your illness has placed you in this position, when you are getting on so well as flag-lieutenant in the Mediterranean. But although I have just made you this promise, I must tell you, which possibly you knew before, that I was trying for Anson last year & should his name be sent in as one of the three by the Admiralty this year, he should have my prior claim.
>
> With renewed good wishes for your happiness, Believe me most sincerely,
>
> Yours, George.[69]

Hoskins replied:

> It was with very great regret that I, and I should say we, heard of your
> renewed illness and that you have been obliged to come home . . . as for the
> Yacht, I don't think you can do wrong in trying for the appointment but it is
> a very uncertain thing to rely on – the appointment is kept very much in the
> hands of high personages . . . I am afraid you over-rate my power of helping
> you, for indeed I can do little in this particular matter. You should see Lord
> W. Kerr, Sir Frederick Richards and the private secretary, and get Sir Michael
> Seymour to write about you.[70]

Hugh and Hilda were married in St Saviour's Church, Walton Place
(behind Harrods), on July the 18th, 1894. Prince George and Princess
May did not attend, having just become the parents of David, the future
Duke of Windsor, but they sent a silver tea set. By the autumn, he was
quite fit enough to show his wife round the family estates of Gnoll
and Llwynmadoc in Wales, and shoot partridges and pheasant. In
November they took passage by P. & O. to Malta, where they set up
home two minutes from Admiralty House in Valletta. As with his
seniority, Evan-Thomas's marital status was another small step towards
the institution of a formal specialization in signals. There was a cost to
be paid for his extended absence, though not an unreasonable one. His
friend Battenberg commiserated:

> I trust it is not too great a disappointment to you to have your promotion put
> back 6 months – 'It is an ill wind &c' – and I dare say Sir Michael will be glad,
> as we all are, not to lose the best of flag-lieutenants.[71]

It was an enviable billet for a newly married couple. Their house still
exists, high above St Michael's Bastion, with a fabulous view across
Marsamxett Harbour towards Sliema. And as ever in Malta, there were
parties, balls, amateur dramatics, and a variety of outdoor social and
sporting activities. (In the '94 Fleet Athletics the C-in-C "won the veterans' race in grand style by almost twelve yards. Burney and Henderson
dead heat for second place."[72]) Whenever the fleet was in harbour, the
admiral and his flag-lieutenant were at the centre of the social whirl, and
Sir Michael and Lady Culme-Seymour were expansive entertainers.

"Very grand people" – sometimes on passage to the East but often
just on holiday – would come to Malta in the winter[73] and would stay
at Admiralty House or in the C-in-C's yacht. The two princesses with
whom Evan-Thomas had sailed in *Osborne*, Victoria and Maud, were
put up by the Culme-Seymours. Lord Cromer was a guest on board
Surprise and enthralled William Goodenough by discoursing at length
on the subject of Egypt. Albert and Theodora Markham (as already
mentioned) stayed for a while, and so too did Clements Markham, the

celebrated geographer. In the possibly careful words of the *Dictionary of National Biography*, Sir Clements (as he became in 1896) "had a genius for friendship with the young . . . above all, young naval officers found in him a tireless friend." The Markham cousins had sailed with William May on the '75 Arctic expedition, and, further back, Albert had been a lieutenant and May a midshipman in Captain James Goodenough's *Victoria* (the name-predecessor of Tryon's flagship, and the last three-decker ever built) in the Mediterranean in the mid-1860s. Both Frederick Inglefield's and William Goodenough's interest in the RGS (of which the former became a council member in 1922 and the latter president in 1930) may be associated with the Markham link.[74]

When Hugh Evan-Thomas finally left the Mediterranean in December 1896, after three and a half years in Culme-Seymour's service, the admiral wrote on his 'flimsy' that "He has great tact and judgement – a thorough knowledge of his duties (signal and otherwise) and both with the fleet in the summer at sea and on shore in Malta has been all that I could wish."[75] His 'haul-down' promotion[76] to commander took effect on January the 1st, 1897.

*

Among the scores of officers of the Mediterranean Fleet whose bridge-watchkeeping hours were spent in thrall to Evan-Thomas's impeccable flag-hoists, was a short stocky lieutenant who had joined *Camperdown* after her repairs in October 1893, with just one year's seniority and no particular distinction.

David Beatty had not excelled, professional speaking, as a very junior officer. His attitude as a naval cadet may be inferred from a *Britannia* photograph: his classmates are sitting and standing more or less formally, but young Beatty lounges, jacket undone and hands on hips.[77] The captain's punishment book shows that he and little Walter Cowan were given six of the best for bullying a first-term cadet[78] (who ran away soon after and was discharged from the Navy). His early reports from sea are generally the monosyllabic minimum,[79] with few of the extra comments of praise typical of Evan-Thomas's. As a midshipman in HMS *Alexandra*, the then Mediterranean Fleet flagship, from 1886 to '88, he preferred his sporting pleasures and social life ashore to hard graft, and was rated "one of the best light weight [polo] jockeys in Malta". At sea, he gained the friendship of Lieutenant the Hon. Stanley Colville, in whose watch he was. Colville was something of a hero to *Alexandra*'s midshipmen, having served in gunboats on the Nile in 1884–5 in support of Sir Garnet Wolseley's belated attempt to rescue General

Charles Gordon from Khartoum. In Rear-Admiral Chalmers's fanciful words, he

> was mad keen on the Navy, and one can imagine the two of them on the bridge in the night watches as the ship ploughed her way through the placid waters of the Mediterranean, exchanging views, over a cup of cocoa brewed by David, on life in general and the Navy in particular.[80]

As a sub-lieutenant studying at Greenwich for his lieutenant's qualifying exams, Beatty's application left much to be desired. He had better things to do. Over twenty years earlier an enquiry into junior officers' education had regretted the choice of Greenwich as the venue for these courses, because of the proximity of "the gaieties, amusements and dissipations of London, so attractive to young men" (typically, James Goodenough had dissented, commending such things as mind-broadening); and true to form, Sub-Lieutenant Beatty spent his weekends on the hunting field and his weekday evenings gadding about town. His room at Greenwich was adorned with "photographs of actresses, some of which were signed in the most endearing terms".[81] Sometimes he would stroll up and down Piccadilly with Walter Cowan, both stony-broke, hoping to bump into a relation or family friend who would buy them dinner. He achieved only 'gentleman's passes' in his exams and more earnest juniors such as Arthur Craig, Edward Phillpotts and Algernon Boyle (respectively of *Barham*, *Warspite* and *Malaya* at Jutland) overtook him in the seniority steeplechase.

Whether he simply didn't care or whether he had an intuitive, arrogant belief that he wouldn't have to struggle like normal mortals – probably a bit of both – historians have remarked on the extraordinary luck which rescued his career and stayed with him thereafter. Back in the Mediterranean, he was transferred in 1895 from *Camperdown* to Rear-Admiral Domvile's flagship, *Trafalgar*, of which Stanley Colville was now XO. It is almost as if fate was pre-positioning him for a most unlikely turn of events.

Early in 1896 General Sir Herbert Kitchener was making preparations to reinvade the Sudan, ostensibly to avenge the death of Gordon eleven years earlier but really to parry an impending French claim to the Upper Nile. The plan would involve the progression of his mainly Egyptian army up the Nile valley, and gunboats were vital to its success. In May he telegraphed Sir Michael Culme-Seymour in Malta, asking for John Jellicoe to lead the river force. At the time Jellicoe was out in *Ramillies* at target practice; and without consulting him Sir Michael telegraphed back that he could not be spared. The admiral reasoned that, given his flag-commander's susceptibility to Malta fever, his health would probably fail him on the Nile; and by the time Jellicoe returned to harbour and learned what had taken place it was too late to remonstrate. He was (in his own words) "deeply disappointed. [And] as a result my old friend Cecil [Stanley] Colville took my place."[82] Colville's experience of the Nile in 1884 made him an obvious alternative choice, and in spite of the early promotion to captain which he gained from the appointment, he and Jellicoe remained the best of friends.[83]

Commander Colville cast about for a team of likely lads, and his young protégé David Beatty, along with Horace Hood, Colin Keppel and Walter Cowan (among others), commended himself.

> Not one naval officer in a hundred had heard shots fired in action; even the generation that had taken part in the bombardment of Alexandria was passing. Colville's half-dozen lieutenants were the only officers out of thousands to be set on the path to glory. Nor was that all, for during the ceaseless skirmishing that went on up and down the river, Beatty received only a bullet through his sun helmet, while Colville had one through his arm, so that Beatty at the age of twenty-five found himself by the fluke of seniority the naval officer in command in action. He made every use of his opportunity and when the campaign ended he was a marked man with a mention in despatches and a DSO – there were captains, and even admirals, without a single ribbon on their chests in that unbemedalled age. And of course when Kitchener gathered his strength for the final advance, Beatty's services were called for again, and he was in command of a gunboat at the victories of Atbara and Omdurman.[84]

The demands which the Nile placed upon Beatty were phenomenal ones for so young an officer; and his capacity to meet them with a cool and level head owed little to his schooling as a junior nobody amongst the battleship routines and *Signal Book* fixations of the Mediterranean Fleet. It might never have come to light had he continued to follow a normal career path in the peacetime Royal Navy, and the ground lost to some of his more diligent contemporaries might never have been recovered.

If there is any truth in Professor Arthur Davis's proposition that "the effectiveness of military leaders tends to vary inversely with their exposure to a routinized military career", or in Maurice Janowitz's that the most decisive officers are "characterized by pronounced unconventionality in their career lines",[85] then the decade of the 1890s could be said to have conditioned Beatty, no rising star hitherto, and Evan-Thomas for their behavioural differences as admirals. Given the binge of expansion soon to beset the Royal Navy, with its consequent knee-high promotion hurdles, both men not only as good as guaranteed their future flags through distinguishing themselves in their radically different ways as lieutenants, but projected into their admiralcies the respective attributes which had brought them the glittering prizes as junior officers.

Left to their own devices, the mechanisms of peacetime preferment would still have denied Beatty the highest rewards of the service – unless overridden by the mechanisms of fantastic chance. On the eve of the Battle of Omdurman, September the 1st, 1898, a young supernumerary attached to the 21st Lancers was strolling along the bank of the Nile

> in company with a brother officer [when] we were hailed from the gunboats which lay 20 to 30 feet from the shore. The vessel was commanded by a junior naval lieutenant named Beatty. The gunboat officers, spotlessly attired in white uniforms, were eager to learn what the cavalry had seen, and we were by no means unwilling to tell them. We had a jolly talk across the stretch of water while the sun sank. They made many lugubrious jokes at our expense [including] offering us hospitality on the gunboat if the worst came to the worst. After a good deal of chaff came the piece of good fortune. 'How are you off for drinks? We have got everything in the world here. Can you catch?' and almost immediately a large bottle of champagne was thrown from the gunboat to the shore.[86]

The missile fell short, and young Winston rolled up his trousers and paddled into the shallows to retrieve it before carrying it "in triumph back to our Mess". Beatty cannot possibly have imagined that he had just thrown champagne (in the desert!) at the man who, by a fluke comparable to that of "an astral collision",[87] would become First Lord of the Admiralty at a critical juncture in his career. The next morning, while waiting to take part in the British Army's last true cavalry charge (a suitably misdirected and bloody one), Churchill watched with admiration as Beatty's gunboats scythed the massed ranks of the dervish army.

16

Regulate Britannia

"The Navy is the first line of national defence and
the chief bulwark of the Empire."

Truth, 10 June 1897

Like all big national anniversaries, the year of Queen Victoria's Diamond Jubilee was a time of taking stock for the British people. What they found, in 1897, surprised and gratified them. First and foremost, they were celebrating the remarkable old lady who had ruled for sixty years. However, as representatives of "one quarter of the inhabitants of the globe came to pay homage",[1] and as her marathon reign had been accompanied by phenomenal "progress and prosperity",[2] they were also, inevitably, celebrating Great Britain.

The formal centre-piece of the jamboree was a massive parade through six miles of the streets of London on June the 22nd (the fourth anniversary, as nobody mentioned, of the loss of HMS *Victoria*); but patriots everywhere got quite carried away with official and unofficial demonstrations.

A grand time was had by all. "Politics were neglected, debates disregarded, disturbing rumours discredited, and even business itself suffered from the general distractions of the public."[3] Towns and villages festooned themselves with flags; school holidays were declared; pubs ran dry; an Oswestry printer sold posters announcing "A MAGNIFICENT INNINGS. SIXTY AND 'NOT OUT'! GOD BLESS OUR QUEEN!" and was arrested for subversion; bonfires were lit on two and a half thousand hilltops from Land's End to John O'Groats; and Victoria was received, wherever she went, with "deafening roars of welcome".[4] Irish nationalists condemned the whole thing. German delegates were heckled by the crowd.[5] And the *New York Times* was nearly moved to revoke independence:

315

The Jubilee has had the effect of increasing the goodwill between Great Britain and the United States. We are a part, and a great part, of the Greater Britain which seems so plainly destined to dominate this planet and has made such enormous advances towards its conquest these last sixty years.

(Today's New Yorkers would more readily connect with a headline-grabbing sideshow:

Few Jubilee incidents have created more interest in America, or touched a chord more readily than the Princess of Wales's dinners to the poor. The accounts of this kindly and womanly charity added to the popularity of the princess, already widely honoured and beloved in the United States.[6])

No sooner had the main events in London passed than the world became aware of another spectacular, in the waters of the East Solent: the Diamond Jubilee Naval Review.[7] Without withdrawing so much as one ship from overseas commands, the Admiralty mustered at Spithead, under the flag of Admiral Sir Nowell Salmon VC (C-in-C Portsmouth), 165 warships – a few more than Jellicoe could field at Jutland – including most of the largest and strongest battleships and cruisers in the world: awesome products of the 1889 Naval Defence Act. It was a display of strength "unparalleled in the annals of our modern steam navy",[8] and which could have engulfed any single foreign fleet. Portsmouth was log-jammed with trippers who came by train from all over the south of England to gawp and marvel with proprietorial pride.

Journalists fresh from watching exotic contingents from every corner of the Empire marching through London's cheering crowds, were not slow to make the connection between Britain's colonial power and the 'Senior Service'. The Fleet possessed (in the words of *The Times*)

a significance which is directly and intimately connected with the welfare and prosperity of the Empire. [It] is at once the most powerful and far-reaching weapon which the world has ever seen. [But] proud as all Britons must be at the unexampled exhibition of national strength, skill and ingenuity, they may be prouder still of the fact that the power which it represents has never been exercised save for the defence of justice and the maintenance of peace.[9]

The Royal Navy was basking, also, in high endorsement from across the Atlantic. At moments of crisis throughout modern history, the link between maritime mastery, on the one hand, and economic, military, political or religious power, on the other, had become apparent to merchants, soldiers, monarchs and popes. But now it had been systematically analysed by an American naval officer, Captain Alfred T. Mahan. *The Influence of Sea Power upon History, 1660–1783* (published in 1890), and its sequel *The Influence of Sea Power upon the French Revolution and Empire,*

1793–1812 comprised an authoritative exposition of Britain's historical debt to the Royal Navy and, as such, found great favour – for reasons chauvinistic as much as intellectual – in British naval circles. For a Yankee to write such books, drawing substantially on French sources, was indeed satisfactory. The British, however, were not the only people to read them; and whereas sea-power had hitherto seemed "a huge mystery hedged in by sea-sickness",[10] Mahan plausibly unravelled its dynamics and sold it to the world.

Theodore Roosevelt, the Secretary of the US Navy, attached great importance to Mahan's work and had sheltered the captain's career while he was engaged in his writing. The Kaiser, already nursing an envy of the Royal Navy and a resentment of the implicit barrier to German colonialism which it represented, read avidly *The Influence of Sea Power* and directed his officers to do the same. And it was by no means overlooked in Japan, France or Russia. These were the very countries which were challenging, and had in some cases already overtaken, Britain in industrial strength. They would no doubt have challenged Britain's naval hegemony before very long anyway, and as the *New York Times* observed of the Jubilee Review, "if other nations have heeded the lesson, the pathway [to] imperial destiny must now be considered clear";[11] but "'Mahanism' became a propaganda tool in the hands of navalists in many countries"[12] and helped to raise the curtain on an age of competitive blue-water expansion.

Among the world's second-rank naval powers the doctrines of coast defence and commerce-raiding yielded to the regal first-rank desideratum of 'Command of the Sea'; and the leading navy was soon to find the rest of the pack steaming hard in its wake. *Pax Britannica* was not essentially about great-power confrontation (unlike *Pax Americana* in the Cold War era); and, in adjusting to the pace of the twentieth century, the courtly old service of timeless legend – joints stiffened and arteries clotted by the comfortable habits of dominion – was to be subjected to immense strategic, organizational and material stresses.

Meanwhile, the visible aura surrounding Britannia in 1897 remained one of serene, unassailable supremacy. Joseph Chamberlain, with premonitions of economic eclipse and strategic overstretch, might describe England as a "weary titan staggering beneath the too great orb of its fate", and no doubt a few naval officers – prophets and alarmists – looked into the future with foreboding; but 'decline-school' theorizing was not a Victorian pastime. With 360 major fighting ships the RN was equal to the next five navies combined, and the blessings of the land which the 'British race' was enjoying all over the world were perceived to be the long-term fruits of its labours. The centenary of Camperdown and Cape St Vincent – two battles which announced the classical age of invincibility – found the service, like the monarchy, in higher esteem and finer fettle than for many years past.

It was in these agreeable circumstances that, six weeks after the review, Sir Michael Culme-Seymour hoisted his flag in Nelson's flagship in succession to Salmon as first among equals of the Royal Navy's three senior 'Home Port' commanders-in-chief. His record of fleet command (Pacific, Channel, Mediterranean) was unique, his standing in the service unequalled. In Portsmouth he found, or gathered around him, familiar faces from the 'Malta clique'.

Fleet-Paymaster Rickard continued to serve as his secretary. Francis Bridgeman served, for the third time, as his flag-captain. Edwyn Alexander-Sinclair, formerly a watchkeeper in *Ramillies*, took Evan-Thomas's place as flag-lieutenant. Staff-Captain Thomas Hawkins-Smith (who had distinguished himself as Master of the Review) commanded *Victory*'s special-service tender *Fire Queen*. Nearby, Prince Louis of Battenberg was flag-captain to Vice-Admiral Harry Rawson in the Channel Fleet's *Majestic*. William May captained *Excellent* (among whose staff was Lieutenant Arthur Leveson). Trevylyan Napier, Sir Michael's future son-in-law, was XO of *Vernon*. And Lieutenant Michael Culme-Seymour was shortly to commence another stint in the royal yacht *Victoria and Albert* (a billet for which R. F. Scott had hopelessly competed[13]). A conspicuous absentee was John Jellicoe: he was about to go out to China as flag-captain to Sir Michael's cousin, Vice-Admiral Edward Hobart Seymour.

Meanwhile in London, Commander Hugh Evan-Thomas took up an appointment as secretary to an Admiralty committee charged with revising the 1889 *Signal Book* "without disturbing the general arrangement, but merely to correct such faults as have been found to exist".[14] It was a task for which he was eminently qualified, the more so since, as Mediterranean 'flags', he had forwarded (over Sir Michael's signature) fifty-five pages of amendments.[15] During this interlude he and Hilda by no means lost touch with the Culme-Seymours – as photographs of Rockingham Castle in their album testify – and a catalytic expedition to the Isle of Wight in the spring of '98 places commander and admiral side by side in the forefront of signalling development.

On a blustery day in May, a small group of naval officers stood huddled in their greatcoats on the grassy cliff-top overlooking The Needles. They were: Sir Michael Culme-Seymour, Commander Evan-Thomas, Rear-Admiral Lord Charles Beresford MP, and Lieutenant Robert Phipps Hornby (of *Vernon*), and they were visiting Guglielmo Marconi's 'station' (a wooden hut) above Alum Bay. Outside the station were two aerials; inside, a 'transmitter' (battery, condenser and induction coil) and a 'receiver' (battery, coherer and ticker-tape machine).[16] Only two years had elapsed since Commander Henry Jackson had first managed to pass a message by electrical, wire-less, means from one end of his ship to another, and the purpose of the present inspection was to see if Signor Marconi could demonstrate the same feat over the fourteen miles between Alum Bay and Bournemouth, where a similar station was manned and waiting.

At the appointed time Marconi (or, perhaps, a yeoman from *Victory*) began manipulating the switch which 'made' and 'broke' the $\frac{1}{4}$kw circuit. After an interval the tape machine came to life and printed the Morse message sent in reply. This cycle was repeated a number of times, and the naval party went home well satisfied. "I have the honour to report", wrote Evan-Thomas to the president of the Signals Committee, Vice-Admiral Sir Compton Domvile, "that on Saturday last (7th inst.) I went to the Needles to witness experiments in signalling without wires, conducted by Signor Marconi." He went on to recommend that, notwithstanding the ease with which signals might be jammed, Marconi equipment should be fitted in two warships for sea trials.[17] In fact, by the time Admiralty procedures had run their course, Marconi had three sets spare, and so the stately old battleship *Alexandra* and two cruisers, *Europa* and *Juno*, were fitted with wireless-telegraphy for the 1899 Manoeuvres, and worked messages at up to sixty miles. Thus was born the Navy's official interest in W/T.

Evan-Thomas's painstaking labour, at the Admiralty, of correcting and amending was duly completed and brought to fruition in the form of the 1898 *Signal Book* (which incorporated within its covers, as Culme-Seymour had suggested, the old *Manoeuvring Book*); and in November 1898 he was appointed to take over the Portsmouth Signal School from its founding CO, Commander Lionel Tufnell. For this billet he was borne on the books of *Victory*, and thus reunited with the congenial group of friends who had come to form his social habitat. It was an enviable place to be, in the naval firmament.

Sir Michael and Lady Culme-Seymour mixed easily with the highest in the land. At least twice they were guests of the Queen at Osborne ("Both she and her husband were very kind to Victoria and Louise at Malta," HM told her journal);[18] they often stayed with Prince George and Princess May at York Cottage at Sandringham, and the Yorks in turn came to stay at Admiralty House, Portsmouth. The Culme-Seymours held frequent dinner parties, sometimes of sixty or more, deployed in intimate groups around small circular tables.[19] The seating plans have survived, and a typical guest list in, say, early 1899, might include the following (here in alphabetical order) with their spouses:

Rear-Admiral Pelham Aldrich
Lieutenant Edwyn Alexander-Sinclair
Commander Charles Anson
Captain HSH Prince Louis of Battenberg
Lieutenant Algernon Boyle (CO of *Malaya* at Jutland)
Lord Brassey (founder of the famous naval annual)
Captain Francis Bridgeman
Captain Stanley Cecil Colville
Miss Mary Culme-Seymour
Lieutenant Michael Culme-Seymour
Lieutenant Sir Charles Cust (equerry to Duke of York)
Commander Hugh Evan-Thomas
Rear-Admiral John Fullerton (permanent CO of *Victoria and Albert*)
Lord Goschen (First Lord of the Admiralty, 1895–1900)
Mr William Graham Greene (private secretary to First Lord)
Lieutenant Lionel Halsey (Jellicoe's captain-of-the-fleet at Jutland)
Captain James Hammett (erstwhile flag-captain to Pompo Heneage)
Staff-Captain Hawkins-Smith
Vice-Admiral Lord Walter Kerr (First Naval Lord, 1899–1904)
Lieutenant Arthur Leveson
Captain William May
Commodore Arthur Moore
Commander Trevylyan Napier (Culme-Seymour's son-in-law designate)
Lieutenant Edward Phillpotts (CO of *Warspite* at Jutland)
Fleet-Paymaster Henry Rickard
Captain Charles Robinson
Admiral of the Fleet Sir Nowell Salmon (CO of E-T's first ship)
Lord Spencer (ex-First Lord)
Commander Ernest Troubridge (we shall meet him again)
Lady Tryon
Captain Rosslyn Wemyss (future First Sea Lord)
Sir Francis de Winton (comptroller and treasurer to Duke of York)
Captain HRH the Duke of York

Sir Michael became First and Principal ADC to the Queen in 1899, and retired, after a career of fifty years, in 1900. A year later the new King, Edward VII, took the singular step of resurrecting, for his benefit, the archaic honorary position of Vice-Admiral of the United Kingdom,[20] which had been abolished by Queen Victoria in 1887 on the death of the then incumbent, Sir Michael Seymour (Culme-Seymour's uncle). The post still exists.

*

Evan-Thomas's stint in command of the Signal School ended in November 1900. He had, in Francis Bridgeman's words, "conducted himself with sobriety & has conducted the Signal School in a most capable manner". His successor was Commander Allan Everett, who would run the establishment for a total of six years between 1900 and 1908, and become acclaimed in the service as the leading signals expert of the Edwardian era. It has already been mentioned how, as a junior officer, Everett had a bee in his bonnet about signalling and exchanged letters with Sir Geoffrey Phipps Hornby, who had sympathized (from retirement) with his precocious view that the *Signal Book* was too complex to be operated conveniently in the presence of the enemy. Everett had subsequently gained accelerated promotion for his efficient service as 'flags' to three successive admirals – Compton Domvile, Sir Henry Stephenson and Sir Harry Rawson (all tram-line authoritarians, and the last two royal favourites) – and had then followed Evan-Thomas's path as secretary to the Admiralty's standing committee on signals before taking charge of the Signal School. Now that this ambitious and able young man was the head keeper (as it were) of the Monster in the Navy's Basement, he was to find – as we shall see – that taming the beast was more easily said than done.

Having handed over the Signal School, Commander Hugh Evan-Thomas returned to the Mediterranean as captain of the third-class cruiser *Pioneer* – at the late age of 38, his first personal experience of sea command. These were splendid, if almost swan-song, days for what was still Britain's premier fleet, when the potential enemies were still France and Russia, and when Admiral Sir John Fisher bestrode the station; but of them, nothing has survived in the Evan-Thomas papers.

After two years in *Pioneer* he was promoted, and then adopted as flag-captain in *Majestic* (1903–4) and *Caesar* (1904–5) by Vice-Admiral Lord Charles Beresford in the Channel Squadron. It is said that Beresford had angled for Captain Percy Scott,[21] but Fisher (as Second Naval Lord) sent Scott to command *Excellent*. One may wonder how future Fisher–Beresford–Scott dynamics might have varied if Lord Charles's wish had been granted.

In terms of personality, Beresford and Evan-Thomas were very different; but both had benefited, as junior officers, from the patronage of Lord Clanwilliam, both enjoyed strong royal connections, and they had been acquainted at least since 'Malta clique' days under Sir Michael Culme-Seymour (whose son Beresford took as flag-commander). In January 1900, when Lord Charles was about to take his first step into flag-rank as second-in-command in the Mediterranean, he had turned to Evan-Thomas (then still at the Signal School) for cramming over certain matters which were held to be of supreme importance for a new rear-admiral:

> My Dear Thomas,
>   I enclose 1/– and ½d stamp which I am in your debt. I am much obliged. I must thank you very much for all the trouble you have taken to instruct me in signals and the new [1898] Book. When I arrive on the station I am certain to feel very grateful to you.
>   Yours Very Truly, Charles Beresford.[22]

Beresford has already featured on the 'obedience' side in the furore which followed the *Camperdown–Victoria* collision, and in due course, as Fisher manoeuvred the highest rewards in the Navy out of his reach, he would work himself into seemingly unrelieved authoritarianism. But in these years he still ranged across the whole Dixonian spectrum. Charlie B. was the greatest character actor (and, in the end, not very much more) on the Edwardian Navy's ample stage.

As a young rake, he had found a wager irresistible. He is alleged to have ridden a pig down Park Lane, and to have walked naked from Hyde Park Corner to St James's (in a carriage with the floor removed and the windows pasted over).[23] Family sources aver that he had the Waterford Hounds tattooed in full cry down his back with the brush of the fox disappearing up his arse, and his sexual misdemeanours lost nothing in the telling. As an increasingly corpulent senior officer he continued to cherish his image as a plunger.

When the Russian Baltic Fleet passed on its hapless, ill-fated way to the Far East in 1904 (having fired on British trawlers in the North Sea, supposing them to be Japanese torpedo-boats), Beresford proposed "on the grounds of chivalry, to attack it with only half of his available ships" – a gesture which, no doubt, turned Nelson in his grave and certainly incensed Fisher. Instead, he shadowed the Russians as they bimbled southwards past Spain and Gibraltar; and while Admiral Zinovi Petrovich Rozhestvensky tried to teach his "fleet of lunatics"[24] how to manoeuvre, Beresford's cruisers taunted him by performing the same evolutions with practised ease on the horizon astern.

The seeds of Charlie B's disastrous schism with Fisher had already been sown in Malta, in 1900. Soon after the then rear-admiral joined Fisher's command, he wished, in the words of his Royal Marine intelligence officer, "to refresh his memory in the elements of the craft" (yes, Captain Hankey was a mason!) and landed some men early one morning on the Corradino parade-ground. There – presumably armed with Evan-Thomas's prompt-notes – he had them "spread out to represent ships in a fleet, and manoeuvred [them] in line ahead, line abreast, quarter-line, and so forth".[25] All went well until the C-in-C made a mortifying signal, read by every ship in Grand Harbour, demanding to know why he had landed men without permission. (Beresford's predecessor, Gerard Noel, had replied to similar rebukes with the menacing information that "I am on my way to see you in my frock coat and sword.") Other incidents followed. In Peter Kemp's even-handed verdict, Fisher "could not restrain his jealousy of Beresford's inherited wealth and aristocratic birth, nor Beresford circumscribe his contempt for Fisher's bourgeois upbringing".[26] Certainly Lord Charles, with his airs and graces, his political and royal connections, tested his senior's patience beyond reasonable endurance, and Fisher's chief of staff, Captain George King-Hall, had to act as "a kind of a buffer between the two",[27] although the legend that they were perennially locked in adversity is incorrect. Now, in command of the Channel Squadron and for the time being out of Fisher's reach, Beresford gained in stature as an effective and 'coming' senior admiral, and from random snapshot evidence, there is much about him to applaud.

For example, he was ahead of his time in proposing that a confidential book should be issued

> embodying the lessons learned in recent fleet exercises as a *guide* to flag and commanding officers on handling ships in action; but Fisher accepted Battenberg's too facile objection stemming from the Victorian Navy's failure to differentiate between 'instructions' issued for guidance and 'orders' intended to be binding.[28]

(Battenberg – Director of Naval Intelligence – feared creating another Byng situation.) It was not until after the Great War that standing *Fighting Instructions* were issued; in the meantime each admiral had to write his own, or endorse his predecessor's, battle-*orders*.

And when two of Beresford's Channel Fleet battleships, *Hannibal* and *Prince George*, collided in 1903, critics attributed the accident "to his 'crazy, new-fangled idea' of manoeuvring his fleet without lights at night, though the Admiralty [under Lord Walter Kerr] acknowledged that he was justified in giving his officers this realistic training".[29]

There is, also, a refreshing letter in Evan-Thomas's papers which places both officers in a modern and constructive light:

> My Dear Thomas,
>
> I have been through the essays written by the officers under your command, on the supposition that Britain & Japan were allied against Russia and France in open hostilities. First allow me to congratulate you most sincerely on the patriotic and clever forethought that prompted you to launch the idea amongst your officers . . . The more younger officers think over and

thrash out details for war the more valuable these officers are to the service and to the state when called upon to occupy high and responsible positions.[30]

However, Lord Charles was already displaying symptoms of the *folie de grandeur* which was to blight his final command of the Channel in 1907–9; he nurtured an extravagant sense of his own position, forswore none of the pomp and circumstance which he considered his due, and behaved like some superannuated and faintly ludicrous matinée idol. "Crowds of MPs and newspapermen came to see him, and it was difficult to get access to him about service matters, and anything arranged was forgotten as soon as you left him."[31] His attention span was short; he became increasingly beholden to the promptings of his subordinates – when he could be induced to listen – and he made mistakes. When leading the fleet out of Lamlash Bay in the Isle of Arran he executed the signal for cruising formation when there still remained an exit course to be done, and chaos ensued.[32]

Evan-Thomas's role as flag-captain must have been midway between master of ceremonies and nanny; and his greatest asset to Beresford was his superlative education, under Sir Michael Culme-Seymour, both in steam-tactics and in how a flagship should be run. Near the end of their time together (after one of Beresford's spats with the new First Sea Lord) Lord Charles freely acknowledged his debt to him.

> I am sorry that I shall not be able to leave my flagship and my fleet in a proper and dignified manner. I look forward to having you with me again in some position before I pipe down and heartily give you all the credit you so richly deserve for making *Caesar* the most brilliantly smart ship on the water.[33]

In two separate notes, both dated March the 6th, 1905, the admiral added for good measure:

> you are certain of a most brilliant career in the service and are sure to become one of Britain's most efficient admirals . . .
>
> Never was an admiral served better or more loyally than by you as flag-captain during our happy and delightful two years together.[34]

There was also a testimonial from below, from Commander Michael Culme-Seymour:

> Dear Tommy,
>   It is difficult for me to tell you how grateful I am to you, not only for being promoted [to captain] but for many other things. The promotion is, I know quite well, due practically entirely to you and the trouble you have taken over it. Also it was entirely you who got me to *Caesar* which made it possible for me to get promoted & where I hope I have learnt a great deal as to how the

duties of the captain of a ship should be performed & nowhere are they better learnt than in *Caesar*.[35]

One might as well add a note from the King's private secretary to Lord Charles, alluding to gunnery trials: "Congratulations to your able flag-captain, on the extraordinary good results."[36]

*

By now the Royal Navy was on the threshold of the turbulent and traumatic changes of the 'Fisher era'. It was as if, to gain admission to the new century, the service had to assimilate half a century's worth of evolution in a dozen years. It had started with the Whitehead locomotive torpedo and the new, efficient, breech-loading rifle. The former killed, and the latter buried, the close-range tactics of the 'ramming era'; and in the late 1890s the Navy went "gunnery mad"[37] (Noel had predicted that officers relieved of the care of sails would have nothing else to do). Owing to the drive and invention of a handful of enthusiasts and prima donnas, most conspicuous among whom was Fisher's friend Percy Scott, many of the obstacles to more accurate, longer-range shooting were systematically surmounted; and from the assortment of battle-formations which had been vaguely mooted for twenty-five years, the fleets dressed back into the beam-firing line-ahead of ancient memory. In 1904 there arrived as 'First Sea Lord' (as the First Naval Lord was now termed) the manic, almost messianic Fisher, poised – contrary to received belief – dramatically to curtail the rebirth of single-line battle-fleets.

*   *   *

Historians spend much time trying to divine patterns in the behaviour of historical figures and groups of whom their understanding is incomplete. In reality, people are much too complex and relationships too variable to be represented two-dimensionally. But the search for explanatory patterns can, at least, be a constructive stimulant of debate.

There are many angles to the conflict of values associated with George Tryon's life and death. The 'climatic' cultural factors which helped to steer the Navy so far on the wrong course (as he saw it) over signalling and manoeuvres have been amply discussed. But the plethora of biographical data and 'snapshot' images in these last few chapters begs some attempt at synthesis. This is as good a place as any to take stock; and, augmented by information hitherto unmentioned, or only lightly touched on, a pattern of at least circumstantial interest seems to emerge.

Those authoritarians – to start the argument tendentiously – who, for reasons of expediency, loyalty or conviction, resisted the informalization of tactics or infiltrated the red-herring of absolute obedience into the *Camperdown–Victoria* affair, featured a disproportionate incidence of one or more of the following four characteristics:

1. previous service on the staff of HMS *Vernon*;
2. ties with royalty;
3. involvement in the Royal Geographical Society;
4. involvement in Craft Freemasonry.

Only a minority of naval officers could possibly have had a tick in the box opposite even one of these items. Yet most of the 'obedience' purveyors could claim more than one, and each additional tick was exponentially less likely. Both Albert Markham and Lord Charles Beresford had a full house. Equally striking is the scarcity of those who had none, although the 'nil return' category must have embraced most of the *Navy List*.

Some fifty officers and a few civilians who enjoyed one or more of the above four biographical qualifications and who are directly or circumstantially relevant to this study (plus a smattering who are not) have been tabulated at the end of this chapter.[38] 'Relevance to this study' was arbitrarily decided by me; and, as item 2 is a matter of opinion, and item 4 unavoidably (for reasons which will be explained) incomplete, the table should be regarded merely as a collation of miscellaneous information whose interest-value the reader may decide for himself. In this exercise normal academic standards of evidence and analysis are impossible.

Few officers were eligible by virtue of rank and seniority to have served as staff members of the pre-1895-ish *Vernon*, and it is noteworthy that Albert Markham, Charles Beresford, William May (Assistant-Director of Torpedoes, 1892–4), Arthur Wilson, Charles Robinson (Markham's *Trafalgar* flag-captain and a member of the *Victoria* court) and Edmund Jeffreys (another member of the court) had all done so – the last three in some degree coincident with Markham's captaincy. Obviously they were liable to share a bond of loyalty with Markham, for *esprit de corps* develops easily amongst pioneers and Old Marco, with his gallant record of exploration and his muscular Christianity, was well regarded. This may be sufficient explanation of their tendency to side with him over the *Camperdown–Victoria* business. But can we take a small precarious step further? Did they actually hold with the *principles* implicit in their sympathy with the rear-admiral? Is there any plausible reason, for instance, why such men should – in contradiction of *Vernon*'s vaunted self-image[39] – intrinsically favour the centralization of authority?

Possibly. The work of the Torpedo School took place on the frontiers of practical physics; the staff formed (at least in their own opinion) a naval scientific vanguard, and their leadership of their profession away from art and into science may have inclined them towards a highly regulated 'Newton's clock' view of the universe, in which the unpredictabilities concomitant with devolved authority had no place.[40]

In explanation of the second apparent coincidence, that of ties with royalty, it could be pointed out that men with royal interest were bound to collect disproportionately in big fleets and flagships and thus have their views (which may have been both deficient and normal) exposed by the light of crisis. Possibly; but that argument already concedes the preferment given to, and anticipated by, officers with Palace connections; and in truth, the 'royalty' factor is best placed within the more general context of the tangled vine of chivalry which clung to, and supported, the edifice of the Victorian social establishment. Beneath its rich foliage, this prolific creeper had many intertwining stalks.

Among them were the learned but basically amateur institutions which blossomed in that quarter of Kensington sometimes known (after the eponymous Prince Consort) as the 'Albertopolis', and of which the Royal Geographical Society is a prominent example. Among them, also, was the hardy perennial of Freemasonry. But first, the RGS.

The Geographical Society was royalized by Prince Albert in 1859, two years before his death. His family took the link seriously, and its formal hierarchy forty years later was:

Patron: Her Majesty the Queen
Vice-Patron: His Royal Highness the Prince of Wales
Honorary President: His Royal Highness the Duke of York
(President: Sir Clements Markham)

As mentioned in Chapter 9, the 'interface' between high-latitude exploration (and hence the RGS) and the RN was considerable, and was ratified by the indulgence of the RUSI.[41] The Navy supplied the Society's expeditions with transport, logistical skill and a pool of fit, disciplined, patriotic personnel. In return, the Society provided the Navy with the trappings of scholarly decorum and with sought-after opportunities for distinction.

After the demand for a North-West Passage had been blunted by the horrifying disappearance of Captain Sir John Franklin's 1845 expedition, and by the realities of hundreds of miles of pack-ice, it is hard to see exactly how humanity benefited from small, ill-equipped groups of Don Quixotes trudging off into the frozen Hell of the polar latitudes, and stumbling back half dead or not at all. Today, when there are sophisticated scientific instruments, the poles no doubt offer unique possibilities for environmental study. But the Nares's and Markhams and Scotts of a hundred years ago, what did they really discover? That "Great God! This is an awful place"[42]? – that was known before they went. Royal patronage suppressed the querying of motives; but the impression is left that, lofty pretences notwithstanding, such expeditions had ceased to be the means to any substantive end, and that the real impetus was the institutional and personal glory of heroic endeavour.

The 'ends of the earth' offered a rare setting for modern "knight-errantry" (Clements Markham's phrase), and the knights-errant had to be, well, *suitable*. There was a strain of snobbery in the Society's efforts to reserve polar exploration for officers of the Royal Navy, to the disadvantage of competitors – such as William Bruce and Ernest Shackleton – from other backgrounds. And "the men in British geographic circles repeated the mistakes of fifty years and condemned British Antarctic exploration to tragedy in the second decade of the twentieth century".[43]

The RGS had two admirals on its Council in the 1890s – Edward Hobart Seymour (Sir Michael Culme-Seymour's cousin), and Albert Markham – and around thirty-five naval officers amongst its Fellows.[44] Some twenty of these naval FRGSs can be linked actively or by association with the 'obedience' side of the *Camperdown* v. *Victoria* conflict, and only three – Gerard Noel, Edmund Fremantle and young Reginald Bacon (while he remained young) – with the 'initiative' side. This, on the face of it, is a high degree of consensus.

As with the '*Vernon* factor', loyalty to Markham must provide part of the answer: loyalty among both institutional colleagues and old Arctic explorers. Captains George Nares and Henry Stephenson had commanded, respectively, *Alert* and *Discovery* on the 1875–6 expedition, and under them had served (in addition to Commander Markham) Lieutenants Aldrich, May, Egerton and Beaumont. Unsurprisingly, these men went on to form the cadre of the Navy's involvement with the Society and all became FRGSs. For further connection, we must look again at the aforementioned 'vine of chivalry' – and, in particular, must try to disentangle the creeper of Freemasonry.

Freemasonry suggests itself as an issue by virtue of the *Victoria* court's gratuitous and unconstitutional exoneration of the local District Grand Master for an appalling accident in which he had literally wielded the manslaughter-weapon. Merely to mention 'the Craft' is to invite slurs of 'conspiracy theorism' in heard-it-all-before tones from touchy masonic apologists – "Oh, that old canard!" – and I was warned by a venerable academic to exercise *caution* (a masonic watchword). No doubt the advice was well meant and *prudent* (another one[45]); however, the generous help received from the United Grand Lodge of England (UGLE)[46] indicates that it was unnecessary.

The dusty cellars of Freemason's Hall in London are the UGLE's ultimate repository of masonic records. The archives are incomplete and geared towards lodges, of which there are thousands, rather than towards individual ordinary members. This means that if, as is quite likely, guesswork fails to locate a name, its owner's status – masonic or not – remains unproven (unless he is famous enough to be boasted in *Military Lodges 1732–1899*, or appendices to later works). Furthermore, an outsider is not allowed free run of the place, and the overworked staff are not there for his benefit. However, they do their good-natured best to help; and by targeting certain lodges, combined with outside reading and serendipity, a good deal of information can be gathered.

For mainly practical reasons, the Craft and the Royal Navy were slow to embrace each other. A lodge looks for regularity in attendance, and members liable to disappear off to sea on long and unpredictable war commissions were not ideal. (Freemasonry remains less common among seaman officers than among shore-loafers such as doctors, dentists, supply officers and reservists.) There were a few attempts in the late eighteenth century to form ship-borne lodges, but officers are not permanently affiliated to their ships (unlike army officers to regiments), and such lodges were short-lived. One of the greatest luminaries of Freemasonry, Thomas Dunckerley, held warrant-rank as a gunner and schoolmaster in the RN until George III accepted him as an illegitimate son of George II (and thus a natural half-uncle) and housed him, with a pension, in Hampton Court – enabling him to devote his time to promoting the Craft.

Arctic explorers and Freemasons alike have claimed Horatio Nelson as one of their own, on rather flimsy evidence: the former on grounds of a three-month visit to Spitzbergen at the age of 14;[47] the latter, of an inscription somewhere in Great Yarmouth referring to 'Brother Nelson' and dated 1801. No documentary records exist ("have survived") to prove Nelson's brotherhood, but it is plausible: in 1801 he stopped at Yarmouth on his way to and from Copenhagen, and the local-boy-made-good may have been serenaded by Norfolk lodges (although one wonders why such an ornament to the Craft was not swiftly raised to grand rank during his time ashore between 1801 and '03).

In the long Victorian peace Freemasonry became popular among non-commissioned ranks (as exemplified earlier by Dunckerley). It naturally suits "a stable society with limited social mobility",[48] and officers probably indulged it as a disciplined – and therefore safe – social activity and conduit of information between senior rates and wardroom.

The 1890s journal of a Petty-Officer Louis Parsons reveals the hospitality extended to naval personnel on the North American & West Indies Station by lodges in Port Royal, Halifax, Bermuda, Montreal, St Lucia, and even Nagasaki, and treats the attendance of officers at fleet masonic functions as both welcome and comment-worthy.[49] At the other social extreme, there were always landed gentry who belonged to 'county' masonic dynasties, such as (within the period of interest to us) the Egertons, the Halseys and the Brownriggs. But two other groups, which were never far apart, helped Freemasonry come of age in the late Victorian Navy: the courtiers and the geographers.

The royal family has been at the head of English Freemasonry for two centuries – indeed has been its safe-conduct through dangerous times (as, for example, when it came under suspicion of Jacobite and American-revolutionary sympathies). Sanctuary was attained in 1787 when the Prince of Wales, later George IV, declared his wish "to be surrounded and served by members of the Craft", and to this end founded the Prince of Wales's Lodge (No. 259). Eighty-five years later, in 1872, the next Prince of Wales, Albert Edward (who was already master of the very superior Royal Alpha Lodge), took his seigneurial place at the head of the lodge which bore his name. The prostration offered to this amiable and somewhat shiftless young man at his installation ceremony indicates how inseparable Freemasonry sought to make itself from royalty:

> We beg to offer your Royal Highness our grateful acknowledgement of the honour you have graciously conferred on this Lodge by kindly assenting to accept the position which was occupied for so many years by your illustrious predecessors.
>
> A close connection between the Throne and the Craft has ever been so distinguishing a feature in English Freemasonry as to have become an established landmark among us, and it constitutes one of the strongest replies in answer to those imputations of evil political and religious designs.
>
> Her Most Gracious Majesty the Queen has herself given public proof of her confidence in the principles of the Craft by extending to it the prestige of her name as patron of one of those flourishing educational institutions of which the Freemasons of England are justly proud.
>
> And when it shall please the Great Architect of the Universe to call your Royal Highness to the Throne of your ancestors, we feel assured that you, Sir, will find the Freemasons of England and especially the members of this Lodge the most loyal of your subjects, devotedly attached to the Person of your Royal Highness, and the staunchest of supporters of the Throne.

'Bertie' concurred, as well he might, and shortly afterwards became Grand Master of England – a position he yielded to his brother Arthur, Duke of Connaught, on becoming King in 1901.[50] His wife, Alexandra, duly followed Queen Victoria as Chief Patroness; and, as already mentioned, he initiated his elder son and heir, Prince Eddy, into the Royal Alpha Lodge in 1885.[51] Freemasonry has remained tucked up with royalty ever since, although the present Prince of Wales, influenced perhaps by his father's lukewarmth towards the Craft and Lord Mountbatten's hostility, is said to have declined to join. One can easily see why, for nearly two hundred years, most courtiers have allegedly been, and allegedly continue to be, 'on the square'. Quite apart from fear of exclusion from a potential forum of backstairs influence, no one who routinely played a part in the order, ceremonies and deference of Court life was likely to have a problem with Freemasonry: these men were vocational royalists whose ritual validation of their seniors fell little short of Divine-Rightism.

At a time of deep naval peace, when social connections were a means to the top, when royal yachts brought career advantage, and when officers had to use whatever leverage they could to stand out from the crowd – when obedience and paintwork, pomp and circumstance, were what made the Fleet tick – it was a simple matter for the Craft to step onto the quarterdecks of the Royal Navy's flagships. And there it found an ample supply of recruits.

The averred purposes of Freemasonry are to promote morality, charity, good-fellowship and humanity. These laudable goals are sought by subjecting would-be initiates to "the strictest scrutiny",[52] and thereafter requiring from them exacting standards of personal conduct – standards which broadly mirrored and exemplified the chivalrous, patrician ethos of Victorian England. Perhaps few masons take these theoretical demands very seriously today, and it would be absurd to suppose that their observance was 100% a hundred years ago – indeed one can think of notable 'brothers' who must have had their fingers crossed when they took their vows; but men (more precisely *gentlemen*) who matched the criteria must, by virtue of their cultural training, have been less rare a century ago than now:

> From the date that the doors of his prep-school close
> On the lonely little son
> He is taught by precept, insult and blows
> The Things that Are Never Done.
> Year after year, without favour or fear,
> From seven to twenty-two,
> His keepers insist he shall learn the list
> Of things no fellow can do.[53]

In brief, Freemasonry was a re-codification of the social codes to which upper-middle-class Englishmen were already well conditioned. This is why officers both humoured it amongst 'other ranks' and (following the example of royal *noblesse oblige*) were easily able to subscribe themselves. And many of the particular virtues and graces to be cultivated by masons were by no means inconsonant with career progress in the late Victorian Navy, for example:

submission[54] (≈ deference, hierarchy, conformity, obedience);

regularity[55] (≈ regulations, routine, conformity, 'Newton's clock');

harmony[56] (≈ conformity, lack of dissent, peer-group values);

obedience[57] (≈ obedience); and

geometry[58] (≈ precision, tidiness, steam-tactics).

It must be apparent by now – at least to the 'profane' reader – that the codes and conventions of the Craft (if taken seriously) harmonize broadly with the 'authoritarian' personality traits defined by Professor Dixon in *On the Psychology of Military Incompetence* and described here in Chapter 9. Masons will resent such an assertion, and to some extent it is an attempt to rationalize the import of the available data: that Freemasonry, like royal connections and the strange case of the RGS, was an authoritarian-group characteristic. But bull, dogma, rituals and codes of honour are all defences against anxiety which make for rigidity of thought and "increase the feeling of dependency which [juniors] have towards their superiors";[59] and it is scarcely controversial to suggest that the rituals and deferences of the Craft had greater appeal to officers who enjoyed ceremony and felt at home in rigid hierarchies, and less appeal to those whose tolerance of such things was low (and perhaps already tested to the limit by their daily service lives). It is, at least, beyond question that many men decline to join because they consider the rituals endemic in Freemasonry to be mumbo-jumbo[60] and the kowtowing childish – and some because they are by nature too arrogant, unclubbable, or just unpleasant, to subscribe to someone else's cult. Whatever the reason, the refusers are likely to be found more on the 'autocratic' than the 'authoritarian' side of the Dixonian personality spectrum.

It was the geographers who broadened and paved the masonic bridge between royalty and the Navy's officer corps. These men – particularly the Arctic explorers – were held in equally high esteem in the RN and the RGS. They repeatedly carried the White Ensign and the Society's illustrious name to the top of the world; and even their famous disasters, such as Captain Sir John Franklin's expedition of 1845, or, two-thirds of a century later, Captain Robert Scott's in the Antarctic, only served to enhance the mystique. It was not, at least while the Markhams were making their names, *de rigueur* to be a mason to participate in polar expeditions: they did not hold extraordinary general lodge meetings in snow-bound bivouacs, although the idea is appealing. Albert Markham himself was not initiated until 1886, when, as already mentioned, Philip Colomb, flag-captain to the local C-in-C, introduced him to Phoenix Lodge (No. 257) in Portsmouth.[61]

Colomb's association with Phoenix is unclear; he may have been a visitor from his mother lodge in Chatham. But the name had a certain piquancy for him. 'HMS *Phoenix*' is known to modern naval personnel as the fire-fighting and damage-control school at Horsea Island in the nether reaches of Portsmouth Harbour: a Dante's inferno of rusty superstructure, troughs of blazing oil, miasmic black smoke and soaking wet fearnought. In 1854 she was a sloop which explored Smith Sound in the Arctic under the command of Captain Edward Augustus Inglefield, and Mate (= Sub-Lieutenant) Philip Colomb[62] was one of her junior officers.

Markham was already captain of *Vernon* when he (along with his XO, Charles Robinson) joined Phoenix, and he progressed rapidly, via the Royal Naval College Lodge (No. 1593) in Greenwich, to the studious Quatuor Coronati Lodge of Research (No. 2076) in London.[63] The founding master of the last-named lodge was, as a matter of interest, General Sir Charles Warren, who ineffectually filled the post of Chief Commissioner of the Metropolitan Police in 1886–8, after the Home Secretary had offered it to another gallant military mason, Captain Lord Charles Beresford.[64] (One wonders if Charlie B. would have caught Jack the Ripper.)

Albert Markham's exemplary masonic attributes, his probity and zeal, rapidly found favour with the Prince of Wales (of whom, in age and appearance, he might have been a twin[65]); for in 1893, the year after his posting to the Mediterranean as second-in-command to Sir George Tryon, he acceded to the Craft Freemasonry post of District Grand Master of Malta – the only naval officer ever to do so – on the death of the incumbent, a Colonel Ramsay. With that elevation came three others, over all of which Albert Edward had patronage: Grand Superintendent of Malta (in Royal Arch Freemasonry), District Grand Master of the Mediterranean (in Mark Freemasonry), and Provincial Prior of the Mediterranean (in the Order of the Knights Templar). There is, as a matter of nit-picking interest, an anomaly concerning Markham's 'patent' as District Grand Master of Malta. It was dated from the date of his predecessor's death – the 6th of March 1893 – whereas there was always a gap of weeks or months between other DGMs. It is scarcely likely that Ramsay died, his passing was telegraphed to the Prince of Wales, and the latter telegraphed back the name of his successor, all on the same day. In reality Markham's appointment was almost certainly made at a later date (between collision and court-martial?) and backdated.

Be that as it may. What about the *Victoria* court-martial? Corruption is enabled by a coincidence of opportunity and motive. To men involved in any form of public affairs, Freemasonry, with its secrecy and unaccountability – its lack of checks and balances – is an opportunity-creative system. Most people would consider tilting the pitch in favour of their interests if they could do so without discovery: the motive is human nature. So, did the rear-admiral's masonic brethren "succour his weakness, relieve his necessities and repel the slanderer of his good name",[66] beneath the awning of HMS *Hibernia* in Dockyard Creek, in July 1893?

Perhaps. It appears that the deputy judge-advocate, Henry Rickard,[67] and at least two members of the court, Captains Charles Robinson and Edmund Jeffreys, were 'on the square'. To this may be added that one of the two officers disqualified at the behest of the *Victoria* defence, Captain Acland, had at least family connections with the Craft.[68] This is short of persuasive. Both Robinson and Jeffreys had other biographical reasons (*Vernon*, shipmates, etc.) to favour Markham, and "logic can very quickly go out the window" – Stephen Knight wisely but unhelpfully reminds us – "if a clear distinction is not made between incidents caused by Freemasonry and incidents merely involving Freemasons".[69] Furthermore, if Markham's predicament was eased by fellow masons on the panel of the court (which it palpably was, although not necessarily *because* they were masons), it was aggravated by that most unlikely of 'brothers', Gerard Noel.

Captain Noel's remark (as a witness) about Markham's option of turning *Camperdown* outwards, instead of inwards into danger, was irrelevant to the question, and the beleaguered rear-admiral could probably have obtained its deletion from the record had he not left it until the next day. Like Robinson, Noel was a member of the Lodge of St John & St Paul (No. 349), which met in Valletta, and Markham was thus unmistakably his masonic as well as military senior. One mason's obligation to another is supposed to constitute "a sure pledge of brotherhood . . . a column of mutual defence and support", and it almost seems as if Noel went out of his way to break faith with these commitments, for had he simply taken an 'anchor-faced' view of the distinction between naval and masonic duty, he could have refrained from making any unnecessary comment at all. In normal terms his behaviour was rude, in masonic terms it was disgraceful.

The bilious, irascible Noel, however, was hardly the masonic model of harmony, restraint and good-fellowship; and from the weight of available information there is little room for doubt that Freemasonry –

whether or not it wilfully steered the *Victoria* findings – was one of the biographical phenomena which characterized the 'obedience' side of the *Camperdown–Victoria* divide. And its popularity was growing among naval officers: indeed the time was ripe for an institutionalized link between Craft Freemasonry and the naval service at large. When the Navy Lodge (No. 2612)[70] was founded in London in March 1896, geographers, and officers recently returned from the Mediterranean, were instrumental in its genesis. Albert Markham was elected first master; and of its 65 founding 'petitioners', two came from unspecified mother-lodges, 19 (one each) from miscellaneous lodges,[71] 14 from Phoenix, 14 from Royal Naval College & United, and 16 from Malta's St John & St Paul. (Gerard Noel was not among them.)

Military lodges were condemned in uncompromising terms by a Past Provincial Grand Master in 1932:

> The formation of masonic lodges in connexion with naval and military units should certainly be prohibited by law . . . I have received on many occasions letters from sailors and soldiers – even from my own sons, one of whom is a sailor, another a soldier – asking how they can be initiated into Freemasonry and what the cost would be, as the only men who secure promotion in either the navy or the army seem to be Freemasons. It should not be possible for such letters to be written.[72]

This is a time-honoured allegation, by no means unknown today, and no doubt the anonymous author had valid grounds from personal experience.

But it is my guess that he was referring to non-commissioned ranks – a serious enough complaint, but not one which concerns us here. I have put forward the proposition that masons among late Victorian officers, through the close correlation of masonic and contemporary values, tended to be card-carrying authoritarians ("there is no organization more reactionary, more establishment-based, than British Freemasonry"[73]). Insofar as this generalization is sound, by the same token these gallant, stiff-collared champions of England and St George were also – in the explicit 'conspiracy' sense of corruption – virtually incorruptible. And among their brothers and cousins were the civil servants who, in running an empire of staggering opportunities and temptations, set standards of integrity which are still remembered as a byword.

(Full oft on Guv'ment service
This rovin' foot 'ath pressed,
An' bore fraternal greetin's
To the Lodges east an' west.[74])

One can also assert that 'profane' autocrats, such as George Tryon,[75] John Fisher or, later, David Beatty, would scarcely have remained silent while their beloved profession was systematically addled by a covert and authoritarian sect (although whether Mountbatten's hostility to the Craft had service origins is not publicly known).

There are however – and this is probably the crux – forms of undue influence for which 'conspiracy' is too pro-active a word, and of which many masons pretend incomprehension: a latent climate of sympathy for one side of a case, for example; an inability to separate peer-group values from the greater common good; and even the absence of any mechanism to challenge peer-group values at source. It can be taken for granted that such ambient forces have been, and in localized ways continue to be, at play in naval Freemasonry over the decades ("I have seen enough of it in [the] service to make me very suspicious"[76]); but with regard to specific cases and more dynamic forms of conspiracy one cannot make assertions one way or the other.

Freemasonry, as it impinges upon this story, was probably more a symptom[77] than a cause: a generally benign, in many ways laudable, occasionally pernicious and, to some, risible, part of the Navy's social scenery. Its practitioners tended to be hierarchically docile, good team players and prominently patriotic. It was from their energy that the Navy League, which powerfully lobbied for naval expansion in the 1890s, drew much of its impetus. It was largely this group, also, which brought into being and supported the Navy Records Society, an institution which satisfied the Victorian 'control' compulsion for indexing, listing and cataloguing,[78] and for which today's historians have reason to be thankful.

It is impossible to place Admiral Sir Michael Culme-Seymour, 3rd Bt., near the centre of this general matrix. Obviously he had strong hereditary royal connections through his courtier-clergyman father and his courtier-soldier brother; and his friend and naval contemporary Prince Alfred, Duke of Edinburgh, had been instrumental in the decision to entrust the court-martial to his presidency in Malta, and probably in his appointment to succeed Tryon. But, unlike (for example) his cousin, Admiral Sir Edward Hobart Seymour KCB,[79] Sir Michael was not a Fellow of the RGS, and has left no record of interest in the North Pole. He was already a senior captain when *Vernon* was first commissioned, and he was, apparently, not a mason (although he was not quite famous enough for his omission from 'trophy' lists of masons to settle the matter). He certainly had close links with high-ranking Freemasons, such as the Earl of Mount-Edgcumbe, Provincial Grand Master of Cornwall, whom he accompanied on a Court mission abroad after Albert Edward became

King, and Prince Arthur, Duke of Connaught, whom his brother and his cousin escorted on a similar assignment; but the fact that he hobnobbed with senior masons and made use of masonic juniors does not necessarily mean that he subscribed to the Craft himself – or, indeed, that he cared a straw for it.[80] The extent to which he was aware of the potential masonic undercurrents in the court-martial over which he presided in 1893, we will presumably never know; although we may note that his purposes were exactly suited by the terms of the verdict.

There is a query over John Jellicoe. One *Masonic Yearbook Historical Supplement* dates his membership from 1895, but it seems that this is a mistake and that he did not in fact join until he was Governor-General of New Zealand in 1922, whence he quickly rose to grand rank.[81] I have not tried to assemble systematic data on naval officers of the 1914–18 war (the task seemed disproportionate to the gain, and the forbearance of UGLE on the ebb), but I collected a few names along the way. There seems to have been a dearth of Freemasons in orbit around Beatty in the BCF (exceptions being: the famously autocratic Captain Reginald 'Blinker' Hall, who, a few weeks into the war, departed from *Queen Mary* to put his talent for conspiracy to spectacular use in Naval Intelligence; *New Zealand*'s Captain Lionel Halsey, who departed to succeed Allan Everett as Jellicoe's captain-of-the-fleet in 1915; and, still there at Jutland, Commodore William Goodenough, whom Beatty had tried to sack more than a year earlier). I gained the tentative impression that a different story might emerge of the Battle Fleet, and, indeed, that the senior officers and admiral's staff in *Barham* could almost have formed a lodge of their own.[82]

*

A Flawed and Incomplete List of Certain Affiliations

The stars under the four headings indicate as follows:

1. On staff of *Vernon* during early years (n/e = not eligible)
2. Linked with royalty[1] († = family link only)
3. A fellow of the RGS and/or Arctic explorer
4. Understood to be a Craft Freemason († = family link, at least)

[1] Junior officer on a royal yacht, or ADC at captain's rank, is not enough for item 2.

	1	2	3	4
Acland, William Dyke		†	*	†
Alcester, Lord (Beauchamp Seymour)	n/e	*		*
Aldridge, Pelham			*	
Aston, George (Royal Marines)	n/e			*

	1	2	3	4
Bacon, Reginald	*		*	*
Beaumont, Lewis		*	*	
Beresford, Lord Charles	*	*	*	*
Bradshaw, Henry (Markham's 'flags')	n/e			*
Brassey, Lord (naval publisher)	n/e		*	*
Bridgeman, Francis		*		*
Brownrigg, Henry J. Studholme	n/e			*
Burney, Cecil				*
Callaghan, George				*
Colomb, Philip			*	*
Colville, Stanley Cecil		*		*
Commerell, John	n/e		*	
Culme-Seymour, Michael (3rd Bt.)	n/e	*		
Curzon-Howe, Assheton		*	*	
Dalton, John Neale	n/e	*	*	*
De Winton, Francis (senior courtier)	n/e	*	*	
Egerton, Frederick				*
Egerton, George Le Clerc	*		*	†
Evan-Thomas, Hugh	n/e	*		*
Gervers, F. T. (Markham's father-in-law)	n/e		*	*
Goodenough, William	n/e	*	*	*
Grant, Alfred E. A.	n/e			*
Haig, Douglas (Army)	n/e		*	*
Halsey, Lionel	n/e			*
Hamilton, Lord George (First Lord)	n/e			*
Hamilton, Richard Vesey	n/e		*	
Hankey, Maurice (Royal Marines)	n/e			*
Hoskins, Anthony	n/e		*	
Inglefield, Edward Augustus	n/e		*	*
Inglefield, Edward Fitzmaurice	n/e		*	*
Jeffreys, Edmund	*			*
Jellicoe, John		*		*
Keppel, Henry		*		*
Key, Astley Cooper	n/e		*	
King, Richard Duckworth				*
Kitchener, Herbert (Army)	n/e			*
Lambton (Meux), Hedworth		*		†
Laughton, John (naval historian)	n/e		*	
Leveson, Arthur	n/e		*	*
Leveson, Edward			*	*
Markham, Albert	*	†	*	*
Markham, Clements	n/e	*	*	†
May, William	*	*	*	
Milne, Archibald Berkeley		*		
Moore, Arthur		†	*	
Nares, George	n/e		*	
Newbolt, Henry (jingoist and naval historian)	n/e			*
Noel, Gerard			*	*

	1	2	3	4
Rawson, Harry		*	*	*
Richards, Frederick	n/e			*
Robinson, Charles	*			*
Rowley, Charles			*	
Scott, Robert Falcon	n/e		*	*
Shackleton, Ernest (RNR)	n/e		*	*
Spencer, 5th Earl (First Lord)	n/e	*		†
Stephenson, Henry		*	*	
Tracey, Richard			*	*
Tufnell, Lionel	n/e		*	
Twistleton-Wykeham-Fiennes, Geoffrey	n/e	*		*
Vander-Meulen, Frederick				*
Warrender, George		*		
Wilson, Arthur Knyvet	*			

Some Naval Officers appointed to Masonic Grand Rank, 1886–1938

Senior Grand Warden: Admiral Baron Alcester, 1890
    -do-   Admiral of the Fleet Earl Jellicoe, 1927
Junior Grand Warden: Captain Lord Charles Beresford, 1886
    -do-   Vice-Admiral Sir Harry Rawson, 1902
    -do-   Commodore Lionel Halsey, 1917
Senior Grand Deacon: Vice-Admiral William St Clair, 1899
    -do-   Vice-Admiral E. M. Rolfe, 1901
    -do-   Vice-Admiral Wilfred Henderson, 1916
    -do-   Admiral A. E. A. Grant, 1926
    -do-   Admiral John Eustace, 1927
    -do-   Admiral Sir Reginald Hall, 1930
Junior Grand Deacon: Commodore Hubert Giles, 1902
    -do-   Captain Claude W. Prenderleith, 1931
    -do-   Captain C. Stevens, 1933
Grand Sword-Bearer: Vice-Admiral H. J. S. Brownrigg, 1938

Grand Master of New Zealand: Admiral of the Fleet Viscount Jellicoe, 1922

17

Ordo ab Chao

"It is convenient for some men to have a nice book of arithmetic to save them the trouble of thinking and the responsibility of acting for themselves."
Saturday Review, 21 July 1894

John Arbuthnot Fisher was England's sufficient if not quite stable answer to Alfred Tirpitz. In retrospect, his historical span seems staggering: he was nominated for the Navy in 1854 by the last of Nelson's captains still on the Active List (Admiral Sir William Parker, C-in-C Plymouth), and the last of the great ships he built (HMS *Renown*) was in front-line service in the year of the atomic bomb. Jacky Fisher, more than any other man, was responsible for the painful transformation of the late Victorian Fleet into the sublime expression of machine-age military power that it was at the end of his six-decade career. As such, he was "more cursed and blessed than any Sea Lord, then or since".[1]

When shadows lengthen in Portsmouth harbour and the tourists have departed, does Fisher's ghost walk the main deck of HMS *Warrior*, listening to the wind in her rigging and sensing her small movements on the tide, "that bulging eye" and dangerous "vacant look"[2] cast acerbically over the rows of fibreglass muzzle-loaders and the racks of replica muskets? Perhaps. Historian Jan Morris claims to have felt his presence.[3] It was in *Warrior* that he first made his mark as a zealot. He arrived in this enormous three-masted ironclad – the fastest and strongest warship in the world – in 1863, aged 22 and fresh from his gunnery course in *Excellent*. There he had spent his spare time walking the South Downs barking out gunnery orders to train his voice, and within a few months he earned the boast of *Warrior*'s men that he was the smartest gunnery-lieutenant in the Fleet. As mentioned in Chapter 10, he also won the friendship of her executive-officer, Commander George Tryon – with whom he once dived overboard to save a seaman who had fallen from aloft – and the two men remained associated.

340

Nearly twenty years later Admiral Sir Beauchamp Seymour ('the Ocean Swell') lumped them together in a state-of-the-Mediterranean letter to Geoffrey Phipps Hornby:

> One has to keep one's eyes open with Messrs Jack Fisher and George Tryon. The first wants everything belonging to other people & the other is about as wide-awake a customer as you know him to be.[4]

At this time Captain Fisher had just brought Britain's newest iron-clad out to Malta. *Inflexible* had been built at a crossroads in the snakes and ladders of battleship development, and her designers had tried, with predictable consequences, to please everyone. But Tryon assured Hornby that "if anyone can make a good ship of *Inflexible*, it is Jack Fisher";[5] and Seymour soon confirmed that he was indeed doing so.

From *Inflexible* he returned to command *Excellent*, which he introduced to the industrial age, and in 1886 was appointed Director of Naval Ordnance. He was "strong and fearless, unscrupulous in [his] methods of attaining great ends",[6] and he wrote to Hornby after a few days at the Admiralty "to report that I am kicking everybody's shins just to let them know I am here":

> I am getting on like a house on fire! I asked for a list of things I was not allowed to have and have got them all but one – then I declined to do any work until I got a new room with *two* windows, the First Lord's carpet and a red leather chair and a short-hand writer – I've got 'em all – I then declined to write on any paper except that allowed to Cabinet Ministers. I'm writing to you on it now! Finally I pointed out to the First Lord that the whole building revolves round the DNO's department. If you haven't got the guns, what's the good of building the ships, and if you haven't got the ships what's the good of entering boys and naval cadets & if you don't enter them what's the good . . . & so on! This is the house that Jack built.[7]

Soon he was stomping the corridors with a placard round his neck proclaiming "I HAVE NO WORK TO DO!" – a state of affairs which many an officer would hesitate to advertise.

Fisher's career owed nothing to family influence or 'old boy' connections. He "despised the class system and laughed at snobbery".[8] The plus side of this was that he stood out as an extraordinarily single-minded and self-sufficient officer at a time when professional fanaticism was unfashionable; the minus side was that he was beyond peer-group restraint, and to the end of his life he remained "a mono-maniac for whom the universe was one storm cloud".[9] When he was appointed Admiral Superintendent of Portsmouth Dockyard, in 1891, he told Hornby:

I think I shall make a good job of it as I know most of the 'Dockyard Mateys' by their Christian names and there's 'honour among thieves'. I shall come and see you directly I come down and unfold my deep laid scheme for making the leopard change his spots (I mean the dockyard matey).[10]

Thirteen years later, as a newly arrived First Sea Lord, his own picaresque spots were unchanged:

I propose a lecture to all the C-in-Cs and Admiral Superintendents whom I am going to have at the Admiralty for an amiable and conciliatory setting-forth of their damned stupidity, pessimism and effeteness, of which I have full and authenticated particulars, and which I shall read out to them and rub their noses in it.[11]

Fisher thought in large brush-strokes and primary colours. His vision was as broad, as grandiose and as ephemeral as Churchill's, when the latter was spurred by brandy, boundless conceit and the resonance of the English language. "Calm, clear, rational analysis and comparison was, like sobriety of judgement, all but impossible for him."[12] He was a man of violent solutions, slobbery affections and fierce intolerances (he once cited a man's being Irish as reason to distrust him, but he may have been joking). He infused his reforming zeal with an Old Testament fundamentalism, and his letters

chiefly took the form of an interchange of Biblical texts, especially those having reference to Smiting, or Coming Swiftly from Behind, or the ruthless and remorseless dealings of Jahveh with his enemies, or the disagreeable things that happened to people who were not found Watching.[13]

In some ways Fisher had been bitten by the same dog as George Tryon, whom he may have adopted as a role model in the 1860s and '70s – indeed, as Norman Dixon points out, there were striking similarities between them.[14] Fisher often spoke of the "sacred art" of delegation, and he defined as the four great Nelsonic attributes: self-reliance, fertility of resource, fearlessness of responsibility, and the power of initiative[15] (a list which amounts to four ways of saying much the same thing, and illustrates the thematic, as opposed to analytical, nature of his mind). 'Playing the Game' was not Fisher's strong suit. He played to win:

If you rub it in both at home and abroad that you intend to be 'first in' and hit your enemy in the belly and kick him when he's down and boil your prisoners in oil (*if you take any*) and torture his women and children, then people will steer clear of you.[16]

His unchivalrous, apocalyptic slogans were not appreciated at the time. In reality – and allowing for charming hyperbole – they merely represented a return to the Basic English of naval warfare, yet one can readily see how (for example) his dictum that "the essence of war is VIOLENCE; moderation in war is IMBECILITY!!" was out of place amongst the white-washed awnings and starched collars, the picnics and polo, and those immaculate fleet manoeuvres of the turn-of-the-century Navy – a slightly disconcerting social gaffe, like mentioning God at the church bazaar. Follow it with "ANY DAMN FOOL can obey orders!!", with its unwelcome tremors from the *Victoria* business, and one can imagine nervous smiles and people edging away. "The new Admiral has just joined the fleet; he is said to be a tremendous scoundrel."[17]

The age of Fisher is a territory of thickets and swamps still being mapped and partitioned by academic exploration and fought over in public debate. For a traveller to hope to pass quickly through without getting enmired or paying heavy tolls is an unlikely proposition. A summary of the Royal Navy's serpentine affairs during these years is beyond the scope of this book and the competence of its author, but it is necessary *inter alia* to ask why Jack Fisher, who railroaded so many radical changes against entrenched opposition, failed to pick up Tryon's 'action-principles' baton and run with it.

Those pro-Tryon officers who made common cause in the immediate aftermath of the *Victoria* disaster – and of whom the Fisher brothers Jacky and 'Uncle Bill' were at least touch-line supporters – had few other interests in common. They were mostly cross-grained and unclubbable by nature, and formed a transient single-issue pressure-group which presently dispersed. Aside from Fisher, only Lord Walter Kerr (whose Tryonism had been passive compliance more than crusading zeal) went on to command the power and prestige to force through reform, but Kerr's "was not a creative mind"[18] and he probably could see no means of keeping faith with the agenda of his late chief, other than by TA – which, in the post-*Victoria* climate, was scarcely an option.

More than a decade after the collision, when the Navy was becoming racked and riven by the Fisher reforms, the Tryonites were mostly in the evenings of their careers and some were vehemently opposed to the radical First Sea Lord for idiosyncratic reasons of principle or prejudice. In addition to his *Life of Sir George Tryon*, Charles Penrose Fitzgerald produced a pamphlet which (in Fisher's view) did "full justice" to the TA system; but he retired without getting higher than second-in-command China, and was considered a garrulous bore to whom few paid much heed.

Gerard Noel, of course, is problematical. Bacon testifies that when he stood in as C-in-C Mediterranean, while Fisher was at the Hague

Peace Conference, he practised the fleet in complicated steam-tactics and called for suggestions for refinements, but discouraged attempts to relate them to war conditions, on the grounds that "he intended them merely as peace evolutions". To Bacon, this revealed a disappointing, peacetime mind-set. But Noel was probably ahead of him, and was using signalled steam-tactics merely for their legitimate 'primary educational' value, with no intention of relying on them in the event of real combat.[19] Noel went on to command the China Squadron (a repository for square pegs), but was incensed, first by Fisher's ill-considered scheme to make interchangeable seaman officers and engineers, and then by the recall of ships deployed abroad,[20] and he took his grievances into retirement.

Reginald Custance served as second-in-command to Compton Domvile in the Mediterranean, and Beresford in the Channel; and as he became implicated in Beresford's hate campaign against Fisher, purgatory was too good for him. Alfred Winsloe served on the 1904–5 ship-design committee which projected the battleship into the all-big-gun era, and then as Fourth Sea Lord; but he commanded only a much-depleted China Squadron, in 1910–13.

Of all Tryon's allies, Fisher was the best placed, through temperament, major fleet command and (ultimately) power at the Admiralty, to resurrect Sir George's campaign to emancipate the fleet from the *Signal Book*. A leather-bound pocket-book, entitled *Notes on Fleet Manoeuvring*, which he issued as C-in-C North America & West Indies in 1899, proves that opinions he had expressed to James Goodenough in 1871 had not fundamentally changed. It took the form of a number of 'dits' and references, "collected at various times for personal use [and which] may be of service to those newly joining the squadron".[21]

It paid tribute to Phipps Hornby, and alluded to four articles written by the great man between 1876 and 1885 on the management of ships in a fleet. It also contained common-sense extracts from Culme-Seymour's *Notes on Manoeuvring* (mentioned in Chapter 15) dealing with the practical minutiae of working in formation. But the booklet's most conspicuous feature was the space it gave to Tryon's manoeuvring with and without signals, which, it said, had been "discredited because a mistake was made and an accident happened when the Fleet was NOT being exercised by TA". Attention was also drawn to Fitzgerald's pamphlet on the subject, and there were two paragraphs extracted directly from Tryon's last proselytizing memorandum of May 1893 – paragraphs which, the booklet remarked, "must impress themselves on every thoughtful mind".

A couple of years later Fisher was arguing that the number of ships available to a wartime fleet would exceed the number which can realistically be handled by one admiral, and that the answer was the command-and-control division of the fleet into two or more lines –

> but what careful and systematic training this requires – what constant practice, what need to consider every eventuality, and for the subordinates to know exactly how to interpret their Commander-in-Chief's wishes at the right moment! More than ever Nelson must be the model for our Admirals.[22]

And as late as 1902 we find Fisher, faithful to his views of thirty years earlier, lamenting to the First Lord, the Earl of Selborne, that "the present *Signal Book* is regarded as sacred as the *Bible*! It's really not up to the *Apocrypha*!"[23]

So why did he not see to it when he had the power to do so?

To some extent the quest for an answer is destined to be unsatisfactory, for known documentary sources offer little help, and we are mostly left with biography and guesswork.

Firstly and most prosaically, it is possible that he made a weather-eye decision that the renewed championship of signal-free manoeuvring would be imprudent ("knowing what happens to the fender when you come alongside with too much weight on"[24]). Fisher-buffs will reject this suggestion: he is said to have lived by the precept that "when you're told that a thing is *impossible*, that there are *insuperable* objections, then is the time to fight like the devil."[25] And in point of fact he did at least make a bid to have the *Signal Book* simplified, a few weeks into his First Sea Lordship in late 1904, when he tried to persuade Beresford to interrupt his sea service to supervise a revision and simplification of the current (1898) *Signal Book*.[26]

At this stage Fisher still thought of the volatile Lord Charles as a potential force for reform, and his reasons for choosing him for this seemingly implausible commission (to which we shall return) were both sincere and, in principle, shrewd. He was paying Beresford a compliment, although, given the fragile nature of relations between them, it was not within his charm to convey it as such. The plan would have entailed Beresford's hauling down in the Channel Squadron a month early and delaying somewhat his accession to the Mediterranean, to both of which he took strong exception. There ensued an ugly interview (opaquely alluded to in Beresford's letter to Evan-Thomas, quoted in the last chapter) in which "all the pent up wrath of the years between the two men broke out".[27] This, however, does not really answer the question.

Secondly and more fundamentally, while instinct and friendship certainly aligned Fisher with Tryon while the latter was alive, their respective talents and obsessions were on different planes. It was said of the period (1883–91) when Fisher was the "moving spirit of the Gunnery Department" that "much was done to improve weapons, but nothing whatever was done to provide for their fighting use . . . it was a materialistic period."[28] This, we know, is an injustice, but it roughly stylizes Fisher's priorities, both then and at later stages of his career. Although he would have agreed with Sir George's incisive distinction between a seaman officer's *primary* and *secondary* educational syllabuses,[29] for example, it was an un-Fisherish articulation. "The use of the Navy more than its practice was his chief occupation. He thought in fleets and seas and where another man might think of firing a salvo he would launch a division." More specifically, he was "no tactician [and] a poor handler of a squadron".[30] He may even have been nervous of fleetwork, although "he liked looking on while other people did it".[31]

It would invite derision to suggest that while he commanded the Mediterranean, in 1899–1902, Fisher was uninterested in tactical themes. "He rattled the fleet about till no one could call his soul his own"[32] and encouraged (in his disruptive way) quite junior officers to explore and expound their own ideas – especially those relating to flotilla warfare.[33] But his main reform agenda took the form of a vigorous drive for mechanical excellence, and he strove above all to bring the technocrat to the fore ("the executive branch can say nothing too bad" about him[34]). His great achievement was to turn his fleet into "a fifteen-knot one without breakdowns, in place of a twelve-knot one with breakdowns".[35] Once ensconced at the Admiralty, he was too obsessed with his ideas of flotilla-defence and of fast monster ships sweeping Britain's enemies off the seas, and with his material, organizational and political battles, to turn his mind to the systematic thinking-through of fundamental action-principles.

There are two further, speculative, angles.

It is possible that in the wake of Culme-Seymour's counter-reformation some senior Tryon-sympathizers accepted that tactical reform through the *Signal Book* had been thwarted, and looked for other ways to approach the problem: they may have seen in the drive to increase gunnery ranges (in response to the growing reach of the Whitehead torpedo) the added benefit of reducing the fleet's dependence on the speed and minutiae of manoeuvring. It is obvious that the influence which an enemy's every twist and turn may have on the tactical dynamics of an engagement diminishes as the range increases, and the need to respond in detail similarly diminishes: great range throws tactics into slow motion – a condition in which 'fleetwork' signalling is under least stress. I am not aware of any primary evidence that construes the failure of TA as a contributory catalyst of gunnery reform; but it may be observed that, after Culme-Seymour's departure, the Mediterranean was commanded for five and a half years (1896–1902) by, successively, Sir John Hopkins and Sir John Fisher, who are both on record as *Signal Book* sceptics and who now indulged and encouraged the fleet's 'Young Turk' gunnery radicals. It may be further noted that, as well as having been successive Directors of Naval Ordnance and Controllers of the Navy, they both went to the Mediterranean from North America & West Indies – a station whose ships were too few and heterogeneous for elaborate steam-tactics. Did Percy Scott mean to imply that Hopkins linked the three subjects when he remarked that he "had ideas of <u>fleet manoeuvres</u>, <u>gunnery</u> and <u>signalling</u> far in advance of any other admiral with whom I had served"?[36]

Carrying on from this, chronologically, is a consideration which calls from the jungle of Edwardian naval politics and which will by no means be recognized by those who tenaciously adhere to a 'Marder-esque' view of the period, but it makes sense of John Fisher's apparent desertion of fleet-action-doctrine 'empiricism'. This is that, with his visions of roving, predatory battlecruisers and blockading submarine flotillas,[37] he went to the Admiralty convinced that battle-fleets were both unaffordable and obsolete, and intending to put an end to them.[38] Why bother trying to reform an entrenched tactical mind-set if it will soon be swept into history by an avalanche of innovation?

If Fisher is credited with the parentage of the 'dreadnought' type, *Invincible* was his love-child and in conception, if not delivery, came first. A veteran observer of government has defined a committee as "a cul-de-sac down which ideas are lured and then quietly strangled";[39] and the all-big-gun battleship was preferred over the all-big-gun armoured-cruiser by Lord Selborne and the 1904–5 Committee on Designs,[40] and Fisher acquiesced, hoping that after one experimental battleship he would be able to convert his colleagues to the idea of super-cruisers alone. However, the internal and external momentum for repeat dread-noughts was to prove irresistible: even before *Dreadnought* herself had been launched, a new design committee (the 'Fusion Committee') deemed the battleship-type for the time being indispensable,[41] and the best the First Sea Lord could manage thereafter was to ride both horses.[42]

The size and composition of the wartime Grand Fleet, the creation of which is mostly and rightly attributed to Fisher, attaches fateful significance to his failure to espouse and implement Tryon's 'action-principles' reform agenda; but, in fact, owing to an obstacle course of pressures and *Realpolitik* compromises, the dreadnought 'Fleet that Jack built' differed fundamentally from the one that Jack had really wanted.

At the time of writing the historical jury still flatters itself to be out on this matter, but recently deep-mined evidence places it, in my view, beyond dispute. When he went to the Admiralty, Fisher had boasted, "It will be Athanasius *contra mundum*; very sorry, but Athanasius is going to win." But in fact it was only a draw. (That his obstruction may have been a blessing in one obvious respect, is an entirely separate issue.)

That still leaves us with the problem of Nelson – readily invoked by Fisher and described as his patron saint by Professor Marder – with all the classically 'Tryonic' tactical values we associate with his famous fleet victories. What exactly was the Immortal Memory to Fisher?

As the extract quoted a few pages back demonstrates, he clearly applauded Nelson's doctrine of tactical devolution, and lamented its absence from the contemporary service. But there was more to it than that. Or, rather, less.

It was rhetorically convenient to him (as to many others before and since) to claim the high ground of naval history. But far from pondering the subject at any sophisticated level, his knowledge of it was poor[43] and his contempt for it "supreme".[44] "History is a record of exploded ideas," he told a Mediterranean Fleet audience, sometime in 1900–2.[45] "History is dead," he announced triumphantly (and perhaps with a wishful note of hysteria) when *Indefatigable* was launched in 1909, "everything is changed".[46] And in his dotage he was still insisting that "there is absolutely nothing in common between the fleets of Nelson and the Jutland Battle!"[47]

At a technical level these dogmatic assertions appear justified: the size of ships, the materials of their construction, the nature of their weapons, the means of their propulsion, and even the colour of their paint, had all changed beyond recognition. Radical new challenges demand radical responses; and in his fight to haul the Victorian Fleet kicking and screaming into the twentieth century, Fisher needed every argument, every handy solecism, to prise loose the tentacles of the past. It all had to go. But he undoubtedly shared the common conceit of midwives of new technology of supposing that their deliveries are so revolutionary as to nullify history's inventory of previous endeavour and experience.

Nelson's main use to John Fisher was as a means of reminding the Navy that violence was its business and its heritage – a device to infiltrate God back into the bazaar. A worthy enough object, perhaps; but for interpreting the past, and assimilating its lessons, he had neither time nor temperament. His manic gaze was fixed on the horizon ahead with scarcely a sternward glance.

*

It is difficult nowadays to understand the extent of the feeling against Fisher, for we look back and perceive him riding the tide of destiny. But there were two general reasons why Radical Jack aroused instinctive and widespread hostility. Firstly, he was, in his personnel reforms and by the standards of Edwardian admirals, virtually a socialist ("This democratic country won't stand an aristocratic Navy!"). And secondly, his full-blooded embrace of new construction from the 'dreadnought' stable – whether battleships or battlecruisers – rendered obsolete the foundation of Britain's maritime supremacy: her towering numerical lead in pre-dreadnought battleships. At best this appeared to be a leap in the dark, at worst a fatal gift to the country's enemies. For whom was 'the Asiatic' (a scurrilous reference to his complexion, and exotic theories about his parentage) really working?

And there were other over-laden applecarts, rocked by his Draconian strategic redeployments, by his scrapping (to release men for service at home) of "160 vessels of war that could neither fight nor run away, and whose officers were shooting pheasants up Chinese rivers and giving tea parties to British consuls",[48] or by his hasty personal animosities and sometimes misbegotten favouritisms. With the clarity of hindsight we may add to his felonies his sponsorship of successive classes of battle-cruisers whose design assumptions would have failed objective analysis (not until aircraft-carriers was his concept of 'HMS Unapproachable' realizable), and his intense but narrow focusing on technology and material to the continued neglect of the less tangible aspects of warfare. A historian has said that "proper tactical and strategic considerations were being ignored because the Navy was now dominated by men of the material school."[49] This may be a travesty of the strategic-reform motives behind Fisher's secretive 'flotilla defence' agenda, but if it refers to the *operation*, as opposed to the *deployment*, of naval power then there is a case to be answered, and it certainly reflects how things appeared to many of the would-be practitioners. Similar complaints in naval memoirs are commonplace.

For example: "obsolete designs and weapons were being replaced by the products of the scientist and engineer at a pace which outran full consideration of their use in war";[50] and

> materialistic skill was responsible for the wonderful development that ensued in our ships and their equipment, but at last, it became a master rather than a servant. It, so to speak, overshot its authority.[51]

To some extent Fisher was taking advantage of the Admiralty's lack of an institutionalized staff system – an analytical, thinking department.[52]

At a personal level he appreciated officers whose sound administrative minds complemented his own predilection for broad, sweeping perspectives, and collected them in his retinue (John Jellicoe, whose mind has been described as a "well-ordered filing system of detail",[53] being the obvious example). But that was a far cry from fostering a free-thinking naval staff which might expose his visionary schemes to the perhaps disenchanting light of analysis. He affected to distrust written arguments on the grounds that a man who writes something down has time to lie (he also, of course, has time to think). His *modus operandi* was "the building of castles in the air and the rearing up of earthly foundations to meet them",[54] and such staff-work as his Fishpond juniors performed for him was merely to rear up the earthly foundations – to connect up the dots – and lacked the integrity of untrammelled analysis.

This state of affairs was assisted by historically rooted structural weaknesses. The second half of Victoria's reign had been the glorious age of the gentleman amateur. Professionally qualified technicians were few, and the esteem in which they were held was tempered by the stigma of 'trade'. Every branch of science was still (considered to be) within the grasp of ordinarily educated men – unlike today, when most people are reconciled to huge areas of non-comprehension. Dilettantism and trial-and-error were the vehicles of progress. In the Navy, career paths such as Gunnery or Torpedoes were 'specializations' only in terms of the incidental amateur skills of professional seamen (and the idiot-proof needs of operational warships); but they had, for many years, been relied upon for the Navy's 'in house' research and development.

As a quite junior officer, Fisher had encountered "a wondrous assortment of brass screws and strings and other things" which had been issued as a circuit-closer at a cost of £7 10s., and promptly made his own from an old tin-can for less than a shilling.[55] Years later, a *Vernon* instructor is alleged to have told his class: "Now, what electricity is we don't rightly know, but this we do know, that Captain Fisher invented it and Captain Wilson improved it."[56] One can only applaud the occasional triumph of ingenuity and common sense, and there will always be a role for extemporization to meet urgent operational needs (good examples being: the use of dissolving aniseed-balls as timers for limpet mines in the Second World War; and the conversion of the revolving base of an office chair into a machine-gun mounting for a helicopter in the Falklands). But as the nineteenth century drew to a close, the time when the Navy's R & D could be entrusted to the garden shed was passing, although the Admiralty's small direct sponsorship of it continued to take the haphazard form of its indulgence of Lieutenant Bacon's interest in pyrotechnics:

I had an inspiration which I thought might be developed, so I made the acquaintance of Sir Norman Lockyer [astronomer], who offered me the use of a laboratory at South Kensington. I obtained leave from the Admiralty for six weeks . . . but never could get the range of my recognition light more than a mile and a half.[57]

Without a dedicated naval staff to define requirements and shape policy in technical matters, and, where appropriate, tap civilian expertise, the Navy was bound for trouble in the twentieth century. It is no doubt easier to see this now than it was then. It happened to be over the problem of long-range fire-control, the 'nuclear physics challenge' of the Edwardian age, that the service first fell victim to the corruptibility and hand-to-mouth nature of the Admiralty's appraisal and acquisition processes – and to Fisher's caprice in matters incidental to his capital-ship revolution.

Mr Arthur Pollen was a technician rather than a scientist, but he had the academic philosophical grounding which was often associated with British scientific pioneering, and the Admiralty's rejection of his inventions was essentially a philosophical failure, made possible by failures of method and integrity.[58] His 'helm-free' system for predicting ranges, based on an analogue computer harnessed to gyroscopic bearing control, was as important a development for gunnery as John Harrison's chronometer had been for navigation 150 years earlier, and had potentially profound implications for the tactical emancipation of Britain's battle-squadrons – for a fleet so equipped could depart from the orthodoxy of two closely controlled lines engaging each other on straight and parallel courses. Explaining these benefits to the Admiralty was as great an obstacle as the nascent technology, and Pollen was not overblessed with tact. His being a civilian, a tradesman, a Roman Catholic, and very clever, did not help him with naval officers either.

In opting for Captain Frederick Dreyer's cheaper, inferior system, the Admiralty, in effect, shelved its campaign to master long-range gunnery and forgot that in 1905 (with the switch to dreadnoughts) it had boldly gambled for qualitative, over crudely quantitative, superiority. Dreyer's cost-saving package prolonged the Royal Navy's submission to the courtly convention of parallel battle-lines, for it was unable to assimilate erratically changing ranges and bearings – and indeed its inventor tendentiously argued that foreseeable tactical needs made such capabilities unnecessary. If he was wrong (and, almost inevitably, he was wrong) British capital ships would find themselves unable to meet the first and third of Fisher's desiderata that they must "hit first, hit hard, and keep on hitting".

*

In basing their respective cases upon assumptions about the future use and practice of British capital ships, both Pollen and (less obviously) Dreyer were exceeding their authority; but, in these catalytic, confusing times, vaunted expertise could be claimed for the asking:

> There was no Staff organization to think out even the general lines on which the weapons so laboriously prepared were to be used, and [to] prepare the gallant men for the set of facts with which they would be confronted.[59]

This state of affairs left the senior officers at sea out on a limb, for much of the professional skill acquired in their first thirty years' service was being eclipsed just as they reached high command. They varied, as men do, in their interests and abilities; and while some could ride the new wave, others could not. They had matured in the old Navy of hemp, tar and canvas, when steam propulsion was still looked upon askance by their superiors, and when 'HANDS TO DANCE AND SKYLARK' was still piped on balmy tropical evenings. Now they found themselves in high command of a Navy of turbines and torpedoes, submarines and wireless, and the first aeroplanes. Exactly how these Wellsian war-machines would shape up in battle, nobody knew.

> It is important to remember that in the victories of Nelson's time, and generally in the eighteenth century, our sea-captains had the same weapons to fight with as had been used for many generations of naval warfare. The capacity and limits of their guns, powder and shots, ships and fleets, were well known. The general tactical form of action was unchanged. What would happen when two ships met and engaged was, as far as materiel was concerned, known within definite limits from handed-down experience and from a hundred sea-fights . . . Nelson knew exactly the risks he ran and accurately allowed for them.[60]

The admirals of the dreadnought years had none of these certainties. They were disadvantaged, as against their predecessors of Nelson's days and their successors of the 1940s, in that they lacked that keel-to-mast-head familiarity with the materiel in their charge. Even at the time of the *Victoria* disaster a newspaper could write that "whenever the next war takes place we shall simply be making a series of the most dangerous experiments that the human race ever ventured upon",[61] and war finally came when *Dreadnought* was less than eight years old and whole divisions of dreadnoughts only five. If the admirals got it wrong they would be pilloried, the country subjugated and the empire dismembered. Much harder, in this climate, to be a Pellew, a Hoste, a Vian or a Cunningham.

> It is not easy to go to school again when you are middle-aged, to find your supremacy as a seaman, based on naval experiences successfully overcome, in

some respects lessened; a new world growing up that disturbs the old train of thought and things, a world which you do not know much about, a time without precedent in naval history, when the junior might know more than his senior about naval technique.

Many older officers, therefore, found it difficult to adapt themselves to the modern ship and its machinery. It needed technical training of a type which they had not had. It was difficult for them to act as a senior officer should, in initiating and stimulating training on new lines which they had not studied.[62]

They responded to this crisis of confidence in two ways: by marinating the material developments of the early twentieth century in the familiar professional ethos of the nineteenth; and by trying to regulate them with rules, standing orders, and comparative statistics.

On the one hand, many senior officers were content to be guided by the shining Victorian lodestar of chivalry, with its quixotic approach to combat. There was much more to Nelson than merely 'engaging the enemy more closely' – "Do not imagine that I am one of these hot-headed people who fight at an immense disadvantage without an adequate object" – but the Edwardian Navy, with its anti-intellectual tradition, still sheltered and promoted men whose repertoire of military skill (when explicit orders defaulted, and sometimes even when they did not) amounted to gallantry, muscle and frontal assault.

On the other hand, the 'scientific' school sought to organize order out of apparent chaos by agency of the Book (or, rather, a plethora of Books). This was, writ large, the old military preoccupation with ensuring an acceptable minimum level of performance by enforcing procedures which unavoidably suppress the maximum level. It militated towards the adoption of one-dimensional 'material' evaluations of tactical problems, and tended to overrate the enemy's strength, for, while he would be credited with his full 'on-paper' assets, one's own circumstantial handicaps were usually too obvious to exclude from the equation.

These alternative nostrums, the 'romantic' and the 'scientific', to what Herbert Richmond called "the supreme business" were poles apart in application, but shared the attraction of appearing to obviate the need for abstract thought or complex judgement *on the spot*. The Great War would provide striking examples of both, and, as a rule, neither was appropriate. The officers were few who could range freely in the middle ground between.

*

A question arising obliquely from the above is whether a reputation for fine seamanship was linked with authoritarianism (which, in Professor Dixon's terms, equates with higher-command incompetence) in the late

Victorian and Edwardian Navy. The haphazard biographical material available suggests that it was.

It would be untenable to suggest that seamanship is somehow inherently incompatible with competent leadership – and would certainly give offence to naval officers prickly about their ship-handling – for some famous autocrats (Tryon, Tyrwhitt, Cunningham, Vian) were celebrated ship-handlers. However, others (Nelson, Fisher, Beatty, Mountbatten) were not; they pushed their way to flag-rank through the display of attributes other than, or additional to, ship-handling and seamanship – attributes which almost necessarily belonged to the seaman officer's secondary educational agenda as defined by George Tryon. In peacetime the odds were against such officers getting to the top (as we shall see, even Beatty was rescued from terminal unemployment only by Churchill's ignoring the Sea Lords' advice to steer clear of him); whereas many admirals were reputed to excel at ship-handling and fleetwork, not just because they had indeed mastered these demanding, if 'primary', skills, but because there was little else to justify their holding flag-rank.

" 'Fine seaman' covered a multitude of shortcomings in those days",[63] and it is noteworthy that Jellicoe sheltered many of his subordinates – men like George Warrender, Cecil Burney, Martyn Jerram, Edward Bradford, Douglas Gamble, Dudley de Chair – on the vague and unhappy grounds of their seamanship. Nelson, in Mahan's words, "was a great general officer; and whether he had the knack of making a ship go through all her paces without a fault mattered as little as whether he was a crack shot with a gun".[64] As Fisher said, "to be a good admiral, a man does not need to be a good sailor. That's a common mistake. He needs good sailors under him."[65] Marder's allusion to Evan-Thomas's reputation as a ship-handler assumes an almost ominous ring.

*

Richard Hough, in *Admirals in Collision*, supposes that Tryon's reform agenda was, within a few years of his death, overtaken by the arrival of wireless-telegraphy.[66] He is wrong. Firstly, the essentials of Tryon's 'action principles' are timelessly relevant to the skills of warfare; and, secondly (if one wishes to confine the argument to fleetwork), formated ships could not be synchronously manoeuvred by non-visual means[67] until the advent of radio-telephony (i.e. direct voice), which the RN did not adopt for general ship-to-ship use until the 1940s.[68]

With Morse-key W/T, "a considerable time is bound to elapse" between the decision to send a signal and its receipt in plain language on the bridge of the recipient ship(s) –

a period which includes the time taken to write out the [message], to transmit it to the wireless office, to code it, signal it, de-code it on board the receiving ship, write it out and transmit it to the bridge.[69]

The total lapse of time will vary from ship to ship, according to the efficiency of the signals staff, pressure of other business, ease of communication with the bridge (which may depend on factors such as whether a vacuum-tube is fitted, whether watertight doors are open or closed, or even whether the upper deck is awash), and so on. This variability precludes using W/T for the purposes of executing

  a. any manoeuvre in unison (such as a turn *together*);

  b. any urgent (= 'immediate execute') manoeuvre; or

  c. a fast sequence of manoeuvres.

Indeed one could say that, had W/T somehow existed in the absence of other means of signalling, the need for Tryon's crusade would not have arisen because *formal steam-tactics could never have progressed much beyond their primitive 1850s condition.*

Besides, as Marconi's invention spread through the Fleet (and notwithstanding its obvious strategic advantages) it had an insidious influence of its own. Officers who had been brought up not to "blow your nose without asking leave, by signal, of the admiral to do so"[70] could now (and often did) use W/T to seek permission from remote seniors for domestic matters of supreme triviality. They were already signals junkies, and their dependency expanded to match the range of the new technology. It created "a difficulty in deciding who the senior officer is",[71] and boundaries of responsibility became blurred. The misuse – as it surely was – of wireless was by no means a one-way traffic, for the Admiralty, too, would succumb incontinently to its temptations. In these ways, legitimate and illegitimate, the early years of the century placed an ever greater premium on signalling and its associated skills.

Meanwhile, to officers struggling to keep their bearings in a blizzard of material changes, the long-familiar visual-signalling system was one of the few constant datum points of their professional world. Fleets, however, were growing in size, due both to the Anglo-German building race and to the gathering of capital ships in home waters. (Whereas the Mediterranean Fleet of the early 1890s had eight to ten battleships, to which, in wartime, the Channel Fleet might have added five, the combined Home Fleets in 1913 had, on their books, thirty-one.) And successive commanders-in-chief found it an increasingly tall order to orchestrate their formations by (what had become) the traditional 'Colombine' means.

In 1910, the then C-in-C Home Fleet, Admiral Sir William May, summarized the lessons of thirty-four recent tactical exercises, and came close to despairing of working his fleet in the presence of the enemy:

It would be almost impossible to get a signal through, on account of the smoke from the funnels and the guns. In many of the exercises carried out in completely clear weather, that is, when the visibility has been 15,000 yards, the fighting arena has been rendered quite misty by smoke: in some cases the repeating ships have been obscured, and this has happened without any guns firing and in a fairly fresh breeze.[72]

These experiences would have pointed a free-thinker towards releasing his subordinates from his halyards – and May indeed began to experiment with divisional independence.[73] Thus, once again, a British fleet found itself approaching the fence over which Tryon had jumped the Mediterranean Squadron in the early 1890s; but, this time, without his goading and spurring, it shied away: Sir William, in the end, merely reaffirmed the confinement of tactics to match the practical limitations of centralized control (an expediency shortly to be abetted by the limitations of the chosen fire-control system). It was left to his successor, the last peacetime admiralissimo, Sir George Callaghan (Home Fleets 1911–14), to begin some tacit, unproclaimed process of recantation.

At the same time the *Signal Book* itself did not remain entirely unchallenged. Fisher's abortive attempt, soon after taking office, to deploy Beresford as a 'de-skiller' of signalling has already been mentioned, and the evidence is that Charlie B., as chairman of the revision committee, would have performed this role effectively, for, not being an expert (as he freely admitted), he saw himself as a consumer, rather than a purveyor, of signalling. Partly because of Lord Charles's refusal to fall in with Fisher's plan, the production of what became the 1906 *Signal Book* assumed aspects of a fiasco.

In 1905, the Signal School stood in high repute within the service. Evan-Thomas's successor as captain, Commander Allan Everett (1900–4), had built on its firm foundations by running voluntary 'fleet-work' courses for senior officers. But after he left, things seem to have gone wrong. Two COs came and went in two and a half years. The first of these, Commander Douglas Nicholson, may have been a stop-gap appointee, for his promotion out of the job was only a matter of months; but he appears to have been landed with the *Signal Book* revision in default of Beresford, and, having produced a draft, went off, in August '05, to be flag-captain to Vice-Admiral Sir George Atkinson-Willes, C-in-C East Indies.

His draft book, meanwhile, was sent out to Malta to be tested by the Mediterranean Fleet; and, after a three-month trial, Lord Charles Beresford rejected it in terms which indicate why Fisher had wanted him to do the work in the first place. It was still cluttered with procedural and administrative matters, and the revisers had sought brevity, not by cutting down on its routine 'trivia' provisions, but by curtailing its explanatory sections and omitting the index. Beresford argued for the proper educational role of a *Signal Book* and pointed out that, in the absence of an index, "an officer or man not conversant with [it] might spend a considerable time trying to find a particular signal". The whole thing was, in brief, a signalman's *Signal Book*, "far too complicated and impractical to be adopted for fleetwork".[74]

Exactly how the 1906 *Signal Book* emerged from this débâcle is unclear. The Signal School's papers are strangely uninformative.[75] William Graham Greene, Principal Clerk of the Admiralty, later said that "the final form was settled in conference between the Commanders-in-Chief of the Channel, Atlantic and Mediterranean."[76] Busy admirals of seagoing fleets have other things to do, and there can be no surprise that the book which emerged was little more than a tinkered-with version of the old. Meanwhile Nicholson's successor at the Signal School, Commander Henry Sandeman, had held the reins for only eight months before an eye infection compelled extended absence on sick leave – for "treatment at own risk and expense" – and although he was declared fit in May '06, he gave up the job in August.[77] It was probably these various regrettable circumstances which caused Allan Everett, now a four-ring captain, to be brought back to the Signal School in 1906 for a unique second term in command. (The school remained thereafter a captain's billet.)

Biographical glimpses show Ev in a sympathetic light. He was a popular officer and celebrated raconteur, who absolutely never took any form of exercise. (Once, when word went round the Home Fleet that he was going to take up golf, a biggish group of well-wishers attended his début, which lasted for two holes.) He has been described by one of his professional successors as "a man of high culture and of independent and original outlook";[78] and it is said that, while he was flag-lieutenant to Sir Compton Domvile, in Culme-Seymour's Mediterranean, he spent some time with a fellow lieutenant exploring philosophy, "with a view to discovering a credo".[79] It would be trite to suggest that he found his creed in signalling, but, having been three times 'flags', and now twice captain of the Signal School, there can be no doubting his status as the Royal Navy's most authoritative signalling expert.

Everett was not long back in Portsmouth before his interests came under renewed assault, from a Captain Cuthbert Hunter, the CO of a minor cruiser. Hunter started by having a go at the long-winded procedure laid down for enemy-reporting by W/T.

"Signals are valuable servants but must not be allowed to become our masters," he said, in November 1907; and submitted his own simple grid-based scheme "by which position, course and speed of enemy's ship or squadron could be signalled with greater accuracy and rapidity than can be done under the present system".[80] He also took the opportunity to deliver a tirade against the signals community in words strongly reminiscent of Tryon's private letter to Phipps Hornby in 1891 (fully quoted in Chapter 10):

> I wish to emphasize how infinitely more important some information is than others and how neither the system nor the routine nor the habits nor any thing else to do with signalling should be allowed for one minute to stand in the way of the rapid transmission of such information as the nature, position, course and speed of an enemy. There are some signals apart from all others in regard to their importance but unfortunately I do not think that our signalmen and signals experts appreciate this.
>
> I may be rash in making this statement, but what is one to think when, on turning to the *Signal Book* – the latest and most modern production of the signals experts – one finds that to tell a division of ships during an action to act independently requires four flags or pendants, while to inform a fleet on a Monday morning that there will be no drill, or to tell a hungry fleet that they can go and feed, requires only one?
>
> The signal expert seems to have an intense dislike of brevity, and useful single-flag signals for action do not exist. The only reason I can think of for this is that the signals expert is a peace expert and has devised a system which is very thorough, and, in relation to peace-work, is good, but by its very rigidity it has made the manoeuvre the slave of the signal, instead of which the signal should be the servant of the manoeuvre.
>
> The above remarks are a digression from the original purpose of this article, but are made to try and save my proposals from that exceedingly valuable but, at the same time, very narrow-minded slave of the system, the signal expert – the ogre who plays the part of 'the Old Man of the Sea' to the 'Sinbad' of tactics, destroying his freedom of movement by his hide-bound rigidity of system.

This barracking, Ev took on the chin. He wasted no time in approving Hunter's quick-reporting scheme, made some modifications of his own, and had it issued to the Fleet.

Having thus cracked the walls of Jericho, Captain Hunter took another breath, in January 1908, and blew his trumpet against the flag-signalling regime. His paper was entitled 'A Criticism on the Present *Signal Book* with Suggestions for its Revision',[81] and he was campaigning for an abbreviated, skeletal system, designed for speed of use in action. Again, his views impart a strong sense of *déjà vu*, and make one wonder if he had not come across a yellowing copy of Tryon's (unmentionable) TA Memorandum:

A close study of the *Signal Book* cannot fail to impress one with a feeling of admiration for the orderliness and simplicity of the system adopted throughout the book. If one, however, thinks more deeply of the reasons for the existence of a signal book, and of the circumstances under which a good system of communication is of the greatest value, then one's admiration dwindles to a low ebb.

Signals are the handmaid of tactics. The supreme test of a system of signals must be its use in action especially and in war generally. An action will probably commence by two organized fleets in good order meeting in more or less clear weather when signals can be easily made and easily seen. [But] in a very short time the ships will be surrounded by water and spray from falling projectiles; the ships themselves will begin to receive considerable damage on deck, funnels will be injured and smoke will obscure the view . . . will our signals satisfactorily meet these conditions?

I contend they will not, but that on the contrary, they will utterly fail. I contend that the *Signal Books* unnecessarily restrict the mobility of the fleet and in a way exercise dictatorship over tactics, which is not the function of the *Signal Book* and *Signal Manual*. I contend that we must provide for the possible as well as the probable – for tactics we would not approve of on the table in the War College, but which might be forced upon us. In war it is the unexpected that will happen and mobility under all conditions will be a valuable possession when the day of battle comes.

Hunter was a bold man to cast aspersions on the regime of steam-tactics under which so many of his seniors had progressed their careers. Whether he thereby compromised his own is impossible to know; but, at a time when as many as fifty per cent of his *Britannia* contemporaries were reaching flag-rank[82] (today fewer than that become commanders), it may be observed that he got no further than captain on the Active List (although he had yet to get into trouble for hazarding *Hermione* in 1909 and grounding *Hampshire* in 1913[83]).

Hunter's paper landed on Captain Everett's desk.

Everett knew the gamut of arguments better than most. Hunter's words can hardly have failed to remind him of the days, more than fifteen years before, when he, as an eager young officer, had pestered the noble and forbearing Sir Geoffrey Phipps Hornby with similar notions. And more recently, in 1902–3, he had been admitted into a small, select Channel Fleet discussion group which formed the earliest traceable roots of the 'off-the-record' journal, the *Naval Review*, and whose prime mover appears to have been Lieutenant (with $2\frac{1}{2}$ rings) Herbert Richmond. In the latter's words:

A few of us felt that while a great deal of attention was being paid to smartness, to drills, to the newly revived matter of gunnery, to wireless, then in its infancy and to what were called Tactics but were actually no more than barrack-yard movements, none was being paid to real tactics or to strategy, and very little to thinking about war or to the training of officers for war. In consequence we started to write papers in which these things were discussed.

There were then four of us: Reggie Hall, Everett, Ogilvy and myself. We exchanged ideas about such things as dividing the fleet *v.* the single line – Ogilvy was particularly keen on this – initiative in place of rigid orders, signalling under conditions of battle, and so forth. We invited each others' criticisms and tried to find out what was wanted rather than to prove our own theories. Then we scattered to various other stations and the thing came to an end.[84]

Apart from the illuminating reference to Frederick Ogilvy (who became a powerful ally of Arthur Pollen, but died of food-poisoning in 1909, at a critical juncture in fire-control politics[85]), exactly who argued what, at these seminars, is unknown. However, Commander Everett's participation and indulgence are remarkable in that he was then two years into his first command of the Signal School and was thus, unlike the others, not a member of the Channel Fleet. He may have been included to provide a 'safe conduct' for a discussion group to which the then C-in-C Channel, Admiral Sir Arthur Wilson, might otherwise have taken exception.

Now, in 1908, Captain Everett personified the Royal Navy's signals establishment; and, while one may guess that he was less than completely at ease with his conversion from would-be poacher into gamekeeper, his reply to Captain Hunter's paper was a strange mixture of confession, endorsement and dismissal. He said, in effect, 'Yes, Hunter has a point, but come back to the real world!':

> Our present *Signal Book* is the gradual growth of the experience of the years of peace, and it must be admitted there is ground for Captain Hunter's contention that war or battle requirements are not the prime consideration of the present code.
>
> Captain Hunter has essayed to produce a signal book, the predominant feature of which is to cater for war and battle requirements, peace facilities being quite secondary. To do this he has started *de novo*, with the result that it would be impossible to tinker with the present books to adopt his main proposals.
>
> New *Signal Books* have only recently been issued, consequently very powerful reasons would have to be appreciated before it was considered necessary to change our present system to such an extent as Captain Hunter proposes. It would therefore be a waste of time on my part to offer any criticisms on the details of his system.[86]

He ended with a disclaimer which sits awkwardly with his brush-off of Hunter's ideas: it was not up to signalmen to impose their views on the

Fleet, he said meekly, it was merely their job to provide for the wants of the seagoing commanders. George Tryon of course had said the same – "I don't think men should be set to construct signal books without they are acquainted with what is wanted" – indeed it goes to the heart of the 'Tryonic' school's grievance against the 'Colombine'.

The Director of Naval Intelligence, Captain Edmond Slade (who, like Ogilvy, happens to have been a committed supporter of Pollen[87]), considered Hunter's arguments to be "very strong", and Everett's "defence of the existing system most damaging":

> he practically admits all that Captain Hunter is contending for. The tendency for signalling methods to be based on peace conditions and to become increasingly complicated has been apparent for some time: it is an almost inevitable corollary of such conditions: and whether anything short of a war will counteract these influences may be doubted.[88]

There seems to have been a delay in sending Hunter's paper out to flag-officers; but their opinions began to come in at the turn of 1908/9, and their responses are instructive. The first two to reply were, as it happened, also supporters of Pollen (it is difficult to decide how far this may be relevant): Lord Charles Beresford and Prince Louis of Battenberg.

From the Channel Fleet, Beresford, who was by now slightly mad (or at least *maddened*) and his support liable to be counter-productive,[89] endorsed Hunter's ideas and made celebration of the fact that

> he appears to have studied the matter historically from the volume of *Fighting Instructions* issued by the Navy Records Society. This alone shows that he possesses a mind capable of estimating the value of such a train of thought in considering methods of handling a fleet in the presence of the enemy.[90]

And from the Atlantic, Prince Louis of Battenberg also approved, reporting that "Captain Hunter's signal book is full of the most excellent ideas and I find myself in entire agreement with most of his suggestions."

From the Home Fleets, on the other hand, Sir Francis Bridgeman did "not concur in the alterations in the *Signal Book* proposed by Captain Hunter", and his successor, Sir William May, agreed that "Hunter's system does not possess sufficient advantage over our present system to warrant a complete change"; while from the Mediterranean, Sir Assheton Curzon-Howe also thought it "too drastic to alter the whole system of signalling which has only recently been revised and corrected by senior officers of great experience".[91]

In the end, Slade's caustic prediction proved correct. There was a further revision of the *Signal Book* in 1912–14,[92] but it was another bout of tinkering and enlargement, and its issue to the Fleet was delayed by the onset of hostilities. Thus, after a century of peace, during which the British Fleet's sense of tactical 'product' was progressively blunted by the creeping interests of signalling 'process', it went to war with *Signal Books* (the eighth or ninth revision of Home Popham's) which, even in the opinion of the conventional, centralizing Jellicoe, were "clumsy, and require great experience before they can be used properly".[93]

*

Perhaps Hunter failed because the ambient climate was against him, and he lacked the rank and standing to sway hostile opinion; but it may be noted that he was challenging more than was strictly necessary – more, even, than Sir George Tryon had taken on. Tryon had introduced his action-system in tandem with, rather than replacement of, the formal signalling system, in furtherance of his parallel *secondary* and *primary* educational curricula. And, if the *Books* retained (as they clearly did) the practical drawbacks which had so troubled Sir George in the early 1890s, the spur for reform of tactical usage could have been driven into the flanks of the Fleet, if not by Captain Hunter, then by the Admiralty (if Their Lordships had been so minded) without overthrowing the *Signal Book* itself, and without raising the spectre of TA.

For example, the umpires in the annual Manoeuvres could have rationed the number of *imperative* signals which flagships were allowed to send – in the same way that they are said to have penalized submariners for firing torpedoes or being submerged – while putting no restraint on the exchange of *informative* signals (which was the purpose for which Popham had invented his Signal Code in the first place). This could have been done by deducting points for executive orders, with the ultimate sanction of 'killing off' flag-deck crews and 'disabling' signal-lamps and W/T aerials. The importance of the Manoeuvres to flag-officers' reputations would have prompted a rush to

1. disseminate, in advance, objectives and priorities;
2. encourage the flow of intelligence; and
3. prime captains and junior flag-officers to exercise their own judgement in the light of (1) and (2).

After a very few years of such disciplines, who can doubt that the Royal Navy's senior officer corps would have been better trained to cope with the vagaries of a major fleet action?

*

There were two reforms – clearly connected – which Allan Everett did feel able to bring about: the abolition of the naval pigeon service,[94] and the institution of an officers' specialization in signalling. Until 1907 an 'S' alongside a name in the *Navy List* denoted an officer employed in surveying. Henceforth it identified one "specially qualified in signalling duties".[95] The qualification was to be gained by attending a 'long course', designed by Everett, at the Portsmouth Signal School. The sanctioning and funding of such an innovation will certainly have involved the First Lord, who will certainly have consulted his naval secretary, Captain Evan-Thomas, whose credentials in signalling were scarcely less conspicuous than Captain Everett's.

Visual signalling had officially come of age as a 'career' technical skill – now on a par with navigation, gunnery or torpedoes. But by the same token it was no longer something which any seaman officer was expected to master: the Navy now provided official wizards, in the master-moulds of Everett and Evan-Thomas, to do it for him (and any flag-lieutenant from outside the coven ran the gauntlet of "Unqualified!"). Its inaccessibility was thus acknowledged and institutionalized – an opposite trend to the radical skill-dilution sought by Tryon, Hunter and (soon) Beatty – and at the same time a defeat for Culme-Seymour's desideratum that every watch-keeping officer must understand signalling inside out.

Most 'experts' seek to hold society hostage in a trap of technicalities and jargon, and then proffer the key in exchange for status and respect (one has only to think of lawyers). That way prosperity lies, at least for them. "There is to be found in all specialized subjects a strong tendency to make a mystery of the particular job."[96] But surely, given the advent and proliferation of wireless, the creation of the 'S' career was one of the Navy's necessary rites of passage into the twentieth century? Not so. The fledgeling W/T branch was, and for the time being remained, the territory of torpedomen (electricians) and of *Vernon*, and successfully resisted unification with the signalmen of *Victory*.[97] Knowledge of W/T was no part of the syllabus for the new S qualification. The only reason, therefore, for the ennoblement and demarcation of (visual) signalling can have been the growing stress placed upon it by the growing size and complexity of fleets – apart, that is, from professional self-aggrandizement. Is it naïve to suggest that it might have been resisted?

The de-skilling of coastal navigation and pilotage in the 1860s and '70s provides a striking (and unusual) instance of movement in the other direction: those essential functions were removed from the time-honoured preserve of professional 'masters' and added to the pool of skills expected of every seaman officer. Before, if the master was ill, the ship did not sail; afterwards, anyone could step into his shoes, decipher his notes, and enable the ship to proceed.[98] As examples of organizational reform, the two cases illustrate opposite principles. Is there a genuine argument which admits of both?

The founding of the formal specialization in signals is celebrated to this day, amid tribal bonding by old hands from HMS *Mercury*,[99] home of the Royal Navy's Signal School from 1941 to 1993. It is also celebrated, unwittingly, by every OOW who fumblingly flashes a two-letter Morse group meaning "WAIT! (while I send for the yeoman)" when he finds himself being flashed by another warship.

*

Just as almost everyone who was anyone in the Navy of the 1880s and '90s had served in the Mediterranean under Phipps Hornby, so most of the senior officers of the Edwardian era had served there under Culme-Seymour. Of the eleven admirals who held the most senior fleet commands in the twelve years between Sir John Fisher's going ashore in 1902 and the outbreak of war in 1914, no less than eight had been associated, through membership or propinquity, with the 'Malta clique' (or Sir Michael's "band of brothers", as one officer called it[100]) – Sir Compton Domvile, Sir Arthur Wilson, Lord Charles Beresford, Sir Charles Drury,[101] Sir Francis Bridgeman, Sir William May and Sir Archibald Berkeley Milne. This is not to say that they must all have shared his opinions on every matter – we have seen that they did not – but his standing in the service was high, and his patronage powerful; and their career ascent through his command-in-chief was a significant common conditioning. The three exceptions were: Sir Assheton Curzon-Howe,[102] Sir Edmund Poë[103] and Sir George Callaghan.

Fisher was succeeded in the Mediterranean by Domvile ("a very poor substitute",[104] and Culme-Seymour's second-in-command in 1894–6), and he in turn by Beresford. The years following Jacky's departure were not, in William Goodenough's words,

> those during which, in the Mediterranean, the greatest progress was made from a professional point of view. It would be idle and wrong not to admit this. Parade of every kind took the foremost place at that time. That the ships were what is known as smart is true; spotless in appearance, the competitive drills admirably carried out, the station-keeping at sea of the highest order. But there was no progress. The movements of ships were still rectangular and at even speed. It should not have been so.[105]

The spoilt young captain of the cruiser *Juno*, David Beatty (whose exotic wife "had taken Malta by storm with her glorious ropes of pearls"[106]), dripped that "everything we do is of the most childish description and not in any single feature can it resemble the real thing."[107] Yet to outsiders, all was well. During the Combined Fleet exercises of 1903, an American journalist was understandably awestruck by the sight of seventy-two battleships and cruisers being manoeuvred perfectly by one admiral. "When these ran in to anchor in eight lines", he reported in admiration, "a straight-edge placed in front of them would not have shown a ship a foot out of position."[108]

> The brains were presumably there [Goodenough continues], the material was improving month by month, the energy of all was ready to move along the line directed, but the directive power was absent. Was it to be wondered at that such a man as Sir A. K. Wilson, coming out to carry out joint manoeuvres with the Mediterranean Fleet, made little disguise of his concern? He was contemptuous. If he, with his strict ideas of what was correct, could be so outspoken, others could be the same.[109]

But they were not. And Arthur Wilson – highly regarded as a tactician though he was – demonstrated how narrow were his ideas for improvement.

> In matters of duty he was as hard as granite, and under his command [1903–7] the Home Fleet became virtually a 'School for Battle'. At sea his ships were kept on a war footing by day, and were often darkened and manoeuvred without lights at night. He was also a tactician who studied tactics by practical use of the Fleet he commanded. The lessons, however, he kept to himself, so, unfortunately, there was no record of them for the education of the younger officers.[110]

One of those younger officers was, again, Beatty, and Chalmers records a minor incident between admiral and subordinate in 1904 or '05:

> On one occasion, when ordered to take up station on the cruiser screen, [Beatty] crossed the bows of the flagship. This being entirely contrary to naval etiquette, the Commander-in-Chief at once asked for his reason. Beatty promptly replied: 'It was the quickest way to my station.' No impertinence was intended: the Fleet was engaged in war exercises . . . [Wilson] made no further comment[111]

– to his credit (but later he did his best to deter Churchill from employing Beatty as naval secretary).

The seagoing admiral most associated with Fisher's first First Sea Lordship is, of course, Lord Charles Beresford. As we have seen, these two wilful and vindictive men had had their differences before, in the Mediterranean and more recently, but their antipathy had remained within bounds and each was prepared to pay tribute to the other when appropriate (as in Fisher's attempt to involve Beresford in the revision of the *Signal Book*). In 1906 Fisher, who knew as well as anyone

Beresford's good and bad points, still tried to accommodate him – even to the extent of recommending him for the upcoming command-in-chief of the Channel.[112] Between then and his taking up that post in 1907, however, Charlie B. seems to have undergone a personality change for the worse. Historian Nicholas Lambert believes that he may have had a minor stroke.[113]

Even his command of the Mediterranean in 1905–7 was marked by (in young Captain Beatty's view) "rigid training and [the] discouragement of initiative";[114] but now, during his command of the Channel in 1907–9 – his final appointment – Beresford presents a Hogarthian figure: resplendent, vain, cantankerous and beset with gout. He flew his flag in the definitive pre-dreadnought *King Edward VII*, whose captain, Henry Pelly, had gained accelerated promotion in the royal yacht (and would fail to gain admittance to the battlecruiser fraternity, as CO of *Tiger* in 1914–16). Needless to say, Beresford "had no superior as a seaman",[115] but

> he had not moved forward mentally with the instruments he wielded and he was inclined to dwell on past days. Never have I known a more 'flagshippy' flagship. Everything centred round the person of the admiral, with whom ceremonial had become an obsession. Our occupation was principally a processional career around the ports of Britain, varied by a few stately and somewhat hackneyed steam-tactics. I do not recall that any very serious problems of war were either attempted or solved [but] Lord Charles received deputations, addressed crowded meetings in his honour, and became Freeman of innumerable cities.[116]

From the end of 1905 the great obstacle confronting Beresford's driving ambition to be First Sea Lord was Fisher's promotion to admiral of the fleet. This postponed Sir John's mandatory age of retirement until 70, and, potentially, his vacation of the coveted post until January 1911 (instead of 1906 as hitherto scheduled). Therefore, short of Fisher's self-retirement or death, Beresford's only way of reaching the top was through his dismissal. This bizarre objective was not so far-fetched, given the power of the pro-Beresford 'Syndicate of Discontent' (which included Reginald Custance, Lewis Beaumont, Arthur Moore[117] and Assheton Curzon-Howe) and Lord Charles was no longer a man to put the interests of service discipline before his own. He duly found his *cause célèbre*.

The mergers and splits, waxings and wanings, of the three home-waters commands, the Channel, Atlantic and Home Fleets, between 1905 and 1909, seem confusing in retrospect; but Fisher's base intention was to surmount a personnel shortage by gathering the Navy's main strength into a multi-layered, collectively massive, organization known as the 'Home Fleets', parts of which would be in varying states of reserve, while the Channel Fleet (a legacy of the days when France was the putative enemy) would wither and fall from the vine. Whether Beresford's tenancy of the Channel gingered Fisher's purpose is a moot point: it was not going to deflect him from it.

Charlie B. set to work advertising the vaunted Home Fleets (currently commanded by his junior in seniority, Francis Bridgeman) as "a fraud on the public and a danger to the state"; and May 1908 found Fisher briefing the First Lord:

> Dear Mr MacKenna,
>
> Here are the papers. As anyone will tell you with Custance and Beresford, there is personal animosity which is ineffaceable and loyalty to Admiralty rulings impossible unless, as I told a High Personage today, you get rid of the First Sea Lord which will be for your own peace and comfort![118]

Beresford expected his Channel Fleet subordinates to join him in his campaign against the Admiralty. One of them, the Fisherite radical and gunnery bore, Rear-Admiral Sir Percy Scott, refused, although "in doing so I fully appreciated that my Commander-in-Chief would be much annoyed".[119] He appreciated correctly. From the friction which ensued, two ludicrous episodes stand out, neither of them diminished by the press.

The first was the 'painting-for-the-Kaiser' contretemps, in November 1907. A visit to the Channel Fleet by the German Emperor was arranged at short notice, and Beresford ordered his squadrons to stop whatever they were doing and see to their paintwork. This caught Scott midway through a cherished programme of gunnery exercises, and he signalled to his cruisers the change of plan in a manner which drew attention to the C-in-C's priorities. He was out of order; and a private wigging might perhaps have been a suitable corrective for a junior driven by pathological zeal. What he got from Beresford was a stage-managed public humiliation on *KE7*'s quarterdeck, and a peremptory (and ignored) demand to the Admiralty that he be relieved of his command.

Eight months later, in July 1908, Scott avoided a '*Camperdown–Victoria*' collision by turning his cruisers in the opposite direction to that ordered by Beresford. At the time Lord Charles endorsed his stand, but then *The Times* got hold of the incident in a manner unflattering to the C-in-C, and set him off again. This time Sir Percy was sent away to South Africa, and departed alleging that in eighteen months he had learned nothing from his chief "except how *not* to manage a fleet".

These affairs were side-shows. Beresford's real feud – one no less acute than that between Keppel and Palliser after the First Battle of Ushant, 130 years earlier – was over fleet organization, war orders, chains of command, more or less anything; and in 1909 Beresford's agitation succeeded in prompting a Prime Ministerial enquiry into (in effect) the First Sea Lord's competence. For this, Charle B. marshalled his forces, putting, among others, Berkeley Milne[120] and Captain Michael Culme-Seymour[121] on standby as witnesses (the latter, at least, must have been greatly relieved when the enquiry disallowed the taking of evidence from nominated supporters).

The findings broadly vindicated Fisher, and Beresford retired to be MP for Portsmouth, deluded and embittered. He was still hugely popular with the public, but the fact is that the revolution forced through by his rival had left him wallowing hopelessly astern.[122] He never commanded dreadnoughts, was not a 'dreadnought era' admiral, and would have been quite out of his depth in the 1914 war, afloat or ashore. His liberal stances on both the fire-control controversy and the simmering *Signal Book* debate are consistent, perhaps, with his flamboyant temperament, but scarcely with his 'obedience' dogmatism at the time of the *Camperdown–Victoria* collision, and serve to remind us that (contrary to what the Beresford–Fisher partisans would have us believe) the internal history of a complex military service is no Spaghetti Western in which the heroes and villains wear colour-coded hats for ease of reference. In December 1912 Lord Charles's name was put forward by Buckingham Palace (like Milne, he was an old favourite of George's) for promotion to admiral of the fleet, but the First Lord's naval secretary, David Beatty, smoothly pointed out that Francis Bridgeman had a better claim, having been First Sea Lord, and no more was heard of it.[123]

*

Although Fisher had survived the Beresford challenge, he was damaged. Calls to end the bickering had been directed at both protagonists, and he was indelibly associated with discord (he "had destroyed the camaraderie of the service: officers were all partisans either of Sir John, or of Lord Charles, and would not speak to each other"[124]). Theoretically he could have stayed on until 1911; but there was a general election in the wind, and with McKenna's doubtful consent he resolved to retire before the possible fall of the Liberal Government (and change of First Lord), having first installed a successor who would keep faith with his policies.

The list of potential candidates was distinguished and unpromising (and came from the generation of lieutenants "whose ignorance and want of interest in the Service" had dismayed Fisher in 1877[125]). The choice of the famously taciturn Sir Arthur Wilson VC appeared to fulfil the basic desideratum. Old Ard Art had come ashore and retired in 1907, aged 65; but his subsequent anomalous promotion to admiral of the fleet had returned him to the Active List. He had kept clear of the Fisher–Beresford brouhaha, but had endorsed Fisher's strategic policies at the 1909 enquiry; and the respect in which he was held as a grisled elder-seadog was universal. He is said to have taken a fleet in thick fog from Liverpool to Plymouth without sighting land and arrived only slightly late – a feat which a modern navigator, disbarred from electronic aids, would regard as almost supernatural. One newspaper acclaimed Wilson, with peculiar apposition, as "one of the most beloved of our naval disciplinarians".[126] Another described him as "strangely conservative", adding enigmatically that he was "supposed to be the only man in the Navy who has not adopted modern nightgear".[127] McKenna had misgivings about him from the start.

"Wilson's undoubted technical flair was marred by a certain narrowness of view and his strength of character degenerated into obstinacy over the years."[128] He had also been out of touch for three years of vigorous development across the spectrum of naval technologies, and it was he "who rejected Pollen's invention in terms which were both arrogant and abusive".[129] Worst of all, perhaps, was his attitude to centralization.

This manifested itself both operationally and administratively. At the time of Manoeuvres in the spring of 1910, soon after his arrival at the Admiralty, Wilson used W/T virtually to usurp tactical control of Berkeley Milne's division of the Home Fleet. Deployed off the coast of Portugal, Milne found his ships being given their formations, courses, speeds, and even expected landfalls, by the unseen hand of the First Sea Lord.[130] It was probably now that Milne made a remark which historians have too easily used against him: "They pay me to be an admiral, they don't pay me to think!"[131] How Wilson would have behaved had a real fleet-action transpired during his tenure of office, we can never know, but the signs are inauspicious.

His refusal to create a naval staff proved indirectly fatal both to him and to his political chief. The denouement came in the wake of a meeting of the Committee of Imperial Defence, called by the Prime Minister in August 1911, to review War Office and Admiralty war plans.[132] As a consequence of the ill-coordinated and head-in-sand nature of such plans as Wilson was able to produce (not to mention his presentational shortcomings), Herbert Asquith put Their Lordships on short notice to get their house in order. Their response was unimpressive, and within a few weeks McKenna was made to swap offices with the young Home Secretary, Winston Churchill.

Appointed to the Admiralty with the express mission of founding a naval staff, Churchill wasted little time in getting rid of Wilson, who was only a few months short of his compulsory retirement age of 70 anyway. In his place, the new First Lord really wanted Lord Fisher, considered Prince Louis of Battenberg (whose German origins told against him), and appointed the "colourless and uninspiring"[133] Bridgeman.

Sir Francis Bridgeman had spent most of his life closely overshadowed by domineering men. As a commander he had been a "martyr to the tantrums of Pompo Heneage"; as a captain he had spent a total of six years as flag-captain to Sir Michael Culme-Seymour; and as Second Sea Lord he had been treated as little better than a sub-lieutenant by Wilson.[134] Now he artlessly and ineffectually tried to resist Churchill's interferences, and before long Winston became strangely solicitous about his health. The hints grew more obvious, and after only a year he was pushed out, amid rancour, in favour of Battenberg, who is widely agreed to have been the best of an indifferent crop of senior officers. Even Beatty spoke well of him.

18

An Example to Our Countrymen

"Teach me to be obedient to the Rules of the Game."
from *Customs and Traditions of the Royal Navy*,
'Manners Ashore and Afloat'

Upon Lord Charles Beresford's hauling down his flag in *Caesar*, back in 1905, Captain Hugh Evan-Thomas was appointed to the command of the Admiralty yacht *Enchantress*, and thence, after a few months, to the post of naval secretary to the First Lord of the Admiralty (he combined the two jobs for a short spell). As naval secretary and professional confidant he served, successively, Lord Cawdor, Lord Tweedmouth and Mr Reginald McKenna, for three and a half of the most tumultuous peacetime years in modern naval history – the Fisher years – and left scarcely a ripple (and very few private papers). He must have seen much of importance to the evolution of naval policy, but of his insights and influence at the Admiralty we know virtually nothing.

There was a place reserved for him in the royal enclosure at the launching of HMS *Dreadnought* in Portsmouth on the 10th of February 1906, but he missed that milestone event due to illness. Fisher afterwards reported ebulliently: "Dear Evan-Thomas, Are you a prophet? Hope you're better . . . all went splendidly."[1] (There is no hint of what the prophecy had been.)

It says much for Evan-Thomas's circumspection that he, who was so readily identifiable with Lord Charles Beresford, travelled unscathed through these hazardous times and even gained Fisher's affable esteem. Many others were not so lucky. He was certainly an 'inside' witness to the machinations of the 'Beresford' troubles, and cannot always have enjoyed the position in which he was placed. For example, in 1907, when misgivings were growing about Lord Charles's appointment to the Channel, Tweedmouth regretted to Fisher that they were more or less stuck with him, although "I know him to be ambitious, self-advertising and gassy in talk".[2] And a year later, at the height of the Beresford–Scott fracas, Evan-Thomas found himself trying to allay Fisher's panic that McKenna was "bargaining privately with Beresford"[3] ("From what the First Lord has told me, I don't think there is any reason whatever to think that he is doing anything else than loyally support you"[4]), and cautioning Lord Knollys against royal intervention:

> with regard to the question you asked me [he wrote to King Edward's private secretary] I think it would be dangerous – as there is no knowing what Lord Charles might make of an audience in his present state of mind. It is a very sad business.[5]

As naval secretary, he enjoyed considerable patronage over captains' appointments, and a perquisite of the job was a sort of *droit de seigneur* over the most desirable ship in the offing at the end of his time. Sure enough, as Captain William Pakenham wrote at the end of 1908: "You have so often been the beneficent deity who has made others happy by giving them ships . . . now you are getting a fine and interesting one yourself." In fact he got the newest and biggest warship in the world, HMS *Bellerophon* (named after the '*Old Billy*' in which he had served as flags to Sir Algernon Lyons), the second dreadnought battleship and in various ways an improvement on the first. She was commissioned in Portsmouth in February 1909, and joined the Home Fleet. At the Spithead Review, that July, she lay second in line behind her famous prototype, which flew the flag of Admiral Sir William May (one of Evan-Thomas's *Ramillies* captains).

The Evan-Thomas Papers do us no more favours over his time in *Bellerophon* than over his Admiralty service. We know, however, that he dined on the 6th of August 1909 with the King and Queen onboard the royal yacht *Victoria and Albert*, and it was probably then that an understanding was reached concerning the future education of their grandsons, the Princes Edward and Albert: a new mission of royal service which would interrupt, for a third time, Hugh Evan-Thomas's career in the Fleet. In the meantime there is record of two episodes concerning his command of *Bellerophon*.

During the 1909 Manoeuvres, Sir William May's mainly pre-dreadnought 'Red Fleet' was chasing Curzon-Howe's 'Blue Fleet', with the speedier *Bellerophon* pushing boldly ahead. Evan-Thomas was acting as a single-ship fast division and, in doing so, overhauled and 'sank' four Blue cruisers: "Not a bad half-hour's work," the *Morning Post* remarked. Pride, however, came before a fall. The next day, in patchy fog,

Bellerophon again ranged ahead of Red, looking for Blue and hoping to repeat yesterday's star performance. The fog suddenly parted, she found herself in close company with six Blue battleships and was "easily defeated and sent to Berehaven" to sit out the rest of the exercise in ignominy. Whether Evan-Thomas took this to heart as a salutary lesson and, if so, how far it may have influenced his attitude towards his command of the Grand Fleet's 'fast division' six years later, one can only speculate.

And, in April 1910, he retarded Britain's pre-war gunnery revolution by reporting unfavourably on Sir Percy Scott's system of 'director-firing' after trials were held in *Bellerophon*.[6] The idea behind central gunnery direction was that one officer would control the main-armament from a position aloft, free from smoke and spray, to coordinate the moment of firing and to obviate the need for each turret to judge its own guns' elevation and bearing. It was the logical sequel to *Dreadnought*'s introduction of single-calibre armament, was essential to salvo-firing and to long-range spotting and correction, and prepared the way for the mechanization of fire-control.

The equipment available in 1910 was primitive, and the trials took place at a temporary and misleading juncture in gunnery doctrine. The RN was trying to shoot its heavy guns with 'continuous aim', by which the layers kept the sights pointing on target in defiance of the rolling of the ship. Continuous aim promised a high rate of fire, for guns could fire when ready, without waiting for a given moment in the ship's roll. It was a difficult task with clumsy hydraulic elevating machinery – nearly impossible in a serious seaway – and it introduced small errors, which were deemed tolerable at the close-ish ranges of around 8,000 yards then in vogue, where the shell's exact throw was not critical.

It was two and a half years before director-firing broke through the practical and prejudicial barriers holding it back, and early wartime experience confirmed that actions might be decided at up to double the ranges previously hypothesized – ranges which made essential both salvo-firing (for ease of spotting) and controlled firing-on-the-roll. In the meantime, Evan-Thomas's findings should be related to their circumstances, although it is worth pointing out both that he must have been aware of Sir William May's hostility to director-firing, and that his ship was chosen by his friend Archibald Moore, Director of Naval Ordnance, at this stage in his career a Beresfordian looking for an anti-Scott verdict.

In November 1909 Sir William May offered Evan-Thomas the plum job of captain-of-the-fleet (= chief of staff), a post which carried with it the substantive rank of commodore and the pay of a rear-admiral. He turned it down, and went instead in July 1910 to command Britannia Royal Naval College in Dartmouth, taking over from Trevylyan Napier. It was a job for which he was, by normal standards, too senior. Fisher was bemused and slightly sour, "but I suppose you obliged the King. Of course it is an excellent thing your going there, for the service but not for yourself."

By now the King was George V, whose approach to parenthood was, to say the least, conservative.[7] The old training hulk *Britannia* had taught him what's what, so the successor-college must be just the ticket for his hapless, low-achieving sons. Hugh Evan-Thomas remained captain of Dartmouth for two years while young Edward (the future Prince of Wales, Edward VIII and Duke of Windsor) and Albert (the future Duke of York and George VI) passed through as "unwilling naval cadets".[8] It has been said that "his ruthless discipline was a byword" at the college[9] – a discipline passed down (one may fancifully trace) from 'Breadfruit Bligh', through Thomas and William Martin, Phipps Hornby and Culme-Seymour. His captaincy was disrupted by two major crises.

In February 1911 the college was struck by measles. The Evan-Thomases (themselves, "to their lasting sorrow",[10] childless) hastily took the two princes out of circulation and into their house at Redlap in Stoke Fleming. Anxious telegrams passed back and forth between Devon and Buckingham Palace. Soon sixty cadets were on the college sick-list and one died (possibly of meningitis). Even in isolation, the princes succumbed to measles, and received every attention, etc., while Captain Evan-Thomas was favoured with remedies from patriotic or mischievous members of the public (hot poultices of boiled onions, for example). At length the danger passed:

> So pleased to hear that both my boys are making such excellent progress but deeply regret the death of poor young Oakley which is most sad. The Queen and I much appreciate all you and Mrs Thomas are doing for our sons.[11]

And Evan-Thomas found himself gazetted ADC.

At the end of March Prince Edward left (to be invested as Prince of Wales and then to go, heavily supervised, to sea). He wrote a farewell letter to his captain, using his *en famille* name of David: "I cannot thank you enough for all your kindness to me at Dartmouth . . . I hope you will have better luck during the rest of your time at the college."[12] Evan-Thomas's luck did not improve in his second year of command, though it was largely of his own making.

King George had presented the college with a dashing statue of himself in naval uniform, and he was going to come down early in March 1912 to inspect this item *in situ* on the quarterdeck, and see young Bertie. Shortly before the scheduled visit a story went round that certain elements were planning to creep out in the night and paint George red. It was only a rumour, but the potential embarrassment was enormous, the more so because (for reasons which will be touched on) red was not the colour to be painting heads of state in 1912.

The gallant captain sought to forestall the unthinkable in true authoritarian style: he ordered his civilian staff to stand guard over the regal sculpture during the hours of darkness. Shiftwork was not in their contracts they said, and went on strike. He sacked them. The college ground to a halt. Young Albert "saw fit to acquaint his parents" with an item in the tabloid press[13] – "My Dear Thomas, What is the nonsense which appeared in yesterday's *Daily Graphic*?"[14] – and the royal visit was cancelled, the matter being conveniently obscured by the onset of the Great Coal Strike which brought the railways to a halt. The would-be (perhaps only might-have-been) pranksters had succeeded beyond their wildest dreams without lifting a finger.

It was not for this triumph but rather because he was next in line that Evan-Thomas was promoted to rear-admiral in July 1912. He may not have savoured the ambiguity in David's letter of congratulations, which solicitously added: "I was so very sorry that my father was unable to visit the college in the spring on account of that tiresome strike & it was a great disappointment to me not to see it again."[15] He handed over Dartmouth to Victor Stanley; served on a committee on Dartmouth entrants; attended a War Course in Portsmouth; and went, for a time, onto half-pay: last in the queue of junior flag-officers awaiting jobs at sea. His prospects were good.

At, say, the turn of 1912–13, the Navy was in the charge of friends. The First Lord of the Admiralty (Winston Churchill) and his naval secretary (David Beatty) might be uncertain quantities, but the First, Second, Third and Fourth Sea Lords were, respectively, Prince Louis of Battenberg (with whom the Evan-Thomases had kept on close social terms[16]), John Jellicoe, Archibald Moore and William Pakenham. And old friends and shipmates promenaded The Mall between Admiralty Arch and Buckingham Palace: as anticipated in Chapter 11, among King George V's equerries were Commander Sir Charles Cust and Captain Bryan Godfrey-Faussett, both 'old ships' from *Melampus* days; and among his 'extra' (= non-vocational) equerries were Rear-Admiral Sir Colin Keppel (who, for reasons which I have not discovered, addressed Evan-Thomas as 'cousin'), and the archetypical royal yachtsman, that "snob of snobs",[17] Vice-Admiral Sir Archibald Berkeley Milne.

It is beyond question that Court influence was brought to bear in the interests of royal favourites among senior officers. Indeed George, because of loyalties formed during his fifteen-year naval career, was less discreet in this respect than his father. We have seen how the Palace tried, in 1912, to secure for Beresford an admiralcy of the fleet (only to be rebuffed by Beatty). In the same year pressure was applied to the First Lord to award three important positions to courtiers and Beresfordians, and it is an unexplained facet of Churchill that he obliged. Fisher, Winston's *ex officio* naval adviser, turned his face to the wall.

The three were: Sir Hedworth Meux (formerly Lambton), another extra naval equerry and Beresford's second-in-command in 1903–6; Sir Reginald Custance, Beresford's second-in-command in 1907–8; and the oleaginous Berkeley Milne.

Meux's preferment as C-in-C Portsmouth would pre-position him, Fisher feared, to be next-but-one First Sea Lord. Custance's selection to preside over an enquiry into the training of cadets and midshipmen would result, in Fisher's paranoid mind, in the dismantling of reforms which Fisher had set in place in 1902. In the event both these appointments proved to be benign; but Arky-Barky's, as C-in-C Mediterranean, did not. Fisher was in no doubt (he never was): he rated Milne "an utterly useless commander" and "a serpent of the lowest order", put it about that he bought his copies of *The Times* second-hand and dubbed him 'Sir B. Mean'. Churchill received a farewell letter:

> I fear this must be my last communication with you in any matter at all. I am sorry for it, but I consider you have betrayed the Navy in these three appointments, and what the pressure could have been to induce you to betray your trust is beyond my comprehension . . . I am going to transfer my body and my money to the United States . . . and it's no d—d use squealing . . . Adieu.[18]

The unlikely pair were back, happily exchanging vitriol, within a month; but the old man's views were (in Milne's case at least) vindicated in the first few days of war.

Whether Rear-Admiral Evan-Thomas's appointment, in December 1913, to be second-in-command of the Home Fleet's First Battle Squadron, under Vice-Admiral Sir Stanley Colville, was smoothed by the Palace is impossible to know. George was clearly under obligation to 'see him right' for his forgoing the captaincy-of-the-fleet in 1910. But it scarcely matters: Evan-Thomas was a strict rule-book officer and a sound seaman with a grasp of signalling second to none among flag-officers – ample passports to success – and his friend the First Sea Lord was himself a grandson-in-law of Queen Victoria.

The Fleet which Hugh Evan-Thomas rejoined as a rear-admiral was one which had remained socially and culturally familiar in spite of the reforms and vicissitudes of the Fisher years (having fended off Fisher's more radical notions). It was a service in which many of the old Victorian criteria of efficiency were still pre-eminent. In Captain Herbert Richmond's scathing view, it was typified by people like Archibald Moore, who

> have been occupied all their lives in making their ships 'smart', burnishing bollards, or overreaching other people in the fleet so as to get out a bower anchor before another man, or swindling at drill, or making record shooting under conditions utterly different from action conditions.[19]

An artificer in *Lord Nelson* in 1913 was no more enamoured of his worm's-eye view of the same syndrome:

> As regards the upper deck and that, especially as we were a flagship, to put it mildly, the spit and polish would drive you crazy. I mean all the brasswork and everything like that was highly polished every day. The decks were scrubbed every morning and when required were holystoned, and the sides of the ship were kept scrupulously clean. You were never allowed to throw anything over the ship's sides on a warship, not even a cigarette end. It's a culpable offence, punishable.[20]

In Gibraltar they sprayed the stockpiled coal with whitewash. There was a reason given: to reflect the sun's rays and slow down the coal's decomposition from heat. But one wonders.

*

It was a service, also, in which the attitudes and ethics of chivalry were at their most voluble (albeit under encroachment from the science of the new materialism). In this, the Navy was reflecting the upper middle classes. The seeds sown and watered by a century of evangelists from Walter Scott to Henry Newbolt were approaching full harvest. The poetry, literature and propaganda of the First World War are thick with the sublime, alluring, lethal images of chivalry;[21] and to understand the unrelenting pull of 'duty' in the face of such unrelenting waste, one only has to ponder the conditioning material.

> In thousands of nurseries and schoolrooms children had been brought up on the exploits in battle of heroes new and old: Hector and Achilles, Horatio holding the bridge, Arthur and his knights, Roland blowing his horn, Richard Coeur de Lion charging the Saracens, the Black Prince at Crécy, Henry V at Agincourt, Sir Philip Sidney at Zutphen, Richard Grenville on the *Revenge*, Prince Rupert charging with his cavaliers, Sir John Moore at Corunna, Nelson at Trafalgar, Wellington at Waterloo, the Charge of the Light Brigade, Nicholson falling at the gates of Delhi, Gordon proudly facing the screaming Dervishes, the heroes of Rorke's Drift, the gallant little garrison at Mafeking playing cricket in the jaws of the enemy . . .[22]

In the last years of peace, furthermore, the champions of chivalry were roused by the threat posed to Britain's neo-Gothic, patrician establishment by the death-watch of socialism. It is not coincidental that 1912 was, as Mark Girouard has pointed out, both a climactic time of social and political change – with constitutional reform, militant trade unions and suicidal suffragettes – and a vintage year for the celebration of chivalric values ("Buchan's heroes are forever saving a threatened society"[23]). Duty, obedience and gallant endeavour were everything.

There opened at the Savoy Theatre in London a (by today's lights) repellently jingoistic extravaganza, *Where the Rainbow Ends*, featuring St George and two Dartmouth cadets defending maidenhood and England against the Dragon King. There must have been an element of parody in this pantomime-with-a-moral, but under that alias it struck a chord and received rapturous reviews. There was no parody in the reverence inspired by the 'Deathless Story of the *Titanic*' and, in particular, by the legendary bearing of First Class male passengers nonchalantly waiting to drown while their families departed in (always) the last lifeboat, or of the band playing until the slant of the deck defeated them – shades of *Birkenhead*, *Victoria*, and the charge of the Light Brigade, transmuted gloriously into the civilian realm. The English notion of manhood had come to be definable in terms of romantic military conventions. "Be British!" the captain (Commander Edward Smith RNR) was implausibly alleged to have told passengers and crew alike.

And there was no parody in the virtual canonization of Captain Robert Falcon Scott.

Scott was first noted by Clements Markham, in the West Indies in 1887, at the unlikely rank of midshipman. The RGS secretary was visiting his cousin Albert, then commodore of the Training Squadron, and he watched a gunroom sailing regatta in which the 18-year-old Scott excelled.[24] He interviewed the boy, and "knew at once" – or so he later claimed – "that he was to be one of the Antarctic heroes".[25] Young Robert remained unaware of his destiny, but ten years later they met again in Gibraltar, when he was a lieutenant, and Sir Clements's earlier impression was enhanced by the discovery that his undeclared protégé had "written a complete section of the *Torpedo Manual*". Two years later he backed him for the leadership of what became the National Antarctic Expedition of 1901–4.[26]

A "subjective element [the usual Victorian mix of class-prejudice and amateur phrenology] entered strongly into Markham's judgement of men", and he "never defined [Scott's] qualifications for leadership except in a generalized way".[27] However, the obituary which it befell Sir Clements to write, twenty-eight years after their fateful first meeting in

St Kitts, leaves little doubt that Scott's appeal was his personification of the ideal of the English muscular Christian – in effect, a facsimile of the two Markhams in their younger days.

Was this criterion appropriate? Scott was really just "an able and conscientious naval officer" – exemplar rather than exception among his contemporaries – who dutifully played out the role in which he had been cast and even followed the approved script. These words of his eerily echo Albert Markham's misbegotten North Pole attempt in 1875:

> No journey ever made with dogs can approach the height of that fine conception which is realized when a party of men go forth to meet hardships, dangers and difficulties with their own unaided efforts, and by days and weeks of hard physical labour succeed in solving some problems of the great unknown.[28]

(A connoisseur's footnote to the 1901 expedition is that both Commander Scott and Lieutenant Shackleton RNR felt moved to become Freemasons a few weeks before *Discovery*'s departure from England.[29])

After his first Antarctic foray Scott returned to his naval career. In 1906 he was Rear-Admiral George Egerton's flag-captain in *Victorious*, and Sir Clements paid them a visit. (Like William May, Egerton was an old '75 hand, and, like Scott, he gave his son the middle name of Markham.) Walking ashore in Majorca, the patriarch of polar exploration talked Scott into readdressing himself to Antarctica. That commitment led, after many delays, to the expedition of 1910 and to the race to the South Pole against the relentlessly professional Norwegians.

Sometime in March 1912, close to death and with frozen fingers, Robert Falcon Scott scrawled a last message to the First Sea Lord: "We are setting a good example to our countrymen, if not by getting into a tight place, by facing it like men when we were there." The heroism of his defeat by Roald Amundsen, and his party's forlorn death, will live for ever in the British national pantheon – indeed it is hard to imagine that his success and survival would have been so honoured. But, as Mark Girouard points out, they shine brightest against a background of presumption that heroism itself is "more important than the intelligent forethought which would make heroism unnecessary".[30]

It is perhaps a marvellous thing that England should have championed a culture – civilized and decent – in which there was no dishonour in losing, as long as you put up a 'good show', and according to which Triumph and Disaster were equal Impostors. Other societies have not generally shared this ethic, which (aside from the dying debate about amateur status in sport) has all but vanished from the modern world. Sportsmanship's encroachment into the military realm has been discussed in Chapter 9. It had its plus points, for it conditioned men to attempt, and sometimes succeed in, unlikely tasks which they would otherwise have declined; but often it led them almost deliberately to court failure. "It may be that Waterloo was won on the playing fields of Eton," a contributor to the *Naval Review* wrote sceptically, in 1913, "but for us it is of more interest to know where Trafalgar was won . . . Probably no class of Englishmen have been less sportsmen than the naval officers of the eighteenth century."[31]

Perhaps Scott's valedictory words to Francis Bridgeman were for his own comfort: a straw of consolation as death stalked closer in the blizzard outside. But they could equally be the sublime epitaph for a number of his peers (indeed, for his Markhamesque generation as a whole). As we shall see, Sir Christopher Cradock and Sir Robert Arbuthnot, not to mention the thousands of men reliant on their judgement, were propelled to unnecessary deaths at Coronel and Jutland respectively by the same gallant, uncompromising, uncerebral imperatives. This is where Mark Girouard's thesis and Norman Dixon's come together, for while, on the one hand, "enterprises the most extravagant in conception, the most difficult in execution, the most useless when achieved, were those by which an adventurous knight chose to distinguish himself",[32] on the other, a hallmark of the authoritarian military personality is "a predisposition towards tasks that are so difficult that failure seems excusable".[33]

*

The historian is hard put to identify many Edwardian natives of the broad territory between the romantic and the materialistic approaches to warfare – the middle ground of strategic insight, exploitation of enemy weaknesses, calculated risk-taking, common sense, flexibility, and occasional bluff – which professional war-fighters should inhabit. The self-advertised 'historical school' of the Edwardian Navy partly comprised officers who merely sought to dignify their discomfiture at technical change.[34] But there are footprints in the sand.

If Sir George Tryon's 'primary' and 'secondary' educational metaphor, for (respectively) seamanship and tactical self-reliance, can be stretched to 'tertiary education', to embrace the strategical aspects of sea-power as laboriously pioneered by Sir John Laughton, Philip Colomb, Alfred Mahan and (latterly, at the Naval War College) Julian Corbett, the primary school graduates who grappled unhappily with the emerging tertiary syllabus included a number of young free-thinkers with radical secondary ideas and keen to apply them. The names of Captains George Ballard and William Boyle, and Commanders Reginald

Plunkett and Kenneth Dewar, suggest themselves; and, above all, that of Captain Herbert Richmond.

Like certain others, Richmond was "critical of the Navy's preoccupation with *materiel* and its neglect of the study of strategy and tactics, an understanding of which, he maintained, could only come through the study of history".[35] But as a historical analyst, he was the rare genuine article. His mistake was to come out as a 'brain' at too early a rank. This was a time when Active List officers were not encouraged to ponder their trade at an intellectual level: those who did so "were regarded as cranks or lunatics, hunters of soft jobs";[36] and as Lloyd George said of the Army, "to be a good average is safer than to be gifted above your fellows."[37] One can understand, perhaps, why the authoritarians sought to sideline Richmond away from the centre of power. He was known to consider the merit-game played by the peacetime rules to be irrelevant as war-training, and the possibility that he might be right was inadmissible. Jellicoe "disagreed fundamentally with [his] approach to practically everything".[38] It was inevitable that Herbert Richmond, when given the chance, would gravitate towards David Beatty.

In late 1911 when Winston Churchill, the new First Lord of the Admiralty, looked about for a naval secretary, he remembered the debonair young lieutenant he had met the evening before Omdurman and found that he was now an unemployed rear-admiral – unemployed, indeed, almost for the two years which would have triggered compulsory retirement. It was not just that bottle of champagne: Churchill was drawn to heroes,[39] and seems to have had a predilection for men whose names began with B.[40] Furthermore he did not share the jaundiced eye with which elders and betters viewed pushy young upstarts – he was one himself. Against the sonorous warnings of Sir Arthur Wilson (still scandalized by Beatty's refusal of the Atlantic Fleet job a few months earlier, if not by the crossing-the-bow incident), he sent for him.

"You seem very young to be an admiral."

"And you seem very young to be First Lord of the Admiralty."

Beatty served as Churchill's naval secretary from early January 1912 until the end of February 1913. To his wife he affected to dislike the job ("Oh dear! I am so tired and bored with the whole thing"), and he appears to have kept a low profile,[41] although from his later effectiveness as First Sea Lord (sometimes in contention with Churchill, when the latter was Chancellor) it may be adduced that he was learning a lot about the corridors of power. He certainly learnt that "you have to have a bloody awful row with Winston once a month and then you are all right."[42]

On the 1st of March 1913 Beatty hoisted his flag over the Battle Cruiser Squadron in succession to Rear-Admiral Lewis Bayly.

It is inconceivable that any alumnus of the Malta clique – Wilson, Bridgeman, Jellicoe or Evan-Thomas, for example – would have acceded in Beatty's casual style to so fabulous an appointment. It certainly bemused his flag-captain, Ernle Chatfield. For several days there was no sign of him.

> Most people, who had been signally honoured with a great command over the heads of others, would have made the occasion one for showing great zeal and attention to duty; even if of no great value, it would have 'created a good impression'. Little did I know the peculiarities of his ways . . . he cared for none of these things.
>
> His Steward, Mr Woodley, who came down to look after the crockery etc., told me he thought the admiral had gone to Monte Carlo. Sure enough, I received a letter from him in a day or two, from that place. He would have his holiday and arrive just when he, and no one else, considered it right and opportune.[43]

Within a couple of weeks of taking over the battlecruisers Beatty started to put his *modus operandi* onto paper – with the able assistance of his staff-commander, Reginald Plunkett. They were fortunate to coincide with the unusually permissive regime of the then C-in-C Home Fleets, Sir George Callaghan, an intriguing figure of whom little is known, but who stands apart from his contemporaries in that he appears to have eschewed both technocracy and slavish centralization, and been guided by empiricism:

> He was no brilliant innovator, he had not graduated in the scientific branches of the service, and would not have pretended to judge the merits of the details of continuous advances in material of all descriptions except by the results which they achieved in practice.[44]

A BCS memorandum of the 15th of April laid down the essentials of Beatty's doctrine. Under the heading "From a study of Great Naval Wars" he wrote:

> It is impressed upon one that Cruiser Captains – which include Battle Cruiser Captains – to be successful must possess, in a marked degree, initiative, resource, determination and no fear of accepting responsibility. To enable them to make the best use of these sterling qualities, they should be given the clearest indication of the functions and duties of the unit to which they belong, as comprehended by the Commander of that unit. They should be completely comprehensive of his mind and intentions.[45]

There was more to follow, and this same memo was to be expanded and revised in February 1915, three weeks after the Battle of Dogger Bank. Beatty cited Clausewitz on the confusion of war and warned that

As a rule, instructions will be of a very general character so as to avoid interfering with the judgement and initiative of captains . . . The Admiral will rely on captains to use all the information at their disposal to grasp the situation quickly and anticipate his wishes, using their own discretion as to how to act in unforeseen circumstances and carrying through every operation with resolution and energy.[46]

Rapidly a battlecruiser lore built up which scythed through a hundred years' accretion of centralization, of geometrical fleet manoeuvres, of 'obey the last order', and of genuflexion to the *Signal Book* – scattering Victorian shibboleths like startled seagulls. Beatty was articulating his "ratcatcher's instinct for war", and he set himself on a subversively informal course which paralleled that of George Tryon.

It is impossible to read the memoranda which accumulated to form BCFOs without images of Tryon's action-principles, his educational agenda and his distrust of the *Signal Book* crowding the mind's eye like a second movie projector flickering on the same screen.[47] Senior officers browsing through BCFOs could not fail to understand that the performance criteria in the battlecruisers differed from the tramline standards regressively imposed on the Battle Fleet by Jellicoe after the outbreak of war. Owing to the deficiencies of their 'secondary education', many would have found the stresses hard to bear, and Beatty tried – with incomplete success – to select personalities who would rise to his demands. (On Archibald Moore: "Well frankly between you and I he is not of the right sort of temperament for a BCS. He is too clever."[48] On Cecil Prowse: "The new Captain of the *Q.M.* is not quite the type of man required for a battlecruiser, too slow in the brain, ponderous, and I fear the ship will deteriorate in consequence."[49]) In stark contrast to Nelson, he was in no position to hand the *Navy List* back to the First Lord with the words, "Choose yourself, the same spirit actuates the whole profession."

Beatty had little inclination for the detailed, boring, unglamorous essentials of efficiency and training: he left that stuff to others. The line between habitual delegation and negligence is a hazy one; but the following generous tribute from William Goodenough was essentially true:

It was not great brains . . . I don't know that it was great professional knowledge . . . It was his spirit, combined with comprehension of really big issues. The gift of distinguishing between essentials and not wasting time on non-essentials.[50]

Whether an admiral's choice of flag-lieutenant could rightly be counted as a 'non-essential' is something which any member of the Malta clique would have disputed. But as suggested in Chapter 6, Beatty sought to liberate the battlecruisers from the *Signal Book* and thus from the priesthood of signals-officers, and his action-doctrine certainly diminished the importance of signalling. It is in this context that his seemingly careless choice of an 'unqualified' flag-lieutenant has to be placed.

When Beatty took over the Battle Cruiser Squadron in March 1913, he briefly kept on his predecessor's efficient and fully trained 'flags', Lieutenant Charles Dix – "no admiral had a better flag-lieutenant", in Sir Lewis's protective view[51] – but they were not a success together, and Bayly wanted his man back for his next sea command anyway. The choice of flag-lieutenant was an admiral's personal prerogative, but Beatty's first mention of Lieutenant Ralph Seymour, after the latter's arrival in *Lion*, has a definite flavour of first impressions about it: "He is a very nice little man and I like him very much," he told his wife.[52] So why Seymour?

Stephen Roskill tries to explain the appointment by alluding to Ralph's aristocratic connections and wondering "whether Beatty placed excessive emphasis on the social duties of a flag-lieutenant, and whether the snobbery to which he and Ethel were subject influenced his choice".[53] Certainly, Seymour had social connections three bags full. He was a great-great-grandson of the 4th Marquess of Hertford; a great-grandson, on the distaff side, of both the 1st Marquess of Bristol and the 2nd Earl of Minto (First Lord of the Admiralty 1835–41); a nephew by marriage of the 5th Earl Spencer (First Lord 1892–5); a first cousin once removed of the 3rd Earl Fortescue, and a second cousin of Captain the Hon. Seymour Fortescue (equerry to King Edward VII). And his father, Sir Horace Seymour KCB, had been Gladstone's private secretary during the Grand Old Man's second premiership (1880–5). But was all this really enough to turn the head of an arrogant young millionaire admiral who was a national celebrity on his own right and who hunted and house-partied easily in the highest circles?

Possibly. But the truth of the matter more likely lies elsewhere.

Ralph Seymour's sister, "the exquisite Horatia",[54] was one of the few very close friends of Miss Clementine Hozier and had been a bridesmaid at Clementine's wedding to Winston Churchill in 1908. So close were they that Horatia was later to live for many years of spinsterhood in a cottage in the grounds of Chartwell. Churchill must have been amused, although not greatly surprised, to find that they were doubly, if distantly, related through the Spencer and Hertford connections mentioned above; and would have known Sir Horace to have been a stalwart of the Liberal Party to which he had belonged since 1904 (Winston's uncle by marriage, Edward Marjoribanks, Lord Tweedmouth, having been Gladstone's chief whip). Winston's rise to First Lord of the Admiralty in Herbert Asquith's administration, his employment of Beatty as his naval secretary in 1912 and his subsequent gift of the battlecruiser command in the spring of 1913, therefore provide a distinctly plausible chain of patronage leading to the appointment of Horatia's brother to Beatty's staff. By 1913 Churchill would certainly have heard about, if not actually met, Lieutenant Seymour, and dinner-table chit-chat probably touched on the fact that he had done his 'short' course in signals in February of that year.[55]

There may have been a further, whimsical, factor – an indirect private debt probably unknown to Clementine – which inclined Churchill to help the young naval officer. When he toured Canada in 1900, he was a guest of the Governor-General, the 4th Earl of Minto, and the latter (Ralph's first cousin once removed) had done his best to further Winston's inept courtship of Pamela Plowden, his first great love.

19

*Commence Hostilities Against Germany**

*Admiralty signal, 4 August 1914

"Damned nuisance missing cricket week."

On Saturday the 25th of July 1914 the Home Fleets' twenty-four dreadnoughts (battleships and battlecruisers) and eight pre-dreadnoughts, with their attendant cruisers and destroyers, were lying in Weymouth Bay under the command-in-chief of Admiral Sir George Callaghan. In the flagship, *Iron Duke*, Assistant-Clerk Rowland Jerram's job on the admiral's staff made him privy to confidential Admiralty signals traffic, and that afternoon he decoded an order for a copy of the fleet's war plans to be delivered forthwith to the Admiralty. As junior dogsbody, he was lurked with this mission.

Callaghan had commanded the Home Fleets now for two and a half years, and was due to be succeeded within four or five months by Vice-Admiral Sir John Jellicoe, the current Second Sea Lord. In requesting his war plans the Admiralty was not entirely levelling with him. Their real destination was not the naval staff, as might have been supposed, but his designated successor; and young Jerram's mission was the first step in Churchill's and Battenberg's (and Fisher's) plan that Sir John should supersede Sir George as soon as war appeared certain.[1]

Jerram hastily packed a bag, collected his packet of papers from Commodore Allan Everett, captain-of-the-fleet, caught a picket-boat to Weymouth and made the 4.30 Paddington train with one minute to spare. In London, a taxi got him to the Admiralty by 9.05, and a porter led him "through the great empty corridors" to the duty secretary – probably either Oswyn Murray or Vincent Baddeley (for the main man, Sir Graham Greene, would hardly be there on a Saturday night) – who told him

to take the papers immediately to the Second Sea Lord at his private residence. So, into a taxi again and across London to 29 Sussex Square, the residence of Admiral Sir John Jellicoe. I rang the bell so violently that the admiral
himself received me at the door so I had to unpack my bag in his hall and
produce my papers from underneath my pyjamas.[2]

Back on board the next day, a signal arrived cancelling the scheduled
dispersal of the fleet (actioning the famous decision taken by Battenberg
while Churchill was absent from London), and the recall of the 1st BS,
"which had already left harbour, caused some sensation". For two days a
state of uncertainty prevailed. Beatty bet Chatfield a fiver that war would
not happen ("he longed for it").[3] And then, on the evening of Tuesday
the 28th, shore leave was cancelled and libertymen were recalled.

> There were about 8,000 men ashore, and the whole of Weymouth, which is
> full of visitors, gathered on the pier to see the men off – they cheered them
> very heartily and the scenes of farewell with sweethearts and wives were very
> moving, as no one knew quite how serious the situation was. They gave the
> message out in the theatre and as the officers and men went out the audience
> rose to its feet and sang the National Anthem. We are a patriotic nation still,
> and it is refreshing to find it so in these trades-union ridden and socialistic
> times.[4]

The next morning the fleet weighed and headed east and then north
towards its secret war-station at Scapa Flow. The Warning Telegram was
received at 6.50 p.m., and as darkness fell the Grand Fleet (as it now
became) entered the Straits of Dover with lights doused and guns
manned against surprise attack by German torpedo-boats. Equally
alert, the Army at Dover Castle probed the darkened ships with searchlights, "a criminal thing to do". War was still six days away.

*

On August the 3rd, Assistant-Clerk Jerram helped Callaghan's secretary
decode the signal ordering the C-in-C to strike his flag in favour of
Jellicoe, who had now joined the fleet, ostensibly as second-in-
command. The Admiralty's reasons for this summary supersession, on
what might have been the eve of battle, have yet to be persuasively
explained. Jellicoe's distress at having to usurp his much-respected chief
has been described many times, and one cannot doubt his private pain,
compounded, no doubt, by fear of unspoken accusation of betrayal.
However, sending six telegrams to Their Lordships over a $2\frac{1}{2}$-day
period, urging them to reconsider or postpone, borders on self-deselec-
tion on grounds of unsuitability: even the nicest fellow with any hunger
to command would have stopped after (say) three. A parallel which
comes to mind is that of the Duke of Medina Sidonia's dismay at finding

himself placed in charge of the *Felicissima Armada*; and it is likely that Sir John was recoiling from the responsibility now facing him.

Throughout his career he had cruised efficiently along, easily gaining with his technical and organizational abilities the admiration of his chiefs. He was a pleasant, tactful man, and a born administrator: an ideal number two. He had all the data at his fingertips. He had watched these ships, this magnificent fleet, take shape in memoranda and blueprints. But his only experiences of command-in-chief were of the squadron-sized, pre-dreadnought Atlantic Fleet in 1910–11, and of half the Home Fleet for three weeks in the 1913 Manoeuvres (whose rules were considered to have been heavily weighted in his favour[5]). It is known that he was in poor health and long overdue for a rest, and yet now, suddenly, on the very cusp of war, he was faced with the highest command of the largest concourse of naval power in the world, and on his slight, tired, anxious shoulders awesome issues would rest.

The comparison with Medina Sidonia, of course, fails examination. Sir John had been groomed for several years for the ultimate command and there is no evidence that he resisted the grooming – Fisher, in Correlli Barnett's splendid words, "unrolled the carpet [and] Jellicoe stepped neatly along it"[6] – whereas the Spaniard, for his part, enjoyed an extensive nautical ignorance and would gladly have remained in his orange groves rather than go to sea at all. However, Fisher's once-stated "absolutely necessary" desiderata that

> those who are designed to act as commanders-in-chief in case of war should in time of peace be kept in constant mental communication with their future subordinates, and, further, that they should be given frequent opportunities for practical command[7]

scarcely obtained in respect of his own long-term protégé in August 1914; and it would be surprising if there were not, dancing amongst Jellicoe's tender remorse for Sir George Callaghan's dignity, fearful, mocking, harlequin doubts. Not so much, as Barnett spins it, doubts about the material quality of the Grand Fleet awaiting him, but doubts about himself – an impostor (as it were) being pushed one precipitate step beyond his immediate competence.[8]

*

Most people in the service expected a major engagement as soon as hostilities were declared, if not before. While soldiers hoped to be home by Christmas, sailors talked of wrapping the thing up by the end of August (but "damned nuisance missing cricket week"[9]). The supposed rituals of pre-combat were taken very seriously.

At home and abroad they removed and landed chairs and tables, civilian clothes and every conceivable item with which they had tried to make their sea-borne lives more comfortable. Docksides were covered in their abandoned non-essentials. It took months and even years to get them back.[10]

It was less easy to discard the mental furniture of peacetime. Both the armed forces started the Great War with "large numbers of loyal, honourable but limited men in positions of responsibility; and although this was all very well when things were going well, it was less good in times of crisis".[11] No doubt there were some of these limited men – Fisher's "regular menagerie of charity admirals"[12] – whose limitations remained undisclosed by the harsh and capricious spotlight of war. Others, including commanders at sea who tried to apply either the purely materialist, or the purely romantic, formula to operational challenges, were not so lucky; although some of the ensuing fiascos were exacerbated by the sharing of executive decisions, in unagreed proportions, between Whitehall and the senior officers 'on the spot'. Their Lordships, particularly the hyper-meddling Churchill, helped themselves to the facilities of W/T but were loath to acknowledge their share of the operational responsibility; while the admirals at sea, uncertain of the provenance or status of Admiralty signals but fearful of blighting their careers, put up with the intrusions.

In the first days of the war Sir Archibald Berkeley Milne, still C-in-C Mediterranean, presided over the escape of the German battlecruiser *Göben* and light-cruiser *Breslau* into the welcoming arms of neutral Turkey.

On August the 3rd, with war looming nearer by the hour, the Great Arch Bark's most pressing task was to shadow, and in the event of hostilities bring to action, these two German ships. The things they were considered most likely to try to do were: disrupt the movement of French troopships between Algeria and Marseilles; and join the Austrian fleet in the Adriatic. These hypotheses had Milne looking in opposite directions from the start. The waters were then muddied by the Admiralty's transmitting confusing instructions (and too many) to this man whose chief forte was implicit obedience to orders.

Milne had under his command a considerable total force consisting of three battlecruisers, four armoured-cruisers and various smaller units; and *Indomitable* and *Indefatigable* were already shadowing the Germans during the last hours of peace. But when the enemy, as they now became on the night of the 4th/5th of August, made use of Italian (= neutral) territorial waters, feinted towards the Adriatic and then made towards Cape Matapan and the Aegean, his uninspired deployments, combined with Rear-Admiral Ernest Troubridge's ignominious decision (based upon a flat statistical analysis by his flag-captain) not to tackle *Göben* with his armoured-cruisers, allowed them to escape. Such was the preamble to Turkey's alliance with Germany and to the dismal misbegotten saga of Gallipoli.

Churchill must share the blame for interference from afar (and, indeed, for Milne's original appointment); and the episode damaged the reputation of Troubridge (who had previously served under Milne in the royal yacht) and wrecked that of Captain Fawcet Wray. But Sir Archibald bore the ultimate operational responsibility, and "his limited and rigid outlook did not allow him to look beyond the difficulties".[13] Fisher would have had him shot.

Seven weeks later there occurred a terrible sacrifice when three armoured-cruisers,[14] *Aboukir*, *Hogue* and *Cressy*, were lost on picket-duty off the Dutch coast. They were quite unsuitable vessels for such an exposed patrol line – big, slow, unnecessary targets – and their deployment, on what was almost close-blockade work, was the product of an unclear chain of command and shoddy strategic staff-work.

The ships were dawdling along on a steady course at dawn on the 22nd of September. Two flag-officers, Rear-Admirals Arthur Christian and Henry Campbell, who might have been present with the squadron, were for mundane reasons absent. It was revealed in the subsequent enquiry that no one at the scene had been briefed on the likely U-boat danger or even exactly why they were there. When *Aboukir* was torpedoed her captain assumed she had struck a drifting mine and ordered *Hogue* and *Cressy* to close to rescue survivors. They approached, stopped, and were torpedoed in turn, with the aggregate loss of 1,400 men. "It does seem childish and just shows how utterly without imagination the majority of our senior officers are," wrote Lieutenant Bertram Ramsay[15] (the future organizer of the landings in Normandy in 1944).

The Admiralty feared embarrassment, and so nobody was court-martialled; the two absentee rear-admirals were merely placed for a while on half-pay. Both were, as it happens, royal favourites: Christian (a midshipman on *Bacchante*'s world cruise) had been captain of Osborne College while the royal cadets were there; and his subordinate, Campbell (a Beresfordian and "a damned sneak", in Fisher's view) had accompanied Prince George on his visit to India in 1905–6 and had lately been 'First Governor' to his eldest son when the latter ventured to sea after leaving Dartmouth in 1911.

The worst blow fell in the Pacific, where the question of how to find and defeat Count Maximilian von Spee's marauding squadron of five cruisers had been exercising the Admiralty since the beginning of the war. Spee's two largest ships, the modern armoured-cruisers *Scharnhorst* and *Gneisenau*, were among the most powerful and efficient 'sub-capital' units in the world and, as always in such situations, the problem was how to intercept them with an adequate force when available ships would have to be spread thinly to find them in the first place (and when borrowing battlecruisers from home waters brought protests from Jellicoe). Von Spee's future movements were variously predicted, and reinforcements sent here and there. When Britain's Japanese allies made the Western Pacific too hot for him he was reported heading eastwards (as Richmond had predicted).

At Port Stanley in the Falklands awaited Rear-Admiral Sir Christopher Cradock. "Tall, handsome, an athlete and sportsman, [and] something of an exquisite",[16] Cradock (knighted for 'personal services' to the King) was "another society person, known not to be up to the mark".[17] He had under his command a force which rated 3:5 in numerical terms against Spee's élite squadron, but more like 3:7, or worse, in military terms. His two most powerful ships, the obsolete armoured-cruisers *Good Hope* and *Monmouth*, had been hastily mobilized with reservist crews who had had little opportunity to exercise their guns. His only efficient unit was the light-cruiser *Glasgow*, although he knew that a pre-dreadnought battleship, *Canopus*, was on its way to join him.

He seems to have sensed the fatal nature of his foray even before it began. Yet he tilted off in search of von Spee, without waiting for *Canopus* (which had almost caught up), and had his antiquated force all but wiped out near Coronel on the coast of Chile, on the 1st of November 1914. Both of his armoured-cruisers were lost with all hands. "It was an absolutely hopeless business from the start – 'the most rotten show imaginable'."[18]

The imperatives which possessed Cradock can only be surmised. What he was doing venturing beyond the narrow waters (and focal point) of the Straits of Magellan is unclear. He was a famously gallant officer with a reputation for both seamanship and impetuosity.[19] In his book *Whispers From the Fleet* (1907) he warned that "a naval officer should never let his boat go faster than his brain", and, again, that "the headstrong unthinking 'dasher' is bound to come to grief before long";[20] so perhaps this was a personality trait of which he was aware. More specifically, he may have interpreted some of the Admiralty's signals (particularly one refusing him further reinforcement) as impugning his resolution, and been anxious to avoid the sort of odium which had attached to Troubridge for the *Göben* débâcle.

For the British public, Cradock's death was only the first part of a heroic 'disaster and revenge' saga, the second part of which came a month later with Sir Doveton Sturdee's swift (and lucky) battlecruiser defeat of Spee off the Falklands; but for Sir Christopher and 1,600 sailors there was no sequel. The propagandist writer Henry Newbolt ("superficially, at any rate, an urbane and sensible man") made celebration of the gallantry of "Christopher Cradock, and all the Company of the High Order of Knighthood".[21] And Rear-Admiral Sir Robert Arbuthnot, Cradock's contemporary and close chum, provided a consoling epitaph: "He always hoped he would be killed in battle or break his neck in the hunting field."[22]

Not everyone would consider Arbuthnot's tribute (for such it was) to be an unmixed blessing, for he was the hardest of the Royal Navy's hard cases, and at Jutland (as we shall see in Chapter 21) he was to lose two armoured-cruisers of his own with all hands and to no constructive purpose. A biographical detour to look at this "very old friend" of Jellicoe is instructive.

Sir Robert, a Scottish baronet, distended the muscular Christian and authoritarian mores of Edwardian England to the point where he was, in a colloquial if not a clinical sense, insane – although, for sure, even in today's armed forces he would be acclaimed for his combative spirit and, from a safe distance, alluded to vaguely as a sound chap. (He kept his motorbike, lovingly polished, in his day-cabin, and went in for gruelling long-distance races in which he pioneered falling off as a means of keeping awake.) In him one can discern the most spartan aspects of Markham, Heneage and Baden-Powell, softened by virtually nothing. He was courteous enough at a social level – though his habit of pushing the table aside after dinner and handing out boxing gloves was not to everyone's convenience – but as a tyrant, bully and physical-training fanatic, Arbuthnot was loathed.

When he was XO of *Royal Sovereign*, in 1900, he proudly published *A Battleship Commander's Order Book* which became an object of merriment in the service. Many a commander's standing orders would comprise a couple of pages on the ship's routines, plus a laconic injunction that everyone was to conduct himself in accordance with *Queen's Regulations & Admiralty Instructions* and the customs of the service. Arbuthnot's definitive 303-page version makes Jellicoe's future GFBOs look like a pamphlet and gives the impression that he was running "a medieval prison hulk".[23] But it was in his overbearing interest in physical fitness that he was at his most disagreeable.

> He was probably the only Admiral of any Navy who regularly boxed his physical training officer, and almost certainly the only one who could be seen on the quarterdeck of the flagship doing three grand circles in succession on the horizontal bar.[24]

While Arbuthnot was a captain, two sailors who were under punishment let it be known that they planned to get their own back. He summoned them to the quarterdeck, issued boxing gloves and knocked them about without mercy. Not surprisingly there came a dark night in Chatham when three of his men hit first. Two of them were taken to hospital.

Everyone around him had to conform with his ideas of health and fitness. It is said that his daughter would give a visitor a display of PT, much as the daughter of any lesser martinet might have been permitted to exhibit her watercolours. A seaman who fell behind on a route march with blistered feet and missed the ship was sentenced to death by him. The Admiralty intervened.[25]

His ships had to be remorselessly efficient. ("He used to throw planks overboard, dead of night, and expect you to be out and pick it up in two minutes. 'E was full of these tricks 'e was. Oh yes, full of that."[26]) But like Walter Cowan, he gives the lie to the Noel Cowardesque cliché that efficient ships are necessarily happy ships, or even well led.

The calamities outlined above are not a balanced measure of the RN's performance in the first few months of the war. In overall strategic terms the story was one of success.[27] A huge array of contingency plans, involving hundreds of ships and tens of thousands of men, was put swiftly into operation – "a triumph of organization, discipline, and general zeal in execution, which left nothing to be desired".[28] The British Expeditionary Force was conveyed to France without a single casualty. The instruments and machinery of economic blockade and 'quarantine' were set efficiently into place. "The red, white and black flag of the German mercantile marine vanished from the oceans. The flow of food and raw materials from overseas, on which Germany was, in the long run, dependent, came to an abrupt halt."[29] As Commander Plunkett said, in the *Naval Review* in October 1914, "the British Navy has achieved, practically without fighting, all that a Navy has ever been expected to perform" (an opinion the more impressive for coming from a battlecruiser luminary and for being above suspicion of post-Jutland special pleading). And there was Beatty's aggressive, one-sided action in the Heligoland Bight – a welcome success which concealed flaws in organization and planning – and Sturdee's Falklands victory.

But the above is a fair reflection of the capacity of the average senior officer to respond to unforeseen or unrehearsed emergencies. Churchill counterpoised the deficiencies of the 'materialist' and the 'quixotic' leadership prescriptions when he urged Beatty to "steer midway between Troubridge and Cradock & all will be well".[30]

In summary, the following might be said of the Royal Navy of 1914:

With few shining exceptions, the performance of our senior naval commanders was dismal. The actions were rife with performances by flag-officers that could scarcely have been worse. Delay and procrastination in the presence of the enemy, faulty disposition of ships, unsound communication practices, disastrous tactical decisions, and utter confusion all contributed to losses of ships and personnel and to missed opportunities to inflict losses on the [enemy].

I know of no case in which any but the highest motives of courage and devotion to duty can be attributed to their actions. In many instances, senior officers hazarded their lives and in some cases lost them. My comments are directed at the system which was responsible for their poor performance, not at the officers concerned. I do not recall ever having taken part [before the war] in an exercise that was other than a set ritual, which, while not without value, certainly did little to prepare us for our wartime activities. The point to be made, and the lesson to be learned, is that, because of this lack of adequate preparation for our senior officers, we lost a large number of ships and men that under different circumstances might have made all the difference between final victory and final defeat.[31]

This sounds like a blend of Percy Scott, Reginald Bacon, Herbert Richmond, Carlyon Bellairs and Filson Young. In fact it is a Captain William Outerson USN, writing of the American Navy at the start of the Second World War. Whether or not his remarks are fully warranted, they are a reminder that the "canker of a long peace" is a creeping sickness to which all professional military forces are susceptible. The Royal Navy's problems in the First World War, however, were certainly exacerbated by the peculiar cultural and circumstantial factors discussed in this and previous chapters: such as the implicit tabooing of moves towards tactical informality, after the *Camperdown–Victoria* collision, and the baleful influence of royalty upon flag-officer appointments.

It cannot be supposed that the Imperial German Navy was free of similar pressures; indeed, in some ways the Wilhelmine Germans were more 'Victorian' than the English: they owed fealty to a much more nearly absolute monarch, and their derivatively Prussian military culture was more authoritarian (the use of the term 'goose-step' by British naval officers in reference to steam-tactics was, of course, an allusion to the idiosyncrasies of German infantry[32]). And it was beyond even the Reichstag to enact the comfortable corporate culture of a long-standing, successful service: the *Kriegsmarine* was built around latent and ultimately critical flaws in personnel management.[33] While the mainly bourgeois officer corps' anxiety to ape their social betters in the Army led to the pretension of an inflated and obnoxious *Kastengeist*, lower-deck conditions were severe, and manning was dependent upon conscripts of uncertain motivational stamina. Even in wartime, officers command, in the last analysis, by consensus; and the reservoir of goodwill was low when hardship and idleness beset the *Hochseeflotte* later in the war.

But the tasks which had faced Tirpitz and Fisher were very different in kind, if similar in scale.

On the asset side, the British started with the chauvinism of centuries and their incomparable seamanship. They took it for granted that they were, in the words of the music-hall ditty (*c.* 1897), the Sons of the Sea:

> Have you heard the talk of foreign pow'rs
> Building ships increasingly?
> D'you know they watch this isle of ours?
> Watch their chance unceasingly?
> ... They may build their ships, my lads,
> And they think they know the game,
> But they can't build boys of the bulldog breed
> Who made Old England's name.

This was powerful magic. Even foreigners – even the German Navy in spite of itself – more than half believed it, and the High Seas Fleet "entered the war with a clearly marked inferiority complex".[34] On the other hand, Fisher had to adapt to meet a strident fleet challenge a large sprawling service whose role for a hundred years had been that of a police force, whose skills related to peacekeeping, and whose traditions and organization could be traced back almost to the Middle Ages.

Alfred von Tirpitz's task appears on paper to have been the more remarkable: to build up a world class navy from a coast defence force in fifteen years. Leaving aside the wider issue of whether their naval rivalry was the main factor which pushed the British into the alliance system ranged against them (and thus cost them the war), it was an error on the part of the Germans – if victory, rather than idle prestige, was their goal – to mount their challenge, at a time of radical new possibilities, in the traditional 'Mahanian' currency of Britannia's supremacy. Fisher, had he been in Tirpitz's shoes, would certainly not have built battle-squadrons. But Tirpitz at least had the chance to create from scratch a logically structured, twentieth-century organization whose avowed purpose was to challenge a specific enemy; and it was in some ways easier to start with a clean slate than to modify long-held attitudes, platitudes, structures and strategies which were clung to by an officer corps discomforted by reform. The *Kriegsmarine* had "the advantage of having nothing to *un*learn".[35]

And it had another 'advantage'. Daunted by the Royal Navy's numerical pre-eminence and historical mystique, it could not allow itself the delusion that it would remain in control of events if the two fleets should meet; and consequently its senior officers were primed to extemporize in the face of the unexpected – *to take their orders from the enemy*, as Sir George Tryon would have said. Tirpitz and his immediate juniors developed realistic tactical exercises for training, stressing that subordinate commanders should be able to handle their squadrons independently when darkness or smoke might prevent the signals of the commander-in-chief from being understood.[36]

It appears that by 1914 this action-doctrine had been discernible to British observers for several years, for Herbert Richmond, William May's flag-captain 1909–11, noted that while "every move [of the Home Fleet] depended on signals, some of us had seen German squadrons being handled without any".[37] Tactical Order No. 1 of the *German Fleet Orders* in force in 1916[38] begins simply, with 'Hints for Battle':

> The following hints are intended to show the aim and object for which everybody should strive, without attempting in any way to circumscribe the free decision and action necessitated by a particular situation.

Tactical Order No. 2 directs that orders during action "are confined to single or at most the two flag signals" and that time is not to be wasted with elaborate procedures of acknowledgement before they are executed. In taking up new formations, furthermore, "special attention" need not be paid to station-keeping. And under 'Leaders Acting On Their Own Initiative' is to be found:

> The leaders of Squadrons, &c, which have been ordered to act independently, or which have become [detached] during the course of the action, are allowed full freedom of action within the experience gained by us . . . Directions for the conduct of independent squadrons, &c, for the further development of the action cannot be given beforehand. They must attack where their support is most needed and where they can most effectively damage the enemy. The one thought, *Annihilation of the enemy's forces, cost what it may,* must reign throughout the Fleet.[39]

Such emphasis on extemporization reflected a real fear of the material panoply of the Grand Fleet – a fear most likely to be borne out if the latter were met as a unified formation in broad daylight. Indeed, for all the brave talk of annihilation, there was little point in the Germans making detailed plans of how to deal with their opponents in a full frontal encounter: an eventuality which they intended to avoid. "It was important for the High Seas Fleet to be good at escaping."[40] But "the fact that at the Battle of Jutland the German battle-fleet was handled much more flexibly than the British was one of the legacies of Tirpitz's work";[41] and the similarity between the meaning of the *German Fleet Orders* and the reputed *modus operandi* of the British Fleet at the Battle of Cape St Vincent (alluded to at the beginning of Chapter 9) is both striking and, to a British historian, uncomfortable.

Sir John Jellicoe, on the other hand, appears to have been informed more by the attitudes of a century earlier – those of the Earl of Torrington, Sir George Rooke, or George Byng (whose family motto was *Leave Nothing to Chance*). It is too easy, perhaps, to caricature the Grand Fleet's C-in-C in this respect; but great worriers are rarely great warriors, and as Jellicoe worried, paper emanated from *Iron Duke*. Late at night he sometimes had to type his personal letters because of cramp from writing memoranda in longhand. Routine 'initiative' injunctions are to be found indeed in his GFBOs – his preface to the section on battle tactics actually declares that it will be "necessary to decentralize command to the fullest possible extent"[42] – but these platitudes (as they had become) were partly carry-overs from George Callaghan's Home Fleet Orders,[43] and now reflected more a dread of losing control than a conviction that central control was impracticable and not to be attempted. "In their broad rationale, [GFBOs] undoubtedly subordinated offensive action to defensive precautions, and the centralization of command was heavily emphasized";[44] and this carefully thought-out catalogue of (in Sir John's own proud words) "the tactics to be pursued by the different units of the fleet in action under all conceivable conditions"[45] gave out the message that any proactive exercise of initiative would be tantamount to disloyalty, a sabotage of the master-plan, indicating loss of faith or lack of *esprit de corps*. "In all cases the ruling principle is that the fleet as a whole keeps together."

Far from conditioning his subordinates to exercise local command during 'PZs' at sea, Jellicoe (like Culme-Seymour twenty years earlier) constantly rehearsed them in the *Signal Book* goose-step. "Training on those principles was bound to induce tactical rigidity and discourage initiative, with unfortunate results in battle";[46] and

> it is possible that he did not realize the extent to which the whole long chain of command with its memoranda, orders and instructions might build a wall of reticence which only the exceptionally strong, independent character would break through.[47]

We have seen, in Chapter 3, how the C-in-C was nervous of headstrong juniors. It could be argued that he had good reason: to bring to bear at the critical juncture the Grand Fleet's crushing gunnery potential would require a high degree of coordination. But there are other ways of effecting coordination, and his distrust of devolution as a 'keynote' theme was abetted by the promise of total control implicit in an elaborate and well-tried (in peacetime) signalling system. One might throw in Fisher's remark, in another context, that the "fogs and short

days and difficult navigation [of northern waters are] very different to
Mediterranean white trousers!!!"[48]

Evidence has recently emerged that there was at the Admiralty
in 1913–14 a renewed debate (to which Jellicoe was privy) about
the relative value of battle-fleets as opposed to flotilla-defence.[49] In
other words, a trend of opinion was rediscovering Fisher's original
vision as First Sea Lord, in spite of the massive and costly dreadnought arms race in the intervening years. Whether this debate weakened Jellicoe's commitment to close battle, and, indeed, assisted the
Admiralty's approval of his self-constraining memorandum of
October the 30th, 1914 (mentioned in Chapter 2), is a matter for
speculation. Either way, for better or worse, most of Britain's naval
'eggs' had been put into the battle-fleet 'basket', and if Britannia was
to defeat the High Seas Fleet it was with the Grand Fleet that she was
going to have to do it – an enterprise from which few of her sailors
saw reason to recoil.

In the longest perspective, the Royal Navy's habits of tactical initiative had turned through an immense 200-year cycle. From the low of
around 1700 they had risen, amid countless knocks and bruises, to the
famous battle-wise high of the early 1800s; and then, in the century of
maritime peace after the Napoleonic War, they had slipped insidiously
down back to the original hidebound point of departure. The 1900s
found the British Fleet's outlook firmly regressed to the age when the
sacred *Signals and Instructions* held sway. And while the British public of
1914 took for granted that another Trafalgar was imminent – indeed
was their birthright – the professional conditioning of the officers in
command of the Royal Navy's mighty dreadnought squadrons made it
more likely that a clash with the High Seas Fleet would be a repeat of
(say) Verez Malaga in 1704 rather than of Trafalgar in 1805. Malaga
served Britain's strategic purpose well enough (by parrying a threat to
Gibraltar), as would Jutland also. The difference was that in 1916 the
world measured naval performance by the standards of Nelson, rather
than by those of Torrington, Benbow and Rooke.

To suggest that the opportunities of Jutland were lost off the coast of
the Lebanon on June the 22nd, 1893, would be to absolve the leaders of
the Royal Navy during the intervening twenty-three years of responsibility for the 'secondary education' of the Fleet's rising officers.
Obviously they cannot be so absolved, and we have seen how discontent with the 'doctrinal' *status quo* kept resurfacing in the confused
waters of the dreadnought era; but by training and by nature they were
ill-disposed towards radical reform: they were having enough of that in
the technical and strategical upheavals which were fully engaging their

attention and their anxieties, and which made the Grand Fleet what it was in material terms.

Realistically speaking, Sir George Tryon was the Navy's best chance before the Great War to get its head straight about the likely conditions of fleet encounters. Had he completed his due tenure of the Mediterranean, and gone on to the Admiralty to be First Sea Lord – he was still just young enough – and thence to instil his action-principles into the service as a whole, who can doubt that the Jutland generation of flag-officers would have been better prepared for the surprises and opportunities of battle? – indeed in some cases different men might have reached the top.[50]

As it was, the professionalism – in the seamanship and the 'account-ancy-management' senses – of the men at the top is beyond question; their mastery of the skills associated with the primary education of a naval officer was admired throughout the world, and the underlying confidence it imparted to the Grand Fleet is impossible to evaluate. Who (apart from a few maverick insiders) could doubt Christopher Cradock's splendid, resonant, idiotic assurance that "the main-sheet still drives the King's ships to windward"?[51] No wonder the Navy could look at its senior officer corps – "the finest set of admirals afloat any country could wish for", in McKenna's words[52] – and suppose that all was well. Who could call such men incompetent? But their brand of competence was only half the story, and the less important half at that. "We had more captains of ships than captains of war," as Churchill – by no means above incrimination himself, as First Lord of the Admiralty (1911–15) – later knowingly lamented.[53]

Hostilities play havoc with peacetime criteria, and before the end of 1914 Herbert Richmond was despairing (with hyperbole born of powerlessness) that "there is no doubt that we are the most appalling amateurs who ever tried to conduct a war."[54]

PART IV

Bringing Scheer to Jellicoe

20

Utmost Speed

"The 5th BS alone would have to entertain
the High Seas Fleet – 4 against perhaps 20."

When the four *Queen Elizabeths*, one after another, executed their 180° turn, forested by German shell-splashes, their massive 15-inch turrets had to train round from port bow to starboard quarter. As the gun muzzles of *Malaya*'s B turret (sited abaft and above A turret) trundled across the bows, the turret officer

> saw that our battlecruisers, proceeding northerly at full speed in close action with the German battlecruisers, were already quite 7,000 or 8,000 yards ahead of us. I then realized that just the four of us of the 5th BS alone would have to entertain the High Seas Fleet – 4 against perhaps 20. The enemy continued to fire rapidly at us during and after the turn.[1]

(The battlecruisers were more like 6,000 yards ahead of *Malaya* – 4,000 from *Barham* – although no doubt in the circumstances it seemed more.)

By a nice irony, while his squadron was still turning, Evan-Thomas hoisted 'TA', the cryptic group for Tryon's controversial battle-cry. In 1916 this by no means threatened the range of possibilities with which Tryon had endowed it: it merely gave warning of unheralded turns-in-succession or changes in speed.[2] This particular juncture (4.55) seems an odd time to make it, although its timing may be mis-aligned by a couple of minutes in the records. It is likely that RA5BS grasped Beatty's wish to have the battleships in line astern of the BCF and, by this signal, was preparing his squadron for *ad hoc* course-tinkering to try to minimize the yawning gap between *Barham* and *New Zealand*.

In fact there was little he could do about it. Beatty had turned the

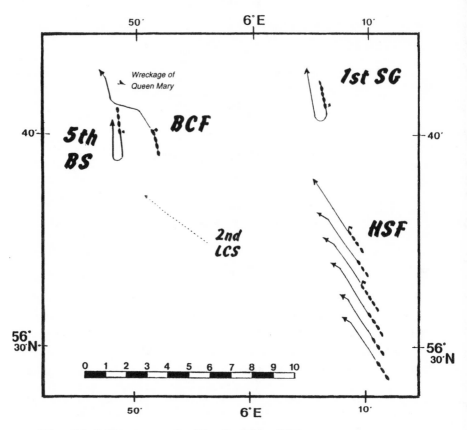

The 5th BS's turn to the North 4.51–5.00 p.m.

BCF up into *Barham*'s grain, but was not prepared to cut his 25-knot speed to enable her (and *König*) to gain ground. Furthermore, Beatty's now-northerly course was not a success, for his ships once again became the recipients of ragged fire from Hipper, who had by now also reversed course; so, he turned away once more to port by 2 points, at 5.0 p.m., hoisting a now hopeless signal to the 5th BS to "PROLONG THE LINE BY TAKING STATION ASTERN". It lay in Beatty's gift, not Evan-Thomas's, to unite the two groups; and as Sir Charles Madden, Jellicoe's chief of staff, flatly declared to Evan-Thomas in 1923, "The fact that you were astern was easily remedied by a reduction in *Lion*'s speed" (adding, "but it was increased & the B-Crs ran out of the action").[3]

Meanwhile the 5th BS had turned 3° or 4° more than a half-circle, and settled onto a course of 000° (true north).[4] We have now reached the first controversy of the 'run to the north'. Evan-Thomas must have been deeply shocked at having witnessed the blowing up of *Indefatigable* and *Queen Mary*, the more so since his powerful squadron, correctly deployed, might have been in a position to forestall at least the former disaster. Now, he had a clear view of the renewed bombardment which the depleted BCF was receiving from Hipper – and which he probably perceived as pushing Beatty off course to the west – and so, in spite of *Barham*'s taking hits, he kept his own course of north, crossed Beatty's wake and embarked upon a protective and gallant foray onto *New Zealand*'s exposed quarter.

This is contentious because every Jutland historian who has published a plan of the action at this juncture places the 5th BS on the BCF's port (= off-side) quarter. I believe they are wrong. A specific anomaly can be demonstrated. Campbell admits that "for 31 minutes the 5th Battle Squadron alone carried on the engagement with the 1st Scouting Group and the 3rd Squadron";[5] yet he echoes the conventional view that "from the period when the BCs had withdrawn from the action, the 5th BS's track lay for the most part about a mile westward of Beatty's." Given the range and bearing of Hipper's force from the two British groups, these statements are incompatible.

If, indeed, Evan-Thomas's track had taken him onto *New Zealand*'s disengaged (= port) quarter, then he would have been further from Hipper than was Beatty (as depicted by the maps of Corbett, Marder, Roskill, Campbell etc.), and there would have been no obvious reason why Beatty's ships should have ceased firing while his own continued. (The difference in range between the Mark V 13.5-inch gun and the Mark I 15-inch was a theoretical few hundred yards.) On the other hand, with Evan-Thomas on *New Zealand*'s exposed (= starboard) quarter at 5.10, and shooting at around (say) 20,000 yards, Beatty is (say) 23,000 yards from Hipper and has little option but to check fire. There is solid evidence that Hipper dropped out of range of *New Zealand*'s shorter-range 12-inch guns at around 5.00, and of the other British battlecruisers' 13.5-inch guns at around 5.08, while remaining within range of *Barham* and *Valiant* for most of the 'run to the north'. It is scarcely plausible that Beatty's people would have come out of their turrets "to stretch their legs and get a little fresh air",[6] with the 1st SG still within striking distance; and one may add that there is a consensus among battlecruiser-witnesses that Hipper actually dropped out of sight in the gathering haze for a considerable period while the 5th BS continued to engage him.

There are at least four pieces of primary (or nearly so) evidence to place the 5th BS on *New Zealand*'s starboard quarter:

1. Years later, in 1923, Evan-Thomas sent to the Director of Training and Staff Duties a sketch which, to make a rankling point about having been made to turn (in E-T's view) the wrong way, greatly exaggerates the degree of turn beyond 16 points, and misrepresents Beatty's course as north rather than NWbyN. But it unequivocally puts the 5th BS fine on Beatty's starboard quarter, and the accompanying text actually says that the extra amount of turn was "necessary in order to get on the enemy side of *Lion*".[7]

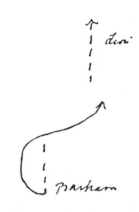

2. In 1926–7, Uncle Hugh "more than once" explained the same movements, demonstrating with matches on the dining-room table, to Lieutenant Geoffrey Barnard.[8]

3. An eyewitness account from one of Goodenough's light-cruisers (*Nottingham*) is illustrated by a sketch which clearly depicts the same thing.[9]

4. Most persuasive of all is the account of *New Zealand*'s own gunnery-officer. Stationed aloft, he had little to do, after Hipper had drawn out of range of his 12-inch guns, except receive 'no damage' and 'ammunition remaining' reports from his turrets and observe the movements of other units. He says quite simply that the 5th BS, having "held on [southwards] longer than the battlecruisers, finally turned up on our starboard quarter, where they now took the brunt of the action, coming under very heavy fire from German battlecruisers and Battle Fleet".[10]

Notwithstanding all expert secondary-source opinions, I have no reservations in crediting Evan-Thomas with crossing Beatty's wake and barging onto his senior's exposed quarter, thus physically intervening between the BCF and the 1st SG, while at the same time trying to fend off the High Seas Fleet astern. This is in fact permitted by the navigational ranges and data in Campbell's narrative (as distinct from his diagrams). Beatty, in his ROP, did not actually claim that the 5th BS took up station on his *disengaged* quarter (he merely said "astern"); it was, rather, one piece of misinformation among many allowed to gain credence after the war. What do Beatty's post-battle track-charts show about Evan-Thomas's relative movements? – they ought to settle the matter. As already mentioned, they fail to feature the 5th BS at all.

Presently, with Hipper's 1st SG thus held at a respectful distance by the 5th BS, Beatty's battlecruisers eased out of the action (and then eased their speed to 24 knots – which did nothing to help Evan-Thomas close the gap).

From the German battlecruisers' perspective,

it was not long before they vanished from our view in the mist and smoke . . .
After [their] gradual disappearance we were still faced with the four powerful
ships of the Fifth Battle Squadron: *Malaya*, *Valiant*, *Barham* and *Warspite* . . .
this part of the action, fought against a numerically inferior but more powerfully armed enemy who kept us under fire at ranges at which we were helpless, was highly depressing, nerve-racking and exasperating. Our only means
of defence was to leave the line for a short time, when we saw that the enemy
had our range. As this manoeuvre was imperceptible to the enemy, we
extricated ourselves at regular intervals from the hail of fire.[11]

While *Barham* and *Valiant* engaged Hipper's 1st SG, *Warspite* and *Malaya* were
busy with the head of Scheer's battle-fleet, which was still pressing hard from
their starboard quarter. In this way (in von Hase's words) "the four English
battleships at one time and another came under the fire of at least nine
German ships, five battlecruisers and from four to five battleships".[12]

Evan-Thomas soon deterred and discouraged Hipper; but there was,
needless to say, a cost to be paid for his gallantry, for he added the gift
of converging courses to the 4,000 yards given to Scheer by the delayed
turn, and the rear ships of his squadron were thus placed in further
jeopardy. Scheer ordered the High Seas Fleet, hitherto in approximate
line-ahead, to turn by divisions to the NNW to bring forward the
moment of his 'closest point of approach'. He was closing for the kill;
and while the BCF was relaxing action-stations, the assault on the 5th
BS was reaching a crescendo. At 5.10 Evan-Thomas ordered an impossible 25 knots and, at 5.14, repented his northerly course and eased
round to the north-west, as if in pursuit of Beatty.

*

While the 5th BS was doing its 16-point turn at 4.55-ish, the four light-
cruisers of Commodore Goodenough's 2nd LCS had been clawing their
way, dodging and weaving, northwards. Their immediate reconnaissance
task – ascertaining and reporting the position, course, speed and
strength of the German battle-fleet – had been done, and now they were
escaping from the killing arena into which they had ventured, on the
flank of the High Seas Fleet. They remained unscathed by dint of their
OOWs 'chasing the splash' (= guessing the enemy's range corrections),
and the German gunnery "was so correct for elevation that, with the
assistance of Providence, it was not difficult to dodge the salvoes".
Nottingham's navigator, whose nonchalance rings less than true, "never
had a more interesting and, in a way, really amusing half-hour than I had
conning the ship at that time".[13] In *Southampton*'s foretop her gunnery-
officer, Lieutenant (later Admiral Sir Harold) Burrough, was twice "half-
drowned by spray from shots falling in the water alongside the ship. The

spray rises to about 80 or 100 feet and then we steam right through the column of falling water. We seemed to have a charmed life."[14]

The threads of loyalties spun under Sir Michael Culme-Seymour's patronage in the Mediterranean in the spacious days of *Pax Victoriana* are interwoven throughout this tapestry of violence in Viking waters twenty years later. As Com2LCS, William Goodenough belonged to the BCF and was directly answerable to Beatty, but he was in no doubt about whom he was serving this afternoon. He had been devoted to John Jellicoe since their sunny 'Malta clique' days, had served him as flag-captain in 1907–8, and had been saved by him from sacking after the Scarborough signalling fiasco. After Jutland he wrote him a letter which could have been penned by any subordinate of Nelson's:

> God Bless you Sir,
>   I never felt so bound to you in affection and respect than at this moment. I trust we gave you the information you wanted, whether it brought you to the spot you so much desired or not . . .[15]

(The remaining 250 words are taken up with the experiences of the 2nd LCS, with not a word about Beatty or battlecruisers.)

Now, soon after 5.0 p.m., Goodenough had caught up with Evan-Thomas's squadron, and he took up station, so to speak, behind his old friend's left shoulder. There, Sir Michael's erstwhile flag-lieutenant and "extra flag-lieutenant" shared a relentless bombardment from the High Seas Fleet. (His son-in-law and another ex-'flags' were pushing out ahead of the BCF with the 3rd and 1st LCSs.) In *Southampton*'s after-control, between the fourth funnel and the mainmast, Lieutenant King-Hall and Sub-Lieutenant Haworth-Booth (the lad who had jumped hospital-ship) had nothing to do but eat corned beef and watch:

> BCs [were] engaged with the German BCs, but we could not see much of this; then came a gap of a couple of miles, then the 5th BS heavily in action with the leading half of the German line. Close to the last ship of the 5th BS was the *Southampton*; sometimes we were 4–6 cables on their disengaged quarter, at other times we were almost astern. Away on our port quarter were some destroyers and the other ships of our squadron. Then followed an hour [5–6 p.m.] in which I can truthfully say that I thought each succeeding minute would be our last. For a solid weary hour we were under persistent 11-inch shell-fire from the rear of the German Battle Fleet, that is to say from all the German battleships who could not quite get the 5th BS and therefore thought they might as well while away the time by knocking us out.[16]

Now, through the voice-pipe, Petty-Officer Barnes's distant mono-tone could be heard reporting, as often as not, "Range hobscured!"; and, like the men in the foretop, King-Hall and his comrades were soon drenched to the skin. The sub-lieutenant – "who was practically speech-less owing to his bad throat" – occupied himself with timing the incoming shells with his wrist-watch. On the twenty-third second he "would make a grimace", and they would brace themselves for a new soaking or worse. "I should say (and this is a carefully reasoned and considered estimate) that 40 large shells fell within 75 yards of us within the hour."[17]

> The fascination of watching these deadly and graceful splashes rising mysteriously from the smooth sea was enormous. To know that the next place where they would rise was being calculated by someone perched up in one of those distant masts, and that he was watching us through a pair of Zeiss binoculars – and I was watching his ship through a similar pair of Zeiss – was very interesting . . . I can – nor could I next day – remember no noise. We were of course not firing ourselves, and it seemed to me that I was being carried along in a kind of dream.[18]

The navigator of *Nottingham* wrote, "All this time we were, needless to say, going full speed, and with the whole German main fleet following it is fortunate that nothing went wrong down in the engine-room."[19]

*

If the story of Jutland were a work of fiction, one of several flaws in the plot would be the manner in which Scheer kept following Beatty in a direction which should have told him that VABCF had some agenda other than straightforward escape. This was the German C-in-C's second 'death-wish' mistake at Jutland. It was as if he was carelessly tempting fate to turn Hipper's *Ausfallsflotte* victory into his own *Risikoflotte* defeat – *quem Jupiter vult perdere, dementat prius* – and it was certainly a failure of staff-work in *Friedrich der Grosse*. (Christopher Cradock once observed that "the time taken by officers to fog out even the simplest problems at sea is occasionally astounding."[20]) But, for the time being, the pursuit appeared to be cost-free; and Scheer was hoping that a British capital ship would (in von Hase's words) "be so damaged as to fall a prey to our main fleet",[21] as had already happened to two destroyers. It was surely this incentive, combined (no doubt) with group pressure on the admiral's bridge, which occluded his judgement and enabled Beatty to lead him by the nose.

In every ship under Beatty's command, the penalty awaiting any one which fell astern was well understood, at least by those aware of the tactical situation. One of *Princess Royal*'s officers wrote that "the only fear [was] that one might get hit in the engine-room, which would drop our speed, so that the ship would fall back and be sunk by the High Seas Fleet following us." The navigating officer of *New Zealand* wondered:

Could we keep them following us long enough [to hand them over to the Grand Fleet], and could we avoid being hit? We had always to think that a ship damaged enough to lose only a few knots' speed would be as good as lost, for she would drop behind into the open arms of the whole German Battle Fleet.[22]

According to a witness in *Tiger*, "we were only firing occasionally now but the great battleships, with their much greater range [untrue!], were hard at it. It seemed they were immune to Jerry's shellfire."[23]

They were by no means immune. *Barham* was hit four times soon after the 16-point turn, allegedly by *Derfflinger*.[24] The first of these, at 4.58, "was one of the most destructive in the battle". The shell plunged through the upper deck, level with B turret barbette, completely wrecked the medical store and the auxiliary wireless office, caused "very severe damage to light structure, and had a very marked incendiary effect". It flashed "down a trunk to the dynamo room and burned all the men there" and upwards, via ammunition hand-ups, to the starboard 6-inch casemate "causing a serious cordite fire and putting [No. 2] gun's crew out of action".[25] There, Lieutenant Robert Porter RNR, who had been caught in the cordite flare-up, "personally superintended the extinction of the fire and the removal of the wounded and remained at his post [until] swelling from burns closed his eyes and rendered his hands useless".[26] A fragment of this same shell

> found its way down to the lower conning-tower, near the bottom of the ship, where the assistant-navigator, Lieutenant [Reginald] Blyth, and his assistant, Midshipman Alex Dodington, were keeping the ship's position plotted. This piece of shell almost severed Blyth's leg and although Dodington did his best to tie a tourniquet, he was much handicapped owing to the lights going out[27]

– and Blyth presently died from loss of blood.

The next shell came down through the after-superstructure at about 5.01, causing major superstructural damage, and severed the aerial feeders to the main wireless. A large splinter entered the already wrecked gunroom, and bounced off the armoured deck there before departing through the port side. A few minutes later another arrived aft, demolishing officers' accommodation and starting fires. The final shell in this series struck close to the first, although its effects were less far-reaching. Either the first or fourth of this series smashed up the boys' forward messdeck and the sick-bay, wiping out medical staff and patients, including the eight boys consigned to bed following their inoculations.[28] Meanwhile the (gunnery data) transmitting-station almost had to be evacuated due to "gas fumes from exploding shells".[29]

The capital ships at greatest risk were Evan-Thomas's rearmost.

"*Malaya* was at first very lucky, and although shells were falling all round and the ship was deluged in spray, she wasn't much hit."[30] The range was still too great for the secondary armament, so Sub-Lieutenant Caslon, in the starboard 6-inch control-tower, remained a spectator. He found it "extraordinarily fascinating":

> The visibility was bad and it was difficult to see the German ships distinctly, but we could see the flashes of their guns with great distinctness, and then after an interval of about 30 seconds the salvoes would fall round the ship.[31]

From B turret, Caslon's shipmate, Lieutenant Patrick Brind, had a similar view:

> The enemy continued to fire rapidly at us during and after the turn, but they did not get really close until about 5.15, when their salvoes began to arrive thick and fast round us at the rate of 6, 8, or 9 a minute. From my position in the turret I could see them falling just short, could hear them going just over, and saw several times a great column of black water fall on top of the turret.
>
> I had counted soon after the turn the number of enemy ships firing at us, and the 9th ship was the rearmost that I thought I saw open fire. I believe that this was at times increased by the German battlecruisers joining in against us, although I cannot say I noticed them myself.
>
> I don't know that I thought about it very much at the time, for I was trying hard to make out our target, but I expected at any moment that we should get a nasty knock, and I realized that if any one of those shells should hit us in the right place our speed would be sadly reduced, and then we should fall behind and probably be sunk.[32]

Malaya's first 'nasty knock' came at about 5.20, when a shell hit the lower edge of the armour-belt abreast B turret.[33] As with other shells which struck armour without penetrating, its whiplash shock was immense. It ruptured the hull below the armour, and caused a projectile to become jammed in the shell-cage feeding B turret's right-hand gun. Brind dashed down to the working chamber

> and we had to work like niggers to clear it. After what seemed an age, but could not really have been long, we succeeded, and by extemporary means managed to get the cage into working order again.

While this was being done, five rounds had to be loaded by 'handraulic' means, but the gun in question "never missed a chance to fire", and the turret crew

> had no thought that we should come off worse than the enemy, but only wanted to know how many German ships were left afloat requiring to be finished off. Many and varied were the benedictions they sent with each round fired.[34]

Meanwhile, *Warspite*, on *Malaya*'s starboard bow, had been taking damage since the turn, although her XO, in B turret, was unaware that it was happening.

> We were firing pretty fast about Green 120°. I distinctly saw two of our salvoes hit the leading German battleship. Sheets of yellow flame went right over her mast-heads and she looked red fore and aft like a burning haystack; I know we hit her hard. Told everybody in the turret that we were doing all right and to keep her going; machinery working like a clockwork mouse, and no hang-up of any sort whatever.[35]

Commander Walwyn noticed a number of heavy shakes, but associated them with the ship's own gunnery, rather than with enemy shells. Then he received a message from the captain saying that the ship had been badly hit aft and he was to go and assess the damage. He was so surprised that he had the message repeated.

He was at once faced with the dilemma of whether to follow the 'safe' route, down through the shell-room and aft through a number of watertight doors, or the quick one, up through the hatch in the turret roof and along the upper deck. Urgency required the latter, so he told his assistant, Gunner Alfred Walkem, to take the low road and join him aft, while he braced himself to take the scenic route. Midshipman Geoffrey Grenfell opened the hatch for him and bowed facetiously as he scrambled out:

> Directly I was on top they banged the hatch to. I didn't waste much time on the turret roof as the noise was awful and they were coming over pretty thick. As I got down the starboard ladder of B, both A and B turrets fired and made me skip a bit quicker. Ran down port superstructure ladder and tried to get into port superstructure; all clips were on [the door], so I climbed over 2nd cutter. [At that moment] one came through the after funnel with an awful screech and spattered about everywhere. I put up my coat collar and ran like a stag, feeling in a hell of a funk.[36]

He finally gained entry through a door which had been kept a chink open, and he went aft along the port side to find nothing obviously amiss, although he was yet to know that the ship had been hit underwater aft and the capstan-engine flat was flooding. He met up with Walkem and sent him off to report to the captain. Walwyn has been described by one of *Warspite*'s midshipmen as "a hot-stuff chap, always here there and everywhere!",[37] and the description is certainly apt in respect of the next couple of hours.[38]

Naval damage-control in the Great War differed from that of today in its generous manpower-supply, in the rudimentary nature of its methods, and in the absence of an 'HQ' organization to prioritize threats to the ship's faculties ('fight/move/float'). Nevertheless, Walwyn's 26-page narrative[39] of his between-decks steeplechase around the battleship's accumulating scenes of carnage – with its terse references to fire, smoke, darkness, chasms awaiting the unwary, escaping steam, electrical shocks, flooding, terrible injuries and incidental absurdities – provides a nightmare glimpse of the realities of modern naval action-damage.

John Campbell's assessment that during the run to the north *Warspite* took no 12-inch hits and only two 11-inch, is strongly belied by Commander Walwyn's testimony, and by his listed total of 31 hits at Jutland as against Campbell's 15.[40] The battleship's XO was in the boys' messdeck when a shell arrived with a "sheet of golden flame, stink, impenetrable dust, and everything seemed to fall everywhere with an appalling noise".

> Several of the fire brigade were sick due to the sweet sickly stench, but there was no sign of poison gas. The shell hole was clean and about the size of a scuttle [port-hole]; big flakes of armour had been flung right across the messdeck wrecking everything. Many armour bolts came away. Flooding-cabinet was completely wrecked and all voice-pipes and electrical leads overhead were cut to pieces. Smoke was pouring up through holes in deck, and it occurred to me the high-angle magazine was very near. [Gave orders] to disconnect all flooding gear from main deck and stand by to flood from middle deck position.
>
> Water from cut fire-mains was pouring below and smoke soon stopped. Plugged fire-mains as far as we could. Everybody busy 'souvenir' hunting and had to put the hose over them to make them take cover below again.

He returned aft to find water flooding the officers' accommodation, and the after middle-deck cabin-flat was soon untenable. This was the result of a 12-inch bursting on the waterline, probably during the turn:[41] "it was obvious the side was blown in below admiral's cabin, the stern was very low due to hard steaming and water was pumping up as we pitched." The nose-cone of another shell went through four bulkheads and came to rest in Temporary-Surgeon Frederick Williamson's bunk. No sooner was Walwyn called away than another one arrived. He hastened back to find his own cabin completely wrecked, with his wife's miniature lying undamaged amid the debris. Then

> there were about four bursts in the lobby. Trunk to steering compartment was wrecked, stanchions cut through, captain's pantry in heaps and everything in a filthy state of indescribable wreckage . . . a column of water, which must have been from 'shorts', was pouring through a hole in deck overhead . . . three stokers were dead in voice-pipe-flat, one having his head blown off and another badly smashed to pieces. Rather a horrible sight, but the burnt ones were far worse.

The noise was appalling and the electric lighting had gone out, although action-candles were quickly lit and daylight streamed in through holes in the deckhead. An unexploded, but broken, 12-inch shell had stopped outside the engineer's workshop, and Walwyn came across "a couple of stokers trying to chip the fuze out. I luckily stopped this little effort."

The genesis of modern damage-control techniques and doctrine is rooted in the experiences of 1916, some of which – like the laminated panelling which splintered into lethal shards, or the polyester clothing which melted onto the wearer, in the Falklands War of 1982 – symptomized a service out of touch with combat conditions. For example, the fire-and-repair parties were hampered by the lead-coated electrical wiring fixed to the deckheads in the main passages: the copper cores transmitted heat some distance from the flames, melting the lead insulation which then dripped onto the heads of the fire-fighters.[42] A temporary solution was found in the wearing of hooded duffel-coats; but, clearly, such cables should have been run along "vertical bulkheads, and never horizontally overhead, as the dripping lead is the devil".

There were other matters for consideration when, and if, they got home. Wire mantlets should be fitted to prevent flakes of armour being flung about by impact shock. Drain-valve wheels located at deck level were impossible to find in flooded compartments, and should have three-foot vertical spindles. Fearnought screens were needed to prevent flash ranging along the secondary batteries. The resin in the Corticine deck-covering melted into an evil, crackling, glue-like substance. Bare wires, broken glass and razor-sharp metal edges "were regular death traps" and called for sea-boots and "thick leather hedger's gloves". More saws should be provided, for cutting wooden shores and battens. More soft-wood wedges, rubber collision-mats and canvas buckets would not come amiss.

Commander Walwyn was by now shaken, grimy and soaking wet (someone had turned on a fire-hose as he passed). He paused in the cooks' lobby and had a cigarette

> – or rather started one, to steady my feelings. Had a yarn with the Pay who was wandering about in a 'kapok' [life-saving] waistcoat using appalling language as to when the Grand Fleet were going to turn up. Had a laugh together anyway. Whilst there, a 12-inch came into WO's galley and blew down though deck. A stoker alongside me looked up and said "there goes my ****** dinner". Everyone was very cheery and anxious for news which I couldn't give as I hadn't the faintest idea what was happening.

Royal Marines in the port (= off-side) 6-inch ammunition supply were playing cards. To one of them, the range of variables was happily limited: "This will mean a drop of leave!" But where the hell *was* the

Grand Fleet? About 30 miles to the north, doing the hardest steaming of its life.

*

The 12.35 signal from the Admiralty's Director of Operations, Captain Tom Jackson, reporting that the High Seas Fleet was still in harbour, has been widely blamed for delaying the battle-fleet's participation in the battle. Professor Marder, for example, talks of the loss of "an hour or two of daylight",[43] and similar statements are common. This idea scores heavy points off the desk-jockeys at the Admiralty, and for that reason is attractive. It is, however, a fallacy, making both a causal error and a mathematical one.

Firstly, the battle-fleet had not been proceeding with haste before receiving the idiotic signal. Pending confirmation that the Germans had actually sailed, Jellicoe was conserving as much fuel as his scheduled rendezvous with Beatty allowed; and, had Jackson made more careful enquiries about the German call-sign DK, all he could have told him was that Scheer's harbour call-sign was in harbour – in other words, there was no new information available. To spur the C-in-C into steaming faster, the Admiralty would have to have sent positive news (which it did not possess) of Scheer's being at sea.

Secondly, the "hour or two of daylight" is obtained by translating time straight into 20 knots' worth of distance, as if Jellicoe had stopped his fleet on receipt of the signal, and remained stationary until he received *Galatea*'s sighting report. It is unnecessary to plot his speed, time and distance, to discover how small a difference it would have made if he *had* received at 12.48 (which was when Jackson's signal reached his hand) a High Seas Fleet direction-find, sighting report or telltale decrypt: he would have ordered steam to be raised for full speed 107 minutes earlier than he did, and would have brought forward by 107 minutes his achievement of 20 knots (say, $6\frac{1}{2}$ knots more over-the-ground, allowing for cessation of zigzag[44]), gaining $11\frac{1}{2}$ miles. He would have arrived 35 minutes sooner at the point where he, in the event, met the High Seas Fleet; but the Germans would not have got there yet, and he would have had to steam on for slightly more than half the time he had saved (say, 19 minutes) before meeting them, six or seven miles further south, at a net gain of only some 16 minutes.

Certainly, his intervention could not be too soon for the besieged 5th BS. A quarter of an hour would have saved lives in *Warspite* and *Malaya*, and would have spared *Warspite* the terrible danger she was to get into when her steering-gear jammed and she circled towards the enemy at the junction of the battle-fleets. But one cannot seriously postulate that it would have made much difference to the dynamics of the main fleet-to-fleet encounter. And anyway, as explained above, even these few minutes are arrived at by invalid reasoning. In reality the buffoon Jackson's mistake made no difference at all to the timing of the fleet engagement. A more plausible consequence was its discrediting of Admiralty intelligence signals.

Galatea's first report to Beatty, at 2.20 p.m., of two enemy cruisers, was 'copied' with interest but no great excitement in the Battle Fleet. It interrupted the afternoon torpor, but alarms like this had happened before and come to nothing. *St Vincent*'s Captain W. W. Fisher teased his Army guest: "This rather puts your presentiments in the shade, Wallace!" "Why?" the clairvoyant pongo replied, "I don't think it does. On the contrary, you'll see there will be more to follow."

And indeed there was.

Within minutes Fisher found himself telling *Iron Duke*, by semaphore, that *St Vincent* was listening to strong (= nearby) Telefunken signals on the 2,600-foot wavelength commonly used by the German fleet. Then a flurry of further messages arrived from *Galatea*, reducing the cruisers to destroyers, giving chase, reinstating a cruiser, and reporting "A LARGE AMOUNT OF SMOKE". Clearly there was a scrap shaping up down south. At 2.35 (as the BCF was completing its turn to the SSE and leaving Evan-Thomas behind) Jellicoe made the flag-signal "RAISE STEAM FOR FULL SPEED AND REPORT WHEN READY TO PROCEED". Zigzagging ceased, and within 20 minutes the battle-fleet had wound up to 18 knots, while *Galatea* reported "SEVEN VESSELS BESIDES DESTROYERS AND CRUISERS. THEY HAVE TURNED NORTH." At 2.52 *St Vincent* flashed *Iron Duke* about more Telefunken intercepts. At 2.57 *Iron Duke* made "RAISE STEAM WITH ALL DESPATCH", and three minutes later came signal BJ: "ASSUME COMPLETE READINESS FOR ACTION IN EVERY RESPECT." Sir John Jellicoe's 100 ships now went through the processes of 'clearing away' and 'closing up' already described in Chapter 7 in respect of VABCF's forces.

In *Indomitable*, the bugler had sometimes omitted the 'G' notes in recent exercises, so when Action-Stations were sounded the initial response was lethargic. In *Hercules* the opposite mistake was made: out of force of habit the bugler started off with two 'Gs', and was sharply ordered, "Belay that, and do as you were told!" The interruption at least set the ship's company listening, and the revised call was greeted by a roar of cheering which welled up through the hatches from the lower-deck messes.[45]

In *Collingwood*, Sub-Lieutenant Prince Albert (the future King George VI), nursing a chronic gastric problem which had been aggravated by *Invincible*'s hospitality on Sunday night, got up from his sick-bed and went to his turret, temporarily cured.[46] One of HMS *Collingwood*'s Jutland battle-ensigns is displayed in the present shore-establishment of the same name; another is among four Jutland ensigns in the possession of Roedean Girls School (the others being from *Hercules*, *Neptune* and *Canterbury*).

A midshipman whose action-station was *Benbow*'s foretop collected a 'battle bag' which he had prepared for such an occasion: a blue jean bag containing "ear protectors, binoculars, a stop-watch, a pistol, a camera, a respirator, sundry scarves, a woollen helmet and so forth", and

> clambered up the starboard strut of the foremast, past the steam siren (which sizzled ominously as one approached it: it is an abominable experience to have a siren actually siren when you are near to it!), through a belt of hot acrid funnel smoke, and finally into the top through the 'lubber's hole'.

He had not been up there long when a profusion of White Ensigns, "large and small, silk and bunting", blossomed above the fleet. "I don't know who started it, but, sure enough, the squeak of halliard blocks announced that we were following suit."[47]

A fanciful story attached itself to *Revenge*. After she had closed up, her bridge personnel heard the sound of a side-drum being played close by.

Who could be practising at a time like this? A Royal Marine bandsman, perhaps, who should be below in the transmitting-station or with his first-aid party? Messengers searched, but although the mysterious rat-a-tatting persisted no culprit could be found. Then someone recalled the legend of Drake's drum, known to every schoolboy through Sir Henry Newbolt's stirring piece of doggerel – that if England were in danger, the sound of Drake's drum would herald his return – and no one in *Revenge* (ninth successor by name of Sir Francis's 1588 flagship) would countenance any other explanation. Elsewhere, needless to say, the story was greeted with ribaldry.

When Jellicoe, pressing southwards as fast as he could, received Beatty's "URGENT. ENEMY BATTLE CRUISERS . . .", the battle-fleet had been at action-stations for more than half an hour. Upper decks had been 'cleared away' and wetted. Forty thousand men were closed up. Equipment had been checked and re-checked. Communications had been tested through thousands of voice-pipes and telephones. Watertight doors and hatches had been clipped shut. Fire-and-repair parties had sorted their hoses and damage-control gear. Turret crews waited by their guns. Then, far to the south, first the light-cruiser *Falmouth* and then VABCF himself reported that Hipper had doubled back towards the south-east. The action was now flowing directly away, and, if it continued to do so, the battle-fleet would have little hope of joining in.

Jellicoe hoisted flags for 20 knots and released Rear-Admiral Hood to forge ahead with his three 25-knot *Invincibles* and join Beatty. Meanwhile, action-stations were relaxed although not formally stood down. Now, with sterns digging in and stern-waves rearing, the battle-fleet settled down to moving faster than it had ever done before. Some ships were fitter than others, and Jellicoe fussed and henpecked. He signalled to no one in particular to "KEEP JUST CLEAR OF THE WAKE OF THE NEXT AHEAD IF IT HELPS SHIPS TO KEEP UP". He invited *Thunderer* to try to overtake *Conqueror* (she did not succeed). And he peevishly reproved the 22-knot *Royal Oak* for sashaying around astern of *Iron Duke*: "YOU MUST STEER A STEADIER COURSE IN ACTION OR YOUR SHOOTING WILL BE BAD" (an oblique legacy of non-gyroscopic fire-control).

Small knots of men now lounged in the weak sunshine on upper decks near their action-stations, savoured the scene, and laughed at feeble jokes. In *Benbow*, a crowd of officers

> assembled on the superstructure and everyone kept one eye on the flagship's signal-bridge . . . *Bellerophon* was charging along behind us pushing the whole ocean in front of her; but in the next division the old *Superb* was so much astern of station that we quite expected to see the *Canada* overhaul her and take her place.

Abeam, the light-cruiser *Blanche* (the 4th BS's repeating ship) was flying Union Jacks from each of her four funnels.[48] In *Marlborough*, Vice-Admiral Burney's chief-steward, Ernest Fox, sat on Y turret roof with the rest of his first-aid party. They watched the thick black smoke, sparks and cinders powering out of the after funnel, and marvelled at the tumbling white stern-wave. "D'you think they'll catch us up?" enquired the admiral's messman.[49]

Then, news of the High Seas Fleet arrived from *Southampton*, and the Commander-in-Chief semaphored to his hard-steaming battle-squadrons: "ENEMY'S BATTLEFLEET IS COMING NORTH." And at 4.51 – even while, far to the south, Evan-Thomas was waiting and waiting for *Lion* to haul down the signal to turn away – he broke W/T silence to tell the Admiralty, "FLEET ACTION IS IMMINENT."

*

At this point Their Lordships should have sent to sea from Harwich, just north of the Thames estuary, the supremely competent Commodore Reginald Tyrwhitt, who was monitoring the airwaves and champing at the bit with his five light-cruisers and eighteen destroyers. Tyrwhitt's famous command (the 'Outer Gabbard Yacht Club', as it styled itself) was the only substantial British destroyer force whose war-training had comprised offensive, independent operations, as opposed to the protective chivvying of capital ships. And Tyrwhitt, like his old friend David Beatty,

> believed in imbuing his officers with an understanding of general principles and then leaving them – or rather, expecting them – to act on their own inter-pretation of these principles in moments of uncertainty or crisis.[50]

His presence at a full fleet encounter – especially in poor visibility when pockets of action might take place on a haphazard basis – might have been of critical value.

Yesterday, when decrypts first revealed that the High Seas Fleet was being ordered to sea (via the Horns Reef), the Admiralty had excluded the Harwich Force from orders to sail, on the grounds that the enemy might at the same time mount a raid by a single battle-squadron, or destroyers, on cross-Channel shipping. This decision should not, perhaps, be criticized, for a Pandora's box of adventurist strategies was expected from the new German C-in-C, and the damage which a raid could have done in the Downs or the Dover Straits was considerable; and until Goodenough's urgent signal of 4.38, it was not known for sure that the main body of the High Seas Fleet had in fact sailed via the Horns Reef (or at all). But once that signal – and Jellicoe's 'fleet action' warning – had been received, the rationale for holding back Tyrwhitt mostly disappears.

Any German foray towards the south-west could now only be small beer, without heavy support; and the routine Allied shipping which might be at risk was of less consequence than the decisive defeat of the German fleet. Tyrwhitt sailed without orders at 5.15, and notified the Admiralty that he had done so. It was far too late for him to join the action on the 31st of May; but, had he been allowed to proceed, he could have been off the entrance to the 'Ems' swept channel by 2.0 a.m., and then scoured north-north-eastwards to fall in with – as fate would have it – escaping German ships or the Grand Fleet. Regrettably, the commodore (in his own words) "might as well have gone on mowing the lawn",[51] for at 5.35 he was peremptorily ordered to "RETURN AT ONCE AND AWAIT ORDERS". Had Scheer subsequently opted for the southerly Ems route as his over-night means of escape, it was an order for which history would rightly have pilloried Their Lordships.

They did, at least, busy themselves with arrangements to receive home a damaged fleet. Signals were sent to hurry ships out of dry docks. The naval authorities at Rosyth, Harwich, Chatham and Dover were told to hold tugs in readiness. Extra patrol vessels were sent to sea from the Forth to keep submarines down. "Everywhere as the long-despaired-of news was whispered through the air and sped along the wires excitement grew."[52] Working parties in Scapa Flow hammered far into the night making coffins.[53]

*

News of the High Seas Fleet ran like wildfire through the Grand Fleet. In *Iron Duke* herself, Paymaster-Lieutenant Lewis da Costa Ricci (better known to the public as 'Bartimeus') witnessed a normally staid leading-seaman "capering, literally capering, along the battery. And as he capered he shouted: 'They're out, lads! They're out! Christ! They're out this time!'"[54] *St Vincent*'s captain gladly ate his words: "Wallace, you are right after all! If they'll only come far enough, they will never get back." Fisher had first thought of sending the major to a place of relative safety, deep down in the ship, but relented and let him go to the maintop (a spectator's position until the ship engaged two targets, or the foretop was hit). Wallace shook the Great Agrippa's hand and dashed below to his cabin for a few moments. On the way he passed sailors busy with hoses, and one of them said to him, "Sir, you *have* brought us luck." Soon he was ensconced aloft, making notes on a signal-pad which he had filched from the bridge. In *Hercules*, Commander von Schoultz, the Russian naval attaché, observed around him "every face radiant with enthusiasm and delight".[55] The British battle-fleet was about to meet its first reckonable enemy since Trafalgar.

The Commander-in-Chief, meanwhile, was becoming increasingly disconcerted by the dearth of information coming from Beatty.

The immediate challenge facing Jellicoe was to bring his massive battle-fleet into the fray, 'deployed' in the most advantageous manner. The 'deployment' was the manoeuvre which would convert the fleet from cruising formation (six divisions disposed abeam, each of four ships in line-ahead) into a single battle-line. The mechanics of this evolution, and the limited range of variations available, will be outlined in the next chapter. But the fear was that a battle-line deployed on erroneous beliefs as to the enemy fleet's bearing, distance and course might have its 'T' crossed and its van decisively hammered; and, for this reason, it was held that the deployment decision must be left until the course and relative position of the approaching enemy were precisely known.

That was the problem. The information coming in from VABCF's forces was hopelessly inadequate as a basis for what may be rated the Royal Navy's most important tactical decision for more than a century. For the paltry details that were sent, and for the many that were not, Goodenough has been too much praised and Beatty too much blamed.

Within 22 minutes of the sighting of the High Seas Fleet, Jellicoe was sent six separate reports.

Three from Goodenough, at 4.38, 4.48 and 5.00, gave Com2LCS's own positions (at odds with each other by several miles[56]) at those times, plus the enemy's bearing and course (the latter, always "North").

One from the light-cruiser *Champion* (leader of the 13th DF) at 4.38 gave another erroneous position and strangely specified the enemy's course as ENE. As Campbell points out, Jellicoe preferred to believe Goodenough, for he told the Grand Fleet that Scheer was "Coming North".

One from Beatty (through *Princess Royal*) at 4.45 was received in garbled form and rightly disregarded.

One from the Admiralty, at 5.0 p.m., was the yield from a 4.09 direction-find, and was quite accurate: it should have gone some way to rehabilitating the Admiralty's intelligence-signals; but as it was an hour stale, and as more immediate stuff appeared to be flowing in, *Iron Duke* may not have bothered to plot it.

The information available to the C-in-C therefore rested, in practice, on the signals coming in from his old friend William Goodenough; and after 5.00 these ceased. Thereafter Jellicoe could only assume that there had been no critical change in the circumstances last reported, and proceed accordingly; but anything could be happening. The silence was so deafening that, after Hood had requested a position from Beatty and failed to elicit a response, Jellicoe himself broke wireless-silence again, at 5.16, to give Beatty his own position, course and speed – though whether *Lion* received this information, through *Princess Royal*, is unlikely.

The accuracy of Goodenough's averred positions can be checked against *Queen Mary*'s wreck, allowing roughly for *Southampton*'s position relative to *QM*, at the time of the latter's loss, and for her subsequent movements. If we start four minutes after *QM*'s demise, with Goodenough's 4.30 signal reporting the cruiser *Rostock*, we have a sequence of four signals in which Com2LCS misrepresented his own position as follows (using magnetic compass bearings, and with declining reliability):

1. His position at 4.30 was given as 7 miles too far EbyS;
2. His position at 4.38 was given as 12 miles too far ESE;
3. His position at 4.48 was given as $8\frac{1}{2}$ miles too far SEbyS;[57]
4. His position at 5.00 was given as $4\frac{1}{2}$ miles too far SE.

It is apparent from this that, having started with easterly error in her DR position, *Southampton*'s directional orientation became slewed clockwise as she closed the German fleet. The scope for plotting errors is discussed in Appendix II. Probably Lieutenant Ireland (the navigator), who was conning the ship, failed to keep Sub-Lieutenant Marsden, the chartplotter, informed of every course-change, and perhaps magnetic courses were plotted as true. Then between 4.48 and 5.0 p.m., as she escaped northwards, she chanced to make amends somewhat by halving the positional error with which *Iron Duke* had to work for most of the next hour. However, the error in Goodenough's last-signalled position was progressively compounded by his leaving Jellicoe with the belief that Scheer was steering *north*, when, in fact, for more than half an hour he was pushing north-west, and forcing Beatty *et al.* to give ground in that direction.[58]

This three- or four-point discrepancy between the High Seas Fleet's reported and actual courses was a major cause of Jellicoe's supposing Scheer to be further east than he really was.

With two squadrons of armoured-cruisers spread out on a 30-mile front ahead of the Grand Fleet, it was near-impossible for Jellicoe to miss the action altogether, but the matter was critical for his forthcoming deployment decision; and for Rear-Admiral Hood (RA3BCS), racing ahead with his three battlecruisers, two light-cruisers and four destroyers, missing was a distinct possibility.

Beatty's token effort to inform his C-in-C of the enemy's whereabouts was a feeble gesture for the senior officer of the Grand Fleet's 'advanced forces'; and it speaks indifferently of Rear-Admiral Brock that *Princess Royal* did not go on reporting off her own bat. They do, however, have the partial alibi – which they were unlikely to advertise

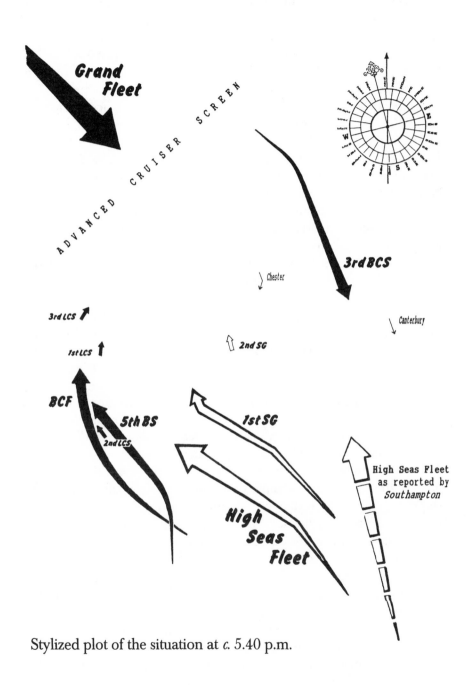

Stylized plot of the situation at *c.* 5.40 p.m.

afterwards – that they had lost sight of the HSF from about 5.00, and then, for some 25 minutes from 5.15, of the 1st SG as well. I say 'partial alibi' because it should not have been beyond their wit to divine, through observation of the 5th BS, the enemy's approximate location. But they also have the excuse that three or four miles astern of them were these four battleships under locally independent command, and four light-cruisers whose dedicated job was reconnaissance, in sight of, and under almost continuous fire from, the German battle-fleet.

Commodore Goodenough did well to have reported the High Seas Fleet three times by five o'clock, but his ensuing silence hardly justifies the plaudits which historians have heaped upon him. The real problem, however, seems to be with RA5BS, senior officer of the loose-ish group of ships remaining in contact with the enemy. Evan-Thomas's failure to report has been remarked upon both by Captain John Harper[59] (normally regarded as 'pro-Jellicoe') and by Arthur Marder,[60] although these historians were presumably unaware of its full irony. This man was one of the RN's highest authorities on signalling 'process'.

In the Mediterranean in 1893–6 he had worked diligently to extend the visual-reporting range of cruisers, and had explored the potential of homing pigeons. In England, in 1897–8, he had serviced the production of a close precursor of the *Signal Book* in use at Jutland. He had witnessed Signor Marconi pass messages between the Isle of Wight and Bournemouth, and, as a consequence, had recommended that W/T be fitted experimentally in HM ships. That he should not now think of signalling to Jellicoe the enemy's position, course and speed, was an abnegation of his specialized career-credentials and an extraordinary testimony of his lack of 'product' awareness. *Barham*'s main W/T had been severed from its aerials, and her auxiliary W/T smashed up; but she was in close company with three perfectly articulate sister-ships, all of whom would presumably have maintained a pointless wireless-silence until the sea closed over them. It may be mentioned that *Warspite*'s captain, Edward Phillpotts, was another one-time Superintendent of Signals Schools (and on this very day four years ago had urged that the Signals Branch and the W/T Branch be merged).

All it needed was a few seconds' semaphoring from *Barham* to *Valiant* to arrange for updates to be sent to the C-in-C every ten minutes. Evan-Thomas's staff-officers – Commander Egerton and Lieutenant Colville – should have been pestering him to approve such a measure. If W/T was not to be made use of at a time like this, what in the world were they carrying it for? Did they suppose that the C-in-C, by virtue of his rank, must know everything? Did they assume that Goodenough was reporting? Or were they too distracted by their own predicament to think about it at all? We can only guess the answers. We do not even know if RA5BS appointed a squadron W/T 'guard ship' to take in signals on his behalf while *Barham* effected repairs. (Organizational and 'tribal' factors which must have disfavoured 'command-awareness' of W/T, will be considered in due course.)

We do, at least, know in graphic detail about the damage being suffered by Evan-Thomas's rearmost two ships, as Beatty's and Jellicoe's respective forces raced blindly onwards on courses misaligned by several miles.

*

During the 'run to the north', even more than during the earlier 'run to the south', the visibility favoured the Germans. To the east, the horizon was obscured by mist or haze,[61] and "low-lying dark grey and purplish clouds", against which the High Seas Fleet and 1st Scouting Group "showed up indifferently"[62] and even intermittently. Sometimes the German ships were identifiable only by their gunflashes. To the west, the horizon was more clearly defined and the British stood out in silhouette like haystacks against the westerly sun, or so it seemed to them. Evan-Thomas apparently calculated that he could see for 12 miles on his disengaged (west) side.[63]

In fact, conditions were worsening for everyone. Occasionally the Germans, also, lost sight of their targets – certainly the more distant BCF – in haze; occasionally they found themselves dazzled by sudden shafts of sunlight. However, "My Dear Mother . . . we had great difficulty in seeing them, but they could easily see us against the setting sun",[64] is an honest, if ingenuous, report of conditions which disadvantaged the British. VABCF's post-battle 'points of interest' committee was quick to think of an antidote which could have rendered the *Queen Elizabeths* less visible to their 'down sun' enemy without impairing their own vision:

> We recommend trials being made of the utility of our own destroyers making smoke on the disengaged side of the large ships to make them more difficult to range or spot on, especially in the event of the enemy having the advantage of light. It should be possible to rapidly control this by signal.[65]

It was too late, by then, to help the 5th BS at Jutland; but if pre-war and early-wartime exercises had been carried out in deliberately unfavourable conditions, ideas like this might have been thrown up and explored by the time it mattered.

As it was, *Warspite* and *Malaya* remained under sustained and accurate bombardment by Scheer's battle-fleet, and both ships came close to being lost before they gained the safety of the Grand Fleet's crowd. German ships, also, were damaged in the 'run to the north'. Rear-Admiral Behncke's leading battleships were hit five times by *Warspite* and *Malaya*, and "were subjected to such a hot fire"[66] that Behncke would eventually be obliged to ease his speed and to turn away somewhat to starboard, presumably to enable all his guns to bear. Meanwhile, the 1st SG was hit thirteen times by *Barham* and *Valiant* and once by *Princess Royal*. Some of the 15-inch hits on *Derfflinger*, *Lützow* and *Seydlitz* did massive internal damage and admitted (ultimately), to the first-named ship, a near-fatal 2,000 tons of seawater. Their military faculties, as a battlecruiser force, were progressively degraded. But they were not under threat of certain execution if they trailed astern: the ships following them were friendly.

By contrast, the *QEs*' Damoclean predicament of being hostage to chance damage to engines or steering-gear, or to major flooding, was unrelieved for nearly an hour and a half. For how long could the dice continue to roll in their favour?

> Sailors are not stupid and they know true danger when it threatens. They can sense it, everyone in the ship can – in the commands that are broadcast inside the ship, in the speed with which people react, in the near hypersense of urgency which exists, at all levels. Imminent risk of explosion, fire and death is a sure way of concentrating the mind.[67]

Still, some people are less disposed to worry than others; and 'The Navy knows what it's doing', however circumstantially implausible, works as a sedative in inverse proportion to rank. The midshipman (name not given) in *Malaya*'s torpedo control-tower was

> slowly beginning to realize that all these projectiles falling a few yards short and over were big ones, and that they were meant for us, and my thoughts, following their natural course led me to think of my life-saving waistcoat, which, like a fool, I had left in my sea-chest down below,[68]

when a 12-inch shell burst on the armoured roof of X turret, about 30 feet directly aft of his position. It dished the turret roof, sprung the armoured bolts holding it in place, threw a hail of splinters up at the tower and skewed off-centre the armoured access-tube. The tower's occupants were knocked into an unseemly heap; and, when they had sorted themselves out and checked for broken bones, they could see the buckled turret roof rocking gently back and forth, and even glimpse the men inside working away as if nothing had happened. The snottie's interest in this phenomenon was curtailed by a salvo fired from the same turret, the blast of which threw him backwards into the arms of an able-seaman and left him dazed for several minutes. Then, at about 5.30, *Malaya* took a hit which "came near to bringing about the destruction of the ship".[69]

Orders for the starboard 6-inch battery to open fire to throw up a screen of splashes between the ship and her tormentors had just reached Sub-Lieutenant Caslon in the starboard 6-inch gun control-tower, when a shell came down through the forecastle deck and burst on No. 3 gun. It wrecked the mounting, wiping out the gun's crew and

killing, also, Lieutenant [James] Young RNR and [Midshipman Henry] Cotton, both very nice fellows. One fragment then passed into the canteen, killing two men that had no right to be there and seriously wounding two others. I think they were dodging work with the sick party. [Meanwhile] the cordite supply for the guns was ignited and a very fierce fire raged through the battery. Some of the burning cordite fell into the magazine, where the chief-gunner and another man threw themselves [onto it], and, although badly burned themselves, saved the ship from going up.[70]

On the shell's bursting, the armoured GCT was

filled with fumes and blue smoke and we were knocked backwards, but it cleared immediately and there was no damage . . . I put my face to the battery voice-pipe to enquire for them, but there was no need to ask: I could hear the most terrible pandemonium and the groans and cries of the wounded men . . . I heard one man call out 'Water! We're burning!'

With permission of the gunnery-officer, Caslon left his post and went down to see if he could do anything. He found that the RNR lieutenant in charge of the port battery, John McCulloch, had come across with some of his men and was working frantically to get the fire under control. "This officer's example [in Captain Boyle's words] undoubtedly had a good effect on the large number of very young men stationed there."[71] There were 102 casualties, most of whom died then or later. Among them was the gunroom steward, whom Caslon had so recently seen laying the table for tea; he was "half burnt from head to foot, the right half of his hair, face, shirt and trousers all gone". The scene, in Caslon's words, was "awful, and best left undescribed".

Orders came for the guns to be got into action as soon as possible "for the Germans were sending a destroyer attack down on us". The two mountings at the extreme ends of the battery, Nos. 1 and 6, were deemed serviceable, and men were drafted over from the port battery to work them amid the slaughter-house carnage. Within ten minutes of the explosion they were ready to open fire, and, as normal means of communication between GCT and battery had been destroyed, Caslon and McCulloch extemporized. The sub-lieutenant found he could shout through the armoured slit to No. 1 gun, and a man from there would run across to the port battery, whereupon another man would run down the port side and through the after athwart-ships passage to No. 6 starboard. It was cumbersome, but it worked.

Meanwhile, below, in *Malaya*'s dressing-stations, they were soon

> far too busy to think of anything but our job, and a good thing too. The wounded began to come down in great numbers, mostly burns and very bad burns they were, entailing very extensive dressings and of course Morphia... I rang up the fore distributing station, much the larger, where the Principal Medical Officer and [Guy] Woodhouse, the junior surgeon, were. Woodhouse told me that the P.M.O. [a senior fleet-surgeon] had had to chuck his hand in. He is a fairly elderly man.[72]

Rear-Admiral Evan-Thomas cannot have known exactly what was happening to the ships astern of him, but he must have guessed from the enemy's fall of shot; and at about the time of this devastating hit he hoisted flags for "UTMOST SPEED" – a term which signalled a state of extremity and called for engine-telegraphs to be put to 'Full Ahead'. This needs explaining.

Normal steaming was done with the engine-telegraphs at 'Half Ahead' and the revolutions-telegraph set for the RPM which would supply the required speed. 'Full Ahead' and 'Full Astern' were reserved for manoeuvring crises when speed of response was critical: they empowered the engine-room to access as many revolutions as possible, as fast as possible. In straight steaming 'Full Ahead' would probably add little to the ship's top speed, for the extra revolutions so obtained were at the steep end of the power *v.* speed curve; but the signal for utmost speed also meant that ships in formation might break station and make use of the small margin of speed hitherto kept in hand for stationing.

The four *Queen Elizabeths* did not actually change their order during the 'run to the north' – there wasn't time – but *Warspite* worked her way up on *Valiant*'s port quarter; and, with their propellers thrusting the North Sea sternwards as hard as their stokers could arrange, the paint on their funnels became browned and blistered with heat.[73] It was very nearly too late for *Malaya*.

Immediately after 'UTMOST SPEED', she received a potentially fatal pair of 12-inch hits below the waterline, level with the forward boiler-room. The midshipman up in the TCT was still gathering his wits after the shock of the 'turret-roof' hit –

> yet still unaware of any desire to be elsewhere – when there came a sudden shudder and lurch through the ship, a frightful din of escaping steam [this was from an unrelated hit, which disconnected the steam-pipe to the siren], and the ship took an uncomfortable list to starboard. There followed tender enquiries from the torpedo flats, switchboard, and other stations below decks as to our welfare, whether we were still alive, and also whether there were still any Huns left. To both questions we replied in the affirmative.[74]

Only one of these shells exploded, but the other one passed right through the ship at an oblique angle of descent, and between them they caused flooding to side compartments and oil tanks. *Malaya* very rapidly assumed an ominous 4° list to starboard, causing the guns to elevate to near-maximum to reach their 19,000–20,000 yard targets;[75] and, most critically, seawater fouled the oil-fuel supply to one of the boiler-rooms, whose fires presently went out. *Malaya*'s speed fell off, and she began to drop astern. This was the nightmare scenario which all but guaranteed the loss of the ship; but a stoker petty-officer smartly shut off the polluted supply and switched to another bunker, and, in spite of hurling everything they could at the briefly lamed duck, Scheer's ships (seven of whom, by Captain Boyle's count, were shooting at *Malaya*) failed to capitalize on their success. It was a heart-stopping crisis, but the battleship clawed her way back towards her sisters, and the list was slowly corrected by pumping fuel over to the undamaged side.[76]

Throughout, Lieutenant Brind, in B turret, had kept one ear listening to the stream of telephone messages for the commander, with whom he shared the 'silent cabinet':

> I heard reports coming through of a fire, later that it was being dealt with; reports that certain compartments had been flooded or water was leaking into others, reports about casualties, dressing-stations being full, the clearing of wounded and dead, and so on. It all came through in the most matter-of-fact way, seeming nothing out of the ordinary, as though we made and heard those sort of reports every day of our lives.

He also heard the turret-sweeper in the gun-house berating his 'oppos' for putting their "****** feet all over the ****** paint-work".[77]

*

The BCF and the 5th BS each had one ship which, through the unaccountable caprice of fate, got off virtually scot-free. *New Zealand*, Beatty's tail-end Charlie after *Indefatigable*'s loss, was hit just once during the whole action and took no casualties at all, although the ship ahead suffered 70 and the ship astern was sunk with more than a thousand dead. For reasons connected with Polynesian witchcraft and given in Chapter 7, the *New Zealanders* affected unsurprise; and, later, when Beatty visited them, he said

> Your escape with so little damage has been little short of miraculous. I hear you believe it is due to that tiki-wiki or whatever you call it, which your captain wears round his neck. Next time if you wish to be so lucky you had better see that he puts the whole uniform on.[78]

It may be mentioned that *New Zealand* wins three other prizes at Jutland. She fired more heavy shells, 420, than any other capital ship (being the only one to expend more than half her outfit of ammunition). Considering that her Mark X 12-inch guns were idle at times when her consorts continued firing, this gives her the battlecruiser prize for rate of fire. However, as she scored only three possible hits (a rate of just 0.7%), she also wins the wooden spoon for accuracy. The protective voodoo, it seems, extended to her targets.

In the 5th BS, *Valiant* was the lucky one. Damaged only by near-misses, she had just one man, a range-taker in an exposed position, wounded by splinters. A boy-seaman, aptly named Keen, even sat atop Y turret throughout the action, polishing periscope lenses, without coming to harm. However, there was another casualty: the ship's mascot, a proud cockerel (as featured on the ship's crest, over the motto *Valiant yet Vigilant*), was stripped of its feathers by gun-blast, and saved from going overboard only by the gallant padre's rugby tackle. Afterwards, a little woollen jacket was made for the dishevelled totem to wear "until a new set of feathers had grown".[79] In the circumstances, it was the least they could do.

*

At 5.33 Beatty's most northerly ship, Rear-Admiral Napier's 3rd LCS flagship *Falmouth*, five or six miles ahead of *Lion*, discerned a large warship in the haze about five miles to the north, and exchanged identities by flashing. The intruder proved to be *Black Prince*, an armoured-cruiser of Rear-Admiral Sir Robert Arbuthnot's 1st CS. Presently, other units – *Defence* and *Warrior* – of Arbuthnot's squadron became apparent, and to the BCF's advanced scouts there could have been no more welcome development. "I can hardly even now describe the thrill we all felt – the Grand Fleet had arrived! It was a wonderful moment, for we felt that at last the High Seas Fleet had been securely rounded up."[80]

It is likely that, on first contact, two unrecorded but important events took place in short order. First, Napier flashed sternwards to *Lion*, *Black Prince*'s identity and bearing; and second, Beatty's staff rapidly deduced from this information that they were approaching the extreme right-wing of the Grand Fleet's cruiser screen, and were thus off-centre by many miles. Although these suggested events are disallowed by Professor Marder[81] (who takes too literally the *Official Despatches* signals list), they merely involve senior officers in doing their job – and, without them, Beatty's ensuing tactics, and the assumptions he appears to have made about Jellicoe's position, are hard to fathom (as Sir Julian Corbett more or less confesses[82]).

Beatty had already warned his ships to be ready to reopen their lapsed engagement with the 1st SG, and he now came round to starboard to close the range and thence to barge Hipper over towards the north-east. It is usually assumed that VABCF was trying to prevent his German opposite from sighting, and giving Scheer early warning of, the Grand Fleet. But it cannot have been clear to him that such a movement would serve that purpose – it might, for all he knew, have had the opposite effect – and it is more likely that he was merely pushing Hipper in the rough direction of Jellicoe's centre, in the knowledge that Scheer must follow in support of his junior.

The task was not difficult, for, unlike Beatty's surviving battlecruisers, some of Hipper's ships were in a parlous condition. The renewed shooting match, at the longish range of about 17,000 yards (which Beatty later tried to insist was 14,000[83]), was fairly perfunctory. Hipper, in von Hase's words, "did not grasp the object of the enemy's manoeuvre"[84] and, fearing that the BCF was trying to cross his T, yielded as required. But he shortly found himself confronted by a fresh squadron of British dreadnoughts which suddenly materialized out of the murk to the east. It was this fortuitous appearance of Horace Hood's 3rd BCS which turned Hipper back onto Scheer and debarred him from performing a vital reconnaissance function.

The Honourable 'Orace had almost got lost. He, like the C-in-C, was working from Goodenough's last reported information; and, although he was some twenty miles ahead, his line of advance had become somewhat offset to the left of Jellicoe's. He was, in fact, about to steam at full speed past the action, when, at 5.36, the light-cruiser *Chester*, stationed at the limits of visibility about eight miles on *Invincible*'s starboard beam, ran into the light-cruisers and destroyers of Hipper's 2nd SG at the close range of around 8,000 yards. There followed an intense skirmish in which *Chester* was badly mauled, with 78 casualties and survivors in the gun batteries (where most of the hits occurred) rendered "stupid from shock",[85] before Hood could intervene. He turned north-westwards (which pointed him towards Beatty) to support the isolated cruiser, and at 5.55 his three battlecruisers – which had been at gunnery practice outside Scapa Flow only yesterday afternoon – emerged from the smog at close range and exacted retribution on the 2nd SG, while destroyers pitched into each other as opportunity allowed.

In three or four minutes three German light-cruisers – *Wiesbaden*, *Pillau* and *Frankfurt* – had been hit, the first-named severely. They threw up smokescreens and fell, or limped, back towards their own battlecruisers; and Hipper, alarmed and bewildered, in turn, circled back on Behncke's van-squadron of the High Seas Fleet. Hood's force of capital ships, dimly discerned to the east and not clearly identified, was the latest 'head' to appear, of what was beginning to seem to the Germans to be the "many-headed hydra" of the British Navy.[86] Who were they, and what next?

Meanwhile the ponderous mass of the British battle-fleet, still in divisions disposed abeam, was inexorably approaching the shrinking gap between Hood and Beatty – although this state of affairs was far from obvious on the compass-platform of *Iron Duke*.

British and German forces were in fact converging – the former, through the machinations of error and luck, from east, west and north; the latter, seemingly spell-bound, from the south – on a patch of sea at 57°N 6°E. Even without early warning of the Grand Fleet from Hipper, it must have dawned on the German Commander-in-Chief that the plot, like the weather, was thickening; and, whatever was happening, he cannot have continued to suppose himself to be in control. Even at this late stage he could have made a fist of extricating his fleet before colliding with Jellicoe. But Scheer steamed on.

Beatty, hitherto the senior British officer engaged, had shrugged off losses which would have destroyed Hipper's 1st SG as a coherent tactical force. Yet he was, once again, setting the agenda – something which, had he been (as Correlli Barnett claims) "a decisively beaten admiral", he could not possibly have done – and he was now within an ace of completing his allotted military task. Although his tactics were less than the master-plan which immediate hindsight could construe them to be, in von Hase's view,

> by completely outflanking us in spite of our highest speed, [he] accomplished an excellent tactical manoeuvre, and his ships carried out an admirable feat of technique. He accomplished the famous 'crossing the T', compelled us to alter course, and finally brought us into such a position that we were completely enveloped by the English Battle Fleet and the English battlecruisers.[87]

Old Packs said much the same thing, with the tact for which he was cherished, in his ROP:

> Nothing now remained but for the Battle Fleet to reap the fruits of a situation brilliantly prepared by the Battle Cruiser Fleet and the Fifth Battle Squadron. Jointly, this body had performed a magnificent feat of arms. Its position relative to the enemy could not have been improved.

Things were, however, not quite as simple as that. There remained to be played out several local squalls of violence in which another 2,100 British sailors would die, before the arena cleared for the Titans to engage. And Beatty had yet to supply Jellicoe with accurate information as to Scheer's whereabouts.

21

The Clash of Battle-Fleets

"The position seemed so advantageous that if the light would only hold for half an hour there would be hardly a German ship left in action."

Shortly before 6.0 p.m., "when the sun was already low and the horizon red with mist and smoke",[1] Beatty's battlecruisers careered out of the mist, broad on the Battle Fleet's starboard bow. Who saw them first, one cannot say: presumably people in the starboard-most column led by Vice-Admiral Burney's flagship *Marlborough*. At any rate, in *Hercules*, the Russian Naval Attaché noted their arrival at 5.55. Further left, in *Benbow*, Sturdee's flagship at the head of the fourth column, Midshipman Roger Dickson, waiting at his periscope in the midships turret, saw them

> suddenly burst through the mist. They were a wonderful sight, these great ships, tearing down across us, their huge funnels silhouetted against a great bank of red cordite smoke and lit up by sheets of flame as they fired salvo after salvo at the enemy whose flashes could be seen in the distance between the ships.[2]

To the group of senior officers on the compass-platform of *Iron Duke*, leading the 3rd Division,

> Beatty appeared out of the mist on the starboard bow [at 6.01 p.m.], leading his splendid battlecruisers which were engaged to starboard with an enemy invisible to us. I noticed smoke pouring from a shell-hole on the port side of *Lion*'s forecastle and grey ghost-like columns of water thrown by heavy enemy shells pitching among those great ships.[3]

Jellicoe at once had "WHERE IS THE ENEMY BATTLEFLEET?" flashed to *Lion* by searchlight. Beatty knew that Scheer's battle-fleet was "closely following" the 1st Scouting Group,[4] at which he was shooting, but the reply he had Leading-Signalman Alec Tempest flash back to

Iron Duke, after a delay of five minutes, merely said: "ENEMY BATTLE-CRUISERS BEARING SE", which was not what the C-in-C needed to know. It began to dawn on Major Wallace, watching the unfolding action from *St Vincent*'s maintop, "that something must have gone wrong".[5] The BCF swept on into the zone close in front of Jellicoe's advancing battle-squadrons: preceded by the 3rd, and accompanied by the 1st, Light-Cruiser Squadrons, and followed at a distance by the 5th BS and the 2nd LCS. The battlecruisers were "a very fine sight: firing very fast [with] projectiles running down around them",[6] and *Lion* was on fire amidships. Through his turret periscope in *Benbow*, Midshipman Dickson looked in vain for *Queen Mary*, his brother's ship.[7]

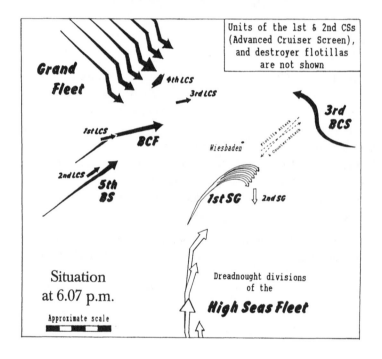

Jellicoe tried again. "WHERE IS THE ENEMY BATTLEFLEET?" This time he got at least some of the information he wanted: "HAVE SIGHTED ENEMY BATTLEFLEET BEARING SSW" – no distance or course. At last, the C-in-C could now unravel his own battle-fleet from cruising formation and 'deploy' it into line-of-battle: indeed to wait any longer would be to invite disaster. The deployment process needs explaining, and there are issues attached to it which have never been properly discussed.

Ideally, as Nelson wrote before Trafalgar, a fleet's "order of sailing" should have been its "order of battle".[8] However, in the age of steam a fleet could be reordered much more rapidly and surely than was formerly the case, and the accepted battle-formation of line-ahead was not always convenient or practical for cruising. As fleets grew in the first few years of the twentieth century, a compact box formation of divisions disposed abeam was adopted for cruising, with the divisions at 'manoeuvring distance' (= their own length plus one ship-space) apart.[9] From this condition, the admiral could form line-of-battle by dint of assigning to a wing division the role of the van, and making the other divisions perform two turns of 90° – the first in-succession, leading ships together, the second in-succession – to snake into its wake. This parade-ground procedure is said to have been developed by Sir Arthur Wilson (after the school of Philip Colomb) in the Channel Fleet in 1903–7, and had been practised in countless exercises ever since. It misleadingly became known as the deployment.

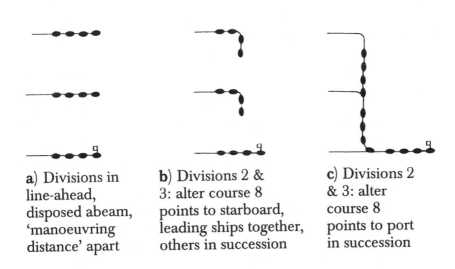

a) Divisions in line-ahead, disposed abeam, 'manoeuvring distance' apart

b) Divisions 2 & 3: alter course 8 points to starboard, leading ships together, others in succession

c) Divisions 2 & 3: alter course 8 points to port in succession

The proper definition of the 'deployment' was "the turn which brings all the battlefleet's heavy guns to bear on the enemy fleet".[10] It did not necessarily have anything to do with cruising formation, being simply a final course-adjustment to put the battle-line onto the optimum course from which to open fire.[11] If cruising formation had not existed, there would still have been a deployment – unless, by luck, the enemy appeared in a manner exactly convenient to the fleet's approach course. This is important, for while the deployment (in this sense of the word) *had* to be left until the distance, bearing and course of the enemy were accurately known to the admiral, there was no need for the fleet to enter the arena still in cruising formation and to have to do its line-forming Corybantic in the presence of the enemy.

Why the two movements became combined is unclear. Perhaps they were combined from the beginning because it was smart to do them together, and because, with the short gun-ranges of the time of Wilson's command-in-chief, there was little danger of the line-forming taking place within enemy range. Whatever the reason, by Jellicoe's time, and certainly in his GFBOs,[12] the 'deployment' concept embraced the action of 'forming line-of-battle',[13] and the two functionally distinct manoeuvres had become united under one signal, by which the speci-fied 'deploy course' would indicate the wing on which the C-in-C wished the fleet to form (a shorthand device which ruled out straight-ahead as an option). Meanwhile, fighting-ranges had increased until they equalled or exceeded normal North Sea visibility, with the result that, if the C-in-C waited until he could see the enemy before com-mencing his line-forming reshuffle, the Grand Fleet would probably have to perform that manoeuvre – which required high concentration and textbook station-keeping, and during which most ships' fields of fire would remain obstructed by other ships – after the shooting had commenced.

There were further dangers in leaving the unravelling, line-forming movement until the last moment. It was possible that a fleet formed in haste into line-astern of the wrong wing-division, would present to the enemy a major convex bend which would both provide an aiming point as each ship paraded through it, and leave the exposed van heavily out-gunned until the bend worked through to the rear. Hence the urgency of Jellicoe's being supplied with early information as to Scheer's where-abouts. A bend *concave* to the enemy would not matter much, because all the main-armament guns of the fleet could bear on the enemy (although each ship's fire-control would be thrown out for a time by its major change of course).

These hazards could be avoided or reduced by 'line-forming' in advance, in which case the choice of wing division would not entail crit-ical risks, and the manoeuvre could take place free of the stress and dis-tractions of a developing battle. The subsequent course adjustment which would probably still prove necessary would present relatively few problems or dangers – and certainly none not incurred in a belated line-forming-*cum*-deployment.

The British had thus institutionalized for themselves a juncture of high drama and vulnerability by carting onto the field-of-battle the

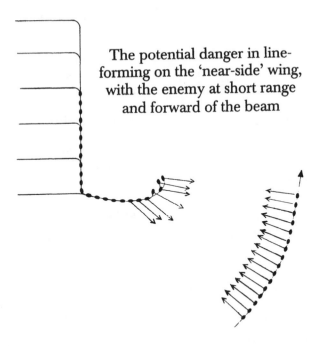

The potential danger in line-forming on the 'near-side' wing, with the enemy at short range and forward of the beam

baggage of a purely housekeeping evolution. The argument that the fleet was safer from U-boat attack in cruising formation than in line-ahead is perfectly correct (that was partly why cruising formation was necessary), but, in reference to the immediate preamble to a fleet action, it is a triviality. The argument that it was more 'professional' to perform both manoeuvres at once (and I suspect this lay at the root of the problem) could, if advanced, be dismissed as a typical peacetime misconstruction of the meaning of 'professional'. Jellicoe could perfectly easily have got the fleet settled into battle-line much sooner – at the latest, when Beatty's reply to his first enquiry proved unsatisfactory – and then 'deployed' (in the strict meaning of the word) as deemed appropriate.[14] This argument he seemed to discover overnight, for, at dawn on June the 1st, he would line-form the fleet against meeting the Germans suddenly at short range.

That having been said, fleets and armies have to fight their battles with the baggage-train of preconceptions which they have brought along into the field. And thus hampered (or not), Jellicoe addressed his deployment decision as German shells – at first probably 'overs' aimed at the BCF by Hipper – began hitting the sea amongst his battle-squadrons. He had already reduced speed somewhat, to enable ships to get back into station; and he had been getting estimates of the visibility in various directions from *Iron Duke*'s range-finders. The results of these enquiries, in the gathering clamp-down, were erratic.

> The visibility varied in different directions and in different localities. It seems that at no time after 6 p.m. was the general average visibility more than 12,000 yards, and as a rule it was less. In exceptional cases, in certain directions, objects could be seen for a short time up to 16,000 yards, but in other directions they could be seen only 2,000 or 3,000 yards away.[15]

However, a weak sun was still spasmodically breaking through from the west, and it was clear that the approaching High Seas Fleet was somewhere in the 'back-lit' hemisphere of vision to starboard, and that was where it must be kept – a position accordant with the objective of getting between the German fleet and its Horns Reef escape-route. The issue facing Jellicoe was whether there was time to deploy on the wing nearest to the enemy (the starboard wing), without having his T crossed before the line was properly formed. Beatty and Evan-Thomas were both clearly under fire from capital ships somewhere on their starboard side (Jellicoe's starboard bow), and perhaps, even now, indistinct silhouettes of German capital ships could be glimpsed in the smog six or seven miles away in that direction.

His moment of decision was graphically recalled by Frederick Dreyer, *Iron Duke*'s captain:

> I heard the signalman calling each word of Beatty's reply . . . I then heard at once the sharp distinctive step of the Commander-in-Chief approaching – he had steel grips on his heels. He stepped quickly on to the platform round the compasses and looked in silence at the magnetic compass card for about twenty seconds. I watched his keen brown weatherbeaten face with tremendous interest, wondering what he would do . . . I realized as I watched him that he was as cool and unmoved as ever. Then he looked up and broke the silence with the order in his crisp, clear-cut voice to Commander A. R. Woods, the Fleet Signal Officer, who was standing a little abaft me: 'Hoist equal-speed pendant SE.'[16]

"As the fleet was actually steering south-east, Woods asked if he could make it a point to port so that it would be clear that the deployment was to be on the port column."[17] Sir John approved, and there rose to *Iron Duke*'s yardarm a three-flag hoist comprised of the long blue-and-white-striped pendant denoting 'Equal Speed', and two rectangular flags (one diagonally quartered yellow, red, blue and black, and the other a cross of St Patrick), denoting the letters C and L, the signal group for SEbyE. Its literal meaning was: "THE COLUMN NEAREST SOUTH-EAST-BY-EAST IS TO ALTER COURSE IN SUCCESSION TO THAT POINT OF THE COMPASS, THE

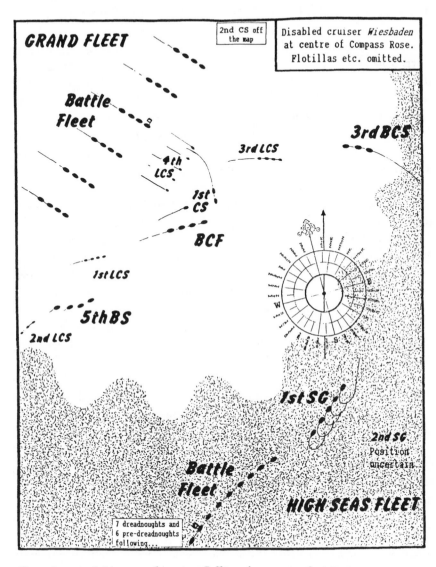

Situation at 6.14 p.m. showing Jellicoe's range of vision

REMAINING COLUMNS ALTERING COURSE LEADING SHIPS TOGETHER, THE REST IN SUCCESSION SO AS TO FORM ASTERN OF THAT COLUMN, MAINTAINING THE SPEED OF THE FLEET." In signalese it was known as 'Equal Speed Charley London', which strange invocation was adopted as the unofficial talisman of the Signal School.[18]

On the signal's execution, the six divisional leaders would turn to port: *King George V*, by only one point (11¼°) onto a course of SEbyE, the others, *Orion*, *Iron Duke*, *Benbow*, *Colossus* and *Marlborough*, by eight points (a right-angle). Then, with each successive minute the 1.1-mile gaps between them would be progressively occupied by their divisional juniors: at minute one, *Ajax*, *Monarch*, *Royal Oak*, *Bellerophon*, *Collingwood* and *Revenge* would come up to their turning-points and swing into line; at minute two, *Centurion*, *Conqueror*, *Superb*, *Temeraire*, *Neptune* and *Hercules*; at minute three, *Erin*, *Thunderer*, *Canada*, *Vanguard*, *St Vincent* and *Agincourt*. (Nine of these ships had Trafalgar battle-honours.[19]) Jellicoe had 'Equal Speed Charley London' hauled down at 6.16. *Iron Duke* sounded two short blasts on her siren ("I AM TURNING TO PORT"), and put her helm over. "I shall never forget" – said a witness in *Warspite* – "the magnificent sight as the squadrons of the fleet swung into line, each ship, as she turned into line, breaking into a ripple of flame from end to end as she opened fire."[20]

Jellicoe's deployment decision became the subject of vociferous criticism from the 'Beatty school' in the 1920s. On this, three overriding comments must be made.

The first is that one must confine his supposed options on *Der Tag* to those encompassed by the Grand Fleet's prevailing doctrine and training. Thus, gifted ideas about deploying on the centre division (a very complicated manoeuvre not then catered for in GFBOs) or deploying into two separate battle-lines, or even my complaint about not having line-formed earlier, are strictly inadmissible. The more fundamental issue of whether, and to what extent, he might have equipped himself with a wider, more flexible range of tactical options will be considered later.

The second is that the very fact of Beatty's driving on across the front of the fleet, rather than trying to take up station ahead of the starboard wing of the cruising Battle Fleet, was hardly likely to persuade Jellicoe that that was the wing towards which he should deploy. If Beatty's movements were calculated to tell the C-in-C something about how to deploy, they were at best ambivalent.

The third is that the compulsion to criticize derives from dissatisfaction with the outcome of the subsequent fleet encounter, and from the belief that if you could somehow throw the dice again at the start, you might get a double six. One may regret that the front of the cruising fleet had not been facing (say) SSE instead of SE, for its deployed course could then have been nearer the enemy by two points. But the reason why Sir John had been steering so easterly a course has been touched on; he did not have to hand an assortment of diagrams and maps depicting the enemy's distance, course and bearing, and was to some extent having to leap in the dark. For a decision taken under great pressure and with a fraction of the information which he had expected to possess, "the manner in which the commander-in-chief worked round the Germans to get good light by putting them to the westward of him"[21] was as good as could have been expected; and wherever it was that Jellicoe went wrong at Jutland – if he went wrong at Jutland – was after the deployment.

Jellicoe brought his fleet into battle in very much better order than did Scheer (that was his forte): the Grand Fleet's battle-line was deployed with its twenty-four dreadnoughts in a compact line of just six miles in length, and with all main gunnery arcs bearing towards the enemy. The High Seas Fleet's sixteen dreadnoughts and six pre-dread-noughts were, by contrast, strung out in a meandering line of around nine miles, and about to have their T crossed. Notwithstanding the literal and metaphorical fog of war, and the nail-biting suspense of the deployment decision, Sir John was (to use modern jargon) in decisive control of the 'battle-space' – although exactly how decisive, he did not appreciate until afterwards. Years later Sir Andrew Cunningham remarked, "I hope I would have had the good sense to make the same deployment as JJ did",[22] and that, insofar as anyone's opinion carries weight, ought to settle the matter.

After the war Scheer affected to blame himself for missing an opportunity to defeat the Grand Fleet while it was busy deploying. This of course reflects the danger of line-forming in the presence of the enemy; but in fact, at the time, Scheer (as his flag-lieutenant later admitted) had scarcely "the foggiest idea of what was happening"[23] – indeed he did not even know that the British battle-fleet was at sea until it was safely in (concave) line-ahead, and he had blundered into the jaws of the trap. The late line-forming thus did not bring disaster down upon Jellicoe; but its lateness greatly compounded the chaos and congestion at what became known as 'Windy Corner', and for this the British paid heavy local penalties.

*

For some fifteen minutes Windy Corner was a navigational nightmare, with a dozen groups of ships, big and small, all set on their own purposes and weaving to reach or maintain their own battle-stations mostly at full

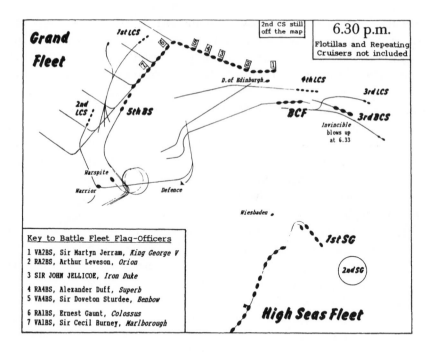

speed and under shellfire. "There was handling of ships such as had never been dreamt of by seamen before."[24] There were several near-collisions, and the sea, beneath its glassy surface, was kicked up into a jumbled cross-swell in which even a 5,000-ton cruiser found it "very difficult to steer".[25] It is impossible to attach a definite sequence to events at this juncture, for so much was happening, so fast, at roughly the same time.

Both the 4th (John Jellicoe's Own) LCS, close ahead of the Battle Fleet, and the 12th DF, screening the starboard wing, found themselves being carved up by BCF destroyers racing to keep pace with Beatty on the latter's 'off' side. "*Faulknor* had to stop engines and several [others] had actually to go astern to avoid a collision. All the time overs and ricochets from the German heavy ships were falling in the middle of our bunched flotilla."[26] Then, charging into this all-British mêlée came Edwyn Alexander-Sinclair's 1st Light-Cruiser Squadron, which had lost bearing on the BCF owing to Beatty's swing to the east, and now found itself increasingly pinched between the Battle Fleet and the battle-cruisers "in the midst of an extremely heavy fire, the whole ocean all round being torn up by shell splashes". As *Galatea* overhauled *Agincourt*, the latter "fired a salvo over us which fairly lifted us in the water. I don't know how many of her fourteen 12-inch guns she fired, but I felt as if my head was blown off."[27]

The 1st LCS belonged with the BCF, but it certainly did not belong here. Alexander-Sinclair sensibly decided to take his quartet through the battle-line and thence to work his way round the back to regain the company of the battlecruisers in the van. Junior ships, according to the 1915 *Signal Book*, "are not to pass through a line or between columns without asking permission". "Bugger that!" was no doubt in the commodore's mind as his light-cruisers (not exactly minnows, by today's standards) selected gaps between the battleships and dodged through at full speed, causing some of the big ships to take evasive action. Even on the other side, they found themselves steaming amongst a profusion of overs, one of which caught *Galatea* in the engine-room.

Bigger fish than the 1st LCS were causing confusion: the archetypal hard-man, Sir Robert Arbuthnot, with three of his large, obsolescent armoured-cruisers (the Grand Fleet's own *Fünf Minuten* squadron) was also doing so. "As soon as the battlecruisers had passed us, we [the deploying battleships] were astounded to see a squadron of our cruisers steaming between them and the enemy on an exactly opposite course."[28] While centre-stage should have been clearing for the leading contenders to engage, here was a supporting actor getting in the way and babbling his own, nonsensical lines. As mentioned in the last chapter, the 1st CS had been screening the starboard half of Battle Fleet's front, and it was the starboard-most ship, *Black Prince*, fifteen miles from 'fleet-centre', which had made the first contact between Jellicoe's force and Beatty's. Now, Arbuthnot had gathered together the other three units and was tilting off into the void between the fleets.

What was he trying to do? It is usually held (for example by Arthur Marder[29]) that the explanation lies in a telling passage in Lord Chatfield's memoirs. One day, during a walk ashore on the Orkney 'mainland', Sir Robert divulged to *Lion*'s captain how he intended to handle his squadron at the beginning of a fleet action:

He was stationed on one of the front wings of the Battle Fleet during the 'approach', as is called the period before the deployment into line of battle. But after deployment his squadron was [supposed to be] stationed in rear of the battle-line. Should, therefore, the Battle Fleet deploy towards the wing on which he was stationed, it would be necessary for him to move his squadron to the opposite flank which would become the rear on completion of deployment, a distance of about five miles. He could, he said, either do this by passing down the disengaged side of the Battle Fleet, which would, he felt, be a dull performance, or he could pass down the engaged side between the opposing Fleets. I said he should go down the disengaged side. If he went between the Fleets he might find himself in a highly dangerous position, but what was even more his smoke might well interfere with the fire of our Battle

Fleet at a critical time. He was inclined to pooh-pooh both these objections and I realized he was determined to go down between the two Fleets, which he said could only take a few minutes.[30]

No doubt Arbuthnot would have done exactly as intimated above, if the Grand Fleet had indeed deployed *towards the wing on which he was stationed.* But it seems to have escaped Marder *et al.* that it did not do so: Arbuthnot's 1st CS was covering the starboard half of the front, whereas the fleet deployed to port, in the direction of Rear-Admiral Heath's 2nd CS.[31] Arbuthnot was thus already not far from his designated station in the rear, which was, in effect, coming to meet him at 17 knots, and he could not realistically have gone round the van and down the *disengaged* side of the fleet even if he had wanted to.

Furthermore, whatever he was doing, he had started doing it well before Jellicoe's commencement of the deployment. Marder offers the alternative idea that he was sacrificing his squadron to cover the Grand Fleet's deployment with a torpedo attack on the German van.[32] The Arbuthnot Clan biographer suggests he was dashing to support Beatty, whom he seriously inconvenienced and whose fire he interrupted.[33] Both these ideas are rather silly and neither can be ruled out.

It appears[34] that the 'innermost' two units, the flagship *Defence* and *Warrior*, with *Duke of Edinburgh* steaming hard to join, had been spurred onwards by the sound of Hood's brief engagement with the German 2nd Scouting Group, and had sighted and engaged those light-cruisers as they recoiled from the 3rd BCS's violent lashing and fell back on their own battlecruisers. Sir Robert had his teeth firmly into the unfortunate *Wiesbaden* and was not going to let go. He steered to close the cripple at full speed, pouring out 9.2-inch shells and dense black funnel-smoke. The fact that Beatty's battlecruisers, pounding across the arena from right to left, were on a collision course, he evidently decided, was not his concern. Nor was the matter of the heavy shells cascading around them.

Defence and *Warrior* compelled Chatfield to veer *Lion* violently to port, and set about the gallant, hapless *Wiesbaden* at close range. "They made one of the finest sights I have ever seen, firing incredibly fast, and one mass of flashes from end to end."[35] Then, Hipper's battlecruisers and Scheer's leading battleships stepped out of the murk and turned their guns onto Sir Robert's elegant antiques at just 8,000 yards' range.[36] "A dull performance" it was not. The two armoured-cruisers "were practically continuously hidden by splashes, and must have been going through hell on earth".[37] Then, for a millisecond *Defence*'s profile seemed to lose its definition, "her sides burst all ways",[38] and the "entire ship was blown into the air, deckplates, bodies, and debris being plainly visible against the smoke".[39] When the smoke cleared there was nothing to be seen. Not a scrap of wreckage.

Warrior now took the brunt of the Germans' attention and reeled under the blows of fifteen heavy shells which killed a hundred men, set her on fire and wrecked her engine-room. *Duke of Edinburgh* was fortunate in having been ill-placed to follow her sisters across the BCF's bows: she had swung into loose station on the battlecruisers' port side and thereafter strained to follow them to the van of the battle-line, making industrial quantities of funnel smoke. The fourth ship of the squadron, *Black Prince*, out on a limb to starboard, had been too far away to get involved in the Windy Corner fiasco, and went to the rear of the battle-fleet in the prescribed manner – possibly damaged, though by whom and how badly is not known, for no one on board survived the night.

There may be weak circumstantial reasons why Arbuthnot's attention was focused so intently on the near-distance. His ships had not been fitted with director-firing, and the turrets would have lost sight of the target had the BCF been allowed to pass in front.[40] Still, when all allowances have been made, cruisers had no business to be messing around in the killing ground between the fleets. Sir Robert was out of his league – something which he was pathologically indisposed to admit in any circumstance. He should have taken note of Beatty's gunfire (as did everybody else) and cleared off out of his senior's way, instead of loitering to dismember carrion in the middle of the most dangerous highway man can devise. Like Sir Christopher Cradock and R. F. Scott, he was upholding Sir Richard Grenville's useless tradition of spectacular, avoidable defeat.

However, it must in fairness be said that had the Grand Fleet's line-forming manoeuvre taken place earlier, the 1st CS's restationing (to the rear) would have been completed before the arrival of the enemy, and Arbuthnot's 'predicament' would not have arisen. Thus he was to some extent a victim of the fleet's entering the fray still in cruising formation – for which Beatty, Jellicoe, the weather, and perhaps to some extent his own neglect of his reconnaissance role may be held variously to blame. By a quirk of history, an earlier *Defence*, a 74-gun ship-of-the-line, had been lost with all hands on the nearby coast of Jutland, in a storm in 1811.

The Germans' transference of fire to Arbuthnot's squadron at least came as a reprieve for the battered destroyer *Onslow*, which had closed to within 6,000 yards to fire torpedoes, and which should not, by rights, have escaped. As it was, Lieutenant-Commander John Tovey was able to get his little ship out of danger, and survived to sink the *Bismarck*, as

C-in-C Home Fleet, a quarter of a century later. And just as *Onslow* was saved by the antics of *Defence* and *Warrior*, so *Warrior*, in turn, was to be saved from the fate of her sister-ship by the unscripted intervention of a more attractive target.

No sooner had Arbuthnot's tragedy been played out, than another drama began in the 5th Battle Squadron – the final scene of the 'run to the north'. Rear-Admiral Evan-Thomas was still clinging doggedly onto Beaty's coat-tails, and as the BCF swung round towards the east he somewhat cut the corner across the port bow of the German fleet in an effort to close the now four-mile gap. A renewed cascade of shelling descended on his battleships. A midshipman in *Valiant* "really thought we might be in the running for the bottom of the sea".[41] The midshipman in *Warspite*'s torpedo control-tower, who had just watched four of his Dartmouth classmates obliterated in *Defence*, chose this moment to become aware "of being well scared and yet at the same time liking it"[42] (as if this was a sixpenny ride in a fun-fair). Then the ships of the 1st Battle Squadron, which comprised the starboard-most divisions of the Grand Fleet's cruising formation, took shape, in the process of deploying, in the murk ahead. "One thing I can express", said an observer in *Malaya*, "is the pleasure it was to see the *Agincourt* suddenly appear in sight ahead, looking more like a Brock's Benefit than a battleship, as she poured out salvoes from her broadside of fourteen 12-inch guns . . ."[43]

At first RA5BS assumed Vice-Admiral Burney's ships to be the van of a Battle Fleet already deployed to starboard, and pressed on after Beatty. But as they drew closer and their bearing broadened on the port bow, it became clear to him that they were still in cruising formation (he may have seen *Iron Duke*'s deployment signal, and its repeats, being hoisted) and that the six-mile front of the battle-fleet was, in effect, trying to slot into the gap between the battlecruisers and the *Queen Elizabeths*. Furthermore, as Captain Craig said in his report,

> the 5th Battle Squadron were now blanking the range for the 1st Battle Squadron, and it was a question as to whether 5th Battle Squadron should endeavour to follow the Battle Cruisers to the head of the line or form astern of *Marlborough*'s Division.[44]

Evan-Thomas promptly chose the latter alternative and has been praised for his initiative ("Another example of a man disregarding Holy Writ, breaking the line etc., I'm not suggesting that Evan-Thomas was a Nelson, I don't think he was"[45]).

In fact, he was *obeying* Holy Writ. Under 'Orders for the 5th BS', GFBOs required him to be "most careful to avoid having his ships between the two battle-fleets when fire is opened, or in such a position that the smoke of his ships hampers the fire on our battle-fleet."[46] The soundness of this standing order is debatable: the *Queen Elizabeths* were more powerful, better armoured, and nearer the enemy, than the ships whose ranges they would successively foul; their oil-fuel smoke was a relatively minor inconvenience; and in this specific instance they were actively supporting Beatty. But there it is. About the time *Warrior* passed, close to starboard, trying to escape destruction, *Barham* wheeled sharply to port by rather more than 90° and reduced speed, to make room for the Battle Fleet and to bring the 5th BS into line astern of the 1st BS.

The manoeuvre was not an unsignalled turn-together (a logical impossibility, to a signals specialist like Evan-Thomas) as stated by Campbell.[47] It was a turn-in-succession – signalled or not[48] – which perforce almost became a turn-together for the rearmost ships. *Valiant* was safely astern of the flagship, but in the 'utmost speed' race to the north *Warspite* and *Malaya* had got themselves into loose echelon on the side to which the turn was being made, and there nearly ensued a barging-match between battleships. *Warspite* turned inside *Valiant*'s port quarter and then found herself squeezed between the latter and *Malaya*'s menacing stem, while their bow-waves clashed in a welter of spray in the narrowing gulfs between them. They were entering a hull interaction nightmare, although little was known about that subject at the time. Captain Phillpotts put his helm over to swing his ship to starboard, to shave close under *Valiant*'s stern and thus escape the trap. In this he succeeded, but the quartermaster had "got a bit rattled and forced the wheel too quick which over-rode [the] telemotor", and Phillpotts found his steering-gear jammed with 10° of starboard rudder on.[49] This was an accident which had been waiting to happen for over an hour.

One of the earlier hits from the High Seas Fleet had distorted the bulkhead between *Warspite*'s aftermost engine-room and the steering-gear compartment, and the steering-engine mounted on that bulkhead had been operating out of true, and overheating, ever since.[50] Now the battleship went on swinging to starboard, and

> so terrific was the noise of bursting shell that no one in the conning-tower could hear the captain's orders, added to which the navigating-officer was temporarily blinded by our gun flash, with the result that the captain himself had to work the telegraphs and use the voice-tubes etc.[51]

Phillpotts tried to use the engines to counteract the helm, but when he found his ship facing the High Seas Fleet with way falling off, decided that continuing the involuntary turn was preferable to presenting a near-stationary target, and so on round they went. Meanwhile, down aft in the steering-gear compartment, they disengaged the seized engine and engaged the alternative one with the same 10° of helm on, with the result that, before the command-team could grasp what had gone wrong, the ship set out on another circuit – this time clean round the fugitive *Warrior*.

Needless to say, *Warspite* received a renewed onslaught of shellfire from the High Seas Fleet, while she thus charged around like a wounded elephant. "Nothing could be seen during this turn except the bursting of shell all around us, and our guns were only able to fire in reply through breaks in the splashes."[52] The main-armament had been put into local control while the gyrations continued, and in Y turret (the Royal Marine turret) Captain Poland

> couldn't find the enemy. I could see his splashes and feel them all over us but I couldn't see him. My 2nd officer was howling for permission to fire at something, but I refused until there was something visible to fire at.[53]

Although the same curtain of splashes partially hid the ship from German spotting-officers, she was hit a dozen times.

Below decks, Commander Walwyn was still rushing from pillar to post in his marathon obstacle course of directing repair parties and trying to keep abreast of new damage. "The noise was deafening and rather nerve-shattering," and he had no idea what was going on outside. He took the opportunity to look out of a shell-hole, and saw a world that was "red, lurid and beastly, heavy firing all round and splashes everywhere, thought we were steaming slow". He was approached by two stokers who

> begged me to take watches, letters etc., found on men who had been [killed]. It struck me as incongruous, as if it mattered a damn as we might all of us go any minute. I told them so but they were insistent about it – Walkem took charge of them.

The most costly hit, in terms of casualties, burst in the starboard battery behind the aftermost 6-inch gun. Several cordite charges were ignited, and although the flash did not, as in *Malaya*, relay along the battery, it badly burned every member of that gun-crew (two, to death), and some members of the next. Fragments went down through the deck and killed a number of men in the lobby below. Walwyn appeared, and took charge. "I was afraid that I should get 'cold feet' at seeing dead men, but was so hardened that I didn't care a rap . . . they were not nearly so frightening as I thought they would be." Hurrying back along the upper deck, he considered the ship's boats "a comic sight . . . smashed to blazes". Passing the meat store, he caught sight of a side of beef which had been forced half-through the grating by blast, and mistook it for a casualty. Forward, the upper deck was well ablaze.[54]

To Commodore Goodenough, in *Southampton*, close astern of the 5th BS, *Warspite* was

a most inspiring sight. Heavily hit, her steering gear disabled, she turned a complete circle. 'There goes your old friend Captain Phillpotts,' said my commander. But it was not so. The proper repairs were made, and, like a dog coming out of the water after a sudden immersion, she shook herself, her course straightened, her guns directed again towards the enemy, and she resumed her position in the line – her speed lessened, her action resolute.[55]

Captain Poland RM now became aware of the presence of the Grand Fleet. "I've never been so thankful for anything in my life. It was like feeling one's feet on the bottom again after being carried away by a strong tide. Lord, they did look fine. I came out and had a look at them." Meanwhile his commanding officer, Captain Phillpotts, tried "to take station astern of *Malaya*, but realized that the ship was still unmanageable, so I withdrew to the northward to shift over steering-gear to some other position".[56] In retrospect, this escapade seems typical of the cussedness for which *Warspite* gained a proud reputation; but had it happened twenty minutes earlier, it would certainly have brought about the loss of the ship. Even now, it was a close thing.

Goodenough, for his part, was under Beatty's, rather than Evan-Thomas's, command, and considered his rightful place to be in the van. But, as others had learnt, the maelstrom between the fleets was no place for cruisers; and, as coal-burners, his ships would have made complete pests of themselves had he attempted to follow the BCF. The commodore therefore resigned himself to sticking with the 5th BS and taking station in the rear.

*

While these things were going on, at the far end of the arena, Rear-Admiral Horace Hood was swinging his detached battlecruiser-squadron (the 3rd BCS), and its attendants, smartly into line ahead of the BCF. We have seen how he had nearly missed the action through advancing too far to the east, and how, by turning west to support *Chester* (which had tangled with the 2nd SG), he had blunted the point of Hipper's reconnaissance spear.

Continuing west, he now sighted, on his starboard bow, the Grand Fleet's van parading towards him ("I shall never forget the grandeur of the spectacle presented by the leading ships as, led by the battleship *King George V*, one by one they emerged from the mist, firing steadily at an enemy who we, of course, could not see," wrote Sub-Lieutenant Phipps-Hornby, in *Chester*). And on the port bow, he could see *Lion* and her consorts charging towards him across the chord formed by the arc of the Battle Fleet, hotly engaged to their starboard. Hood was, at last, perfectly placed to combine with Beatty, and it was obvious that, rather than add to the congestion between the BCF and the converging battle-line by trying to squeeze in astern of the former, he should turn round now and take station ahead. Hood thus waited only until Trevylyan Napier's light-cruisers had careered past, at about 6.21 p.m., and then turned through 16 points to place himself about two miles ahead of Beatty. As he did so the shapes of Hipper's battlecruisers became apparent within easy range to the south-westwards. *Invincible*, *Indomitable* and *Inflexible* trained their 12-inch guns round from port to starboard and opened an extremely accurate fire on the 1st SG at just 9,000 yards.

For several minutes the Germans could see nothing of their new assailants, and fired ineffectually in the general direction of Hood's gun-flashes, while *Lützow* and *Derfflinger* were hit again and again – the former eight times in eight minutes, and her ultimate loss may be attributed substantially to damage she received now from *Invincible*. Hood called up the voice-pipe to his gunnery-officer, Commander Hubert Dannreuther, in the foretop: "Your fire is very good. Keep at it as quickly as you can. Every shot is telling!" However, with battlecruisers engaging at such ranges, something cataclysmic was liable to happen, sooner rather than later; and at around 6.30 "the veil of mist in front of [the Germans] split across like the curtain at a theatre"[57] and Hood's ships were briefly lit up in sharp relief. Now, with clear targets, Hipper's battlecruisers replied to devastating effect. A salvo engulfed Hood's flagship, with a shell penetrating one of the midship turrets, bursting inside and relay-igniting the magazine.[58]

The explosion cut the ship in two, evidently removing a substantial midships section, and causing the bow and stern sections to collapse inwards and downwards. Of *Invincible*'s company of 1,032, just six men were selected, by the unaccountable lottery of war, to survive. From half-way up the foremast, Commander Dannreuther made an exit befitting the composer Wagner's godson, which he was. As the water rose to meet the subsiding foretop, he merely stepped out into it. The story that he alighted, dry-shod, onto a wooden target which had broken free of its stowage, appears to be untrue, although the target may have been the 'raft' of which he and three others made use. A young marine, Private Bill Gasson, had a miraculous escape from the offending midships turret: he was simply blown out of it and found himself in the sea, badly burned but in one piece. In his later career he ran the Officer Training Corps (latterly the Combined Cadet Force) at Malvern School for twenty-six years, and was presented to the Queen at the commissioning of the present *Invincible* in 1980, at the age of 85.[59]

The destroyer *Badger*, on *Lion*'s off-side, was flashed by Beatty to "PICK UP SURVIVORS FROM WRECK ON STARBOARD SIDE". Expecting to rescue hundreds of Germans, her first-lieutenant hastily mustered an armed guard as she dashed out into what seemed like no man's land. They arrived to find the two ends of a great ship standing vertically out of the water like tombstones, each resting on the bottom, acres of float-ing kitbags and hammocks, and just six survivors: four on a raft, and two a short distance away. *Badger* hove-to alongside the raft, and while her whaler (armed with a revolver) went off to retrieve the two swim-mers, the first-lieutenant was appalled and astonished to embark an RN commander, as "self-possessed as if he was joining a new ship in the ordinary course of events" and much taken with the armed guard.[60] *Badger* steamed slowly around for a while, looking vainly for further sur-vivors, while German shells fell sporadically nearby and the van of the Grand Fleet swept by.

*

By now the Battle Fleet was drawing clear of its deployment clutter. The last division had turned the corner onto the deploy-course of SEbyE (111° true), and *Barham*, *Valiant* and *Malaya* had formed astern of *Agincourt* ('the Gin Palace'). There had been some overlapping and jockeying, owing mainly to Jellicoe's having to reduce speed to 14 knots for a time, to help the BCF and the wretched *Duke of Edinburgh* pass clear ahead and to ease the congestion of lesser ships at the head of the line. And *Warspite* had gone meandering off somewhere. But by around 6.40 p.m. the Battle Fleet was in one straightish line,[61] its composure – never seriously ruffled – was restored, it had the advantage of position, and it now numbered twenty-seven dreadnought-battleships. Every-thing seemed organized to vindicate the careful planning in Grand Fleet Battle Orders and all those thankless months of fleetwork training. But what of the enemy?

In fact Reinhard Scheer had already turned his fleet away.

So uncertain was the visibility, and so focused were British officers on close-quarters manoeuvring and local squalls of violence, that the German Commander-in-Chief's horrifying moment of crisis had passed unguessed, and his remedy virtually unobserved.

The deploying Grand Fleet had opened fire raggedly from 6.17, as targets appeared and arcs of fire allowed. In his position aloft in *St Vincent* Major Wallace found the blast "enough to blow one's cap off".[62] The funnel-smoke of Beatty's ships, big and small, crossing the arena caused much interference, and no organized target-distribution was possible. But if, as battle-fleet shooting went, the results were sporadic and piecemeal, it did not seem so to the enemy. The conditions of light which earlier had so favoured the Germans now hampered everybody, but the High Seas Fleet more than the British. The first German units to glimpse what lay in store were Hipper's battlecruisers: at around 6.20 p.m. "we came under heavy fire. It flashed out on all sides. We could only make out the ships' hulls indistinctly, but as far as I was able to see the horizon, enemy ships were all around us."[63] By around 6.30 most British battleships had opened fire, and now the leading German battleships found themselves facing

> the belching guns of an interminable line of heavy ships, [and] salvo followed salvo almost without intermission, an impression which gained in power from the almost complete inability of the German ships to reply, as not one of the British dreadnoughts could be made out through the smoke and fumes.[64]

"The shock to Scheer was stupendous."[65] While he strove to grasp the situation, Hipper was pushed round towards the south and heavy damage was inflicted on the leading battleship, *König*, in which Rear-Admiral Paul Behncke was wounded. The impression Scheer sought to give after the war, of cool calculation at this juncture, is belied by the stark fact that he had managed to get his T crossed at a decisively close range with the High Seas Fleet strung out in an extended line, and if he persisted on his present course, his fleet's continued existence as a cohesive organization was measurable in minutes.

He was not long in a dither, for at 6.35 he ordered a 'battle turn-around' (*Gefechtskehrtwendung*) which was efficiently obeyed by his fleet under urgent and difficult circumstances: each ship putting her helm over as soon as the one astern was seen to begin turning. Within a few minutes the entire German fleet was steaming westward, although this was far from apparent to Jellicoe. In the shifting banks of smog rolling slowly towards the British line, no more than three or four enemy ships had ever been visible from *Iron Duke*'s bridge, and, as firing petered out at around 6.45, Sir John attributed the enemy's disappearance to the thickening mist – although he did turn his divisions one point to starboard (from 111° to 122° true), onto a course of south-east (which was the deploy-course he had wanted in the first place).

*

When the big guns checked fire, few on the British side doubted that this was a mere hitch: that Sir John Jellicoe was fully in charge, and the High Seas Fleet was still somehow 'in the bag'. The long-awaited reckoning was only just starting, and the Germans had scored no hits on the Battle Fleet, whose gunners were just getting into their considerable stride.

The still-floating *Wiesbaden* had acted as the pivotal point (at a five-mile radius) of the Grand Fleet's deployment; and now, with nothing else to do, William Goodenough, like Arbuthnot before him, found her lure irresistible and took his squadron out into no man's land to assault her.

In the battleship *Colossus*, Rear-Admiral Ernest Gaunt felt moved to make an inspiring signal. For some moments he was lost in thought, then he told his 'flags' what he had in mind. Lieutenant David Joel tried to dissuade him, "but the admiral over-ruled me, as admirals do"; and presently there stood out in the breeze above Captain Dudley Pound's ship: "REMEMBER BELGIUM AND THE GLORIOUS FIRST OF JUNE."[66]

As usual, no authentic news had been available below decks for some considerable time, and a trickle of people emerged to see what they could see. Of the enemy fleet, there was no sign, which some attributed to their own remarkable gunnery. An inspiring sight was presented by *Acasta*, one of four destroyers which had been attached to the 3rd BCS. Almost an hour earlier, at the time of Hood's engagement with the 2nd SG, Commander Loftus Jones, in *Shark*, had led them out to parry a German destroyer attack and "things very quickly became unpleasantly warm" – the more so when Hipper's 1st SG intervened.

Shark was soon smashed up, and *Acasta*, herself hit forward, closed her senior to offer assistance. As she approached, she received "two big ones through the after engine-room", which cut steam pipes, wrecked the steering-gear and destroyed the dynamo. Thus it was that, helpless either to steer or to stop, *Acasta* steamed slowly down on the British line, "guided by Providence" with siren wailing and 'not under control' signal aloft. She passed close in front of *Lion*, receiving the benefit of a salvo intended for Beatty, and blundered on through a shoal of hard-steaming 'friendly' destroyers. She finally came to a halt in the grain of the Battle Fleet, down by the bows, with her engine-room untenable, and her crew mustered aft in life-preservers; and while the captain, Lieutenant-Commander Barron, waited to be run down, they

> held a very fine review of the Grand Fleet as ship after ship passed us, some to port and some to starboard. The men were very excited and cheered each ship as she passed, particularly the Commander-in-Chief in *Iron Duke*.[67]

To one witness they seemed like any crowd gathered to watch the King pass. "Perfectly MAGNIFICENT! Thank God I'm an Englishman!"[68]

A future king was passing. In *Collingwood*'s A turret, Prince Albert had been banging away at *Derfflinger*, and this mild-mannered and rather poorly youth noted that "all sense of danger and everything else goes, except the one longing of dealing death in every possible way to the enemy." Now he sat out on the turret roof, to get a break from the cordite fumes and the smells of hot oil and blistering paint.[69]

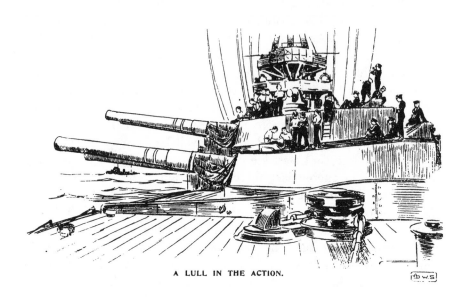

A LULL IN THE ACTION.

Meanwhile a number of torpedoes were heading for the rear of the British line. It is unclear exactly who fired them (perhaps the still-floating and extraordinarily tenacious *Wiesbaden*, and/or miscellaneous torpedo-boats, since departed to the west), but most of their tracks were seen clearly and they were easily avoided. One, which was not seen, struck *Marlborough* at 6.54, deep down and level with the bridge. It destroyed some thirty feet of hull plating and made the ship jump.[70] Two men were killed in the starboard dynamo compartment and containable flooding occurred in a boiler-room, where the fires had to be drawn. At Chief-Steward Fox's first-aid post, in a lobby down below armour, they felt the ship lurch over to starboard, and looked at each other in a moment of near-panic, causing the surgeon-lieutenant to seat himself forbiddingly at the foot of the ladder.[71] The list stopped at about 8°, and *Marlborough* was able to maintain her position in the line, apparently unimpaired apart from her unnatural starboard lean – although her speed was now confined to 17 knots, and there were problems with the hydraulics in the $13\frac{1}{2}$-inch gun-turrets.[72]

Meanwhile, Jellicoe flashed astern to Burney, in *Marlborough*, "CAN YOU

SEE ANY ENEMY BATTLESHIPS?", and received the reply "NO". He now realized that the enemy's disappearance was due to more than the weather, and turned the fleet another four points (45°) to magnetic south (167° true). This was the product of puzzlement as much as of aggression, and would not have rediscovered the High Seas Fleet if Scheer, having effected his escape, had continued to behave rationally. Jellicoe's tactical inhibitions will be discussed later; however, one may regret that, with the enemy out of sight somewhere to the south-west, he did not at least adopt south as a new base-course, and get the fleet into line-ahead on it. Clear arcs of fire were vital in a fleet action, and it must have been obvious that he was not going to go back to SEbyE (the deployment 'single line-ahead' course) and fight the battle on that base-course.

The matter was complicated by the fact of divisional leaders already being on a one-point line-of-bearing, which would have made turning-in-succession awkward (although it was considered practicable with a line-of-bearing of up to 15°). But he could, alternatively, have ordered the fleet to re-form into line-ahead/astern of *Iron Duke*, and left its flag-officers to sort themselves out ("RESUME PREVIOUS ORDER" might have done it). Either way it would have taken about twenty minutes to complete: although if there was ever a time to re-dress his battle-line, this was it. However, at 6.55 he turned *by divisions*, four points to starboard, and in doing so substantially undeployed the Grand Fleet, more than half-way returning it to divisional cruising formation.

The manoeuvre came as a deliverance to the helpless *Acasta*, which was all but lost to sight beneath the flare of *Marlborough*'s port bow before the wounded battleship started to swing to starboard. It also caused the 3rd and 4th Divisions to combe either side of the bow and stern sections of *Invincible*. *Benbow* passed so close to the wreck that

> we could almost have chucked a heaving line aboard her. She was broken in two with her bows and stern sticking out of the water. *Benbow*'s men jumped up on top of their turrets and cheered heartily. The idea that it could be any other than a German ship had never entered their heads. Then we passed about half a cable distance and saw her name, and the cheering ceased suddenly . . . Our admiral [Sturdee] was very upset about it – she was his flagship in his last great fight off the Falklands.[73]

An engineer-officer in a passing destroyer often ruminated, in later years, "on how many people were imprisoned alive in some of the watertight compartments lying at the bottom of the sea". Other witnesses, high up on the bridges of passing dreadnoughts, became haunted by the thought that the mass of objects in the water, through and over which they steamed, may have been men, rather than the

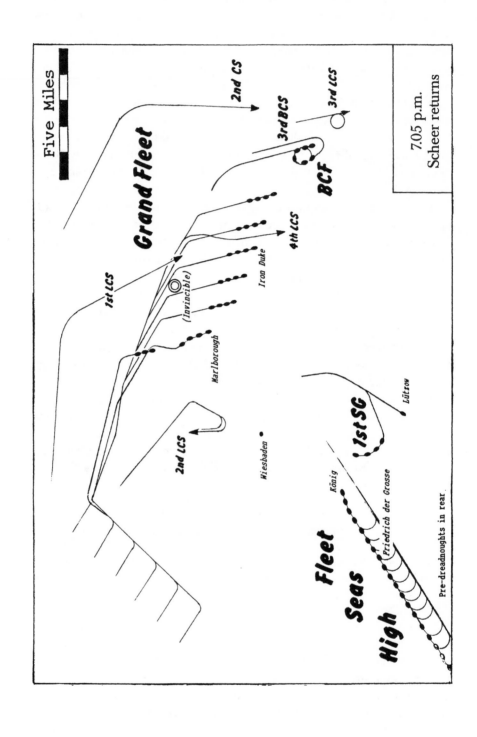

Five Miles

Grand Fleet

2nd CS

3rd BCS

3rd LCS

BCF

1st LCS

(Invincible)

4th LCS

Iron Duke

Marlborough

2nd LCS

Wiesbaden

1st SG

König

Lützow

Fleet

Seas

High

Friedrich der Grosse

Pre-dreadnoughts in rear.

7.05 p.m.
Scheer returns

kitbags etc. alleged after the battle. In fact, testimony from *Badger* shows that it was not so.

About this time, Captain Ernle Chatfield left *Lion*'s bridge to see for himself the damage to his ship.[74] In particular, he inspected the horror of the gutted Q turret, and must have thought of the turret explosion in his father's ship *Thunderer*, in 1879. He may also have begun to appreciate Warrant-Officer Grant's insistence upon magazine safety regulations (Grant, at any rate, ended his career as a captain). In his absence from the bridge there occurred a problem with *Lion*'s steering which was to assume surreal proportions in the post-Jutland bickerings. The BCF flagship turned a full, lazy 360° circle. She probably put helm on, in conformity to the Grand Fleet's four-point turn to starboard, and left it on. The battlecruisers astern followed her round, while the two ahead (*Inflexible* and *Indomitable*) turned in imitation and took the opportunity to tag on to the end of the line. Napier's 3rd LCS, also ahead, copied the circle.

The loop allowed the Battle Fleet to reduce the gap on the BCF, and caused the latter to lose bearing on the enemy (briefly out of sight). Beatty later insisted that it never happened, claiming it was a double turn to close the enemy, to starboard and then back to port, and tried to ban the circle from the battlecruisers' track-charts. But *Lion*'s navigator, Commander Strutt, included it in his running commentary down the voice-pipe to Lieutenant Chalmers in the chart-house below the compass-platform,[75] and *New Zealand* defiantly left it on her track-chart. How could such a thing happen by mistake? It scarcely matters, but Beatty made such a fuss about it that it invites our attention.

In calm, sunless conditions, and with no scenery (in the form of land or shipping), it is just about possible for an inattentive officer-on-the-con to turn a circle; but not all of these conditions applied. Lord Chatfield's reference to it in his memoirs is deliberate, and carefully worded: before leaving the bridge, he put starboard helm on while handing over the con to Beatty's chief of staff, Captain Rudolf Bentinck. Chatfield clearly wanted his naval readers to know that it had nothing to do with him. But it was pretty shoddy to hand over with helm on – and why to Bentinck, who was not in *Lion*'s lawful chain of command, rather than to Strutt? In fact Bentinck was due to supersede Henry Pelly in command of *Tiger* in a few days' time, and it was no doubt thought a good idea to let him 'have a go'. Perhaps the chief of staff was thrown by the gyro-compass failure which *Lion* reported after the battle; but the course change was in *magnetic*-compass points, and, with more than a dozen nearby ships (including, briefly, the van of the Grand Fleet) tracking across his field of vision, not to mention A and B turrets training back and forth, the manoeuvre suggests a rare absence of mind. Had 'tactical rudder' been used, and had *New Zealand* been out of station, there might have been a collision.

*

Meanwhile, as Jellicoe was executing his four-point divisional turn towards the south, several miles to the west Scheer was reversing the course of the High Seas Fleet and heading back into exactly the mess from which he had so promptly extricated himself. This was his third 'death-wish' decision at Jutland, and it may never be convincingly explained. He later alleged, ludicrously, that he wanted to rescue the crew of *Wiesbaden*.

It is unclear how much of the British battle-line Scheer, near the centre of his own line in *Friederich der Grosse*, had seen, and it may be that he still did not appreciate that the whole of the Grand Fleet was present. Furthermore, when the 2nd SG had found themselves confronted by Hood's battlecruisers, to the east, at around 6.0 p.m., *Frankfurt* had reported her formidable assailants as battleships – the Germans subsequently wished it into their heads that *Invincible* had been *Warspite* – and, at 6.45, the battlecruiser *Moltke* had flashed to Scheer that the "ENEMY'S VAN BEARS EbyS", which, at the time, was four points too far south for *King George V*, and two points too far south even for the BCF.

Therefore when Scheer turned round, onto a course of EbyN, he may have been calculating that he would pass across the stern of whatever British force was present. "This is the explanation that best maintains, or detracts the least from, Scheer's reputation as a skilled tactician."[76] On the other hand, every mile to the west meant getting pushed, aimlessly, further and further out into what had suddenly become a horribly British North Sea, and it may simply be that his brain had entered into a state of denial of the way events had turned against him twenty minutes earlier.

Whatever his logic, he marched the High Seas Fleet, headed by Hipper's battered and relatively thinly-armoured battlecruisers, straight back into the worst trouble that it lay in his gift, as C-in-C, to contrive.

*

Goodenough's light-cruisers served as the trip-wire which announced the return of the High Seas Fleet. Having stepped forward to deal with *Wiesbaden*, they discovered that "she was [still] covered by the rear ships of the enemy fleet".[77]

Suddenly out of the mist behind her came an absolute rain of shells. We could not tell what it was we had run into, but it must have been the tail of the German battle-line. There was nothing for us to do but retire. As the *Southampton* turned, a salvo of big shells landed all around her, and the *Dublin*, turning in her wake, was missed only by inches. We [*Nottingham*] turned inside the wake of *Dublin* and just missed the salvo which would have obliterated us.[78]

The 2nd LCS's extraordinary luck held, and once more it dodged back out of harm's way, merely shaken-up and drenched. While thus under fire, Goodenough observed the Germans' second reversal of course and reported it by W/T to Jellicoe, although long before his signal was decoded its import was apparent from the renewed thundering of heavy gunfire.

Those Grand Fleet personnel who had come out to goof on the upper deck tumbled back to their action-stations. Some were quicker about it than others. Prince Albert was still sitting on his turret roof when a shell shrieked over *Collingwood*, and he was sharply told: "Come down before you get your head blown off!"[79]

The smoke from the Germans' earlier advance was still being carried down onto the Grand Fleet, and the vagaries of the visibility meant that the resumption of British fire was initially sporadic, but it quickly grew in volume as the enemy emerged into view. And while Jellicoe hastily sought to reshuffle his divisions into line-ahead, the German van was much more seriously bunched up and not fully under command. Hipper and his staff had disembarked from the crippled *Lützow* and were steaming about in a destroyer trying to find a battlecruiser in a fit state to take them. The battlecruisers themselves were physically obstructing the 3rd Squadron astern of them, causing the battleships to reduce speed and, in some cases, even stop. And now, German disorganization turned to chaos as, for a few terrible minutes, British salvoes rocketed in, thick and fast, from battleships virtually indiscernible to the east.

Hipper's ships took the brunt: they were, in Commander von Hase's words, *"in absoluten Wurstkessel!"*[80] The already crippled *Lützow* and *Seydlitz* were each hit five times, *Von der Tann* once. *Derfflinger* was shattered by fourteen hits, having two of her gun-turrets gutted (as per *Lion*'s Q turret earlier) and most of their 140 men killed.[81] Of the battle-fleet, *König*, *Markgraf* and *Helgoland* were each hit once (*Helgoland*, eleventh in the line, probably by an 'over'), *Kaiser* twice, and *Grosser Kurfürst* seven times. (One wonders if anyone in *Grosser Kurfürst* remembered that the last ship to bear the name had been sunk in a collision on this date in 1878.) As they jockeyed for clear arcs of fire and manoeuvred under full helm, they fired back desperately at gunflashes, but

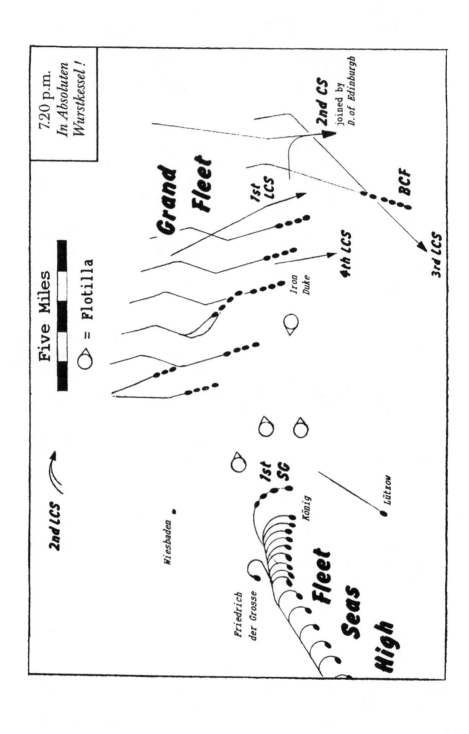

7.20 p.m.
In Absoluten
Wurstkessel !

Five Miles

◯ = Flotilla

Grand Fleet

1st LCS

4th LCS

Iron Duke

2nd CS
joined by
D. of Edinburgh

BCF

3rd LCS

2nd LCS

Wiesbaden

1st SG

König

Lützow

Friedrich der Grosse

High Seas Fleet

with no means of spotting their fall-of-shot and almost completely without effect.

On the British side, *Colossus* took either two or three non-serious hits (probably from *Seydlitz*) which wounded five men. One shell caused a brief flare-up among 4-inch ammunition boxes, and another entered just above the waterline and exploded near the admiral's quarters.[82] There were near-misses whose splashes soaked bridge personnel in several ships, including the Russian naval attaché in *Hercules* ("How you say? – Bugger!").[83] And splinters came aboard *Agincourt* and broke open a hutch in which Lieutenants Cunninghame-Graham and Egerton kept five white ferrets.[84] But that, apart from the piecemeal dodging of a few real and imaginary torpedoes, was all. The 'Square Law of Attrition', by which an initial advantage compounds itself in favour of the superior side, was beginning to tip the High Seas Fleet down a steepening slope to oblivion.

Once again, Scheer had to extricate his fleet as fast as possible.

At 7.14 he wirelessed to the 1st SG a signal whose literal meaning was "AT THE ENEMY, STAKE ALL. SHIPS ARE TO ATTACK WITHOUT REGARD FOR THE CONSEQUENCE"; and Captain Hartog of *Derfflinger* (acting in Hipper's absence) was marshalling the battlecruisers to carry out this 'suicide order' when Scheer partially reprieved them by amending it to "OPERATE AGAINST THE ENEMY'S VAN". Meanwhile the German C-in-C called for a mass destroyer attack on the Grand Fleet, and the German battle-line carried out another about-turn (a shambles, compared to the first), and retreated behind smokescreens, with the 1st SG trailing behind.

*

The German Navy's claims of victory at *Der Skagerrak* are at their least credible in the light of the High Seas Fleet's two precipitate flights (more especially the second) from the 300 heavy-guns of the Grand Fleet. However, Jellicoe did not know for certain what Scheer had done with his fleet, of which only a few ephemeral shapes in the mist had been apparent from *Iron Duke* (HMS *Erin*, the fifth ahead of *Iron Duke*, never opened fire at Jutland). His immediate concern was the mêlée of destroyers in the middle ground, and the torpedoes which must now be heading towards his line in unknown quantities. He altered course together, two points to port, to SSE, at 7.23, and then a further two points, to SE, two minutes later.[85]

The torpedo attack itself was rather less than a half-cock affair. Only three out of six and a half flotillas were in a position to comply, one of those was so slow to do so that it had to be recalled, and some of the boats of the remaining two had already shot their bolts in penny packets

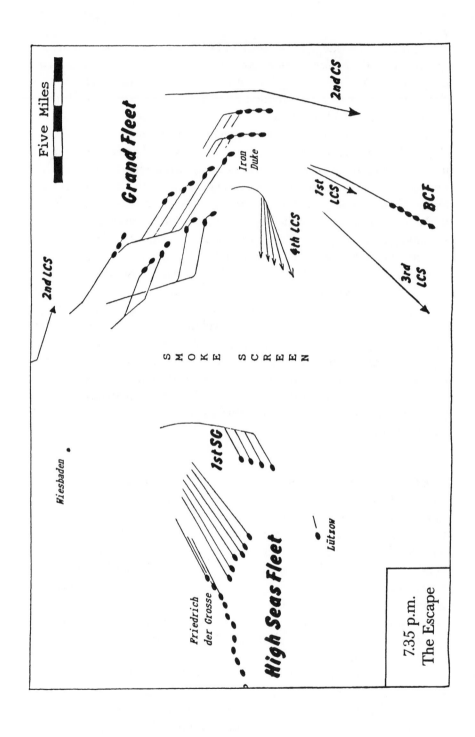

Five Miles

Grand Fleet

2nd CS

2nd LCS

Iron
Duke

1st
LCS

4th LCS

BCF

3rd
LCS

S M O K E   S C R E E N

Wiesbaden

1st SG

Lützow

Priedrich
der Grosse

High Seas Fleet

7.35 p.m.
The Escape

at the Grand Fleet or, earlier, at Hood's 'battleships', and carried no reloads. They also met harassment from John Jellicoe's Own light-cruisers, and some of his destroyers, which sank one of their number and damaged two others. In all, in this attack, the Germans put thirty-one torpedoes into the sea.

Jellicoe's evasive action caused many of them to run out of range short of the Grand Fleet. But several crossed the line, and there were some heart-stopping moments as individual dreadnoughts twisted and heeled under full helm to avoid them. The tracks were conspicuous, and it was usually the men in the spotting-tops (of, for example, *Marlborough*, *St Vincent* and *Neptune*) who saw them first and alerted the bridges. From *Marlborough*'s foretop, they watched torpedoes pass ahead, astern and underneath. In *Neptune*, the gunnery-officer bellowed "HARD A-STARBOARD" down the voice-pipe, and the helmsman fortunately (though incorrectly) obeyed it.

> We began to turn rapidly [to port], but the torpedo got closer and closer. From the foretop we were craning our necks over the metal side, while the whole top was groaning and vibrating under the strain of the ship turning at full speed with full helm on. We looked down on the tops of the turrets and the decks below, and could see our shipmates working down there quite unconscious of the immediate peril. The torpedo was now dead astern following exactly in our course, but going faster than our fastest speed, and coming closer and closer, until our view was blanketed by the mainmast. *We* could do nothing, of course, but wait and wait, mouths open . . . Nothing happened. An enemy salvo splashed down close on our starboard bow, but nobody heeded it. Then somebody laughed, and breaking the spell, we knew that it was somehow all right. The miracle, for it really seemed miraculous, was accounted for in *Neptune*'s report: 'Torpedo was either deflected by the wash from *Neptune*'s propellers, or ran its range out. The latter is more likely.'[86]

Meanwhile, the Germans were lost to view in the pollution from guns, fires, funnels and smoke-generators, mingling with the gathering mist, and once again firing petered out.

As a means of defeating the torpedo attack, Jellicoe's manoeuvre was a complete success, and, had it occurred much earlier in the day, would be acclaimed as a skilful dodge to disarm the High Seas Fleet's destroyers. But, although it was (as we shall see) only brief, it also granted success to Scheer's extrication-bid, and, with sunset only forty minutes away, has assumed the proportions of the defining moment of the fleet-to-fleet encounter. By it, Sir John was widely held to have forsaken the Royal Navy's opportunity for unambiguous victory. "Mistakes may be forgiven, but God himself cannot forgive the hanger-back."[87]

*

The 1775 *Fighting Instructions* said:

> If the Enemy be put to the Run, <u>and the Admiral thinks it convenient</u> the whole Fleet shall follow them, he will make all the Sail he can himself after the Enemy, and take down the Signal for the Line of Battle, and fire two Guns out of his Fore-chase; and all the Flag-ships are to do the same: Then every Ship in the Fleet is to use his best Endeavour to come up with the Enemy, and lay them on Board.[88]

It was to be a source of bewilderment, both to the British public and to a sizeable section of the naval service, that at 7.35 p.m. on May the 31st, 1916, the admiral did not think it convenient.

At this juncture Edward Hawke or Adam Duncan (and, perhaps, David Farragut) would have turned the Grand Fleet, by divisions, towards the enemy. This manoeuvre could have been done before the torpedoes arrived, greatly reducing the fleet's total target-profile and affording individual ships lateral room to 'combe the tracks'. Upon rediscovering the enemy's rear (as it now was) divisions could have been turned far enough to port or starboard to reopen gunnery arcs. Two or three ships might have caught torpedoes, but, as Hawke and Duncan demonstrated, at Quiberon Bay (1759) and Camperdown (1797) respectively, victories will not be won late in the day without radical action and a disregard of incidental risks.

Jellicoe's turn-away has been defended almost as strongly as it has been attacked,[89] and no doubt some of the criticism has been misinformed. But to spare the enemy from one's primary weapon-system through fear of his secondary weapon-system does seem, *prima facie*, an unsound proposition. Furthermore all three of Sir John's squadronal vice-admirals (Burney, Sturdee and Jerram) had misgivings about the turn[90] (Beatty's people were furious). And as Jellicoe allegedly blamed himself, in his post-battle depression, for missing "one of the greatest opportunities a man ever had",[91] and as he later (and more sensibly) pondered whether he should not have turned the fleet *towards* by divisions,[92] even by the 'Jellicoe-school' yardstick, there is a case to answer.

We have already considered (in Chapter 2) the heavy responsibilities which weighed on Sir John's shoulders: how the High Seas Fleet, although a thorn in Britannia's flesh, was relatively benign in grand-strategic terms, and its destruction considerably less important than the preservation of the Grand Fleet 'in-being'. For Britain in 1916, the naval *status quo* was sustainable. Jellicoe was not a man to lead the Grand Fleet into any sort of ambush; and, even today, we study Jutland in the lee of the Royal Navy's command of the sea (or, at least, of those seas necessary to the Allied war effort) in 1914–18.

We also understand something of the cultural provenance of his authoritarian preoccupation with order and control.

What is less accessible is the evolution, in the higher echelons of the Royal Navy, of perceptions regarding 'flotilla' warfare. It has recently emerged that, although Fisher's original agenda for superseding battle-ships with torpedo-carrying craft had been frustrated by the momentum which gathered behind dreadnoughts, the matter was under reconsideration in the months before Jellicoe left the Admiralty to take over the Grand Fleet in 1914.[93] (This recantation was presaged by the enhancement of secondary batteries from 4-inch to 6-inch in capital ships after 1911 – a compromise of the all-big-gun principle, pointing to ships whose size and expense threatened to become prohibitive.)

There is also a 'fantasy' problem with Grand Fleet Battle Orders. While Jellicoe correctly understood that a fleet action would have to be forced upon Scheer – that was obvious – the conception in GFBOs of the ensuing tournament was that the High Seas Fleet would fight it as a set-piece duel, by steering a parallel course and awaiting the pleasure of British gunnery-officers, like coconuts in a shy. Insofar as Jellicoe had considered the possibility that the Germans might try to escape such a contract, he had (as his letter to the Admiralty of October the 30th, 1914, demonstrates) resolved not to pursue. This we know was consonant with his command-and-control outlook, his over-dependence on signalling, his fire-control assumptions, etc. But with this stricture as a cornerstone of doctrine, Jellicoe's staff must have known among themselves that the chances of a decisive pay-off rested on the High Seas Fleet's behaving in a manner contrary to its own best interests, and were therefore more remote than the rank and file of the Grand Fleet were encouraged to believe. Part of the shock of Jutland was the discovery of this mismatch of expectations, which, to some (the bullish and the strategically naïve), seemed little short of a betrayal.

The 'Admiralty letter' brings us to the specific, material reasons for his reluctance to pursue a retreating enemy: fear of a submarine trap, fear of mass attacks by destroyers, and fear of floating mines.

> There can be no doubt whatever that they will endeavour to make the fullest use of these weapons in a fleet action, especially since they possess an actual superiority over us in these particular directions.

The 'submarine trap' idea (disregarding its detailed difficulties) is hardly applicable to Jutland, since, as Jellicoe knew perfectly well, Beatty had been steering Scheer for an hour and a half before the battle-fleets met. The torpedoes and mines, however, both amounted to *idées fixes* in the Commander-in-Chief's mind.

The growing respect for flotilla warfare, at the Admiralty in 1914, has just been mentioned. There was, also, more than a semantic difference in the fact that the Germans had *torpedo-boats*, whereas the British had torpedo-boat *destroyers*; and Jellicoe calculated that the Grand Fleet would face eight flotillas (88 boats), and 440 torpedoes, all at once. To seal the matter, the new German C-in-C, Reinhard Scheer, was a torpedo specialist by trade, and Jellicoe's own torpedo people had told him – they would, wouldn't they? – that 35% of torpedoes fired indiscriminately at a fleet in close order would hit (which might be true if no one took avoiding action).

To counter this onslaught, the ploy of turning away held big defensive advantages over turning towards: the missiles would be approaching at a 30-knots slower relative speed, making them much easier to avoid, and some of them might (as they did) run out of puff before they reached the fleet. All this rationalization made detailed, on-paper sense. But while it is the job of staff-officers to foresee hazards, it is the role of the admiral to review their warnings in the wider context (at Matapan, Cunningham listened patiently to his staff and then damned them for a "pack of yellow-livered skunks"). Jellicoe was himself a natural staff-officer, and his caution compounded theirs.

Then there was the question of floating mines. The origins of this terror are obscure – perhaps the number of useless mines which had broken loose from their moorings in the early days of the war – but Jellicoe believed that the Germans, in retreat, would strew in their wake masses of mines, and that the water through which they had passed must therefore be avoided at all costs. The High Seas Fleet carried no mines.

A more recent naval warrior, Captain Christopher Craig (commodore in command of British naval forces in the 1991 Gulf War, and no relation of Evan-Thomas's flag-captain) has made a remark which seems appropriate to Jellicoe's wariness of closing the enemy at Jutland: "It is axiomatic in risk-taking that you should always concentrate upon dealing with the threat you *know* to exist, rather than those you *imagine*."[94] This is perhaps a little too glib. Craig's own primary task in the Gulf was that of preparing the way for American capital ships by overseeing mine clearance, a business in which threats are assumed to exist on a percentage scale of probability until proved otherwise. And it was partly mines (and wholly underwater threats) which Jellicoe was assuming to exist after Scheer's second turn-away.

But what we can say for certain is that this career-technocrat was misled by 'rationalist' doctrine (for which he was ultimately responsible) into getting grossly wrong the threat-percentage in regard to both mines and torpedoes. His sleepless nights were visited by a fearful array of underwater weapons, and, as a consequence, for seventeen critical minutes, while the fate and future of the High Seas Fleet – or, at least, of a substantial part of it – hung in the balance, he helped Scheer to disengage.

*

After steering south-east (twelve points at variance from the enemy's course) for ten minutes, Jellicoe turned back, five points to SbyW, expecting to find the High Seas Fleet where he had left it. There was no sign of it, and he realized that something had gone wrong, although he did not yet know what, and nobody was telling him anything. At 7.40, after another five minutes, he turned a further three points to southwest – a course which might have been of some use at 7.23. Still nothing. Scheer was still drawing away, albeit more slowly. Presently a signal came in from Goodenough reporting the enemy heading west, and another from Beatty (at the south end of the line) reporting them north-west of the BCF, and so, at 8.0 p.m., seven minutes before sunset (*Iron Duke* time), Jellicoe at last turned four more points to due west.

In this period there occurred another 'Beatty' incident. VABCF was not actually in sight of the enemy at around 7.40, but knew where he must be and was keen to press ahead towards the west, although he was rightly reluctant to do so without the close support of a few battleships. To the north-east of him was Sir Martyn Jerram's van squadron, trailing its coat rather aimlessly, or so it seemed from *Lion*. A range of insubordinate signals was mooted on *Lion*'s compass-platform, but they settled for a moderate (and verbose) "SUBMIT VAN OF BATTLESHIPS FOLLOW BATTLECRUISERS. WE CAN THEN CUT OFF WHOLE OF ENEMY'S BATTLE-FLEET". This was sent by W/T to Jellicoe at 7.47, but did not reach his hand until 8.01, by which time the C-in-C was in the process of turning the fleet west. Jellicoe responded to Beatty's request by ordering Jerram to close the battlecruisers, which the vice-admiral did, turning two points back to port to do so.

The 'Jellicoe school' later deplored Beatty's posturing (as they saw it) and pointed out that by the time the signal was received it was redundant and that it had the unfortunate result of diverting Jerram somewhat away from the enemy.[95] These calculations, as far as they go, are correct. But the delay in the signal's reception (owing to internal processes in *Iron Duke*) cannot be put in the balance against Beatty, and does not invalidate his perception of an opportunity being lost at 7.47. The matter was to rankle on both sides of the debate for several years.

Scheer, meanwhile, could not afford to be driven further out to the west. He now knew that he was dealing with the whole of the Grand Fleet, and, although increasingly comforted by the clamp-down of visibility, knew that he had to get his fleet into friendly waters by day-break. He gradually altered round to the south-west and then south. His pre-dreadnoughts had been placed in the van by the reversal of course, and his half-demolished battlecruisers, having to some extent cut the corner, were now between them and the enemy. There were no more head-on clashes, but there were a few brief, disjointed outbreaks of firing in which the Germans were rebuffed off their southerly course.

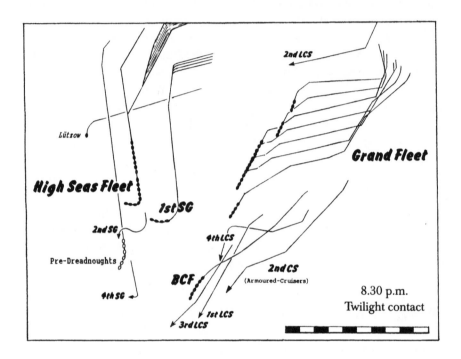

The sporadic gunfire on the peripheries proved to Jellicoe that the High Seas Fleet (or some of it) was still close, although its formation, course, speed and readiness for battle were all unknown. Were the fog suddenly lifted and daylight miraculously restored, the enemy would be clearly seen, just over there, within easy range of $13\frac{1}{2}$- and 15-inch ordnance. But in the prevailing conditions, with lanes of visibility alternating erratically with almost total clamp-down, to carry on advancing would be like taking heavy cavalry into a hostile terrain of woodlands and hedgerows; and the Grand Fleet was in no kind of predicament which could justify such recklessness. The predicament was all Scheer's. Jellicoe therefore eased round towards south-west and then south, as dusk crept forward by the minute.

*

Somewhere to the north, *Warspite* wirelessed to RA5BS that she had regained possession of herself and was good for 16 knots, and would rejoin the fleet if she knew where it was. As the fleet was steaming away from her at 17 knots, Evan-Thomas told her to go home. So she set course west, and presently came across the destroyer *Defender* (which had a 12-inch shell lodged under one of her boilers) with *Onslow* in tow. *Defender*'s captain briefly attempted to fall in with the battleship, but the latter soon drew ahead and out of sight. The two disabled destroyers, the halt and the lame, would reach Aberdeen nearly two days later. Not far away the seaplane-carrier *Engadine* was starting the same long haul with the huge deadweight of *Warrior* behind her.

Also far astern of the action was the wallowing *Acasta*. After the close-shaves and near-misses of her 'journey' through the fleet, her surroundings seemed like (as indeed they were) the site of some big public event after the crowds had gone, leaving behind litter and stillness. One or two strays were still picking among the debris. *Fearless* and *Galatea* both came by to offer help, but were waved off, and they hurried away. In the distance, a *Queen Elizabeth* could be made out, turning circles, but she, too, poked off after a while, leaving the little destroyer "feeling rather lonely". A periscope was sighted and fired at vigorously, but it was only a piece of wreckage. Below decks, stokers, waist-deep in water, laboured by candlelight on the unlikely project of reconnecting the steam supply. During the night sufficient repairs would be made to limp at 3 knots, and in a rising sea John Barron, too, would point his battered ship towards Scotland.[96]

Meanwhile, in the hiatus following Scheer's second withdrawal, there had been another easing of action-stations. Souvenir hunters came out and searched for shell-splinters. In *Colossus*, "orders were sent for ratings to go to the galley and collect bully-beef sandwiches and cocoa, which was very welcome. Torpedo people grew very bored and lay down on the deck where they could find space."[97] An officer in *Indomitable* resolved to allow only one gramophone into his turret next time: they had

> one in the gunhouse and one [below] in the working chamber, and during every lull in the action these two were started playing simultaneously, each with a different record. The result was one of the real horrors of the war.[98]

Well, it may have seemed so to him.

In ships mauled in the 'battlecruiser phase' they were still struggling to surmount damage and tend their wounded. As in *Warspite*, localized parts of *Barham*, *Malaya*, *Lion* and *Tiger* were abandoned as irredeemable outside a dockyard. *Malaya*'s main dressing-station was crowded with burns victims of the cordite fire. In *Lion*, Chatfield's bathroom was being used as an operating theatre and "was an awful sight [with] bits of body and arms and legs lying about".[99] (Bathrooms made good operating theatres, because they had fresh water, tiled floors and drain-holes.) In the same ship, a stoker whose leg had been blown off was distraught at losing the wad of money in his sock and made his first-aiders go back to find the missing limb.[100]

Midshipmen were sent on errands. The 'young gentleman' in *Malaya*'s torpedo control-tower took the opportunity to visit the starboard 6-inch gun battery.

> Everything was dark chaos. Most of the wounded had been taken away, but several of the killed were still there. The most ghastly part of the whole affair was the smell of burnt human flesh, which remained in the ship for weeks.[101]

From *Lion*'s foretop Anthony Combe was sent down to scavenge for some food. Dodging around the repair parties, he went aft and purloined a ham from the wardroom pantry, buttoned it into his monkey-jacket and made his way back to his eerie. Beatty caught sight of him sneaking up through the bridge, ham protruding from jacket, and, guessing that he had lifted said item from the admiral's pantry, called out, "Hey, you young blighter!" But Combe skipped up the foremast ladder and away, and Beatty's attention was drawn to some other matter. The sobriquet of 'The Snotty who Stole the Admiral's Ham' was not strictly deserved, but brought with it a certain kudos.[102]

Perhaps Beatty's attention had been drawn to the rediscovery, to the west, of the 1st SG. Hipper was trying to transfer from his destroyer to *Moltke*, his only still-sound battlecruiser, and his squadron had no way on. This plan was hastily shelved as once again $13\frac{1}{2}$- and 12-inch shells bowled in from almost invisible opponents to the east, hitting *Derfflinger* and *Seydlitz*. Some of Rear-Admiral Mauve's pre-dreadnoughts, beyond the 1st SG, also came into view, and *Schleswig-Holstein* and *Pommern* were both hit before they could melt back into the mist, although they made a spirited reply and scored an 11-inch hit on *Princess Royal*.

The Germans were seen by at least a few people in the van of the Battle Fleet astern of the BCF. In the "leading turret of the leading ship in the leading squadron of the Grand Fleet" (= A turret of Jerram's flagship, *King George V*) Sub-Lieutenant 'Smiler' Cunliffe

> saw the silhouettes of three battleships in the mist about 8,000 yards away on the starboard bow and positively identified them as German by the distinctive cranes between their funnels. He reported them to the bridge, but no action was taken and the chance slipped away.[103]

And it was about now that, in *Orion*, the subordinate flagship of Jerram's 2nd BS, Arthur Leveson's flag-lieutenant turned to the rear-admiral and said,

> 'Sir, if you leave the line now and turn towards, your name will be as famous as Nelson's.' But like Evan-Thomas, Leveson [who, long ago, had walked down *Victoria*'s side with John Jellicoe] had been schooled to obey; after a moment's hesitation he answered: 'We must follow the next ahead.'[104]

The Germans slipped away into the gloom, and Beatty declined to follow. This was to be the last engagement between capital ships until *Renown* opened fire at *Gneisenau* on April the 9th, 1940.

As the Germans retreated, they introduced the Grand Fleet to their superlative star-shells – an innovation unknown to the British – by firing one to signify their disengagement. In one of Beatty's light-cruisers, a junior officer of unusual mental detachment thought it

> really lovely . . . after all the furious deep red displays of pyrotechnics we had been treated to for over three hours, this gentle, cool, pure white Star of Bethlehem was quite like the spirit of peace coming to brood over us.[105]

It augured badly for the approaching hours of darkness.

22

Night Inaction

"It looked lovely in the dark, and three ships blew up. It was a pretty sight, watching the illuminations in the sky."

As dusk advanced, Sir John Jellicoe had no intention of seeking to re-engage, and almost nobody has suggested that he was wrong. The Grand Fleet's crushing mathematical preponderance was only realizable (only *organizable*) in good visibility, and night-fighting has always been the resort of the side disadvantaged in daylight. The Royal Navy's first experiments in gunnery by searchlight had taken place back in 1885, in the Mediterranean,[1] and had not proceeded by leaps and bounds since. The British fleet had little incentive to plan for, or engage in, conditions which favoured it least (although some senior destroyer officers must have recalled the days, before the flotillas became servants of the Home Fleet, when they had trained for little else, and many of their ships were still painted black). Even Beatty's standing orders, of 1918, said: "Owing to the risk from torpedo fire, it is undesirable for heavy ships to engage at night if it can be avoided";[2] and Sir John had long reconciled himself – had he not? – to leaving off action, should he meet the enemy late in the day, and to finishing the business at leisure in the morning.[3]

For its part, the High Seas Fleet, which *had* to some extent trained for night combat, and whose inferiority would have mattered least in the close-quarters anarchy of darkness, was set on the single project of getting home. Through right or wrong causes, therefore, the two commanders-in-chief were once again united in uneasy consensus: for the next six or seven hours, both wished for a battle-fleet truce.

For the meantime, Jellicoe did not seriously doubt that he could

472

remain in control. His giant battle-fleet was still fresh, virtually unscathed and supremely confident, and it blocked the enemy's best escape route. By any criterion other than that of active engagement, the Germans' position was a desperate one. And if Sir John had trained his juniors to shadow and dog the enemy during the night, to take charge of localized events without the orders which distant seniors could scarcely issue and signalling scarcely deliver, and to report and report again by wireless – and if he were favoured with reasonable visibility at dawn – then the matter was still as good as in the bag. But the Germans had twice eluded him with disconcerting ease. And there were those brooding, critical 'ifs'.

How should Jellicoe dispose his fleet overnight? The sun would rise a few minutes after 3.0 a.m. Where should the Grand Fleet be then? How would the High Seas Fleet seek to escape the *Wurstkessel* during its nocturnal stay of execution?

Placing himself in his opponent's shoes was not one of Jellicoe's strong points, but logical reasoning was; and, as darkness enveloped *Iron Duke*'s bridge, the problem probably looked like this:

1. In darkness, after several hours of skirmishing (with the consequent degradation of his DR plot), and perhaps with compasses put out by gunfire, Scheer would hardly try to find the seaward end of some secret swept-channel through the Heligoland Bight minefields.

2. With damaged and crippled ships (which he undoubtedly had), the long haul up through the Skagerrak and round Denmark was unlikely to attract him; and, besides, there was little Jellicoe could do about it if the Germans absconded to the north: he couldn't be everywhere.

3. Sir John therefore need concern himself with two possible lines of escape for the High Seas Fleet:

a. The 'Horns Reef route' 80 miles to the south-east. This was clearly the most immediate solution to Scheer's predicament, were it not for the stark fact of the Grand Fleet's sitting massively in the way.

b. The 'Ems route' along the Frisian coast 150 miles to the SSW. This would negate Jellicoe's 'Horns Reef' advantage of position, but there would be twice as far to go to reach safe water. The Grand Fleet might be able to turn the tables again, and any crippled ships Scheer was nursing would almost certainly be overtaken by Beatty tomorrow morning.

4. Although Scheer might choose the Ems route, for Jellicoe to go rushing off on that assumption would be to leave wide open the door to the Horns Reef, and might well involve barging into the High Seas Fleet by mistake in the dark.

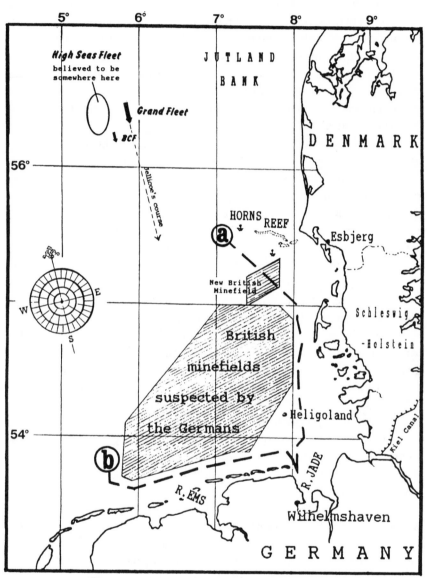

How would Scheer get home?

The choice facing the British Commander-in-Chief in second-guessing Scheer, and the value-scale of consequences of his being right or wrong, may be depicted in the form of a decision-tree:

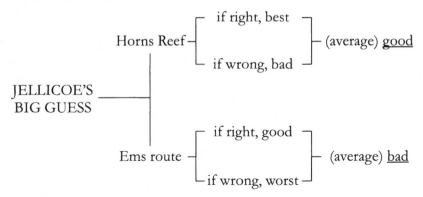

The decision might have been slightly easier had the Harwich destroyer force been motoring towards the entrance to the Ems route, instead of languishing in Harwich; but, even so, Jellicoe made the rational choice, although his solution was a partial compromise. With the High Seas Fleet somewhere close to the west, and its most desirable objective to the south-east, he would continue steaming south, and prepare to renew action at dawn. At the same time he would not lose much ground on the enemy if the latter went for the Ems after all.

In one respect his formula was flawed: his continued speed of 17 knots would outpace the German pre-dreadnoughts (not to mention damaged units) and cause him to draw slowly ahead of the High Seas Fleet. In fact nobody had reported the older battleships, and Sir John may have been unaware of their presence. Also, the last daylight exchange of heavy gunfire, that between Beatty and Hipper/Mauve, in the two fleets' respective vans, probably gave both Cs-in-C the impression that the other's main fleet was further south than was really the case.

*

At 9.17 p.m. Jellicoe ordered the Battle Fleet to take up night-steaming formation, with squadrons disposed abeam, one mile apart. This compact formation has been criticized as presenting a concentrated target-area for torpedo attack, and prohibiting radical evasive action.[4] In fact Jellicoe's main concern was to avoid 'friendly-fire' incidents in the night, and this was the reason why he sent the Grand Fleet's destroyer flotillas to take up station a full five miles astern. (In the 1913 Manoeuvres, his destroyers had tried to torpedo his battleships.) Even as these changes were being effected, there was a brief flare-up of small gunfire to starboard, as the German 7th and the British 4th Destroyer Flotillas brushed together and quickly parted.

Apart from the breakup of the line-of-battle into squadrons, and the relegation of the destroyers, the night-time arrangement was mostly a case of living with existing dispositions. Owing to *Marlborough*'s speed problem, which grew worse during the night, her division of the 2nd BS (in the BF's left-hand column) fell progressively astern until it was level with the 5th BS, which was following the main fleet with Goodenough's 2nd LCS on its own starboard quarter. Following somewhere astern of everyone was the armoured-cruiser *Black Prince*, last seen heading off into the yonder, allegedly damaged, from Windy Corner. Ahead, and to the south-west of the Battle Fleet, ten miles out on *Iron Duke*'s starboard bow, Beatty's six battlecruisers, the 2nd CS, and the 1st and 3rd LCSs conformed to Jellicoe's course and speed. The minelayer *Abdiel* was sent off to the Horns Reef channel.

Most of the capital ships now fell out from action-stations and closed up defence watches, with the main-armament only partially (although the secondary armament fully) manned. Many people were able to take a break, get some sort of a meal and, where applicable, start sorting out the mess.

In the three leading battlecruisers, "some of the scenes between decks in the vicinity of shell bursts beggar description" and the night "was spent in frenzied work on repairs".[5] In *Lion*, at the southern end of the fleet, the navigator, Commander Strutt, repaired to his cabin to find it completely gutted by fire. His only surviving possessions were the remains of his prized golf-clubs: a small pile of iron heads in the corner. Another officer was shaken to see the carnage of some of the living-spaces, regretted looking into the captain's bathroom, and then stepped into an immaculate wardroom, still laid out neatly for tea.

In *Princess Royal* the dead were laid out in the stokers' bathroom, so that their mates could identify them without disturbing the sick-bay.[6] "The duty which was found most difficult was that of collecting the dead, and the portions of the dead and wounded, after action." (*Chester*'s CO formed the view that "officers found it less difficult than did the men to steel themselves to carry out these duties . . . the morbid feeling of horror is more marked in the less educated mind."[7]) In *Tiger* a group of bodies was discovered some time after the fighting had stopped –

> bad hats, [who] stowed themselves away, instead of going on watch in the boiler room. They found a lonely and deserted spot in the middle of the ship and thought themselves safe, but a shell found them out . . . What a moral![8]

In the same ship there were still wiremen (electricians) stuck in a switch-board compartment with the flat above flooded and no other means of escape. They would be there for many hours yet.[9]

The other three battlecruisers and most of the Battle Fleet had no comparable traumas, but "there was an awful litter of stuff everywhere between decks, made by the shock of our broadsides dislodging loosely stowed gear". *Neptune*'s gunnery-officer was observed gazing speechlessly into his cabin: his tin hip-bath had broken from its deckhead stowage and demolished the electric radiator, while "all the drawers had shaken out, and his clothes were in a mêlée on the floor"; worse, in an excess of zeal, the fire-brigade had hosed the cabin with seawater and thoughtfully filled the bath.[10] In *Hercules* the Russian attaché's marine servant had spent the action down in a 12-inch magazine, and

> had not the faintest idea about the course of the battle. But certain occurrences had led him to the conclusion that we had sunk several enemy ships and suffered a number of hits. When I invited him to go and look for these he said he thought the repair parties had already repaired them.[11]

In *St Vincent*, the captain-of-the-foretop had fallen down a ladder and broken his nose – "which was a large one, so that, with it bandaged, he was a source of fun to his part-of-ship".[12]

In *Malaya*, at the rear of the fleet, when emergency lighting was finally provided to the starboard battery,

> it was a scene which cannot easily be forgotten – everything burnt black and bare; the gallery, canteen and drying-room bulkheads blown and twisted into the most grotesque shapes, and the whole deck covered by about 6 inches of water and dreadful debris; and permeating everywhere the awful stench of cordite fumes and of war.[13]

Meanwhile, below, the medical teams were losing burns cases. Surgeon-Lieutenant Lorimer was at his wits' end:

> I don't quite understand the immediate cause of death. We talk vaguely of shock, but I don't know that this explains it. A man will walk into a dressing station, or possibly be carried in, with face and hands badly scorched, not deeply burned or disfigured. One would call it a burn of the first degree. Very rapidly, almost as one looks, the face swells up, the looser parts of the skin become enormously swollen, the eyes are invisible through the great swelling of the lids, the lips enormous jelly-like masses, in the centre of which a button-like mouth appears. I have an idea that it must be due to the very high temperature of the burning cordite applied for a very short time. It is quite unlike any burns I have ever seen in civil life, and would be very easily avoided by using asbestos gloves and masks, or similar anti-fire substance.

(*Tiger*'s XO made a similar observation in his report, and white cotton anti-flash balaclavas and gauntlets became standard issue after Jutland.)

> The great cry is water. Not much pain, and that is easily subdued by morphia. There is then great and increasing restlessness, breathing rapid and shallow, and final collapse. The bodies stiffen in their twisted attitudes very rapidly. The scorched areas are confined to the exposed parts, face, head and hands; hair, beard and eyebrows burnt off. The skin of the hands, the whole epidermis including the nails peels off like a glove. In many cases one has to look twice to be certain that one is cutting off only the skin, and not the whole finger. In very few cases does the burning go any deeper than this. And yet they die and die very rapidly. Cases looking quite slight at first become rapidly worse and die in an appallingly short time.[14]

In *Barham*, Midshipman Royer Dick 'fell out' from the transmitting station and returned to the gunroom, hungry and exhausted, probably hoping to find tea still on the table. He found instead that a shell had exploded inside the compartment, and it was a total shambles. One detail impressed him: the gunroom butter-dish was embedded intact in the steel bulkhead, the butter still inside.[15]

Astern of the three *Queen Elizabeths*, the four light-cruisers of the 2nd LCS were still marvelling at their survival, unscathed, of an hour and a half of heavy shelling. In *Southampton*, Lieutenants Stephen King-Hall and Harold Burrough extemporized arrangements for controlling the guns in a night encounter, and then King-Hall curled up on the canvas cover of a signal-lamp, in a corner of the bridge.[16] It was dark, a fairly heavy mist was coming down,[17] and, for a time, all was quiet. "If only I had gone to my cabin [Goodenough afterwards remarked], had a glass of port and quietly thought out what the enemy was likely to do."[18]

Suddenly the navigator, Lieutenant Ralph Ireland, whispered to the commodore that they had company: against the faint after-tone of light to the west could be made out a line of ships, alarmingly close. King-Hall ran back to the after control-tower, to be greeted by young Haworth-Booth saying, "There are five Huns on the beam. What on earth is going on?"

The strangers – cruisers evidently – were converging. The nearest one was only about 1,000 yards away and had three funnels. There were seven three-funnelled light-cruisers in the Grand Fleet, and someone mentioned the armoured-cruiser *Donegal* (which had recently left the Grand Fleet). Who *were* they?

*

About the time Jellicoe ordered his night dispositions, Scheer marshalled his fleet as best he could (some of the battlecruisers seemed to

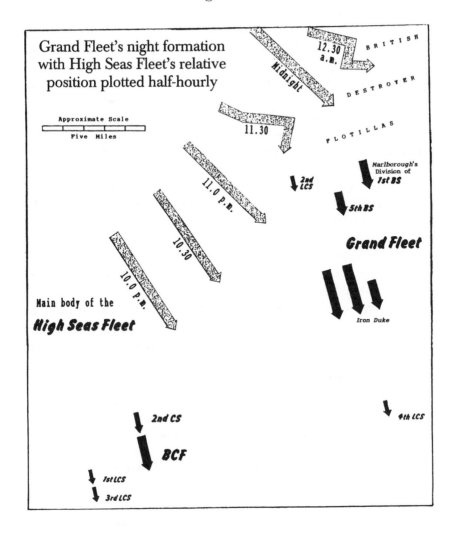

Grand Fleet's night formation with High Seas Fleet's relative position plotted half-hourly

Approximate Scale
Five Miles

have gone astray) and altered from south to a course of $SSE\frac{1}{4}E$, which led directly to the Horns Reef. It is not clear what was in his head at the time. He was opting for the escape route which could bring the earliest, and most complete, success, but which was the least likely to succeed. Historians argue as to whether he was being very cool or had gone into auto-pilot. He said the former, his flag-lieutenant the latter. There is certainly something of the 'riderless horse heading for home' about the High Seas Fleet's nocturnal movements; and if choosing the Horns Reef was not in itself an error, Scheer's making a bee-line for it was his fourth 'Jutland' decision which could, had the British been on the ball, have cost him his fleet.

Nobody knew the overall picture, or anything like it, but the High Seas Fleet was now astern of Beatty, and obliquely crossing the area between Beatty's wake and Jellicoe's formation, bearing down on the latter's rear. The two opposing battle-fleets were "steaming down the sides of a very long, very slender V",[19] with the Grand Fleet slightly further down its side than the High Seas Fleet. The most eastward German units, out on Scheer's port bow, were the five light-cruisers of Commodore Ludwig von Reuter's 4th Scouting Group. These were the ships trying to occupy the same water as the 2nd LCS.

Finally, Goodenough said, "I can't help who it is – fire!"[20]

The action is said to have lasted for three and a half minutes, though I doubt anyone timed it. *Dublin*, the ship next astern of *Southampton*, actually opened with guns and searchlights a second before the flagship. King-Hall saw shells slam into the target, 800 yards away, and caught a bizarre glimpse of a compartment inside her as her plating opened up. Powerful searchlights blazed back, straight in the eyes of the British gunlayers, followed by a hail of shellfire. German searchlight-and-gunnery coordination was one of the many unpleasant lessons of Jutland. *Southampton* was soon well alight with ammunition fires, one virtually under the bridge, and her upper-deck personnel were felled by splinters. King-Hall tried to summarize the indescribable:

> . . . then I tasted and experienced war in its elemental state. It was not nice. Then it was that for the first time in my life I had men killed and mangled at my side. One instant they were God's image, the next a mass of bloody flesh. These were men one knew, liked, had lived with for long monotonous months. Until 10.30 p.m. on May 31st I didn't really know what war was. I thought I did, but I didn't.[21]

With thirty-five killed and forty-one wounded, and burning like a beacon, *Southampton* reeled away to port, expecting to be finished at any moment. But the enemy's fire was petering out: *Nottingham* and *Birmingham* had left their own searchlights off and, as a result, had enjoyed undisturbed rapid shooting, and the Germans, too, were veering away. Furthermore, *Southampton* had put a torpedo 'in the post', almost as an afterthought, and there was a big underwater explosion and the leading German's lights went out. *Frauenlob* capsized and sank, leaving five survivors out of a company of more than three hundred.

Apart from *Southampton's* fires, darkness and silence took over once more. On paper, the British had won this squall of killing – if only by virtue of that torpedo – though to describe anyone as the victor of such an affair has little meaning.

*

Historians have different ideas of how the chaotic events astern of the Grand Fleet on that short, moonless night may be divided into separate spasms of violence; and analyses appear to range from three to fourteen. It doesn't matter much for our purposes. Nobody was in control. All involved could only respond to events – often with only a few seconds' warning – and try to sell themselves as dearly as they knew how. And there were several collisions: British-German, British-British, and German-German.

The British were disfavoured (for several ships, fatally) by inadequate practice in night-fighting. The Germans had got hold of the Grand Fleet's two-letter challenge signal,[22] and used it back, whereas their own recognition sign was an array of coloured lights (briefly switched on) which was impossible to replicate. And British destroyers stood out in dayglo-black in the glare of German star-shell. But the worst defect was, perhaps, the sheer lack of information: most flotillas had been stationed on the off-side of the battle-fleet during the daylight clashes and had thus seen nothing of the enemy, and it would have helped if Jellicoe had issued a situation appraisal (and 'night intentions') at nightfall. The picture was just about clear enough to have most look-outs watching to starboard to start with, which was better than nothing.

The most prolonged session erupted shortly before midnight (GMT), when the night was already more than half over. This was when the left side of the V butted into the right, and began to push its way through. It started in a way similar to the 2nd LCS's brief engagement, described above.

Captain Charles Wintour, in the destroyer *Tipperary*, was leading the 4th DF and keeping loose station on the 5th BS, dimly discernible ahead of him, when to his west a line of huge darkened ships materialized, evidently on a converging course. Again there was the awful hanging question of who they were. In reply to her challenge *Tipperary* received a deluge of 5.9- and 3.5-inch shells from the port-side secondary guns of the battleships *Westfalen* and *Nassau*, augmented by the light-cruisers *Rostock*, *Elbing* and *Hamburg*, which found themselves between the German dreadnoughts and the British flotilla.

"The first salvo swept away *Tipperary*'s fore bridge and bow gun",[23] and "a huge shower of sparks and flames shot up, absolutely enveloping the ship from our sight".[24] In a few seconds she was blazing and drifting in a cloud of smoke and escaping steam. For a couple of vital minutes the next senior officer, Commander Walter Allen in *Broke*, was convinced that this was an appalling 'friendly-fire' mistake, but then *Westfalen*'s searchlights strayed onto one of her own consorts and resolved that issue. Meanwhile, *Tipperary*, *Spitfire* and one or two other units got off torpedoes, and the Germans turned away. There is disagreement as to whether *Elbing* was, or was not, now struck by a torpedo. The Germans say not – an assertion hotly disputed by *Spitfire*:

> much to our joy and relief [our torpedo] was seen to get the second enemy ship between the after funnel and the mainmast, and she seemed to stop firing, heel over and all her lights went out; but instead of the violent explosion we expected to see there appeared a kind of dull red glow, and then fire seemed to spread forward and after from where she was hit.

Garland's torpedo-crew also claimed it: their torpedo hit the target, they said, "just beneath her mainmast, causing her searchlights to go out immediately".[25] *Sparrowhawk*'s crew claimed it as well.

The issue is neither here nor there for the future of *Elbing*. She veered away, into the path of the dreadnought fleet, and was rammed by the battleship *Posen*. With both engine-rooms flooded, and listing badly, she drifted helplessly away 'down' the German line.

The German searchlights were switched off, and for a short time there was darkness, except for the blazing pyre of *Tipperary*, towards which *Spitfire*'s Lieutenant-Commander Clarence Trelawney now steered with the idea of helping. Other eyes, however, were attracted to the beacon, and, as Trelawney regained his night-vision, he realized that there was a large ship bearing down on him for the purpose of ramming. He "ordered 'Hard-a-starboard. Full speed ahead both', and, leaning over the bridge screen, shouted 'Clear the foc'sle.'"[26] The ships connected port-bow to port-bow.

The impact rolled the battleship *Nassau* several degrees to starboard, causing the salvo now fired by her forward turret at maximum depression to pass over the destroyer, although the blast reduced the latter's upperworks to a tangle of scrap-iron and killed most people on the bridge. For her part, the destroyer was rolled "over to starboard as no sea ever made her roll", and then scraped her way down her assailant's side while boats, davits, etc., were torn away. As fast as the crisis had arisen, the little ship found herself alone, on fire in several places, with every electric alarm-bell ringing at once and twenty feet of German plating on her foredeck.

They started to pull themselves together. The captain was discovered "alive though badly knocked about", having been blown from the bridge onto the upper deck. With fire-hoses playing around him and without anaesthetic, the young surgeon-probationer set to amputating the leg of a seaman who had also been found alive, but badly injured, amongst the wreckage. Then somebody shouted, "Look out!", and, bearing down on them at full speed was another huge ship, a vision from Hell:

a mass of fire from foremast to mainmast, on deck and between decks. Flames were issuing out of her from every corner. She [missed *Spitfire* by a few feet, and] tore past us with a roar like a motor roaring up hill in low gear, and the very crackling and heat of the flames could be heard and felt.

Because of her two widely spaced funnels, they took her for a German battlecruiser, but she must have been *Black Prince* with her centre funnels missing. (She is thought to have tried to take station on German battleships by mistake.) Soon afterwards, "there came an explosion from the direction in which she had gone".[27] There were no survivors.

Meanwhile, command of the 4th DF had devolved to *Broke*'s Commander Allen. It was a brief reign. He pressed in for another attack. Again, there was an identification problem, and *Broke* was hammered before she could gain a firing position. Careering out of control, she collided with *Sparrowhawk*, cutting half-way through the ship, and they lay locked together, still under fire. A sub-lieutenant from *Sparrowhawk*'s upper deck found himself thrown onto *Broke*'s foc'sle. ("Who are you?" asked someone in the dark.) An element of farce entered the proceedings. Each captain supposed his ship to be sinking and gave orders for his crew to get onboard the other. "About 20 of our ship's company went into *Broke* and about 15 men from *Broke* came across into us." While they were thus engaged, *Contest* piled into *Sparrowhawk*'s stern, irretrievably jamming the latter's rudder hard over.[28] Presently they drifted apart, still lit by the burning *Tipperary*.

Not far away, another German light-cruiser was left crippled, with her boiler-rooms partly flooded. Command of the 4th DF had further devolved onto Commander Reginald Hutchinson of *Achates*, who with great tenacity had led the six remaining units back in a third attack in which *Ardent* and *Fortune* were efficiently demolished at close range, but which put a torpedo into *Rostock*.

> Soon after midnight the van of the German battlefleet reached a point which the British fleet [= the two rearmost groups, led respectively by *Barham* and *Marlborough*] had passed hardly a quarter of an hour earlier, and then entered the gap between the latter and its [destroyers], without anybody in either the British or German battlefleets becoming aware of this circumstance.[29]

Among the most unaware was Commander Malcolm Goldsmith of *Lydiard*, leading the combined 9th & 10th half-flotilla. He was even unaware that his original group of five destroyers had attracted so many strays that he was now actually leading a line of twelve. He was, in addition, convinced that the 4th Flotilla flare-up to the west had been a ghastly all-British affair. When he sighted the towering, shadowy masses of a line of dreadnoughts, he assumed they were the 5th BS and shaped a course to pass ahead of them, with the intention of taking station on their starboard side. The manoeuvre was well calculated for five ships, all right even for ten, but the last two units, *Petard* and *Turbulent*, found themselves being trampled down by the van of the High Seas Fleet.

Petard rang-on full-ahead and managed to swerve across, although the Germans opened a blaze of searchlights and shellfire at her as she tried to speed away into the night. *Turbulent* was run down by *Westfalen*, with no survivors. Goldsmith, in the only really conspicuous British lapse of 'destroyer' initiative, failed both to turn round and attack, and to report by wireless to Jellicoe.[30]

In fleet terms, a few destroyers, plus or minus – even the odd cruiser – made little difference. For the British, the main issue was the failure to interpret what was happening and inform the Commander-in-Chief – in the destroyers themselves, certainly, but, even more pointedly, in those battleships in the rear of the Grand Fleet which had a grandstand view of the show and nothing else to do.

*

On the compass-platforms of the 5th BS and *Marlborough*'s division of the 1st BS officers watched the fireworks and drank cocoa. ("'Course, they 'ad Cadbury's, not like the Pusser's stuff" which ratings had to drink.[31])

Malaya's Captain Boyle saw "enemy big ships" and identified a *Westfalen*-class dreadnought battleship.[32] Sub-Lieutenant Caslon was on the bridge with him. They watched an attack

> almost astern of us, at about 12.45 a.m. Firing suddenly broke out, and it was soon obvious that it was a destroyer attack on larger ships. The large ships were firing hard and a few minutes later one destroyer blew up. Then a lot of guns fired together, and in the flash we saw that the large ship had cranes between the masts [denoting a German battleship]. I was on the bridge at this time, as this was my night station, and there was a general cry of 'Hun!' The same flash illuminated the destroyers – I could see them lying quite close to the Germans – the one which blew up was the *Turbulent*, and, as I watched, the next in line (the *Petard*) was badly hit. [They must have been *Ardent* and *Fortune*.]
>
> Immediately afterwards the leading German ship put a searchlight on us. It was only on us for a few seconds, but at once he altered course right round to port, and the whole line followed and were lost to sight. I don't know to this day what ships they were. We certainly thought they were battleships, but at night time everything is distorted in regard to size and distance, and they may have been the new cruiser, which also had cranes.[33]

From B turret, Lieutenant Brind

saw and heard several of our destroyer attacks on the Germans. One especially, we had an extremely close view of. Some of the German shell fired at our destroyers fell among us. I have a vivid recollection of these destroyers dashing into blinding searchlights and into a perfectly furious fire. The leading boat was hit badly & was soon ablaze from stem to stern. The others seemed to make good their escape after firing their torpedoes. We saw and felt heavy explosions as though a torpedo had hit, and one ship was actually seen to sink. One of these explosions actually lit up the whole sky. It seemed almost impossible to know what was going on around us, and which was friend or foe. But as so much was happening, we thought it absolutely certain that we should meet the enemy in the morning.[34]

One of these explosions registered on the paper roll in *Malaya*'s barograph.

Valiant's Captain Woollcombe saw "heavy firing" on three separate occasions, and identified two German cruisers "apparently steering to the eastward at a high speed".[35] His navigator, Commander Geoffrey Freyberg, heard "a terrific noise of gunfire to starboard" at about 11 p.m.

Flashes of guns and searchlights told him that it was the HSF crashing through the destroyer flotillas that were guarding the Grand Fleet's rear. There could be no question at the time that it could be anything but the High Seas Fleet. 'We thought "Ah! We've got them again!" Our guns were sighted: we were within easy range – provided we didn't hit our own ships as well as the enemy.' But no orders came to engage. No orders came even to turn and cut off the German fleet which was clearly making for the northern channel.[36]

And, in Lieutenant Duthy's words, "the sky was brilliantly lit up by the flashes of the guns".[37]

Barham's Captain Craig alluded to "constant attacks by torpedo craft on ships, first to the westward, and then to the northward, and about 0.45 a.m. an immense explosion to the NNE".[38] Rear-Admiral Evan-Thomas recorded

heavy firing [at 10.15] a little abaft the starboard beam, which I surmised to be attacks by enemy destroyers on our light-cruisers and destroyers . . . At 10.39, heavy firing was observed on the starboard quarter, and destroyers appeared to be attacking the cruisers. At 11.35, a further attack was seen further off nearly right astern.[39]

A petty-officer thought "it looked lovely in the dark, and three ships blew up. It was a pretty sight watching the illuminations in the sky."[40]

We will return to *Barham*. There were other spectators.

As the night wore on, and the Germans pushed their way from one alarm to another across the rear of the Grand Fleet, *Marlborough*'s foursome (to port of the 5th BS) became the closest to the action. A witness in the foretop of Vice-Admiral Burney's flagship later wrote of

> signs of actions being fought to starboard or astern of us most of the night. There was firing on our starboard beam at 10.15 p.m., and again at 10.40; and 11.40 gunfire was reported astern, and at 12.10 a very heavy explosion, like a ship blowing up, was seen and heard, accompanied by heavy gunfire.

And in *Agincourt*, the rearmost ship of that group, Lieutenant Cunninghame-Graham

> could see and hear heavy firing on our starboard quarter and we also saw a large ship passing down our starboard side. This as far as I know was not reported to the C-in-C by anyone. Looking back it seems quite extraordinary that this single and obvious duty was neglected.[41]

Even battleships in the main body, six or seven miles further away from the fighting and formed around *Iron Duke* – *Vanguard, Conqueror, Colossus* and *Bellerophon* – certainly saw the loom of gunflashes and starshell astern and some of them lined up their guns, although, for reasons of distance and mist, details were not discernible; and ships in close company can be forgiven for not reporting what must have been visible to the flagship.

The critical failure was the omission of those senior officers in the rear of the Grand Fleet, who were in a position to observe, to alert the Commander-in-Chief to the possibility that this was more than just his destroyers defending the fleet from German torpedo-boats; and on those officers must rest much of the blame for Scheer's blundering through the rear of the British fleet 'undetected'. So compelling is it to condemn them, that one keeps looking for some mitigating circumstance.

Jellicoe's criticism was muted. He always tried to be loyal to subordinates (notably to Evan-Thomas), and he was, of course, incriminated through his failure to train them in their wider duties. He ventured that "Captain Boyle of *Malaya* should have reported sighting enemy large ships",[42] but directed disproportionate ire at the Admiralty for withholding ("*almost hourly*") information which, he claimed, "would have led me to alter course during the night for the Horn reef".[43] (The Admiralty told Jellicoe Scheer's correct course and speed at 10.41 p.m., and although the execrable Captain Jackson failed to pass on certain 'follow-up' decrypts, the picture did not fundamentally change during the night. Jellicoe was exaggerating the Admiralty's omissions and his respect for its data.)

In fact Algernon Boyle *did* report the heavy ships – to his own senior officer – by shaded lamp via *Valiant*,[44] and we know that *Barham*'s damaged wireless had been restored to working order, for she had exchanged signals with *Warspite* earlier.

Nearly twenty years later, *Barham*'s captain was goaded into writing this defence of RA5BS in the *RUSI Journal*:

> It is doubtful whether the various observations of enemy ships made by ships of our battlefleet ought to have been reported to the C-in-C. I was on the bridge all night with my Admiral, and we came to the conclusion that the situation was known to the C-in-C and that the attacks were according to plan. A stream of wireless reports from ships in company with the C-in-C seemed superfluous and uncalled for. The unnecessary use of wireless was severely discouraged as being likely to disclose our position to the enemy. The same reasoning probably influenced the *Marlborough*'s division. This may have been an error of judgement but cannot be termed 'amazing neglect'. In any case the impression in the 5th BS was that the enemy were following astern of our fleet and that we were in the best position to resume action at daylight. It is very doubtful whether, if the C-in-C had got the reports from the *Malaya* and the *Valiant*, he would have been in a position to conclude definitely that the enemy were making for the Horns Riff.[45]

He went on to argue that, anyway, the fog off the Horns Reef the next morning would have made a fleet intervention "exceedingly difficult" – which is probably correct but sublimely irrelevant to *Barham*'s failure to keep Jellicoe informed at midnight.

Notwithstanding the blame which may be attachable to certain senior officers, we should also look critically at the specialized business of wireless-telegraphy at Jutland.[46]

Years later, Admiral Sir Angus Cunninghame-Graham wrote a combined condemnation of those senior officers and exoneration of W/T and of signals specialists. If only the former had had more regard for the latter (he would have us believe) all would have been well.[47] Sir Angus was a career signaller and had an agenda. After the battle, he qualified in signalling and served as a flag-lieutenant, and subsequently commanded the Signal School. He had to adopt a position from which

a. there was nothing wrong with W/T as a means of communication,

b. no blame was attachable to qualified signals personnel, and

c. the entire blame must therefore be placed upon the senior commanders.

With regard to (c) he has a strong and obvious case, but what about (a) and (b)?

Some signals of critical importance at Jutland took uselessly long periods of time to be delivered. We had two examples in the last chapter: when Goodenough's warning about the return of the High Seas Fleet (at around 7.0 p.m.) reached Jellicoe's hand, the Germans had been and gone; and Beatty's controversial invitation to follow the BCF, also, was overtaken by events before the C-in-C read it.

These delays were, as already suggested, largely due to internal 'processing' congestion in *Iron Duke*. There is also evidence that external conditions were, at times, extremely difficult and success very uncertain. The destroyer *Faulknor* tried to report, soon after 2.0 a.m. (the very last chance for the Grand Fleet to cut off the enemy), but her transmissions were jammed by the Germans, and her officers had much else on their plate. And a telegraphist in one of Goodenough's light-cruisers later said that

> as the fleets were in very close proximity, the noise in the headphones was absolutely deafening. So much so that we had to keep relieving the operators after a stint of about ten minutes' duration. Many ships were transmitting at full power at one and the same time, so it became almost impossible to either send or receive a complete message.[48]

But underlying these problems was an organizational weakness which has been mentioned in Chapter 17 and which handicapped communications 'attitude'. At the time of Jutland, while qualified signallers (who, by then, included most flag-lieutenants) were the products of the Signal School in *Victory*, qualified W/T operators were still the products of *Vernon*; and "the dominant conception was still of W/T as apparatus allied to other electrical equipment, rather than an instrument of command."[49] As in *Titanic*, four years earlier, the correct dynamics between the work of the W/T office and the business conducted on the bridge had yet to be fully acknowledged.

The W/T people had resisted amalgamation on the grounds that their best ratings would tend to be 'borrowed' to augment the personnel on the bridge (an occurrence not unknown today), and that standards could only be guaranteed through continued independence. The most recent attempt to merge the two specializations had been made by Edward Phillpotts (now of *Warspite*) when he was captain of the Signal School in 1912, and defeated on the ever-statesmanlike grounds that 'the time is not ripe'.[50] The tribal separation of the 'sparkers' and the 'bunting-tossers' meant that, while the signals-officer (or chief-yeoman, in ships without a qualified (S)[51]) held professional authority over all signals emanating from his ship, and the W/T branch was under his executive thumb, his qualifications denoted his mastery of visual signalling rather than any knowledge of wireless, and the torpedomen (augmented by marines[52]) of the W/T sub-branch were not his divisional responsibility. Those privileged, waistcoated communicators who mingled with the senior officers on the bridge, therefore, had no compelling brief for wireless-telegraphy, and were not there by virtue of it.

These circumstances must have assisted the Royal Navy's exemplary wireless silence in the First World War, but, if so, that was a positive deriving from a larger negative (and the way to ensure perfect 'emission control' is not to take the gear on board in the first place).

With regard to the reporting failures at Jutland, Cunninghame-Graham blamed the habitual non-participation of COs and flag-officers in wireless 'enemy-reporting' exercises in harbour. But one may guess that many signals-officers and flag-lieutenants were remiss in representing W/T's true importance. How closely Lieutenant (S) Colville pressed Evan-Thomas to send signals, we cannot know; but one may mention the testimony of a young wireless-telegraphist in *Iron Duke* to the effect that an important signal which came in during the night – possibly from the Admiralty – was not passed to Jellicoe because he was having a nap, and his staff (who included three 'long-course' communicators) did not wish to wake him.[53]

We can therefore attribute the many reporting failures at Jutland to a cocktail of factors, including: (a) lack of initiative, and 'seniority knows best'; (b) fear of being direction-found; and (c) insidious organizational flaws. Perhaps all senior officers, not just Goodenough, should have gone to their cabins at nightfall on the 31st of May, had a glass of port, and thought through the enemy's options. But that would have been venturing into what Tryon had tried to reintroduce as their 'secondary-syllabus' duties, whereas all too many of them owed their rank to their 'primary' accomplishments.

*

Although the German battle-fleet was passing astern, and all the pyrotechnics seemed to be happening in that direction, there were other ghostly monsters prowling silently around the Grand Fleet. In the collision-avoidance manoeuvring at the time of *Southampton*'s battle at 10.45, *Moltke* and *Seydlitz* (the former now flying the flag of Rear-Admiral Franz Hipper) had become separated from the formation, and each made her own way eastwards, some distance to starboard (south) of the main body of the High Seas Fleet.

Seydlitz was critically damaged, listing and down by the bows, and her stability was so reduced that she had started to loll with each major helm-movement. By pure chance, while the 4th DF's drama was taking place to the north, she wandered into the Grand Fleet astern of Jerram's 2nd BS (comprising the right-hand column of the main fleet) and ahead of the 5th BS, which was half-trying to keep station on *Marlborough* (not realizing the latter's problems) and thus widening the gap ahead. Carrying on eastwards, *Seydlitz* found *Marlborough* looming on her port bow, and turned away in a three-quarter circle to starboard which took her down between Evan-Thomas's group and Burney's, and then on round, across the latter's wake.

During this gyration her dim outline was sighted by *Marlborough*, *Revenge* and *Agincourt*, though none of them could know what she was. *Agincourt* "did not challenge her so as not to give our division's position away".[54] *Marlborough*'s gunnery-officer lined up his 13.5-inch guns,

> put a range of 4,000 yards on the sights and a deflection of 24 right, then asked the captain for permission to open fire. He replied 'No', as he thought it was one of our own ships. Of course what I ought to have done was to have opened fire and blown the ship out of the water and then said 'Sorry'.[55]

We know – which Captain George Ross did not – that it was *Seydlitz* and that any medium-sized nudge would have got rid of her. But Ross may have been discouraged from taking on an unknown intruder partly by his own ship's deteriorating condition: at 2.0 a.m. Sir Cecil Burney would be reporting to Jellicoe that *Marlborough* could make only 12 knots, and would be told to send her home (which he did, at daybreak, with *Fearless* as an escort, having transferred himself and his staff to *Revenge*). In the meantime, another torpedo would probably have been terminal.

While *Seydlitz* was wandering drunkenly through the Grand Fleet, *Moltke* was probing for a way through, further ahead (in Grand Fleet terms). Three times, at 11.30, 11.55 and at 1.20 a.m. (GMT), she found herself approaching Jerram's battleships, and each time "the menacing dreadnoughts came up starkly against the eastern sky, Captain von Karpf gave the order to swing away . . . and the ship faded into the blackness".[56] *Thunderer* sighted her, but refrained from opening fire for reasons which are, by now, familiar. Finally, von Karpf simply piled on the speed and headed southwards, before crossing well ahead of the Grand Fleet.

*

At ten minutes past two, there was a very big explosion a long way astern of the fleet. Some twenty minutes earlier, Captain Anselan Stirling, leading the 12th Flotilla in the destroyer *Faulknor*, had sighted a line of enemy battleships to starboard, and manoeuvred his group at high speed to reach a firing position. The Germans spotted them coming in the brightening twilight, and tried to evade, but lost them again, and Stirling anticipated the evasion.

"It was already too light for the battleships to be able to use their searchlights to advantage, but it was sufficiently dark and misty for the destroyers to deliver a surprise attack"[57] – and, as there were German torpedo-boats milling about, the recognition dilemma, for once, belonged to the enemy. By the time the High Seas Fleet had made a major turn away, four destroyers, *Faulknor, Obedient, Marvel* and *Onslaught*, had delivered their attack, and one, or two, torpedoes struck the pre-dreadnought *Pommern*, detonating her magazine. She erupted in a clap of thunder and a massive red fireball, and broke in two. There were no survivors. *Onslaught* was hit by a shell which wrecked her bridge and killed her captain, Lieutenant-Commander Onslow.[58]

So ended the last major destroyer engagement of Jutland. The British had lost five destroyers during the night and had several badly damaged. The German had lost one 'torpedo-boat', to a "mysterious" explosion which blew her bows shortly after Stirling's attack, described above, although *Moresby* claimed to have torpedoed her (somebody did it). Never again would so many destroyers and so many potential targets be found in a hundred-square-mile patch of sea. Never again would the fog of war be quite so thick, or 'situation awareness' of such short radius. Notwithstanding many extraordinary acts of bravery (and feats of seamanship in getting some of the wrecks home), it had not been a defining night for flotilla warfare, although it had been a graphically educational one.

The German official historian was lyrical about the High Seas Fleet's torpedo-boats, and scathing about those of the Grand Fleet – alluding to the latter's "few successes and disproportionate losses".[59] Some of his criticisms of training and coordination are justified; but British light-forces, for all their technical and doctrinal defects, proved rather more dangerous in the dark than did their German equivalents. Admittedly, Scheer obliged by bringing his big fat ships right in amongst them, but they torpedoed (or otherwise caused the loss of) a pre-dreadnought battleship, three light-cruisers and a possible destroyer – a respectable exchange in its own right, and one comparable in hardware terms to Cunningham's at Matapan or Beatty's at Heligoland Bight and Dogger Bank combined – and Captain Stirling's flotilla attack was as close to 'textbook' as one can find in the 1914–18 war.

Furthermore, the Germans had no moral claim to the high ground: their own torpedo-boats might as well not have been there, and their avoidance of losses was proportional to their ineffectuality. They, too, had technical and doctrinal limitations, which must be accounted against their expertise in night-fighting (which mainly boiled down to illumination techniques). Apart from a possible hit on *Turbulent*, they failed to torpedo anything. Campbell alludes vaguely to defects observed "in the running and depth-keeping of some German torpedoes".[60] But, whereas the most moderate curiosity would have discovered the nearest squadrons of the Grand Fleet, German destroyer commanders displayed no sense of mission to seek out and destroy. The 7th Flotilla, ordered forward for this purpose, restricted its speed to 18 knots for fear of funnel sparks (from inferior coal) betraying its presence, and, thus shot in the foot, had little chance of finding major targets and none of gaining a firing position. Worse, the ten large (1,300-ton), powerful boats of the 2nd Flotilla actually removed themselves from the mêlée and went home by the scenic route, through the Skagerrak and round the north of Denmark, taking fifty-seven torpedoes with them: their superior officer, Commodore Paul Heinrich, had allowed this, "SHOULD [THE] RETURN JOURNEY TO GERMAN BIGHT APPEAR INADVISABLE".

It almost beggars belief – certainly Jellicoe's set of beliefs – that the nocturnal demons in the High Seas Fleet's most modern destroyers were afraid of the dark in the approaches to the Horns Reef, and strongly suggests that the Germans had developed their night-fighting techniques for self-preservational, rather than offensive, purposes.[61] It is also indicative of the 'fugitive' mind-set which pervaded every section of Scheer's fleet that night, and which the German Official History was not inclined to advertise. It was, as Sir Robert Arbuthnot would have said, a dull performance.

*

Shortly after the destruction of *Pommern*, as the first streaks of the new day were creasing the sky to the north-east, the Germans incurred a batch of losses from accumulated damage. Of these, by far the greatest – indeed their greatest of the war – was that of the battlecruiser *Lützow*, although it stands much to the credit of Captain Harder and his crew that her demise had been postponed until now. Savaged by an estimated twenty-four heavy shells during the daylight action, and with 150 casualties, she had wandered off at 7 knots, attended by four torpedo-boats, and lost contact with the main German body. Bulkheads gave way, electrical power was lost, and, by 12.30 a.m.,

> the bow was so low in the sea that the waves began washing round the fore turret and flooding the forward boiler room. An attempt to proceed stern-first, so as to relieve the pressure, had to be abandoned when the propellers came out of the water and the draft forward increased to fifty-six feet . . .[62]

There was no option but for the destroyers to take off her crew, which was done in orderly manner, wounded first, and then to despatch the great ship with torpedoes.

About now, nearly fifty miles to the north-east, the remarkable light-cruiser *Wiesbaden*, the Grand Fleet's Aunt Sally at the time of the deployment, finally capsized and sank. One survivor was picked up after thirty-eight hours on a raft. About now, also, some seventeen miles to the south-south-east of *Lützow*, most of the crew of *Elbing* were transferred to a destroyer, leaving a handful of men to try to half-sail, half-drift their ship towards the Danish coast. It was a short-lived attempt, for, when hostile ships were sighted, they gave up, set scuttling charges and took to their cutter. Further south still, *Rostock* was similarly scuttled a short while later.

The British, too, had loose ends to tie or cut early that morning. A hundred and twenty miles to the north-west, *Engadine* lost the battle to tow home the waterlogged *Warrior*, and, in worsening sea-conditions, patiently took off the armoured-cruiser's 650 surviving crew (an operation for which her Channel-ferry rubbing-strake proved an asset). "The *Engadine* fellows were awfully good to us. They gave up all their cabins to us, where we were billeted in twos and threes, and the wardroom was made into a hospital."[63]

The surviving men of the much-collided-with *Sparrowhawk* were rescued from their hulk by the destroyer *Marksman*, but not before the derelict *Elbing* had given them a turn: the German cruiser, imperceptibly succumbing to her scuttling charges, drifted out of the mist nearby, causing them to man their one working gun and fear the end. Nothing happened. Then, as they watched in astonishment, their supposed nemesis rolled over and sank. Far away, *Warspite* had spent the night plugging holes in the deck and side-plating in an attempt to 'darken ship' (a project eventually abandoned). Meanwhile *Acasta*, *Onslow* (in tow of *Defender*), *Broke*, *Spitfire*, *Garland*, *Contest*, *Porpoise*, *Onslaught* and now *Marlborough* were all struggling homewards: a ragged trail of deformity and endurance, each ship with varying injuries and varying prospects, against a rising north-westerly. *Onslaught* was navigating with bits of a chart stuck together, and a boat's compass.

*

At 2.30 a.m., with daylight gaining strength, Jellicoe turned his fleet round towards the north. It was a misty morning; "visibility [is] awful [and] we don't know where the enemy are though doubtless the Admiral does."[64] He did not, but he supposed them to be somewhere to the north-west (Beatty supposed them to be south-west; in *Tiger*, the money was on the Skagerrak). Anyway, the C-in-C wanted to gather together and redeploy his destroyers: a process which proved more protracted than he had expected, so scattered and disorganized had the flotillas become during the night.

At 3.0, a few minutes before sunrise, he reverted the fleet to 'action-stations', and re-formed it from squadrons disposed-abeam into line-of-battle: "in order to be ready for the enemy's Battle Fleet if suddenly sighted"[65] (and having learnt yesterday's deployment lesson).

For a while nothing happened, and then a Zeppelin appeared and hovered at a range of three or four miles, at the edge of visibility. Starting with *Revenge*, a number of battleships emptied their guns at it, at extreme elevation. A dozen miles away a salvo from this sport fell into the sea not far from *Malaya*, causing Captain Boyle to shout "Where are they? Where are they?", a question which nobody around him was able to answer.[66] Now, the significance of the Zeppelin dawned: it must be telling Scheer where the Grand Fleet was, reducing to zero the chances of renewing the battle; and presently a decrypt came in from the Admiralty reporting that the High Seas Fleet was even now approaching the Horns Reef swept-channel. The disappointment, in the words of *Valiant*'s navigator, "was acute".

Zeppelin L11 did indeed report that the British fleet was some thirty-five miles to seaward, steaming north. "To the great regret of all concerned", wrote the German official historian (winning the Jutland prize for creative writing), "it was too late for our Fleet to overtake and attack them."

With a new fleet-encounter ruled out, the usual fear of the U-boat menace now resurfaced, and Jellicoe re-formed his fleet in cruising formation, and then led it hither and thither for a few hours, raking through the wreckage, the oil-slicks and the bodies of the battleground, looking for survivors to rescue or stragglers to sink. As regards the former, *Acasta* was found, struggling against a head-sea, and was taken in tow by the destroyer *Nonsuch*; as regards the latter, the Germans had done the work already. At length, there was nothing for it but to turn *Iron Duke*'s bows towards Scapa Flow; and, at the prosaic bugle-call to "RETURN STORES", the Grand Fleet's sixty thousand men fell out from action-stations, subdued and cheated. It was only now that Jellicoe learnt from Beatty of the fate of *Indefatigable* and *Queen Mary*. It was a bewildered and angry Battle Fleet which butted homewards through a northerly gale – but angry at exactly what, no one really knew. They had a better idea in the Battle Cruiser Fleet, which had borne the brunt of the losses, and recriminations were already taking shape.

Jellicoe, meanwhile, occupied himself by worrying about U-boats. The Germans had signalled to their submarines off the Grand Fleet's bases to stay on station for another day, if their endurance allowed.

Some of those which could have complied, did not receive the message, but the Admiralty did, and the airwaves were full of warnings. Most at risk were the cripples, particularly *Warspite* and *Marlborough*; and Jellicoe ordered destroyers out of Rosyth to meet the former, and told off four ships of the Harwich Force to find and escort the latter. Both battleships kept their secondary-armaments on hair-trigger alert, and made preparations, as best they could, for saving life in the event of abandoning ship. In *Warspite*, as "every boat in the ship had a hole in it, messtables and stools were got up on deck and lashed together to form rafts".[67] Both battleships were narrowly missed by torpedoes as they approached the British coast.

Men reacted differently to their battle experience, though those under Beatty's command had rather more to deal with than most of those in the Battle Fleet. In *Lion*, Midshipman Combe watched the dead being taken out of Q turret. "Nasty sight", was his tight-lipped comment.

In *Warspite*, Captain Poland RM was quite willing to admit that he had been "in the most dreadful state of terror the whole time . . . I don't think I'm a warrior by nature. Too easily frightened."[68]

In *Chester*, Sub-Lieutenant Phipps-Hornby found himself desensitized. Picnicking in the captain's cabin (the wardroom being wrecked) he

> was regaled by the cook – a true cockney – with how he had found his mate lying dead with the top of his head neatly sliced off 'just as you might slice off the top of a boiled egg, Sir'. By that time I had become so inured to death and wounds and blood that I was able to listen unmoved, continuing with my meal the while.

A midshipman in *Malaya* thought that "although most of us were in a way scared, we would all have given our souls rather than have missed being in the action."[69]

Many were tired and emotional (in that phrase's literal meaning), and conversations trailed off in mid-sentence. Opinions on the battle fluctuated wildly, with senior officers on the whole more downbeat than their juniors, and tempers frayed. In *Southampton*, one of the most traumatized of the surviving British ships, Lieutenant Stephen King-Hall several times found himself approaching tears for no immediate reason, and nearly thumped Commander Rushton when the latter's appraisal of events differed from his own.

During the afternoon, Beatty visited *Lion*'s chart-house.

> Tired and depressed, he sat down on the settee, and settling himself into a corner he closed his eyes. Unable to hide his disappointment at the result of the battle, he repeated in a weary voice, 'There is something wrong with our ships', then opening his eyes and looking at the writer [Lieutenant Chalmers],

he added, 'and something wrong with our system'. Having thus unburdened himself he fell asleep.[70]

*

That evening, some of the dead were committed to the deep. The Battle Fleet slowed down and ensigns were half-masted while those few ships which needed to – *Barham*, *Malaya* and a number of destroyers – performed this necessary task. Even from a distance, *Benbow*'s Midshipman Dickson was moved: "The seas were coming on board some of the ships and spray was sweeping along the decks. Surely no men ever had a wilder burial."[71] Midshipman Royer Dick, of *Barham*, remembered it as "a real Boy's Own scene".[72]

In *Malaya*, they laid to rest

> the poor unrecognizable scraps of humanity from the explosion [in the battery]. It was a gloomy scene, the grey sky, the grey sea, the stitched up hammocks, the Padre with his gown blowing in the breeze. The Last Post was sounded by the marine buglers, and our shipmates plunged into the sullen waters.[73]

"There was not a soul without a lump in his throat, and quite a lot of the officers and men standing on the upper deck were very near to tears."[74]

A hundred miles to the south, the BCF flagship launched overboard the bodies of six officers and eighty-seven men.[75] "I saw only one man break down and weep, an officers' steward. He apologized and said 'I cannot help it, I have a brother on the *Queen Mary*.'"[76]

A hundred miles further south still, *Chester*, struggling towards the shelter of the Humber, buried eleven.

> As the chaplain was among the dead, the captain read the burial service, standing at the head of the ladder that led up from the starboard waist. He made an impressive figure, as he himself had been slightly wounded. His head was bandaged, and blood stained his greying beard . . . The captain's bob-tailed sheepdog had also been wounded, in the leg, but happily not seriously.[77]

*

There was no let-up for the medical teams in badly damaged ships. *Barham*'s Fleet-Surgeon Ernest Penfold, bruised and shaken from nearby bursts, "tended the wounded with unremitting skill and devotion for forty hours without rest".[78] At about 2.0 a.m. on the night of the 1st–2nd of June, *Malaya*'s Surgeon-Lieutenant Lorimer RNVR fell down. He had been dressing and re-dressing burns cases for most of the last thirty-three hours, and had been feeling great pain in his legs, through standing in one place so long. I discovered that my legs and ankles were swollen like a case of severe dropsy. Fortunately it was my last case that I collapsed, so we were able to get a rest. I had asked the wardroom wine caterer, who was one of our best helpers, to leave a double whisky behind the flower pot in the wardroom. I could not walk, and had to go the length of the ship on my hands and knees, and a jolly difficult thing it is to climb up and down ladders on your hands and knees. I got to the wardroom, collected the whisky, sank into a chair and lighted a cigarette. The next thing I remember was getting shaken by some attendant to go to some case. The whisky was undrunk, the cigarette had burnt to my fingers.[79]

*

Warspite was the first in, on the afternoon of Thursday the 1st of June. After gamely trying to ram a U-boat, she limped into the Forth, fussed about by destroyers, and was eased into Rosyth dockyard, whence her sister, '*Big Lizzie*', was extracted.

> There was a poignant scene as crowds of dockyard workers gathered on the dockside to watch the dead and wounded being carried over the gangways. The ship's male-voice choir, led by their conductor, a Welsh stoker, sang 'Comrades in Arms' while this was being done. Many a strong man broke down and wept.[80]

Later, Midshipman Bickmore "personally counted over 150 holes in the ship . . . the funnels were like colanders",[81] but, in reality, her damage was more spectacular than structurally critical, and her casualties – fourteen killed, thirty-two wounded – incredibly light (many a destroyer suffered much worse), as most of her company had been behind effective armour-plate. When Commander Walwyn's wife saw her husband's cabin "she burst into tears . . . shambles . . . she had decorated it".[82]

Early on Friday morning the battlecruisers came in, followed by *Engadine* with *Warrior*'s survivors. *Princess Royal* and *Tiger* went straight into the dockyard, while *Lion* secured to her buoy, and almost at once, along with *New Zealand*, *Inflexible* and *Indomitable*, commenced coaling. "The men were nearly dead by the time we were finished."[83] Later, a barge came alongside and, with infinite care, the wounded were hoisted out. During the afternoon "heaps of telegrams were sent from Dalmeny post-office to relations etc."[84] That evening the battlecruisers re-ammunitioned.[85]

In the middle part of the day the bulk of the Grand Fleet arrived back in Scapa, to coal/oil ship, re-ammunition, and discharge the remaining dead. (There was some small concern that they might be ordered back to sea with bodies still on board.) A hospital-ship came alongside to take off the wounded, a tug to collect the dead: as the latter steamed down the line "all ships half-masted and sounded the Last Post".[86] That evening John Jellicoe, who had lost six thousand men as against Reinhard Scheer's two and a half thousand, reported twenty-four dreadnought battleships ready for sea. Scheer could muster ten.

Meanwhile the men of the Grand Fleet had to endure a shock, if anything, greater than the savage losses of Jutland: the German version of the battle.

In Wilhelmshaven and Berlin the spin was obvious and easy: the High Seas Fleet had met the Grand Fleet in battle, sunk four capital ships (they claimed *Warspite*) while losing no dreadnoughts of their own (they did not admit *Lützow*, or, for that matter, *Rostock* and *Elbing*). Scheer had won "a brilliant victory," and could point to prisoners-of-war, mainly survivors from BCF destroyers, to prove it. One can understand, now, the desperate need for good war-news, in June 1916, with the relentless wastage of lives in France, and the privations already being felt in the Fatherland. Telegraph wires hummed with it. After a hundred years of strutting the world stage, Nelson's navy had been routed. "The spell of Trafalgar has been broken," a euphoric Kaiser told his fleet; "the English were beaten. You have started a new chapter in world history."[87] Bells rang, flags flew, and public holidays were declared.

The sensational news sped to England from neutral Switzerland, and arrived on British breakfast-tables on the morning of Friday the 2nd of June, when the Grand Fleet was still at sea. The *Daily News* spoke of "a defeat". The British public, innocent and chivalrous, and still unadjusted to the notion that 'propaganda' was part of the armoury of war, took it as fact. Even men-of-affairs, who should have suspended judgement, gave it credence. At about the time *Lion* was securing to her buoy in Rosyth fairway, the physicist Sir Joseph Thomson arrived at the office of the Board of Invention and Research ('Intrigue and Revenge'), close to Trafalgar Square, to find Lord Fisher

> pacing up and down the room more dejected than any man I have ever seen. He kept saying time after time, 'They've failed me, they've failed me! I have spent thirty years of my life preparing for this day and they've failed me!'[88]

To the returning ships, the discovery that they had been judged *in absentia*, by those for whom they had held the ring and on their enemy's say-so, hurt deeply. As Beatty wrote, "my poor sailors were terribly upset at first at the injustice."[89] The Admiralty's initial statement on the battle, strictly honest about British losses and unavoidably vague about the Germans', would make things worse;[90] and the Royal Navy's pathological mistrust of the media may be traced to Friday the 2nd of June 1916.

In Scapa Flow that night, Lieutenant Oswald Frewen of *Comus* (4th (JJO) LCS) wrote in his diary:

> I am nothing. Beatty is nothing. Jellicoe is nothing, the 5,000 gallant fellows who have lost their lives are nothing. We *all* pass on, whether in a chariot of fire to Heaven, or in our beds. It is the NAVY that matters. The Navy, who has lost no battle since decadent Charles reigned – if then. The NAVY, on whom the Empire and the civilized world leans, the Navy, Nelson's NAVY, Drake's NAVY, whose trustees we are, and it is the NAVY, whose good name has been flung a prey to dirty Teuton woman-butchers, to supercilious neutrals, as though it were not more than the good name of a harlot. And I have seen it.[91]

The next morning, Saturday the 3rd, *Malaya* went down to Invergordon to take *Emperor of India*'s place in the floating-dock there. The dockies, having read the papers, and now confronted with the evidence of her damage, gave her a mixed reception.[92] *Barham* set off south for Devonport, and Evan-Thomas travelled by train to Rosyth to hoist his flag in *Queen Elizabeth*. That day, Lieutenant King-Hall managed to get away for a couple of hours from the awful scenes and smells in *Southampton*, now lying in Rosyth basin, a tourist attraction to battle-cruiser personnel, with dockyard foremen clambering about, and went into Dunfermline. There he found the population in a state of excitement, with nobody taking a blind bit of notice of his uniform. The explanation? A local league semi-final between Loanhead Mayflower and Broxburn Athletic. What else.

PART V

Aftermath

23

Something Wrong With Our System

"There is no tradition in the 'tradition' arguments, except the tradition
of 100 years of peace in which war was forgotten."

On the morning of Monday the 5th of June, Surgeon-Lieutenant
Lorimer left HMS *Malaya* at Invergordon and travelled to Aviemore
to join his wife for a few days' leave. He found that she had taken the
children off for a picnic in the woods, and he went to find them.

> I had just left the turmoil of the ship, my hands were still deeply stained
> yellow from the picric dressings; my ears were deaf with the noises of the ship
> and the guns; I still smelt the stench of the dressing station; I was wearied and
> tired to a degree, and here in the midst of a pine wood I met the family. I shall
> never forget the peace of that scene.[1]

The peace was local. That afternoon an unseasonal north-easterly gale
lashed the Far North, and dusk heralded "the dirtiest night we had seen
in Scapa" with dreadnoughts, anchored in what was normally the lee of
Hoy, bucking at their cables and shipping seas on deck. Duty-watchmen
peering out from oilskins and duffel-coats were surprised to see the
armoured-cruiser *Hampshire* weigh and head for the gate in Hoxa Sound,
and were thankful it was not them. Few of them knew she was carrying
the Secretary of State for War, Field Marshal Lord Kitchener, on his way
to North Russia. He had stopped off to visit Jellicoe and be debriefed
about the battle, but had rejected the proffered advice to delay sailing.

The Commander-in-Chief had personally changed the cruiser's initial
route north, from the customary east side of the Orkney islands, to the
west. His motive was to limit his old friend's discomfort during his first
few hours at sea; but the gale tricked them by backing to the north-west,
and soon the waves were such that her brace of escorting destroyers
were unable to keep up and were sent home. Not long after that,

503

Hampshire struck one of *U-75*'s mines off Marwick Head and foundered in the raging gale, drowning Herbert Kitchener and most of her company of 650. A handful of men somehow got ashore, clinging to rocks and inching up the cliffs in the dark, to reach remote crofts and raise the alarm.

Jellicoe was racked by guilt. The Germans can scarcely have been expecting to bag a lone cruiser setting out northwards (via the wrong side of the Orkneys) for Archangel, but the tragedy had the appearance of an assassination,[2] and set Scapa buzzing with rumours of spies and saboteurs. Coming, as it did, less than a week after Jutland, it brought Sir John's morale to its lowest ebb. His health had been in the balance for many months, he was terribly tired, and beset by self-doubt over his leadership in battle. The solitary burden of high command had taken its toll: "I often feel that the job is more than people over 55 can tackle for very long,"[3] he told the First Sea Lord, perhaps preparing an alibi[4] and an honourable exit. He should probably have been ordered ashore now, at least for a rest-cure; but so soon after Jutland, it would have savoured of summary dismissal, and that was unthinkable. So, for the time being, he stayed.

*

It did not take the Germans long to be found out over *Lützow*, *Elbing* and *Rostock*. The British public began to grasp that there had been two 'battles' over Jutland, a physical one and a public-relations one, and came round to crediting at face value the measured asseverations of Their Lordships – the more so as collateral testimony trickled in from neutral sources. A few lucky survivors from *Frauenlob*, for example, had been picked up by a Dutch ship and taken to Holland, where they were interviewed by a Press Association representative. The German light-cruiser had entered the fray in company with the High Seas Fleet, so her crew knew little of the battlecruiser action, and, of course, nothing of the German post-battle publicity claims. They talked freely.

> They stated that half the German Fleet had been engaged with five units of the British Fleet. The British sailed north accompanied by light-cruisers and a number of torpedo craft. They were hopelessly outnumbered by the large German squadron amongst which were the latest German dreadnoughts. The Germans thought them easy prey but suddenly the Grand Fleet arrived, and the Germans could only save themselves by flight. They did so.[5]

As the days went by, the British press began to make amends. "It is not customary for a victor to run away"[6] was now the tenor of editorials; and people began to talk of undoubted, if less than Nelsonic, victory. The 'Sailor King' also rallied round by visiting Scapa, Invergordon and Rosyth, and assuring "all ranks and ratings that the name of the British Navy never stood higher in the eyes of their fellow countrymen whose pride and confidence in their achievements are unabated". The unpalatable truths remained, however, that British ships and 6,000 lives had been traded cheaply in the exchange of battle, and that the RN had failed to obtain a result accordant with its heritage – and immune to the mendacious constructions of journalists.

From this derived an implacable determination to give the Germans short shrift 'next time', and thus set the record straight. Attention was focused on what had gone wrong. In the capricious test of real battle, as distinct from the scripted war-gaming in Grand Fleet Battle Orders – and with the partial exceptions of the BCF light-cruisers – *nobody*'s operational role had been entirely fulfilled, or their practices vindicated. And, while the damaged ships were being patched up, no time was wasted in setting up a range of technical committees of enquiry.

Reports of all kinds were called in and analysed.[7] Some of the damage-control lessons were basic and remain relevant today. Pakenham indented for 150 extra fire-extinguishers per ship. The captain of *Chester* warned that

> watertight doors should be properly closed. If a door is closed by [only] one or two clips and a shell explodes in its vicinity it will be blown away bodily and will act as a very large splinter, being hurled the length of the compartment and killing everyone in its way.

Gunnery-officers agonized over the likely causes of the cataclysmic magazine explosions, and took steps to put their house in order: there was presently issued a memorandum detailing twenty-six measures to improve 'flash-tight' practices, with particular regard to the stowage and handling of cordite. The armour-plate provision for the battlecruiser *Hood*, building in Clydebank, was substantially enhanced. A 'double salvo' variant of the fast German 'ladder' system of finding the initial range was adopted in September, in place of the more deliberate 'bracket' system.[8] And there was the matter of defective armour-piercing (AP) fuzes. Jellicoe pestered the Admiralty to commence the mass-production of exact replicas of the German AP fuze (of which several samples were brought home to Rosyth).[9] The Admiralty demurred, but eventually brought out a new British fuze which reliably exploded its shell fifteen to twenty feet behind armour-plate. The efficiency of the AP shells themselves was not questioned until German gossip reached the Grand Fleet via neutral diplomats some months later; but, after much delay, that too would be rectified.[10] These changes, in Jellicoe's estimate, "certainly doubled" the effectiveness of the Grand Fleet's heavy artillery.[11]

A programme of night-fighting practices was introduced in July. For battleships, these involved 'sub-calibre' firings (small, blank-firing guns screwed into the breeches of heavy guns) and battery-control exercises in the less populous reaches of Scapa Flow. During one such exercise without navigation lights, in late August, *Valiant* realistically rammed *Warspite* and did considerable damage to both ships.[12]

The main latent gunnery weakness, or at least the one with direct tactical ramifications – that of fire-control – was not addressed. Frederick Dreyer, whose inventions the Navy had adopted before the war, was Jellicoe's flag-captain, and would soon follow him to the Admiralty to serve as Director of Naval Ordnance. In these circumstances, it was, as Roskill says, "highly improbable that any step would be taken to replace the system for whose introduction he had been responsible and which bore his name".[13] This matter would not be put right until after the war, when Beatty was First Sea Lord,[14] although he would start the ball rolling in 1918 by setting up a Grand Fleet committee to report into the 'future development of fire-control tables', which was seriously critical of the Dreyer system.[15]

The Battle Fleet's heavy dependence on signals for command-and-control – allegedly, one every sixty-seven seconds during the daylight action[16] – underlined the unpleasant discovery that "flag signals were a most uncertain method of communication",[17] while W/T suffered both from neglect and from a lack of doctrine as to priorities,[18] and was hostage to deliberate or accidental jamming. Jellicoe, as we shall see, was to make one particular command-and-control 'innovation' (for so it was for him) towards mitigating the first problem. Meanwhile, a Grand Fleet W/T Committee reported that

> In all future capital ships the Auxiliary W/T Office, Auxiliary Coding Office, Cipher Office, Sound Telegraph Office and Distribution Office should be situated immediately below the conning-tower, in direct communication with each other and centred on the Intelligence Office, all well protected by armour[19]

– a recommendation which may be said to form one of the tentative roots of the Plotting Organization (later the Action Information Organization) which would become standard in British warships in the inter-war years.

*

Innovation also followed the wounded on their pain-racked journeys to hospitals and nursing-homes. A young surgeon from St Bartholomew's Hospital in London, a New Zealander named Harold Gillies, was prompted by severe facial-burns cases to develop the 'tube pedicle' method of transferring tissue from one part of the body to another, and thus made pioneering advances in plastic surgery.[20]

*

Meanwhile, there were a number of organizational reforms initiated by, and at, the Admiralty. For the Grand Fleet, the most important was the resolution, taken at a conference of Jellicoe, Beatty and the Sea Lords on June the 25th, that the two parts of the fleet must be united at a common base, and that that base could only be the Firth of Forth. This decision would take well over a year to implement, for the space necessary to protect the entire fleet from U-boats required storm-proof boom defences to be stretched across the outer part of the Firth, and that meant a huge commitment of buoyage, nets, ground-tackle and defensive minefields. But at least a start was made.

It took a year, also, to prise the W/T Branch from *Vernon*'s jealous grip, and to transfer it to *Victory*. But on June the 20th, 1917, wireless-telegraphy ceased to be a byline of torpedomen, and became, instead, the departmental and administrative property of the Signals Branch. From now on, to qualify for the coveted 'S' after his name, an officer would have to pass daunting examinations in W/T; and, as more and more seagoing flag-lieutenants were S's (a rule boosted by this very reform), wireless would become, for the first time, tribally and knowledgeably represented on the bridge.[21]

Other reforms were internal. A month after the battle, with the service still stinging from its defeat by German propaganda, it was proposed that there be formed a Naval Publicity Department under a rear-admiral – a measure which would, it was imagined, avoid the sort of presentational mistakes which had been made in dealings with the press after Jutland. In the memoranda generated by this faintly caddish suggestion, John Buchan's name was thrown up as a potential writer of semi-official communiqués. The chief naval censor, Captain Sir Douglas Brownrigg, felt that Buchan's ignorance of the sea and his pretentious style, combined with the fact that he was already helping the Foreign Office, militated against him, and suggested Julian Corbett (historian at the Naval War College) for the serious stuff and Rudyard Kipling for the lighter. It appears that, in the event, both Corbett and the ubiquitous journalist Filson Young (to whom no RNVR rank was now attached) were employed as consultants.[22]

At about the same time, the First Lord's naval secretary, Captain Charles Bartolomé, the officer most involved with the administration of flag-officer appointments, circulated a memo which observed that it certainly seems curious that so much trouble is taken to obtain reports on junior officers, whose responsibilities and opportunities for doing harm are small, while no official record of any sort exists in the case of flag-officers, unless they receive Their Lordships' satisfaction or otherwise. Their fitness for command is never even mentioned.[23]

Whether this was triggered by Jutland, or merely made more timely by it, one cannot say; but the First Lord, Arthur Balfour, laconically noted "Agreed", and commanders-in-chief were thereafter directed to submit, on certain specified occasions, confidential reports on all rear-admirals serving afloat, assessing their fitness

1. for their present commands, and
2. for further employment.

Thirdly, the "almost criminal ineptitude" in the misuse of signals intelligence at Jutland led to the *de facto* confiscation of Room 40 from the Directorate of Operations, and its transfer to the realm of Naval Intelligence (a move made *de jure* in 1917). There, under the benign autocracy of Blinker Hall, the Room grew from a cryptographic service into a full-blown operational-intelligence centre.[24]

The Royal Navy was learning.

*

All the flaws in warship *matériel*, and all the flaws in Admiralty organization, could not come close to exculpating the failure to deal decisively with the High Seas Fleet. And, however minutely the post-battle committees might check over the physique of the Grand Fleet, it was inevitable that its *brain* should also come in for criticism, and that the most acerbic critics would be in the Battle Cruiser Fleet.

The immediate correspondence between the C-in-C and VABCF was carefully supportive. Jellicoe wrote:

> Please accept my sincere congratulations on the action of the forces under your command under the difficult and disadvantageous conditions of light which existed for you. Your ships inflicted very severe damage to the enemy. Words cannot express my deepest sympathy with the relations and friends of the gallant officers and men who have gone under.[25]

Beatty wrote:

> I want to offer you my deepest sympathy in being baulked of your Great Victory which I felt was assured when you hove into sight. I can well understand your feelings and that of the Battle Fleet, to be so near and miss is worse than anything. The cussed weather defeats us every time.[26]

But Beatty did not really blame the weather. He "was terribly disappointed that when Jellicoe arrived he did not go in and take the High

Seas Fleet by the scruff and sink them in line";[27] and, indeed, the dangers into which Jellicoe had declined to turn his battle-fleet must have seemed minor compared to the gauntlet which the BCF had run. When Commander Hubert Dannreuther, *Invincible*'s senior survivor, arrived back in Rosyth in *Badger* on June the 2nd, he received a signal to report to *Lion*. There, Beatty interviewed him alone in his cabin. "I was with him for at least an hour, and I always look back upon it as one of the most painful hours I have ever spent in my life. He was in a state of frenzy almost." He was convinced he had been let down by Jellicoe, and walked up and down the cabin ranting against him. "I was only a young commander at the time, and I was feeling awfully uncomfortable."[28] Thereafter, Beatty never wavered in his belief that Jellicoe had thrown away "a tremendous opportunity by not risking for once a departure from the plan of manoeuvre which (Beatty admitted) he had always made clear he would follow";[29] and, in writing of the battle, Sir David never failed to mention that he brought the enemy "into the jaws of our fleet",[30] and Sir John never failed to labour the weather. Jacky Fisher helpfully chipped in, with the dogmatism of one who never commanded a fleet in war, that "rashness in war is prudence, as prudence in war is criminal."[31]

Thus began the long, sorry saga of the 'Jutland controversy'. And while the acrimony between flag-officers remained muted until the Armistice (which ended hopes of a proper fleet action, for which Jutland would have been a mere dress-rehearsal), from the start, the Battle Fleet and the Battle Cruiser Fleet held widely differing corporate perceptions about their respective roles on the 31st of May.

The personnel of the Battle Fleet knew little of the hard fighting done by some of Beatty's units, and considered that, if they had over-reached themselves, their own "swollen headedness" was to blame.[32] In the words of Lord Mountbatten, who joined *Lion* as a midshipman soon after Jutland, they somehow

> thought the battlecruisers had let them down and failed to carry out their prime duty to keep the C-in-C informed of where the High Seas was and what it was doing. Obviously, I thought, this was a 'cover up' for their failure to get properly into action.[33]

For their part, the BCF "felt that the Battle Fleet did not make their best speed during the approach to the battle",[34] and, of course, could never accept with either equanimity or charity Jellicoe's allowing the High Seas Fleet to escape. In the 1950s, when Captain Stephen Roskill tried to question Lord Chatfield on the subject of relations between the BF and the BCF, the admiral was evasive; but even an 'outsider' – Roger

Keyes (of future Zeebrugge fame), arriving to succeed Michael Culme-Seymour in command of *Centurion* a month after the battle – was shocked to find RA2BS, Arthur Leveson, unperturbed at the failure to deal with the German battle-fleet, on the pedestrian grounds that "We will still win the war."[35]

So well known was the ill-feeling that, at the beginning of August (near the end of the period of grace afforded by the bulk of the High Seas Fleet's known repairs[36]) Jellicoe was driven to arrange for the BCF to visit Scapa, and for the fatted calf to be killed. Battlecruiser officers were "inundated with invitations to dine", with the subject of Jutland evidently tabooed. Beatty "was not quite sure that it is all quite sincere". At dinner in *Iron Duke*, Old Packs made some remark about the battle, causing "a sudden hush, followed instantly by a Babel of tongues on diverse subjects".[37]

*

In the weeks after Jutland, Beatty attempted two (arguably) self-serving campaigns, both of which Jellicoe parried with the Admiralty's help.

First, he sought to dictate the manner and extent to which his formal despatches should be placed before the public. He favoured Jellicoe and Balfour with the advice that "I am not unduly sensitive to criticism"[38] (a sure preface to an exercise in paranoia) and regaled them with a catalogue of past grievances. His Heligoland Bight ROP had been rendered almost unintelligible, he said, and the editing of his Dogger Bank ROP had made him look like a "rotter of the worst description [who] ought to have been shot with the shade of Byng standing by as a witness". Now, after Jutland,

> I have already been the subject of a considerable amount of adverse criticism and I am looking to the publication of the despatches to knock it out. It is hard enough to lose my fine ships and gallant pals, but to be told that I am [a] hare-brained maniac is not quite my idea of British fairness and justice. So I ask you to have my story published.[39]

The First Lord replied, with absolute right, that officers should not have publication in mind when they write despatches, and that despatches so written would be of little use to the Admiralty. Meanwhile the C-in-C did his best to accommodate his petulant subordinate, by submitting for publication in the *London Gazette* extracts as generous as secrecy and non-repetition permitted, but Beatty still made an eleventh-hour attempt to nobble the diagrams. "I do not understand [his] attitude in regard to the despatch," Jellicoe complained to Sir Henry Jackson, the First Sea Lord.

It is surely not his business to edit it or to have anything to do with the plans which it is proposed to publish. The telegram sent me yesterday in which he asks to see the new plan before publication astonished me. I did not think it right to suggest a reply to him, but my view would have been for the Admiralty to have told him that the plan was none of his business.

I am afraid the term Battle Cruiser 'Fleet' has given him the idea that his position is different to that of other admirals . . . I will let him understand the position should I find it necessary.[40]

Beatty's triangular relationship with Jellicoe and the Admiralty was, by now, already under stress as a result of his other campaign. A direct consequence of Jutland was the clipping of the BCF's wings, in terms of its roving commission away from the battle-fleet, and while VABCF continued to campaign for the permanent secondment of Evan-Thomas's command to his own, Jellicoe redoubled his determination to prevent it. In furtherance of their respective aims, they interpreted the 5th BS's role at Jutland in ways which caricatured their pre-battle opinions, but which were (ironically) barely compatible with their respective stances after the war.

Beatty's assertion was that

The presence of the Fifth Battle Squadron made it possible for touch to be maintained with the enemy High Seas Fleet. Without the Fifth Battle Squadron, in reducing visibility, it is certain that the Battle Cruisers would either have been destroyed or would have had to haul off, in which case the enemy battle-fleet would not have been brought into the jaws of our Grand Fleet.[41]

Jellicoe's position, on the other hand, was that the battle had proved that

the 5th Battle Squadron is not fast enough to get away from the German 3rd Battle Squadron and cannot therefore be used as a backing-up force for the Battle Cruiser Fleet, far from the main fleet[42]

– indeed, it was liable to be "a source of embarrassment and risk".[43]

This dispute should have ended at the meeting at the Admiralty on the 25th of June, when the Sea Lords came down in support of Jellicoe;[44] but Beatty did not willingly accept their verdict and continued to bicker over the 5th BS, contriving this or that reason for the issue to be reopened, until he was more firmly put in his place at the end of August. He was to get even.

*

In the immediate aftermath Beatty was fulsome to Evan-Thomas:

Just a line to thank you from the bottom of my heart for your gallant and effective support on Wednesday. It was fine to see your fine squadron sail down as it did. I hope your grand ships were not too much knocked about. *Warspite* will not be long – nothing serious. Your coming down in support and poor Bertie Hood's magnificent handling of his squadron will remain in my mind for ever.[45]

The comradeship of shared danger was one thing; getting the story down on paper for public analysis, whether in 1916 or later, in a manner agreeable to David Beatty was another. Even as he wrote he was final-izing 'master' track-charts which depicted the BCSs, with their attend-ant destroyers and light-cruisers, Hipper, Scheer and Jellicoe, but from which the 5th BS was conspicuous by its absence.[46] In the 1920s Evan-Thomas was to read and reread the above letter with a mounting sense of bewilderment.

As private correspondence spread outwards from the Grand Fleet, apprising very senior officers and elder sea-dogs of the salient features of the battle, Evan-Thomas received many other plaudits. Old Sir Gerard Noel wrote to him, as did Sir William May and, from Admiralty House, Portsmouth, Sir Stanley Colville. The latter alluded to his own nephew:

My Dear Evan-Thomas, let me congratulate you more than warmly on your handling of the finest squadron in the world and having made the Huns fly home after receiving much damage. Hope the flag-lieutenant is well, give him my blessing.[47]

Perhaps the most highly prized letters, both for Evan-Thomas and for Jellicoe, came from Wadenhoe House, Oundle, from Sir Michael Culme-Seymour. The octogenarian sailor wrote to Jellicoe, his former flag-commander:

I cannot help sending you a line of congratulations on your late fight and to say what pleasure it gives me to see my old friend doing so well. I am told the way you commanded the fleet both before, during and after the battle was 'splendid', as I knew it would be. My old Flag Lt. seems to have had a good chance and to have done as we knew he would.[48]

And he wrote to the old flag-lieutenant: "My Dear Evan-Thomas, I must send you a line of hasty congratulations on the part you took in the fight. I am told that you have reason to be proud of yourself and of your squadron."[49]

Jellicoe replied:

Thank you so much for your kind words. I appreciate them exceedingly from my old chief <u>from whom I learned so much</u>. The weather was most unkind to us and it was heart-breaking that we could not finish the job off. Evan-

Thomas's ships got a good many hits on board, but they are very tough . . . If Mrs Trev is with you please tell her I never saw Trev [Trevylyan Napier] looking better in his life.[50]

Evan-Thomas replied:

We much wish we had been a bit closer to Beatty at the start – in which case Von Hipper would no longer be in existence . . . Anything that I may know about a fleet or a squadron was taught to me by you – so if I did help a very little when Beatty was in a tight place it was your fault![51]

Meanwhile Sir Michael's source of information, his son and name-sake, made sure he entertained no degenerate notions about the Battle Cruiser Fleet:

My Dear Pappy, Beatty was <u>never</u> in action with the German Battle Fleet at all. Tommy with his 4 took on the entire German Battle Fleet for $1\frac{1}{2}$ hours till we came up, and to him is due all the credit that is to be got out of the affair.[52]

*

Starting on the 1st of July, the attention of the British people became engaged by something larger and more distressing than an inconclusive twilight shadow-boxing of fleets in the North Sea.

Herbert Kitchener was fortunate, perhaps, not to have lived long enough to know how the semi-trained and ill-equipped volunteer army, which his *Your Country Needs You!* posters had recruited, fared at the Battle of the Somme. The first day brings to mind his famous victory at Omdurman, only this time the infantry falling like corn before the scythe of mechanization was British. Captain Wilfred Nevill famously led his company of the East Surrey Regiment across no man's land dribbling a football. ("True to the land that bore them, The Surreys play the game."[53]) Young Nevill and most of his men and nearly 20,000 others were killed.

In that summer of 1916, six years after the death of the King for whom it was named, the 'Edwardian era' finally died. Conscription, total mobilization and the Somme, each in its own way a harbinger of a stark and uncompromising world, were all part of the process. No longer would playing the decent, codified, sublimely amateurish game of chivalry be enough. The lingering mirage of Camelot had vanished for ever: images of 'Deep England', with which propagandists and advertisers have sought to stir the national subconscious over the last three generations, hark back to a period before that summer. The loss of innocence was a milestone on Britain's path of centuries; and Jutland too, in its more internalized, corporate way, was part of it. The sudden

disproof of the reassuring, structured assumptions about the formula
for naval mastery, which had accumulated during the untesting age of
Victoria, was real enough for the RN's senior officer corps.

> But naval men are not so inventive as to be capable of altering their methods
> radically upon the doubtful and confusing results of a brief, indecisive action
> fought in a North Sea haze in failing daylight. Jutland was a turning point, and
> not a revolution.[54]

*

At the other side of the North Sea, despite the official euphoria, the
German High Seas Fleet's 'private' assessment of *Der Skagerrakschlacht*
was by no means as up-beat as its publicized claims made out. It was
only the icing on the cake that was sweet. For a start, some of their
grotesquely wrecked ships took far longer to repair than the damaged
British units (a total of 650 dry-docking days as against 350), and their
visible condition was, in a sense, more harmful to morale than ships
'cleanly' sunk and rubbed off the *Navy List* ("It is wonderful how sailors
put these things out of their mind almost immediately," Beatty said,
after *Vanguard* blew up in Scapa Flow, in 1917[55]). But more important
was the spectre of irresistible coercive power which mere glimpses of
the Grand Fleet had left in the minds and memories of German
officers. "Intoxicated with victory" though they were (in the words of
the Austrian Naval Attaché),

> they do not deny that they were extraordinarily fortunate, and that if the
> action had been prosecuted with energy on the British side, and if the
> 'Nelson touch' had been in evidence, things might have gone very badly for
> Germany.[56]

One officer wrote that "On 1st June, 1916, it was clear to any thinking person that this battle must, and would, be the last one.
Authoritative sources said so openly."[57] Another admitted, after the
war, that the men "are not fools about the things they can see, and the
way we were crushed from the moment your battle-fleet came into
action took the heart out of them. Another hour of daylight would have
finished it."[58] When *Kriegsmarine* personnel had toasted *Der Tag* with
such bravado all those years, a disorderly rush for somewhere to hide
was not what they had been visualizing. The most telling testament
comes from Vice-Admiral Scheer's own confidential report to Wilhelm
II. Here he made the tendentious, and highly questionable, assertion
that "even the most successful outcome of a fleet action will not force
England to make peace", and he advised the All Highest that "a victorious end of the war within a reasonable time can only be achieved

through the defeat of British economic life – that is, by using the U-boats against British trade."[59]

The French had come to an equivalent conclusion after Trafalgar, and it was a thinly disguised back-pedal to the views of Scheer's less swashbuckling predecessor, Hugo von Pohl. It amounted to a multiple confession that

a. the 'victory' had changed nothing to Germany's strategic benefit;

b. the Grand Fleet may as well be awarded the status of 'undefeatable';

c. the High Seas Fleet would not be seeking a repeat engagement.

The Kaiser's Navy, too, received an education in the summer of 1916.

*

The German fleet did, however, venture beyond the defensive minefields of the Heligoland Bight on three occasions after Jutland: twice in 1916 and once in 1918. The most adventurous of these forays, and the only one which raised the near-possibility of another fleet action, was the first, which took place on the 18th/19th of August.

With his battleship complement (although not his battlecruiser force) restored to strength after repairs, Scheer set in motion the original bombardment plan which had been scheduled for the 31st of May but which had, on that occasion, been cancelled because of insufficiency of Zeppelin reconnaissance. The agenda was that Hipper, with his two serviceable battlecruisers *Moltke* and *Von der Tann*, augmented by three of the most modern battleships, would bombard Sunderland and then attempt to draw Beatty into the embrace of the High Seas Fleet. The German C-in-C was satisfied that this time his "elaborate reconnaissance arrangements",[60] with Zeppelin scouts and U-boat trip-wires, would prevent his being surprised by the Grand Fleet and having the scheme backfire on him.

As usual, Room 40 alerted the Admiralty to an impending operation, and the Grand Fleet was at sea well before the Germans. Jellicoe, who was taking a much-needed rest at Kinpurnie Castle, his father-in-law's place near Dundee, intercepted the Battle Fleet in a cruiser assigned to him for that purpose, and regained command from Sir Cecil Burney. A full inventory of five *Queen Elizabeths* (this was before the *Valiant–Warspite* collision) brought his battle-line to a total of twenty-nine – double that which Scheer could now field – while Beatty was on a short lead of 30 miles ahead.

At around dawn on the 19th, the British submarine *E-23* torpedoed the battleship *Westfalen*, which Scheer sent home under escort, while, some two hundred miles to the north, *U-52* torpedoed *Nottingham*, which sank. The loss of one of Goodenough's gallant quartet of light-cruisers was not a major factor in the half-blindfold chess game between the opposing fleets, but Jellicoe's reaction to it *was*, and calls into question his mental robustness. He feared that *Nottingham* had been mined, and that the Grand Fleet was heading, Beatty-first, into a mine-field-trap; and so he reversed the course of the entire Grand Fleet for two hours, until the situation clarified sufficiently for him to feel able to resume his southerly direction. Various excuses have been made for him;[61] but the fact remains that four hours were lost, and that he could have frustrated any mine-trap (or U-boat ambush) by sidestepping the Battle Fleet to the east for (say) an hour, without necessarily comprom-ising his future position *vis-à-vis* the High Seas Fleet.

Nevertheless, there was still a good prospect of the fleets meeting, as confirmed by *E-23*'s W/T report of the *Westfalen* incident, which Jellicoe received after he had turned southwards once more; and by 2.0 p.m. the Grand Fleet was at action-stations, fully anticipating a fleet action with many hours of daylight in hand to finish the job. Another hour would have secured Jellicoe's position astride the High Seas Fleet's line of retreat; but fate intervened again.

The Harwich destroyers, by now racing up from the south and about level with Cromer, were sighted by a Zeppelin which mistook some of them for battleships, and so reported them to Scheer. Presented with the apparent opportunity to defeat an isolated battle-squadron, Scheer abandoned the plan to bombard Sunderland, and turned his fleet south towards Tyrwhitt and away from the approaching, but still unsuspected, Jellicoe. At 2.35 the German C-in-C suddenly abandoned this new project and turned for home. His reasons, about which he was later evasive, were surely not unconnected with the startling news, received from *U-53*, that Jellicoe's massive force was only sixty-five miles to the north, steaming south. "Once again the Grand Fleet returned to harbour in a state of bitter disappointment"[62] – losing *Falmouth* to another U-boat on the way.

The episode throws up two grounds for criticizing Jellicoe, who was (in his own words) "quite played out" by the strain of continuous command.[63] The first, his turning about and steaming away for two hours, has been discussed above. It seems almost an abnegation of the human spirit.

The second criticism is one of strategic priorities. It seems that Jellicoe, in following a track relatively close to the English coast, was more concerned with protecting coastal towns than with cutting off the High Seas Fleet, and was thus being driven by the enemy's agenda. This puts Scheer, notwithstanding his subsequent obfuscation of the issues, in the position of being the clearer prioritizer, for he readily abandoned his bombardment plan when the chance appeared to offer itself of defeating an isolated British battle-squadron. Sir John should have hardened his heart in respect of the inhabitants of Sunderland (or wherever) whilst manoeuvring to seawards to block Scheer's retreat – and bring to an end the threat of future bombardments. And while the likelihood may have been small of the Grand Fleet's being able to approach the enemy entirely undetected, with Jellicoe in firm possession of the geographical 'weather gauge', and with searoom restricted by various known minefields and the Dogger Bank's 'shallow patch', there would have been limited scope for evasion on Scheer's part.

*

Soon after the August near-miss, there was published the list of honours and awards won at Jutland. Conspicuous among them were KCBs announced for Evan-Thomas and Pakenham ("You made history, I did not!" the latter wrote), and, posthumously, for Arbuthnot and Hood. Goodenough was promoted to rear-admiral, but remained in his ship, with Commander Rushton promoted into the job of flag-captain (a difficult arrangement for both officers); and also promoted was *Warspite*'s Commander Walwyn. These rewards were universally celebrated,[64] but caustic comment was provoked in BCF circles by the Battle Fleet's seemingly over-rewarding itself for steaming in line and obeying orders. Beatty, who was himself promoted within the Order of the Bath to the rank of GCB, was "woefully disappointed at the inadequacy of the rewards meted out to the fine fellows who supported me so gallantly".[65]

Certain 'BCF' senior officers, such as Goodenough, had not helped by taking the austere view (which Cunningham shared after Matapan) that people should not get prizes for doing their jobs, and indeed, "when all did well, it is hard to individualize".[66] But in *Southampton*, for example, it was felt that the failure to honour their navigator (who had conned the ship unscathed through heavy shellfire for an hour and a half), their torpedo-officer (who had sunk *Frauenlob* at close range in the dark) or their gunnery-officer (who had controlled the guns from the bridge while a fire raged beneath him), stood in unjust contrast to the gongs handed out to officers of the BF, who, it seemed, had merely been present.[67] *Shannon*'s GO was recommended for "not opening fire".

*

On the 11th of September 1916, Sir John Jellicoe published his amended Grand Fleet Battle Orders "as revised in the light of the lessons of Jutland";[68] and, four days later, the Admiralty brought out an 'addendum' to the 1915 *Signal Book*.[69] The addendum contained a flag to trigger the complicated business of deploying into line on a centre column. The new GFBOs included a list of four ways in which the C-in-C might respond to a massed torpedo attack (one of which was to turn towards), with a wordy, noncommittal discussion of their relative pros and cons. There was also, in reference to initiative, a new provision in GFBOs, the full import of which has (unsurprisingly) slipped past historians, but which, in the context of our particular interests, has great significance. Under 'Battle Tactics' we find that the C-in-C "may make the signal 'MP'".

MP was a vacant group in the *Signal Book*. Now, Jellicoe warned that he might hoist it when conditions made it "very difficult to control the movements of the whole battle-fleet", and that it enjoined flag-officers to

> manoeuvre their squadrons independently whilst acting in support of the squadron or division to which the fleet flagship is attached. It is in no way intended to imply that such decentralization is not to take place unless the signal 'MP' is made. If made, it merely points out that decentralization has become essential for the time being.

What is remarkable about this is, of course, that a signal tailored to the same requirement had been provided in the *Signal Book* for thirty-eight years, and could be found under the cryptic group 'TA'; and Jellicoe's avoiding it now can only have been because it still carried unsettling, or controversial, associations – either for him personally (a survivor of *Victoria*) or for the Navy at large.[70] By the same token, he must surely have been aware of the supreme irony that he, an honours graduate of the school of Sir Michael Culme-Seymour, had been compelled to acknowledge, from bitter experience, that the shaky premiss on which British fleets had, for two generations, been practised and led – the assumption that tactical signals could be relied upon to 'get through' in action – was fallacious, and that conditions might obtain in which manoeuvring without signals would "become essential".

We need not imagine that John Jellicoe was a sudden willing convert to manoeuvring without signals. The keynote of GFBOs continued to be the detailed choreography of battle-tactics, around the base-desideratum of action between fleets on parallel courses; and there is no evidence that, in the short time remaining to him as C-in-C, Jellicoe ever practised his flag-officers in 'MP' manoeuvring. He was at best taking one uncertain step into doctrinal schizophrenia. But his introducing his own 'TA-type' signal into the Grand Fleet was an unadmitted vindication of Sir George Tryon. That it had taken the fog and failure of real combat, with issues of grand-strategic importance at stake, and rare opportunities squandered, to bring home what derided fundamentalists had been asserting for decades, was also a sorry indictment of the naval profession's capacity to manage its business. Only time would tell whether it was not, in this war, too late.

The detailed matter of how, if he waited until signalling was difficult before hoisting MP, the fleet was supposed to know it was in force, is a question which Jellicoe would not have welcomed. The complete, Tryonic solution would have been to make TA implicit in the deployment signal, and to train his squadrons to function thereafter with a minimum of orders. But that would have been two long, doctrinal, strides too far.

*

One day at the end of November 1916, Midshipman Charles Arthur was loafing on the quarterdeck of the battleship *King George V*, in the presence of the flag-captain –

> an unsound thing to do, I admit, but he was on one side of the deck and I was on the other. Anyway, this chap – Captain Field [First Sea Lord, 1930–3] – he beckoned me over, and I doubled across and came to attention and said 'Yes Sir?' And when I looked at him there were tears rolling down his cheeks. He said 'Arthur, you may as well tell the gunroom that Sir John Jellicoe has been superseded'.[71]

Jellicoe's relinquishing the command of the Grand Fleet, and his accession to the post of First Sea Lord, had less to do with his diminishing fitness to remain in supreme command afloat, than with mounting public and political disquiet at the comatose state of the Admiralty under Arthur Balfour and Henry Jackson, and the consequent wish to sweep its hallowed corridors with (what was anticipated as) a stimulating sea-breeze. The war was in a state of stalemate of which there was no end in sight, and sweeping changes at highest Government-level were in the wind. Indeed, the wisdom of replacing a lacklustre First Sea Lord with an exhausted one was not, at the time, an issue. Jackson was reconciled to going; Jellicoe was nationally known and admired, he understood the wartime Navy better than any other senior officer and (unlike the demonic 75-year-old Fisher, still plotting vainly in the bushes) enjoyed near-universal goodwill. He felt, furthermore, that he could bring to the Admiralty fresh ideas about how to deal with the new U-boat offensive – which was becoming recognized as more important than the outstanding matter of the High Seas Fleet.

Who was to step into his shoes? Correspondence – sometimes ill-natured and awkward – about his possible successor had been taking place since September.[72] The appointee, for reasons of experience and credibility, would have to come from the Grand Fleet's inventory of vice-admirals, of whom there were five: Sir Cecil Burney (SO1BS), Sir Martyn Jerram (SO2BS), Sir Doveton Sturdee (SO4BS), Sir David Beatty (SOBCF) and Sir Charles Madden (Chief of Staff).

Burney was "an old and trusted friend [and] a fine seaman"[73] who, as second-in-command, would have taken over had Sir John died at sea. But he was tired, uninspiring and increasingly arthritic (he "has always been ill", in Lady Beatty's diagnosis); and he owed his retention thus far to Jellicoe's patronage.

Jerram, although competent in 'primary' detail, was another uncharismatic, tramline disciplinarian, and there was that lingering doubt as to whether he had, or had not, turned towards the west in support of the BCF in the gathering dusk at Jutland (Beatty had cut him dead when the battlecruisers visited Scapa, and is reputed to have requested his court-martial[74]). No more than Burney, would Jerram be acceptable.

The remaining three were better material, but Jellicoe's implacable distrust of Sturdee (noted in Chapter 3) was as great as his, now considerable, phobia about Beatty, and he tried to debar them both – the vice-admirals with the most combat experience – from the succession. This left him in the less than ideal position of backing Sir Charles Madden (another future First Sea Lord), who was not only his brother-in-law, but was also the most junior candidate and the only one with no direct experience of high command at sea.

The First Lord, the stolid elder-statesman Arthur Balfour, was unswayed by Jellicoe's petitioning. From Whitehall (and, indeed, Downing Street[75]) the view was clearer than from *Iron Duke*, and Sir David Beatty was duly offered both the command-in-chief and the acting-rank of admiral. One concession which Jellicoe did win, exercising a long-standing grievance, was the downgrading of the BCF's title from Battle Cruiser Fleet to Battle Cruiser *Force*, although by now it was partly a case of shutting the stable door after the horse had been promoted.

To be appointed First Sea Lord was hardly ignominious, but it cut Jellicoe deeply to pack his bags and go ashore, and he carried with him a sense of failure. It would not, now, befall him to redress the missed opportunities of Jutland; and his abilities as a fighting admiral would forever be defined by that anti-climactic event ("The press will get me now and I am finished," he said to Beatty[76]). His nominee for the succession had been spurned; and, above all, there was the parting from the great fleet which he had organized, nurtured, trained and humoured through the privations and trials of war, for twenty-eight months. Never again would he stand in the icy wind on *Iron Duke*'s compass-platform and watch the great, lumbering shapes around him as they jockeyed for perfect station, flag-hoists billowing, bursts of spray tossing over their foc'sles. "I could not have felt the parting more, I believe, even if I was leaving my own children," he confided, in some distress, to Hugh Evan-Thomas.[77]

*

There have been a few items of news, within living memory, of which it is said that people can remember where they were and what they were doing when they heard them. For the men of the Battle Fleet, one of the big ones was the supersession of Sir John Jellicoe. Even the thousands who knew him only by sight, thought of him as a friend – a modest, honest, decent man – as well as a definitively professional commander-in-chief; and even Jutland had not dulled the dogged faith induced by his presence. "The cries of distress that went up from ordinary seamen on his leaving the Grand Fleet at the end of 1916 were deeply felt." It is small exaggeration to compare Jellicoe's departure with Nelson's death 111 years earlier, when hardened sailors who had "fought like the Devil, sat down and cried like a wench". Indeed, one officer in *Iron Duke* averred that he "never saw so many men blubbing, before, as on the day you left the ship",[78] and another, that "the men stayed on deck watching the barge until she was lost to sight".[79]

The reverse of the coin was that his successor was regarded with widespread suspicion – outside the ranks of junior officers, some of whom were bored or astute enough to welcome a chief who "had in him some elements of a bounder".[80] When Beatty arrived in Scapa to take over command,

> there was no spontaneous cheering to greet him, and had not Admiral Sir Cecil Burney, second-in-command, realized what was happening and signalled an order to 'cheer ship', there would have been no welcome. As it was, the formal cheers were nothing compared with the roar of cheering with which the Grand Fleet said goodbye to Jellicoe.[81]

Lord Fisher, as erratic and muddled (or devious and ambitious) as ever, was quick to rally to his former protégé:

> I have yet a forlorn hope you may go back – sooner or later. I ought to say that my opinion [of Beatty] has greatly altered because of the Jutland Battle episodes, whatever high opinion I might have previously had.[82]

*

A desultory auction of senior officers had commenced between Beatty, Jellicoe and Balfour in the North British Hotel, Edinburgh, on Saturday the 24th. In Beatty's not unreasonable view, it was "most desirable that officers who fill the important commands under me should be those with whose personal capabilities I am acquainted and in whom I had perfect confidence";[83] but in truth there was not much material for radical appointing, and the flag-officers of the 'Beattyite' Grand Fleet would be those men whom Beatty could tolerate at sea, and Jellicoe did not want to take to the Admiralty. Jerram fell into neither camp, struck his flag and was not further employed. Burney went with Jellicoe to the Admiralty to be Second Sea Lord.

The new C-in-C's patronage did not extend quite as far as he wanted, but to replace Burney as the Grand Fleet's second-in-command he sensibly chose (in spite of his beard, which he disliked) Sir Charles Madden. This was a palliative to the Jellicoe camp, and, after the man himself, no one knew better how the fleet worked. To replace Jerram in the 2nd BS, Beatty 'imported' Acting Vice-Admiral Sir John de Robeck, who had shown his abilities in the Dardanelles. As his chief of staff, Beatty took Rear-Admiral Osmond Brock from the 1st BCS, replacing him with another Dardanelles veteran, Rear-Admiral Richard Phillimore. And to step into his own shoes as SOBCF, he appointed Sir William Pakenham, replacing him in the 2nd BCS with Rear-Admiral John Green (lately CO of *New Zealand*).

It was expected that Sturdee would resign his post as VA4BS, in high dudgeon at having both Beatty and Madden promoted over his head, and the Admiralty rather pointedly wrote to ask his intentions. But he stayed – "the nation being at war, I feel it is my duty to place my services entirely at the disposal of Their Lordships" – and thereafter did his loyal best to serve his new boss. Beatty, in return, referred to him archly as "The Victor of the Falklands Battle"[84] and told Lady Beatty that "Poor Sturdee is very *piano* but is eating out of the hand and ready to help all he can."[85]

In addition to Cecil Burney, Jellicoe took with him to the Admiralty three officers: Rear-Admiral Alexander Duff, to be Director of the new Anti-Submarine Division; *Iron Duke*'s Captain Frederick Dreyer, to be Duff's assistant and, later, Director of Naval Ordnance; and *Warspite*'s Edward Phillpotts, to be First Sea Lord's Naval Assistant (JJ to Evan-Thomas: "Forgive me for taking Phillpotts"[86]). Rear-Admiral Michael Culme-Seymour was already there as Director of Mobilization. They would shortly be joined by *Queen Elizabeth*'s Captain George Hope.

There is no suggestion that Beatty considered getting rid of Sir Hugh Evan-Thomas (to Lady Beatty: "Madden, Evan-Thomas . . . are alright"[87]). Apart from there being no obvious substitute worth the disruption the 5th BS was widely understood to have saved the BCF at Jutland,[88] and summarily to sack its gallant senior officer would have expended every ounce of credit Beatty enjoyed with his new command. And, in fact, the changes afforded Evan-Thomas a degree of functional promotion, for now, when his squadron worked with the Battle Cruiser Force (as it would from time to time), he, being senior to Old Packs, would be in overall command[89] – the sensible force-command arrangement which would have obtained at Jutland had Bayly or Sturdee been given the job of SO5BS in the first place.

Evan-Thomas adapted to the change in leadership with impeccable loyalty and pragmatism, writing privately: "Our chief is of course a very great loss, but he is badly wanted in Whitehall where he will be invaluable just now. <u>Our new chief will be first rate</u>."[90] He was not to know that his first-rate new chief had yet to spring an unpleasant surprise over the matter of his flagship.

*

Beatty inherited a fleet which ran like clockwork: an enormous, complex, orderly community, efficiently supplied, rigorously practised, spoiling to settle accounts with the High Seas Fleet, and as reconciled to its barren surroundings as could be wished. These legacies of Jellicoe's command were tremendous assets, and of the two main management tasks facing the new C-in-C, the first was simply not to squander Jellicoe's work and to maintain the fleet's high morale in the face of what might be many more months of waiting for action. The second was to institute his own ideas as to how the fleet should be run, trained and led.

In the eyes of the men of the Battle Fleet, Sir John Jellicoe's act seemed an impossible one to follow. Many ratings, in particular, would continue to regard the fleet as his, as if Beatty were merely borrowing it. Those in the '*Duke*' never wavered in their loyalty to Jellicoe, even long after he had departed,[91] and did not take kindly to Beatty's intrusion. In a memoir which surely contains both hyperbole and geographical confusion, Joe Cockburn, the young torpedoman who had made ship models for Jellicoe, echoed a comparison common among his shipmates:

> At sea, Sir John, a figure in a duffel coat and sometimes wearing a white cap cover would come through the messdecks with an 'Excuse me', and that would be Sir John making his way to the bridge. When Beatty came on board it was 'CLEAR LOWER DECKS' and a file of marines wearing short-arms with Beatty in the middle. We never liked him. [He] never moved without a file of marines.[92]

And while Beatty's letters show his mirth at the tons of his predecessor's office equipment which he evicted from the flagship ("my predecessor loved detail, I hate it!!"[93]), Cockburn scathingly recalled the removal of Jellicoe's tactical-gaming table and its replacement with "a thing like a Turkish bath, getting the heat from dozens of electric lamps". This was Beatty's Electric Light Bath, which he had had built in *Lion*, and in which he used to sit, of an evening, when he was cold. (Once Filson Young, having knocked and heard "Enter!", went into Beatty's cabin to find an apparently empty room, and got a fright when he noticed the admiral's head protruding from the furniture.[94])

Before long, in Cockburn's analysis, Beatty "sensed that he was not welcome and transferred his flag [and Electric Light Bath] to the *Queen Elizabeth*"; and, indeed, Beatty admitted privately that "there was too much Jellicoe about the *Iron Duke*, so I thought a change would be for the best."[95]

It was understandable for a new C-in-C to want a flagship unassociated with his predecessor (although in 1800 St Vincent hoisted his flag in *Royal George* exactly *because* of her company's fondness for the departed Bridport), and it was his prerogative to use whatever ship he liked. But his insistence on *Queen Elizabeth* is highly debatable; and, since he mentioned to his wife just before Christmas that he was "having a little trouble on the *Queen Elizabeth* question, and it may come to a struggle",[96] he evidently met with resistance from the Admiralty. The ship comprised one-fifth of the Grand Fleet's fast battle-squadron, and to take her away meant reducing that force to the 'Jutland four' and, periodically, to just three units – a cut which could have ramifications for Evan-Thomas in a future encounter with enemy heavy groups at sea, and even jeopardize his capacity to 'turn the enemy's line' in the prescribed manner.

Beatty explained away his choosing *Queen Elizabeth* by asserting, with majestic humbug, that "she had the speed to enable him at short notice to get to the most favourable position for exercising supreme command in battle".[97] It is impossible to take this seriously. To award himself a 'roving commission' in a fleet action would distract him from the correct use of the Battle Fleet; and, with all of four knots' extra speed, he would either mask successive battleships on his way to 'have a look for himself', or he would have to pass behind them where he would be able to see nothing. He could very easily have chosen one of the new 15-inch *Revenges*, which were still joining the Fleet and which were fully the equals (some would say the superiors) of the *Queen Elizabeths* in all military qualities except speed – and barely two knots slower. As late as mid-January '17, his staff-commander, Reginald Plunkett, was indeed expecting that he would transfer his flag from *Iron Duke* to *Ramillies*.[98]

But Sir David had coveted *Queen Elizabeth* at least since November 1914, when the First Lord of the Admiralty had imprudently promised the class to him; and it looks very much as if he was determined to fly his flag in what he considered to be the most prestigious warship in the world, come what may. *QE* went into Rosyth dockyard to have an assortment of flagship-like modifications (extra voice-pipes, a pole-mast for an admiral's flag, crutch-blocks for his barge, etc.[99]), and then, on the 16th of February 1917, one year and ten months after Churchill's promise was retracted by Jellicoe, Beatty's habitual flag-captain, Ernle Chatfield, ousted Captain George Hope from his ship, and the Cross of St George ascended her new pole-masthead. RA5BS, through upwards-loyalty or self-preservation, appears to have made no protest, although it may be noted that Jellicoe promptly employed Hope at the Admiralty, as Director of Operations.

Among the *Lion* hangers-on who moved into '*Big Lizzie*' were two midshipmen, the future Lord Louis Mountbatten and "my great friend Frank Bradford". They were heralds of overcrowding, of flagship routines, and of their ship's exile from the élite club of the 5th Battle Squadron, and they received "a poor welcome" in the gunroom:

> The battleship midshipmen made it clear that they didn't like battlecruiser midshipmen. The feeling against Beatty hoisting his flag in the *QE* and crowding the ship's officers out with his staff found expression in a popular song at a concert in the *QE* just before Beatty came. This was often sung by the other members of the *QE* gunroom:

> > We want to keep our cabins,
> > Our cabins, we do.
> > We don't want to sling in hammocks,
> > And wear stiff collars too.
> > For a gilded staff may be jolly fine,
> > But with us you'll all agree,
> > That more or less the 5th BS
> > *Is* the old *QE*![100]

*

Shortly after Beatty's accession, Lieutenant-Commander Ralph Seymour, now the incumbent of the most prestigious flag-lieutenancy in the world (to the chagrin of the Grand Fleet's qualified 'S's), was able to report to Lady Beatty that

> All the admirals came to dinner the other night. A very different appearance to the last time I saw all the admirals of the Grand Fleet together, none deaf or in any way aged or infirm ... My best love to you all for Christmas.[101]

Beatty and his followers brought a sense of a new dawning to the fleet's higher strata. While he himself cannot be ranked among the most prominent military brains of this century, he grasped, as Tryon had, fundamentals of naval warfare which had not been taken on board by some of his technically more proficient, or career-serving, seniors and contemporaries. At any rate, he made use of – certainly gave rein to – a number of officers, such as Reginald Plunkett, Osmond Brock and Herbert Richmond, who *can* be counted among the Royal Navy's emerging doctrinal thinkers. Indeed, *Lion* had been a focus of mild sedition for some time before the change of high command.

Three weeks after Jutland, when unauthorized thinking was still something of a clandestine activity, Sturdee had sent Beatty (to whom he was at that time still senior) a long paper which would certainly have offended Jellicoe. It addressed the maladies which he saw besetting the Grand Fleet. "There can be no doubt", he said,

> that our system of peace training has not been ideally suited to the requirements of modern war . . . It is almost inevitable now that we must reap what we have sown, but anything that can be done to foster and encourage [qualities of initiative and bold leadership] will, even now, be of infinite value to us.[102]

A month later, Captain Richmond, languishing in comparative exile in command of the pre-dreadnought battleship *Commonwealth*, based on the South Coast, wrote to Commander Plunkett on the need for better professional general education, and asked: "Are the younger men beginning to think that they haven't known enough about the conduct of war, and to recognize what a lot of shortcomings there are? I hope so."[103] Richmond knew that Plunkett was a postal address for Beatty, and, indeed, the latter "read Richmond's proposals with interest", and, upon becoming C-in-C, arranged for him to be given command of the battleship *Conqueror* in the Grand Fleet.[104] Meanwhile discussion papers were emerging into the unaccustomed daylight.

On the change in high command, Plunkett was quick to produce one entitled 'General Principles and their Application'.[105] It consisted of a collage of truisms about the nature of warfare, without much on how they were to be applied in practice; but at least the truisms were getting aired. He followed it in January 1917 with a longer paper full of unspoken blame for Jellicoe, Jerram and Evan-Thomas:

> The occasions for caution are many, great risks must be taken very seldom but they are justifiable when they promise great results which cannot otherwise be achieved. Thus it may be suggested that strategy may be cautious, but almost inevitably there comes a time before the climax is reached

when caution must be thrown to the winds – or at least must cease to be a dominant factor.

Each subordinate leader must know his C-in-C so well that he will know exactly what he would wish if he were himself present at the moment when a decision must be made. The subordinate must then use his initiative and seize the opportunity that presents itself, in the manner that he believes the C-in-C would wish. To wait for orders or to ask for orders may well be justified by the printed instructions, but both mean wasting time and waste of time is almost inevitably fatal to success.[106]

The issue of squadronal (or 'divisional') action was an obvious barometer of tactical doctrine, and on the prima facie evidence, Jutland had not been an advertisement for it. Every major British ship loss (with the possible exception of that of *Queen Mary*) could be said to have come about through squadrons departing from the strictures of GFBOs and getting embroiled ill-advisedly, beyond proper support; and Evan-Thomas may have had this in mind when (as mentioned in Chapter 3) he told Richmond in July 1917 that he viewed independent action "with alarm" and considered "any separation dangerous".

This was a misconstruction of the proper meaning of squadronal action, which was that junior flag-officers should manoeuvre to take advantage of any passing opportunity to damage or disrupt the opposition, and, upon their doing so, all suitable forces within supporting distance must move in support. Freedom to attack, and obligation to support. It did not mean 'go tilting at anything in sight', and was as much a matter of 'secondary education', calling for alertness, interpretation, judgement and decision-making, as one of sheer aggression. Nevertheless, while the radicals were justified, in principle, in pushing for fastest progress towards devolution, Beatty had to operate with the personnel to hand, and reform at the right speed for Herbert Richmond would have been too fast for many others in the Grand Fleet – and in some ways too fast for the C-in-C himself. For example, to the disappointment of some of his advisers, he continued to support the traditional single-line ahead "until the enemy's fleet has been disorganized and broken up",[107] but he wanted there to be no hesitation, among his divisional leaders, in adopting 'manoeuvre' tactics, as soon as the cumbersome battle-line risked the loss of offensive opportunities.

Beatty started by sending his admirals out from Scapa to get used to manoeuvring their squadrons without supervision;[108] and then, in March 1917, he effectively transfused his BCFOs into the wider Grand Fleet by overriding GFBOs with two "commendably brief" pages of Grand Fleet Battle *Instructions* (GFBIs), setting out the principles of decentralization and anticipation which would henceforth govern the conduct of the fleet.[109] This innovation, of course, harks back to Richmond's pre-war complaint (mentioned in Chapter 4) of how the RN had forgotten the distinction between mandatory *orders* and guiding *instructions*.

Meanwhile, one may discern the workings of squadronal action in the new concentration-of-fire measures introduced in 1917. First flashing lamps, and then short-range W/T, were used to direct the fire of a whole division, and October 1917 found Beatty reporting to the King that

> we have got through a very heavy gunnery programme and have I think made considerable strides in increasing their efficiency. So much so, that we are now able to produce a concentration of 4 [underlined twice] ships on one target without any loss of efficiency in the individual ships, or in the rapidity of fire, indeed we have increased both, by a system of combination and inter-communication which has worked very well.[110]

Finally, on January the 1st, 1918, Beatty abolished GFBOs – or, rather, divided their contents into two separate volumes: an expanded version of his new GFBIs; and Grand Fleet Manoeuvring Orders (GFMOs). In the latter were consigned all those practical minutiae, collated by Jellicoe, about the handling of squadrons and flotillas, in various conditions and formations, which should by now have been common knowledge to the senior officers involved. In the former were "the guiding principles which are to be observed by all arms of the fleet when obtaining contact, and when in action, with the enemy", and they were to be brought to the notice "of all officers of the rank of lieutenant and above". Among the guiding principles we find the need to apply crushing force to any section of the enemy's line which might present itself, and the warning that it may be necessary to turn towards a massed torpedo attack in order to maintain gun-range. And here, given new prominence, were his own and Jellicoe's previous initiative provisions, augmented by an injunction which had featured in Sir George Callaghan's pre-war standing orders, but which Jellicoe had discarded:

> Whenever flag or commanding officers find themselves without special directions, either from inability to make out or receive signals, or from unforeseen circumstances rendering previous orders inapplicable, they are to act as their judgement dictates in making every effort to damage the enemy.[111]

There has been some misapprehension concerning Beatty's tactical reforms: Professor Marder both overstates them in detail[112] and underestimates them in general. More important, perhaps, than the reshuffle of words between various titles, was the subtle but significant change in the role of the Grand Fleet's standing orders, for it was now GFBIs (if anything) which the captain would leave open on the pelorus, to the annoyance of the navigator, not the full volume of GFBOs (now GFMOs). A parallel may be drawn, at least in principle, with Tryon's putting the *Signal* and *Manoeuvring Books* "to one side" in action and using instead his back-of-an-envelope tactical system. Indeed, it may be said that while GFMOs still catalogued the Colombine 'primary' skills which Beatty expected of his Grand Fleet COs and flag-officers, GFBIs summarized the Tryonic 'secondary' principles by which he meant them to be guided.

The successive modifications to the orders/instructions themselves, the change in their role implicit in the new nomenclature, and the innovations in the training and practices of the Grand Fleet, which took place between Jellicoe's post-Jutland amendments and (say) the beginning of 1918, can justly be rated a cumulative revolution.

Steadily, therefore, Beatty made clear that, whereas Jellicoe had expected a battle to conform to the script in GFBOs, he, for his part, expected his flag-officers to respond to the ebb and flow of the action: to take their orders from the enemy (as Tryon would have said), and not, on any account, to let go of him.

By this time Herbert Richmond – delighted to find himself under a chief who "sees so much beyond his own arm"[113] – was conspiring with Reginald Plunkett (now Plunkett-Ernle-Erle-Drax) to harness Beatty as a force against the cultural teredo which had eaten so deeply into the service's timbers. In a letter to Plunkett, scribbled on a signals pad in September 1917, he defined their objective as being to

> pull to bits the 'tradition' arguments, by showing that there is no tradition in them, except the tradition of 100 years of peace in which war was forgotten. I think if we resolutely set ourselves to work along these lines we could interest B. enough to have him on our side.[114]

*

In June 1917, King George V visited the Grand Fleet. He was, in a sense, on business, having a backlog of honours to invest, and it had the characteristics of a state visit. Beatty's relationship with the Monarch (as he liked to call him) was adequate but never close. They had served together in *Alexandra*, in the late 1880s, when George was a sub-lieutenant, and the Beattys had been guests at Abergeldie or Balmoral on five separate occasions between 1906 and 1914;[115] but the two men were, at best, wary of one another. Their differences in personality could hardly have been greater, and if the King, with his staid ideas about conduct, did not actually know that Beatty was carrying on with the wife of one of his equerries, he probably suspected that that was the sort of thing he might do. Now Beatty told his own wife:

> The Monarch arrives Thursday, he really is a nuisance and adds much to the labours, and is to remain until Monday. He is to be accompanied by Pressmen and cinematographers. It appears he is anxious that the world should know that he is doing something. But it does not help the war.[116]

Beatty, however, had a gift for 'taking charge', and he now did so in his forthright style. When the King arrived aboard *Queen Elizabeth* after a gruelling trip across the Pentland Firth, on a bitterly cold day, he was promptly "popped" into the Electric Light Bath,[117] and he thereafter submitted to the programme arranged for him. Every day he was farmed out to one flagship or another for lunch (very desirable, in Beatty's view, since George had tediously forsworn alcohol for the duration); and *Queen Elizabeth* took him to sea for gunnery demonstrations with the 5th Battle Squadron.

The highlight of the visit was the investiture of honours. Owing to inclement weather, this took place in *Queen Elizabeth*'s wardroom flat, which was closely packed with naval officers, recipients-to-be, a guard of honour and gentlemen of the press (who, last seen being hoisted aboard in limp condition after their sea-crossing, now mysteriously reappeared). After a false start, when a bearded admiral's resemblance to the King caused the marines to salute and the band to strike up the National Anthem (Madden did this from time to time), His Majesty arrived to distribute the awards – of which the most senior was Beatty's GCVO – from a table "ablaze with insignia, ribbons, stars and crosses".[118] The show, however, was stolen by Beatty himself, in a manner which was both dramatic and ironic, when Hugh Evan-Thomas came forward to be dubbed.

Sub-Lieutenant Prince Albert (now serving in *Malaya*) had just positioned the hassock for the rear-admiral to kneel upon, when there was "something of a thrill" as Beatty suddenly stepped out and drew his sword, handing it, hilt-first, to the King. Thus was Evan-Thomas knighted with Sir David Beatty's sword, in the battleship which Beatty had requisitioned from his command. It was a splendid, chivalrous gesture, which was universally acclaimed as "a striking compliment from the Commander-in-Chief to the man who gave him such invaluable help at the Battle of Jutland"[119] – and this may, indeed, have been Beatty's sole motive. But it is permissible (at least in view of his later conduct towards Sir Hugh) to allow a smidgen of cynicism to intrude.

Sir David's flagship had been invaded by a man (one of very few) who eclipsed him in precedence, and who was the main focus of the attendant press reporters. George was on familiar – almost familial – terms with some of Beatty's subordinates: Evan-Thomas, of course, but also in varying degrees Goodenough, Leveson, Napier and Pakenham. These officers, along with Commander Sir Charles Cust (present as ADC), formed a loose 'courtier' group, bonded by friendships which went back many years, and of which Beatty was not himself a member. What more brilliant way than by this marvellous Elizabethan piece of theatre to reassert dominance in his own territory?

*

Beatty's showmanship was a vital factor in maintaining the Grand Fleet's morale amid the tedium of endless training and endless waiting for action. His defiant, rakish image, his energy and outward self-assurance fostered an endurance of purpose and commitment which a less charismatic officer (even Jellicoe) could not have discovered. He never missed an opportunity to attend the fleet's sporting events or theatrical productions, and he always spoke to the assembled audience afterwards. The message was always the same: "Soon they will have to come out, and there is only one thing for us to do. Annihilate them." Always, he was cheered to the echo. Privately, he wondered if it would ever happen: "I keep saying to myself, 'Patience, just have patience', but it is hard to live up to that."[120]

Even at the time of the change of command, the focus of the naval war was shifting to the Western Approaches and to merchant shipping. The 'unrestricted' U-boat campaign against trade had got under way after the High Seas Fleet's abortive August foray, and, in Beatty's first month as C-in-C, and Jellicoe's as First Sea Lord, the mercantile tonnage sunk was three times higher than at the time of Jutland – and three times higher than the rate of replacement-building. The situation got progressively worse in the early months of 1917. By April, a dozen ships (Allied and neutral) were being sunk every day. At this rate the war would soon be lost.

Jellicoe had gone to the Admiralty partly to get to grips with the U-boat menace. He failed. The Admiralty had long set its face against that old eighteenth-century solution, convoying, partly through doubts about the abilities of merchant ships to keep station (the fine tuning of speed was the anticipated problem), but partly, also, because of a statistical misconception which over-represented the scale of the escorting task by a factor of fifteen.[121] Jellicoe and the new, unassertive First Lord, Sir Edward Carson, lapsed into a mind-set of defeat.

The issue became the subject of an extraordinary tussle of will between Their Lordships and a handful of comparatively junior officers, of whom three stand out: Captain Herbert Richmond, Commander Reginald Henderson and Lieutenant-Commander Joseph Kenworthy. The last-named (later the 10th Lord Strabolgi, and not a serious career naval officer) appears merely to have enjoyed unofficial links with Lloyd George and to have kept him informed of junior-officer opinion about the Admiralty. Richmond's deep perceptions of eighteenth-century convoying enabled him to see the issues in terms of method and cost-efficiency. Jellicoe tried to discredit him as "just a paper man", and while the Admiralty obtusely wasted precious months looking to technology for a solution to the crisis, hundreds of merchant ships went to the bottom.

Reginald Henderson, a brilliant young commander of the Anti-Submarine Department, has been described as the "chief architect"[122] of the convoy system. At the Admiralty in 1917, he had experience of organizing the coal trade between South Wales and France, and, like his friends Richmond and Kenworthy, worked behind the backs of his seniors to reach the ear of the Prime Minister. It was disgraceful, and it does David Lloyd George's judgement credit that he encouraged it (the all-seeing, all-knowing secretary of the War Cabinet, Colonel Sir Maurice Hankey, was not uninvolved). Most of the above is a digression. But it illustrates how Britain was saved from defeat in 1917 by a handful of quite junior mavericks of the sort which Jellicoe cordially disliked, and which armed forces usually try to suppress. Most, if not all, of them were at some stage and in some manner connected with Beatty.[123]

The climax came at the end of April 1917, when the Prime Minister, in effect, read the riot act to Their Lordships, and ostentatiously visited the Admiralty (unprecedented!) to underscore the point. Convoying took a while to get right, but, as the summer months of 1917 progressed, the loss-curve turned decisively downwards. As galling for the Admiralty as Lloyd George's intervention was the appointment, in early June, of Sir Eric Geddes as Controller of the Navy (and honorary vice-admiral): a dynamic Scottish railway engineer who had worked miracles with the military transport system in France, Sir Eric was a man after the Prime Minister's driven Celtic heart, and anathema to the Admiralty's gentlemanly, anxious regime. There was soon friction.

At the end of July, Carson was 'kicked upstairs' to the War Cabinet by Lloyd George, and Geddes, after only seven weeks as Controller, was moved to the highest Admiralty post of First Lord. Then, a few days later, the "worn out and obstructionist" Sir Cecil Burney was forced out of the post of Second Sea Lord over Jellicoe's protests, to be replaced by a relative unknown, Vice-Admiral Sir Rosslyn Wemyss. 'Rosy Wemyss' (or 'Old Biddy', as he was sometimes called in royal circles[124]) was a monocled officer of impeccable social graces and limited war record. Jellicoe thought him "such a nice fellow to work with",[125] and wondered why he was given the new title of 'Deputy First Sea Lord'. Inevitably, before long, Geddes made Jellicoe's removal a condition of his own staying on, and, in December, Sir John was dismissed ("very curtly", he considered, "without any reason at all being given"[126]) with a junior peerage as a sop to his wounded pride, and Wemyss stepped into his shoes.

Some sections of the service were scandalized. Others, mainly those around Beatty, were delighted: "Jellicoe has fallen," Richmond wrote. "One obstacle to a successful war is now out of the way."[127]

All this while the Grand Fleet had been waiting and training and waiting, up at Scapa Flow. "How many months are we to wait?" Beatty ached to know.

> I would not mind how many if I knew at the end we would get them, but it is the haunting fear that we never shall and the Grand Fleet will never be able to justify itself, that is the fly in the ointment . . . Indeed we would all lie down and turn up our toes if we thought for a moment there was a possibility of it being possible.[128]

In December 1917 a squadron of four, later five, United States battleships joined the Grand Fleet, to form the 6th Battle Squadron. After initially viewing each other with wariness the two nationalities blended easily. The 'dry' American officers soon discovered that there was an open bar in the nearest British warship, and the British appreciated tinned peaches. The 6th BS became integrated with a degree of harmony which was all too soon forgotten after the war:

> So completely did our squadron merge into their fleet that we became a part of it, and ceased to be held as anything else. In our ships we served tea, had dinner late, spoke in abbreviations, signalled drilled and maneuvred in the British way as nearly as we could. In British ships, the officers were organizing jazz bands, dancing jazz, using our slang, drinking iced drinks, shouting our Navy yells and discussing our fire-control. The Grand Fleet had become no longer that of Britain alone. It was the Grand Fleet of the English speaking nations.[129]

Privately Beatty feared that the prospects for a German fleet victory had by now slipped so far into the realms of fantasy that they would certainly never come out again; and after the fleet moved south to Rosyth, in April 1918, he would go up to Edinburgh to try to extract some joy out of a fortune-teller named Josephine. Meanwhile the waiting, and the training, and the futile forays to sea went inexorably on.

We know from a hundred previous experiences what these sweeps are. You see nothing but bad weather. There is as much chance of seeing a Hun as there is of our flying. I suppose old Nelson's crowd had the same show off Toulon, but under more unpleasant circumstances. And even then, young chaps used to go meandering off in brigs and sloops and cutters, and have the deuce of a time.[130]

An American officer later testified to the spirit of the Grand Fleet, in words which do Beatty's leadership much credit:

the outstanding characteristic of British Sea Power was its extraordinarily high morale in the face of great handicaps . . . When Allied military morale was at the breaking point, and the refusal of the German High Seas Fleet to come out and fight imposed heavy burdens, Grand Fleet morale was at such a peak that it was a joy to serve in it.[131]

As the war drew to an end on the rutted, debris-strewn roads of north-western Europe in the autumn of 1918, hopes briefly rose of a face-saving foray by the High Seas Fleet, but the same German sailors who, "on May 31st, 1916, had fought with the utmost gallantry and steadiness in the face of heavy odds, broke into open mutiny rather than go out and seek battle again".[132] And, as it became inescapably apparent that Beatty's magnificent fleet of fleets had gone on honing its efficiency and maintaining its good humour for no appeal to a higher court of battle, then Jellicoe's supposedly missed opportunities at the costly, half-cock engagement of May 1916 assumed their historical perspective. Germany's collapse into disorder and disaffection found Beatty in the sourest of tempers:

The Fleet, my Fleet, is broken-hearted, but are still wonderful, the most wonderful thing in Creation, and although it would appear that they can never achieve their hearts' desire, they preserve a cheerfulness that is extraordinary . . . I had most of my Captains and Admirals on board this morning, and with them to support me, I feel we could go anywhere and do anything. All suffering from a feeling far greater than disappointment, depressed beyond measure . . .

[As for the Germans,] the only thing to do is to sail into their poisonous country and wreck it and take what we want and put the fear of God, Truth and Justice into them, represented by the British Tommy.[133]

The Allies had scotched the snake, not killed it: "there will be another war in twenty years, and Japan will be on the other side."[134]

Beatty's sentiments were not, in fact, universally shared in his fleet. Not everyone was broken-hearted. One midshipman called the war's end "the most wonderful day since the world cooled down",[135] and the impromptu letting off of pyrotechnics and playing of ragtime went on far into the night.

The Admiralty, unsure of who now wielded authority in Germany, managed to contact von Hipper's High Command and arrange for an envoy to be sent over to Rosyth to 'negotiate' the terms of the naval armistice. Rear-Admiral Hugo Meurer (who had commanded the pre-dreadnought *Deutschland* at Jutland) and a small staff duly arrived in the cruiser *Königsberg*, which entered the Firth of Forth without ceremony on November the 15th, and was directed to anchor close to the island of Inchkeith.

Technically, the state of war was suspended rather than ended, and the first formal meeting between British and German officers was stage-managed with every ounce of Beatty's flair and malice. ("You would have loved it," he told his mistress, "it was Dramatic and Tragic to a high degree."[136])

From his anchorage, Admiral Meurer and his small group were brought by destroyer, through thick fog, the twelve miles to *Queen Elizabeth*, past seemingly endless rows of British and American dread-noughts whose great bows loomed out of the drizzle, duty-watchmen calling out challenges, fog-bells clanging. On the flagship's quarterdeck, the Grand Fleet's largest Royal Marines silently lined their path, capes, bayonets and steel helmets glinting in the light of arc-lamps positioned above. The German officers were ushered forward into the comman-der-in-chief's day cabin, where they received the full chill of British *froideur*.

Beatty, with his senior staff and his interpreters, sat, stony-faced, along one side of a baize-covered table, beneath a portrait of Nelson. Meurer's credentials were unhurriedly examined, and then the long cat-alogue of internments and U-boat surrenders was read through, with little scope for negotiation. Cowed by their straitened circumstances and by sheer *force majeur*, the Germans' protestations were feeble and mostly futile: if this or that ship was unable to sail because her crew had deserted, or her engines were defective, then another must be found to take her place. In such stilted conversation as there was, Meurer's tale of privation and disorder in his homeland was heard without sympathy ("Thank God for the British Navy," Beatty told himself, "this is your work"[137]). During an interval the German admiral was spotted in the pantry, pocketing a wedge of cheese.

Presently, he departed with his instructions. And on the morning of the 21st of November, Rear-Admiral Ludwig von Reuter, whose light-cruisers had tangled with Goodenough's on the night of Jutland, losing *Frauenlob* and raking *Southampton* with shellfire, brought the still-serviceable units of the High Seas Fleet – seventy ships in all, shabby and unkempt, and without breech-blocks in their guns – to an appointed rendezvous off May Island. There they were met by Beatty and 370 Allied warships, all at action-stations and waiting for just "one shot to start the whole show again". To the Germans, the silent lines of British battleships were endless: "the spectacle was stupendous, overpowering."[138]

When the High Seas Fleet was at anchor in the lee of Inchkeith, Beatty signalled: "THE GERMAN FLAG WILL BE HAULED DOWN AT SUNSET TODAY, AND WILL NOT BE HOISTED AGAIN WITHOUT PERMISSION." The Germans had come, under the terms of the Armistice, to be 'interned'. In insisting that they strike their colours, Beatty was, in effect, claiming their surrender. It was illegal, even dishonourable; but what was honour to a fleet which had refused combat and claimed victory – claimed, indeed, to have wrested the trident from the Navy which "had ruled the oceans when Berlin was a mud-streeted village"?[139] Von Reuter protested miserably, but, under 'house arrest' by political agents aboard his own ship and surrounded by Allied naval power immeasurably greater than his dishevelled and disarmed squadron, the issue was a sophistry.

At sunset the men of *Queen Elizabeth* gave Sir David three deafening cheers. "I always told you they would have to come out," he said in reply. In *Iron Duke*, they thought Jellicoe's absence from this climactic event, and the way Beatty took all the credit, "was the most disgraceful thing that ever took place".[140] Another absentee was Vice-Admiral Sir Hugh Evan-Thomas: on October the 1st, 1918, after three years leading the 5th Battle Squadron with vigorous efficiency (if not, on every occasion, with imagination), he had handed over command to Rear-Admiral Arthur Leveson, and gone ashore.

The Imperial German Naval Ensign was in fact hoisted once more in the High Seas Fleet. Seven months later, on the morning of June the 21st, 1919, as the terms of the peace settlement were being finalized in Paris – terms which would see the German ships shared out among the victorious powers – their depleted crews hoisted ensigns, opened seacocks to admit the waters of Scapa Flow, and took to the boats. As the great warships settled, to sink or capsize, a party of Kirkwall schoolchildren, reviewing the fleet from a fishing-boat hired for the purpose, supposed it to be a show put on for their benefit.

24

Dirty Work Somewhere

"Publicity, controversy, politics and ostentatious ballyhoo."

Sir Rosslyn Wemyss was in an unenviable position as interim First Sea Lord between Jellicoe and Beatty. Although he had presided over the ultimate defeat of the U-boat campaign, he could not be said to have had the 'unreserved confidence of the service' – the customary platitude – if only because he was not widely known. His predecessor's supporters, of whom many remained at the Admiralty, suspected him of playing a part in the manoeuvres which had removed their beloved chief from office, and, as soon as the Armistice was declared, Beatty's partisans resented his obstruction of their hero's advancement.

Old Biddy had started his naval career seven years senior to Beatty but owing to the latter's post-Egypt promotional boost they had both got their brass-hats in 1898, and, owing to his service in China, Beatty had subsequently eased a couple of years ahead. In 1905 Wemyss succeeded Beatty in command of the cruiser *Suffolk* (later implying that he found her in a state of "inefficiency and discontent"[1]), and Beatty thereafter regarded him as his natural junior – only First Sea Lord now because, during wartime, Britain's foremost fighting admiral was required at sea. There could be no question but that Beatty's succession of Wemyss was merely a matter of time – indeed, Sir Eric Geddes, as First Lord, had given him a verbal undertaking that the First Sea Lordship would be his as soon as the war ended.

But the war had ended, the former High Seas Fleet was relegated to Scapa Flow, the American battle-squadron departed, Christmas came and went, Geddes was succeeded by Sir Walter Long, and still Beatty's flag flew over the Grand Fleet as it swung around its anchors in the backwaters of world affairs. The problem was that while Wemyss lacked

Beatty's charisma and high public profile, he was a man of urbane political and diplomatic skills, and the Prime Minister, David Lloyd George, wanted him to stay on at least until the peace negotiations in Paris were complete. His proconsular retention of office triggered a form of paranoia in his heir-apparent, who was unaccustomed to being thwarted and now behaved like a spoilt child. "I think that some consideration is due to an officer in my position, and that I should not be kept 'backing and filling' indefinitely to suit your convenience,"[2] Beatty notified his professional senior.

On April the 3rd 1919, Beatty became, at 48, the youngest admiral of the fleet in history, when he and Jellicoe were promoted to the highest naval rank by special Order in Council. For four days his Union Flag flew at *Queen Elizabeth*'s masthead, and then the Grand Fleet dispersed and Admiral Sir Charles Madden hoisted his cross of St George as C-in-C Atlantic Fleet.

Sir David thus 'came ashore' for the first time for six years. First, he went to Paris, which was busy with statesmen, diplomats and generals. There he received many French honours, and complained – not for himself, but for the great service which he personified – of being ignored by the British delegation. He contrasted the French Government's loan of a special train, with the Admiralty's refusal of a travel warrant for his wife's maid, and worked on his sense of grievance. Then he went out on a well-earned holiday.

Accompanied by his wife, her niece Gwendolen Field, Commander Ralph Seymour (who had been granted special leave[3]) and a small staff, Beatty embarked in Lady Beatty's 700-ton steam yacht *Sheelah* in Marseilles, and set out on a Mediterranean cruise during which he was fêted at every port of call. Meanwhile he monitored days-old copies of British newspapers, for, with his evident complicity, a campaign about the First Sea Lordship had been launched by the Northcliffe press – *The Times*, *Daily Mail*, *Daily Mirror* and *Evening News* – which was little short of insulting to the incumbent.

Once back in England, Beatty resumed his petulant correspondence with the Admiralty, fulminating about being 'unemployed'. By mid-June Long was writing to the King's private secretary that he

> has behaved very foolishly and if he does not mend his ways I think he will make it very difficult for him ever to become First Sea Lord. Meanwhile Wemyss has strengthened his position immensely by the dignified way in which he has borne these most undeserved attacks.[4]

It was fantasy to pretend that the next First Sea Lord could be anyone other than Beatty, but the problem now for Long was how to contrive

Wemyss's departure in a manner which did not appear a craven surrender to Beatty's blustering. Meanwhile, Sir Rosslyn stayed put.

In August Beatty's vanity was appeased somewhat when he was elevated to the peerage. It was satisfactory that he got an earldom (to match that of Field Marshal Haig), whereas Jellicoe had received a mere viscountcy. It was also satisfactory that the titles themselves – Viscount Jellicoe of Scapa, Earl Beatty of the North Sea – suggested that whereas the former had spent his time holed up in harbour, Beatty had spent his out searching for the enemy (although statistically speaking the balance lies rather more the other way[5]).

*

Meanwhile, the Admiralty's Director of Navigation, Captain John Harper, had been assigned by Sir Rosslyn Wemyss to produce a digestible record of Jutland based only on formally documented, or otherwise verifiable fact, with little commentary and no value judgements. It is easy to say now that it was too early to attempt an 'official' version of the battle – "too many Jutland veterans were still alive, still engaged in a longer running fight, the promotion battle, still anxious to clear their individual yardarms"[6] – and that the Admiralty should merely have released an anthology of documentary evidence (which it partially did, in the form of the *Official Despatches*, in December 1920). In reality, however, the primary sources were so riddled with inconsistencies and conflicts that expert adjudication was necessary if the public was to make sense of it.

Harper set to work, commencing his task by sending out the minesweeper *Oakley* to locate the wreck of *Invincible*, so that Beatty's and Jellicoe's navigational plots could be reconciled. Then he painstakingly squared the mass of reports and tracings into a coherent narrative. The proofs of his restrained and matter-of-fact study came back from the printers in October 1919 and were approved for publication by the Board of Admiralty a few days before Lord Wester Wemyss (as he had become) retired. A copy lay on the First Sea Lord's desk when Beatty finally took over on November the 1st, 1919.

Beatty had conquered the utmost peak of his profession: admiral of the fleet, an earldom, now First Sea Lord and Chief of Naval Staff. He was the foremost naval hero of the Great War; the American press had rated him greater than Nelson (and the US Navy had copied his customized version of the British naval uniform). Since lieutenant's rank the newspapers had eaten out of his hand, and he was unaccustomed to public criticism. With the end of wartime censorship, however, he became aware of revisionist murmurs about aspects of his performance at Jutland and elsewhere, and he now found that the *Harper Record* failed to endorse in every respect the battlecruisers' Jutland folklore. It was a simple matter to block its publication and tell its author to clarify a number of points in a suitable manner.

It was less easy to get him fully to comply. Harper soon gathered that the First Sea Lord, and, prominently, Rear-Admiral Chatfield (Fourth Sea Lord, 1919; Assistant Chief of Naval Staff, 1920) were seeking to minimize the role of the Battle Fleet, and to disguise the facts

> that Admiral Beatty had seriously neglected the duty of giving his Commander-in-Chief frequent and precise information of the position of the enemy; that he had failed to inflict damage on a greatly inferior enemy owing to incorrect dispositions of his ships and faulty signalling; and that the shooting of his battle-cruisers was far below the standard expected, at that time, in the Royal Navy.[7]

Harper was now, in effect, being asked to take Lord Beatty's word that certain ranges, timings and other details, which he had patiently distilled from masses of navigational, gunnery and signals data, were wrong, and to attach his name to Beatty's preferred alternatives. Furthermore, Harper's name as the author of the report had been given out in Parliament, so the product would forever be connected with him personally, however 'institutionalized' it became in redrafting. A matter of integrity was at stake, and while there is a stylized element of 'David and Goliath' about his view of the dispute, he had been given (initially) untrammelled terms of reference, and came to feel that the honour of Jellicoe *et al.* depended upon him (as it did, to some extent). It was natural for Harper to defend his work, even if his mission acquired the obsessive logic of mild paranoia.

Beatty's accessory, Ralph Seymour, had accompanied his master to the Admiralty, first as 'additional naval secretary', and then as assistant to Chatfield; and for a time the First Sea Lord made use of the commander as a go-between in dealings with Captain Harper, to whom he unwisely confided that "we do not wish to advertise the fact that the Battle Fleet was in action, more than we can help."[8] The captain cooperated to the extent of making several minor, innocuous alterations, but flatly refused to make certain other changes without an order in writing (which would absolve him of intellectual responsibility for the result). This Beatty could not issue. Among the disputes which stand out in pettiness and rancour was the admiral's claim to have engaged the enemy more closely than he really did, at around 5.45 p.m., and the vexed business of whether the BCF turned through a circle or through an S-bend at 7.0. In defiance of what Harper held to be persuasive evidence,

Beatty would not countenance the record's depicting him as looping-the-loop, and went to the length of forging an 'original' track-chart – only to make a hash of his pre-ennoblement signature.[9]

Meanwhile the world was waiting for the promised 'official' account of Jutland, and Members of Parliament were getting restive about the delay: did the Navy, after all, have something to hide? It was embarrassing; Beatty was not wholly in control, and the First Lord was by no means in his pocket. Anyway, Harper couldn't be sacked without the likelihood of the reasons for his dismissal becoming public. Stalemate.

The partisans of each side sought to discredit their opponents (and, as usual when retired officers are locked in controversy, the snide dismissives, "so-called — " and "armchair — ", were exercised as required). Within a few months of Beatty's taking office, John Harper was targeted by Commander Carlyon Bellairs MP. In his preface to *The Battle of Jutland, the Sowing and the Reaping,* Bellairs (a *Britannia* contemporary of Beatty's) found it necessary to inform the reader

> that Captain Harper has never been a staff-officer. He was navigating officer of the Royal Yacht from June 6 1911 to February 10 1914, and then assistant Harbour-Master at Portsmouth. The performance of these honourable services does not demand any knowledge of war[10]

– in contrast, presumably, to the business of being a Member of Parliament. And before long both Harper and Jellicoe found themselves receiving the attentions of the ever-obliging Northcliffe press.[11]

Jellicoe, meanwhile, was doing his best, as an Admiralty outsider, to help Harper fight his corner. He had read the *Record* and was anxious for its publication – he looked forward to its effect on "those so-called naval experts who write articles for money" (an unattractive and snobbish slur which could never have come from the pen of his career-sponsor, Lord Fisher) – but was constrained from writing to the papers himself by his disdain for vulgar publicity. On a number of occasions Viscount Scapa travelled up from his home in the Isle of Wight to keep track of developments:

> I went to the Admiralty yesterday and knocked up against Captain Harper in the passage, very angry with the *Daily Mail* for an attack on him. I have not read the article as that is a paper I don't read. I fancy the First Lord is taking up the matter in the House [he did no such thing]. I mentioned to him the delay in publication & am seeing him again next week when I intend to go into the question of alterations in the report.[12]

Time was running out, for he was soon to go out to New Zealand to be governor-general (for which service he would finally get his earldom) –

a circumstance which no doubt heightened Harper's sense of trustee-ship, for the gallant captain was himself a New Zealander. Jellicoe had at least half an ally in the First Lord, Sir Walter Long, who was quite aware of what was going on (having dissuaded Harper from suing Bellairs for libel, for example) and who was trying to keep his perch on a narrow and rickety fence; and although disputed matters were far from resolved when Jellicoe sailed for the Antipodes in August 1920, he had extracted an undertaking from Long (repeated in Parliament, in less forthright terms) "that no changes would be made without his concurrence".[13]

*

Negotiations remained deadlocked. Press and Parliament wanted to know why the "missing *Harper Report*" was apparently being sup-pressed;[14] and its author's nerves were, understandably enough, becom-ing "badly frayed".[15] It is said that in the late summer of 1920 Harper had a nervous breakdown[16] (although he was fit enough to command *Resolution* in 1922). Where the bones of contention involved *Lion*'s sig-nalling efficiency, Ralph Seymour, also, must have found himself in an acutely difficult position; and as the tiresome business ground on, Beatty began to appreciate less and less his former flag-lieutenant's wartime services. It was probably about this time that he confided to someone that Seymour "lost three battles for me" – oblivious, appar-ently, of his vicarious responsibility for his junior's recurring errors.

It was not the most propitious moment for the commander to want to marry Beatty's niece. Flag-lieutenants not infrequently married into their admirals' families: indeed that possibility was sometimes a factor in their selection. But when Ralph had the temerity to try to betroth himself to Gwendolen Field – a beneficiary, like Ethel, of the vast Marshall Field fortune – the First Sea Lord's wildcat wife "rose in Hell's fury to break [the] engagement", and the admiral was disposed to indulge her. Seymour ceased to be *persona grata* with the Beattys. He was, according to Sir Shane Leslie, "severely reprimanded"[17] (although for what exactly, it's hard to imagine), and despatched to Portsmouth, in November 1920, to be XO of the Royal Yacht *Victoria and Albert*. Gwenny was packed off to Rome.

Ralph had served Beatty continuously for almost eight years, had basked in his friendship and patronage, and had made the admiral "his god". Nothing had equipped him for these bitter, simultaneous, blows to his aspirations and self-esteem. That winter and spring his mental health was in the balance. In May 1921 he had a nervous break-down. His service record merely states that he was admitted to Haslar naval hospital on June the 20th, suffering from 'psychasthenia', but Commander Stuart Bonham-Carter (C-in-C Malta, 1943) had already stepped into his shoes in the royal yacht three weeks earlier. In the 1920s 'psychasthenia' was a handy label for conditions which doctors didn't really understand. Even today, it is rather nebulously defined as a

> psychoneurosis marked especially by lack of self-control, in consequence of which the patient is dominated by morbid fears or doubts, impulsion to unreasoning and consciously wrong or foolish acts.[18]

Seymour was in and out of RN hospitals at Haslar, Portland and Great Yarmouth for nearly a year. In May 1922 he was allowed three months' "leave of absence on probation", and in early September was simultaneously discharged and retired from the Navy as medically unfit.[19] He signed up for that faithful resort of would-be gentlemen-farmers, Cirencester Royal Agricultural College, and went home to Brighton to stay with his widowed mother at No. 19 Chesham Road for the few weeks remaining before term began.

The doctors who discharged him could not, perhaps, have been expected to allow for the prospect of his having to meet Beatty again, at a civic luncheon to mark the unveiling of Brighton's war memorial, on Saturday the 7th of October. On the morning of Wednesday the 4th, it appears that Ralph left Lady Seymour's house and walked the two hundred yards, by way of Chesham Street or Chichester Place, to the seafront where he turned left and took the inclining cliff path towards Rottingdean. Taking a constitutional along the cliffs was a holiday-maker, a Mr William Swain, secretary of the Watford Brewery. Near a place known as the Black Rock (since re-sculpted for the Brighton Marina) the visitor noticed a youngish man walking very fast and got the impression that he was trying to reach a certain spot before him. As he watched, the stranger took the slope leading to the cliffs at a run, steadied himself for a moment, then raising his hands above his head took a header over the edge as if diving into a swimming pool.

The next day, Thursday the 5th, *The Times* reported that "An unknown man aged about forty threw himself over the cliff at Black Rock Brighton." On Friday it gave the name of the deceased, on the same page as an article lamenting that the terms of the Naval Treaty of Washington precluded the preservation of HMS *Lion* as a national shrine. That day the inquest at Rottingdean was told merely that Commander Seymour had

> suffered a breakdown resulting from war strain. For some months he was in hospital . . . Since then he had appeared brighter. Ten days ago, however, he was invalided out of the Navy, being one of those affected by the reduction in

the establishment. He seemed to feel very deeply leaving the profession in which he had had a distinguished career . . . He was 36 years of age and had latterly complained of sleeplessness.

This was sufficient. It was not uncommon, in the 1920s, for 'demobbed' officers – ex-Army, usually – to take their own lives,[20] and a verdict of suicide during temporary insanity was returned on Beatty's "roly-poly flag-lieutenant" whose companionship and court-jesting had once so commended him to his chief. ("Flags is my Food Dictator & is very arbitrary," the admiral had told his wife, with pretend-forbearance, in 1917.[21]) The next day Earl and Countess Beatty's limousine was hauled through Brighton's cheering crowds by the men of Sussex Division RNVR, and the First Sea Lord received the freedom of the borough.

Lady Seymour blamed Beatty bitterly for her son's death, and sent the admiral what was described (by Shane Leslie) as "an atrocious letter" and (by Ralph's sister Horatia) as "a real stinker". In 1926 she published a biography of the commander, based on a selection of his letters, which portrays an intelligent and lively officer and makes no reference to the causes of his final 'illness'. After the book had gone to print, Horatia found a 'flimsy' which Beatty had written on her brother in 1919. He had

> conducted himself entirely to my satisfaction – has served with me for over six years, assisted me greatly in the work of his department of signals and communications in an ever-growing command which called up qualities from him of a high order & he never failed.[22]

Whatever view one may adopt on the above testimonial – and its ending certainly grates – the sense of bewilderment and hurt left in the Seymour family over the seemingly savage way in which Beatty had turned on his protégé may readily be understood. That Beatty is said by his recent biographer to have been placed under stress by Seymour's death arouses limited sympathy. Ralph was not to be the only post-war victim of the Earl of the North Sea, and, indirectly, casualty of the Battle of Jutland.

*

Meanwhile, the Admiralty, thwarted by its internal dissident, had been offered an apparent means of escape from its Jutland-history problem. As part of its 'Great War' series, the Committee of Imperial Defence (CID) had commissioned an official history of naval operations from the accomplished historian Sir Julian Corbett, and in late 1920, his publishers, Longmans, argued that Sir Julian's work (more precisely, Volume

III) would be, to some extent, scooped if the *Harper Record* were published. This petition was thankfully embraced, particularly by Sir Walter Long; and it was decided that Harper's work would be made available to Corbett, while the Admiralty would produce, instead, an analysis, or 'staff appreciation', of the battle in the form of a confidential book for internal naval consumption. While these developments successfully sidelined the obstinate Captain Harper, they also transferred the Harper controversies into the jurisdiction of a court over which Beatty had little influence (and indeed Sir Walter – no fool he – may have had this in mind in promoting the new arrangement).

At the Naval Historical Branch the Dewar brothers – Captains Alfred and Kenneth (the latter of whom, as flag-captain of *Royal Oak* in 1929, would be caught in the flak after the admiral called the band-master a bugger[23]) – thus set to work on the Staff Appreciation of Jutland "on the lines desired". The Dewars, at least in their own estimation, belonged to a new Shining Path of naval intellectuals.[24] At any rate, their "capacity for original thinking and literary talents always held an appeal for Beatty",[25] and they now set about putting those skills to use on Beatty's behalf. In Captain Oswald Frewen's words, they "sailed gaily in, but got bogged down in a month among the masses of Battle-Cruiser contradictory signals and reports". Frewen had been Harper's navigation assistant in the compilation of the embargoed report and was thus, in his own words, "a link in the chain of knowledge of the secret history of the history of Jutland". He later recounted to Evan-Thomas, with more than a dash of *schadenfreude*, the Dewars' difficulties:

> they obviously couldn't go to Harper to get disentangled, *I* was known as a hostile witness, so they went to young Pollen, nephew of A. H. Pollen the scribe [and fire-control inventor], who was the only other person who knew the battle inside out at that time, and who was helping Sir Julian Corbett in his *Naval Operations*, with our *Harper Report* track-charts. I called on Pollen soon after, who told me the story, & he said 'I disentangled them alright, and got them back to the bare bones of fact – & of course, when you've cut out all the cackle and *do* get down to the bare bones, you are left with – the *Harper Report*".[26]

The project was completed in September 1921, and Beatty was delighted with it. It was full of "far-reaching and astringent criticism of Jellicoe",[27] and was unfit even for internal distribution: they dared not issue to the Fleet a book "that would rend the service to its foundations".[28] Sir Julian Corbett, who had been favoured with a proof copy (presumably to counteract the *Harper Record*'s baleful influence upon him), read it with increasing wonder till at last I felt it my duty to convey to the Admiralty that such a grotesque account of the battle certainly ought not to go out as their considered verdict. I don't know if my hint had any effect, but a few days later all the proofs were recalled and I understand it was to be drastically revised before publication. I was allowed to retain my copy and the more I studied the battle the more grotesque did the Dewar account appear.[29]

The Staff Appreciation was classified 'SECRET' and extant copies were confined to lock and key. It was now necessary to produce a 'de-venomized' version which could be given the circulation from which the original had been disqualified. The Directorate of Training and Staff Duties was charged with this task. Thus was born the *Admiralty Narrative* of the Battle of Jutland.[30]

*

The first draft of the rewrite took several months to complete, and was then sent by surface mail to Lord Jellicoe in Wellington. By March 1922 the Governor-General was confiding to Frewen that he had

> filled over 20 sheets of foolscap in pointing out inaccuracies which were obvious. The diagrams I have not had time to tackle properly yet, but they are also in many places inaccurate, whether judged by Harper diagrams, by Captains' & Admirals' reports or by gunnery data.[31]

The passages with which Jellicoe took issue included matters of detail which impugned the reputations of some of his subordinates, and "attacks on his officers, like that on Admiral Sir Hugh Evan-Thomas, upset him considerably."[32] In June, he wrote to Sir Hugh, back in England, warning him that

> I had to enter a strong protest against the manner in which the authors of the 'staff appreciation' of Jutland insinuated that blame was attachable to you for the opening of the distance between the BCF and the 5th BS to 10 miles between the time of *Galatea*'s sighting the enemy and the BCs being in action. I pointed out very clearly that this was due to signals being made by flags at a great distance and not by W/T or by SL & that if there was any blame, it lay elsewhere. I've not yet been told what alterations will be made in the appreciation, but nothing will induce me to agree to such a distortion of facts.[33]

Jellicoe finished his critique of the Staff Appreciation, as he incorrectly called it – he may have been unaware of the completion and suppression of the original – early in November (in which month he – "unfailing ally of every charitable or philanthropic impulse"[34] – was, as a matter of no interest, installed as Grand Master of New Zealand). "Much delay [had] been caused by the necessity for checking every statement and every part of each diagram" and he had had to do all the work himself "at a time when my duties as Governor-General absorbed a great deal of my time".[35] Now, at last, he told Frewen,

> it will be on its way home shortly with my comments on it, which are nearly as voluminous as the appreciation itself. The carelessness and inaccuracies of this document are extraordinary and the charts and diagrams are even worse. It is necessary now perhaps to 'take the gloves off'. The staff appreciation is of course a BCF account, looked at through BCF eyes.[36]

To Their Lordships, he was scarcely less blunt:

> My observations will reveal the fact that I take exception to a great deal of the *Narrative* and to many of the diagrams. The *Narrative* is inaccurate as to fact in many numerous instances. It is also most misleading in deductions drawn ... the ideas attributed to me are in many cases entirely unjustified and many insinuations are made to which I take the strongest exception.[37]

But Viscount Scapa was working under a new disadvantage (in addition to those of dignity and distance): the capable and effective Sir Walter Long[38] had departed from the Admiralty in February 1921 and been succeeded by Lord Lee of Fareham, and Lee in turn by Mr Leopold Amery in October '22; and neither of the two newcomers had either Long's familiarity with Beatty's gerrymandering ways, or his will to curb them. And there was another loss to contend with, that of Sir Julian Corbett, in September 1922:

> The death of Sir Julian is a sad blow for history. I have lost a friend in him of long standing & the Navy has lost its great historian. It will be impossible to replace him ... what will happen to his Volume III, I can't imagine.

Soon Jellicoe was conducting a heated correspondence by wire with Leo Amery. In July 1923 he was threatening to resign from New Zealand, if the Admiralty went ahead and published the *Narrative* without his comments or remarks, and return to England to publish the truth.[39] In October the Admiralty's grudging list of revisions (along with a catalogue of refused revisions) arrived in New Zealand, and another dissenting telegram duly travelled the 12,000 miles to London, only to be ignored.

Meanwhile, Volume III of the late Sir Julian Corbett's *Naval Operations* – which included a competent and (seemingly) uncontentious account of Jutland[40] – had been brought to publication by the Historical Section of the CID. The Lords Commissioners of the Admiralty had a statement inserted in the front of the book disclaiming responsibility for it, and adding the insinuative information that they "find that some of the principles advocated, especially the tendency to minimize the importance of seeking battle and of forcing it to a conclusion, are directly in conflict with their views".

*

An imaginary round-up of gold-braid, entitled "Some Sea Officers of the Great War", painted in 1921 by Sir Arthur Cope and currently in storage in the National Portrait Gallery, aptly represents Jellicoe's powerlessness in these years. It depicts him seated, clutching a newspaper (presumably containing critical reports on Jutland) and looking pensive; while Beatty stands commandingly in centre-stage. Evan-Thomas blends passively into the second-rankers of the supporting cast.

*

Admiral Sir Hugh Evan-Thomas had succeeded Sturdee as C-in-C The Nore in March 1921. 'The Nore' – the East Coast command area based on the dockyard town of Chatham in Kent, and named after a Thames-estuary sandbank where the admiral's guardship once flew his flag – was one of the Royal Navy's three elder-statesman Home Port commands (the others being Portsmouth and Plymouth). They were collectively regarded as the pinnacle of a distinguished sea-dog's career.

These were not inspiring days for the Fleet, with economies and payings-off, especially after the Treaty of Washington early in 1922. It was difficult to devise realistic training, motivate personnel or maintain standards of efficiency. But equally, they were not times of great workload. A page of instructions, drawn up for the benefit of Evan-Thomas's flag-lieutenant, Robert Fitzroy (by, one imagines, a head-gardener on a Welsh estate), explains in graphic detail how to prepare a rose-bed: a 3-inch layer of horse manure to be well trodden in at a given depth[41] (probably the admiral's garden had been turned over to cabbages during the war). It was later said of Sir Hugh in Chatham that "All who knew him locally regarded him as one of 'Nature's Gentlemen'."[42]

Sir Hugh should have been riding high. He had received decorations, including the Croix de Guerre with palms, from five countries; and it will have meant much to him that he had been honoured in his native Wales, becoming an honorary doctor of law at Profysgol Cymru, Bangor, in 1920, and High Sheriff of Glamorgan in 1922. But "it was known to his family that *something* was worrying him very much indeed"; and he was, of course, worrying about the Admiralty's evident intention to "slant" the official version of the "operations of the battle-cruisers and 5th BS, without consulting him or calling for his comments, although he was within easy reach, and was the flag-officer mainly concerned".[43]

It is clear that while he had not been asked for his views on the *Narrative*, he had obtained a draft copy of that document – probably spurred by Jellicoe from afar. And in April 1923 he sought advice on his predicament from Sir Charles Madden, who told him that

> your view of the case is moderate, the facts are more strongly favourable to you . . . I have no wish to revive the controversy which is so harmful to the service . . . but it is so very important to get the facts firmly stated in the official account that I hope you will urge your views on the Admiralty, & I trust will succeed.[44]

Accordingly, he went to see Amery, in mid-July, and then pressed the latter's naval secretary for any results of his visit. The reply from Rear-Admiral Hugh Watson (in the process of handing over to Rear-Admiral Michael Hodges) was less than satisfactory:

> I saw 1st Lord yesterday. He told me he had seen you on the matter you spoke to me about, and that he had already looked into the point you spoke about. 1st Lord told me to tell you that if he thought it necessary after further study of the papers he would ask you to come and see him. I have explained the matter privately to Hodges who has also seen this letter.[45]

At this, Evan-Thomas sent his chief of staff, Captain Herbert Hope (brother of the captain of *Queen Elizabeth*, in the 5th BS), hotfoot up to London. Hope reported back that

> the 1st Lord considers there is nothing in the narrative you could take exception to except the fact of the 5th BS not immediately following the *Lion*'s motions [at 2.32 p.m.] as mentioned . . . I understand from you that it was not a question of not seeing a signal, but that the signal was expressly not sent to the 5th BS, and that it was due to this, coupled with the only information you had as to the enemy's movements, which induced you not to immediately follow motions.[46]

Evan-Thomas now wrote both to Hodges and to Captain Vernon Haggard (Director of Training and Staff Duties) recapitulating the catalogue of *Lion*'s mistakes and *Barham*'s alibis at 2.35-ish and 4.50-ish (discussed, more or less, in Chapters 6 and 8). Yet, as the weeks went by, Jellicoe's situation reports from New Zealand conveyed a rising note of frustration. "The worst features of the whole narrative are contained in the insinuations," Viscount Scapa confided early in November, adding three weeks later that he had obtained no concessions on the two main episodes concerning the 5th Battle Squadron. (Of the second of these, "the Admiralty say that the signal to turn 16 points was hauled down before *Barham* passed *Lion*, & say there is ample proof of this, but don't give me this proof!!!"[47])

"Amiable, kind, well-wishing, easily crushed",[48] Sir Hugh was ill-equipped by nature to do battle with the Admiralty over a matter which had implications for the integrity of the professional head of the service and half the naval staff. But at length he steeled himself to take the bull by the horns and demand a formal request for his version of those events at Jutland which concerned the 5th BS. To this end he booked another interview with Leo Amery, for the morning of the 3rd of December 1923.

Beatty was forewarned of his visit. Perhaps Amery, who seems to have been fairly under his thumb, mentioned it; perhaps the First Lord's naval secretary, Michael Hodges (who had commanded *Indomitable* and *Renown* in the BCF), tipped him off. Anyway, as Evan-Thomas went into Amery's office, the First Sea Lord "appeared from nowhere" and followed him in. It would be gratifying to report that Beatty – "nice mannered boy", Queen Victoria had thought him – behaved with the decorum befitting an Earl of the North Sea, and took the opportunity to discuss C-in-C Nore's grievances. But such is not the case. He demanded the First Lord's urgent attention on some other matter, and (in Sir Hugh's words) "pushed me" out of the room, "for fear that I might tell the truth".[49]

The only records of the encounter derive from Evan-Thomas, and their choice of words varies.[50] "Pushed" and "bundled" are presumably dramatic licence, but it is reasonable to infer that physical contact might have ensued had Evan-Thomas tried to persist with his interview with the First Lord, and that for this reason he did not do so. Nothing in his forty-eight years' service had prepared him for scrapping with the First Sea Lord in an Admiralty corridor, and "that little fool Amery" did nothing to intervene.[51]

So, gallant, defeated Sir Hugh made his unhappy way back to Chatham, seething with outrage and injustice. By 2.30 p.m. he was very ill, and specialists were summoned from London.[52] He had had a partial stroke, which compelled his early retirement from the Navy four months later,[53] and put him in and out of nursing homes for the next two and a half years.

Three days after Evan-Thomas's collapse, and as yet unaware of it, Lord Jellicoe sent Amery another long telegram which made no discernible impression on the recipient. By Jellicoe's later (February 1924) account to Sir Hugh,

> I related the facts at length as to the failure to signal to you by SL or WT . . .
> I then pointed out that any delay in turning the 5th BS to the north was due
> to the *Lion*'s signal not being hauled down until after you had passed her.
> Further I drew attention to the omission to comment on the fine shooting of

the 5th BS as recorded by Scheer and Von Hase . . . I am fully determined that I will under no circumstances agree to anything being published that reflects upon you without a published protest and corrections from myself.

I am, I confess, both surprised and disgusted that those responsible at the Admiralty should have tried to get such a perversion of facts made public . . . Old Chap, I hope that we shall meet on the golf links next year to renew old combats of *Ramillies* days.[54]

*

Upon his turning over his command (to Goodenough) at the beginning of March 1924, custom enjoined Evan-Thomas to see the King. He wasn't up to it. The naval secretary explained to Lord Stamfordham that his "doctor had advised him not to hang about in London", and that the admiral had

> asked me whether I could suggest that instead of his name being submitted in the ordinary course of events with a view to his being received by the King, such a visit to His Majesty might be postponed until the summer . . . Although he declares that he is quite fit again, his appearance, at least to one like myself who had not seen him since his illness, hardly confirms his statement.[55]

The formality appears to have been waived, and Sir Hugh retreated to Devon to convalesce.

The King was not unaware of his old friend's troubles, and it can have been no coincidence that the 1924 Birthday Honours List upgraded him to the Grand Cross (the senior class of knighthood) of the Order of the Bath — an award which was hailed in valedictory terms by the *Manchester Guardian* as

> one of the most popular naval honours that could possibly have been gazetted, for although [Admiral Evan-Thomas] is comparatively unknown to the general public, he has a great reputation in the Service in addition to being one of the best-loved officers on the flag-list. Entering the Navy in 1875, he has always been a tremendous slogger but troubled very little about popular notice . . . For [the Battle of Jutland] he received his knighthood and was steadily promoted until he was generally regarded as having the best chances of the plums of the Navy. Unfortunately, continuous over-work as Commander-in-Chief of the Nore brought on an illness which has practically spoilt all chances of further promotion although it does not stop his getting about at his Devonshire home.[56]

(There were only two possible forms of "further promotion" for the commander-in-chief of one of the Home Ports, and while there have been less likely admirals of the fleet, it is quite impossible to imagine Evan-Thomas as First Sea Lord — even had the post been vacant — and there is no suggestion that he, or anyone on his behalf, ever harboured such an ambition.) His receipt of the GCB at Buckingham Palace was postponed until he was fit enough to travel. Almost a year passed.

Meanwhile, in June 1924, the *Admiralty Narrative* came out. It acknowledged Lord Jellicoe's complaints with extraordinary meanness of spirit: they were consigned to an appendix and punctuated with graceless Beatty-ite refutations. Evan-Thomas was "too ill to be allowed to read it".[57] Jellicoe wrote to Hilda, expressing his deep regret that "I have failed to get the Admiralty to do justice to your husband":[58]

> I tried to get [Amery] to cable out to me the note that the Admiralty intended to make on that portion of my remarks which concerned Sir Hugh. He refused either to do this or to alter the narrative so as to make it clear that the actions of Sir Hugh were quite correct. He refused also to publish the cables exchanged between us, which in themselves would have been sufficient to clear Sir Hugh . . . I confess that I could not believe that any gentleman could have taken such a line. But he is a weak man and he is working under influence.
>
> [Vice-Admiral] Sir Michael Culme-Seymour [4th Bt., 2nd Sea Lord], as perhaps you know, tried to get things right at the last minute & I was quite prepared to leave it to him and to Admiral Madden whether I should with-draw my comments . . . [but] he wired to say that it was too late, as the book was being published. I only hope that nothing [further] untoward has occurred to Sir Hugh's health as the result, as if it has I should hold the Admiralty accountable . . .

On the 2nd of May 1925 Evan-Thomas had recovered enough to travel to London to receive his GCB, and "had the honour of being received by His Majesty".[59] In fact, George V gave him a private audience of half an hour and listened to his account of his ordeal at Beatty's hands.

There can be little doubt where the King's sympathies would have lain, had he been a free agent: Evan-Thomas and he were 'old ships' from long ago days in *Britannia*, *Bacchante*, *Melampus* and *Osborne*, and their friendship had endured across the years. Sir Hugh had looked after George's sons at Dartmouth, and had attended Prince Albert's wedding to Lady Elizabeth Bowes-Lyons, now the Queen Mother, in 1923. George, for his part, was godfather to Sir Hugh's niece, 'Georgie' Dalton – as he was to both Jellicoe's son and Markham's daughter – and the ancient and cantankerous Sir John Dalton, who still exercised a shadowy thrall over his former royal pupil, may have made representations on his brother-in-law's behalf.

So 'Sprat' sat down with 'Old Voice' for one last time and patiently heard him out. However, George's well-known loyalty to old friends found itself in conflict with his heavy sense of public duty as head of state. He was distressed for the future of the Royal Navy – his own Alma Mater (from which he had never technically retired[60]) – and, in this era of League-of-Nationism and cutbacks, when the dorsal fins of disarmers, economists, air-power prophets and jealous American navalists were circling the depleted Fleet, Beatty's assertive leadership was at a premium. The previous year the King had been so troubled by rumours of the First Sea Lord's impending resignation as to "beg" him (by Beatty's own account),

> for the good of the Service and the State, to remain at the Admiralty. The Navy was the only thing left and it would soon crumple up if I left. He was very nice and complimentary and very much moved and asked me to treat our conversation as private.[61]

Now George assured Evan-Thomas "that he quite appreciated the situation and how B played the fool – but he thought it better for the nation that there should be no more controversy".

*

Evan-Thomas in his short fretful years of retirement was absent-minded and preoccupied, aged beyond his years, as he pottered about from one country house to another while his in-laws and relations sought to keep him busy. Sometimes he stayed at Cople in Bedfordshire, sometimes with his brother Llewellyn at Pencerrig near Builth Wells, or with his nephew Henry Evan-Thomas at Llwynmadoc. He shot partridges and pheasants at Llwynmadoc on October the 1st 1925, a date – the tenth anniversary of his hoisting his flag in *Barham* – which must have prompted a renewed onset of brooding. His game-book has no further entries.

The sorry saga of the history of Jutland continued to gnaw. His stress was heightened by his typical, and possibly misplaced, wish to shield Hilda from the sordid details; though he did at least rehearse episodes of Jutland, with the aid of matchsticks, to his naval nephew. He was consoling himself with the hope that

> we are having so much truth from the Germans that it is becoming difficult for the Beatty party to keep up the lies they spread, to try and hide the two awful mistakes of their Chief – by trying to shift it on to others . . . Now the Germans, especially Hipper, my especial enemy, have published so much, I am wondering if the master and crew of the Pirate will try to find something different to lie about to keep their face up.[62]

Then, two events early in 1927 prompted the whole business to boil over again: the publication of Winston Churchill's *The World Crisis, 1916–18*; and the retirement of Rear-Admiral John Harper.

Churchill's 'line to take' on the subject of Beatty, with, on the one hand, his 1912–13 career sponsorship of the admiral, and on the other, his inside knowledge of the unhappy Seymour saga through Horatia (who was now a 'grace and favour' resident of the Chartwell estate), might not have been a simple matter. However, "the public demands elocution rather than reason of those who address it. It rejoices in sweeping statements, confident assertions, bright lights and black shadows."[63] Winston perceived this better than most and nobody could brighten or blacken more plausibly than he.

World Crisis, on Jutland, is not pathologically anti-Jellicoe; it does, after all, contain that much-quoted line, which has delimited censure for all time, about the C-in-C's being "the only man on either side who could lose the war in an afternoon".[64] But, apart from this caveat, Churchill's tone and his treatment of evidence are unremittingly Beatty-ite; and he makes clear his agenda and his justification right at the start:

> The dominant school of naval thought and policy are severe critics of Sir John Jellicoe. They disdain all personal grounds or motives; they affirm that the tradition and future of the British Navy join in demanding that a different doctrine, other methods and above all another spirit must animate our captains at sea, if ever and whenever the Navy is once again at war. They declare that such an affirmation is more important to the public than the feelings of individuals, the decorous maintenance of appearances, the preservation of a superficial harmony, or the respect which may rightly be claimed by a Commander-in-Chief who discharged an immense and indeed inestimable responsibility.

Missing this argument (or dis-missing it), *Truth* counter-asserted that

> it is not likely that when Mr Winston Churchill got down to write his version of the Battle of Jutland he contemplated doing any disservice to the reputation of his particular hero. For Mr Churchill belongs whole-heartedly to the 'Beatty School'. In his book *World Crisis*, he claims to have 'discovered' the Admiral. He records with characteristic self-congratulation, how, despite having been warned . . .[65]

There was probably much in Churchill's account to which Evan-Thomas, as a card-carrying Jellicoe disciple, took exception; but the part which directly impugned and offended him related to the causes of the 5th BS's delay in following the BCF's turn to the SSE at the beginning of the action. This passage of some fifty lines[66] is devoted almost entirely to explaining why Evan-Thomas was at fault, and what the consequences were, with only two lines given over to the possibility that there were counter-arguments, and not a word about contributory errors on Beatty's part. By comparison, the section dealing with *Barham*'s delayed reversal of course at 4.50[67] is almost conciliatory – "perhaps the rear-admiral, having been slow in coming into action, was inclined to be slow in coming out" – and confuses the act of displaying an imperative flag-signal with its execution (implying that *Lion* kept the signal aloft until *Barham* obeyed it). But overall, the partiality of *World Crisis* was a bitter pill for Evan-Thomas to be expected to swallow. What was he to do?

> All through his life he [had] really believed in 'the silent service', and that the interests of the nation and his beloved Navy were not advanced by publicity, controversy, politics or ostentatious 'ballyhoo';[68]

but then, as Oswald Frewen was to say, "when the gentlemen are silent with a self-seeker loudly advertising himself in their midst, the ignorant public are apt to be deceived",[69] and Sir Hugh's reticence and discretion had been too much presumed upon already. Ultimately there comes a time to cut cards with the Devil, and, although his family tried to stop him, he finally wrote to the papers.

His letter in *The Times* of the 16th of February condemned *World Crisis*'s treatment of Jutland as "a mixture of armchair criticism, want of vision from a sailor's point of view, an utter disregard of the effect of smoke, gunfire and fog added to a terribly partisan account". He answered Churchill's version of 'the turn to the SSE' with a summary of the '5th BS' perspective, and he confronted the public, for the first time, both with *Lion*'s neglect of Grand Fleet signalling procedures and with the fact that, during the Admiralty's post-war forays into authorship, "no remarks from me have ever been asked for either by the Chief of the Naval Staff or those under him".[70]

The first to congratulate him was his brother Llewellyn:

> Although I wrote to you suggesting you should avoid writing to *The Times*, I couldn't help a feeling of satisfaction in reading your letter today.
>
> One of my chief reasons for asking you to avoid controversy was that it isn't good for you as it is always a worrying job however much you are in the right. Anyhow I expect you will be feeling a lot better now you have got it off your chest and I know you will have the sympathy and backing of the majority of naval officers although they can't join in and say so. Bless you old man and love to Hilda.[71]

The Times letter had a catalytic effect, although the admiral confessed to Oswald Frewen (who reintroduced himself enthusiastically, having served under Evan-Thomas in 1904 as a midshipman) that he had still felt obliged to pull his punches:

> The worst part of the whole thing, I couldn't put in my letter, was that Beatty prevented me from seeing the First Lord when I went up from Chatham to

ask that I might be asked for my report, before the first part of Jutland was written. I was so angry and worried at this that I got a partial stroke and after three years of it I am only just fully well again. However, Winston, having given me the chance, I have let it off and feel much better . . . What a horrible & disgusting affair this whole business is . . . my feeling is the same as yours that there has been some dirty work somewhere.[72]

Meanwhile, Sir Hugh having nailed his colours to the mast, other Battle Fleet champions rallied to his cause. *Truth* carried an editorial on "Beatty's Blunder at Jutland", asked why it was that no remarks from Evan-Thomas had ever been asked for by the Chief of Naval Staff, and supplied its own rather obvious idea of the answer:

The Chief of the Naval Staff, of course, is Lord Beatty himself. He has held that position since 1919, and therefore all the work on the Official History was done during his regime. Is it unfair to guess that one reason why Sir Hugh Evan-Thomas has never been called upon to make any remarks was the possibility that he might have made some such remarks as he has now made in *The Times*? With this in mind the question inevitably recurs why the *Harper Report* was never published.[73]

In the *Daily Mail*, Admiral Mark Kerr (one-time flags to Sir Anthony Sir Iley Sir Oskins, in *Victoria*) rated his ex-shipmate's riposte to Churchill "unanswerable" proof that

the smashing up of our battlecruisers was due to the Vice-Admiral, Sir David Beatty, racing off without giving any instructions to the 5th Battle Squadron, which was attached to him for the very purpose of strengthening him in the event of his meeting the enemy battlecruisers or part of the High Seas Fleet.[74]

The *Star* published a letter from Major-General Sir George Aston RM (another shipmate) on Churchill's injustice to Jellicoe;[75] and the *Morning Post* featured a long article by Rear-Admiral Harper condemning the Churchill–Beatty axis.[76]

Harper, who was privately (and not very convincingly) blaming Beatty for spiking his naval career, was free to enter the public fray, and was even now finalizing a book-length record-straightener on Jutland. Under the heading "FRESH NAVAL REVELATIONS" the *Evening Standard* put its readers on stand-by with the information that

A book will be published in about six weeks time replying to Mr Winston Churchill's comments on the Battle of Jutland. It has been written by Rear-Admiral J. E. T. Harper CB who was head of a committee appointed by the Admiralty to report on the Battle of Jutland. This report has never been published though frequent requests have been made for its production by

Members of Parliament. Admiral Harper is now bringing out his own book and is very unsparing in his criticism. It is likely to cause some agitation in Whitehall.[77]

Harper's, indeed, was not the only anti-Churchill book in preparation, for a panel of greyheads was putting together *World Crisis by Winston Churchill – A Criticism*. The project was led by Lord Sydenham, and the chapter on Jutland was written by Admiral Sir Reginald Bacon (who had already produced the polemical *Jutland Scandal*, in 1924).

In spotlighting his hero, Churchill had, it seems, merely illuminated the target for Jellicoe's battle-line of retired and disgruntled flag-officers (even in 1926 Evan-Thomas addressed Jellicoe as "My Dear Commander-in-Chief"); and, in the last few months of his eight-year tenure of office, the First Sea Lord suddenly found himself under bombardment. His own supporters still had the advantage of position, and fired back by contriving to have it placed on record in *Hansard* that (as the *Evening News* put it) "signals from Lord Beatty which Sir Hugh said he never received were entered in the signal log of the *Barham* as having been received".[78]

This manoeuvre took place in the House of Commons on the 15th of March 1927; its details are as follows. In reply to a question from Commander Carlyon Bellairs (who else?) the First Lord of the Admiralty – now Mr William Bridgeman (no relation of Sir Francis B.) – stated that

> the [destroyer restationing] signal is in the signal log of HMS *Barham* as received at 2.30 p.m., by searchlight from *Lion*, the text being as follows: 'take up position now to form submarine screen when course is altered to SSE'. The executive signal to turn is recorded in *Barham*'s signal log as received at 2.37 p.m. by flags, from *Lion*, the text being as follows: – 'alter course, leaders together, remainder in succession, to SSE, speed 22 knots'. I may add that between these two times the *Barham* had signalled to her own destroyers: 'take up station for screening on altering course to SSE'. This signal is timed at 2.34 p.m. in the log of HMS *Fearless*, senior officer of the flotilla.

If this was designed to throw a spanner in the works, it certainly does that. Even without the words underlined by me, its implications (as mentioned in Chapter 6) make trouble for Evan-Thomas. The underlined bit is discordant with our whole understanding of the 'turn to the SSE' episode, and for it to be true, Evan-Thomas's command-organization would have to have been seriously dysfunctional.[79]

Maybe there is a simple explanation. Perhaps when *Barham*'s signals staff came to write up the "fair" log, they listed the searchlight-repeat as the flag-signal which it originally was, and fudged the timing to minimize the delay. Perhaps the log had been, as Evan-Thomas suggested to his nephew,[80] "tampered with" by the Naval Historical Branch. We can never know the truth behind Bridgeman's statement; Sir Hugh "made no public reply",[81] and the Historical Branch obligingly destroyed the Jutland fair signal logs ("monstrous", in Sir Angus Cunninghame-Graham's succinct opinion).

Bridgeman added, in reply to further questioning, that the Admiralty still had no intention of publishing the *Harper Record*. Six weeks later he changed his mind. Harper points out that this volte-face took place directly after the preliminary notices of *The Truth About Jutland* had been issued by his publisher (John Murray), and connects the two events. It is also worth mentioning that Beatty was about to be succeeded by Jellicoe's brother-in-law and Grand Fleet chief of staff; and just as Madden had all accessible copies of the Staff Appreciation destroyed, he would certainly have had *Harper* published.

So in the end, the public got both the *Harper Record* (Cmd 2870) and *The Truth About Jutland*. The latter is a readable, layman's version of the former, augmented with Harper's pro-Jellicoe (but surprisingly restrained) opinions, and prefixed with a précis of the story of the *Record*. Inevitably, it was dismissed in Beatty circles as a 'grudge book'. Someone at the Admiralty penned a confection entitled 'The Truth About Harper'.[82]

For the Jellicoe school, it was (like Jutland) a victory of sorts; although with the previous year's General Strike, and all the other political, economic and cultural diversions of the 1920s, one can only be surprised that the matter still commanded so much public interest.

*

There are three dimensions to the Byzantine, and sometimes Borgian, 'secret history of the history of Jutland'.

The first is that of the motives and methods of the warring factions. Here, academics have tried to be even-handed between the two groups, as if wisdom can be arrived at by halving the difference (the eternal fallacy of British diplomats). This might happen to work with the two particular command-and-control fiascos involving the BCF and the 5th BS (studied in Chapters 6 and 8), for, when the detailed faults on both sides are weighed in the scales against each other, there does appear to be a strange balance of blame. But with regard to the broader historiographical agendas of the two partisan groups, it is a considerable injustice to the Jellicoe school.

To some extent we can see the Jellicoe-ites (certainly Evan-Thomas) retaliating in kind against simplistic assertions and selective evidence.

And it may be that Jellicoe himself, isolated from the naval community, on the far side of the world, allowed conspiracy fears to loom larger in his mind than was really warranted. The observation that a high-status professional élite which accepts the bouquets must also be prepared to take the brickbats, is a deserved reproof to both factions; but the self-serving attempts to steer the public's perceptions of Jutland, and deny other men their due credit, took place overwhelmingly on Beatty's side. Indeed, it must reveal character flaws of a scale which one can only contemplate with sorrow that, at a time when he had his work cut out leading the Royal Navy in its peacetime battles against enemies in half a dozen guises – enemies collectively more threatening, and more successful, than the German High Seas Fleet – the First Sea Lord should expend time and temper trying to suppress evidence that (for example) his flagship turned a circle instead of an S-bend at a certain unengaged juncture of the Battle of Jutland.

Jellicoe's own insipid apologia, *The Grand Fleet 1914–1916: Its Creation, Development and Work* (1919), had been 'platitudinized' by a patrician loyalty to his erstwhile subordinates as a group. And by no yardstick, other than BCF mythology, was the *Harper Record* a scurrilous document: if Beatty had had sufficient good humour to allow its publication to proceed in 1919 or '20, the Jutland partisans would never have withdrawn into diametrically opposite encampments, and a gesture would have been made for the unity and morale of the beleaguered profession of which he was chief. Powerful and effective First Sea Lord though Beatty was, he lacked some of the skills of kingship.

The second dimension is that of the specific claims and counter-claims which each side put forward to support their preferred versions of events. Many are tendentious, some are entertaining, others tedious. Those bearing on the 5th BS's interaction with the battlecruisers have been detailed in their rightful contexts, and a few others have been mentioned in passing. A systematic reappraisal of the whole lot may be reserved by the naval-historical community for punishment of one of its number found guilty of some horrible offence.

The third dimension has been neglected by recent historians – the 'even-handed' thing gets in the way – although Churchill clearly introduced it in *World Crisis* (with conviction or artifice, as may be). It concerns the conflicting action-principles which underlie, or appear to underlie, the arguments of the two partisan groups. Picking through their assertions, it can be discerned that they were basing their respective cases on irreconcilable doctrinal premisses. It would, indeed, have been surprising if the implicit differences between GFBOs and BCFOs had not become projected, thinkingly or unthinkingly, in dogmatized form into the post-war squabble. This third dimension connects with the first (in the sense of the diametrically opposed positions) and with the second (in that it may subjectively influence our preference for one side over the other); but a discussion of it belongs to the next and final chapter. Suffice it to say here that, within its framework, Beatty's side comes out, in my view, much more strongly than Jellicoe's.

*

On May the 31st, 1928, Vice-Admiral Arthur Craig Waller (formerly Craig) wrote to Evan-Thomas "to greet you once more on the evening of Jutland, twelve years gone". He talked of that dramatic day they spent together on *Barham*'s bridge, and of "the short hours of darkness which seemed so long".

> How quickly it is forgotten. To the great B.P. it is chiefly memorable as an acute controversy. You will I hope put away any thoughts of those acrimonious arguments of the ill-advised staff 'report' and remember the warm tribute to yourself and to the squadron paid by the Battle Cruiser Force admiral in his official despatches. I trust the world goes well with you . . .[83]

Sir Hugh slipped his moorings three months later, on August the 30th, an old man of only 66, at Cople in Bedfordshire. A memorial service was held in Eglwys Oen Duw parish church, close to Llwynmadoc in the deep green silences of mid-Wales. There, a brass plaque remembers him with Psalm 121:

> I WILL LIFT UP MINE EYES UNTO THE HILLS
> FROM WHENCE COMETH MY HELP
> MY HELP COMETH FROM THE LORD
> WHICH MADE HEAVEN AND EARTH

The following year, at a reception in Glamorgan, the Mayor of Neath told Earl Jellicoe that Gnoll, the local estate where Hugh Evan-Thomas was born, had been bought by the corporation to serve as a public park, a war-memorial and a tribute to the town's most distinguished son. Jellicoe replied, with permissible hyperbole, that

> If I had one loyal and splendid supporter during the Great War in the Grand Fleet, one who never failed me, one who led his ships magnificently, and not only led them magnificently, but brought them to a pitch of efficiency that was a pattern to the whole of the Grand Fleet, it was Admiral Sir Hugh Evan-Thomas. We were associated from our earliest days in the Navy . . . Throughout his life, I am glad to say, we were the greatest possible friends. No one regretted his death more than myself. His life was a pattern to every naval officer and every Christian gentleman in this country.[84]

Jellicoe lived for another six years. Early in November 1935 (having meanwhile succeeded Earl Haig as President of the British Legion) "he caught a chill while planting poppies",[85] and died a fortnight later. At the time of his funeral, Beatty was worn out by his long and disputatious stint as First Sea Lord, by the demands of his impossible wife, by falls in the hunting field, and perhaps in some small measure by the Jutland controversy. And he had flu. But he defied doctors' orders, to act as pallbearer on a bitterly cold, showery day ("What will the Navy say if I fail to attend Jellicoe's funeral?"[86] – what indeed), and he himself died four months later, aged just 65. Today the bodies of the Earls of Scapa and the North Sea lie (in Captain Roskill's words) "close to Nelson's in the crypt of St Paul's".[87]

That same winter, King George V also passed away. While going through Sir Hugh's effects, in 1930, Lady Evan-Thomas had found an envelope containing nineteen cedar of Lebanon seeds collected nearly fifty years earlier by Midshipman Evan-Thomas of HMS *Bacchante*. She planted them at Pencerrig. Five germinated and she sent one of the saplings to Sprat a few days before his death in January 1936.[88]

25

Perspective

"I don't give a damn about your bloody rules, this is how it is going to be done."
Sandy Woodward, during a staff meeting in *Hermes*
in 1982, *One Hundred Days*, p. 241

A few years ago I came across a French print of the Battle of Trafalgar, in an antique shop in Brittany. It had all the usual stuff – clouds of smoke, fallen masts, tangled rigging, man in water clinging to spar – and it bore a sublime caption: "*Grande Bataille de Mer! Héro Anglais Tué!*" It was out of my price range. I mention it to illustrate that victory is a flexible concept, especially soon after the event, when powerful issues of public morale, national pride, loss of face, etc., come into play, and that 'spin-doctoring' is but a modern term for one of the oldest professions in the world.

For the British battle-fleet, Jutland hardly justifies the term 'battle'. It had only a few intermittent minutes of shooting at shadowy silhouettes, and (splinters aside) was not hit once by the German battle-fleet. Indeed, in terms of casualties in the main battle-line – two men killed, five wounded – Scheer's "brilliant victory" could have been absorbed, unnoticed, into the Grand Fleet's quarterly returns of accidental injuries. Had another fleet encounter taken place, in Jellicoe's time or in Beatty's, it is unlikely that anyone would care much who 'won' Jutland. The imperative to attach to it the label of 'victory' – and even to describe it as a great battle – derives at least in part from its being the only meeting of the two fleets in the entire war.

For their part, the Germans could claim victory in *Ausfallsflotte* terms – that is, in terms of an erosion of British numerical superiority. The fright of their lives, but an *Ausfallsflotte* victory nonetheless. They had traded one battlecruiser for three, and had inflicted 10% casualties on the 60,000 British sailors present, in exchange for some 6% of their own. However, the concept behind *Ausfallsflotte* was to bring about an equalization of forces towards an ultimate trial of strength, and claims of victory are conditional on that future battle. The Germans knew on the day after Jutland that there must be no such event, hence their need to claim that *Der Skagerrak* had been *Der Tag* – by which more demanding yardstick it was a strategic defeat.

A rational society supports a navy for the purpose of achieving or safeguarding certain strategic ends. The Grand Fleet in 1916 had a heavy and obvious 'safeguarding' task, and Jutland reaffirmed and enhanced its dominance. By contrast, the Kaiser's fleet – scarcely the product of rational strategic policy – was faced with an implausible 'achieving' task, and *Der Skagerrak* subjected its pretensions of battle-fleet adequacy to a harsh and irrevocable exposure. But then, if the original purpose of the HSF had been to deter the British from joining an alliance against Germany, it had failed (and lost its relevance) long before Jutland.

Many wise things have been said about the Battle of Jutland,[1] and much work has been done, and continues, on technical comparisons of the two fleets.[2] In terms of *matériel* the British are generally held to have been inferior,[3] and in view of the terrible, inexcusable facts that British magazines were easily detonated by German shells, and that most deaths on both sides were caused by British explosives, this truism would require massive German defects to balance the scales.

However, in many respects British technology did well at Jutland. To start with, British signals intelligence was more advanced and far more productive. Then, British fuel endurance was greater; British propulsive machinery was more reliable; British armour-plate (inch for inch) was better; British torpedoes were more efficient and left a less conspicuous track; British central direction of gunnery was considered by the Germans to be better; and the British had at least set out on the fire-control computerization trail, although they had not (as some thought) reached the destination. Most importantly perhaps, at least some of the ingredients of the 'deadly cocktail of defects' (referred to in Chapter 3) which related to magazine vulnerabilities, were amenable to fairly speedy rectification.

But any differential in technology – whichever side it favoured – was not the all-important issue in the combat relationship between the Grand and High Seas fleets. To Scheer (allegedly, the only man on either side who could win the war in an afternoon), the question was irrelevant. Had the mist lifted ahead of him to reveal a shadowy six-mile line of cardboard cut-outs crossing his T, he would have done his emergency *Gefechtskehrtwendung* just as smartly as he did at Jutland. The British could not know it for sure until November 1918, but the

German Navy was never going to put into practice the 'risk fleet' threat of a naval Armageddon: the idea had been a dead letter since its deterrent bluff had been called in August 1914, and thereafter in German minds it carried the appeal of mass suicide. Whatever it was made of, the Grand Fleet was plausible enough to the enemy.

*

It cannot be said that the Grand Fleet really gave Jutland its best shot, or that Sir John Jellicoe filled "each unforgiving minute with sixty seconds' worth of distance run". Did he need to? This, for the British, is the real Jutland debate.

The heavy grand-strategic responsibilities which so burdened Jellicoe have been discussed. His book, *The Grand Fleet 1914–1916*, and Reginald Bacon's vitriolic *The Jutland Scandal*, are implicitly full of them. The sub-text is that his sense of responsibility as a strategist rightly constrained his freedom of action as a tactician – and it is, indeed, logically sound for the mathematically superior side to seek a decision through the controlled application of force, and refuse, if it can, the anarchy of manoeuvre warfare. If the odds favour you, deliberation makes sense. Lord Louis Mountbatten, a card-carrying 'battlecruiser' snotty by origin, was fully converted at the Tactical School in the 1930s:

> I completely changed the immature emotional views I had absorbed about [Jellicoe] when I was a midshipman. I now realized what an outstandingly competent, brave and brilliant man he was, though I could still have wished he had steered for the Horns Reef.[4]

And Howard Kelly, one of the few officers to come out of the miserable *Göben* affair with credit, is often quoted as saying, "Get your bravery over young, before you command the British Fleet."

However, Beatty managed to reconcile Jellicoe's strategical caution with his own more robust tactical doctrine, and Jellicoe was widely and plausibly blamed for failing to reach out for the decisive tactical victory which fate seemed to be proffering. "His actions have got to be sifted and explained. They are in the same class as the failures of Byng and Matthews, which resulted in court-martial."[5]

Jellicoe's actions at Jutland can all be explained, more or less, and sifting them will yield nothing indictable. When the Earl of Torrington was court-martialled in 1690 for timidity at the Battle of Beachy Head, he was found to have broken no rule, and no more did Jellicoe (the rules being his, approved by the Admiralty). Anyone re-fighting the battle as a war-game will find it difficult to behave differently unless they cheat by empowering themselves with departures from the tactical doctrine, standing orders, and battle-training which prevailed in the Grand Fleet at the time. That is really the point. The way Jellicoe fought Jutland had to be consistent with the action-principles with which he had imbued his forces, and with the narrow range of tactical options he had made available to himself thereby. To hope to achieve a significantly different result one would need to change the rules in tendentious and perhaps contemporarily discordant ways. As far as the 31st of May 1916 (on its own) is concerned, inspired ideas, like conjurors' rabbits, must be ruled out of hat.

Jellicoe's tactical doctrine and formalized ideas of battle were in accord with his strategic responsibilities; and tactics, it is alleged, must always be the servants of strategy. So far, so good. However, war is infinitely unpredictable in detail, nobody can expect to control it, and the power of a military force must include its capacity to respond rapidly and effectively to unscripted eventualities. Jellicoe's battle-orders bear some fanciful resemblance to a tedious naval board-game called 'The Duel', which Philip Colomb invented in 1879 for two players and an umpire.[6] In 1916 the High Seas Fleet disregarded the rules, and where the hell was the umpire? Jellicoe's main fault was that 'control' was a contract he tried to make with fate: he feared losing it, sublimated the possibility that he might do so, and imposed a doctrinal regime which seemingly presumed to govern the very nature of warfare. Even Fisher, his main career-sponsor, thought him "saturated in discipline".

Close analogy with Torrington – of whom, as it happens, Colomb was an admirer – would be seriously unfair to John Jellicoe, but 'Tarry in Town' (coiner of the 'fleet-in-being' phrase) believed in playing safe, stuck to the letter of Navy law, and shared with Jellicoe a dread of "being caught in some situation in which the book would not help him".[7]

Further, those officers with whom Jellicoe surrounded himself and who benefited from his patronage in the Battle Fleet conformed without obvious exception to the authoritarian mould. One of them (Herbert Heath) was alleged by Richmond to have had "a pumpkin on his shoulders" instead of a head.[8] Autocrats are unpredictable and have the unsettling capacity to function without supervision. There were not many around in 1914–16, but, to smooth the centralization of command in a fleet several times larger than that which George Tryon had considered too unwieldy for centralization, John Jellicoe avoided employing them. (In 1915 he defended his retention of the "deaf and absent-minded" Vice-Admiral Sir George Warrender on the incredible grounds that he was "excellent as a squadron admiral in peace".[9])

Sir George Rooke's fleet leadership, in the War of the Spanish

Succession, was another precedent to which Jellicoe could have related: a brave and much-honoured officer, Rooke "lacked any flexibility of tactical thought. He fought his naval battles on rigid lines, and reprimanded any captain who tried to achieve a tactical advantage by departing from them."[10]

Jellicoe's desire for control and centralization caused his command style to be as signals-orientated as that of Phipps Hornby, Culme-Seymour or Arthur Wilson. "A ceaseless stream of signals from the flag-ship was required to regulate the movement of the fleet"; and, as Jellicoe himself implicitly acknowledged after Jutland, "in the smoke, confusion and uncertainty of battle the process was far too elaborate."[11] The 'communications lobby' set out their stall of excuses and mitigations. There were many, battle-conditions being among them, but the chief one was

> the shortage of trained signalmen and telegraphists brought about by the wartime expansion of the Navy, and the rapid development of wireless telegraphy ... The strength of the signal personnel of the Grand Fleet was therefore inadequate, and the responsibility for reading important signals often fell upon boys still in their teens, whose contemporaries in other branches were carrying a charge to a gun or trimming coal. Important duties, no doubt, but mistakes made in such duties could not have the far-reaching effect of a mistake made in making or reading a signal.[12]

What the communicators did not discuss was the long-term misrepresentation of the dependability of signals by those with vested interests in promoting signalling culture. For half a century they had been saying 'We can do this. Trust us!', and had resisted attempts to de-skill signalling or reduce its role in fleet-tactics. Now, when their wizardry had at last been put to the empirical test of a fleet-action, and when "the attempt to centralize in a single hand the whole conduct in action of so vast a fleet [was perceived to have] failed",[13] they were claiming that it was not their fault because the task was, after all, so difficult. Clearly what was needed was not a lament at the shortage of skills impossible to supply in large quantity in wartime, but a dilution of the skills on which the fleet's cohesion depended, as Tryon, Hunter, Callaghan and Beatty had variously pursued over the past twenty-five years.

In reality, signalling did not "fail" quite as dramatically as implied by Churchill, above; but its practical limitations had already made necessary a set of tactical constraints which would partially conceal failure. The same could be said of the Dreyer fire-control system, which Jellicoe had been instrumental in procuring before the war.

It bears emphasis that Captain Dreyer's gear was not 'helm-free', and could not, in practice, carry over information about a given target from one own-ship course to another: rather it would have to start again and build a fresh database to establish the new rate of change of range. If this starting-again process took five minutes[14] then any significant course alteration would lose the Grand Fleet a total of 120 ship-minutes of firepower. The problem was more important at long ranges, where, owing to steep shell trajectories, only the exact range would hit the target. And had GFBOs' forecast of the nature of a fleet-action – opposing fleets on straight courses – proved accurate, it would not have mattered much anyway. But that is the point: the Dreyer system abetted an inhibition about one's own movements, at the expense of a proactive interest in those of the enemy, and compounded the Grand Fleet's psychosomatic command-and-control constraints.

The over-centralization of British command-and-control at the time of Jutland is commonly attributed to the Victorian cultural conditioning of a service which had "forgotten what war was".[15] There is much in this, and my several chapters on 'The Underlying Reason Why' provide strong evidence to support it. Most pertinently, John Jellicoe's mid-career discipleship of a highly authoritarian Commander-in-Chief of the Mediterranean Fleet has been outlined in Chapter 15. However, the main thrust of Part III was the controversy which periodically surfaced about the Royal Navy's *Signal Book* doctrine; and the deterministic 'blame-their-parents' alibi fails to acknowledge an impressive record of protest.

Philip Colomb's 1874 *Manual of Fleet Evolutions* – the operational epitome of the Victorian Fleet – appeared to define the skills required of a seaman officer in the industrial age, and its goose-step doctrine was consonant with Victorian notions of order and propriety; but I have found only two statements by senior practitioners implying unqualified faith in its combat utility, in the forty years after its production: Sir Geoffrey Phipps Hornby's inaugural memorandum to the Mediterranean Fleet in 1877, and Sir Michael Culme-Seymour's booklet of 1895.

Perhaps, since the system was 'Admiralty-issue', praise was superfluous. Perhaps certain officers (Compton Domvile and Arthur Wilson, for example, or Hugh Evan-Thomas) thought its merit self-evident, and if they could be questioned more closely, strong endorsement would be thrown up. But both Hornby and Culme-Seymour, the definitive goose-steppers themselves, may be counted among those who, at some stage or other, confessed to reservations – as may Sir George Tryon, Sir John Hopkins, Sir John Fisher, Penrose Fitzgerald, Gerard Noel, Lord Charles Beresford, Nathaniel Bowden-Smith, Robert Harris, Alexander Buller, Cuthbert Hunter, Prince Louis of Battenberg, (by inference) Sir George Callaghan, Sir David Beatty, and even, to some extent, Malta-cliquist Sir William May.[16] To this list might be appended Tryon's flag-captain Maurice Bourke, May's flag-captain Herbert Richmond, and Beatty's staff-commander Reginald Plunkett. As a generalization, therefore, the seagoing community was fairly united in disquiet about the *Signal Books*, and the rift lay not between groups *for* and *against*, but rather between *Doubters* who supposed the system to be remediable by amendment, and the more disruptive *Dissenters* who did not.

These misgivings lacked the unity and empirical authority to have Colomb's regime dislodged as the determinant of British battle-tactics until its frailties became a matter of record after Jutland. But between 1891 and '93, it had looked likely to be unseated by the Mediterranean Fleet, and its reprieve came about only through the fluke of the *Camperdown–Victoria* collision. Had Tryon not made a simple mistake, or had Albert Markham been equal to his little command-crisis, it is likely that Sir George's 'doctrine-based doctrine' would have continued to gather momentum, and the background scenery of customs and practices in 1914 might have looked somewhat different. Therefore, while the problem itself certainly took root in the cloying soil of Victorian culture, the valiant attempts to deal with it came from Victorian brains, and only through a tragic and fantastically unlikely set of circumstances does the Grand Fleet's tactical strait-jacketing appear the inevitable product of historical trends.

So there was a strong element of personal choice – or, at least, of personality – in Jellicoe's choosing the authoritarian, control-intensive line he did, when he took over the dinosaur in 1914 and tried to run it from one central, and indifferently connected, brain: he was by no means merely a victim of his times. And it is not profoundly ahistorical to suggest that he (or another officer in his place) might have trained his subordinates along more functional, more artful, lines of interpretation and mutual support, to endow his fleet with the flexibility to respond to a wider range of contingencies; and that, when the "suitable conditions"[17] were not forthcoming, or when the enemy departed from the optimum British text, he could (had he wished) have made use of that flexibility. For example, if one imagines a scale of thickening mist (from 1 to 10), whereas he was more or less obliged to disengage at, say, 3, he could potentially have held on to the enemy until it reached 4 or 5 before releasing his grip. Most of Beatty's innovations, both in technique and in doctrine, were designed to raise the threshold of 'unsuitable conditions'.

*

A strong case can be made to the effect that the Royal Navy's classical achievements (usually when outnumbered) had established performance criteria which transcended those required by the strategic situation in 1916. And if Jutland failed to measure up to victory by Nelson's standards, it was victory by those of Rooke or Benbow. Even Alfred Mahan, the godfather of twentieth-century battle-fleet strategy, decried

> the 'sterile glory' of fighting battles, and still more of running risks, the object of which is not worth the possible loss . . . [If sea-control] can be attained equally well by other means, the battle-fleet should be preserved as both a political and military factor of the first importance.[18]

Perhaps refraining from adventurism, and preserving the unassailability of British sea-power, was the RN's greatest possible gift to the Allied war effort. But the likelihood that the Grand Fleet could, if trained and led on fundamentalist action-principles, have had its strategic cake and eaten it, in 1916, will forever rankle.

*

At the end of the last chapter I left hanging the statement that historians have missed something fundamental about the unhappy post-war Jutland controversy.

What they have missed is that the two sides were resting their respective cases on incompatible doctrinal manifestos – which each held to be self-evident truths in a manner which precluded compromise between them. For example:

1. *On one hand*: "Isn't it one of the fundamental principles of naval tactics that an admiral makes sure that his orders are understood by distant parts of his fleet before rushing off into space, covered by a smokescreen?"[19]

On the other: "An Admiral commanding a squadron sighting the enemy would anticipate that his supporting squadron would close without further orders."[20]

2. *On one hand*: "The smashing up of our battlecruisers was due to Sir David Beatty racing off without giving any instructions to the 5th Battle Squadron."[21]

On the other: "Beatty had every right to suppose that the 5th Battle Squadron would conform to his movements."[22]

3. *On one hand*: "Beatty's staff should have known that because of the distance and the smoke, their signal was not clear, because it was not answered."[23]

On the other: "A sudden alteration of course by the ship sighting the enemy is seen far more rapidly than any signal could be sent, and, being an almost certain indication of an enemy having been sighted, should be acted upon immediately."[24]

4. *On one hand*: "The failure, in the *Lion*, to convey the executive order to turn to the *Barham* still further delayed the time at which those powerful battleships could come into action."[25]

On the other: "It has been proved again and again that nothing is more fatal than 'waiting for orders'."[26]

5. *On one hand*: "Owing to the delay in receiving the alter-course signal, the distance of the 5th Battle Squadron from the battlecruisers was increased to ten miles."[27]

On the other: Initiative/disobedience is a "duty owed by juniors towards senior officers that it is well for officers to ponder over and digest".[28]

6. *On one hand*: "Effective communication links are essential to successful command-and-control."[29]

On the other: "It is essential that commanders and their staffs have a clear understanding of the higher commander's intentions so that they can take appropriate action in the absence of timely direction."[30]

Both sides were bludgeoning their audience with hyperbole; and for either to budge an inch in these dogmatisms would be to admit into the court-room some prejudicial aspect of the other side's case. The confrontation caricatured the respective cadences of Jellicoe's GFBOs and Beatty's BCFOs (and his subsequent GFBIs), and was a re-manifestation of the *Camperdown–Victoria* dispute, of the earlier tensions between Philip Colomb and George Tryon, and even of the differences between the Duke of York and Prince Rupert in the seventeenth century.

Was the confrontation symptomatic of a naval hothouse of tactical debate? To some extent, yes – at least in the case of some of the 'Beatty school' – but to a large degree, the position an officer adopted was governed more by temperament and whose gang he belonged to, or aspired to, than by abstract thought. Reginald Bacon is a case in point: his dogmatism about orders and signals in support of Jellicoe, is quoted under item 5 above; so is his marvellous endorsement of initiative in support of Tryon. These opinions were published just one year apart. Which set of rules did he really believe in? Did he even notice the conflict? Probably not. Thus is illustrated the unsystematic nature of the thought-habits of British naval officers, and the glaring scope for their 'secondary education' – even at times when organic controversies offered much (perhaps too much) stimulant for debate.

However, once allowance has been made for anger, yardarm-clearing and overstatement, the Beattyites (the 'On the other hands', above) were overwhelmingly in the right. For example, contrary to Evan-

Thomas's assertion (under item 1), the punctilious conveyance of orders has nothing to do with the "fundamental principles of naval tactics": it is merely a desideratum which achieves 'essential' status in peacetime – especially in those navies which cede power and influence to suppliers of communications services. But more important, the Beattyites were, for whatever motives, at least propping open the door to the concept that there were serious empirical lessons to be derived from Jutland; and, as Bellairs wrote, "there is little hope for the Navy of the future unless we are going to think with resolution and clarity concerning this battle."[31]

*

It is likely that, even without the lessons of the Great War, a minor ground-swell of doctrinal rebellion would have rolled steadily up the flag-list in the 1920s and '30s. A degree of restiveness in the middle ranks of the service had been discernible before August 1914, as the historical (or 'post-materialist') school began to speak out. "It is in the study, not of the instrument, but of its use that we are deficient; in the study of strategy, tactics and war, and war as a whole," Alfred Dewar had written in 1913.[32] Furthermore, as Professor Jon Sumida has persuasively argued,[33] there were other factors pulling in the same direction: the growing prospect of numerical inferiority (always a stimulant of fighting technique), for example, and technological stagnation deriving from financial constraints. However, when Sumida refers collectively to the "tactics of the First World War", he fails to differentiate between the respective doctrines of Jellicoe and Beatty, as commanders-in-chief, and his words would certainly be qualified by senior officers who served in the Grand Fleet under both.

There was undoubtedly a collaboration of influences beckoning the British towards the tactics of manoeuvre and the devolution of command in the inter-war years, but it was the irrefutable failure of "our system" at Jutland which gave the waiting radicals, from Beatty down, the moral authority (and career security) to urge their doctrinal views on the fleet. Beatty's heartsick comment to Lieutenant Chalmers, before falling asleep on the settee in *Lion*'s chart-house, became implicitly if imprecisely understood by an up-and-coming generation of officers who would not otherwise have carried the banner of reform. The 'rationalism' accrued during the century of peace had to yield to empirical evidence on the irresistible scale of that of 1914–16.

The Royal Navy between 1919 and 1939 came to be dominated by BCF values. That is not to say that Jellicoe's legatees did not hold high commands and high offices: his Jutland chief of staff (Madden) and three Battle Fleet captains (Frederick Field, Roger Backhouse and Dudley Pound) held the post of First Sea Lord. But Beatty and his former flag-captain, Lord Chatfield, between them occupied that position for two-thirds of the inter-war years; most commanders-in-chief were influenced by the views of Sir Reginald Plunkett-Ernle-Erle-Drax (formerly Beatty's flag-commander), and there was, anyway, 'for the good of the service', a degree of rapprochement between the two groups whose polemicists had so exacerbated the *Harper Record* controversy. "We made many mistakes," Beatty said in a speech (written for him by Richmond) in 1919, "and it is our business today to see that the lessons have been taken to heart."

The keynote of the operational reform of those years could be said to have been the maximization, through technique, of available technology – at least as far as surface warfare was concerned.

> Between 1916 and 1939 the lessons of Jutland were taken to heart and steps taken to exercise and improve the Plotting Organization. The strategical situation was separated from the navigational chart and kept on a plotting sheet, thus aiding the Command by providing a separate picture which could be studied without interfering with the requirements of the Navigating Officer for the safe navigation of the ship . . . After 1933 all Instructor officers and Schoolmasters did a course in plotting at HMS *Dryad* and were allocated for plotting duties in the ships in which they were borne.
>
> The increased attention to night fighting and destroyer searching and striking forces soon made it necessary to keep a plot in destroyers. This led to a further increase in the requirement for trained officers, which was met by including instruction in plotting in the Sub-Lieutenants' Navigation course. Also for the first time a requirement arose for ratings to be employed on the plot . . .[34]

Thus it was that, by 1939, every 'private' ship, even a humble destroyer, had systematic appraisal facilities – in the form of automatic plotting-tables, internal communications and trained personnel – far superior to those of *Iron Duke* or *Lion* at Jutland. Subsequently, during the Second World War,

> new weapons were in use at sea and new counter-measures were required to deal with them. Fighter direction was introduced and made effective by use of an air plot fed in the main by warning air Radar . . . In the process many new ideas and much new equipment were introduced, some of which could be adapted for the surface plots. Great strides were made in the development of W/T direction-finding and the 'Y' service, both of which began to give more information to the Command than before. Different fleets had different problems. All [adapted] their plotting organizations to great advantage [but] a universal organization was needed which could be adapted to the needs of the moment.

To this end the Action Information Organization came into being. There is nothing inherently new in it. It sets out to unite under the control of the Command all the sources of information, the plots and the means of appreciation and execution which modern naval warfare demands. In addition, it provides a meeting ground upon which Navigation, Radar, Gunnery, Torpedo, Anti-submarine, Communications, and the Air can pool their separate resources for the common good.

The order in which the purposes of the AIO are listed is significant:

The primary object is to serve the Command by providing a picture of the tactical and strategical situation, both surface and air, which is up to date, comprehensive and readily intelligible.

The secondary object is to direct the weapons, including the air weapon, on to their targets.[35]

The terms 'primary' and 'secondary', be it noted, are used above in the opposite way to that meant by George Tryon: here primary means 'more important' (he used it to mean 'elementary'), and secondary means 'subordinate' (he used it to mean 'more advanced'). To use both frames of reference in one breath is to invite hopeless confusion, but one can assert that an AIO, whose main object was the clear presentation of "the tactical and strategical situation" must, by its mere existence, greatly have enhanced the 'secondary' awareness (in the Tryonic sense) of every commanding-officer – if only because the possession of knowledge carries with it implicit responsibilities. What had been thought of as exclusively 'admiral's business', in 1916, was now everybody's business. This was one of the many subtle but constructive manifestations of the retreat of tramline military deference.

In the 1950s, it would be a comparatively minor step in practical terms (although controversial in traditionalist ones) for the captain to forsake his action-station on the bridge and fight his ship from the operations room.[36] Today, every ship in a task-group is linked, with pooled information, integrated tactical picture and delegated tasks. Their various systems-computers are constantly chattering. Thus equipped, *Barham*'s ops room would have known in real time about *Galatea*'s sighting and Beatty's new course at 2.35; *Iron Duke* would have taken in *Lion*'s plot before the Grand Fleet's deployment, or *Malaya*'s picture of the goings-on astern at around midnight.

While these innovations were still at an early stage, Beatty's administration had brought into service the Admiralty Fire Control Table (AFCT) Mark I. "The new machine was capable in theory of producing a highly accurate firing solution rapidly even when the target and firing ship were converging or diverging at sharp angles and high speed" –

indeed it owed so much to Arthur Pollen's pre-war ideas that Their Lordships were compelled to make a substantial settlement for breach of copyright.[37] The AFCT was installed in the new battleships *Rodney* and *Nelson*, and in older capital ships as and when they underwent major refits. At the same time, by the early 1930s, British admirals were exploring the possibilities of manoeuvre-warfare and night-fighting. Taking the lead in these enquiries were two successive Commanders-in-Chief Mediterranean, Chatfield and Sir William W. Fisher (CO of *St Vincent* at Jutland).

> By 1934 the Royal Navy was investigating situations in which the battle-fleet purposefully sought out night action with enemy capital units. Under successive commanders of the Mediterranean Fleet, night-fighting was established as standard.[38]

The easy 'hindsight' charge has been made that "a future Jutland fought against the Japanese fleet in Far Eastern waters befogged the Royal Navy's thinking over the entire horizon of maritime warfare in the years before the Second World War."[39] If this means that the Royal Navy wanted to refight a Jutland-scale battle along tactical principles unchanged from those of May 1916, then the accusation is nonsense. If it means that the Navy was preparing itself for future battle-fleet action, in which the perceived mistakes of Jutland must not be repeated, then there is truth in it. It may be seen in the building of what were, ton for ton, the world's most heavily armoured battleships (and carriers, and cruisers) in the late 1930s. And it may be justified by the First Lord's projection that, while the fleets of France and Italy would, he thought, continue to cancel each other out,

> Germany and Japan would be level-pegging with Britain in commissioned capital ships by 1941, and by 1944 would be in the lead. By the end of 1946 he was looking at $34\frac{1}{2}$ capital ships for Germany and Japan (the *Deutschlands* each counting for a half), as against 29 for the Royal Navy. With such mathematics in the offing only a fool would have consigned the era of big-gun fleet-action entirely to the dustbin of history[40]

– and, indeed, the experience of Jutland was potentially a tremendous asset.

The curve towards squadronal tactics was not a constant incline. Sir Dudley Pound's command of the Mediterranean in 1936–9 appears to have been a retrogressive step as regards the fostering of initiative. Pound was an archetypal centralizer, as his First Sea Lordship was to demonstrate in 1939–43. It may be mentioned that he had distinguished himself as a flag-lieutenant in the Channel Fleet at the turn of the century, and had served Evan-Thomas as flag-commander in the 1st BS in 1913, before commanding *Colossus* in the Grand Fleet. Stephen Roskill later said, with the authority of having belonged to *Warspite* when she flew Pound's flag, that under his command

> the tendency for excessively detailed orders and centralized command reappeared. When Sir Andrew Cunningham took over [the] fleet he scrapped [Pound's] system, insisted on all operation orders being extremely simple, and encouraged flexibility and initiative by his subordinates.[41]

An American cruiser CO (accustomed to reams of printed paperwork) was introduced to Cunningham's methods of command when he reported for orders in 1943. The admiral drew a map with his finger in the dust on the side of his staff-car, and then asked if he had any questions.[42]

Cunningham did not serve at Jutland. But among those who sailed at nightfall on the 30th of May 1916 confident of their abilities and methods, and who returned to harbour on the 2nd of June, discontented, cheated, and in varying degrees receptive to the view that there was "something wrong with our system", were no less than eight future First Sea Lords.[43] Two more missed the battle by a cat's whisker.[44] And even the 1939 *Fighting Instructions*, which were jointly signed by the authoritarian Sir Dudley Pound and by Sir Charles Forbes (another Grand Fleet battleship captain), bear a strong resemblance to Beatty's 1918 GFBIs, with glimpses of Tryon thrown in, as the following extracts indicate:

> The Admiral will control the movements of the battlefleet as a whole . . . until the moment of deployment, when the Senior Officers of divisions will automatically control their divisions.

> After the battlefleet has deployed, Divisional Commanders have full authority to manoeuvre their divisions so as best to achieve the destruction of the enemy.

> In low visibility . . . the Divisional Commander who first sights the enemy has full authority to act without waiting for orders . . .

> The Admiral and other Divisional Commanders will manoeuvre their divisions to support the division engaged, developing the maximum volume of gunfire as soon as possible.

> The Admiral will control the division in which the fleet flagship has taken station. The movements of this division and the signals made by the Admiral must be watched carefully at all times, so that other Divisional Commanders can appreciate and anticipate his wishes and conform generally to the Admiral's movements.

To enable Divisional Commanders and Captains to direct their full attention to fighting the enemy, close and accurate station-keeping is not necessary.

Immediately the Captain of any ship considers he can damage the enemy by opening fire, he is to do so whatever may be the class of ship concerned. He is never to wait for an order to open fire or for a fire distribution signal.

If the enemy turns away, it is the Admiral's intention to keep him under effective gunfire and accept the position of torpedo disadvantage.

If the signal 'Chase' is made, each Divisional Commander will make the necessary signals to his division. Faster ships should be allowed to pass ahead of the slower or to quit the line in order to make full use of their speed to stop the enemy.[45]

*

If the 1914–16 Grand Fleet's doctrinal roots lay in the structured 'rationalist' certainties of the late Victorian Mediterranean Fleet, those of the Royal Navy of the Second World War lay in the empirical lessons of the First World War: and were instrumental in helping Britain survive a combination of maritime enemies by whom she should, rationally speaking, have been defeated. Lessons, however, have to be systematically rehearsed over and over again. Naval history has not ended. Nor do the skills of naval mastery form a non-slipping ratchet of performance, with each generation of practitioners starting where the last left off. Because the RN forgot this before 1914, it took a dismal series of disasters, fiascos and failures to remind an efficient, gallant and highly committed service what war was about.

*   *   *

The basic import of this book is how, while the Royal Navy was undergoing its fifty-year conversion from oak and canvas to steel and turbines, its once-clear, empiricist understanding of 'product' was pilfered from the lay-apart store by the vested interests of 'process', and how both the symptoms and the cost of that felony may be discerned, in various ways, at Jutland in 1916.

To insist, glibly, that history always repeats itself is to reduce it to a set of unintelligent, negative superstitions.[46] However, history, at the least, comprises an echo-chamber in which past and present voices can mingle; and, no less than any other human activity (and more than most), the military professions are susceptible to enduring pressures and syndromes.

At first sight, the question of whether the story told here serves as a cautionary tale, a rustic parable, of relevance to today's naval scenery of satellites, smart missiles and management-strategies, appears to depend on how far it was shaped and conditioned by, on the one hand, influences peculiar to the late Victorians, or, on the other, influences endemic in peacetime. In practice, these two categories are impossible to separate, for the Victorian era was the definitive era of peace – certainly of peace at sea – and its cultural, political and 'security' characteristics were all consonant with that condition. Nevertheless, there may be those inclined to dismiss the saga as belonging wholly to the former category, as a means of consigning it to the museum.

They will probably invoke the technocrat's nostrum which has worked so well in the past: 'Everything is changed, history is dead!' And having persuaded the Navy of the novelty of its predicament – assisted by an impressive array of jargon – they will proffer solutions of their own convenience. Thus we may expect to hear: "the situation confronting [commanders] at sea today is a world apart from that facing their counterparts of twenty or thirty years ago"[47] (the alleged revolutionary time-scale is sometimes a matter of months) – statements which are usually true in a narrow sense and behind which there is an agenda. In the land of the blinded-by-science, the one-eyed man can be king.

Of course, in both the Navy and the wider world, the technical changes over the last generation *have* been revolutionary – almost as revolutionary as those assimilated by the late Victorians. For example, to a computer programmer, a shop steward, or a redundant spot-welder, vehicle assembly-lines have changed beyond recognition. But while the fact that complex tasks are performed in seconds by microchipped robots is of crucial interest to those directly affected, in terms of what is being achieved it is merely incidental, and to a 'lay' member of the human race a car assembly-line of today still more closely resembles, in form, function and product, its predecessor of twenty years ago than anything else one could think of.

So it is, and will remain, with naval technology and naval purposes. And a 'long-view' perspective of this story appears to be that the conflict of naval action-doctrines has been a recurring one, that the dichotomy has persisted in cycles of varying length for four hundred years, and that spasms of technical change from the carrack to the aircraft-carrier did nothing to diminish it: indeed technological patent-remedies merely compounded the problem by purporting to have transcended it while broadening its scope. In our quest to extract doctrinal lessons from the patterns of the past we do not have to jump to attention every time a technocrat speaks – a rediscovery of a view which was gaining support among the better-read of naval officers on the threshold of the Great War.[48]

That having been said, today's Royal Navy is not officered by neo-late-Victorians. The service has to master and integrate immensely sophisticated systems, and scientific methods of analysis are an inseparable part of the formulation of operational doctrine. 'Operational Analysis' (OA) grew out of the operational research at the Air Ministry and Admiralty (most notably Western Approaches Command) in the Second World War. In anticipation of combat, warriors and theorists have always attempted rudimentary forms of OA in their heads, or on their blotters. The Americans who built frigates to fight decisively outside the reach of the carronade must have used such a process. Laird Clowes's analysis, in 1894, of seventy-four attempted rammings is another example – as is Tryon's calculation about the tactical costs inherent in flag-signalling when two fleets were manoeuvring at given speeds and distances.

Today OA is a formalized system of gathering a database of cases and propositions and subjecting it to rigorous mathematical and computer-model analyses. It could be termed 'Virtual Empiricism', and the story of the peacetime Victorian and Edwardian Navy is an eloquent testimony for the need for it. Untrammelled OA would surely have cut the supposedly 'scientific' high-ground from under Philip Colomb's feet, and precluded the acceptance into doctrine of his system of fleet-tactics. As it was, the goose-step's rebuttal rested on Tryon's rather disorderly articulations and on Fitzgerald's and (later) Beatty's seemingly Luddite appeals to common sense and the 'tactician's eye'. OA could potentially also, of course, have exposed to Jellicoe the frailties of over-centralization of command, while at the same time reining in the Don Quixotes like Cradock and Arbuthnot, and focusing Beatty's attention on tiresome matters such as force-dispositions and 'upwards' information-flow.

OA cannot be infallible. Its integrity will for ever be susceptible to agendas ('situating the analysis'), to short-cut assumptions, and to the selection of input-data. But its integrity increases, and dirigibility declines, with its accessibility to the full spectrum of ideas and interested parties. OA 'without walls' is science acting as it should: as servant rather than master; and it can only narrow the potential (and sometimes fatal) gulf between 'rationalists' and practitioners.

*

Are the syndromes (for want of a better word) underlying the story told in this book acknowledged as issues, implicitly or explicitly, in today's service? Has the Royal Navy's stock of empirical wisdom, hard won-back in two World Wars, been allowed once again to waste away during its subsequent fifty-year technical transformation?

I can only summarize what I consider to be those syndromes, and

dinates by signal before charging off over the horizon (and so tactical legitimacy is bestowed by us signallers).'

The servant having thus achieved mastery, (10) *Innovations adopted in accordance with peacetime doctrine, may lock the Fleet into both systems and doctrine which will fail the empirical test of war* – for "the harsh lessons of combat will always be a world away from theorizing and simulation".[53]

In the analysis of Captain Stephen Roskill (a gunnery specialist), the Royal Navy's various technical deficiencies in the Great War had their roots in "the excessive dominance of the executive or 'line' officer over the specialist".[54] His meaning is not absolutely clear, for, as discussed in Chapter 17, many of the specialists in the Navy were 'line' officers; but I submit that the cause of the problem was almost exactly the opposite: the *excessive deference* given to vaunted expertise. Why this state of affairs should have prevailed is a matter for sociological debate (partly pre-empted in Chapters 9 and 18) – in my guess, the English upper classes' disdain for 'industry' led to their yielding gladly to anyone perverse enough to claim technical territory – but the consequence was a set of sanctuaries whose inmates, in effect, enjoyed benefit of clergy and were spared the gauntlet of robust debate.[55]

For example: Jutland was the wrong time to discover that tactical signalling could, after all, fail; that an unobstructed chain of cordite led to the magazine; that the 'bracket' method of finding the range was too slow; that the fuzes in British armour-piercing shells did not work; that the fire-control system would fail to track a target unless the latter cooperated; that searchlights, like guns, have to be centrally directed; that wiring fixed to deckheads could drip molten lead onto the heads of fire-fighters. Yet all these systems, and many others, had been explicitly or implicitly guaranteed by Roskill's specialists, who, had their judgement been queried, would have stood on their dignity and blustered (occasionally it was, and they did).

One might suppose that these errors were the products of the bad old days before there was a proper naval staff, and so they were; but the syndrome lived on. The Germans found out off Norway in 1940 that their U-boat torpedoes did not work; the Americans had a similar surprise in the Western Pacific in '42; the British were under air attack in Falkland Sound in '82 before they discovered the terms on which Sea Wolf missile-computers would accept a target,[56] and their ships had to burn before the Ministry of Defence would acknowledge that polyester clothing can melt onto the wearer.

It is a BGO, and no less than human nature, that (11) *Purveyors of technical systems will seek to define performance criteria and trials conditions.* This is known as 'situating the estimate', and the Treasury can become a powerful accomplice when marginal cost-savings are scented. The lesson appears to be that (12) *A service which neglects to foster a conceptual grasp of specialized subjects, will have too few warriors able to interrogate the specialists.* This is especially important in spasms of technical change, for it is then that specialists get furthest ahead of general knowledge of their subject, and can make the most expansive claims. Unfortunately, the conceptual explanation of technical matters is not a strength of the armed forces, for it requires the cooperation of the very people whose mystique it threatens and whose career-ticket is obscurantism.[57]

*

This brings us back to signallers: the specialist interest-group which launched and sustained the manoeuvring system by which British fleet-tactics were hamstrung for more than forty years. We have seen that the seminal event in this process was Popham's *Vocabulary Code* (adopted as the 1816 *Signal Book*), not for its author's intentions, but because of its potential capacity and the use to which it would be put. As Lord Charles Beresford said in 1905, "the subject of signalling [is] perhaps one of the most difficult possible to grapple with, and one on which opinions can hardly be expected to be unanimous."[58] However, there are imperative grounds for contending that (as Martin Van Creveld has said, of Vietnam)

> while up-to-date technical means of communication are absolutely vital to the conduct of modern war in all its forms, they may, if understanding and proper usage are not achieved, constitute part of the disease they are supposed to cure.[59]

And without decrying the colossal benefits of cost-efficiency brought by modern signalling to the use of naval resources at many levels, a debate on the cumulative impact of the 'Popham–Colomb–Morse–Marconi' quartet on signalling culture must recognize several related and well-authenticated propositions.

The first, that (13) *The volume of traffic expands to meet capacity*, is remarked upon by Captain Barrie Kent in his history of signalling in the Royal Navy.[60] Coming from an ex-CO of the Signal School, it amounts to a confession and a caution – the more so the latter as new technology is forever expanding the range and capacity of communications.[61] This Parkinson's Law was apparent in the Colombine manoeuvring system, although Lieutenant Inglefield's resort to simple invention, to help his 'buntings' keep up with Sir John Baird's frenetic flag-signalling, illustrates it more precisely. But it was wireless-telegraphy, and the growth of Allied networks in and after the Second World War, which gave the syndrome real scope; and now "the capacity of modern communications systems is outpacing the ability of the 'user' to absorb it all".[62]

The British like to blame the Americans, with whom systems, procedures and practices have been progressively integrated since the inception of NATO in 1949 (or, indeed, of the British Pacific Fleet in 1944[63]). In the Korean War, British warships received US broadcasts from Guam, as well as British ones from Singapore, and the former, in the opinion of Lieutenant Raymond Dreyer, 'flags' to the British admiral, were "full of much useless and incredible garbage, resulting in serious delays to traffic".[64] The reasons for this state of affairs were variously mooted, but self-protection on the part of US staff-officers was perceived to be one – on the lines of 'If I notify everyone about everything, blame will slide more surely outwards when something goes wrong'. It has been suggested to me that this is a military manifestation of the peculiarly American paranoia about litigation, by which the mere existence of signalling has generated a compulsion to send signals – although it should be noted that Americans absolutely cannot be blamed (more's the pity) for the 2,000 signals routed daily through Malta during the Suez misadventure in 1956.

In the last generation or so, with the increases brought about in radio capacity by automated formatting, on-line encryption and computer-queuing (not to mention high-speed transmitting and satellite linking), these signals abuses have combined to comprise a scale of organized incontinence which Van Creveld has termed the 'Pathology of Information'; and even Captain William Pakenham, a former Director of Naval Signals (and a cousin of Old Packs), admits that "the success of the communications system in delivering an increasing flood of message traffic means that operational staffs may now be overwhelmed by the sheer volume of information to be digested."[65]

I have been a 'signals-flood' victim, albeit on a Mickey Mouse scale, in Royal Naval Reserve minesweepers. For one example, on a NATO exercise in the late 1980s our radio personnel comprised one petty-officer radio-supervisor (RS) and one junior radio-operator (RO2), and as we plodded up and down our stretch of coastal sea-lane, we were favoured with a hundred signals per day of which perhaps half a dozen had bearing on our military task. There were signals about 'Orange' movements in the Baltic, about frigates fuelling in the Hebrides, about amendments to rates of lodging allowance, about drinks parties in Gibraltar, and signals about signals. All had to be sifted by a watch-keeping officer who filed the relevant ones and might as well have thrown the rest overboard. If he averaged sixty seconds assessing each signal, the task took him almost two hours at a time when he was already stretched with defence watches and departmental work, and soon RS, RO and WKO were dizzy from lack of sleep. The siege of signals became an extra straw for the camel's back of the ship's efficiency and endurance.

I was not at the time aware that we were acting out a living heritage (to which the Americans were late-comers). The shortage of trained signalmen in times of mobilization was predicted by Phipps Hornby in 1885. Wireless-telegraphy was deemed "most inefficient" after the 1906 Manoeuvres, "not because it didn't work, but because of the enormous number of useless and obsolete messages transmitted".[66] And in 1913 Vice-Admiral Jellicoe found the "interpretation and distribution of signals" to be handicapped by shortages of qualified personnel and on-board office facilities.[67] Most of our problem was caused by our ship's being automatically listed among the 'info-addressees' of other people's business; but it was an insidious little assault on product by process, which it should have been somebody's job to prevent. One supposes that if each signal-address had entailed some modest cost to the sender – £2, say, or a low-voltage electric shock – greater selectivity might have been discovered.

The petty adversities of a since-disbanded RNR squadron will not cut much ice, but they illustrate a threat of dysfunction which has troubled much bigger fish: (14) *Signals 'capacity' tends to be defined by how much the senior end can transmit, rather than by how much the junior end can conveniently assimilate.* In Operation Corporate, the campaign to recover the Falkland Islands in 1982, in spite of 'MINIMIZE' – a debased ritual-call for restraint in signalling – HMS *Hermes* is said to have handled the jaw-dropping figure of 170,000 signals in two and a half months (which by my count equals one every thirty-nine seconds), of which 62,000 (one every 107 seconds) called for 'flag-action', and 4,500 (one every twenty-five minutes) 'special handling'.[68] The Task Group commander, Rear-Admiral John Woodward, formed "a full-time Staff Intelligence Cell", and was fortunate to have had a highly competent, and presumably hyperactive, staff-officer who relieved him "of a vast quantity of unnecessary detail and hassle-factor". Still, he worried

> about the horrendous volume of signals required to keep the whole act together, not just locally in the south, but between the task groups and the UK. The whole communications system was grossly overloaded and could come to a grinding halt if we had a major operational problem.[69]

Nine years later the commander of British naval forces in the Gulf War, Commodore Christopher Craig, in the destroyer *London*, found his team of one chief-yeoman, one RS and seven ROs handling more than 1,000 incoming signals each day and transmitting an average of 70 – a totally unacceptable load. Cries of 'minimize signal traffic at sea' achieved nothing. Ready-formatted US signals with hundreds of addresses threatened to clog the system.[70]

The Gulf War saw a refinement to the clogging of the system which may be compounded by the "elaborate command structure" of coalition warfare,[71] but which might have been extrapolated from the 1906 report on W/T (if not from *Lion*'s flag-deck at Jutland): (15) *Signals' prioritizing mechanisms become dislocated in times of overload.* Owing to the backlog of signals which quickly built up after fighting began in January 1991, messages properly classified as 'Routine' were competitively uprated to 'Priority', 'Priority' to 'Immediate' (and presumably 'Immediate' to 'Flash'); and the congestion shifted progressively upwards. The result was the confusion of urgent and non-urgent traffic, and unplanned burden to the victim-addressees; and all this loss of composure came about without an enemy spanner within throwing distance of the works. The Gulf War also illustrated the syndrome (named the 'Schwartzkopf syndrome' by John Ferris and Michael Handel) which delayed Jellicoe's deployment decision: (16) *Incoming traffic can act as a brake on decision-making*, by reason that the next signal, due in any minute, might contain intelligence or analysis relevant to the decision you should be taking now.[72] Even if it does, by the time you have found out, the shelf-life of some earlier item may have expired, leaving you, relatively speaking, no better off – and late.

In December 1995, as the American C-in-C Europe (NAVEUR) was gearing up to support the NATO presence in the former Yugoslavia, his communicators were claiming a need for seventy-nine more channels than there were in existence.

Needless to say, (17) *The more signals, the more the sun shines on signallers.* Jutland's 'flag-signal every sixty-seven seconds' (during the daylight action) represented a gratifying market for signalmen, and was partly the result of supplier-induced demand. And one notes, in passing, from the separate testimonials of two captains of the Signal School (Cunninghame-Graham and Kent) and from miscellaneous items, that signallers tend to measure, and advertise, their performance by volume of traffic. Syndrome No. 17 is undeniably at work today. However, communicators are merely providers of a service for various agencies, none of whom wish to be thought inactive in a crisis; and short of paying signallers in the proverbial manner of Chinese doctors – in inverse proportion to the need for their services – one cannot expect them to want to disoblige clients who have varying degrees of influence in the higher defence structure.

Nevertheless, part of the 'communications package' remains a duty of care to the 'outboard' recipients, for whom the whole shebang exists; and if that duty is shirked, because it appears too difficult or disruptive of 'process', then the job is not being done. (18) *The 'centre' must subject its own transmissions to the strictest self-denying ordinance*, and, in this, seniority is critical. Admirals no doubt imagine that they are always curbing signals traffic (or, at least, delegating the task to signallers, which is not at all the same thing); but their failure to enforce compliance is manifestly more the rule than the exception. Unfortunately, there is a powerful disincentive for the politico-military centre to self-impose signals restraint: (19) *Signalling promotes the centralization of authority.*

Popham started it, unintentionally. His revolutionary *Signal Book* brought a new formality to command relationships by reducing the need for collaborative conferences, with all their 'in your face' nuances of comprehension, in favour of the terse, formatted signalese for which the Royal Navy still admires itself. Then came the regimentation of steam-tactics and Colomb's manoeuvring system. Then, wireless-telegraphy arrived to elasticate the strings of seniority and create issues of operational command which return to hamstring the Royal Navy.

The persistence of the problem today is partly a legacy of the Battle of the Atlantic and of the subsequent Cold War. The organization which oversaw victory in the Atlantic in 1941–4 left a deep impression. The processing of vast quantities of wireless-intelligence, the directing of (at any one time) dozens of convoys and hundreds of warships and aircraft, and the constant work of operational research, could not have been performed by a lesser outfit than the 1,000-strong headquarters of the C-in-C Western Approaches at Derby House in Liverpool. Small wonder, then, that when Britain's naval role in NATO focused increasingly on anti-submarine warfare and the sea-control of the North-Eastern Atlantic, and when the ships available as Home Fleet flagships frequently offered inadequate command facilities, the business of fleet-command moved ashore: first, in 1952, to Pitreavie in Fife, and then, in 1953, to Northwood in Middlesex.[73] There it has remained, under the purview of a full ('four star') admiral, serviced by increasingly complex communications.

Over the ensuing three decades the RN's practice and culture of operational command at rear-admiral and vice-admiral (two and three star) levels atrophied. For a whole generation this seemed of little consequence: the Navy had merely moved with the times. But when the era of super-bloc confrontation, upon which defence planning had long been predicated, came to an end in the late 1980s, the service sailed into a future of limited 'operations other than all-out war' with heavy-duty, centralized command institutions purpose-built to subsume local senior officers – and with the latter ill-equipped to take back the weight.

Conditions which genuinely demand a four-star level of command may in due course re-emerge, but in present circumstances it seems that, as with Sir Arthur Wilson and Sir Archibald Berkeley Milne in 1909, or Churchill and the same unfortunate in 1914, or Churchill and Sir Charles Forbes during the Norwegian campaign in 1940, the issue of the centre's correct usage of remote communications hangs in a doctrinal void.

The matter was illustrated again before the end of the Cold War, in the Falklands conflict of 1982. The campaign in the South Atlantic was run from Northwood by Admiral Sir John Fieldhouse who, as Task Force Commander, exercised command over not only Rear-Admiral John Woodward (the Task Group Commander) but also the land forces, the amphibious forces and the hunter-killer submarines. Woodward was thus just one of Fieldhouse's operational subordinates, and he could find major pieces being moved around what he reasonably considered to be his chessboard for purposes which were not always agreed or even apparent.

A crisis-point was reached on the 1st–2nd May, when the Task Group appeared threatened by an Argentine pincer-movement and the one submarine, *Spartan*, which should have been in a position to locate, and perhaps sink, the Argentine carrier, to the north of the Falklands, had been sent off on some other mission by the Task Force Commander. But for a freak absence of wind which prevented the launch of the carrier's strike-aircraft, the consequences could have been dire for the Task Group; and the organizational conflict over the command and deployment of the submarines might stand out in retrospect as the fatal British weakness. As it was, Woodward's urgent signal to *Conqueror*, to the south of the islands, to ATTACK BELGRANO GROUP, was a direct order to a unit not under his command. Northwood quickly took the signal "off the satellite, in order that *Conqueror* should not receive it",[74] but it had the intended effect in England.

The generally successful working relationship which obtained between Fieldhouse and Woodward in 1982 owed much to their earlier acquaintance as submariners, and was more a case of extemporized method surmounting higher-command organization than it was a vindication of that organization. The command structure risked disaster, and with other personalities in the key positions it might have become inoperable. The considered opinion of some senior officers is that the inconvenient command-and-control lessons of Operation Corporate have been disregarded.

Emergencies, by definition, happen rarely, [and] planning to deal with them receives few tests. While the rest of life hurries along this aspect of human affairs lies dormant for decades at a time, then is sharply exercised. If, in the crisis, it survives, it has proved itself and is perpetuated.[75]

In the 1991 Gulf War, again, the British naval command regime was an inappropriate response to the scale and nature of the problem. Royal Navy forces ultimately numbered twenty-six ships, and performed vital roles in the most dangerous waters in the van of the main Allied forces. The military profile of the task, and the need for entry to the high-level councils of our Allies (whose understanding of mine-warfare was not all it might have been) would have justified a two-star flag-officer, and the command facilities of an *Invincible*. Instead, British forces seemed to be regarded by Northwood and Whitehall as merely an enlarged Armilla Patrol (by which the RN had policed the Gulf of Oman since 1980), and remained under the control of a one-star officer, Commodore Christopher Craig, who was much handicapped by cramped conditions and inadequate support facilities in the destroyer *London*.

If they are not already doing so, space-systems will soon be able to include Northwood in the tactical 'ops room' data network of a task-group at sea, and thus technically empower CINCFLEET to 'fight' it himself. The idea is, of course, counter-instinctive: a trip into the Twilight Zone, with robotic ships remotely controlled by a computer-gamer (whom sci-fi convention enjoins us to portray as mad) safe in a concrete bunker; and it would find no support in the newly published *Fundamentals of British Maritime Doctrine*. But one can certainly name one First Sea Lord, Sir Arthur Wilson, who would have seized upon such a facility with relish, and another, Sir Dudley Pound, who might have found its temptations irresistible.

Sir Andrew Cunningham, as a 'four star' ashore, could technically have intervened in the Battle of Sirte in March 1942. Every signal and sighting report was monitored in Mediterranean Fleet HQ in Alexandria, where the unfolding action was plotted on the operations table. Cunningham was mortified to find himself "behind the scenes while others were in action against vastly superior forces",[76] and paced up and down, declaiming on what Rear-Admiral Philip Vian and his captains ought to do next. As signals were 'copied' showing them doing it, he would add "There you are!", "That's correct", or "Good boy!", but he forbore to interfere.[77] When the action was over, he sent a signal suggesting a convoy disposition which Vian was about to order anyway. One would like to believe that the future Royal Navy will take its command-and-control principles more from 'ABC' than from 'Old Ard Art' – although that rather begs the issue of 'two star' competence, in which respect Cunningham and Wilson were very differently served. Another circle.

Calls for the re-devolution of command-and-control might be condemned as traditionalist and sentimental. And signalling, with all its levels and data-links, is now so inextricably involved with issues of command that many may be inclined to confuse the two and (not for the first time) abandon the whole subject to communications theologists. But there are very good reasons – aside from the self-inflicted handicaps mentioned in recent pages – why to do so would be unsound.

First, by the Royal Navy as a whole – and this no doubt applies to other navies and other services – an essential principle continues to be under-acknowledged: (20) *There is an inverse law between robust doctrine and the need for signalling.*

This 'law' should be a BGO (although Jellicoe understood it only after Jutland) – and is not a bad litmus test of doctrine. The historical evidence to support it is overwhelming at both strategical and tactical levels. It underlay the fleet-training doctrines of Jervis, Nelson, Tryon, Beatty and Cunningham, and it has many striking illustrations from this century – including, of course, every act of constructive disobedience.

The other side of this coin is that (21) *Heavy signalling, like copious orders, is symptomatic of doctrinal deficiency,* and is often the preamble to disaster. Forces without an understood common doctrine, especially those extemporized from diverse commands and different navies (such as the Franco-Spanish fleet in October 1805, or the Allied squadron in the Java Sea in March 1942), tend to go to war in a lather of signals, ordering dispositions, explaining procedures, clearing up and causing misunderstandings. They are, of course, doing their best to sort themselves out, and the agency of signalling might enable them to scrape by – but that merely reflects the local positive side of a general negative: for, as in the case of Victorian steam-tactics, (22) *The promise of signalling fosters a neglect of doctrine.*

This, of course, connects with Popham's obviating boat-transfers, at the beginning of the nineteenth century; and, in a sense, 'doctrine' may be tainted by association with primitive levels of articulacy, especially if communications 'process' is honoured above military 'product'. However, "improved signalling capabilities [were] part of the downfall of doctrinal development",[78] and "the ability to communicate has led to a position where some of the lessons of the past, such as the use of a sensible degree of delegation, are in danger of being lost".[79] There is much to be said for a culture of selective signalling inarticulacy.

There is one part of the Royal Navy which could teach the rest of the

Fleet something of communications attitude. Submariners covet their capacity to work with the minimum of supervision: indeed, once 'on task', their ability to receive and transmit traffic is only spasmodic, and they will leave signals unanswered for days if it suits them. Although the communications dynamics of submarines tend to be much simpler than those of other warships (for they usually work alone), submariners operate habitually from doctrine, and thus serve as a present reminder that it can still be done – and done with unrivalled competence. One senior submariner, fulminating about the surface Fleet's profligate signalling culture, suggested to me that as a matter of house-training ('good for you') much routine administrative traffic should be saved up and sent by mail, adding, with disarming quaintness, "It's more writers we need, not more signallers!"

Then, there are practicalities. While "naval communications are undoubtedly very reliable under normal conditions there must remain a worrying question mark over their capacity in war." (We must rebel against the definition of peacetime as 'normal conditions' for any military system.) Indeed, their frailties are such that our dependence on them for command-and-control functions is admitted by Captain Pakenham to be cause for "grave concern".[80] A whole range of injuries – some of them new, others old hat – may be inflicted by the enemy or by circumstances, and, as Tryon and Beatty more or less clearly understood in ways applicable to their own times, (23) *War-fighting commanders may find themselves bereft of communications faculties on which they have become reliant in peacetime training.*

Most forms of radio-transmissions can be eavesdropped, jammed, 'spoofed', direction-found, and disrupted by direct attack on equipment. "Electronic warfare is taken extremely seriously at all levels in modern navies and it is often said that the EW battle at the outset of an engagement will largely determine the overall outcome."[81] Perhaps the most serious Achilles' heel is the dependence of our command-and-control system on satellite communications, "long and successful reliance [on which] without any serious attack being mounted has engendered unprecedented complacency".[82]

Satellites can fail from integral causes (as did the British Skynet I, in 1974). They can be taken out by physical attack, by electromagnetic pulses (which follow high-level nuclear bursts, and can now be replicated by other means[83]) "and probably in future by laser weapons".[84]

The Argentines, in 1982, may not have possessed the capacity to attack our satellite communications, but "it is a matter of open record that Iraq had the means at her disposal" in 1991, and a mystery that she failed to use them.[85] It is only a matter of time before the 'Western

Allies' are confronted by an opponent with both the means and the sense to attack their satellites, for

a. the necessary technology is becoming increasingly accessible to medium powers, and we must expect its proliferation;

b. it is cheaper than the sort of order-of-battle necessary to defeat us on our own military-hardware terms; and

c. politically, communications-warfare is mostly below killing-warfare on the 'bodybag' spectrum of conflict.

At the shipboard end, the issue of communications vulnerability evokes ready historical parallels. Just as signalmen might have been mown down by shell splinters in the 1880s, and as W/T operators were killed in *Barham*'s auxiliary wireless-office at Jutland, so they can be killed in the year 2000. As action-damage for a time deprived *Lion* and *Barham* of wireless faculties, modern radio systems may be disabled. As halyards were severed in the running fights of the First World War, proximity-fuzed shells can be burst over a ship for the express purpose of trashing her aerials.[86] And equipment (as well as its user–maintainer) can malfunction for mundane reasons unconnected with enemy action. The Maritime Warfare Centre could do worse than hang on its wall Ralph Seymour's bemused apologia for the fiasco at Dogger Bank:

> Signals went through like clockwork . . . when I say they went like clockwork I mean until the clock stopped, which it did at the critical moment when we really wanted to signal. We were reduced to two pairs of halliards, no W or searchlights, all electrical supply having failed, so when we hauled out of line could do nothing as our flags were completely concealed by smoke.[87]

So great (although unquantifiable) are the potential frailties of long-range signalling, that the 'Northwood' system of centralized control may prove, under test of the next major crisis, to be a command-and-control 'Maginot Line' which a resourceful enemy could outmanoeuvre and defeat, leaving our forces in disarray.

Van Creveld's analysis of American command in Vietnam prompted him to remark that "To study command as it operated in [that war] is almost enough to make one despair of human reason; we have seen the future, and it does not work."[88] Twenty years later the largely fortuitous circumstances of the Gulf War provided a teasing new glimpse of the American ideal of victories without bodybags, and has sent mega-dollars tumbling down the Alician rabbit-hole of 'Information Warfare', in pursuit of the "delusion that the mere possession of information can somehow have the same deterrent effect that once had to be achieved through hard-earned military powess".[89]

"The important thing about the so-called 'communications industry' is that it is basically concerned with merchandising."[90] Every profession would like to lock the world into deepest clienthood, but the danger with military communicators being allowed to do so lies in their implicitly promising something which may be unsustainable or useless in war conditions. They have done it before: they were happy to see the Fleet's dependency on their services approach hostage-status in the years preceding the Great War, while they kept implying 'This will work. Trust us!' And having won the coveted S after their names, and accelerated their careers, they were found to be wrong – as certain boorish officers with attitude had predicted all along.

The future is not necessarily the cyberspace asylum feared by some and eagerly fostered by others. Most of the problems were created by, or at least evolved with, wireless-telegraphy, and it may be that the continued growth of the same will start the pendulum moving back. As long ago in cyber-prehistory as 1982, Sandy Woodward found that the availability of a satellite secure-speech 'natter net' was doing something genuinely almost new for operational control. It enabled senior commanders hundreds or even thousands of miles apart to converse in a way which resembles more the face-to-face meetings of ancient folklore than the stilted signalling argot of the last 150 years.

> No other form of communication is as good as a telephone conversation for dealing with complicated subjects or difficult decisions. This is partly because, as we all know, both meaning and nuance can be conveyed by speech in a way that is impossible in written communication.[91]

The logical projection of this is that the telephone-assisted seawards return of 'community of thought' will lessen the detailed dependence on more formal communications. The desideratum of 'common doctrine, common picture' is becoming more independent of time and space than ever before.

Moving ahead in time (an officer at the Signal School in 1908 predicted that wireless-*telegraphy* would be eclipsed by wireless-*telephony* within two years – a remark presumably motivated by anti-*Vernon* sentiments), we come to the possible consequences of the 'digital revolution', which, although still "in its infancy is [allegedly] about to change the ground rules of modern warfare". "Because of the increasing tempo of conflict and the greater dependency on computer-assisted processing and data-capture", digitization may lead the military planning process "to become less centralized and hierarchical and more distributed and cooperative".[92]

Technology itself may therefore assist the evolution of the role of Northwood towards a regime by which CINCFLEET (or the new

Permanent Joint HQ, also situated at Northwood) issues policy directives and rules of engagement to the task-group commander at sea, while making available a library service of briefings, information and analyses which he can download as and when he wants them. And then, if satellite links become disrupted during operations at sea, there will at least be senior officers 'on scene' fully organized for, and doctrinally accustomed to, the exercise of independent command, and the dislocation will be to a major dimension of the fleet's sensory capacities, rather than to its central nervous system. (24) *Properly disseminated doctrine offers both the cheapest and the most secure command-and-control method yet devised by man.*

Elsewhere the first breaths of a new, critical, breeze seem to be disturbing the antennae of communications culture. Now that the proliferation of multi-media and modem-linked computer systems in business and domestic usages has passed the 'honeymoon stage', laymen are no longer easily seduced by vaunted wizardry,[93] and are increasingly inclined to think critically of functions and roles. The real world, after all, still exists outside cyberspace. In the armed forces, too, with technology now able to supply counter-productive volumes of traffic, and with military analysts and policy-makers browbeaten by

> jargon impenetrable by the normal devices of the English language . . . [by] a bewildering array of concepts . . . [and by] nonsensical images of sets and subsets at presentations on future warfare, each concept shown as a subset of the rest in seemingly hopeless confusion,[94]

the cry must at last be turning from 'More please!' to 'What does it really do?' More than a hundred years ago George Tryon said of the naval communications of his day: "We want signal books to give us what we want, we do not want to be dragooned by signal books."[95] In today's communications-intensive naval environment, it remains as vital as ever that signalling be confined to the role of the servant of operations.

*

One of the people who read part-drafts of this book told me that I have depicted British naval officers of the late nineteenth century as remarkably stupid. I pointed out, rather feebly, that theirs was a strongly chivalrous culture which did not equate cleverness with courage, or stupidity with cowardice; and that, by their own standards, he was, to some extent, applying the wrong yardstick. Nevertheless, the charge took me aback, for I had no such intention and no such general opinion.[96]

Furthermore, there are grounds for supposing that, far from being peculiar to the Victorian Royal Navy, the compulsive deferences to hierarchy and the institutional 'stupidities' encountered in this study could be found almost anywhere in peacetime military life, in many cases in greater measure; and readers from other glasshouses would be wise to leave that stone unthrown. (The officers who formation-wrecked seven destroyers on the California coast in 1923[97] were neither British nor Victorian.) However, as I count myself an opponent of the 'bloody fools' school of history, my critic found a nerve. Perhaps I have failed adequately to honour the criteria by which these men were measured in their own time: but then the paradigm shift is one of my themes. Perhaps I have failed to appreciate the pressures on honest men to conform to the corporate tenets of a sole-employer profession – less a case of fools, than of men made fools of – but this, if it is admitted as a personal alibi, must be acknowledged as an institutional liability.

Probably at no other time in history has the RN's officer corps been so uniformly moulded in its cultural self-image as in 1914. They thought they were good, but, in ways that mattered, they were not. They thought they were ready for war, but they were not. They would have reacted with high indignation to the suggestion that they were not every bit as good and ready as they thought they were. The idea that the predictable, controlled conditions of peace (on one hand), and the erratic, ungovernable demands of war (on the other) favour different sorts of officers is a commonplace with a respectable history, although one which the Edwardian Navy completely failed to assimilate. At the turn of the century Fisher delighted in quoting "golden words" of Alfred Mahan:

> Those who rise in peace are men of formality and routine, cautious, inoffensive, safe up to the limits of their capacity, supremely conscientious, punctilious about everything but what is essential! Yet void altogether of initiative, impulse and originality.[98]

Part of the problem had always been that, with no 'bloody wars and sickly seasons' to decimate the *Navy List*, with no combat opportunities to establish reputations and disrupt the social certainties, the only plausible way to progress in the service was to obtain the patronage of the Establishment by gratifying and reaffirming its values. The Navy, for its part, responds as would any other hierarchy: it invests in future conformity

> by moving the obedient individual up a niche in the hierarchy. This is a doubly ingenious ploy, because the individual is rewarded for his obedience and feels motivated to climb to the next niche, and the hierarchy itself is preserved and strengthened.[99]

In this way is established a self-sustaining circle of dependency. It is sobering to reflect that, in order to get into a position where his higher-command abilities become an issue, (25) *Every proven military incompetent has previously displayed attributes which his superiors rewarded.*

Almost every device of authoritarianism and 'accountancy' management is designed to shorten and lower the focus of loyalty of an intelligent and patriotic serviceman from the distant horizon of national interest, down to his immediately superior officer, standing career-menacingly in front of him. This, as shown in Chapter 9, was the mid-Victorians' gift to the armed forces. The consequence is the conditioning of officers "to see a pin but not a mountain",[100] for initiative and moral courage can be equated, by mediocre, anxious seniors, with disloyalty – and correspondingly penalized. The armed forces' macho 'Can Do' ethos is not in every instance as heroic as it sounds. Richmond deplored "the system which denies officers opportunity to think or express their ideas. I hate this slavish habit of naval officers & this false idea of loyalty, which is generally not loyalty at all, but cowardice."[101]

Peacetime military hierarchies tend to lapse into a way of imagining (as the Edwardians certainly did) that a military incompetent will obligingly exhibit other behavioural characteristics which will assist his identification (like the previously mentioned colour-coded hats). To the narrow-minded and the lazy, this conceit has much appeal: their prejudices can be given free rein in the detection of the give-away characteristics. They can happily disqualify officers with unorthodox methods, colourful private lives, the wrong sort of accents or the wrong sort of wives: officers like Nelson or Beatty. Or Reginald Henderson, who was mentioned in Chapter 23 in connection with the introduction of convoys.

Commander Henderson was the full 'Dixonian' definition of an autocrat, and he would certainly not have prospered in the peacetime Navy, then or now, had he run his ship the way he ran the battleship *Erin* between 1914 and 1916. He made a pact with the crew: he didn't care what they, or she, looked like, so long as they shot better, and coaled faster, than anyone else in the fleet. In Scapa Flow, for some reason, *Erin* usually found herself moored next to *Agincourt*, whose XO took a more conventional view of discipline and would get his men up at 5.45 a.m. to scrub the decks, rain, snow or shine, summer or winter. Having thus stowed their hammocks and worked for an hour and a half, *Agincourt*'s people would suffer the gall of hearing Reveille being sounded in *Erin* next door, and feelings ran high at least till lunchtime.[102] In the 'rearmament years' of the late 1930s Henderson served under Chatfield as Third Sea Lord and Controller of the Navy (perhaps the most effective this century), in which capacity his expansive ideas of self-auditing left the Treasury occasionally speechless, and the Navy a few percentage points larger than it would otherwise have been. He died in office in 1938. One may reflect that, for all the Edwardian era's authoritarianism, the large mesh of the pre-1914 promotion-filter allowed a few good men – lateral thinkers with the courage of their convictions – to squeeze through.

During the Second World War, Nevil Shute Norway (the novelist known by his first names) was in a position to observe the Navy's institutional habits, as an RNVR lieutenant-commander at the Admiralty. He had had earlier dealings with the Air Ministry, and so was not taken wholly by surprise by what he found. He and his fellow VRs discovered that

> in many instances the only way to get things done quickly was to short-circuit the system, getting verbal authority by telephone and letting the paperwork tag along three weeks later. These methods required senior officers of the regular Navy to give verbal decisions which might involve expenditure of thousands of pounds without any paper cover and naturally made us very unpopular.
>
> Now and again we would find some cheerful young commander or captain who was as brave in the office as he was at sea. Commenting on such an officer and on his way of doing business we would say 'He's a good one. I bet he's got private means'. Invariably investigation proved that we were right. The officers who were brave in the Admiralty were those officers who had an independent income, [and] could afford to resign from the Navy if need be without bringing financial disaster to their wives and children. It started as a joke with us, then it turned into an axiom. These were the men who could afford to do their duty in the highest sense.[103]

Every complex organization needs administrators, and every naval officer has to exercise administrative skills, as a matter of routine, from quite early in his career. The need for officers suited to the bureaucratic and political processes in the 'corridors of power' is also an obvious and compelling one: stronger, for the Royal Navy, after the Admiralty's loss of its own historic, and jealously regarded, civil service in 1964, when the service departments were merged into one 'neutral' administration in the Ministry of Defence.

> The officer who performs well before a Congressional committee, who is good at staff work, and who has a knack of saying what he has to say in a way that does not offend his seniors, may be regarded in a more favourable light by them, in spite of the fact that these characteristics are not the ones that are best for a commander at sea. This tends, in peacetime, to tip the scale somewhat in favour of admirals who are good staff officers rather than good

fighters . . . The question ultimately becomes: how can we assure ourselves that we have a reasonably adequate mix of the two? Both are needed, but at different times. The naval service – and the country – cannot help but suffer if the mix becomes badly unbalanced.[104]

Sight can be lost of the fact that the public supports the service for its war-fighting capacities – and other desiderata, however ineluctable, are subservient and *circumstantial*, rather than *essential*. "A fighting service should always keep a good proportion of operational, and preferably fighting, experience amongst its highest-level decision makers."[105]

We know clearly enough what sort of officer the pre-1914 Navy produced, encouraged and rewarded. Albert Markham was an example. In addition to his celebrated 'polar' accomplishments, he helped to pioneer new technology, excelled at all forms of outdoor sport (beware the fitness fanatic!), was abstemious, chivalrous and almost pathologically deferential to authority. At the time of writing, a fine portrait of him adorns the wardroom staircase in HMS *Dryad*.

Hugh Evan-Thomas is another. The efficient, amiable lieutenant in Malta displaying his golfing trophies with an air of studied nonchalance personified the late Victorian ideal of the young men who would inherit the world's greatest empire, with all its privileges and solemnly perceived obligations. Later, as he approached flag-rank, his matchless 'primary' competence brought him the unqualified approval of the Edwardian military establishment – in all the professional and personal nuances which that coveted condition implied. By what criteria could a military profession, becalmed in peacetime, have denied these officers promotion and senior command? And they are needed. They are conspicuous for the tidiness of their desks/ships/personal habits and excel in the controlled, predictable, cash-constrained conditions of peacetime: they maintain the service's hierarchical fabric, oil the wheels of its process machinery, and tend to be first-rate training-officers.

But in wartime the ratcatchers are needed, as well as the regulators, and needed at senior operational level. Captain William Outerson, USN, might have had the late Victorians in mind when he wrote, in 1981, that battle skills

are not capabilities that an officer automatically acquires when he achieves flag rank, nor are they capabilities that are already possessed by all officers who become admirals. We cannot assume that the officer finding himself in [real combat] situations will be able to resolve them correctly simply because he wears broad gold stripes. They are capabilities that must be cultivated.[106]

Were one to enquire at some official level about the criteria for senior officer selection in today's Royal Navy, one would probably receive in reply the same prickly blend of 'Never fear!' and 'Mind your own business' which one would certainly have received before the First World War. And on the evidence of 1982, today's officers know a good deal more about warfare than did their forebears of 1914. Furthermore, in this supposedly 'post-deferential' age, the British armed forces are much more self-questioning, and less complacent about the authoritarian certainties, than they were before the Great War – that itself was one of the yields of that war, as OA was of the next.

Nevertheless, apart from a few intense weeks in 1982, a few intense days in 1991, and one or two isolated incidents in the late '40s, the Navy has now been at peace (albeit not the deep peace of the nineteenth century) for fifty years, and its processes and motivations have been those of peacetime. And if history has anything to tell us on this subject it is that (26) *Peacetime highlights basic 'primary' skills to the neglect of more advanced, more lateral 'secondary' abilities, the former being easier to teach, easier to measure, and more agreeable to superiors.*

If it is in the interests of the country that our military professionals should direct their brains and their talents towards some loftier object than their immediate seniors, if it is desirable that "some potentially fine wartime commanders are [not] lost to the Navy by voluntary separation",[107] then there is needed a system which measures ability by a wider range of criteria than merely those agreeable to the 'accountancy' culture of a pyramid hierarchy.[108] Other things being equal, the officers who will be least disorientated (and thus stressed) by the sudden, erratic, demand-led conditions of war are unlikely to be those whose careers have thrived in opposite conditions in peace. Unfortunately, as an American rear-admiral has said, "present Navy leaders can hardly be expected to admit (whether or not correct) that they would not function well in wartime. Nor can we expect them to damn the system which produced them."[109]

*

My research into procurement policy in the 1930s brought me to the conclusion that (27) *The key to efficiency lies in the correct balance between organization and method.*[110] I was not expecting to find my way back there at the end of this very different book – mainly because I was not thinking in the same frame of reference – but the conflict between centralization and doctrine is merely another way of expressing the same dichotomy. In the former study, the inter-service supply regime, designed mainly by Admiral Chatfield under the roof of the Committee of Imperial Defence (CID), was successful because it shared and exemplified the collaborative, informal characteristics of Colonel Hankey's unique style of organization. After the Second World War, the CID was to some extent made the scapegoat for the catastrophic trend of Britain's strategic fortunes in the late 1930s by senior officials who feared that they would be blamed if the organization was not. Nonetheless, the CID was a rare example of a higher military organization providing the permissive context for effective method – a balance which military career hierarchies are ill-equipped to get right.

The circumstantial pressures in favour of over-organization and against method are woven deeply into the fabric of the military professions, to whom the precise defining of responsibility is an obsessive activity. 'Wiring diagrams' with jobs in boxes proliferate, resulting in structures designed to achieve (at best) one exact template-task very well, but no others. Worse, morale becomes hostage to the ambitious, middle-ranking officer who needs to establish and reaffirm his reputation as a mover-and-shaker. In each new job he has two years (eighteen months, really) to do it, and whereas organizations can be impressively represented on one side of paper, methods cannot. The consequence is the frenetic reorganizer: "an enthusiast for initiatives, he creates a dust-storm of change at the start of every job, moving on before the consequences come home. Everyone knows him for a fraud, yet he thrives."[111] In reality, the chemistry is as important as the physics. "Organization charts – Draw them in pencil. Never formalize, print and circulate them. Good organizations are living bodies that grow new muscles to meet new challenges. A chart demoralizes people."[112]

The tension between organization and method is equally apparent at sea, not just in the syndrome of "ageing lieutenant-commanders" (by whom Woodward's fleet would have been organized to a standstill[113]), but more importantly in the Victorian conflict between the *Signal Book* goose-step on the one hand, and tactics of doctrine and opportunity on the other, and in the differences between Jellicoe's and Beatty's respective methods of leading the Grand Fleet.

Organization will forever be at the core of the military. It is essential to basic training; and the need to condition diverse civilian recruits to a trade in which lives will depend on their procedural drills, their teamwork discipline and their responses to danger, ensures that the armed forces must remain the most highly organized part of human society. In combat too, there are circumstances in which organization is the sole tactical key to success – as when the enemy's behaviour is almost entirely predictable. Nelson, before attacking the fixed defences of Copenhagen, issued precise ship dispositions; 'Operation Neptune' in 1944 (the naval side of the invasion of Normandy) was the triumphant epitome of detailed organization. But circumstances are rare in which the enemy's scope for initiative is virtually zero. And Nelson famously demonstrated (and Tryon and Beatty understood) that the higher combat skills demanded by 'manoeuvre warfare' can be attained only by 'method' (or 'doctrine', or 'action-principles').

In an age when military operations are overwhelmingly likely to be

a. remote from the 'centre',

b. joint (= inter-service) and

c. combined (= international),

it is more important than ever that the Royal Navy sets the 'doctrine' agenda and makes clear the doctrinal terms under which it will operate – the more so as the British probably have a unique cultural predisposition towards method, accustomed as they are to the role-playing implicit in an unwritten constitution, evolved through centuries of empiricism, as against (for example) the explicit definitions of a written, rationalist one, drafted by lawyers.

*

(28) "*Doctrine draws on the lessons of history*," says Admiral Sir Jock Slater, introducing *The Fundamentals of British Maritime Doctrine*. He's right – inasmuch as history has lessons as opposed to approximate precedents. And in long periods of peace historically informed analysis can act as a restraint on the creeping values of authoritarianism and the self-promotional claims of rationalists.

Regrettably, today's Royal Navy seems content to regard its past as merely a cue for bouts of table-thumping at Trafalgar Night Dinners – content to imagine that the great practitioners of the past prevailed because they were ten feet tall, rather than because of the study they devoted "to the strategy and tactics both of contemporary and of earlier battles and campaigns".[114] The edge which the Trafalgar heritage gave to the British at Jutland, Dunkirk, Matapan, the Falklands, is unmeasurable, and any other navy would sell its soul for such a legacy. But if it carries with it the conceit of imputing, by association of heredity, extra stature to today's wearers of the dark blue, and thus relieves them of the bother of addressing their professional provenance (bother which the technocrats will have them believe would be a waste of time anyway), it is as poor a preparation for combat today as it was in 1914.

*

The war-graves of Jutland have been colonized by crabs and congers and shoals of whiting. They snag the nets of fishing-boats which work too close to them, and skippers from Hvide Sande, Torsminde and Thyborøn know exactly where they are – in some cases miles from the positions averred by British records – and could drop dan-buoys at bow and stern of almost any of them without difficulty, if suitably prompted.

Most of the big British wrecks, broken by catastrophic internal explosion, lie in large sections upside-down, with their superstructures, upper decks and armament compressed into the seabed. Permission to dive on them is not normally given, and, lying at over fifty metres, they are reasonably safe from souvenir hunters (though who's got *Queen Mary*'s propellers?). Only the after part of Jacky Fisher's prototype battlecruiser *Invincible* is the right way up, having fallen back that way onto the seabed after standing up on end. The huge fingers of X turret loom menacingly in the opaque green stillness, the turret-roof blown off, the breeches closed and the guns presumably loaded and waiting for Commander Dannreuther to 'make' the circuit to trigger the next salvo at *Lützow*. On the seventy-fifth anniversary of the ship's loss, divers from the Royal Artillery secured a White Ensign on the teak quarter-deck which Horace Hood, like Sturdee before him, used to pace.[115]

Two thousand miles away lies HMS *Victoria*, the grave of Sir George Tryon and so many of his shipmates, of two monster $16\frac{1}{4}$-inch guns, of Commander Jellicoe's paint pots and the late Victorian Navy's one major bid for tactical reform. She has not been visited since the waters of Tripoli Bay closed over her in the midsummer of 1893, and, at around a hundred metres, perhaps never will be. The best memorial to this once-proudest flagship would be for the service to remember the reformation her admiral was dedicated to bringing about. And why.

APPENDIX I

Time and Space at Jutland

Notwithstanding the asseverations of many witnesses and historians, there are few absolute certainties of time and space at Jutland. After the battle Edwyn Alexander-Sinclair told the elderly Admiral Sir Arthur Moore something which every policeman knows: "no two people seem to see things alike even when standing beside one another, and everyone's notion of time varies extraordinarily."

The potential pitfalls of time and space may be grouped under the following headings:

1. *Log-books*

Log-books (along with track-charts) are often regarded as the most thoroughbred of primary sources. Yet, in battle, the men responsible for them could easily be distracted from their upkeep, which would rank low in immediate priorities. Rear-Admiral Royer Dick, a Falklands, Jutland and Matapan veteran, made a comment about signal logs which holds true of logs in general during periods of pressure:

> I am an awful cynic about these things; I mean, logging the signals is the sort of thing you do afterwards and by that time you make it up – on the line of 'My God, if I don't get something in here, I'm going to be in trouble'.

Today's naval officer will be relieved to learn that his role-model forebear was just as likely to fudge the log after the event as he. In fact, for a generation to whom the transfers of data from 'rough' to 'fair' logs was commonplace, such an exercise did not necessarily carry connotations of forgery. In summary, log-books are most accurate when they least matter.

2. *Time-keeping*

Celestial navigation depended on extremely accurate chronometers (three in number) which were jealously guarded by the navigator and tended by his 'tanky' (= turnkey). But outside the navigation department, precise time was less important to daily life in 1916 than today, and the synchronization of time-keeping, both within fleets and within ships, much less accessible.

Most departments, and most log-books, would be governed not by the NO's rarely seen chronometer but by a departmental clock or even someone's pocket-watch. In an era before internally broadcast time-checks, was it anyone's job to see that every such time-piece was synchronized? Practice probably varied from ship to ship. The record of the *Victoria* court-martial has a comment by Rear-Admiral Markham to the effect that (then visual) signals would be logged according to the clock in the signals office, which might well differ, by a minute or two, from that on the bridge. The arrival of wireless did not change this circumstance.

There are half a dozen Jutland W/T signals listed as received in *Iron Duke* some minutes before they were sent by the BCF, which gives rise to the probability that the BCF (or, at least, *Lion* and *Galatea*) was a few minutes ahead of 'Grand Fleet time'.

3. *Helm orders*

At the time of Jutland, and for some years after, port and starboard helm orders were expressed the other way round. At an early age I wondered why First-Officer Murdoch 'starboarded' *Titanic*'s helm if the iceberg was on his starboard bow – no wonder he hit it. The custom derived from the fact that the tiller of a sailing vessel is put over away from the direction of the turn, and the jargon persisted into the era of steam when tillers retreated below decks and out of the seaman's consciousness.

The matter was modernized in the mercantile world as a consequence of American pressure, in 1930, and the Royal Navy conformed. Since then the jargon has reflected the movement of the rudder: an officer wishing to turn his ship to port, has given a port helm order and the helmsman has moved the top spokes of his wheel in that direction.

Primary accounts of Jutland are unlikely to contain errors on this account, but original narrators, to whom the old system was second nature, may not have taken the care over wording necessary for modern readers. For example when *Queen Mary* blew up, *Tiger* and *New Zealand*, astern of her, took evasive action by putting their helms to starboard and port respectively, to turn to port and starboard (in accordance with the custom relating to their numbers, 4 and 5, in the line). Hastily taken notes could confuse anyone.

4. *Track-charts*

This subject is dealt with separately, in Appendix II.

5. *Courses and directions*

Another possible source of confusion. Charts are aligned towards true north and most major warships had north-seeking gyro-compasses by 1916. But lesser vessels (and aircraft) whose electrical supply was generated by their main propulsive machinery, and was therefore not constant, were still dependent upon magnetic compasses; and the age-old practice of giving courses by magnetic compass 'points' (a point=$11\frac{1}{4}$°, a division of 360° by 32) was still in use. Thus course alterations tended to be by cardinal or sub-cardinal points, a custom which died out with the universality of gyro-compasses and repeaters. To a modern sailor with his gyro-compass, a magnetic course of NWbyN would mean $326\frac{1}{4}$° plus or minus the local magnetic *variation* (= the number of degrees by which magnetic north lies east or west of true north). This sounds complicated, but only from our standpoint: for navigators and helmsmen with only a floating magnetic compass card to work from, a simple compass point was easier to read than the exact number of degrees (clockwise from north).

Variation is itself a problem for Jutland historians, especially in view of the fact that the Navy was in a transitional phase between magnetic and true courses and directions. In the east central North Sea in 1916, variation was $+13\frac{1}{4}$° (meaning that magnetic north was $13\frac{1}{4}$° west of true north), and the two gradations were calibrated as follows:

Mag	True	Mag	True	Mag	True	Mag	True
N	$346\frac{3}{4}$°	E	$076\frac{3}{4}$°	S	$166\frac{3}{4}$°	W	$256\frac{3}{4}$°
NbyE	358°	EbyS	088°	SbyW	178°	WbyN	268°
NNE	$009\frac{1}{4}$°	ESE	$099\frac{1}{4}$°	SSW	$189\frac{1}{4}$°	WNW	$279\frac{1}{4}$°
NEbyN	$020\frac{1}{2}$°	SEbyE	$110\frac{1}{2}$°	SWbyS	$200\frac{1}{2}$°	NWbyW	$290\frac{1}{2}$°
NE	$031\frac{3}{4}$°	SE	$121\frac{3}{4}$°	SW	$211\frac{3}{4}$°	NW	$301\frac{3}{4}$°
NEbyE	043°	SEbyS	133°	SWbyW	223°	NWbyN	313°
ENE	$054\frac{1}{4}$°	SSE	$144\frac{1}{4}$°	WSW	$234\frac{1}{4}$°	NNW	$324\frac{1}{4}$°
EbyN	$065\frac{1}{2}$°	SbyE	$155\frac{1}{2}$°	WbyS	$245\frac{1}{2}$°	NbyW	$335\frac{1}{2}$°

It cannot be guaranteed that no Jutland source has either expressed a magnetic direction numerically, without allowing for variation, or picturesquely portrayed a true direction in cardinal or sub-cardinal terminology. It is essential for a historian both to be aware of this possibility and to make clear what directional currency he himself is using. I therefore use compass points only in reference to magnetic directions (unless qualified by 'true'), and numerical degrees only in reference to true directions. I sometimes put one in brackets after the other to underline the difference.

It is noteworthy that many sources – forgetting that we know where the wrecks are – place *Queen Mary* too far to the right, from the viewpoint of *Indefatigable*, by an angle close to the prevailing variation, suggesting that some of them have transferred, without adjustment, magnetic courses onto a true plot.

APPENDIX II

Track-Charts

The movements of various British squadrons at Jutland were published with the *Official Despatches* in 1921 in the form of an assortment of track-charts. These charts were drawn up by ships' officers and flag-officers' staffs in the days immediately following the return to harbour. Historians have relied upon them, as proof of this or that, without testing their credentials as historical evidence. As a rule track-charts were submitted only by flagships, but each of the four battleships of the 5th BS submitted one, as did three of the four surviving battlecruisers of the 1st and 2nd BCSs (which composed the BCF before the 3rd BCS rejoined at the start of the main fleet action).

The only way to fault a single track-chart in isolation is to study its time notations to see if unlikely or impossible speeds are implied. Throughout the period in question the *Queen Elizabeths* steamed at close to their formated maximum speed, which may be taken as about $23\frac{1}{2}$–24 knots. Their track-charts show a general consensus towards this speed, but only *Warspite*'s is consistently credible: at various times we find *Malaya* claiming an impossible 27, *Barham* $16\frac{1}{2}$ and *Valiant* 14. With the 26-knot BCF there are similar anomalies. These are straightforward errors of draughtsmanship which are sufficient to discredit the track-charts as reliable evidence. But there is a better way of testing them – even if a negative one – and that is by a process of like-with-like comparison.

The two heavy groups under Beatty, the BCF and the 5th BS, provide the perfect opportunity for critical track-chart comparison, for each remained in close formation throughout the afternoon. At first sight, however, their charts hardly lend themselves to comparison, such is the variety of scale and the lack of unanimity as to true or magnetic orientation. This calls into question the use for which track-charts were intended by the C-in-C or Admiralty, for much unnecessary work with pantographs and tracing paper would have been been required to combine them. In the age of clever photocopiers, it is much easier.

606

If we select 4.00 p.m. GMT as a time-datum, and combine the several charts of each group by standardizing the scales and time notations, aligning them all to true north and placing them in correct station in relation to each other, the afternoon quickly goes to pieces.

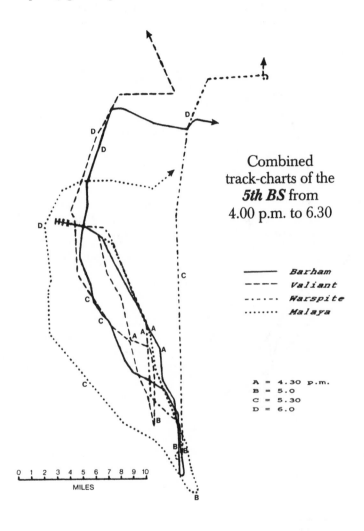

Combined
track-charts of the
5th BS from
4.00 p.m. to 6.30

——————— *Barham*
– – – – – *Valiant*
–·–·–·– *Warspite*
············ *Malaya*

A = 4.30 p.m.
B = 5.0
C = 5.30
D = 6.0

0 1 2 3 4 5 6 7 8 9 10
MILES

The above diagram (synthesizing the track-charts of the 5th BS) finds *Malaya*, tail-end Charlie of the 5th BS, 6 miles ahead of *Valiant* after less than an hour; and at 6.00 p.m., according to our 5th BS master track-chart, some of the ships are scarcely in sight of their sisters. *Malaya* and *Warspite* are 13½ miles apart (which puts *Malaya* 26,400 yards out of station), and by no means are they all proceeding in the same direction. At 6.30 *Valiant* and *Malaya* are steering courses which diverge by some 80 degrees. *Malaya* apparently settled on a course 3 points west of her consorts' when the squadron turned away from the

High Seas Fleet at around 5.00 o'clock, while *Warspite* went off on a solitary expedition towards true north until 5.40. Clearly, this is nonsense.

With the surviving battlecruisers a similar picture emerges (see below) – with an exotic variation. As if to compensate for the lack of a track-chart from *Tiger*, Rear-Admiral Pakenham, who flew his flag in *New Zealand* as RA2BCS, submitted a chart of his own in addition to the ship's one.

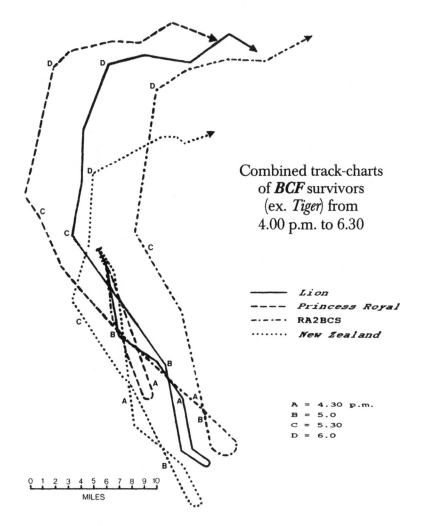

Combined track-charts
of *BCF* survivors
(ex. *Tiger*) from
4.00 p.m. to 6.30

────── *Lion*
─ ─ ─ ─ *Princess Royal*
─·─·─· RA2BCS
········· *New Zealand*

A = 4.30 p.m.
B = 5.0
C = 5.30
D = 6.0

0 1 2 3 4 5 6 7 8 9 10
MILES

Thus we have one track-chart for *New Zealand*'s upper bridge where Pakenham, his flag-lieutenant and Captain Green spent the action, and one for her conning-tower where the navigating officer, his junior-assistant and the chief quartermaster were stationed. By the time of the turn to the north at 4.40 *Princess Royal* has only steamed 11 miles, whereas *New Zealand*'s conning-tower has gone more than twice as far. At 5 o'clock we find *Princess Royal* $10\frac{1}{2}$ miles from *New Zealand*'s navigator, who now is estranged from the people upstairs by 4¾ miles. By 5.30 *Lion*, *Princess Royal* and *New Zealand*'s admiral have settled down on an east–west line with a spread of 8½ miles, and there they remain. *New Zealand*'s navigator, meanwhile, has taken a line-of-bearing SW of her own admiral at 7 miles – a distance which increases to 11 miles by 6.30. At this time both bits of *New Zealand* are out of station on *Lion* by 6 or 7 miles, but in almost opposite directions.

These track-chart errors have nothing to do with discrepancies in the ships' geographical reckonings. I have removed this factor by unifying the tracks at 4.0 p.m., with each group in its correct formation. Track-chart errors derive from deficiencies in the data on which they were based: those details of speeds and course changes which found their way – or not – into the notebooks of the officers-of-the-watch.

It could be objected that these men had better things to do – such as con their ships and fight a battle – than worry about their records for the sake of armchair tacticians. That is the point. The presence of the enemy did not relieve the navigator of his obligation to keep an accurate record of the ship's movements, but the conflict of interests lay not on an interface between seamen and historians, but internally in the realm of the former.

During a battle, the demands made on the navigator were exacting. *New Zealand*'s navigator later wrote:

> The noise of our own salvoes, and the shrieking of the enemy's shells falling over or short and throwing up great sheets of spray, left one with little time to think of any-thing except the work in hand. I personally was fully occupied in keeping station on the next ahead together with plotting our position on the chart, for we were being led by the flagship along a snake-like course.

The navigator of *Southampton*, Lieutenant Ralph Ireland, was more distracted. The senior ship of the 2nd LCS avoided being sunk by the High Seas Fleet by virtue of "the very clever manner in which our navigator zigzagged the ship according to where he expected the next salvo would fall". Although he was repeatedly drenched by the cascading splashes from the "fifty or sixty shells [which] fell within 100 yards of the ship", his success can be measured by the fact that not one direct hit was sustained. It is unlikely that he made copious notes while this was going on.

At one stage an explosion under *Lion*'s bridge put the BCF's navigational reckoning in jeopardy. Lieutenant Chalmers

> was working on the chart in the Admiral's Plotting Room when I felt the deck under my feet give a sudden heave. At the same moment the chart table, over which I was leaning, split in the centre and the windows fell in, exposing the chart and myself to the full blast of the wind.
>
> I placed both hands on the chart, but the wind was too quick for me, and before I could realize what had happened, the chart was torn in two, and the business half of it flew through the window. I last saw it fluttering over the sea like a frightened seagull.
>
> I climbed on to the compass platform and reported the incident to the navigating officer, who was keeping the reckoning in his notebook, but could not leave the

compass. He handed me the book and told me to get another chart and plot it all over again. D.B., who was standing beside him, having heard the order, turned to me and said, 'Mind you get a check from the *Princess Royal.*' This was typical of Beatty's coolness and clarity of mind in the height of action.

In similar vein, when *Barham*'s assistant-navigator, Lieutenant Blyth, was mortally wounded about an hour into the action, the keeping of the navigational record for the squadron flagship devolved on to his midshipman-assistant. And although this traumatized youth, who tried to stanch his senior's loss of blood with the lights temporarily out, performed his unexpected task "in a highly creditable manner under difficult circumstances", Captain Craig regretted, in his report, that "the recording of details [was] not so full or accurate as I should have wished".

In all ships (though more especially flagships) senior officers would, every so often, barge into the chart-house, elbow out of the way the navigating officer, grab the dividers and stare at the chart, while the hapless NO (or his assistant, if he was on the con) stood aside and answered staccato questions as best he could while trying not to forget whatever calculation or piece of draughtsmanship he was in the middle of doing. These disruptions further eroded the accuracy of the navigational record, and were to lead directly to the genesis of the Plotting Organization, whereby an additional plot for use of 'the command' was kept separately. Indeed, in his Jutland report, Craig asked that in future an extra assistant-navigator be borne for the purpose of keeping the flagship's reckoning and noting tactical data.

The shortcomings of the track-charts therefore derive mostly from the conditions under which the component information was recorded, aggravated (in many obvious cases) by careless post-battle draughtsmanship in the placing of time labels. No doubt the track-charts requirement was regarded as an irksome chore, and most were probably delegated by exhausted navigators to the nearest 'dogsbody' (as *Valiant*'s was, to an RNR lieutenant).

APPENDIX III

Time and Space at the 'Turn to the North'

Primary sources – ships' logs, *Official Despatches*, eyewitness evidence in Fawcett & Hooper, plus a few less ingenuous bits and pieces – provide about twenty separate accounts of the time-relationships of events at the 'turn to the north', most of them incomplete and all of them at odds with each other in one way or another. A few are so impossibly mixed up that they have to be disregarded altogether.

For example, Fawcett & Hooper reject *Lion*'s gunnery-officer's statement that the reversal of course happened at 4.40 and attach a footnote saying, "this turn was more probably 4.46." Yet they retain the same officer's estimate of 4.48 as the time of *Lion*'s passing *Queen Mary*'s wreckage. If *Lion* had put her helm over at 4.46, she would have been coming out of the turn at 4.48, and *Queen Mary*, which had been stationed 1,200 yards astern, would have to have blown up just 30 seconds earlier for *Lion* to have been passing her wreckage then. In their anthology of often contradictory first-hand accounts, F & H have picked the wrong piece of data to argue with, for it is obvious that however far the BCF travelled between the loss of *QM* and the 180° turn, it must be allowed to return over the same distance before revisiting the site of her loss. (*Lion* in fact passed it approximately half an hour after her sinking.)

A key item is the observed 'transit' of *Barham*, *Lion* and *Lützow*. This was the moment when Beatty barged between the 5th BS and its targets, and the British battleships had briefly to check fire after loosing off a blind last salvo over the BCF. A transit as dramatic as this is a most valuable item. The scope for a mistaken observation is nil, and in this case the transit must have occurred only a few seconds after *Lion* was abeam of *Barham*. We can construct a tentative time, speed and distance argument, using

- *Barham*'s alleged distance astern of *Lion* at the time of Beatty's turn;
- the speeds of the two groups as discussed in Chapter 7; and
- the probable 14 minutes between *Queen Mary*'s loss and *Lion*'s turn.

It is obvious that

a. *Barham* passed *Queen Mary*'s wreckage when she had made up her distance astern at the moment of loss.

b. *Barham* and *Lion* passed each other on opposite courses when they had between them closed *Barham*'s distance astern at the moment of *Lion*'s wheel-over.

Therefore

1. Between *Queen Mary*'s loss and her own wheel-over (W/O), *Lion* travelled for 14 minutes at 26 knots = 6 miles.

2. At *Lion*'s W/O *Barham*, at 8 miles astern, was 2 miles short of *Lion*'s position at the time of *QM*'s loss, and 1.4 miles short of *QM*'s wreckage (assuming *Queen Mary* to have been in station). *Barham* therefore passed *QM*'s wreckage $3\frac{1}{2}$ minutes after *Lion*'s W/O (the time taken to travel 1.4 miles at 23.7 knots).

Taking the problem through Lion's *turn and up to the moment of* Barham's *passing,*

let us accept the following propositions:

1. That *Lion* took about 2 minutes to complete the turn.
2. That the turn reduced *Lion*'s speed from 26 to 18 knots.
3. That *Lion* then regained speed at a rate of 4 knots per minute.

Starting at *Lion*'s wheel-over, and straightening out the other course alterations (those immediately before and after the turn being about equal) the relative movements of VABCF and RA5BS pan out something like this:

	Barham has travelled	*Lion* has travelled	Distance to point of passing
after 1 minute	790yds	–	15,210
after 2 minutes	1,580	–	14,420
after 3 minutes	2,370	666	12,964
after 4 minutes	3,160	1,466	11,374
after 5 minutes	3,950	2,333	9,717
after 6 minutes	4,740	3,200	8,060
after 7 minutes	5,530	4,067	6,403
after 8 minutes	6,320	4,934	4,746
after 9 minutes	7,110	5,801	3,089
after 10 minutes	7,900	6,668	1,432
after 11 minutes	8,690	7,535	–225
after 10 minutes, 52 seconds			*zero*

A 'London Underground' type diagram (not to scale) of distances between the *Lion* and *Barham*, from the time of *Queen Mary*'s loss until the moment when *Lion* passed in front of *Barham*, is shown opposite.

This is how to produce an apparently exact result from approximated ingredients! Obviously the exercise is based upon items of 'alleged' or 'probable' data – assumptions about this or that – but the important thing is the broad compatibility of the proportions. The elements support each other in a manner which would cause the whole lot to fall down if one prop were removed. Someone disputing one item has to supply an alternative plausible structure for everything else.

The time-table of events put forward in Chapter 7 may now be augmented as follows:

Loss of *Indefatigable*	4.02
Loss of *Queen Mary*	4.26
Lion's wheel-over for reversal of course	4.40
Barham (southbound) passes *QM*'s wreckage	4.43½
Flagships pass	4.51

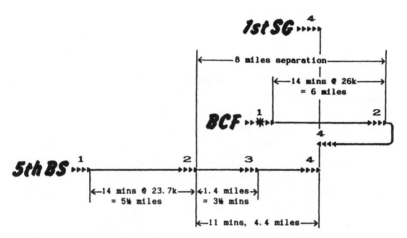

Key: –

1 = moment of *Queen Mary's* loss
2 = moment of *Lion's* wheel-over
3 = moment of *Barham's* passing *Queen Mary's* wreckage
4 = moment of *Lion's* passing *Barham* (*Lützow* in transit)

APPENDIX IV

German Targeting at the 'Turn to the North'

As mentioned, and disputed, in Chapter 8, N. J. M. Campbell (*Jutland: An Analysis of the Fighting*) admits of no German battleships firing at the 5th BS while they were going through their delayed turn at around 4.55 p.m. He has some shooting at Beatty, others at Goodenough, but none at Evan-Thomas.

He identifies eleven of Scheer's battleships opening fire at the 2nd LCS between 4.48 and 4.52. By 4.52 six have, for unstated reasons, stopped, leaving five (*Kaiser, Ostfriesland, Nassau, Kronprinz* and *Thüringen*). At 4.56½ *Kaiser*, too, stops, leaving four. A few of the ships which thus gave Goodenough a break at the time of the 5th BS's reversal of course, apparently remained idle until recommencing at Goodenough between 5.00 and 5.12. Of the seven ships which, according to Campbell, suspended fire at Goodenough, three were divisional leaders (which had the clearest fields of fire), whereas no divisional leader was amongst those which continued.

The target-groups of Scheer's sixteen dreadnought-battleships, at 4.55-ish, as alleged by John Campbell, can be represented diagrammatically by the 'shape' of each ship (round for BCF, square for 2nd LCS), as shown in the diagram opposite. This requires us to believe that, with Goodenough's four light-cruisers bold as brass within easy range and with favourable light conditions for range-finding, the divisional flagships of Scheer's dreadnought battle-squadrons simply stopped shooting, while some of the ships astern of them carried on at slightly longer range.

Common sense says that between 4.52 and 4.56½ some of the German battleships which were firing at Goodenough, including three divisional leaders, shifted their aim a few degrees right to a more important target: Evan-Thomas. (In my time calibration, at 4.56½, when *Kaiser* apparently stopped shooting at Goodenough, the 5th BS was spread around the hub of the turn, bunched-up through loss of speed under helm, with *Warspite* presenting a broadside target.) Some of the following ranks of German battleships were

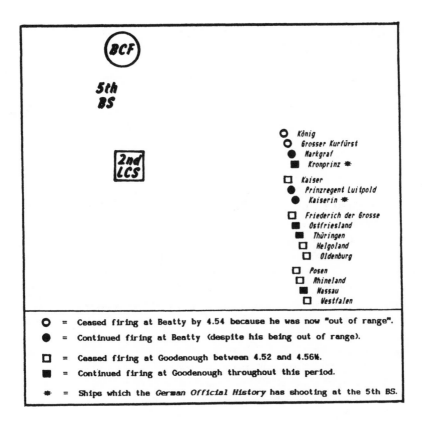

unable to get a clear view of the new targets and so continued to shoot at Goodenough.

Meanwhile, some or all of those ships which Campbell claims continued to fire at the out-of-range and departing Beatty, actually shifted their aim slightly left and, with little interruption in their rate of fire, took up with the 5th BS. Campbell tells us that *König* – the northernmost battleship and closest to both British heavy groups – checked fire at 4.54; but this may have been noted originally as 'Engaged battlecruiser until 4.54', from which Campbell (or some intermediary) has inferred a cease-fire.

Geoffrey Bennett, in his salty and sensible account of Jutland, considers that the 5th BS's turn-in-succession "drew the fire of the enemy battlefleet from Goodenough's light cruisers". And the German Official History says that

Kronprinz (whom Campbell has continuing to shoot at Goodenough) and *Kaiserin* (whom Campbell has continuing to shoot at Beatty) "opened fire at *Barham* at 4.50 and continued to engage her 'effectively' until she turned to the north at 4.58, at which time she received two hits". Leaving aside the time discrepancies, the naming of only these two ships, each the rear (furthest) ship in her division, must be a symptom of the haphazard nature of the records – which are sufficiently wanting to allow Campbell to draw wrong conclusions.

In summary, I put forward the following counter-scenario:

1. The ships which according to Campbell were engaging the 2nd LCS and inexplicably stopped firing for several minutes, in fact shifted aim a few degrees right to the advancing/turning 5th BS. These include flagships *Posen*, *Friederich der Grosse* and *Kaiser*. The German Official History adds *Kronprinz*, who Campbell has continuing to shoot at Goodenough.

2. Some of the ships which were engaging the distant BCF shifted aim, between 4.54-ish and 4.57, a few degrees left to the 5th BS. Among them were Behncke's flagship *König*, *Grosser Kurfürst*, *Markgraf* and *Prinzregent Luitpold*. The German Official History adds *Kaiserin*, whom Campbell has continuing to shoot at the BCF.

3. Neither of these target transferences involved significant interruption to the Germans' rate of fire, and so "cease fire – open fire" sequences (with naming of new targets) failed to find their way into German notes.

4. When the *QEs* had drawn clear of the turn-trap and were regaining speed northbound, some of those German battleships which were least favourably placed, in terms of range and arcs of fire, to continue to engage them, redirected their attention to Goodenough's 2nd LCS.

This proposition need be *only partially right* to rescue several German battleships (including three flagships) from a strange lapse of interest in the enemy, to explain *Warspite*'s and *Malaya*'s version of events, and to justify Captain Boyle's deviation from Evan-Thomas's turning routine. There ought to be two ways of testing it.

Firstly, is it permitted by the known ranges? To discover this, one would have to adopt a known range from early in the 'run to the north' and work the relative-velocity problem backwards to the turn, allowing for Rear-Admiral Behncke's angle of convergence and his offset from Evan-Thomas's course, and various other factors. The task would be fairly straightforward if the available navigational information was equal to it. It is not. And neither are the gunnery ranges. According to Campbell, Behncke's ships (in order of sailing) eventually opened fire on the 5th BS as follows:

König	at 5.10	at 18,600 yards
Grosser Kurfürst	at 5.00	at 19,000 yards
(*Margraf*		not mentioned)
Kronprinz	at 5.08	at 18,600 yards
Kaiser	at 5.10$\frac{1}{2}$	at 17,900 yards
Prinzregent Luitpold	at 5.08	at 19,100 yards
(*Kaiserin*		not mentioned)

Even ignoring the problem of why *König* should have held her fire until the ship astern had been shooting for ten minutes, these ranges are incompatible: *Kaiser* was fourth ship-astern of *König* and slower; she cannot possibly have got closer to *Malaya* by 5.10.

It is perfectly possible to construct a plot, using the *Kaiser* range and selected measurements from the plethora of primary and secondary charts and diagrams, to demonstrate that most of the 3rd Squadron of the High Seas Fleet had *Malaya* in range as she turned. Equally, someone wishing to prove the opposite could do so by adopting the *König* range and fishing around for obliging data in the worm-jar of statistical assertions. Either exercise would be fairly worthless as forensic evidence – not least because the idea that the 5th BS was open-fired upon by the HSF at times listed above is in fundamental dispute.

Secondly, what do German primary sources say about the High Seas Fleet's targeting at this juncture of the Battle of Jutland? (The German Official History has already been quoted.) Campbell does not supply source-notes, but in his bibliography cites "war diaries and action reports of German ships engaged in the Battle of Jutland", and claims that "these are, in general, far better than the corresponding British reports." A perusal of the *Kriegstagebücher* of Behncke's squadron shows this assertion to be insupportable. They share (if anything, in greater measure) all the shortcomings of British reports. Some of their timings are seriously at odds – *König* and *Kaiser* place Behncke's 'fire-distribution' signal at 4.46, *Prinzregent Luitpold* at 4.40, *Kronprinz* at 4.30 – and their target identification is outstandingly poor. They conjure up an image of junior officers going round, a day or two later, pestering exhausted and irritable (or, perhaps, light-headed with relief) seniors for something to write down. (They are also, to a British eye, disfigured by dramatic exclamations, which would, in themselves, place in doubt their documentary detachment.)

Taking them from the top:

The British capital ships first seen from *König* are identified, by bridge-consensus, as *Lions*; but the 5th BS and the BCF then become inextricably mixed in the cursory narrative. Whichever group *König* engaged, her officers appear to have identified the foremost as a *King George V*, and the rearmost as an *Iron Duke* or a *Queen Elizabeth* (all battleship classes). Campbell tells us that *König* first opened fire on the 5th BS at 5.10; but *König*'s own account says that at 5.10 – because her guns could no longer reach the leading (= northernmost) ship of the target group (= *Barham*?) – she transferred her aim to the rearmost (stated again to be an *Iron Duke*).

Grosser Kurfürst's version is the most compatible with Campbell's. She claims to have opened fire at the second ship of a northbound formation – "apparently a cruiser of the *Lion* type" – at 4.49. (The time is out of kilter with my working time-table, by which the best range on a *Lion*-class target occurred at 4.42–3; but several German timings are around 6 minutes fast of British timings.) Sometime after 4.58 the range then becomes too great, so *Grosser*

Kurfürst switched to a battleship, the third ship from the left (implying a change of target-group, since in both groups the second ship from the north and the third from the left were the same).

Markgraf only mentions firing at a battlecruiser of the *Lion*-type, but does not check fire until 5.25, by which time the BCF was well out of the action and only the 5th BS receiving fire.

Kronprinz's account strongly supports my hypothesis. She opens fire (at an unstated time) at a *Southampton* on a bearing of 289° at 17,000m. The time of 4.51 then appears in the margin. Without explanation the target is now described as "the first from the left of four ships of the *Queen Elizabeth* class". Firing stops at 5.0 p.m. "after nine minutes". For eight minutes *Kronprinz* holds her fire for unstated reasons, and then reopens, at *Malaya*. Only this second session at the 5th BS, from 5.08 until 5.21, is acknowledged by Campbell.

Kaiser reports only light-cruisers and *Queen Elizabeths* (describing the latter very accurately). She opens fire at a *Southampton* at 4.48, at 14,600m, and stops at 4.50, allegedly because the range was now 19,000m. It is impossible for Goodenough to have opened the range by 4,400m in 2 minutes, likely that words are missing from the records, and that, in fact, fire was transferred to the 5th BS at 19,000m. Later, at 5.07, fire reverts to the light-cruisers, before opening (again?) at 5.10 at the last *Queen Elizabeth*.

Prinzregent Luitpold's officers apparently identified their targets in retrospect, after the battle: at the time they were by no means sure. At 4.48 she opened at "a cruiser of the *Lion* class". She fired eight salvoes and checked at 5.04. At 5.08 she opened at "a cruiser of the *Indefatigable* class [and] at least three hits were obtained". This is nonsense, for, quite apart from considerations of distance, by then the 5th BS had fouled the range between *Prinzregent* and the BCF (see Chapter 20). Campbell, presumably rightly, interprets the '*Indefatigable*' as a *Queen Elizabeth*; but what about the earlier '*Lion*'? Anyway, there is some target information missing, for German gunners did not need 16 minutes to fire eight salvoes.

Kaiserin is stated by Campbell to have fired only at *New Zealand*, yet the *Queen Elizabeths* are the only big ships her diary mentions. When they

> reached 6 points on the port bow they suddenly reversed course and opened fire. 4.50: fire was opened on the furthest left ship on 295°, at the great range of 19,200m. In one overwhelming salvo hits were observed in several places at once. At that moment the enemy began to disengage, ship by ship . . . 4.58: the range became too great and fire was stopped. Despite disengaging the enemy trailed astern [*Malaya* did this (see Chapter 20)], but regained its position.

*

Of Campbell's assertion that "contrary to the usual accounts, none of the 3rd Squadron was firing at the 5th BS, while they were making their turn", four things may therefore be said:

1. A consensus of competent British eyewitnesses (as sampled in Chapter 8) contradicts it;

2. Documented British circumstantial evidence (*Malaya*'s early turn – see Chapter 8) contradicts it;

3. A commonsense appraisal of the High Seas Fleet's targeting options calls it into question;

4. The German ships' war-diaries, which comprise very poor testimony in respect of these issues, do not support it.

APPENDIX V

Tryon's formal explanation of his Tactical Doctrine

Sir George Tryon's official letter explanatory of his Temporary Memoranda A
B and C, in his Report on 'A System of Fleet Manoeuvres With and Without
Signals', of 21st November 1891, is reproduced here in full (even to the extent
of preserving the original's two paragraphs numbered 6) (from ADM 1/7057).

Before leaving Malta on the 15th October I issued the enclosed Memorandum
[Temporary Memoranda A B and C], with a view to carry out the existing system of
Fleet Manoeuvres as established in the drill books, viz: the *General Signal* and the *Fleet
Manoeuvre Books*, at a time when it would not be practicable to carry out the instructions therein in their entirety; (1) because it would be impossible to maintain an adequate staff of signalmen in exposed conditions; and (2) because the delay occasioned
by having to wait till signals were repeated and answered, even supposing it could be
done, would be unendurable.

2. I have long been impressed with the importance of exercising a fleet from the
point where the drill books leave off, and to test the existing system by greatly increasing the rapidity with which a fleet can change its direction and its order without entail-
ing disadvantages.

3. Signal masts and halliards, signalmen, helm signals and speed signals, are all liable
to be swept away, and to my mind it is clear that at the very outset of an engagement,
at least some of the ships will have suffered in the above respects with a result, if the
drill practice is alone exercised, that embarrassment might be expected; and, clearly,
the movements of a fleet would be greatly delayed, and probably even an opportunity
to obtain an advantage that might not recur again would be lost; again, a signal might
be made executive at a wrong time, should the halliards be shot away while a signal is
flying.

4. It is necessary that a fleet should be able to move in any direction, with all the
rapidity that is consistent with safety to its component parts, so that a leader may be
able to manoeuvre against another who may have adopted quite different methods
based on a different system; in other words, the system established in a drill book,
when carried out to the fullest extent, should be such as to leave the fleet in the hands
of its chief, plastic, and free to move in any direction without delay.

5. It is also desirable that signals should be so few and so simple that it would rarely be necessary for officers to refer to a book, save when there is time and the opportunity to do so.

6. It is apparent to me that a fleet that can be rapidly manoeuvred without having to wait for a series of signal repetitions and replies will be at a great advantage to one that cannot manoeuvre with signals rapidly because it is subject to the restraint they impose.

6. The system I have now practised provides for the free movement of the fleet in any direction its guide may direct without any signal at all. It places somewhat increased responsibility on leaders of columns, but no more than was the case during the old wars, and at no time are the fractions of the fleet (the divisions or sub-divisions) thrown beyond the proper distance for supporting each other, while the units of the fleet simply follow their guide and support him.

7. By the employ of a single flag the Admiral can form his ships in single line, divisions, sub-divisions, or the ships in line on their guides; and he can alter course together, or re-form, using a single flag.

8. With but slight modification, the principles of the existing systems, established in the drill books, are carried out.

9. Should officers continue to be practised only under the existing rules and regulations with the manoeuvre signals, repeats and replies, established in the drill books, at a time such as I have already referred to, and when that which is to me inevitable, viz., when we are deprived of the present methods of communicating freely with the fleet, they will be unprepared, from want of experience and practice, to manoeuvre without signals, or when a very few flags are employed.

10. An effort is now made to provide what is required, and it is unquestionable that officers practised and experienced in manoeuvres so conducted, will be able to handle their vessels with confidence, and far greater safety to each other than they would be if no previous arrangements are made to meet what is certain to take place. (*See* paragraph 3.)

11. Instead of endeavouring to maintain a number of signalmen in exposed positions (and with the very limited space that can be protected against quick-firing and machine guns of light calibre, it would not even be possible at any time to carry out the system of signalling as ordinarily practised), we require for the conduct of the ship –

(1) The Captain, who commands and has an eye over everything.

(2) The Navigating Officer, who supervises the steering of the ship, and in narrow waters, watch in hand, attends to her safe navigation: no more important duty can fall to man; it requires constant practice and incessant vigilance; now, more than ever in history, are experienced practical navigating officers required who are identified with the task.

(3) The helmsman.

(4) One selected man to watch incessantly the guide (a signalman).

(5) One man to look out in the opposite to (4) (a signalman).

(6) Two others to attend to directors, voice-pipes, telltales &c.

(7) Three signalmen, who may be on the deck below, to hoist signals and replies (usually one flag).

12. In this we approach to a number to whom it is practicable to give some protection, even if all cannot be placed within the conning-tower. The officers and men told off to meet casualties should be stationed at hand, but should be so placed as to avoid,

as far as possible, the liability to the same chances that may occur to those whom they are told off to relieve in case of necessity.

13. I have found so far, in this fleet, that it takes from 2 minutes 30 seconds to 3 minutes 50 seconds before a general signal is repeated and answered under circumstances of every advantage. At 10 knots this means a distance of between, say, 840 and 1,290 yards is traversed while waiting to give effect to a signal, and a change of bearing is effected at 1,000 yards of, say, 4 points, or at 2,000 yards of, say, 2 points; difference in bearing and space that illustrates the importance of time in manoeuvring, and should the speed of vessels passing be doubled, viz.: if ships passing in opposite directions each steam 10 knots, the changes of bearing will be magnified to a corresponding extent, and still further show the necessity of the case and the problem involved.

14. While speaking confidently as to the necessity of reducing the time occupied in manoeuvring to a minimum, and also of largely reducing the employ of signals, it is certain that the desired result can only be obtained after considerable practical experience in the working of the system elaborated in drill books, the object of which should be to lead up to free and rapid movement with sufficient precision for the safe conduct of a fleet, and for giving mutual support.

15. While this suggestion does not supersede anything, it provides for conditions when the present system would not be workable. Should a flag officer require more elaborate movements and changes, or the stationing of divisions and sub-divisions, or ships, in some special way, he can only do so when there is room and space at his uninterrupted disposal; then the ordinary methods of signalling can be employed without detriment.

G. Tryon, *Vice-Admiral.*

Notes

Introduction

1. Fifty-five of the British dead were washed up in Sweden (file in ADM1/8327).

2. This refers to the brief action between the two battle-lines, and does not count the many hits sustained in the 5th Battle Squadron during the 'battlecruiser phase', the two hits on HMS *Colossus* by Hipper's battlecruisers, or the torpedo hit on HMS *Marlborough*.

3. Stephen Roskill, *Earl Beatty*, p.184.

4. W. S. Chalmers, *Life and Letters of David Beatty*, p.221.

5. See Macintyre, p.113.

6. See Bennett, p.87.

7. Early drafts of this work were circulated to selected readers under the working-title of *Conflict of Style*, and it has been referred to under that title, in well-meaning anticipation, in at least two publications.

Chapter 1: *A Ship which can do Everything*

1. Rear-Admiral Royer Dick, interview 29.6.89.

2. See S. W. Roskill's *HMS Warspite*.

3. Malcolm Brown & Patricia Meehan, *Scapa Flow*, p.69. For a thumbnail guide the light-cruiser *Southampton* took in 69,000 tons of coal during the war (MRDN 1/3).

4. Oscar Parkes, *British Battleships*, p.562.

5. See Jon Sumida, *In Defence of Naval Supremacy: The Pollen Papers*. The Admiralty was forced to make amends in the 1920s, after it had abandoned Dreyer's system in favour of its own version of Pollen's, with a substantial breach of copyright settlement.

6. Filson Young, *With the Battle-Cruisers*, p.1.

7. Beatty was aided and abetted in this by his flag-commander, Reginald Plunkett, who wrote in 1913: "the battle-cruiser is really a fast battleship: it possesses all the qualities of such a vessel, while resembling a cruiser only in the quality of speed . . . The battlecruisers, then, are a flying squadron of fast battleships" (DRAX 1/2). He was sharply to revise this view after Jutland.

8. Section XXIV, paragraph 7.

9. Carlyon Bellairs, *The Battle of Jutland*, p.53.

10. Post-Jutland BCF committee on construction, 23.6.16; *Beatty Papers*, Vol.I, p.358.

11. Ruddock Mackay, *Lord Fisher of Kilverstone*, p.323.

12. Parkes, p.562.

13. *World Crisis*, Vol.I, p.99, n.2.

14. Sumida, pp.59–60.

15. Unveiled to flag-officers at a meeting at Cromarty in May ('Battle & Cruiser Squadrons, Programme', ADM1/8383/179).

16. John Winton, *Captains and Kings*, pp.18–19.

17. *Signal Book: New Issue, 1912–14*, ADM1/8274.

18. For narratives of Churchill's 'names' battles, see Winton, *op. cit.*, or Robert Massie, *Dreadnought*, p.781.

19. *Ibid.*; Parkes, p.562; Tony Gibbons, *The Complete Encyclopedia of Battleships and Battlecruisers*, p.206. On 8 August 1914 Churchill decreed that "departments should proceed on the assumption that the war will last one year, of which the greatest effort should be concentrated on the first six months; and all arrangements for the construction of works and vessels, supplies, etc., should be made with this period in view." In May 1915 he circulated a revised working-assumption that the war would not be over before the end of 1916 (ADM1/8388/235).

20. See Richard Hough's *The Big Battleship*.

Chapter 2: *The Grand Fleet*

1. Journal of Surgeon-Lt D. Lorimer RNVR (IWM).

2. John Horsfield, *The Art of Leadership in War*, pp.112–15.

3. Arthur Marder, *From the Dreadnought to Scapa Flow*, Vol.II, p.10.

4. William Sims, *Victory at Sea*, p.5.

5. G. H. Bickmore (IWM).

6. J. Cockburn (IWM). Admiral Sir George Tryon had used a tactical table with models in HMS *Victoria*, of which Jellicoe had briefly been commander in 1893; and Fisher had kept such a table in a spare room in Admiralty House, Malta.

7. Horsfield, p.115.

8. Roskill, *Earl Beatty*, p.173.

9. Correlli Barnett, *The Sword Bearers*, p.125.

10. Beatty to Churchill, –.11.14, BTY/3/2/3.

11. 1st German Navy Law.

12. 1.5.15, 'Translated Letters of Admiral von Pohl', CAB 45/288.

13. A few weeks before the torpedoing of *Lusitania* he wrote: "Although I regret the loss of lives, it would be a good thing if a liner was included. That would strike home" (31.3.15, *ibid.*). Five months later, he wrote: "since the submarine campaign has become impracticable on account of the restrictions which have been ordered, I beg to be relieved of my post as chief of the High Seas Fleet" (3.9.15, *ibid.*). (He remained at his post until January 1916.)

14. Lt Stephen King-Hall in Louise King-Hall (ed.), *Sea Saga*, p.441.

15. *Official Despatches*, Appendix IV.

16. William Goodenough, *Rough Record*, p.59.

17. *Jellicoe Papers*, Vol.I, p.74.

18. Jellicoe to Jackson, 12.4.1916: *ibid.*, p.232.

19. Graeme Spence to TLCs, 4.6.12, quoted by Malcolm Brown & Patricia Meehan, in *Scapa Flow*, pp.11–12 (order of paragraphs changed).

20. Horsfield, p.121.

21. Stephen King-Hall, of *Southampton* (a light-cruiser attached to the Battle Cruiser Fleet and normally based in the Forth), *Sea Saga*, p.449.

22. Brown & Meehan, p.228.

23. Admiral Sir Angus Cunninghame-Graham, papers (NLS).

24. Rear-Admiral Hugh Evan-Thomas to his wife, 30.12.15 (Llwynmadoc papers).

25. Brown & Meehan, pp.63, 64, 86, 89, 155.

26. R. K. Dickson, Acc.13509 (NLS).

27. William Manchester, *The Last Lion*, Vol.I, p.485.

28. Lord Chatfield, *The Navy and Defence*, p.100.

29. C. S. Forester in introduction (p.xxi) to W. S. Chalmers, *Life and Letters of David Beatty, Admiral of the Fleet*.

30. *Ibid.*, p.xxiv.

31. Roskill, pp.43–5.

32. Shane Leslie, unpublished draft narrative, SLGF 10/1.

33. Paraphrase of Roskill, p.147.

34. Chatfield, p.103.

35. Roskill, p.95; *Beatty Papers*, Vol.I, p.164.

36. Roskill, p.134.

37. *Dictionary of National Biography* (Chalmers).

38. Marder, Vol.II, p.17.

39. Filson Young, *With the Battle-Cruisers*, p.15.

40. Marder, Vol.II, pp.8–9.

41. Chatfield, pp.43–5.

42. See G. A. H. Gordon, *British Seapower and Procurement Between the Wars*.

43. Horsfield, p.129.

44. King-Hall (ed.), p.376.

45. Roskill, p.147; see also King-Hall (ed.), p.423.

46. Beatty's flag-lieutenant used these terms in private correspondence.

47. Not quite literally true: the 2nd BS, under Vice-Admiral Warrender, glimpsed German cruisers between rain squalls on the day of the Scarborough raid; but this paltry exception underlines the point.

48. "We all wished we were in the battle-cruisers": Commander Bonham Faunce (midshipman, *Hercules*, 1916), interview 30.5.91.

49. King-Hall (ed.), p.448.

50. Rear-Admiral Stephen Tillard (IWM).

51. Penrose Fitzgerald.

52. John Winton, *The Death of the Scharnhorst*, p.30.

53. King-Hall (ed.), p.376.

54. This information comes either from BCFSOs or from *Rosyth Naval Directory, 1917* (the latter is in Dunfermline Public Library).

55. Filson Young, p.113.

56. Filson Young, pp.113–14.

57. King-Hall (ed.), p.426 (two sentences combined).

58. Ruddock Mackay, pp.26 & 34. Admiral Hope acquired Midshipman Fisher as a

sort of 'pledge' from Captain Charles Shadwell of HMS *Highflyer*. When Shadwell was wounded fighting Chinese pirates and had to be invalided home, his parting request to the admiral was to "take care of that boy!" (Robert Massie, *Dreadnought*, p.412).

59. Goodenough, p.94.

60. Filson Young, *With the Battle-Cruisers*, p.77.

61. H. J. W. Fisher, *Indomitable* (IWM). It is tempting to suppose he was playing Richard Hannay, from John Buchan's 1915 best-seller *The Thirty-Nine Steps*, but the Forth Bridge was added to that story in 1935 by Alfred Hitchcock.

62. James Morris, *Pax Britannica*, p.425.

63. Filson Young, p.113.

64. King-Hall (ed.), p.421.

65. *Ibid.*, p.495.

66. *Ibid.*

67. Royer Dick, interview.

68. G. H. Bickmore, *Warspite* (IWM).

69. William Seymour, *Battles in Britain*, Vol.II, p.30.

70. Interviews in connection with the Jutland 75th anniversary diving expedition.

71. Chalmers, pp.151–2. On the BCS's return to Scapa, the battleship *Orion* sent a party over to help the light-cruiser *Southampton* coal, a gesture which may be unique.

72. Letter of 16.11.14, *Jellicoe Papers*, Vol.I, p.92. The cancelled sixth *Queen Elizabeth* was to have been considerably faster than her nominal sisters.

73. Reply of 18.11.14, *Jellicoe Papers*, Vol.I, p.96.

74. Letter of 30.11.14, *Beatty Papers*, Vol.I, p.169.

75. Letter of 2.12.14, *ibid.*, p.171.

76. Roskill, pp.106–7.

77. *Jellicoe Papers*, Vol.I, p.141.

78. *Ibid.*, p.143.

79. 26.4.15, *ibid.*, p.157.

80. A similar idea had appeared in his 'War Orders' when he was second-in-command Atlantic Fleet in 1912.

81. Corbett, *Signals and Instructions, 1776–1794*, p.13; see also pp.112 & 157.

82. Memorandum of 15.4.13, DRAX 1/2, cited Roskill, p.67; a memo of 10 days earlier has it worded slightly differently: "forming the *first* division of a battle-fleet in a general action": *Beatty Papers*, Vol.I, p.59.

Chapter 3: *The Fifth Battle Squadron*

1. Colville to George V, 3.9.15, Royal Archives: RA GV Q832/395.

2. ROSK 3/3; also Add.MSS 52506.

3. Letters in possession of Commander Martin Bourdillon.

4. Arthur Marder, *From the Dreadnought to Scapa Flow*, Vol.II, p.441.

5. *Jellicoe Papers*, Vol.I, p.212.

6. Roskill, *Earl Beatty*, p.155.

7. Marder quoting Goodenough, *Dreadnought*, Vol.III (2nd ed.), p.43.

8. Rear-Admiral Royer Dick, interview.

9. See Marder, Vol.II, p.168.

10. *Western Mail*, 14.5.29, Evan-Thomas papers.

11. Evan-Thomas's photograph album (courtesy of Martin Bourdillon).

12. William Goodenough, *Rough Record*, p.67.

13. Marder, Vol.II, p.441.

14. *Ibid.*, pp.10–11.

15. Roskill, p.126; Roskill, *Churchill and the Admirals*, p.38; Chatfield, *The Navy and Defence*, p.128.

16. This was Charles Marmaduke Evan-Thomas, son of Hugh's brother Algernon. Another nephew, Lieutenant Charles Lindsay Evan-Thomas, son of brother Llewellyn, was serving in a Portsmouth-based destroyer.

17. Redmond McLaughlin, *The Escape of the Goeben*, p.21.

18. As a midshipman in 1878, for example, Sturdee came 1st out of 201 competitors (George Warrender came 4th, William Pakenham 56th).

19. John Horsfield, *The Art of Leadership in War*, p.115.

20. Marder, Vol.II, p.12.

21. *Jellicoe Papers*, Vol.I, p.169.

22. Letter to Jackson, 7.8.15, *Jellicoe Papers*, Vol.I, p.177.

23. Letters to Jackson, 29.4.16 & 21.5.16, *Jellicoe Papers*, Vol.I, p.241.

24. Letter to Lady Beatty, 13.5.17, *Beatty Papers*, Vol.I, p.430.

25. From Richmond diary, in Arthur Marder, *Portrait of an Admiral*, pp.262–3.

26. *Beatty Papers*, Vol.I, p.287.

27. *Ibid.*, p.291.

28. *Ibid.*, p.294.

29. *Ibid.*, p.295.

30. *Ibid.*, pp.297–9.

31. "He replied with an abject apology": Roskill, *Earl Beatty*, p.140.

32. *Beatty Papers*, Vol.I, p.299.

33. 9.3.16, *Jellicoe Papers*, Vol.I, p.227.

34. *Beatty Papers*, Vol.I, p.229.

35. This appears to have been something of a syndrome among First Sea Lords; it may be that some First Lords avoided selecting effective debaters for the Navy's most senior appointment.

36. Bonham Carter, quoted Marder, Vol.II, p.290.

37. Letter of 7.3.16, *Jellicoe Papers*, Vol.I, p.226.

38. Jackson MSS, letters of 5, 8, 9 & 13.3.16.

39. W. S. Chalmers, *Life and Letters of David Beatty*, p.207.

40. See for example letter to Jellicoe of 21.11.15, *Jellicoe Papers*, Vol.I, p.188.

41. As he demonstrated in a BBC interview in 1941.

42. Diary of Lt Stephen King-Hall (*Sea Saga*, p.437).

43. Chatfield letter to Capt. Phillimore, 24.2.15 (Capt. the Hon. P. G. E. C. Acheson, *Inflexible*'s Commander, IWM).

44. My thanks to Eric Grove.

45. Peter Padfield, *The Battleship Era*, p.241.

46. See N. J. M. Campbell, *Jutland, An Analysis of the Fighting*.

47. For example, letter of 7.5.16: Chalmers, p.222n.

48. Jellicoe to Jackson, 5.3.16, *Jellicoe Papers*, Vol.I, p.225.

49. Geoffrey Lowis, *Fabulous Admirals*, pp.157–8.

50. *HM Rosyth Dockyard* (ROS, Dunfermline Public Library).

51. Chalmers, p.218.

52. Letter to Fisher, 2.12.14, *Jellicoe Papers*, Vol.I, p.101.

53. Jellicoe to Beatty, 29.1.16, *Jellicoe Papers*, Vol.I, p.205; see also ADM1/8446/17, with correspondence between Fisher and the Prime Minister.

54. Roskill, p.107.

55. *Ibid.*, p.184.

56. *Jellicoe Papers*, Vol.I, p.225.

57. Marder, Vol.III, p.41n.

58. King-Hall, *Sea Saga*, p.435.

59. If her log is to be believed, *Inflexible* split the difference and put her clocks forward by half an hour.

60. R. H. C. F. Frampton, *Barham* (IWM).

61. Royer Dick, interview.

62. A. H. Ashworth (IWM). This illustrates the squadron's subdivisional organization. The 5th BS comprised the 13th and 14th subdivisions of the Battle Fleet. The composition of the subdivisions was a matter internal to the 5th BS, relating to captains' seniority. Normally the 13th subdivision comprised *Barham*, *Warspite* and *Malaya*, and the 14th, *Queen Elizabeth* and *Valiant*. But the absence of one ship could alter the whole thing. When *Queen Elizabeth* was away (as at Jutland) *Barham* and *Valiant* comprised the 13th subdivision, while *Warspite*, now the senior private ship, took charge of *Malaya* to form the 14th.

63. R. B. Fairthorne.

64. Ashworth (IWM).

Chapter 4: *The Grass Was Never Greener*

1. This is speculation on my part, but there is testimony that men would pull for miles just to admire (in particular) the matchless lines of HMS *Tiger* (see Oscar Parkes, *British Battleships*, p.553).

2. BCFOs (Drax papers).

3. Leading Signalman Fullbrook (IWM).

4. A. H. Ashworth (IWM).

5. Interview, 19.9.91.

6. Vice-Admiral Sir Francis T. B. Tower's entry in *Who's Who* mentions only a marriage in 1937. This marriage in 1916, to one Esther Keyden, is confirmed by the Scottish Records Office.

7. R. H. C. F. Frampton (IWM).

8. E. Roynon-Jones (IWM).

9. ROSK 3/3 (CCC).

10. Captain Herbert Richmond disinterred it in 1913, and coined the concept of "conditional obedience" (*Naval Review*, 'Orders and Instructions', original pagination 281ff.)

11. Beatty to Fisher, November 1914, *Beatty Papers*, Vol.I, p.150. Beatty's flag-lieutenant confirms that BCS memoranda "were not known to officers outside the squadron" – with the exception of Jellicoe (Lady Seymour, *Life and Letters of Commander Ralph Seymour RN*, p.138).

12. Geoffrey Bennett, *The Battle of Jutland*, p.61.

13. *Beatty Papers*, Vol.I, p. 304.

14. William Pakenham, 17.1.08, in file on 'Responsibility of Board of Admiralty for Naval War Direction', ADM1/7992.

15. There are two legal angles which VABCF should have considered. Firstly, if,

while the 5th BS was under the same tactical direction as the BCF, Evan-Thomas let the side down by failing to act in a manner indicated in BCFOs, Beatty would be unable to prove (in the words of today's Naval Discipline Act) "that the order contravened was known to the accused or that he might reasonably be expected to know of it". Secondly, Evan-Thomas was senior to both Brock and Pakenham, and therefore if Beatty were killed in action, or *Lion* knocked out of the fray (as at Dogger Bank), tactical command over the BCF would have devolved onto Evan-Thomas's shoulders (as it did when the 5th BS worked with the BCF after Pakenham had succeeded Beatty). Yet he could hardly be expected to make the battlecruisers work properly if he hadn't read the instructions.

16. Notes of a conference at the Admiralty on 26.6.16, *Beatty Papers*, Vol.I, pp.367–8.

17. Lady Seymour, *Life and Letters of Commander Ralph Seymour RN*, p.153.

18. Filson Young, p.223.

19. Rear-Admiral W. S. Sims USN, *The Victory at Sea*, p.303.

20. William Laird Clowes, *The Royal Navy, a History*, Vol.VII, p.426.

21. Claude Wallace, *From Jungle to Jutland*, Chapter 11.

22. For example, W. S. Chalmers, *Life and Letters of David Beatty*, p.218.

23. This story sounds fishy, but is to be found in, among other places, Prince Louis of Battenberg's notes in the Milford Haven papers in the IWM, although Battenberg admits that he had left the Admiralty shortly before it was supposed to have happened.

24. Sir Angus Cunninghame-Graham, essay on signals, Acc.4198 (NLS).

25. Arthur Marder, *From the Dreadnought to Scapa Flow*, Vol.II, p.420 (citing Naval Staff Monograph No.31 (1926)).

26. *Ibid.*, p.444.

27. Jellicoe to Henry Jackson, 12.4.16, *Jellicoe Papers*, Vol.I, p.233.

28. *Jellicoe Papers*, Vol.I, p.254.

29. Boy 1st Class Hawkins (IWM).

30. ADM101/399.

31. *Sunday Telegraph*, 29.5.66.

32. Midshipman Archibald Dickson, letters home, Acc.13589–90 (NLS).

33. P. F. E. Cox, *Warspite* (IWM).

34. G. H. Bickmore (IWM).

35. T. F. Bradley (IWM).

36. Stephen King-Hall ('Etienne'), *A Naval Lieutenant 1914–1918*, pp.125–6.

37. Malcolm Brown & Patricia Meehan, *Scapa Flow*, p.95.

38. *Official Despatches*, pp.1–2.

39. Boy 1st Class Hawkins (IWM).

40. Owing to the confusion of time-zones, and *Barham*'s having moored apart from the rest of the 5th BS, it is difficult to be sure of the order in which the heavy ships proceeded.

41. T. F. Bradley (IWM).

42. Midshipman Dickson (NLS).

43. R. H. C. F. Frampton (IWM).

44. D. Lorimer (IWM).

45. Extracted from 'Bartimeus' (*The Navy Eternal*, pp.48–59) by Bennett, p.63.

46. Frampton.

47. King-Hall, p.126.
48. 'Bartimeus', *The Navy Eternal*, p.48.
49. Bennett, p.63.

Chapter 5: *Another Wild Goose Chase*

1. J. Ruberry (IWM).
2. *Jellicoe Papers*, Vol.I, p.131.
3. George E. Haigh (IWM Sound).
4. Frampton (IWM).
5. *Barham*'s log, ADM53/34796.
6. A. S. Tempest (IWM). Tempest does not specify gambling debts, but that is the most plausible way a humble stoker could have accumulated a "wad" of notes.
7. This may be a numerical exaggeration, but the essence of the story is permissible from *Barham*'s casualty lists: eleven boys and ordinary-rates aged 16–18 were killed apparently at or near the "fore medical station" (MO's Journal, ADM101/406).
8. This is shown by the position of *Indefatigable* (which was lost at 4.02).
9. *Barham*'s navigator confirmed this in a letter to Evan-Thomas in 1923.
10. *From Jungle to Jutland*, Ch. 12.
11. Patrick Beesly, *Room 40*, p.155.
12. See graph showing 'Safe Distance which can be Run', in Battle-Cruiser Force War Records, ADM137/2135.
13. Stephen King-Hall ('Etienne'), *A Naval Lieutenant 1914–1918*, p.127.
14. Arthur Gaskin (IWM Sound).
15. John Ouvry (IWM Sound).
16. Fawcett & Hooper, *The Fighting at Jutland*, p.7.
17. *Sunday Telegraph*, 29.5.66.
18. MSS 13586 (NLS).
19. Chalmers, *Life and Letters of David Beatty*, p.225.
20. I am indebted to notes made by Robert Church in the early 1970s (IWM).
21. Arthur Marder, *From the Dreadnought to Scapa Flow*, Vol.III, p.40.

Chapter 6: *Failure to Concentrate*

1. Reginald Bacon, *Earl Jellicoe*, p.260.
2. Cdr R. H. C. F. Frampton, *Barham* (IWM).
3. GFSOs.
4. Arthur Marder, *From the Dreadnought to Scapa Flow*, Vol.II, p.441.
5. Cdr R. H. C. F. Frampton, *Barham* (IWM).
6. The *Admiralty Narrative* deduces '6 minutes' from the claim in *Barham*'s report-of-proceedings that the turn SSE happened at 2.38, but admits that the logs of *Valiant*, *Warspite* and *Malaya*, plus *Warspite*'s track-chart, all place the turn at 2.40 (p.12n.).
7. Corbett's comment that *Lion* was now "hull-down" from *Barham* is the kind of embellishment which Jutland can do without. The horizon's distance in nautical miles is 1.15 × the square root of height-of-eye in feet which, in the case of *Barham*'s bridge, results in slightly over 10 miles, so *Lion* was almost exactly on it. In order to have been literally 'hull-down', with only upperworks visible, *Lion* would have to have been 13 or 14 miles away.

8. Sir Lewis Bayly, *Pull Together*, p.146.

9. BCF No.017 of 18.2.15 (reprint of BCS 015 of 17.7.13).

10. Marder, *Dreadnought*, Vol.III, p.5.

11. Add.MSS 49014.

12. Evan-Thomas papers.

13. Madden to Evan-Thomas, 19.8.23, Evan-Thomas papers.

14. Evan-Thomas's comments on a report by Capt. Hope, –.7.23, Evan-Thomas papers; letter to *The Times*, 16.2.27.

15. Letter to Admiral Hodges, 14.8.23, Evan-Thomas papers.

16. *Official Despatches*; Frampton (IWM).

17. Hansard, 15.3.27, First Lord's answer to a question by Commander Carlyon Bellairs MP (see Chapter 24).

18. W. S. Chalmers, *Life and Letters of David Beatty*, p.225.

19. *Handbook of Signalling*, 1913 (ADM186/667), under 'Hints to Signalmen'.

20. The matter is less obvious than one might suppose, for semaphore requires a background of sky; however the port bridge wing is specified in the *Handbook of Signalling* (*op. cit.*) as the position from which to semaphore to recipients on the starboard bow or the port quarter.

21. Writer P. Blanche (IWM Sound).

22. See James Goldrick's *The King's Ships were at Sea* for the most authoritative accounts of these two episodes.

23. U-boat-itis was at its most acute in the early months of the Great War, but has been a recurring feature of naval warfare ever since. In the South Atlantic in 1982, Rear-Admiral Woodward is said to have lost his patience with it and declared: "I'm not going to alter course every time a shrimp farts." Beatty is implausibly alleged to have ordered the Grand Fleet's 'torpedo' flags destroyed after he became C-in-C (Rear-Admiral W. S. Sims USN, *The Victory at Sea*, p.217).

24. *Beatty Papers*, Vol.I, p.154.

25. *Jellicoe Papers*, Vol.I, pp.110–12.

26. Battle Orders for 1st BCS, 17.7.13 (in DRAX 1/2, and DRAX 4/1 section P). This item disappears from BCFOs in the month after Dogger Bank.

27. Lady Seymour, *Life and Letters of Commander Ralph Seymour RN*, p.153.

28. *Rough Record*, p.93.

29. Chalmers, p.210.

30. *The King's Ships were at Sea*, p.304.

31. *Jellicoe Papers*, Vol.I, p.110.

32. Marder, Vol.II, p.140.

33. *Great War at Sea*, p.128.

34. Roskill, *Earl Beatty*, pp.156–7; the reference for the Jellicoe quotation is 'Remarks given to the USA Captain' of December 1920, Dreyer papers 6/9.

35. Madden to Evan-Thomas, 19.8.23, Evan-Thomas papers.

36. *Beatty Papers*, Vol.I, pp. 367–8.

37. Unsigned memo (probably 1934) in Chalmers papers, quoted in Marder, Vol.III, p.54.

38. *Jellicoe Papers*, Vol.II, p.36.

39. Madden to Evan-Thomas, 19.8.23, Evan-Thomas papers.

40. Chalmers, p.268.

41. *Jellicoe Papers*, Vol.II, p.447.

42. Cowan, *The Sound of the Guns*, p.133.

43. Roskill, p.155 (see fn. 6).

44. Compare with the battle-cruiser *Renown*'s keenness to have a go at *Bismarck* on the evening of the 26th May 1941, before the Home Fleet battleships could arrive. The Admiralty felt it necessary to signal her to haul off.

Chapter 7: *The Battlecruiser Duel*

1. Fawcett & Hooper, *The Fighting at Jutland*, pp.9–10.

2. Stephen King-Hall ('Etienne'), *A Naval Lieutenant 1914–1918*, p.128.

3. Fawcett & Hooper, p.92.

4. C. Caslon (IWM).

5. Fawcett & Hooper, p.23.

6. G.M. Eady (IWM).

7. Rear-Admiral Royer Dick, interview.

8. H. Walwyn, in Phillpotts (IWM).

9. G. H. Bickmore (IWM).

10. W. J. Eddy (IWM).

11. Oliver Hill (IWM).

12. T. F. Bradley (IWM).

13. Cdr A. B. Combe (IWM).

14. In accordance with a temporary memorandum introduced because of the similarity of the Imperial German Navy Ensign to the White Ensign.

15. R. Frampton (IWM).

16. Mid. G. M. Eady (IWM). The story that a stoker shinned up the bridge-ladder, took a dekko at the captain, and returned to his stokehold saying, "It's oright! 'E's got 'em on", if true at all, must relate to Dogger Bank.

17. See Desmond Young, *Rutland of Jutland*. In spite of Young's claims, it is difficult to imagine *Campania* making much difference to the course of events: neither technology nor operational doctrine was sufficiently robust.

18. Phillpotts papers (IWM).

19. Fawcett & Hooper, p.111.

20. Cdr Georg von Hase, *Kiel and Jutland*, pp.142, 144.

21. Milford Haven papers (IWM). There was a cine-camera in action in *Orion*, but its negative film was "so underexposed that no positive could be made" (Grand Fleet Secret Packs, Vol.66, ADM137/1946).

22. Von Hase, p.148.

23. *Ibid.*, pp.148, 153–4.

24. In Burrough (IWM).

25. A witness in *Tiger*: Fawcett & Hooper, p.31.

26. Von Hase, p.150.

27. Victor Hayward, *HMS Tiger at Bay*, p.111.

28. W. S. Chalmers, *Life and Letters of David Beatty*, p.231.

29. W. E. May, via Antony Preston.

30. Christopher Craig, *Call for Fire*, p.96.

31. N. J. M. Campbell, *Jutland, An Analysis of the Fighting*, p.41.

32. 'Extracts from a report made by Admiral Hipper to Admiral Scheer', Part I, item 35, 'Battle of Jutland', CAB 45/269.

33. Campbell, pp.49, 61.

34. *Ibid.*, pp. 64, 65.
35. Hayward, p.103. This was probably the Norwegian barque *Candace*.
36. Cdr Walwyn in E. M. Phillpotts (IWM).
37. 20.7.15, Evan-Thomas papers.
38. RA5BS's ROP, *Official Despatches*.
39. Campbell, pp.60–1.
40. Arthur Marder, *From the Dreadnought to Scapa Flow*, Vol.III (2nd ed.), p.57.
41. Cdr Walwyn in E. M. Phillpotts (IWM).
42. *The Truth about Jutland*, p.59.
43. See, for example, Campbell, pp.44, 57.
44. Roskill, *Earl Beatty*, pp.158–9.
45. C. Farmer (IWM Sound).
46. Von Hase, p.164.
47. 'Extracts from a report made by Admiral Hipper to Admiral Scheer', *op. cit.*
48. Midshipman in TCT, Fawcett & Hooper, p.93.
49. Otto Groos, *Der Krieg in der Nordsee.*
50. Campbell, pp.49, 48.
51. *Ibid.*, pp.78, 94.
52. *Ibid.*, pp. 79–84, 103, 135.
53. Von Hase, p.143.
54. Rear-Admiral Royer Dick, interview.
55. A certain amount of speed-trial information for *Queen Elizabeth*, recorded between 1922 and 1928, may be found in ADM136/10, Part 4.
56. Campbell, p.102.
57. *Remarks on Handling Ships & c.* (1904), p.32, ADM186/631.
58. Letter to the author.
59. Chalmers, p.217.
60. 'Points of interest gathered from all ships of the BCF and 5th BS', Milford Haven papers (IWM).
61. For example, in Fawcett & Hooper, although some of the photographs are composites.
62. Item 33, GFOs, ADM137/4052. In 1910 Jellicoe's flagship *Prince of Wales* was one of two ships selected to host the RN's first trials of a repeating gyro-compass (A. E. Fanning, *Steady As She Goes*, p.177).
63. Von Hase, pp.154–5.
64. Von Hase, p.161.
65. Campbell, p.47.
66. Fawcett & Hooper, p.31.
67. Notes for Capt. Pelly's draft "Reminiscences", 1937/8, and Diary extracts, both in Capt. Roynon-Jones (IWM).
68. Francis (NLS).
69. Hayward, *Tiger at Bay*, p.104.
70. A Cdr Suetsugu Nobumasa was in *Colossus*, and a Lt-Cdr Inamura Shinjiro was in a light-cruiser. (My thanks to David Evans and Mark Peattie.)
71. This calculation is based upon *Indefatigable*'s position as given in the *Harper Record*, and *Queen Mary*'s position as fixed by SatNav by the 1991 diving expedition. It allows approximately for the following factors: *Indefatigable*'s veering out to starboard before exploding; *Queen Mary*'s stationed distance ahead of *Indefatigable*;

Beatty's course alterations between the two disasters; and the 0.3kn. NNW'ly tidal stream.

72. Hayward, p.108.
73. Beatty's bearing from *Derfflinger* shifted aft from green 47° at 4.27 to green 105° at 4.33.
74. Von Hase, p.164.
75. Marder, Vol.III (2nd ed.), pp.225–6.
76. Letters of Admiral von Pohl, CAB 45/288.
77. William Goodenough, *Rough Record*, p.95.
78. Chalmers, p.237.
79. *Ibid.*
80. Fawcett & Hooper, p.40.
81. Antony Preston.
82. Stephen King-Hall in *Sea Saga*, pp.365–6, 453.
83. Fawcett & Hooper, pp.75–6.
84. Goodenough, p.95.
85. *Dreadnought to Scapa Flow*, Vol.III, p.72.

Chapter 8: *Standing into Danger*

1. Cdr A. B. Combe (IWM, and separate testimony).
2. *Life and Letters of David Beatty*, p.283.
3. Stephen Roskill, *Earl Beatty*, p.148ff.
4. Ashworth (IWM).
5. NLS.
6. Ashworth.
7. Appendix II, 'Record of Messages'.
8. Beatty's report, *Official Despatches*.
9. Arthur Marder, *From the Dreadnought to Scapa Flow*, Vol.III, p.46.
10. *Official Despatches*.
11. Evan-Thomas to Capt. Vernon Haggard, 14.8.23, Evan-Thomas papers.
12. *Official Despatches*.
13. Footnote in paper on *Errors Made in Battle of Jutland*, Jellicoe Papers, Add.MSS 49014.
14. Chalmers, *Life and Letters*, pp.220 & 239.
15. *The Navy and Defence*, p.144.
16. Notes made by a midshipman in the conning-tower, Fawcett & Hooper, p.22.
17. *Official Despatches*, Signals List.
18. Under *Lessons of the 31st of May*, BCOs, No.38 (Marder, Vol.III, p.221; Drax papers).
19. Evan-Thomas to Haggard, *op. cit.*
20. Later the 3rd Viscount Colville of Culross, the nephew of the Stanley Colville who gave young Beatty his original career break in the Mediterranean Fleet in 1896.
21. Letter from the Hon. Anthony Colville to the author, 30.4.91.
22. *Grand Fleet Orders*, article 500, 10.6.16 (ADM137/4052).
23. Since disposed of, but quoted in *Harper Record*; a copy (not quite a facsimile) exists in the Drax papers.
24. H. S. Fulbrook, Leading Signalman, *Malaya* (IWM).
25. Campbell, *Jutland, An Analysis of the Fighting*, p.98.

26. Brodie, *A Guide to Naval Strategy*, pp.271–2.

27. Marder, pp.73–4.

28. Milford Haven papers, DS/Misc/9 Reel III (IWM).

29. Marder, Vol.III, p.73; Bennett, *The Battle of Jutland*, p.87.

30. (Source untraced at time of publication.)

31. Frampton (IWM).

32. IWM.

33. *Warspite* departed from the custom of allocating X turret to the Royal Marines.

34. Letter of June 1916 to his brother, published in *Naval Review*, April 1985.

35. Fawcett & Hooper, *The Fighting at Jutland*, p.95.

36. F. J. Arnold, Ordinary Wireless-Telegraphist, *Malaya* (IWM).

37. Fawcett & Hooper, p.115. A similar account by Lt Brind, in slightly different words, is to be found in the journal of Surgeon-Lt D. Lorimer RNVR.

38. C. Caslon (IWM).

39. *Official Despatches*, p.217.

40. *Admiralty Manual of Navigation*, Vol.I, 1938, gives typical data for a battleship's turn through 180° at 15 knots with 15° of helm. Original course 360°; intermediate course (bearing of place where new course is arrived at) = 67°; intermediate distance = 870 yards. This must have been based on either a *Queen Elizabeth* or a *Revenge*. Also, *QE*'s 'ship's book' says: "it has been found necessary in the Atlantic Fleet to use a tactical diameter of 800 yards" (ADM136/10).

41. Campbell, p.98.

42. *Ibid.*

43. Campbell, pp.98–9.

44. Appendix to (British) *Official Despatches*.

45. My thanks to Bundesarchiv, Freiburg im Breisgau, Germany; and to Gaby Timko for so kindly going there for me.

46. This may need qualification in one nit-picking respect. A turn-in-succession is a godsend to a ship astern of station, for by judiciously turning inside the wake of the next ahead she can make up lost ground. The war-diary of one of Rear-Admiral Behncke's battleships, *Kaiserin*, remarks that the *Queen Elizabeths* appeared to be as much as 1,000 metres apart (I have allowed 800 yards in the text). *Kaiserin's* diary may be confusing the BCF and the *QEs* – see Appendix IV – but it is possible that, while *Malaya* was forced to turn early for external reasons, *Valiant* and *Warspite* – most plausibly the former (for reasons explained) – also did so, to regain station; and instead of being exactly fixed, the turning-point was receding slowly northwards.

47. It was not *de rigueur* for an admiral and his flag-captain to be in the same location, and practice at Jutland appears to have varied; however, Craig marked the 12th anniversary of the battle by writing to Evan-Thomas a letter which referred to their being together on the bridge.

48. ROP.

49. Midshipman Bostock. This is quoted to represent the generally alleged sequence of events, not to make claims about hits on the HSF.

50. Captain Boyle's ROP.

51. Fawcett & Hooper, pp.113–14.

52. Roger Keyes, *Naval Memoirs*, Vol.I, p.42.

53. *Ibid.*, pp.40, 43.

54. Lewis Bayly, *Pull Together*, p.156.

Chapter 9: *The Long Calm Lee of Trafalgar*

1. Sir Julian Corbett, *Fighting Instructions, 1530–1815*, pp.134–5.

2. For a narrative of this rich and complex story see Brian Tunstall (ed. Nicolas Tracy), *Naval Warfare in the Age of Sail: The Evolution of Fighting Tactics, 1650–1815*.

3. Don Domingo Perez de Grandallana, quoted by Sir Julian Corbett in *Fighting Instructions, 1530–1815*, pp.267–8.

4. Admiral Francis Geary to his flag-captain, *c.* 1780.

5. Hugh Popham, *A Damned Cunning Fellow*, p.128.

6. Leslie Gardiner, *The British Admiralty*, p.208.

7. Quoted by Popham, p.125.

8. The NELSON CONFIDES story is variously said to have stemmed from Pasco's assistant, Lt George Brown, or from Capt. Thomas Hardy (Edward Fraser, *Sailors Whom Nelson Led*, p.223). Patriotic historians have hailed the enforced changes as fortuitous, but the original would have cut more ice in the fleet.

9. Including the telegraph flag which indicated Popham's code, the message took 32 flags. Every word except DUTY had a three-flag group from the lexicon. *Duty* had to be spelt, *D* with one flag, *U T* and *Y* with two each.

10. *Book of Signals and Instructions for the Use of His Majesty's Fleet*, 1816.

11. Michael Lewis, quoted by Popham, p.129.

12. Captains of sloops in the Pacific were told to refrain from sticking the Union Jack on every island and coral atoll they came across.

13. Alfred Friendly, *Beaufort of the Admiralty*, p.246. The secondary quotation is from Rear-Admiral George Richards's *Memoir of Hydrography*.

14. Friendly, p.255.

15. *Ibid.*

16. E.g. *Fairy* in the North Sea in 1840.

17. John Duncan & John Walton, *Heroes for Victoria*, p.77.

18. Parry resigned in 1829 to take up a lucrative job in Australia. His great-grandson, Edward Parry, commanded the New Zealand-manned cruiser *Achilles* at the Battle of the River Plate in 1939.

19. *Tales of the Sea from Blackwood* (1970), p.12 (from *Good Hunting in the Bight*, by 'Shalimar' (1947)).

20. See Amanda Foreman's M.Phil. thesis *Politics or Providence: Why Parliament abolished the Slave Trade in 1807* (Oxford, 1993).

21. Gardiner, p.218.

22. Raymond Howell, *The Royal Navy and the Slave Trade*, pp.36–7.

23. Reginald Bacon, *A Naval Scrap Book, 1877–1900*, p.103. See *inter alia* Philip Colomb's *Slave Catching in the Indian Ocean* (1873); papers on the slave trade in MLN/199/26 & 63. There are a dozen books on the subject, the most recent being Howell's, cited above.

24. Gardiner, p.218.

25. Admiral Sir George King-Hall, in *Sea Saga*, p.277.

26. *Ibid.*, p.218 (order of sentences changed).

27. Donald MacIntyre, *Jutland*, p.17.

28. Jan Morris, *Rule Britannia*, p.146; see also Geoffrey Lowis's *Fabulous Admirals*, p.145.

29. Gardiner, p.296.

30. The Reverend C. M. Ramus's proposal, in the 1870s, for a rocket-propelled

planing missile-float, for which he predicted 275 m.p.h. and 3 miles' range, is one of the more exotic examples (see ADM11/167).

31. See D. K. Brown's *Before the Ironclad*; Andrew Lambert's *Battleships in Transition*.

32. Ruddock Mackay, *Lord Fisher of Kilverstone*, p.96.

33. E. S. Turner, *Gallant Gentlemen*, p.261.

34. Richard Hough, *Admirals in Collision*, p.44. A classic if sociologically biased text for this subject is Geoffrey Penn's *Up Funnel, Down Screw*.

35. Oscar Parkes, *British Battleships*, p.260.

36. See C. C. Penrose Fitzgerald, *From Sail to Steam*; or, for a brief summary of the issues Parkes, *British Battleships*, p.260.

37. William Goodenough, *Rough Record*, p.28.

38. Clanwilliam to Phipps Hornby, 16.4.90, PHI/120C.

39. Bacon, *A Naval Scrap Book, 1877–1900*, p.33, see also pp.87ff.

40. *RUSI Journal*, Vol.XXXV, pp.733ff.

41. Goodenough, p.21.

42. The 1873 *Gunnery Manual* specified three ways of ascertaining range:

    1. Measuring with a sextant the angle between the enemy's masthead (whose height you have to guess) and his waterline, and finding his distance from tables provided;

    2. Climbing aloft, measuring the angle between the enemy's waterline and the horizon, and referring to tables based on your height above sea level;

    3. Counting the seconds between the flash and the report of the enemy's guns and multiplying by 380 yards.

The second method was officially preferred, presumably because it was the least convenient. 1,800 yards was the longest range considered to be of any interest.

43. See Humphrey Hugh Smith, *A Yellow Admiral Remembers*, pp.27–8. When grey livery came in in 1902, the Admiralty provided paint for eight coats, and in so doing removed a suppressant of gunnery.

44. Percy Scott, *Fifty Years in the Royal Navy*, pp.60–1.

45. King-Hall, p.266; Scott, p.297. I have been told a scurrilous tale of a frigate, in the late 1970s, dumping Sea Cat missiles rather than have a scheduled firing blister the paintwork before a visit to an American port.

46. *RUSI Journal*, Vol.XXXVIII.

47. Goodenough, p.21.

48. Duncan & Walton, p.107.

49. Quoted by Gardiner, pp. 269–70.

50. Gardiner, p.293.

51. *Ibid.*, p.272.

52. Lord Cork & Orrery, *My Naval Life*, pp.12–13.

53. See *Uniform Regulations*, 1879 (43 pages of regulations, followed by 42 colour plates); *Uniform Regulations*, 1890.

54. Cork, p.15. See also Smith, p.57 for a lament for the days of fancy clothing; and section on uniform in the article 'The Seamen of the Royal Navy: Their Advantages and Disadvantages as Viewed from the Lower Deck', in *Tracts Relating to Naval Affairs* (1867–1902).

55. Eugene L. Rasor, *Reform in the Royal Navy*, p.42.

56. *Ibid.*

57. Cork, p.14.

58. Geoffrey Lowis, *Fabulous Admirals*, p.235.

59. Goodenough, pp. 28–9.

60. S. W. Roskill, *Earl Beatty*, pp.21–2.

61. Cork, pp.12–13.

62. Seymour Fortescue, *Looking Back*, p.19.

63. Anonymous article: 'The Seamen of the Royal Navy . . .' (*op. cit.*).

64. *Saturday Review*, 21.7.94.

65. "A smart royal-yard man would be allowed to go on shore when he liked, come on board when he liked, and be as drunk as he liked, so long as he was always on the top line when there was work to do aloft" (Smith, p.51).

66. This book is amongst the papers (Rockingham: WR(S) 212) of Sir Michael Culme-Seymour (CO of *Temeraire* and *Monarch* in the Mediterranean in the late 1870s), but it contains entries for the Channel Fleet to which he did not, at the time stated, belong.

67. 4.7.93.

68. Dudley de Chair, *The Sea is Strong*, p.21.

69. This happened in *Canopus*'s after-turret on the night of the 7th of December 1914, when the ship was in Port Stanley in the Falklands – with the consequence that the first salvo it fired at *Gneisenau* the next morning consisted of two practice 'bricks', one of which skipped off the sea at extreme range and hit (Richard Hough, *The Great War at Sea*, p.112).

70. Dudley Pope, *Life in Nelson's Navy*, p.198.

71. Lewis Bayly, *Pull Together*, p.66.

72. Smith, p.56. See also Seymour Fortescue, *Looking Back*, p.40.

73. 'Manning the mast' was still a regular evolution for junior seamen in 1975 (Turner, *Gallant Gentlemen*, p.261).

74. Cork, pp.10 & 20.

75. My thanks to Andrew Lambert.

76. Macintyre, p.17.

77. See *Fabulous Admirals*, by Geoffrey Lowis; or the chapter on 'Lunatics at Sea' in Stanley Bonnett's *The Price of Admiralty*.

78. Lowis, pp.85–6.

79. Bonnett, p.142.

80. Mary Egerton, *Sir Geoffrey Phipps Hornby*, p.305. This story is verified in its essentials by the log entry for 2.1.79 of Tryon's *Monarch* (ADM53/11565).

81. Lowis, p.32.

82. Dixon, *On the Psychology of Military Incompetence*, p.178.

83. Letter to Tryon, 31.5.71, quoted Mackay, p.93.

84. Culme-Seymour papers, WR(S) 242. As Ward-Hunt's secretary, Captain Sir Michael Culme-Seymour witnessed at close hand this inauspicious policy-reversal.

85. See Alfred Mahan, *Types of Naval Officers*, pp.446–7.

86. Duncan & Walton, p.55.

87. 22.5.92, *RUSI Journal*, Vol.XXXV, pp.733ff.

88. See Dixon, p.348.

89. William Manchester, *The Last Lion*, pp.70–1.

90. Sir Walter Scott, quoted by Mark Girouard in *Return to Camelot*, p.33.

91. Girouard, p.49.

92. "Although feudalism and chivalry are not synonymous, approval of one tended to go with approval of the other" (Girouard, p.240).

93. Almost. Utilitarianism and some forms of political radicalism were incompatible with chivalry.

94. Information for candidates, from the *Universal Book of Craft Masonry*.

95. Masonic historians would claim it to be the other way round. Numerous tomes have been written, mostly in the late Victorian period, purporting to prove that Freemasonry pre-dates Noah. But few masons take this seriously.

96. Girouard, p.143.

97. In the poem *My Last Words* on the last page of Kingsley's *Alton Locke*.

98. Girouard, p.233.

99. *Ibid.*

100. *Ibid.*, p. 176.

101. Jacqueline Bratton in *Imperialism and Popular Culture* (ed. John MacKenzie), p.73.

102. J. F. C. Fuller, *The Army in My Time*, pp.76 & 78.

103. Rudyard Kipling, *The Lesson*.

104. My thanks to Andrew Lambert.

105. Nigel Rees, *Dictionary of Phrase and Allusion*, p.259.

106. *Dictionary of National Biography* (Sir John Laughton).

107. Hornby to Lieutenant Allan Everett, 31.10.91, MER/55.

108. Letter quoted by Mrs Frederick Egerton in *Sir Geoffrey Phipps Hornby*, pp.81–2.

109. See, for example, 'Our Peril Afloat, or Collisions and How to Avoid Them' (in *Tracts Relating to Naval Affairs*, 1872); or 'The Manoeuvring Powers of Steamships and the Avoidance of Collisions' (in a course of papers for the Shipmasters Society, 1895).

110. Article XXXII of the 1859 *Signal Book* warned: "It will always be necessary to pay particular attention to the different velocities with which different ships perform their evolutions, without which, there may be just danger of their running on board each other."

111. 1889 *Signal Book*, p.3.

112. In an undated 1900s memorandum (in MER/55), signals expert Commander Allan Everett defined these laws as follows:

1. Ships moving at equal speed and steering the same course can never meet, and must always preserve their distance and compass bearing.

2. Any ship moving at the same speed as another, and steering at any given moment for the position occupied by the other, must, on arrival at that position, be the same distance apart as originally.

3. If equal numbers of ships (columns) retain the same formation, and the distance they are apart is not less than the length of the line they occupy, they can rely on law (2) as long as the angle between their manoeuvring courses is 90° or over.

113. Hough, p.44.

114. *Dictionary of National Biography* (Sir John Laughton).

115. D. M. Schurman, *The Education of a Navy*, Ch. 3.

116. 1874–7 flag-captain on China Station, where the fleet rarely, if ever, operated as a united squadron; 1880 captain of *Thunderer* in Mediterranean; 1881–4 Captain of the Steam Reserve, Portsmouth; 1884–6 flag-captain (in the base-ship *Duke of Wellington*) to C-in-C Portsmouth.

117. *Dictionary of National Biography* (Sir John Laughton).

118. *Ibid.*

119. Letter of 6.3.77 (from PHI/120), quoted by Mackay, in *Fisher of Kilverstone*, p.132.

120. G. P. Hornby VA & C-in-C, HMS *Alexandra* at Malta, 26.3.77, PHI/132 Part 1. Hardy's contribution was small: he added a few practicalities concerning lights to the 1826 *Signal Book* (my thanks to Andrew Lambert).

121. Mackay, p.140 (order of sentences changed).

122. Smith, p.66.

123. Letter to Captain Gerard Noel, 20.8.93, NOE.

124. Hough, *Admirals in Collision*, p.46. I have not verified the "14,000 variations", but Hough gets the figure (presumably) from Bacon's *Life of Lord Fisher of Kilverstone* (p.152).

125. My thanks to D. K. Brown for a horse's mouth account of the clip story, written in 1940 by Rear-Admiral Sir Edward Inglefield.

126. Hough, pp.46–7.

127. Hough, p.44.

128. MLN/198/4B10.

129. A biographical trivia item is Captain William Dowell's membership of the enquiry into the *Mary Celeste*, in Gibraltar in 1873.

130. Confidential memo 'Revision of the Signal Book', tentatively dated 1885, MER/209; also in Signals Committee, ADM116/59.

131. Barrie Kent, *Signal!*, p.239 (from MER).

132. Hornby to Lieutenant Allan Everett, 31.10.91 & 19.12.91 (MER/55).

133. ADM116/60.

134. ADM116/62.

135. A caustic comment about these yachting trips was made from time to time in the House of Commons (my thanks to Mary Cross).

136. Cork, p.17.

137. Bacon, *Scrap Book*, p.50.

138. Seymour Fortescue, *Looking Back*, p.33.

139. Lazenby (IWM Sound).

Chapter 10: *Sir George Tryon's Action Principles*

1. An American newspaper, quoted by Richard Hough in *Admirals in Collision* (1958), p.14. No historian can deal with the subject of George Tryon without paying fulsome tribute to Hough.

2. *Montevideo Times*, 1.7.93.

3. Hough puts Rowley on Tryon's side, and adds, as a participant, Rear-Admiral J. N. East (Rtd), who, like Philip Colomb, was really an umpire.

As a matter of interest, Baird's grandfather, General Sir David Baird, had been friend and co-adventurer of Captain Home Popham in campaigns in 1806 in South Africa and South America (as had Colonel William Carr Beresford, Lord Charles Beresford's half-great-uncle).

4. PHI/132 Part 5.

5. Hough, *Admirals in Collision*, p.19.

6. CAB 37/22 (item 24).

7. William Goodenough, *Rough Record*, p.37.

8. *Talk*, 5.7.93.

9. Clayton letter to wife, September 1885 (in custody of Mary Cross, whom I thank for help in this and other matters).

10. His family were high Tories, and he had benefited from political 'interest' in his early career. (My thanks to Andrew Lambert.)

11. At this time the RNR comprised vocational seafarers who, at the time of the annual manoeuvres, augmented the RN skeleton crews of the Reserve Fleet.

12. See *United Service Magazine*, May 1890; Arthur Marder, *British Naval Policy, 1880–1905*, p.91. The matter was next raised in 1905: see 'National Indemnity or Insurance of the War Risks of British Shipping', CID paper 69B, 15.11.05 (CAB 4/2).

13. Hough, p.53.

14. *Ibid.*, p.46.

15. C. C. Penrose Fitzgerald, *Sir George Tryon KCB*, pp.334–47.

16. George Aston RM, *Memoirs of a Marine*, p.120.

17. Andrew Lambert, *Battleships in Transition*, p.88.

18. Quoted in Ruddock Mackay, *Fisher of Kilverstone*, p.88.

19. PHI 120(B), quoted in *ibid.*, p.175.

20. See, for example, letter to *The Times*, 8.8.93.

21. 1889 edition of the *General Signal Book*.

22. 21.4.91, Signals Committee, ADM116/62.

23. C. C. Penrose Fitzgerald, *Modern Naval Tactics*, p.20.

24. Memorandum of 9th October 1805.

25. (Source untraced at time of publication.)

26. Letter to *The Times*, 18.8.93.

27. My thanks to Captain Barrie Kent.

28. Letter to *The Times*, 18.8.93.

29. Tryon's down-to-earth approach to station-keeping is evidenced in his *Corrections and Additions to Temporary Memorandum A*, issued in September 1892. Against the possibility of compasses being damaged in action,

> lines should be scored on the deck so that they can be readily referred to immediately after a turn has been made, to ascertain the relative bearing of a ship on which station is to be maintained. They will be found of much use when no compass is available. (Files of Standing Committee on Signals, ADM116/64)

30. This is actually taken from the revised Temporary Memorandum A, of 18.10.91 in ADM1/7057. The wording here is doctored slightly, for simplicity or to conform to terminology used in the Jutland chapters of this book.

31. Seymour Fortescue, *Looking Back*, pp.165–6.

32. In fact in this TA experiment, repeating ships also used 23 flags, and answering addressees 42. But as repeating and answering were not essential to TA, these were disregarded in assessing the results.

33. *Dictionary of National Biography* (Vincent Baddeley).

34. Kerr to Tryon from HMS *Trafalgar*, 5.11.91, ADM1/7057. Three subordinate clauses have been omitted here, without prejudice to the meaning.

35. PHI/120. The allusion to *"Alabama & Kearsage"* refers to the fratricidal duel between a Confederate schooner and a United States sloop, off Cherbourg on 19.6.64.

36. Troubridge to Watson in HMS *Bellerophon*, 22.2.92, ADM1/7057.

37. Files of Standing Committee on Signals, ADM116/64.

38. Nicholson to Admiralty from HMS *Raleigh*, 15.3.92, ADM1/7057.

39. ADM116/64.

40. ADM116/64.

41. ADM116/64. See ADM1/7075 for his own, earlier misgivings about the use of the *Signal Book*.

42. Hough, p.53.

43. Goodenough, p.37.

44. Hough, p.53.

45. Fitzgerald, *Sir George Tryon KCB*, p.352.

46. Tryon to Phipps Hornby, 23.12.91, PHI/120.

47. Noel to Mahan (23.12.90): "I am not given to flattery, so I trust that you will believe me when I say that I have never before read or seen any work on naval matters more full of interest, more clearly written, or displaying fuller and more accurate knowledge of the subject than *The Influence of Seapower upon History* . . . Accept my sincere thanks for the pleasure your book has given me." Mahan replied politely (24.1.91) that he knew of Noel by reputation (NOE 1A/II).

48. *The Gun, Ram, and Torpedo* (1874), published as the first essay in an anthology of the same name; 2nd, updated, edition published in 1885.

49. Lewis Bayly, *Pull Together*, p.160.

50. In July 1891 Noel and Hornby were riled by anti-seamanship "rubbish" which Fitzgerald "had lately written [in the *United Service Magazine*] to flatter the engineer". They consoled themselves with the hope that if Fitzgerald were "given enough rope he will soon hang himself" (NOE/1A). Noel also sided with Johnstone against Fitzgerald's and Fremantle's idea of making seamen and engineers interchangeable, a scheme which Fisher later espoused.

51. Bourke to Noel, 22.8.93, NOE.

52. Humphrey Hugh Smith, *A Yellow Admiral Remembers*, p.62.

53. Mediterranean letter of 21.11.91, ADM1/7057.

54. PHI/120D.

55. Letter to Markham, MRK/35.

56. Taken from two letters to Markham quoted in Rear-Admiral Sir Edmund Poland's first draft of *The Torpedomen: The Story of Vernon* (PLND/2).

57. See Edward Bradford's biography of A. K. Wilson.

58. Hough, p.23.

59. Ian Cameron, *To the Farthest Ends of the Earth*, p.111.

60. For 1,000-page report, see *Accounts and Papers*, 1877, Vol.LVI, p.557ff.

61. Cameron, p.114.

62. *Lloyd's Weekly Shipping List*, 24.7.85.

63. *The Times*, 31.7.85; 3 & 4.8.85. *Hecla* turned to port and rammed *Cheerful* amidships on the port side. Colomb's 'Collision Diagram' could have been cited to demonstrate that, at such close quarters, the only way for *Hecla* to avoid a collision was to turn towards (and 'inside') the approaching steamer.

64. Hough, pp.27–8. Hough's source appears to be Sir Sydney Fremantle's *My Naval Career*, p.43.

65. Standing Orders for *Active* in 1886, Johnstone papers (JOH).

66. M. E. & F. A. Markham, *Life of Sir Albert Markham*, p.253. (Edmund Henry Jellicoe took his own life in 1904, while a lieutenant on the China Station.)

67. These matters are discussed in greater detail in Chapter 16.

68. Sir Sydney Fremantle, *My Naval Career*, p.63.
69. John Duncan & John Walton, *Heroes for Victoria*, p.162. The unfortunate subject was General Sir Redvers Buller.
70. The phrase is Lloyd George's, describing careerist Army officers of 1918 (*War Memoirs*, p.2041).
71. Clayton to wife, March 1885 (Mary Cross).
72. WRS/papers, Rockingham.
73. ADM1/7172. The actual wording of Major-General Arthur Wellesley's General Order was "... moral *impossibility*", and from its context (a retort to a court-martial verdict acquitting an officer of disobedience) it appears that he was adopting a position on initiative exactly opposite to that imputed by Sir George Tryon. (My thanks to Evan Davies.)
74. Lord Charles Beresford to Phipps Hornby, 1.8.93, PHI/120D.
75. Aston, p.138.
76. Smith, pp.40–1.
77. Hough, p.53.
78. Goodenough, p.41.

Chapter 11: *Meanwhile, by Royal Appointment*

1. Strictly speaking there was a third yacht: the small non-residential *Alberta*, used for shuttling the Queen between Portsmouth and Cowes when she was visiting Osborne House; plus an even smaller despatch vessel, *Elfin*.
2. Reginald Bacon, *A Naval Scrap Book, 1877–1900*, p.141.
3. William Goodenough, *Rough Record*, p.30.
4. Introduction to Godfrey-Faussett papers, BGGF.
5. "Albert saw no harm in whipping them – his daughters as well as his sons." Dennis Friedman, *Inheritance*, p.34.
6. Ben Pimlott, *Hugh Dalton*, pp.7–8.
7. Harold Nicolson, *King George V*, p.8.
8. Melvyn Fairclough, *The Ripper and the Royals*, p.207.
9. James Pope-Hennessy, *Queen Mary*, p.246.
10. Pimlott, p.9.
11. Nicolson, p.7.
12. John Winton, *Captains and Kings*, p.7, referring to George's hapless sons' experience of Dartmouth (under Evan-Thomas's captaincy).
13. Llwynmadoc papers.
14. *Ibid.*
15. 29.1.78, *ibid.*
16. 31.1.78, *ibid.*
17. In possession of Commander Martin Bourdillon.
18. *The Times*, 22.7.78.
19. *The Times*, 6.8.78.
20. 26.7.78.
21. Bertram Chambers, *Salt Junk*, p.92.
22. Pope-Hennessy, p.421.
23. Llwynmadoc papers.
24. Ponsonby, quoted by Nicolson, p.19.
25. Nicolson, p.24.

26. *Ibid.*, p.18. Among Dalton's advisers was Lord Charles Beresford.

27. 'A Ranker', *Life in the Royal Navy*, p.93.

28. Percy Scott, *Fifty Years in the Royal Navy*, pp.36–7.

29. Minutes of debate on Arctic exploration, in the *RUSI Journal* (1895), p.592.

30. Queen Victoria's journal, Royal Archives.

31. Nicolson, p.28.

32. Pimlott, pp.9–10, 11.

33. Fitzgerald at RUSI 1883, quoted (wrongly dated 1887) by Oscar Parkes, *British Battleships*, p.260.

34. For example, Victoria's letter to the First Lord, 7.2.81, Royal Archives.

35. Mark Kerr, *Prince Louis of Battenberg*, pp.79–80.

36. *Ibid.*, p.75.

37. 'A Ranker', p.123.

38. 18.12.81, Add.MSS 52504.

39. 6.6.82, Prince George's diary, Royal Archives.

40. Pimlott, p.10.

41. Theo Aronson, *Prince Eddy and the Homosexual Underworld*, pp.78–9.

42. Georgina Battiscombe, *Queen Alexandra*, p.190.

43. Victoria's favourite daughter Vicky was Crown Princess of Prussia.

44. 23.9.83, Llwynmadoc papers. The presence at Sandringham in August 1883 of "a naval lieutenant kept on shore by a bad knee" is mentioned in a letter of James Stephen's quoted in James Vincent's book *HRH The Duke of Clarence* (1893). Michael Harrison, in his *Clarence*, jumps to the conclusion that it was Lieutenant F. B. Henderson (Rtd) whom Vincent names as a contemporary of Eddy's at Trinity College. Henderson was an ex-*Bacchante* sub-lieutenant of whom I have discovered little; but the presence at Sandringham of two *Bacchante*-ites with leg injuries would have been remarkable.

45. Harrison, *Clarence*, p.76.

46. *Ibid.*, p.92.

47. Llwynmadoc papers.

48. *Ibid.*

49. Dalton to Ponsonby, 23.3.84, RA, PP Vic 1884/18888.

50. RA, GEO V AA 6/314 and RA, GEO V AA 6/327.

51. 17.7.86, Add.MSS 52504.

52. Service Record, ADM196/20.

53. Pimlott, p.12.

54. Nicolson, p.7.

55. Pope-Hennessy, p.192.

56. Stephen Knight, *Jack the Ripper: the Final Solution*.

57. Melvyn Fairclough, *The Ripper and the Royals*. Some of these theories may have been promoted by Joseph Sickert, in a tortuous effort to establish his own royal descent.

58. *History of the Royal Alpha Lodge No. 16*, by Colonel Shadwell Clerke.

59. Friedman, p.61.

60. RA Z 475 18, quoted by Pope-Hennessy, *Queen Mary*, p.193.

61. Battiscombe, p.188.

62. Pimlott, pp.10–12.

63. Fairclough, Ch. 10.

64. According to the *London Gazette* nine royal or serene highnesses were present at his death.
65. Nicolson, p.44.
66. Letter to Dalton, 1.3.93, RA GEO V AA 6/413.
67. 26.2.92, RA GEO V AA 6/412.
68. RA GEO V AA 6/363.
69. Reginald Bacon, p.139. It may be added, by way of illustration, that Geoffrey Phipps Hornby had served his father successively as flag-lieutenant and flag-commander; and as late as 1928, Reginald Tyrwhitt did not forbear to employ his son, as flag-lieutenant.
70. *Western Mail*, 10.7.16, Llwynmadoc papers.
71. 18.5.89, RA GEO V AA 6/382.
72. Mark Kerr, *Land, Sea and Air*, p.69.
73. HET to home from Patras, 31.2.91, Llwynmadoc papers.
74. Llwynmadoc papers.
75. *Victoria*'s log, ADM53/16466. They may have known of the duke's death by commercial news telegram before the official 'wire' arrived.
76. Admiralty correspondence, January–February 1892, ADM1/7114.
77. Michael Harrison, in *Clarence*, names an equerry, Captain the Hon. Alwyne Greville, as "Eddy's constant companion since first joining the [naval] Service" (p.210). In fact, Greville was a soldier.
78. 12.4.92, RA, GEO V AA 6/416.
79. RA GEO V A 2582/7.
80. 9.6.92, RA GEO V AA 6/417.
81. *Globe*, 25.6.92.
82. *Ibid.*
83. Diary 15.1.92, BGGF1/25.
84. David Thomas, *Royal Admirals*, p.132.
85. Nicolson, p.47.
86. George's diary, 8.8.92, Royal Archives.
87. Royal Archives.
88. Undated, Llwynmadoc papers.
89. 4.11.92, from Marlborough House, Pall Mall, Llwynmadoc papers.
90. S. W. Roskill, introduction to Godfrey-Faussett papers (BGGF).
91. See SLGF 2/1.
92. Admiral Sir Frederick William Fisher, *Naval Reminiscences*, pp.208, 282. Prince Louis of Battenberg may have turned down *Osborne* for the same reason (King-Hall, *Sea Saga*, p.294), and/or *Victoria and Albert* (Thomas, *Royal Admirals*, p.106).
93. Arthur Marder, *Fear God and Dread Nought*, Vol.II, p.21.
94. Redmond McLaughlin, *The Escape of the Goeben*, p.25.
95. Stanley Bonnett, *The Price of Admiralty*, p.142.
96. McLaughlin, p.25.
97. Geoffrey Lowis, *Fabulous Admirals*, p.35.
98. McLaughlin, p.27.
99. Llwynmadoc papers.
100. 7.1.93, Llwynmadoc papers.
101. Dear Dad, 2.5.93 Add.MSS 52504.
102. Battiscombe, p.199. They were "lethargic, uneducated and childlike, not to say

childish, in their tastes and amusements". Victoria, furthermore, was "delicate, hypochondriacal and already slightly embittered".

103. Duncan Crow, *Edwardian Women*, p.70.
104. Log, ADM53/14837 (14838 after 30.4.93).
105. Pope-Hennessy, p.229.
106. Nicolson, p.49.
107. Pope-Hennessy, p.253.
108. Hough, *Admirals in Collision*, p.55.
109. *Ibid.*, p.55.
110. Lord Sydenham of Combe, *My Working Life*, p.120.
111. Penrose Fitzgerald, *Sir George Tryon KCB*, p.348.
112. Files of Standing Committee on Signals, ADM116/64.
113. Letter from *Nile* at Marmarice, 12.6.93, NOE24/G.
114. Edward Bradford, *A. K. Wilson*, p.123.
115. Mrs Noel to Noel, 23.6.93, NOE/1B.
116. Hough, p.110.

Chapter 12: *Nemesis*

1. See Humphrey Hugh Smith, *A Yellow Admiral Remembers*, p.68.
2. Mediterranean Fleet's printed Summer Cruise programme, BCK/13/15B.
3. The ships were: *Nile, Edinburgh, Collingwood* and *Edgar*. Tryon's orders to Noel may be found in NOE/12; *Nile*'s signal log is in NOE/20A.
4. JOH/30; Admiral Johnstone's obituary, *The Times*, 5.12.27.
5. Alfred Winsloe to Phipps Hornby, 16 (or 18).8.93, PHI/120D.
6. Brackenbury to Mrs B., 23.6.93, BCK/13/15B.
7. Under 'Anchoring in Company' the 1987 *Navigation Manual* says: "The anchoring formation should be taken up in good time, so that alterations of course can be made by turns together, a much simpler procedure than wheeling" (Vol.I, p.402).
8. Mark Kerr, *The Navy in My Time*, p.30.
9. The idea that *Dreadnought* had a tighter turning-circle than *Victoria* is problematical. Richard Hough found it somewhere, and a letter in Arthur Moore's privately printed biography shows that Moore firmly believed it to be true: he puts *Dreadnought*'s diameter at 450 yards, *Victoria*'s at 670, and *Camperdown*'s at 800 (Marjorie Moore, *Adventures in the Royal Navy*, p.87). This, however, is contradicted by 'Turning Trials in HM Ships' (1890, ADM116/444), which states *Dreadnought*'s and *Victoria*'s diameters at half-speed to be 3.7 lengths (= 395 yards) and 2.6 lengths (= 295 yards) respectively. The terms and conditions of the trials are not stated, but presumably they were consistent between ships. The issue is further confused by the court-martial's acceptance of *Camperdown*'s turning-circle as 660 yards (at 9 knots and full helm), while Noel gave *Nile*'s diameter as 550 yards – and clearly believed it to be smaller than *Victoria*'s.
10. Court-martial evidence, ADM1/7171.
11. A. B. Jenkins had been Fisher's XO in *Inflexible*.
12. Wilson to Markham, MRK/41.
13. Richard Hough, *Admirals in Collision*, p.8.
14. Hough, p.89.
15. Captain Gerard Noel's eyewitness evidence, ADM1/7172.
16. Hough, p.94.

17. Captain Noel's eyewitness evidence. Noel's ship, the closest to the spot where *Victoria* sank, fixed her position with horizontal sextant angles from Rankine Lighthouse of the following charted features: El Mina (31°25'); Tower of Lions (41°33'); Tripoli Castle (47°4'); extension of rocky shore marked "129 feet" (73°17').

18. This tally ignores any non-complement civilians, such as Maltese servants, Italian bandsmen or Chinese laundrymen, who were on board.

19. Sir George Carew, in *Mary Rose* at Spithead in 1545; Sir Clowdisley Shovell, in *Association* in the Scilly Isles in 1707; Sir John Balchen, in *Victory* on the Casquets in 1744; Richard Kempenfelt, in *Royal George* at Spithead in 1782; Sir Hyde Parker in *Cato* in the South Atlantic in 1782 (or early '83 – nobody knows); Sir Thomas Troubridge in *Blenheim* off Madagascar in 1807; and Robert Reynolds in *St George* on the Jutland coast in 1811. Sir Howard Kelly almost joined the list in 1931 when he was shipwrecked in his official yacht HMS *Petersfield* in the China Sea, but got ashore safely.

20. Jellicoe's saviour was Midshipman Philip D. R. West, who received the Royal Humane Society Medal.

21. Bourke to Phipps Hornby, 6.7.93, PHI/120D. *Victoria* had run aground (for a second time) in 1892, for which Bourke had been reprimanded – an experience which was said to have turned his hair white (*Hawk*, 27.6.93).

22. Winsloe, court-martial prosecutor, to Phipps Hornby, 16 (or 18).8.93, PHI/120D.

Chapter 13: *Court-Martial*

1. *Sheffield & Rotherham Independent*, 8.7.93.

2. *Morning Post*, 1.7.93.

3. Brackenbury to Mrs B., 23.6.93, BCK/13/15B (also see to Hornby, 23.6.93, PHI/120D Part 2).

4. George Aston, *Memories of a Marine*, p.151.

5. Marjorie Moore, *Adventures in the Royal Navy* (privately published biography of Admiral Sir Arthur Moore), p.90.

6. *Saturday Review*, 1.7.93.

7. Bill Fisher to Gerard Noel, 29.6.93, NOE/1B.

8. Bourke to Noel, 22.8.93, describing an emotional interview with Hoskins (who "completely broke down") upon his return to England, NOE/1A.

9. See for example: Bourke to Noel, 22.8.93, NOE/1A; Fleet Paymaster Charles Gifford (Clanwilliam's secretary) to Noel, 26.6.93, Captain Swinton Holland to Noel, 1.7.93, NOE/1B.

10. Lord Spencer came close to abetting the 'drunk' rumour, when he told Queen Victoria: "It is impossible to avoid the feeling that Sir G. Tryon must have had something overhanging him which for the moment obscured his ordinarily clear intellect" (undated, Royal Archives, E56/113). The Queen must have known that the senior naval career of her son Alfred had been perennially overhung.

11. Mrs Noel to Noel, 19.7.93, NOE/1A. She added: ". . . I forget if I told you this before. Aunt Leila came here today full of it, she having heard it from a quite different direction." There are at least four other occult tales connected with the disaster.

12. Fitzgerald to Bourke, repeated by Bourke to Noel on 22.8.93, NOE/1A.

13. 29.6.93, NOE/1B.

14. Diary of PO Louis Parsons (BRNC Dartmouth).

15. Reginald Bacon, *A Naval Scrap Book*, Vol.I, pp.162–3.

16. *Ibid.*, p.155.

17. A phrase from Rudyard Kipling's account of the '97 manoeuvres (see *A Fleet in Being*).

18. Bacon, p.156. Bacon wrongly dates these events 1891.

19. 27.8.90, PHI/120C.

20. Rockingham archives, WR(S) 537; the newspaper is unidentifiable.

21. My thanks to Mrs Priscilla Napier, the admiral's granddaughter-in-law.

22. King George V (as he then was) wrote to Sir Michael in February 1911: "I am grieved to think that you, but more especially Mrs Napier, should have been subjected to the pain and annoyance of appearing in the witness box in a court of justice in order to refute this scandalous lie which now for nearly twenty years has gained credence with a certain class all over the Empire" (Rockingham: WR(S) 234).

23. Queen Victoria's journal, Royal Archives.

24. The Prince of Wales's visit, with his three daughters, to the opera was criticized in the press as in poor taste.

25. Queen Victoria's journal, Royal Archives.

26. *Ibid.*, 25.8.00.

27. *Hawk*, 27.6.93; gossip columnist writing under 'My Dearest Mollie'.

28. Llwynmadoc papers.

29. Queen Victoria's journal, 21.7.93, Royal Archives.

30. "My Dear Dad" of 30.6.93, Evan-Thomas Papers, Add.MSS 52504.

31. *Dictionary of National Biography* (Sir John Laughton).

32. 30.6.93, Evan-Thomas papers.

33. 1.7.93, Llwynmadoc papers.

34. 24.11.93, *ibid.*

35. 1.9.92, Godfrey-Faussett's diary, CCC.

36. NOE/1B.

37. *Morning Advertiser*, 4.7.93.

38. See, for example, *Leicester Morning News*, 27.6.93; *Birmingham Argus*, 3.7.93.

39. 15.7.93. *QR & AI* (article 634) stipulated that courts-martial "shall be public and all persons shall be admitted". It is not only the press who have, on occasion, suspected the Admiralty of evasion: Commander Alastair Mars, faced with court-martial in 1952, reckoned that "If it were held aboard Nelson's flagship at Portsmouth, it would be a public trial and I would be bound in consequence to get a fair deal. But I knew how easy it would be to ship me to some such spot as Scapa Flow where I could be court-martialled in obscure isolation, be given whatever punishment they fancied, and the world, not knowing, would not care" (Alastair Mars, *Court Martial*, p.14).

40. 4.7.93.

41. 4.7.93.

42. By Mr Henniker Heaton (Canterbury) on 3.7.93, and Sir Alfred Hickman (Wolverhampton North) on 6.7.93. It may be mentioned that, owing to the First Lord's being a peer, Shuttleworth's burden in the Commons, in effect, equated with that of the Admiralty's political head.

43. 6.7.93.

44. *Admiralty & Horse Guards Gazette*, 22.7.93.

45. LC2/129.

46. 23.6.93, LC2/128 (exclamation in original). The three admirals of the fleet were Lord John Hay, Sir Geoffrey Phipps Hornby and Sir John Commerell. A sombre naval aspect of the wedding was the display to the public of George and May's immense collection of wedding presents "at so much a head for the benefit of the *Victoria* Fund" (Pope-Hennessy, p.265). The Mediterranean Fleet's collection for a present went down with the ship.

47. 23.6.93, LC2/128. In LC2/129 is a black-list of a dozen or so names, apparently sent to the Lord Chamberlain's office a week before the event.

48. *Hawke*'s log ADM53/13865.

49. Mars, *Court Martial*, p.202.

50. Winsloe to Phipps Hornby 16 (or 18).8.93, PHI/120D.

51. *Ibid.*

52. There was no teleprinter at this date, but the Morse-key equipment in use had a speed of 30 to 40 words per minute (my thanks to Cable & Wireless's museum curator). Markham was criticized in the press for sending his despatches to London by courier rather than by telegraph.

53. *Illustrated Police News*, 8.7.93.

54. Letter of 5.7.93 to Noel from a British resident in Greece, NOE/1A.

55. NOE/1B.

56. 20.7.93.

57. 8.7.93.

58. 4.7.93.

59. 4.7.93, see also 28.6.93.

60. 28.7.93.

61. 4.7.93.

62. 8.7.93.

63. *Saturday Review*, 1.7.93.

64. Letter to Mother, 23.6.93, Add.MSS 49039 pp.65ff. On the day after the disaster Arthur Wilson (who had adopted young Edmund Jellicoe while *Trafalgar* was in refit) had had JJ transferred from *Nile* to *Sans Pareil* where he had a cot rigged for him in his own cabin.

65. Culme-Seymour, Winsloe (prosecutor), Jellicoe, and Lt Sydney Fremantle ('officer of the court') "made up a four for racquets and usually went off for an hour's sweat immediately after the court had risen at four o'clock" (Sydney Fremantle, *My Naval Career*, p.61).

66. *Admiralty & Horse Guards Gazette*, 15.7.93.

67. Richard Hough, *Admirals in Collision*, p.147.

68. M. E. & F. A. Markham, *Life of Sir Albert Markham*, p.239.

69. 8.7.93.

70. 5.7.93.

71. 27.6.93, MRK/41.

72. 23.6.93, MRK/41.

73. Culme-Seymour to Hoskins, 21.7.93, Rockingham: WR(S) 213.

74. Culme-Seymour to a Mr Barrington, 15.7.93; Culme-Seymour to Hoskins, 21.7.93; Rockingham: WR(S) 213.

75. Canon David Markham and his family had to be in residence in Windsor for two months every year. (Albert Markham, *Life of Sir Clements Markham*.)

76. 19.7.93.

77. ADM1/7171 & 7172. Or ADM121/14: *Mediterranean Station Records*, Vol.61 (many of the diagrams relating to the loss of *Victoria* have been removed from this file and placed in MP11/93).

78. Winsloe to Phipps Hornby, 16.8.93, PHI/120D.

79. Mrs Noel to Noel, 21.7.93, NOE/1A.

80. Mrs Noel to Noel, 25.7.93, NOE/1A.

81. Norman Dixon, *On the Psychology of Military Incompetence*, p.112.

82. Admiral Bertram Chambers, *Salt Junk*, p.201.

83. Vander-Meulen had been promoted rear-admiral on 23rd June for reasons unconnected with the collision. While in command of *Inflexible* his XO (as a matter of interest) was the famously despotic George Cherry.

84. 24.7.93, NOE/1B.

85. See Clowes to Brackenbury, 2.5.07, BCK/10; also Clowes, *The Royal Navy, a History*, Vol.VII (1903), p.426.

86. Hough, pp.162ff., and *Daily Telegraph*, 26.6.93. The Markham–Clowes–Hough solution was endorsed in 1989 by a Cdr M. D. Dewar (who should have known better) in *Collisions at Sea – How?*

87. The definition of the meaning of the Compass Pendant (the flag which denoted a turn-in-succession) on p.15 of the 1889 *General Signal Book* (in the National Maritime Museum). Another reference to the matter may be found in Signals Committee correspondence (ADM116/62).

88. The definition of the meaning of the Compass Pendant on p.9 of the 1898 *General Signal Book* (ADM186/646). The italics are in the original.

89. A. K. Wilson's vain hope, on June the 22nd, that "an arrangement had been made for one division to circle round the other" illustrates the point. Consider also Noel's dismissal, while giving evidence at the trial, of the 'circle round theory': "Such an evolution could hardly have been made without some further communication by signal."

90. Tryon to Hornby, 23.12.91: "Equal speed is in my opinion absolutely called for in manoeuvres unless you want to have a ramming match."

91. "If possible, plan on a long run-in on the final approach course to the anchorage. This gives other ships plenty of time to settle down in their station" (1987 *Navigation Manual*, Vol.I, p.402).

92. The ship's doctor, who had seen him a few minutes before the disaster, testified that his leg ulcer (which was on the mend) was the only thing visibly wrong with him, and that he appeared neither deranged nor drunk.

93. *Dreadnought*, p.393.

94. Edward Bradford, *A. K. Wilson*, pp.125–6.

95. Mark Kerr, *The Navy in My Time*, p.31.

96. Winsloe to Phipps Hornby, 16.8.93, PHI/120D. Winsloe was tempted to allude to it as a means of putting Tracey in the witness box, but decided that it would only tarnish Tryon's reputation and make harder his task of prosecuting.

97. Bouverie Clark to Commander Spencer Login, 13.7.93, in MRK/41.

98. 1976 edition, Vol.IV, para.0141.

99. 1987 edition, Vol.I, p.402.

100. 1976 edition, Vol.IV, para.0144.

101. After a collision between two ships of Beresford's Channel Squadron while exercising at night without lights in November 1903, the Admiralty conceded that hazardous training was necessary.

102. My thanks to the (1994) Deputy Chief Naval Judge Advocate.

103. 22.7.93.

104. One of the incidental ironies of the disaster is that several years before, during Phipps Hornby's tenure of the Mediterranean, while prosecuting at the trial of a Captain Lindsay Brine for causing a collision, Tryon's cross-examination of the *other* captain included the following: "You were on the bridge of your ship, you saw that a collision was imminent, why did you not starboard your helm [i.e. turn to port]?"

105. Bacon, p.187.

106. 22.7.93.

107. These words are not Markham's but Captain William Dyke Acland's, when he made common cause, at the trial, with Markham over the interpretation of the signal.

108. Freddy Noel (brother?) to Noel, 30.7.93, NOE/1A.

109. 8.7.93.

110. Question No. 1598, ADM1/7172.

111. ADM1/7172; *Officers of the Royal Navy Tried by Court-Martial, 1880–1903*, HMSO (1905).

Chapter 14: *Their Lordships' Predicament*

1. This, at least, was Winsloe's impression, reported by Philip Colomb to Phipps Hornby (8.8.93, PHI/120D). In fact Noel had dinner with him at least once.

2. Winsloe to Phipps Hornby, 16.8.93, PHI/120D. On the day after the collision John Brackenbury had written to Sir Geoffrey that Markham was "absolutely blameless" (*ibid.*), and to his wife that "the fault was entirely the commander-in-chief's as we were all obeying his orders" (BCK/13/15B).

3. 3.8.93.

4. 28.7.93.

5. *Saturday Review*, 25.11.93.

6. 31.7.93, Althorp papers, K437.

7. 8.8.93, *ibid.*

8. 28.7.93.

9. 28.7.93.

10. 29.7.93.

11. Letter of 13.8.93, NOE/1A. (As a matter of sublime inconsequence, among the crew of Custance's *Phaeton* was a boatswain named Earl Spencer.)

12. Mrs Noel to Noel, 31.7.93, NOE/1A. One reform which did follow from the disaster was the institution of compulsory swimming tests.

13. 11.7.93, NOE/1A.

14. 6.8.93, NOE/1A.

15. MRK/41, rough copy in NOE/1A/II.

16. Noel's diary mentions the following social companions: Tryon, Markham, Acland, Brackenbury, Custance, Karslake, Moore and Wilson (NOE/32).

17. Noel's 1876 Naval Prize essay was entitled *The Best Types of War Vessels for the British Navy*, and touched on the turning powers of ironclads and the risk of collision. Johnstone's 1884 Naval Prize essay was a discussion of how best to organize and distribute the personnel of the Navy on the outbreak of war. (*RUSI Journal*, Vols.XX & XXVIII).

18. NOE/1B.

19. 10.8.93, NOE/1A.

20. Markham to Noel, undated: "I cannot permit your sneer at the ability of Captain Johnstone to pass unchallenged . . . I have the greatest confidence in his skill and ability to handle his ship and the utmost faith in his prudence and loyalty" (NOE/1A).

21. Marjorie Moore, *Adventures in the Royal Navy*, p.86.

22. 3.8.93, MRK/41.

23. 29.7.93. In 1852 the troopship *Birkenhead* was wrecked on the coast of South Africa with heavy loss of life. Victorian myth-makers rushed to promote the consoling legend that the troops had stood patiently to attention on deck as the water rose round them – a scenario which is questionable.

24. Lord Fisher, *Memories*, p.66. Gamaliel was St Paul's Pharisee teacher; Fisher did not specify whom he had in mind as St Paul.

25. 6.7.93, PHI/120D.

26. Phipps Hornby to Culme-Seymour, 30.6.93, Rockingham: WR(S) 248.

27. Hoskins to Hornby, 27.6.93: "Your letter was duly appreciated and considered but I believe arrangements have already been made for sending out a new commander-in-chief. The name of course cannot be published until the Queen's sanction has been given" (PHI/120D). The only precedent of an admiral of the fleet commanding afloat was that of Earl Howe in 1796.

28. Mary Egerton, *Sir Geoffrey Phipps Hornby*, p.392. In 1863 when Tryon was commander of *Warrior* (and Fisher her gunnery-officer) Hornby was captain of *Edgar*, both ships taking part in the Channel Squadron's round-Britain cruise of that year. Like Tryon, Hornby was the beneficiary of Conservative political interest.

29. Brackenbury to Phipps Hornby, 23.6.93, PHI/120D.

30. *Review of Reviews*, 15.8.93; see also Colomb's letter to Noel of 20.8.93 (NOE/1A).

31. Clements Markham to Phipps Hornby, 10.8.93, PHI/120D. A fortnight earlier Mrs Noel had written to her husband: "I hear Mrs Clements Markham has shut herself up and won't receive anybody – silly woman!" (26.7.93, NOE/1B).

32. Lake to Phipps Hornby, 16.1.94, PHI/120D. Among the few instructions which Hornby left for his own funeral was the wish that FitzRoy, Winsloe Lake, and a Captain James Bruce should be present.

33. Rockingham: WR(S).

34. *United Service Gazette*, 12.8.93.

35. Charles Benedict Davenport, *Naval Officers, their Heredity and Development*, p.101.

36. He was unconscious for three weeks, during which he "dreamt that he was commanding a fleet in the Baltic. Never had there been such successfully executed manoeuvres, never such cheery dinner parties, never so much fun and chaff, and all his favourite captains had been with him" (Mary Egerton, p.388).

37. Colomb to Hornby, 8.8.93 (see also 3.8.93), PHI/120D.

38. Peter Kemp, *Oxford Companion to Ships and the Sea*, p.308.

39. Letter to Phipps Hornby, 11.3.91, PHI/120C.

40. Letter to Phipps Hornby, 1.8.93, PHI/120D.

41. Hough, *Admirals in Collision*, p.109.

42. Geoffrey Bennett, *Charlie B*, p.188.

43. M. E. & F. A. Markham, *The Life of Sir Albert Hastings Markham*, p.245.

44. Beresford to Phipps Hornby, 1.8.93, PHI/120D.

45. Fisher to Spencer, 29.8.93, Althorp papers, K441. Admiral Sir John Hay is not to be confused with his kinsman Admiral of the Fleet Lord John Hay.

46. 20.8.93.
47. Article XXXVII in the 1816 *Signal Book*, XXXIII in the 1859 *Signal Book*, and XVI in the 1867 *Manual of Naval Evolutions*.
48. Article XX, under 'Instructions For the Conduct of a Fleet'.
49. This, a reference to the loss of *Fittleton* in 1976.
50. 28.7.93.
51. 14.7.93.
52. 5.8.93.
53. *The Times*, 31.7.93.
54. Hough, p.160.
55. Letter to Markham, 26.7.93, MRK/41.
56. 31.7.93.
57. Letter to wife, 23.6.93, BCK/13/15B.
58. E.g. *Admiralty & Horse Guards Gazette*, 5.8.93; Custance's letter to Noel of 13.8.93: "Colomb's letter was most unfortunate and I am extremely sorry that it should have been written. The view which he wished to put forward might very well have been stated without making it appear as a personal attack on Sir G. Tryon . . . It will make no end of bad blood."
59. *The Times*, 12.8.93. Fitzgerald had "felt inclined to say a great deal more nasty things than I did say, but restrained my militant ardour for the sake of appearances". *The Times*, normally able to publish letters at 12 hours' notice, withheld his from publication for more than a week (letter to Noel, NOE/1A).
60. *The Times*, 12.8.93; also quoted in Hough, p.161.
61. NOE/12.
62. 20.8.93, NOE/1A.
63. This is more strongly conveyed in Colomb's letter of 7.9.93. There may be a seed of truth in his almost-claim to have invented TA, for he may have been instrumental in inserting the TA message in the 1878 *Signal Book* (although then it was labelled '184', rather than TA).
   The introduction of this item in the 1878 book appears to give rise to doctrinal confusion, for the same book retained an older permanent article (XIII under 'Instructions For the Conduct of a Fleet') which lays down that "When the Admiral makes any movement without a signal, the ships of the Fleet are to regulate themselves thereby . . . unless the Admiral makes the signal that his motions are no longer to be attended to."
   If this is a standing instruction, then 184 is superfluous. The article disappears in the 1889 book (which redesignated 184 'TA'), with the result that the duty to conform to the admiral's unsignalled movements had been turned, over a succession of two *Signal Book* revisions – both much influenced by Colomb – from the normal state of affairs to a deviant one requiring special notification.
64. And he was not even that expert: his *Manual of Fleet Evolutions* contains the assertion that a reduction in engine revolutions while under helm will tighten the turn, and an increase will widen it. In fact, insofar as propellers thrust onto rudder surfaces, the opposite is true. (This error stood for 22 years before someone – Rear-Admiral Edmund Fremantle – pointed it out.)
65. One sentence from an earlier part of this letter has been transplanted into the fifth paragraph quoted here, with no alteration to Fitzgerald's meaning.
66. 22.9.93, NOE/1B.

67. Letter in *The Times* of 18.8.93.
68. Commander Robert Noel to Noel, 7.9.93, NOE/1A.
69. *Truth*, 3.8.93.
70. When asked by Dr MacGregor, MP for Invernesshire, on 6.7.93.
71. The full text of Bowles's question was:

> I ask the Secretary to the Admiralty whether all orders given by a superior officer in Her Majesty's Navy to a Captain of a ship are always subject to the present condition 'with due regard to the safety of Her Majesty's ships'; and in case obedience to such an order would entail a collision with a friend or endanger a ship in any other way, is it the duty of any such Captain to avoid that danger by forbearing to obey such an order; is it a Regulation in Her Majesty's Navy that in case it appears to a Captain of a ship that the course ordered by his superior officer would endanger his ship, it is the Captain's duty (such orders notwithstanding) to take such steps as may be necessary to avoid any such danger, and is not the responsibility for so doing thrown entirely on the Captain; and is it, further, the Captain's duty, when time or circumstances do not admit of the Admiral's permission being obtained, to take such steps without such permission? [*Hansard*, 10.8.93.]

Kay-Shuttleworth's brief, evasive answer was repeated on the 24th, but thereafter the question was not asked again. (The eventual Admiralty Minute on the verdict presumably sufficed for an answer.)
72. Winsloe to Phipps Hornby, 16 (or 18).8.93, PHI/120D.
73. Hoskins to Spencer, 3.9.93, Althorp K446.
74. – evidently without success. Bourke to Noel, 22.8.93, NOE/1A.
75. M. E. & F. A. Markham, *Life of Sir Albert Markham*, p.102.
76. See MRK/41.
77. 12.8.93.
78. Volume 10 of Signals Committee files, ADM116/64.
79. Mark Kerr, *The Navy in My Time*, p.29.
80. Hough, p.8.
81. Fisher's words, *Memories*, p.142.
82. 29.8.93, K441.
83. UK-S to Spencer, 3.7.93, Peter Gordon, *The Red Earl*, Vol.II.
84. *Admiralty & Horse Guards Gazette*, 4.11.93.
85. That it met in *Enchantress* in Chatham is stated in Lord Spencer's memo of 13th of October. The 26th of September was the only eligible day the ship was there: she had just brought Their Lordships round from Portsmouth, whither she returned on the 27th (*Enchantress*'s log).
86. *Records*, pp.50–1.
87. Spencer's memo of 13.10.93, ADM1/7172.
88. A phrase used by the *Nautical Magazine* in connection with Lord Mersey's enquiry into the *Titanic* disaster in 1912.
89. 12 & 15.10.93, Althorp papers, K437.
90. 24.10.93, Althorp papers, K437.
91. 28.10.93, (NMM) MRK/41.
92. ADM1/7172; *Officers of the Royal Navy Tried by Court-Martial, 1880–1903*.
93. 4.11.93.

94. 4.11.93.

95. 9.11.93, Althorp papers, K437.

96. 16.11.93, Althorp papers, K437. Culme-Seymour's letter to Markham, of the 15th of November, is to be found in MRK/41.

97. JOH/35.

98. Letter of 5.11.93, JOH/34.

99. M. E. & F. A. Markham, *The Life of Sir Albert Markham*, p.245.

100. 3.11.93, MRK/41.

101. Beaumont to Markham, 3.11.93, MRK/41.

102. 22.11.93, MRK/41. The best known example of Their Lordships refusing to revise a decision was over the dismissal of Admiral Sir Dudley North for allowing French destroyers to pass through the Straits of Gibraltar unchallenged after the fall of France in 1940. After the war five admirals of the fleet, including three former First Sea Lords, petitioned the Admiralty to reopen his case, to no avail. "The Admiralty would preserve its venerable privilege of doing as it thought fit with officers of the Royal Navy" (Leslie Gardiner, *The British Admiralty*, p.383).

103. 2.12.93, Althorp papers, K437; see also Hoskins to Spencer, 7.12.93, K446.

Chapter 15: *Counter-Reformation*

1. *Sans Pareil*'s log, ADM53/15565; Noel's diary, NOE/32. Owing to the lack of space in Grand Harbour, the fleet almost certainly exited in reverse order: hence the signal for steam-tactics so soon after the flagship's slipping.

2. 21.7.93, WR(S) 213. Photographs *c.* 1895 show *Sans Pareil* with a light foremast stepped immediately abaft the bridge. Perhaps it was added, for signalling purposes, by Malta dockyard at the behest of Culme-Seymour.

3. Oscar Parkes, *British Battleships*, p.356.

4. PHI/120C, quoted in Ruddock Mackay, *Fisher of Kilverstone*, p.203.

5. Had the original plan held good, *Camperdown* (and Captain Johnstone) would not have been leading the 2nd Division on the fateful 22nd of June; and *Royal Sovereign*, with her greater reserve of buoyancy, could probably have survived such a blow.

6. 30.6.92, RA King George V's Diary.

7. Evan-Thomas's gamebook, Llwynmadoc papers.

8. 22.8.93, Althorp papers, K437.

9. NOE/1.

10. Marjorie Moore, *Adventures in the Royal Navy*, p.90.

11. Letter to Noel, 3.8.93, NOE/1B.

12. 5.7.93, NOE/1A. Culme-Seymour had not left England when this was written, but *Nile* was away from Malta cruising independently.

13. 25.8.93, NOE/1A.

14. *The Times* of 19.8.93.

15. *The Times* obituary, 5.12.27.

16. Quoted by M. E. & F. A. Markham in *Life of Sir Albert Markham*, p.253.

17. Richard Hough, *Admirals in Collision*, p.171.

18. Lord Chatfield, *The Navy and Defence*, p.80.

19. p.71, ADM186/631 (extract slightly truncated). A similar statement is to be found in Christopher Cradock's *Whispers from the Fleet*.

20. *Ramillies*'s log, ADM53/14828.

21. PHI/120D. Fisher (himself financially strapped) suggested to Hornby that Jellicoe might prefer not to have "pecuniary assistance" (letter of 10.8.93).

22. Correlli Barnett, *The Sword Bearers*, p.130.

23. Evan-Thomas's obituary, *Sheerness Guardian*, 8.9.28.

24. William Goodenough, *Rough Record*, p.38.

25. Frederick Dreyer, *Sea Heritage*. Jellicoe was of slight build, and the savage kick of the Martini-Henry must have been a disincentive to rapid-fire.

26. May was given the additional title of Chief of Staff, presumably as a palliative for succeeding an officer who was junior to him.

27. *Sheerness Guardian*, 8.9.28.

28. Jellicoe Papers, Add.MSS 49038.

29. Mark Girouard, *Return to Camelot*, p.21.

30. *Ibid.*, p.224.

31. Now in possession of Commander Martin Bourdillon.

32. Goodenough, p.41.

33. Phipps Hornby to Culme-Seymour, 30.6.93, Rockingham: WR(S) 248.

34. George Aston, *Memoirs of a Marine*, p.149.

35. 13.7.94, WR(S) 213.

36. Undated fleet circular, WR(S) 238.

37. William May, *The Life of a Sailor*, p.60. When May first reported to Culme-Seymour to learn what his 'staff' duties would be, he was unable to shift the admiral from the subject of tandem bicycling.

38. Reginald Bacon, *A Naval Scrap Book*, Vol.I, p.162.

39. *Ibid.*, pp.186, 258.

40. *Ibid.*, p.258.

41. Now in Rockingham: WR(S) 457.

42. 22.9.93, NOE.

43. W. S. Chalmers, *Life and Letters of David Beatty*, p.16.

44. Humphrey Hugh Smith, *A Yellow Admiral Remembers*, p.67.

45. *Ibid.*, p.54.

46. Sir Percy Scott, *Fifty Years in the Royal Navy*, p.73. Scott's view is endorsed by Kenneth Dewar (*The Navy from Within*, p.24).

47. 16.5.95, CUR/20.

48. In a passage designed to celebrate the efficiency of signallers, 'Taffrail' (Capt. Henry Taprell Dorling) depicts the flagdeck crew of a dreadnought getting a repeat to the masthead within 45 seconds of the signal's appearance in the flagship (*Carry On!*, p.19).

49. In 1902, a Captain Arthur Moggridge argued that each ship should automatically form on the next ship forward of her beam, that the 'guide of the fleet' should be the ship forward of everyone else's beam, and that the admiral should be in the centre but able to take over 'guide' by signal if he wished. This system, admitted Moggridge (who had been Fisher's master-of-the-fleet in *Renown*, in the West Indies), would require at each end of the line captains of proven tactical "appreciation" ('Remarks on lessons learned from the Tactical Games worked out at the R.N. College', FISR 5/10, F.P.4208).

50. ADM116/66, Vol.14 of Signals Committee files; Sir Michael's arguments about 'leader' and 'guide' are also in MER/209.

51. *Ibid.* At about this time (*c.* 1895) Beresford explained to a friend, using match-

sticks on a table, how he would advance upon an enemy fleet: "he would approach in line abreast and at a given moment turn into line ahead to the right or left" (Henry Spenser Wilkinson, *The Brain of the Navy*, p.195). It would be interesting to know his position on the 'guide/flagship' question, for to have the option of turning either way, he must have been prepared not to be leading after the turn. But then again, as he admitted to Evan-Thomas in 1900, he had manoeuvred a squadron for no more than two hours in his life.

52. George King-Hall, *Sea Saga*, p.301.

53. Files of Standing Committee on Signals, ADM116/64.

54. Letter of June 1895, WR(S) 213.

55. Notes sent by Barnard to Marder (ROSK 3/3, also Add.MSS 52506).

56. 5.9.93 from Barrie Kent, *Signal!*, p.241.

57. See long paper by Aldrich in WR(S) 238.

58. Chalmers, p.16.

59. A sophistication of William Martin's Mooring and Manoeuvring Board, in the form of a trigonometrical slide-rule which gives the true course (for a given speed) to any new station in a moving formation.

60. Hoskins to Evan-Thomas, 24.11.93, Evan-Thomas papers, Add.MSS 52504–6.

61. Kent, *Signal!*, p.236.

62. 27.10.93, Llwynmadoc papers.

63. Aston, p.139.

64. Llwynmadoc papers.

65. Protheroe to Noel, 29.4.94, NOE/1A.

66. 29.4.94, Llwynmadoc papers.

67. Llwynmadoc papers.

68. There is a hint in Prothero to Noel, 29.4.94, that Hilda had visited Malta during the winter.

69. Llwynmadoc papers.

70. 20.7.94, Llwynmadoc papers.

71. First page and date missing, Llwynmadoc papers. The Admiralty machine may have taken a year or more to produce this decision.

72. Prothero to Noel, 29.4.94, NOE/1A. For Burney to be in the veterans' race, the age qualification must have been 35; Sir Michael was 58. The Henderson referred to was William Henderson, Acland's successor as captain of *Edgar*, the future founding-secretary of the *Naval Review*, and the uncle of Reginald Henderson (Third Sea Lord in the late 1930s).

73. C. C. Penrose Fitzgerald, *From Sail to Steam*, p.183.

74. See Goodenough, p.36.

75. Llwynmadoc papers.

76. Although falling into disuse, 'haul-down' promotions of subordinate staff members on flag-officers' relinquishing important commands were not abolished until 1913. William Goodenough was a beneficiary of the practice in 1904 ('Promotion of Officers etc.', in ADM1/8327).

77. My thanks to Evan Davies. The photograph is too badly damaged to be worth reproducing in this book.

78. 13.4.85, *Record of Conduct Book 1876–1887* (BRNC Dartmouth).

79. BTY 1/1.

80. Chalmers, p.12.

81. *Ibid.*, p.13.

82. Unpublished Jellicoe autobiography, Jellicoe Papers, Add.MSS 49038. Kitchener's connection with Jellicoe is unclear.

83. In 1914, in the event of his own death, Jellicoe would have preferred Colville as his successor as C-in-C Grand Fleet, even though seniority had relegated Admiral Colville to a shore appointment. In my view Colville should have been given the job in the first place (see Chapter 19, n.8).

84. C. S. Forester in foreword (p.xix) to Chalmers's *Life and Letters of David Beatty*.

85. Janowitz, *The Professional Soldier*, p.35 (including extract from Davis, 'Bureaucratic Patterns in the Navy Officer Corps', in *Social Forces* (1948)). Janowitz's *Psychology and the Military Establishment* must also be mentioned.

86. *My Early Life*, pp.186–7. This extract has been slightly shortened here.

87. Forester (in Chalmers, p.xx).

Chapter 16: *Regulate Britannia*

1. *New York Times*, 28.6.97.

2. *The Times*, 1.7.97.

3. *Annual Register.*

4. *Ibid.*

5. The following dead-pan item appeared in *Truth*, on 8.7.97:

> A member of the Naval and Military Club, who was present when the Jubilee procession passed, is anxious to make it known that the unfavourable reception of the German Emperor's representative was the work of the crowd on the pavement and not of the occupants of the club premises. It is my correspondent who has introduced the name of the Naval and Military into the case, not I; but if the German representative was hooted when passing, it is well that the club should be relieved of responsibility for it.

6. *New York Times*, 24.6.97.

7. Evocatively described by Robert Massie in the introduction to *Dreadnought: Britain, Germany and the Coming of the Great War.*

8. *The Times*, 26.6.97.

9. *The Times*, 25.6.97.

10. Fisher, *Memories*, p.110.

11. 28.6.97.

12. Antony Preston, introduction to *The Influence of Sea Power upon History, 1660–1805* (illustrated, 1980), p.9. Mahanism still held sufficient thrall over historical perceptions, in the 1960s, to channel Professor Marder's interpretation of Edwardian naval politics into an almost exclusively 'battlefleet' framework.

13. Reginald Pound, *Scott of the Antarctic*, pp.23–4.

14. Signals Committee Files, Vol.16, ADM116/67. There appears to have been, in the 1890s, a standing signals committee which acted as a mail-box for suggestions and amendments, but which was upgraded in 1896 to produce a new revision of the *Signal Book*. Initially, Lt Allan Everett acted as 'revision' secretary, until superseded by Cdr Evan-Thomas.

15. Signals Committee Files, Vol.13, ADM116/65.

16. Sir Arthur Hezlet, *The Electron and Sea Power*, pp.29 & 31.

17. Report of 10.4.98 by Commander Evan-Thomas, ADM116/523. Lt Phipps

Hornby submitted a separate report to the CO of *Vernon*. Jackson's early experiments had been carried out while he was CO of the Plymouth torpedo school. Why were torpedomen so concerned with wireless? Electricity is most of the answer, but, also, W/T was perceived as an invisible means of controlling torpedo-boats at night (see A. J. L. Blond, 'Technology and Tradition: Wireless Telegraphy and the Royal Navy, 1895–1920', University of Lancaster PhD thesis, 1993).

18. Queen Victoria's Journal, 28.1.98 & 25.8.00. The Queen was probably confusing Louise, who had married the Duke of Fife in 1889, with Maud.

19. WR(S) 240.

20. Leslie Gardiner, *The British Admiralty*, p.39.

21. Geoffrey Bennett, *Charlie B*, pp.256–7.

22. Beresford to Evan-Thomas, 15.1.00, Llwynmadoc papers.

23. Shane Leslie, *The Film of Memory*, pp.79, 80.

24. *Naval and Military Record*, quoted by Arthur Marder (*From the Dreadnought to Scapa Flow*, Vol.I, p.110).

25. Lord Hankey, *The Supreme Command*, I, p.20.

26. *The Oxford Companion to Ships and the Sea*, p.79.

27. *Sea Saga*, p.313.

28. *Oxford Companion*, p.261.

29. Bennett, p.260. In fact both Fisher and Wilson had manoeuvred their fleets without lights at night.

30. Beresford to Evan-Thomas, undated, Llwynmadoc papers. Evan-Thomas probably learnt this practice during his time under Sir Anthony Hoskins.

31. His NO, Cdr Henry Oliver, quoted by Bennett, p.257.

32. It would be interesting to know more of this incident: presumably some of his captains disobeyed to avoid grounding their ships.

33. Beresford to Evan-Thomas, 23.12.04, Llwynmadoc papers.

34. 6.3.05, Llwynmadoc papers.

35. Llwynmadoc papers.

36. Knollys to Beresford, 4.2.05, *ibid.*

37. Gardiner, *The British Admiralty*, p.287.

38. The table could have been expanded to include certain other factors – membership of the Royal Yacht Squadron, Brethrenship of Trinity House, for example – which would share a degree of commonality with some of the items chosen here. On the other hand, the 'So What?' factor would have loomed progressively larger.

39. See Rear-Admiral E. N. Poland's *The Torpedomen*. *Vernon*'s unofficial motto is said to have been *Swing it till Monday*.

40. My thanks to Eric Grove, who edited the above.

41. Clements Markham gave a paper on Arctic exploration, at a RUSI meeting presided over by Philip Colomb, in 1895. The link with the RN was naturally emphasized.

42. R. F. Scott's diary comment on the South Pole.

43. T. H. Baughman, *Before the Heroes Came*, p.114 (extract truncated).

44. My thanks to Miss Jayne Dunlop, of the RGS library.

45. "The emblem of prudence is the first and most exalted object that demands our attention in the lodge. It is placed in the centre, ever to be present in the eye of the Mason, that his heart may be attentive to her dictates, and steadfast in her laws; for prudence is the rule of all virtues; prudence is the path which leads to every degree

of propriety; prudence is that channel whence self-approbation flows for ever . . ."
etc., etc. (Robert Macoy, *A Dictionary of Freemasonry*, p.631). Is this suitable stuff for
our naval warriors?

46. Particularly from Mrs Jowett and Mr Ashby, and, through them, the Board of
General Purposes.

47. "It should always be remembered that the list of naval Arctic explorers is
headed by the name of Horatio Nelson," Colomb told the RUSI (*Journal*, 1895,
p.592). It's (just) possible he was being humorous.

48. Stephen Knight, *The Brotherhood*, p.23.

49. Journal of PO Louis Henry Parsons (BRNC Dartmouth).

50. Edward continued to attend masonic functions in regalia after becoming King.

51. Among Navy-related names in the nineteenth-century Royal Alpha Lodge may
be found: Hedworth Lambton, Tennyson D'Eyncourt and Studholme Brownrigg
(Shadwell Clerke, *History of the Royal Alpha Lodge No. 16*).

52. Robert Macoy, *A Dictionary of Freemasonry* (published in the late nineteenth
century), p.458.

53. Rudyard Kipling, *The Waster*.

54. "Your obedience must be proved by a close conformity to our laws and practices, and by perfect submission to the Master and his Wardens." Macoy, p.677.

55. "In every order the spirit of regularity should reign and more especially in the
order of Freemasonry." *Ibid.*, p.607.

56. "A habit of debate prevalent amongst the brethren is an evil which carries ruin
in its train; divisions disunite the brethren and mutual distrust is the mildest consequence to be expected." *Ibid.*, p.490.

57. "To be obedient is one of the great duties of a Freemason." *Ibid.*, p.601.

58. "Masonry is an art founded on the principles of geometry. Freemasons ought to
make themselves intimately acquainted with geometry." *Ibid.*, pp.518, 520.

59. Norman Dixon, *Psychology of Military Incompetence*, see pp.183, 193.

60. Some, like Beresford (who gives a farcical account of his initiation – *Memoirs of
Admiral Lord Charles Beresford*, p.108), may join in spite of it.

61. It is necessary to specify the number because there were half a dozen other
'Phoenix' Lodges on record, and lodges are indexed by number.

62. Colomb appears not to have been initiated until 1867, when he joined the
Pentangle Lodge (No. 1174) in Chatham.

63. Information from *Representative British Freemasons* (1915).

64. Beresford immodestly sponsored the Lord Charles Beresford Lodge (No. 2404)
in Chatham, *in absentia*, in 1891. It comprised marine 'other ranks', stokers, artificers,
etc., and hints at the spell of *noblesse oblige* which he cast around him. He joined it
himself in 1893, after coming home from Tryon's Mediterranean to command the
Chatham Steam Reserve.

65. Remarked upon at least by Richard Hough in *Admirals in Collision* (p.23).

66. From 3rd degree ritual (Martin Short, *Inside the Brotherhood*, pp.177–8).

67. Rickard at the least had close family links with Freemasonry.

68. William Acland's physician father had been a colleague, in royal service, of the
surgeon Sir William Gull (over whom a shadow has been cast by Jack the Ripper theories), and his brother had both written Gull's biography and married his daughter.

As a matter of record, the only 'brother' among *Victoria*'s dead mentioned by
name in *The Freemason* (and so presumably the most senior in masonic rank) was a

Warrant Officer Samuel Leonard, Past District Grand Registrar of the Malta Grand Lodge.

69. Stephen Knight, *The Brotherhood*, p.98. In the same context one might wryly allude to Alexander McKee's law: academics are so afraid of ridicule by rival scholars that "if two possible theories present themselves the one only moderately boring, the other infinitely dreary, then it is the latter, invariably, which they will favour, because this establishes them as serious scholars in the eyes of other scholars"! *Verb. sap.*

70. I have not sought access to the records of these lodges (Nos. 197, 303, 338, 357, 358, 720, 1159, 1165, 1174, 1205, 1428, 1615, 1616, 1724, 1924, 2076, 2418, 2424 and 2465) in search of other naval officers.

71. The future King George VI and his son-in-law Prince Philip were initiated into the Navy Lodge in 1919 and 1952 respectively.

72. *Freemasonry – The Greatest Bluff of the Age*, pp.18–19.

73. Stephen Knight, *The Brotherhood*, p.3.

74. Kipling, *The Mother Lodge*.

75. Tryon's son became a mason, which suggests that there was no family hostility to Freemasonry.

76. Barry Domvile, *From Admiral to Cabin Boy* (1943), p.157.

77. However statesmanlike, there is an impossible horse-and-cart sophistry about labelling everything as a 'symptom', for one can end up bereft of 'causes' – unless it is acknowledged that a pool of vaunted 'symptoms' can collectively amount to a 'cause'.

78. Professor Wayne Kostenbaum of Yale thinks that an obsession with lists may be a symptom of latent homosexuality. No doubt work remains to be done in this field.

79. It has been mentioned that Edward Hobart Seymour was on the council of the RGS. To this it may be added that he had applied for command of *Discovery* in the '75 Nares–Markham Arctic expedition, but, owing to a wound, was turned down as medically unfit (Henry Stephenson got the job).

80. The diary of PO Parsons conveys the sense that, as C-in-C Channel, Culme-Seymour made few, if any, concessions to fleet masonic social events, in contrast to the practice on the North American Station.

81. My thanks to the Grand Secretary of the Grand Lodge of New Zealand.

82. For example, Commander Henry J. S. Brownrigg was to become Grand Sword-Bearer in 1938 (when he was a vice-admiral), and was the first naval officer to be so appointed.

Chapter 17: *Ordo ab Chao*

1. Geoffrey Lowis, *Fabulous Admirals*, p.95.
2. Redmond McLaughlin, *The Escape of the Goeben*, p.27.
3. *Fisher's Face*, pp.40–1.
4. 11.1.82, PHI/120C.
5. 12.12.81, PHI/120C.
6. Filson Young, *With the Battle-Cruisers*, p.2.
7. 26.11.86, PHI/120B.
8. Richard Ollard, *Fisher and Cunningham*, p.39.
9. Young, p.2.

10. 15.4.91, PHI/120C.

11. Leslie Gardiner, *The British Admiralty*, p.305.

12. Ollard, p.27.

13. Young, p.14.

14. Norman Dixon, *On the Psychology of Military Incompetence*, p.268.

15. See Fisher's *Memories*, p.124.

16. Letter of 22.2.05, quoted by Arthur Marder, *Fear God and Dread Nought*, p.51.

17. Lord Hankey, *The Supreme Command*, p.14.

18. *Dictionary of National Biography* (Vincent Baddeley).

19. (Reginald Bacon, *Naval Scrap Book*, p.240.) In his biography of Fisher, Bacon actually states that, in Noel's view, evolutions "were merely to be regarded as tactical gymnastical exercises for practising officers in the handling of their ships" (Vol.I, p.128). This, of course, is pure Tryon.

20. See 'C-in-C China, Sir G. H. U. Noel, Criticism of Board Orders', June 1905, ADM1/7811. An attractive light is shed on this famous old curmudgeon, as C-in-C China, in his 'specially recommending for promotion' Cdr Philip Colomb (Jnr) in 1905 (Colomb's Service Record, ADM196/42).

21. CUR/22.

22. 'Remarks on Tactical Exercises, 1901–1902', FISR 8/2 F.P.4703. (My thanks to Jon Sumida.)

23. Marder, *Fear God*, Vol.I, p.250.

24. A phrase he used when declining to involve himself in another controversy; quoted by Ruddock Mackay, *Lord Fisher of Kilverstone*, p.194.

25. William Goodenough, *Rough Record*, p.58.

26. Fisher to LCB, 30.11.04, SELB 42/f/35. (My thanks to Nicholas Lambert.)

27. George King-Hall diary entry for 3.3.05, *Sea Saga*, p.326. The stormy interview must have taken place in the third week of December 1904.

28. Admiral Sir William Henderson in the *Naval Review* (1930), quoted in Mackay, p.227.

29. We can discern that he agreed, from his quotation of Mahan in one of his Mediterranean lectures in 1900/2: "Those who rise in peace are men of formality and routine, cautious, inoffensive, safe up to the limits of their capacity, supremely conscientious, punctilious about everything but what is essential! Yet void altogether of initiative, impulse and originality." (Extracts from confidential papers, 'Mediterranean Fleet, 1899–1902', FISR 8/1 (CCC).)

30. Young, p.3.

31. Humphrey Hugh Smith, *A Yellow Admiral Remembers*, p.149.

32. *Ibid.*, p.148.

33. Bacon, *Scrap Book*, p.241ff.

34. Hankey quoted in Mackay, p.225.

35. George King-Hall in *Sea Saga*, p.322.

36. Percy Scott, *Fifty Years in the Royal Navy*, p.74 (underlining added). As mentioned, Scott had not served under Tryon, but his 'Tryonic' concerns about tactical signalling are evident in correspondence, *c.* 1898, with Assheton Curzon-Howe (CUR 10/b). (My thanks to John Ferris.)

37. The most authoritative analysis of this is in Chapter 2 of Jon Tetsuro Sumida's *In Defence of Naval Supremacy*. Since publication of that seminal book in 1989 further confirmatory work has been done by Sumida and by Nicholas Lambert.

38. A pocket-guide to the differences between Arthur Marder *et al.*, and the revisionists can be found in Jon Sumida's review of Robert Massie's *Dreadnought*, in (USNI) *Proceedings*, December 1992, pp.113–15.

39. Sir Barnett Cocks, *New Scientist*, 1973.

40. Sumida, p.34.

41. *Ibid.*, p.59ff.

42. Fisher's intention that all eight units of the 1909 programme be battlecruisers was defeated by (among others) Francis Bridgeman. Ample signposts to Fisher's preferred agenda can be found in Marder's *Fear God and Dread Nought*, Vol.II (see for example Fisher's letter to Arnold White on pp.188–9).

43. As Marder has pointed out, Fisher's famous suggestion that Britain should "Copenhagen the German fleet *à la* Nelson" confused James Gambier's surprise attack in 1807 with Nelson's slogging-match in 1801.

44. Marder, *Portrait of an Admiral*, p.49. Richmond's verdict on Fisher's acquaintance with history was blunt: "ignorance could go no further" (p.52).

45. Extracts from confidential papers, 'Mediterranean Fleet, 1899–1902'.

46. (Source untraced at time of publication.)

47. *Memories*, p.149.

48. *Ibid.*, p.42.

49. It was Stanley Bonnett, in *Price of Admiralty* (p.183), but it could have been any of several.

50. W. S. Chalmers, *Life and Letters of David Beatty*, p.85.

51. Lord Chatfield, *The Navy and Defence*, p.xi.

52. The question of a naval staff had been exercising thinking officers – such as Phipps Hornby – at least since the 1870s (see Nicholas Rodger, *The Admiralty*, p.113). It is virtually *de rigueur* for historians of the Edwardian Navy to labour the lack of such an item, as if it was an obvious-to-any-fool panacea to all ills; one sometimes wonders if they know clearly what they mean. Most of the military fiascos of this century have been supervised by higher organizations luxuriant in 'staff'; and strategy by committee can be as disastrous as by maniac and is never as brilliant as by (rare) genius.

The mere act of setting up a staff-system is liable to confuse and disrupt lines of accountability, and is a far cry from conjuring up a senior officer corps trained and disposed to make use of it. But leaving that aside, what might a naval staff have been expected to do?

It could, *in theory*, have thought principles, evolved doctrine, explored ramifications, spotted pitfalls, assimilated intelligence, and done much planning spadework. This is wildly ambitious for (say) 1910; but then, on the other hand, this historian's flexible friend can do whatever you like.

53. Correlli Barnett, *The Sword Bearers*, p.123.

54. Fisher's own words quoted by Ollard, p.21.

55. Mackay, p.122.

56. Goodenough, p.26.

57. Bacon, *A Naval Scrap Book*, pp.163–4.

58. See Sumida, *In Defence of Naval Supremacy*; Anthony Pollen, *The Great Gunnery Scandal*.

59. Young, pp.9–10 (sequence changed but sense unaltered).

60. Chatfield, p.149.

61. *New Zealand Herald*, 1.7.93.

62. Chatfield, p.x.

63. Admiral Sir William James, letter to Arthur Marder, quoted in *From the Dreadnought to Scapa Flow*, Vol.II, p.441.

64. *Types of Naval Officers*, p.447.

65. *Memories*, p.45.

66. Richard Hough, *Admirals in Collision*, p.171.

67. I say 'non-visual' rather than 'non-flags', because it can (almost) be done by switching off searchlights in near-instantaneous relay down a line of ships, although this has to be set up in advance. As a matter of interest, a conference held in *Vernon* in 1907, on the use of W/T, found that communication between ships should continue to be by visual means (ADM11/1061).

68. Why this was the case, when the RAF adopted it for ground-to-air control in 1918, has not been adequately explained.

69. Percy Scott, p.208. Jellicoe, in *The Grand Fleet, 1914–1916*, claims that whereas "At the beginning of the war ten minutes to a quarter of an hour would elapse before I could be sure that all ships had received a manoeuvring signal addressed to the whole battlefleet", owing to his training programme "in 1916 the time rarely exceeded two to three minutes [and] I could handle the Battle Fleet by wireless with as much ease and rapidity as by visual signals" (p.59). This must be taken with a very large pinch of salt, for it reflects performance attainable in the laboratory conditions ("incessant practice in harbour") in which he drilled his fleet, rather than in those arising in the midst of battle.

We know from 'Jutland' anecdotal evidence that the din in W/T headphones, from the transmissions of two huge nearby fleets, was such that many signals were hopelessly drowned out, and that stressed-out operators had to be relieved every ten minutes (this, quite apart from certain key ships having their W/T disabled by action-damage). And indeed, later on in *Grand Fleet*, when dealing with Jutland, Jellicoe confusingly admits that "a varying but considerable time is bound to elapse" between a wireless signal's being authorized and its receipt on the bridges of addressees, and that "the interval is greater with wireless than with visual signals" (p.318).

70. Penrose Fitzgerald, *From Sail to Steam*, p.181.

71. Scott, p.199.

72. Memo of 17.5.10, in 'Report of Home Fleet Exercises' (ADM1/8120).

73. See for example 'Notes on Tactical Exercises, 1909–11' (NLMoD Eb.012). (My thanks to Jon Sumida.) Marder exaggerates May's commitment to divisional tactics, and loses credibility in declaring his reforms to have been discontinued by his successor, Sir Francis Bridgeman (*Dreadnought*, Vol.I, pp.396, 399). Bridgeman, for all his faults, *preceded* May; and it appears to have been May himself who discontinued his divisional experiments.

74. Report of 16.12.05, ADM1/7811.

75. MERcury collection. (My thanks to Alan Giddings of NMM Manuscripts, for his help.)

76. 16.4.08, ADM116/1068.

77. Service record, ADM196/43.

78. Barry Kent, *Signal!*, p.245 marginalia.

79. Sydney Fremantle, *My Naval Career*, p.64.

80. Memo from HMS *Edgar*, 11.11.07, ADM1/7987. (My thanks to John Ferris.)

81. Files of Signals Committee, ADM186/661. The original of Hunter's proposed signal book is in ADM116/1069.

82. This remarkable statistic represents R. F. Scott's term, which was two years later than Hunter's. These were the cadets who benefited most from the expansion of the Navy during their middle careers.

83. Service record, ADM196/42.

84. Richmond to Vice-Admiral Thomas Drew, 27.9.44 (Australian War Memorial collection 124, 4/12). (My thanks to John Ferris.)

85. Sumida, p.175.

86. 13.3.08, ADM186/661. As his letter was sequentially dysfunctional, the extracts quoted here have been rearranged.

87. Sumida, p.137.

88. 29.04.08, ADM116/1068.

89. As happened in the case of Pollen (Sumida, pp.168–9).

90. 28.12.08, ADM116/1068. (The hand of Sir Reginald Custance, his Channel second-in-command, may be discernible in this lofty reply.)

91. ADM11/1068. Curzon-Howe was amplifying the findings of a committee which was chaired by Rear-Admiral George Callaghan and included Capt. William Pakenham.

92. ADM1/8274.

93. Jellicoe's report after the 1913 Manoeuvres ('Miscellaneous Papers', ADM116/3381).

94. All the main naval bases had pigeon lofts, and under the Royal Naval Pigeon Reserve 1,000-odd members of the Pigeon Association had undertaken to place (an average of) 10 birds each at the disposal of the Admiralty in war-time (ADM1/7992).

95. In the Seniority List, not the Ship List.

96. Stephen King-Hall was referring to his violin teacher (*Sea Saga*, p.440) but it suffices – and, indeed, could be applied to certain technical 'experts' among naval historians.

97. The issue appears to have been raised in 1903, 1906 and 1912. See Barry Kent, *Signal!*, pp.30ff.; A. J. L. Blond, 'Technology and Tradition: Wireless Telegraphy and the Royal Navy, 1895–1920' (University of Lancaster PhD thesis, 1993), pp.144ff. In clinging to their not very rational independence, the wirelessmen were doing their own defensive barricading: they feared that, if they were absorbed into the signalling branch, the best W/T men would tend to be filched for work on the bridge (a wedge whose thin end was allowed, anyway, by Admiralty order in July 1910). In small ships this is sometimes still an issue.

98. Paraphrased from Fisher paper (FP 4754), 3/06, quoted Mackay, p.427.

99. My apologies to Captain Barrie Kent, author of *Signal!* (and to whom I am indebted).

100. Sydney Fremantle, *My Naval Career.*

101. Drury (an FRGS) had submitted written 'expert' evidence in support of Markham at the *Victoria* trial.

102. Curzon-Howe (FRGS) was a royal favourite from a courtier dynasty. (As a collector's item, he "shared with King Edward VII and Lord Charles Beresford the

idiosyncrasy of always having his trousers creased down the side instead of down the front": Lionel Dawson, *Gone for a Sailor*, p.158.)

103. Poë attended Prince Arthur, Duke of Connaught on a Court mission to Japan in 1912. The Poë and Domvile families were related by marriage.

104. Bertram Chambers, *Salt Junk*, p.284.

105. Goodenough, p.51.

106. Chambers, p.314.

107. Letter to wife, 3.10.02, BTY/17/10/11–15.

108. Quoted by Geoffrey Bennett, in *Charlie B*, pp.257–8.

109. Goodenough, p.51.

110. Chalmers, p.86.

111. *Ibid.*

112. My thanks to Nicholas Lambert.

113. His handwriting distinctly worsened, and contemporary references implicitly acknowledge that a change had taken place: even a midshipman formed the view that "by the year 1907 (which was when I became an insignificant officer in his flagship) the peak of his curve of service had then passed" (Dawson, p.130).

114. Stephen Roskill, *Earl Beatty*, p.41.

115. Dawson, p.135.

116. *Ibid.*, pp.131, 133.

117. Moore had applied to retire in July 1908: "He gives no reason, but I fear it is the very strong feeling that he has against the Navy having anything to do with the press . . . The Service can ill afford to lose men of the stamp of Sir Arthur" (Evan-Thomas to Knollys, 7.8.08, RA W59/48).

118. 11.5.08, in file 'Responsibility of Board of Admiralty for naval war direction', ADM1/7992.

119. Scott, p.211.

120. Beresford to Milne, 22.4.09, MLN.

121. Beresford to Culme-Seymour, 23.4.09, Rockingham: WR(S).

122. As evidenced by a letter he wrote to *The Times* on 7.7.14: "a submarine . . . must frequently come into harbour to replenish its electric batteries" (quoted Scott, p.278).

123. Roskill, *Earl Beatty*, pp.53–4. Concurrently Beatty's boss was clashing viciously with Beresford in the House of Commons – which no doubt outweighed the fact that Winston's widowed aunt-by-marriage had remarried to Lord Charles's brother.

124. Opinion expressed by Sir Edmund Poë to Sir George King-Hall (*Sea Saga*, p.328).

125. Mackay, p.132.

126. *Daily Graphic*, 28.2.12.

127. *Daily Chronicle*, 9.7.06.

128. E. N. Poland, *The Torpedomen*, p.34.

129. Ollard, p.38.

130. Balfour's private secretary to Balfour, reporting conversation with Bridgeman, 7.3.10 (Add. MSS 49766 – cited by Nicholas Lambert in chapter on Bridgeman in *The First Sea Lords* (M. Murfitt ed., Praeger, 1995)).

131. Letter from Peter Kemp to Richard Hough, quoted in Hough's *The Great War at Sea*, p.84.

132. CID 114th, 23.8.11, CAB 2/2 (worth reading!).

133. Roskill, p.52.
134. Bonnett, p.194.

Chapter 18: *An Example to our Countrymen*

1. 12.2.06 (last word may be wrong). Evan-Thomas papers.
2. 8.6.07, letter 135/Box A, Tweedmouth Papers.
3. Fisher to Lord Esher, 12.7.08, quoted in Arthur Marder, *Fear God and Dread Nought*, Vol.II, p.183.
4. Evan-Thomas to Fisher, 15.7.08, FISR 1/6 320 (also quoted in Marder, as above).
5. Evan-Thomas to Lord Knollys, 27.7.08, RA W59/39.
6. 'Director Firing Gear . . . Report of trials in *Bellerophon*', ADM1/8145.
7. See Dennis Friedman, *Inheritance*, p.79.
8. *Ibid.*, p.77.
9. Post-Jutland biography in unknown newspaper (Llwynmadoc papers).
10. Sir Geoffrey Barnard, notes on Evan-Thomas, ROSK 3/3 and Add. MSS 52506.
11. 17.2.11.
12. 30.3.11.
13. John Wheeler-Bennett, *King George VI*, pp.54–6.
14. George V, 29.2.12.
15. 17.7.12, Llwynmadoc papers.
16. Evan-Thomas's papers include several invitations from the Battenbergs to dine, to shoot, to stay.
17. Reginald Pound, *Scott of the Antarctic*, p.160.
18. Marder, *Fear God*, Vol.II, pp.451–2.
19. Quoted by Arthur Marder in *Portrait of an Admiral*, p.50.
20. Gilbert Adshead (IWM Sound).
21. Chivalry conveniently type-cast the enemy as dragon-like, fit only for slaying; but very occasionally he too was awarded laurels, as in the case of Captain Karl von Müller, of the German cruiser *Emden* (paper by Philip Cordier, Annapolis 12th Naval History Symposium, 1995).
22. Mark Girouard, *Return to Camelot*, p.281.
23. Paul Webb, *A Buchan Companion*, p.xix.
24. Pound, p.18; see also Ian Cameron, *To the Ends of the Earth* (a history of the RGS, 1830–1980).
25. Francis Spufford, review of Baughman's *Before the Heroes Came*, in the *Guardian* of 1.2.94.
26. Among Scott's other backers were Admiral Sir Anthony Hoskins, Admiral Lord Walter Kerr, and Captain George Egerton.
27. Pound, p.27.
28. Quoted Pound, p.77.
29. Scott on 9.4.01, into the Drury Lane Lodge (No. 2127); Shackleton on 9.7.01, into the Navy Lodge. Scott's interest in the Craft was to continue on his return, while Shackleton's (like his rapport with the RGS) distinctly waned – although masonic honours were showered upon him after he was knighted.

As a further curiosity, it may be noted that in 1902 Scott christened a mountain at 83°S 'Mount Markham' (sometimes given as Mount Clements M., sometimes as

Mount Albert M.) – in near-perfect latitudinal symmetry with the 'Markham Inlet', named by Nares in 1875, at $82\frac{1}{2}°$N.

30. Girouard, p.14. As a matter of interest, in 1913 a bronze statue of Captain Smith was commissioned from sculptress Lady Scott – R.F.'s widow – and Beresford gave a stirring speech at its unveiling (Gary Cooper, *The Man who Sank the Titanic?*, pp.144–9).

31. Capt. William Boyle, on 'Individual Preparation for War', pp.77–8 (original pagination).

32. Girouard (quoting Sir Walter Scott), p.33.

33. Norman Dixon, *On the Psychology of Military Incompetence*, p.380 (tense altered), see also p.246.

34. Beresford declared that *Dreadnought* "indicates a decadent tendency to rely on powerful material rather than on skill and grasp of the art of war" (file on Beresford–Fisher feud in ADM1/7992; Fisher detected Custance behind this statement). While this sort of lofty remark lies close to the debate about the lack of a naval staff, it steps over the line between comment and cant. Firstly, it supposes that material excellence and martial skill are mutually exclusive; and, secondly, it implies that the speaker possesses the skill and insight whose non-application is so lamented.

35. Peter Kemp, *Oxford Companion to Ships and the Sea*. For Richmond, see Marder's *Portrait of an Admiral*.

36. Filson Young, *With the Battle-Cruisers*, pp.9–10.

37. *War Memoirs*, p.2041.

38. Daniel Baugh in James Goldrick & John Hattendorf (eds.), *Mahan is Not Enough*, p.17.

39. See Anthony Storr's psychological profile in *Churchill Revised*, pp.268–9.

40. As noted by Ernest Rodway, *Churchill: Your Questions Answered*, pp.25–6.

41. Fisher, in his conspiratorial (almost clandestine) meetings with Churchill in *Enchantress*, seems not to have noticed Beatty.

42. As he told his relief, Dudley de Chair (quoted in Roskill, p.58).

43. Lord Chatfield, *The Navy and Defence*.

44. Sydney Fremantle, *My Naval Career*, p.163.

45. 15.4.13, DRAX 4/1.

46. 18.2.15, DRAX 1/3.

47. BCF 017 of 18.2.15 contains what is almost a direct crib from Tryon's TA memorandum of November 1891: "In special cases where ships are required to turn together as quickly as possible, Blue Pendant will be hoisted singly at the yard-arm towards which the turn is to be made." (DRAX 1/3.)

48. Beatty to Jellicoe, 8.2.15, *Jellicoe Papers*, Vol.I, p.144.

49. Beatty to Lady B., 26.11.14, *Beatty Papers*, Vol.I, p.168.

50. William Goodenough, p.91.

51. Lewis Bayly, *Pull Together*, p.131.

52. *Beatty Papers*, Vol.I, p.58.

53. Roskill, p.60.

54. Mary Soames, *Clementine Churchill*, p.48.

55. Service Record, ADM196/50, Part I, p.26.

Chapter 19: *Commence Hostilities Against Germany*

1. Jellicoe was not apprised of his destiny, merely believing that he would be appointed second-in-command.

2. Diary of Sir Rowland Jerram (NMM).

3. Lord Chatfield, *The Navy and Defence*, p.120.

4. Jerram Diary. As a matter of irrelevance, this day saw the first successful aerial torpedo drop, by Lt-Cdr (later Air Chief Marshal Sir) Arthur Longmore in a Short 81 seaplane (A. B. Sainsbury, *The Royal Navy Day by Day*).

5. So considered, at least by the chief umpire, Admiral of the Fleet Sir William May, and by Rear-Admiral Beatty (from evidence in May's report in 'Miscellaneous Papers . . .', ADM116/3381).

6. *The Sword Bearers*, p.126.

7. 'Remarks on Tactical Exercises, 1901–1902', FISR 8.2.4703.

8. My choice for C-in-C Grand Fleet? Sir Stanley Colville, after leaving Callaghan to serve his full term. Why? 1) Colville had commanded the 1st BS in the Home Fleet from 1912–14; 2) Like Beatty, he was well accustomed to working with Callaghan's less formal standing orders (and had, incidentally, been a friend and career-sponsor of young Beatty in the 1890s); 3) He was senior to Jellicoe and slightly younger. In my view he was well positioned to succeed Callaghan in wartime, and his appointment ashore as C-in-C Orkneys (1914–16) was a waste.

9. Privately printed, *Diary and Letters of Alexander Scrimgeour RN*, p.6.

10. Stanley Bonnett, *The Price of Admiralty*, pp.191–2.

11. Girouard, *Return to Camelot*, p.269. James Goldrick points to an apparent watershed at around the rank of captain and remarks that, in this respect, the war came ten years too soon (*The King's Ships were at Sea*, p.30). If he has in mind men like Tyrwhitt, Chatfield, W. W. Fisher, Stirling, Richmond, and the two Kellys, one can only agree.

12. Fisher to Jellicoe, 18.11.14, *Jellicoe Papers*, Vol.I, p.100.

13. Redmond McLaughlin, *The Escape of the Goeben*, p.99.

14. Strictly speaking, the term *armoured-cruiser* was incorrect usage after January 1913. Then, the plethora of 'cruiser' categories and sub-categories was rationalized into just three: Battlecruisers, Cruisers and Light-Cruisers (ADM1/8327). Although incorrect, I use *armoured-cruiser* because of the generic imprecision of *cruiser*.

15. Quoted by James Goldrick, *The King's Ships were at Sea*, p.134. Goldrick's Chapter 6 provides the best account of what was known as the 'Broad Fourteens' disaster.

16. Bertram Chambers, *Salt Junk*, p.283.

17. *Political Diaries of C. P. Scott*, p.111.

18. Marder, *Fear God and Dread Nought*, Vol.II, p.113.

19. *Ibid.*, p.110.

20. These and many other homely cautions are to be found in *Whispers from the Fleet*.

21. Girouard, pp.281, 289.

22. Geoffrey Bennett, *Naval Battles of the First World War*, p.80.

23. Bonnett, *Price of Admiralty*, p.143. In addition to his *Order Book* (for which he acknowledged help from Captains George Warrender and Edward Inglefield) Arbuthnot published *Details and Station Bill for a Battleship* in 1901. Together they are a rich source of routine trivia about daily life in the turn-of-the-century Fleet, although the *Order Book* mostly refers to things which would have been done anyway, because it was someone's departmental job to do them. He was so joshed about this tome that he prevailed upon the compilers of *Who's Who in the Navy* (a one-off, in 1913) to suppress the fact of his authorship.

24. See Geoffrey Lowis, *Fabulous Admirals*, pp.139, 125.

25. Bonnett, p.144. This 'blistered feet' story has also been connected with Cecil Burney.

26. Arthur William Ford (IWM Sound, 000719).

27. See Jellicoe's *The Grand Fleet, its Creation and Work*; Sir Julian Corbett's *Naval Operations*, Vol.I; James Goldrick's *The King's Ships were at Sea*; Paul Halpern's *A Naval History of World War I*.

28. Sydney Fremantle, *My Naval Life*, p.171.

29. V. E. Tarrant, *Jutland, The German Perspective*, pp.20–1.

30. Churchill to Beatty, 22.11.14, BTY/3/2/2.

31. Captain William Outerson USN (Rtd), 'Peacetime Admirals, Wartime Admirals', USNI *Proceedings*, April 1981.

32. Sir Geoffrey Phipps Hornby and Arthur Moore were guests at German Army Manoeuvres in 1890 and, to their amusement, "saw for the first time the famous goose-step" (Marjorie Moore, *Adventures in the Royal Navy*, p.77).

33. See Holger Herwig, *The German Naval Officer Corps*.

34. Marder, *Fear God*, Vol.II, p.19.

35. Penrose Fitzgerald, *From Sail to Steam*, p.181.

36. Peter Kemp, *Oxford Companion to Ships and the Sea*.

37. Richmond letter to Admiral Drew, 27.9.44 (Australian War Memorial collection 124, 4/12). (My thanks to John Ferris.)

38. ADM186/17.

39. *Taktische Befehle der Hochseeflotte* (1914), ADM137/4326.

40. Richard Hough, *Dreadnought*, p.155.

41. Kemp, *op. cit.*

42. GFBOs, Section VI; ADM186/595.

43. DRAX 1/9.

44. Roskill, *Earl Beatty*, p.81.

45. Viscount Jellicoe, *The Grand Fleet, 1914–1916*, p.49.

46. Roskill, *Earl Beatty*, p.81.

47. Marder, *Dreadnought*, Vol.III, p.221, quoting Edward Althem's *Jellicoe*, p.116.

48. Letter of 17.2.07, quoted in Marder, *Fear God*, Vol.II, p.117n.

49. Nicholas Lambert, 'British Naval Policy, 1913–14: Financial Limitation and Strategic Revolution', *Journal of Modern History*, Vol.67, No.3, September 1995, pp.595–626.

50. Lord Sydenham who had known Tryon personally, and been secretary to the CID in 1904–7, considered that "if at the Admiralty before August 1914, there had been anyone possessed of his clear insight and grip on the larger naval problems, much would have happened differently" (*My Working Life*, p.120).

51. *Whispers from the Fleet*, p.viii.

52. McKenna to Jellicoe, 31.10.11, *Jellicoe Papers*, Vol.I, p.22.

53. Churchill, *World Crisis*, Vol.I, p.93. Winston had probably read Captain William Boyle's words in the *Naval Review* in 1913: "The fact that we know how to handle our ship and manipulate her armament does not indicate that we are ready to play our part in war" ('Individual Preparation for War', p.78).

54. Diary quoted by Marder, *Portrait of an Admiral*, pp.315 & 23.

Chapter 20: *Utmost Speed*

1. Fawcett & Hooper, *The Fighting at Jutland*, p.115.

2. 'Conduct of a Fleet in Action', GFBOs: "in any formation other than line ahead, course cannot be altered without signal".

3. Evan-Thomas papers, Add.MSS 52504 (the "increased" is not supportable).

4. *Valiant's* ROP, *Official Despatches.*

5. N. J. M. Campbell, *Jutland*, p.102.

6. (*Princess Royal*) Fawcett & Hooper, p.22.

7. Evan-Thomas to Haggard, 14.8.23, ROSK 3/3.

8. In Vice-Admiral Barnard's notes for Arthur Marder, in ROSK 3/3.

9. Fawcett & Hooper, p.70.

10. Fawcett & Hooper, p.26.

11. Georg von Hase, *Kiel and Jutland*, pp.172–3, 174.

12. *Ibid.*

13. Fawcett & Hooper, pp.70–1.

14. IWM.

15. Add.MSS.

16. King-Hall in *Sea Saga*, from p.453.

17. Burrough (IWM) (also in *Sea Saga*).

18. Stephen King-Hall ('Etienne'), *A Naval Lieutenant 1914–1918*, p.131.

19. Fawcett & Hooper, p.71.

20. *Whispers from the Fleet*, p.17.

21. Von Hase, *Kiel and Jutland.*

22. Fawcett & Hooper, pp.40–1.

23. Victor Hayward, *HMS Tiger at Bay*, p.113.

24. The German Official History attributes *Barham's* first two hits at this juncture to *Kronprinz* and *Kaiserin*. Captain Craig, in his ROP, names *Derfflinger* as the culprit, and Campbell chooses to side with him. Perhaps they are right, but I would like explained why *Derfflinger* was ignoring Hipper's order of 4.57 to pair off with *Princess Royal*. It may also be mentioned that a BCF witness described the 1st SG, at this juncture, as "firing with much less regularity and precision than an hour earlier" (Fawcett & Hooper, p.21). Campbell's seemingly pro-Hipper agenda is the subject of Appendix IV.

25. Campbell, p.126.

26. Grand Fleet Secret Packs, Vol.66, ADM137/1946.

27. Richard Frampton (IWM).

28. Boy 1st Class Henry Hawkins (IWM).

29. Frampton.

30. Vice-Admiral Caslon (IWM).

31. *Ibid.*

32. Lt Eric Brind, Fawcett & Hooper, pp.115–16.

33. Campbell says the shell hit abreast A turret; Lt Brind, the OIC B turret, says B turret (Brind narrative in Lorimer (IWM)).

34. Fawcett & Hooper, pp.116–17.

35. Walwyn in Phillpotts (IWM). (Also, Fawcett & Hooper, p.138. The time divisions inserted in Walwyn's testimony in F & H are the editors' and not Walwyn's.)

36. Phillpotts papers (IWM). In the version in Fawcett & Hooper the word 'hell' has been replaced by 'deuce'. (Deuce is used a lot in F & H.)

37. Richard Fairthorne, interview, 1992.

38. In recommending Walwyn for promotion after the battle, Captain Phillpotts actually said that he "managed to be everywhere".

39. Phillpotts papers (IWM).

40. In Phillpotts (the list is not in the much-shortened version of Walwyn's account in Fawcett & Hooper). Some, but not all, of the difference may be accounted for by Walwyn's including, and Campbell's excluding, 5.9-inch hits. With shell-bursts perforating and buckling decks and bulkheads over wide and overlapping radii, perhaps compounding damage to already distorted structures, it is unlikely that either of them are accurate, by any definition.

After the battle Jellicoe received from Rosyth a report of damage sustained by the battlecruisers and *Warspite* at Jutland (dated 16.6.16, 'Grand Fleet Secret Pack No. 66', ADM137/1946). This states that the battleship "received five or six hits abaft Y turret (which blew out a huge part of the ship's side in Admiral's after cabin and office flat . . . made holes in armour, admitting water from Y turret to stern between main and middle decks)". Campbell elects to dismiss this (Campbell, p.178), allowing only one hit abaft Y turret between 4.45 and 6.15, and only two between 6.15 and 7.0 p.m. So, even by a dockyard assessment, he is two, or three, hits short – and this only in the aftermost 100 feet of the ship. Despite citing Walwyn in Fawcett & Hooper, he pays little heed to 'at the scene' testimony.

There is another problem with Campbell's list of 13 hits alleged to have been taken between 6.15 and 7.0 p.m.: while he must be right to aver that those received from *port* happened when *Warspite*'s helm jammed and she circled out of control, neither he nor anyone else who was not present can be sure that none of the five or six received from *starboard* occurred earlier.

41. In Walwyn's list of 31 hits, this is No. 1. Phillpotts (IWM).

42. This is borne out by 'Damage sustained by *Warspite*', report of 16.6.16, Grand Fleet Secret Packs, Vol.66 (ADM 137/1946): "In the vicinity of a large number of shell-bursts the lead casing and insulation had been completely melted off all electrical circuits, leaving only bare wire." The problem of finding an insulating material which can resist the heat conveyable by copper wire is an enduring one.

43. *Dreadnought*, Vol.III, p.48.

44. A zigzag of 2 points either side of base-course increases distance by only about $7\frac{1}{2}\%$.

45. Bonham Faunce, interview 30.5.91.

46. John Wheeler-Bennett, *King George VI*, p.93.

47. Fawcett & Hooper, p.191.

48. Roger Kirk Dickson, Acc.13509/13586 (NLS).

49. Ernest Fox, IWM Sound (and Arthur Sneesby, in Brown & Meehan, *Scapa Flow*, p.95).

50. Temple Patterson, *Tyrwhitt of the Harwich Force*, p.176.

51. *Ibid.*, p.163.

52. Sir Julian Corbett, *Naval Operations*, Vol.III p.349.

53. C. H. Petty, Shipwright, Scapa Flow (IWM).

54. *The Navy Eternal*, p.184.

55. Von Schoultz, *With the British Battlefleet*, p.118.

56. Even allowing for Goodenough's movements, which we can roughly plot but *Iron Duke* could not, his positions are at odds.

57. Marder's map (which drew from the 'pro-Beatty' *Admiralty Narrative*) and

Corbett's map (which drew from the 'pro-Jellicoe' *Harper Record*), plot Goodenough's position at 4.48 as, respectively, 11 and 9 miles from *QM*'s wreck, on a true bearing of 140°. This approximate consensus works.

58. The mismatch of plots has been blamed entirely on a mismatch of DRs: *Iron Duke*'s allegedly being four miles too far east, and *Lion*'s seven miles north-west. We know from the wreck of *Indefatigable* that Beatty's DR at around 4.0 p.m. was surprisingly accurate, and although Appendix II explains why major errors may be expected in the plotting of ships engaged with the enemy, more blame should be placed on Jellicoe's ignorance of Beatty's and Scheer's north-westerly course for about half an hour after about 5.10 p.m.

59. *The Truth about Jutland*, p.78.

60. *Dreadnought*, Vol.III, p.91.

61. Primary accounts have not made the meteorological distinction between mist and haze, the former comprising water droplets held in suspension, the latter, solid particles of dust or pollution. Later in the battle, smog (a combination of the two) is probably the appropriate word.

62. King-Hall, in Harold Burrough (IWM).

63. Mentioned in Jellicoe to Beatty, 4.6.16, *Beatty Papers*, Vol.I, p.319.

64. Lt A. E. D. C. Duthy, *Valiant* (IWM).

65. Plunkett Committee, Milford Haven papers, DS/Misc/9 (IWM).

66. V. E. Tarrant, *Jutland, The German Perspective*, p.109.

67. Sir John Woodward, *One Hundred Days*, p.282.

68. Fawcett & Hooper, p.94.

69. Campbell, p.132.

70. Lorimer (IWM).

71. Recommendations for decoration, Grand Fleet Secret Packs, Vol.66, ADM137/1946.

72. Lorimer.

73. H. J. W. Fisher (IWM).

74. Fawcett & Hooper, p.94–5.

75. Enclosure 'A' to Captain Boyle's ROP. Is this evidence that the ship was not discernibly rolling (for, otherwise, through dint of firing on the back-roll, they could have cancelled the gunnery handicap of a 4° list)?

76. By Caslon's testimony, these two very serious incidents – the gutting of the starboard battery, and the reduction of the ship's speed – occurred in the reverse of the order given here (and as specified by Campbell). It has to be said that in circumstantial ways this makes sense. First, the need for the 6-inch guns to come into action would have loomed larger after the ship lost speed; and second, Caslon would hardly have noticed the list-and-speed problem while he was busy trying to sort out the battery (though it is not clear that his narrative of the 'list-and-speed' hit was based on his own observation).

77. Fawcett & Hooper, p.117 (including the blanks).

78. G. M. Eady (IWM). Beatty was himself strongly superstitious. He regularly consulted fortune-tellers; and he would bow three times to the new moon, to the discomfiture of people around him on the bridge.

79. H. B. Sweetman, as reported in the *Yorkshire Post*, 31.5.66.

80. Fawcett & Hooper, p.103.

81. *Dreadnought*, Vol.III, p.97.

82. *Naval Operations*, Vol.III, p.355.

83. After the war, Captain Harper (Director of Navigation) calculated that the range at re-engagement must have been about 17,000 yards and said so in his post-war draft 'Record'. In consequence he and Beatty had "a first class row" and he was ordered to reduce the range to 14,000 yards, which he refused to do. Marder, despite drawing heavily from the Beatty-ite *Admiralty Narrative*, agrees with 17,000 yards. According to Campbell, *Princess Royal*, the only battlecruiser to score a hit during this short exchange, did so at 16,500 yards. Pelly's ROP says that at "4.50 [*Tiger*] recommenced firing at *Derfflinger*. Long range, 18,000 yards, and enemy very indistinct. Only two salvoes fired."

84. Von Hase, p.172.

85. *Chester*'s post-battle damage report, 13.6.16, Grand Fleet Secret Packs, Vol.66, ADM137/1946.

86. Otto Groos, *Der Krieg in der Nordsee*.

87. Von Hase, *op. cit.*

Chapter 21: *The Clash of Battle-Fleets*

1. Von Schoultz, *With the British Battlefleet*, p.129.

2. Roger Kirk Dickson, Acc.13509/13586 (NLS).

3. Dreyer, quoted Bennett, *The Battle of Jutland*, p.105.

4. ROP, *Official Despatches*.

5. Claude Wallace, *From Jungle to Jutland*, p.242.

6. Evidence from *Conqueror*, Fawcett & Hooper, *The Fighting at Jutland*, p.197.

7. Roger Kirk Dickson, Acc.13509/13586 (NLS).

8. 'Trafalgar Memorandum'.

9. Actually the Grand Fleet's divisions cruised closer than this, and were moved out to 'manoeuvring distance' at 3.10 p.m.

10. As given in 1939 *Fighting Instructions*.

11. Captain Geoffrey Bennett supports this by inference. Jellicoe, he says, "had surprised Scheer before [Scheer] could deploy his fleet. Obliged to make the long passage of the swept channel from the Jade to the Horn Reef with his three battle-squadrons in line ahead, he had maintained this formation as he followed Hipper northwards" (*The Battle of Jutland*, p.111).

12. Section VI, ADM186/597.

13. In 1917 Beatty wrote: "The word 'deployment', though in constant use, needs a definition to make the meaning perfectly clear; it is at present closely connected with deploy *into line*." Sturdee wanted a specific pendant denoting deployment, but thought 'Battle Order Pendant' would be a better name for it than 'Deployment Pendant', because the former "would be descriptive of what is intended in the Battle Orders, besides being a Naval and not a Military term". (File on 'Deployment Signals', in Grand Fleet Secret Packs, Vol.80, ADM137/1965.)

14. A by-line to the 'deployment' issues is a provision in GFBOs (Section VI, para. (c)) empowering the leader of a wing division to initiate the deployment off his own bat, if he should sight the enemy "at close quarters" in low visibility. Whether Burney, when he first glimpsed the High Seas Fleet at around 6.05, considered invoking this clause and pre-empting Jellicoe's decision is not known. Whether Sturdee, in his place, would have done so, is perhaps a more realistic question (Sturdee always held that Jellicoe should have deployed to starboard at Jutland).

15. John Harper, *The Truth about Jutland*, p.22.

16. *Sea Heritage*, p.146.

17. Barrie Kent, *Signal!*, p.55. It is unclear why the wing could not have been indicated by the position (superior or inferior) of the Equal-Speed Pendant.

18. 'Charley' is so spelt in the phonetic alphabet in 1915 Grand Fleet Signal Orders (ADM137/266).

19. At the time of writing (and aside from HMS *Trafalgar*) there is just one commissioned warship, HMS *Swiftsure*, in the entire RN with a Trafalgar name – a state of affairs which may be explained by the existence of a Ships' Names and Badges Committee.

20. Midshipman Bickmore (IWM).

21. *Southampton's* gunnery-officer, Lt Borrough (IWM).

22. Marder, *Dreadnought*, Vol.III, p.105.

23. Hearsay, quoted in *ibid.*, p.225.

24. Testimony from *Falmouth*, Fawcett & Hooper, p.283.

25. Stephen King-Hall (in *Southampton*), *Sea Saga*, pp. 457–8.

26. Fawcett & Hooper, p.130.

27. *Ibid.*, p.134.

28. Roger Kirk Dickson, Acc.13509/13586 (NLS).

29. Vol.III, p.114.

30. Chatfield, *The Navy and Defence*, pp.145–6.

31. It beggars belief that GFBOs did not allow for the deployment-wing cruiser-squadron to take the lead, and the other to go to the rear, whichever way the fleet deployed. As things stood, a deployment to port was very much simpler for the armoured-cruisers than one to starboard, and this may be a symptom (like the stationing of Jerram's powerful squadron on the port wing) of a predisposition on Jellicoe's part towards deploying to port.

32. Vol.III, p.114n.

33. *Memoirs of the Arbuthnots of Kincardineshire and Aberdeenshire*, pp.326–7.

34. From plot-sketches made in *Duke of Edinburgh's* foretop (*Official Despatches*, Chart 11a).

35. Witness in *Conqueror*, Fawcett & Hooper, p.197.

36. Godfrey staff-college lecture notes (1930), CAB 24/269.

37. Account from *Neptune*, Fawcett & Hooper, p.192.

38. A conglomerate quotation from two midshipmen: one in *Warspite* (Fawcett & Hooper, p.128) and one in *Benbow* (Dickson).

39. Wallace, p.242.

40. Evidence from an officer in *Cochrane* (sister-ship to *Warrior* etc.) of the 2nd CS (Fawcett & Hooper, p.289).

41. Duthy (IWM).

42. Fawcett & Hooper, p.95.

43. *Ibid.*

44. *Official Despatches*. The fact of Craig's mentioning this may hint that he did not wish to identify with the rear-admiral's decision (as he had tried to expedite Evan-Thomas's response to Beatty's turn at 2.35-ish).

45. Royer Dick, interview.

46. ADM186/597.

47. p.153.

48. Evan-Thomas in his ROP said it was not signalled; signal lists (*Official Despatches*, Godfrey lecture notes etc.) say it was.

49. Some accounts (e.g. Fawcett & Hooper, p.147) say 15°.

50. Walwyn account in Phillpotts papers (IWM); also account from another *Warspite* officer in Fawcett & Hooper, p.148. John Campbell rejects this scenario and provides his own explanation (Campbell, p.179), which the reader might prefer – with the caution that Campbell appears committed to playing down *Warspite*'s hits in the earlier part of the run to the north (see Chapter 20, n. 40).

51. Fawcett & Hooper, p.147.

52. *Ibid.*

53. Letter to brother, published in *Naval Review*, April 1985.

54. Walwyn in Phillpotts papers (IWM).

55. William Goodenough, *Rough Record*, p.96.

56. ROP.

57. Von Hase, *Kiel and Jutland*, p.183.

58. One may as well mention that a close observer in the light-cruiser *Gloucester* could not accept that *Invincible* was destroyed by a shell hit: he was convinced that all German shells were falling well short. Letter to Harper in CAB 24/269.

59. Malvernian Society.

60. Fawcett & Hooper, pp.249–50.

61. *Valiant*'s ROP reports a "bad kink in rear of our line of battle" at 6.35, and "line straightened" at 6.40.

62. Wallace, p.243.

63. Von Hase, p.177.

64. German Official History.

65. Marder, Vol.III, p.118.

66. Kent, p.63.

67. Fawcett & Hooper, p.420.

68. *The Jutland Battle, by two who took part in it*, pp.7–8.

69. John Winton, *Captains and Kings*, pp.43–5.

70. Fred Morris (boy, in *Marlborough*'s port battery) (interview).

71. Ernest Fox (IWM Sound).

72. Campbell, p.180.

73. Roger Kirk Dickson, Acc.13509/13589 (NLS).

74. Chatfield, p.147.

75. Admiral Chalmers' memo in Roskill MSS, quoted Marder, p.130n.

76. Marder, Vol.III, p.112.

77. From *Southampton*, Fawcett & Hooper, p.275.

78. From *Nottingham*, Fawcett & Hooper, p.275n.

79. Winton, pp.43–5.

80. See Campbell, Chapter 11.

81. Von Hase, pp.187–8.

82. Wallace, p.247. The last-mentioned hit appears to be unknown to Campbell. Major Wallace was shown the damage by Rear-Admiral Gaunt after the battle, and his account is so specific that there can be little room for error.

83. Cdr Bonham Faunce, interview 1991.

84. Sir Angus Cunninghame-Graham, Acc.4198 (NLS).

85. The most authoritative analysis of this juncture (albeit one designed to defend

Jellicoe) is that of Captain John Godfrey in his 1930 Staff College lectures (notes in CAB 24/269).

86. Midshipman in *Neptune*, Fawcett & Hooper, p.213.

87. William James, *The Eyes of the Navy* (biography of Reginald Hall), p.202.

88. Article XXVI, underlining added.

89. Defended in varying degrees by (for example) Reginald Bacon, John Harper and John Godfrey.

90. Burney and Sturdee, from post-battle evidence (in Marder, Vol.III, pp.133–4). Jerram, whose van squadron was the least threatened by the torpedo attack, anticipated Jellicoe's turn-back by a few minutes.

91. Beatty hearsay, via both Beatty's son and Leopold Amery, the Beatty-ite First Lord, 1922–4 (Marder, Vol.III, p.237n.)

92. 'Errors made in Battle of Jutland' (1932), in *Jellicoe Papers*, Vol.II, p.447.

93. Nicholas Lambert, 'British Naval Policy, 1913–14: Financial Limitation and Strategic Revolution', *Journal of Modern History*, Vol.67, No.3, September 1995.

94. *Call for Fire*, p.77.

95. See Godfrey's lecture-notes.

96. Fawcett & Hooper, pp.241–2.

97. N. E. White, Electrical artificer, *Colossus* (IWM Misc 1010, 65/3).

98. Fawcett & Hooper, p.248.

99. Anthony Combe (family testimony).

100. Alec Tempest, Leading Signalman, IWM (also in *Naval Intelligence*, p.124).

101. Fawcett & Hooper, pp.95–6.

102. Combe, *op. cit.*

103. Obituary, *Daily Telegraph*, 11.12.90.

104. Bennett, p.126.

105. *The Jutland Battle, by two who took part in it*, p.5.

Chapter 22: *Night Inaction*

1. A. B. Sainsbury, *The Royal Navy Day by Day*.

2. GFBIs, 1.1.18, ADM137/4055.

3. Letter of 12.4.16 to Henry Jackson (quoted in Chapter 4).

4. Also, eight-ship squadrons one mile apart were at half-manoeuvring distance, and could not have 'line-formed' without first opening out.

5. Fawcett & Hooper, *The Fighting at Jutland*, p.86.

6. A/B D. T. Thomson (IWM).

7. *Chester*'s CO's ROP, *Official Despatches*.

8. Stephen King-Hall in King-Hall (ed.), *Sea Saga*, p.417.

9. G. J. Ellison (IWM).

10. Fawcett & Hooper, p.195.

11. Von Schoultz, *With the British Battlefleet*, p.148.

12. Henry Short (IWM).

13. Fawcett & Hooper, pp.95–6.

14. Journal of Surgeon-Lieutenant D. Lorimer RNVR (IWM).

15. Interview. A piece of ship's side from *Barham*'s gunroom is in the Imperial War Museum (no butter-dish).

16. *Sea Saga*, p.461.

17. Midshipman Roger Dickson, HMS *Benbow*, Acc.13569 (NLS).

18. Testimony of Commander Colin Buist (sub-lieutenant in *Southampton* in 1916), Roskill MSS, quoted Marder, *From the Dreadnought to Scapa Flow*, Vol.III, p.170n.

19. Langhorne Gibson and John Harper, *The Riddle of Jutland*, p.219.

20. William Goodenough, *Rough Record*, p.96.

21. *Sea Saga*, p.450.

22. It is often said that they acquired it at dusk, from *Princess Royal*'s reminding *Lion* of what the current challenge was (*Lion* having lost it) and using an unshaded light. This seems to me implausible, for reasons of range, bearing, signalese, language etc., but, even if true, there is evidence that they had it already, and they would certainly have got it as soon as they were challenged.

23. John Campbell, *Jutland, An Analysis of the Fighting*, p.286.

24. Fawcett & Hooper, p.348.

25. *Ibid.*, p.333.

26. *Ibid.*, p.340.

27. *Ibid.*, p.343.

28. *Ibid.*, pp.350–3.

29. *Der Krieg in der Nordsee*, p.368.

30. This brief account, like some others, derives from an assortment of published sources.

31. George Haigh (IWM Sound).

32. ROP, *Official Despatches*.

33. Caslon (IWM).

34. In Lorimer (IWM).

35. ROP.

36. *Sunday Telegraph*, 29.5.66.

37. A. E. D. C. Duthy (IWM).

38. ROP.

39. ROP.

40. E. Phillips (IWM).

41. Sir Angus Cunninghame-Graham, Acc.4198 (NLS).

42. 'Errors Made in Battle of Jutland', *Jellicoe Papers*, Vol.II, pp.451–2.

43. *Ibid.*

44. Marder, Vol.III, p.180.

45. Vice-Admiral Arthur Craig Waller, 'The Fifth Battle Squadron at Jutland', *Royal United Service Institute Journal*, November 1935.

46. Battleships had 'Type I' sets: 3 spark, high power, 1,000-metre wave on which all ships kept watch. Smaller ships had weaker 'Type II' sets. All ships had a low power buzzer set, worked by a rotary spark wheel, used in Scapa (Cunninghame-Graham).

47. Cunninghame-Graham, Acc.4198 (NLS); see also *Random Naval Recollections*.

48. G. F. Spargo, telegraphist, *Dublin* (IWM).

49. A. J. L. Blond, 'Technology and Tradition: Wireless Telegraphy and the Royal Navy, 1895–1920', University of Lancaster PhD thesis, 1993, p.154.

50. ADM116/1210.

51. As a rule, in flagships and destroyer-leaders the 'signals officer' was a qualified (S); in private ships he was any officer detailed to administrate the department as divisional-officer. In the latter case (as with Lt Cunninghame-Graham in *Agincourt*) he would have some other job to do at action-stations, and the senior professional signalman on the bridge would be the chief-yeoman.

52. Royal Marines needed to know W/T to coordinate landing parties. The 5th BS's staff W/T instructor was a Royal Marine captain.

53. Bill Piggott (interview, 1991).

54. ROP.

55. *Admiralty Narrative*. For this brief account of the adventures of *Seydlitz* and *Moltke*, I rely substantially on Marder and on Tarrant (*Jutland, the German Perspective*) – who also owes much to Marder (Vol.III, p.183).

56. Tarrant, p.195.

57. *Ibid.*, p.219.

58. It is said that Arthur Onslow had requested HMS *Onslow*, but the Admiralty clerk had got confused and sent John Tovey to that ship and Onslow to *Onslaught*.

59. *Der Krieg in der Nordsee*, p.388.

60. Campbell, p.404.

61. The German Official History alludes to "the training that [Scheer's] fleet had received in repelling destroyer attacks" (*Der Krieg in der Nordsee*, p.368).

62. Tarrant, p.226.

63. Fawcett & Hooper, p.442.

64. Dickson, Acc.13569 (NLS).

65. *Grand Fleet*, p.384.

66. C. Caslon (IWM).

67. J. Hazelwood (IWM Sound).

68. Letter to his brother, reprinted in *Naval Review*, April 1985.

69. Fawcett & Hooper, p.97.

70. Chalmers, p.262.

71. R. K. Dickson, Acc.13586 (NLS).

72. Interview.

73. Lorimer (IWM).

74. Fawcett & Hooper, p.97.

75. *Lion*'s log, ADM53/46846.

76. F. W. Dagenhardt (IWM).

77. A/S/Lt Windham Mark Phipps-Hornby (IWM).

78. Grand Fleet Secret Packs, Vol.66, ADM137/1946.

79. Lorimer (IWM).

80. Collins, ERA *Warspite* (IWM).

81. Bickmore (IWM).

82. Fairthorne, interview, 19.9.91.

83. Combe (IWM).

84. Lt Edwin Downing, *Lion* (IWM).

85. *Lion*'s log, ADM53/46846.

86. PO Edward Phillips, *Barham* (IWM).

87. Quoted (from where?) by Tarrant, p.247.

88. Sir J. J. Thomson, *Recollections and Reflections*, p.219.

89. To Eugénie Godfrey-Faussett: Roskill, *Earl Beatty*, p.204.

90. Saturday June 3rd: "Among our losses were the heavy battlecruisers *Queen Mary*, *Indefatigable*, *Invincible*, and the cruisers *Defence* and *Black Prince* were sunk. The *Warrior* was abandoned by her crew. Eight destroyers were also lost. The enemy losses were serious. At least one battle-cruiser was destroyed, two seriously damaged and one battleship sunk. One German light-cruiser [actually four] and six destroyers

were sunk and two cruisers disabled. A German submarine was rammed and sunk [not true]." (When Their Lordships denied losing any battleships, Midshipman Fairthorne's naval father "had an uneasy feeling that for the purpose of this denial, the Admiralty was classifying *Warspite* as a battlecruiser".)

91. Frewen papers, Add.MSS. Is this piece of writing a little too well-crafted to have been written on that exhausted first night in?

92. F. J. Arnold (IWM).

Chapter 23: *Something Wrong with our System*

1. IWM.

2. *U-75* appears to have laid her mines in the wrong place, having mistaken Marwick Head for St John's Head on Hoy, fifteen miles further south; but, still, *Hampshire* passed through both the intended and actual mine-lay areas.

3. Marder, *Fear God and Dread Nought*, Vol.III, p.237.

4. History has many examples of older and bolder admirals who made lighter weather of high command than did the 56-year-old Jellicoe. Kempenfelt was 63 at the Second Battle of Ushant, as was Rodney when he broke the French line at The Saints; Howe and Alexander Hood were 68 and 67 at the Glorious First of June; Duncan was 66 when he dismantled the Dutch fleet at Camperdown, and Jervis 62 at Cape St Vincent.

More recently, the regulation of career structures has institutionalized 'ageism' in the armed forces (although the USN's Rickover somehow escaped the net until 81); but still, Somerville was 58–60 when he made Force H the most cost-effective standing task force in history, Cunningham was 58 at Matapan, and Ramsay 61 when he organized and commanded Allied naval forces at D-Day. One might mention again Cowan's joining the Commandos at 71, though whether he was more of a hazard to friend or to foe is a moot point.

The real issue is not age but robustness of attitude, and in this respect Jellicoe had probably always been 'too old' to lead the Grand Fleet to a great victory: too burdened with what might happen, too immersed in staff details to 'leave something to chance' – and perhaps too nice a chap. Beatty called him "always a half-hearted man" (Roskill, *Earl Beatty*, p.220) – and, as usual, the libel was leavened with an element of truth.

5. Reported in *Edinburgh Evening News*, 3.6.16. *Frauenlob* was survived by five men.

6. The First Lord's words, quoted in the *Dunfermline Press*, 10.6.16.

7. Grand Fleet Secret Packs, Vol.66, ADM137/1946. See also ADM1/8463/176, 'Cause of explosion in British Warships when hit by Heavy Shell'.

8. ADM137/4822.

9. *Jellicoe Papers*, Vol.II, p.28.

10. See 'Projectiles in HM Fleet, etc . . .' ADM137/3834–7. The failures of British armour-piercing shell are persuasively analysed by John Campbell in the final chapter of his *Jutland, An Analysis of the Fighting*. However, a note of restraint is suggested by the detailed report of an Austrian Naval Attaché who toured the High Seas Fleet at Wilhelmshaven within two weeks of the battle and found that "the enormous piercing power of [British] shell at great distances aroused [the Germans'] admiration", and, again, that "the British shells have great penetrating power, and from all reasonable distances the main armour was generally pierced clean through . . . [the shells] pierced everything in their course and often went right through the whole ship." (CAB 25/269.)

11. Marder, *Fear God*, Vol.III, p.263.

12. A striking account of this incident, by *Valiant*'s NO, Commander Geoffrey Freyberg, is in *Scapa Flow* (Malcolm Brown & Patricia Meehan, pp.119–20).

13. Roskill, *Earl Beatty*, p.192. See also Jon Sumida, *In Defence of Naval Supremacy*, pp.307–8.

14. Sumida, pp.315–16.

15. ADM186/241.

16. Marder, *Fear God*, Vol.III, p.228n. (from William Tennant's Jutland lectures).

17. Marder, *Fear God*, p.175.

18. A. J. L. Blond, 'Technology and Tradition: Wireless Telegraphy and the Royal Navy, 1895–1920', University of Lancaster PhD thesis, 1993, p.307.

19. *Ibid.*, p.311.

20. See Sir Harold Gillies, *Plastic Surgery of the Face*, p.356; also Antony Wallace's *The Influence of Jutland on Plastic Surgery*.

21. ADM116/1210.

22. ADM1/8462/170. (Corbett's role in drafting a press release is mentioned in ADM137/1946.)

23. 30.6.16, ADM1/8462/166.

24. Roskill, p.194.

25. In Pelly papers (IWM).

26. *Jellicoe Papers*, Vol.I, p.277.

27. Sir Shane Leslie's notes for a biography of Beatty, SLGF 12/1.

28. Michael Wolff, 'Jutland by 10 Men Who Were There', article in *Sunday Telegraph*, 29.5.66. The version of this interview, in a private letter from Dannreuther to Marder (in Marder's *Fear God*, Vol.III, p.238) differs somewhat in its wording. It is not clear whether Wolff was misquoting Marder (whose book came out in 1966), or quoting another source.

29. Temple Patterson, in introduction to *Jellicoe Papers*, Vol.II, p.5.

30. For example a letter of 6.6.16 to Admiral Meux, which found its way into the newspapers (*Dunfermline Press*, 10.6.16).

31. To Beatty, 9.6.16, SLGF 12/1.

32. Admiral Sir Alexander Duff's diary for 6.10.16 (NMM), quoted in Roskill, p.196.

33. 'Some remarks written by Admiral of the Fleet, the Earl Mountbatten of Burma, 51 years after the event', Milford Haven papers (IWM). Midshipman Mountbatten had joined *Lion* a few weeks after Jutland, and quickly absorbed all the partisan beliefs of his messmates.

34. Leading Signalman Alec Tempest, *Lion* (IWM).

35. Roger Keyes, *Naval Memoirs*, Vol.I. p.36.

36. 'Report of Damage done to German High Seas Fleet . . .', ADM137/3839.

37. Beatty to Lady B., 8.8.16, quoted in Marder, *Fear God*, Vol.III, p.247.

38. To Balfour, 21.6.16. To Jellicoe, he was "not particularly sensitive".

39. Beatty to Jellicoe, 20.6.16, *Jellicoe Papers*, Vol.I, pp.288–9.

40. 5.7.16, *Jellicoe Papers*, Vol.I, p.290.

41. To Jellicoe, 27.7.16, *Jellicoe Papers*, Vol.II, p.33.

42. Jellicoe to Jackson, 14.6.16, *Jellicoe Papers*, Vol.I, p.278.

43. 31.7.16, *Jellicoe Papers*, Vol.II, p.34.

44. Roskill, *Earl Beatty*, p.195.

45. 4.6.16, Evan-Thomas papers, Add.MSS.

46. See, for example, *Official Despatches*, Chart 8a.

47. 7.6.16.

48. 9.6.16, *Jellicoe Papers*, Vol.I, p.276.

49. 7.6.16, Evan-Thomas papers.

50. 12.6.16, WR(S) 257 (Rockingham).

51. 16.6.16, *ibid.*

52. 8.6.16, *ibid.* This crossed Sir Michael's letter to E-T, and must have been junior's second letter home about the battle.

53. Epitaph, quoted by Mark Girouard in *Return to Camelot*, p.286.

54. Sir Henry Newbolt, *Naval Operations*, Vol.IV, p.17.

55. *Papers*, Vol.I, p.448.

56. Report of Austrian Naval Attaché, 17.6.16, CAB 24/269.

57. *Berliner Tageblatt*, 18.11.18, quoted by Jellicoe in *Grand Fleet*, pp.411–12. Other translations of this vary slightly (e.g. in Tarrant, p.250).

58. Carlyon Bellairs, *The Battle of Jutland*, p.82.

59. Translation in ROSK/3/5 (cited in Roskill, p.188; Tarrant, *Jutland, the German Perspective*, p.250).

60. Temple Patterson, *Jellicoe Papers*, Vol.II, p.4.

61. Marder, *Fear God*, Vol.III, pp.290–1.

62. Roskill, p.198.

63. Marder, *Fear God*, Vol.III, p.288.

64. Aside from Sir William Pakenham's congratulations, Sir Hugh received others from Goodenough, Arthur Craig, Hubert Brand, George Aston ("I often think of the time at Malta when the future looked so black for you on the doctors' reports and how well you stuck it out"), Arthur Leveson, Martyn Jerram, Lionel Halsey, Godfrey-Faussett, John de Roebeck, Colin Keppel and Arthur Christian.

65. Roskill, p.204.

66. Paraphrase of *Malaya*'s Captain Boyle, in Grand Fleet Secret Packs, Vol.66, ADM137/1946.

67. King-Hall, *Sea Saga*, p.477.

68. *Jellicoe Papers*, Vol.II, pp.47ff.

69. ADM186/699.

70. The new MP signal was not included in the 15.9.16 addendum to the *Signal Book* – why should it be? The book already had TA. When the next revision of the *Signal Book* came out in September 1917, while Jellicoe was First Sea Lord, we find that his 'MP' signal is still omitted (the group MP being put to another use), and that the 'TA' signal has been transferred to group 'NP' (1917 *Signal Book*, ADM186/729), suggesting that he would have made do with the 'TA' signal in his GFBOs revision, if only its cryptic group had been changed to something else.

71. As told to, and recalled by, his term-mate Richard Fairthorne (Fairthorne interview, 19.9.91).

72. See *Jellicoe Papers*, Vol.II, pp.77–82.

73. *Grand Fleet*, p.413.

74. Shane Leslie, SLGF 12/1.

75. Roskill, p.200.

76. SLGF 12/1.

77. 17.12.16, Add.MSS 52504.

78. Surgeon-Captain Robert Hill to JJ, 1.8.17, *Jellicoe Papers*, Vol.II, p.192.

79. Halsey to JJ, 29.11.16, *ibid.*, p.105.

80. King-Hall, *My Naval Life*, p.222.

81. G. H. Bickmore (IWM).

82. Fisher to JJ, 1.12.16, *Jellicoe Papers*, Vol.II, p.107.

83. To Balfour, 27.11.16, *Beatty Papers*, Vol.I, p.381.

84. See, for example, Seymour to Lady B., 22.12.16, BTY 13/34.

85. 4.12.16, *Beatty Papers*, Vol.I, p.384.

86. 17.12.16, Add.MSS 52504.

87. 4.12.16, *Beatty Papers*, Vol.I, p.384.

88. There is a story that Beatty had made a speech telling the men of the BCF to take off their caps to the men of the 5th BS, if they should meet them ashore, for they had saved their bacon at Jutland. One can only speculate as to whether such a scene took place, but a surer cue for a punch-up can hardly be imagined.

89. As he was at the time of the 'Battle of May Island' on 31.1.18, when the BCF ran down a flotilla of K-class submarines in fog.

90. To wife, Evan-Thomas papers, December 1916.

91. In May 1917 every officer, man, and boy in *Iron Duke* subscribed to a silver model of the ship, guns trained on Green 60, to mark the anniversary of Jutland. They got round the regulation designed to outlaw gifts to senior officers by presenting it to Lady Jellicoe (Dreyer letter to JJ, 30.5.17, *Jellicoe Papers*, Vol.II, p.165).

92. J. Cockburn (IWM). The praetorian guard of marines is well documented elsewhere.

93. DB to Eugénie Godfrey-Faussett, quoted by Roskill in *Earl Beatty*, p.205.

94. Filson Young, *With the Battlecruisers*. If we combine this scene with Beatty's strange propensity for pulling faces, then Young might, indeed, have had cause for alarm.

95. DB to Eugénie, quoted Roskill, p.206.

96. 21.12.16, *Beatty Papers*, Vol.I, p.388.

97. Chalmers, p.275.

98. Paper in DRAX 1/18.

99. Ships Book, ADM136/10 Part 2.

100. Milford Haven Papers (IWM).

101. 22.12.16, BTY 13/34.

102. 21.6.16, *Beatty Papers*, Vol.I, p.344.

103. Richmond to Plunkett, 21.7.16, DRAX 1/61.

104. Daniel Baugh, in John Hattendorf (ed.), *Mahan is Not Enough*, pp.17, 14.

105. DRAX 1/18.

106. *Ibid.*

107. GFBIs ('General Principles', para. 3), *Beatty Papers*, Vol.I, p.457 (also ADM137/4055).

108. Roskill, p.206.

109. *Ibid.*, p.213; *Beatty Papers*, Vol.I, p.379.

110. 16.10.17 (RA GV Q832/375).

111. GFBIs ('General Principles', para. 19).

112. Marder (*Dreadnought*, Vol.IV, p.38) presents as a Beatty innovation an 'initiative' injunction which featured verbatim in the GFBOs in force at the time of Jutland.

113. Diary, 22.9.17, Richmond Papers (NMM).
114. 27.9.17, DRAX 1/61.
115. Information from Royal Archives.
116. Beatty to Lady B., 19.6.17, *Beatty Papers*, Vol.I, p.443.
117. Beatty to Lady B., 22.6.17, Chalmers, p.318.
118. Unknown paper, Llwynmadoc papers.
119. *Daily Chronicle*, 7.7.17.
120. Beatty to Lady B., 1.3.17, *Beatty Papers*, Vol.I, p.407.
121. The Admiralty brandished a set of figures of all arrivals and departures from UK ports. This included all cross-Channel and small coastwise traffic, instead of merely ocean-going traffic. (The affair, of course, was not quite as simple as this, and is lucidly discussed by Arthur Marder in *Dreadnought*, Vol.IV.)
122. Marder, *Dreadnought*, Vol.IV, p.154.
123. Henderson's service as Third Sea Lord was under Chatfield's First Sea Lordship.
124. See, for example, George to Evan-Thomas, 13.9.91 (Llywnmadoc).
125. Jellicoe to Beatty, 4.8.17.
126. Letter to Dudley de Chair, 29.12.17 (*The Sea is Strong*, p.236).
127. Marder, *Dreadnought*, Vol.IV, p.344.
128. Beatty to Lady B., 24.5.17, *Beatty Papers*, Vol.I, p.433; Beatty to Lady B., 9.7.17, *ibid.*, p.446.
129. Francis Hunter, *Beatty, Jellicoe, Sims and Rodman*, p.170.
130. Stephen King-Hall, *Sea Saga*, pp.480, 432.
131. Quoted from USNA's *Shipmate*, January 1964, by Marder, *Dreadnought*, Vol.V, p.129.
132. Introduction by Hector Bywater to Ludwig Freiwald's *The Last Days of the German Fleet*, p.x.
133. Letter to 'a friend' (presumably Eugénie Godfrey-Faussett), 12.11.18.
134. SLGF 12/1.
135. Basil Jones (HMS *Emperor of India*), quoted in Roskill, *Earl Beatty*, pp.275–6.
136. Letter to Eugénie Godfrey-Faussett, 26.11.18 (quoted in Roskill, p.277).
137. *Ibid.*
138. Ludwig Freiwald, *The Last Days of the German Fleet*, p.286.
139. James L. Stokesbury, *Navy and Empire*, p.320.
140. Cockburn (IWM).

Chapter 24: *Dirty Work Somewhere*

1. Goodenough's interpretation of passages in *Life and Letters of Admiral of the Fleet Lord Wester Wemyss*, review article, *RUSI Journal*, 1935 (Vol.LXXX).
2. 1.3.19, *Beatty Papers*, Vol.II, p.25.
3. Service Record, ADM196/50, Part 1, p.26.
4. 14.6.19, RA GV G.1474/3.
5. There are several reasons why this was so. Neither the Germans' policy of playing safe with the High Seas Fleet, nor the Admiralty's signals intelligence early-warning system, was clearly established in the early months. The Grand Fleet's harbours were more secure in Beatty's time. There was a near-critical shortage of oil-fuel in 1917. (*Southampton*'s war-mileage illustrates the point: 1914 = 20,720; 1915 = 24,055; 1916 = 21,538; 1917 = 19,299; 1918 = 21,331 (MRDN 1/3).)

6. Leslie Gardiner, *The Royal Oak Courts-Martial*, p.82.

7. Introduction to Harper's 'Facts Dealing with the Compilation of the Official Record of the Battle of Jutland and the Reason it was not Published' (reproduced as an Appendix to the *Jellicoe Papers*, Vol.II).

8. Seymour to Harper 18.12.19, *Jellicoe Papers*, Vol. II, p.465.

9. *Ibid.*, pp.465–6, 473, 478n. The circle business came to a head at the Admiralty on the 4th or 5th of August 1920. Interestingly, a Harper letter of 6.8.20, telling Dreyer of "the latest development", reveals that the naval secretary "strongly" advised Harper to stick to his guns (DRYR 6/2). The naval secretary was Rudolph Bentinck, who had been Beatty's chief of staff at Jutland and (according to Chatfield's memoirs) took over *Lion*'s con while the disputed manoeuvre was in progress – a circumstance which Harper almost certainly did not know in 1920. To me, this is the clincher.

10. Carlyon Bellairs, *The Battle of Jutland*, p.xi. He was not doing strict justice to Harper's 'action' record, as the latter had served with distinction in South Africa and the Ogaden. As a matter of interest, Harper had been 'master' of the 1914 Naval Review.

11. Primarily the *Daily Mail* in early February 1920.

12. Jellicoe to Oswald Frewen, 12.2.20, Add.MSS 53738.

13. Roskill, *Earl Beatty*, p.330. The commitment in Parliament (4.8.20) was less surely worded: ". . . shall certainly ensure that he [JJ] will see the final form before publication".

14. *Daily Telegraph*, 18.12.20; see also *Daily Mail*, 28.10.20. The matter was raised in Parliament on 27.10.20; 1, 4, 15, 22.11.20, and 1, 8.12.20.

15. Roskill, p.330.

16. Frewen to Evan-Thomas, 22.2.27, ROSK 3/3 (also Llwynmadoc).

17. SLGF 10/1.

18. *Stedman's Medical Dictionary.*

19. Service Record, ADM196/50 Part 1, p.26.

20. See E. S. Turner, *Gallant Gentlemen*, pp.294–5.

21. Letter of 1.3.17, *Beatty Papers*, Vol.I, p.408.

22. SLGF 10/1. This may have been the recommendation which got Seymour his Cross of St Michael and St George (CMG) "for valuable services as Fleet Signal Officer" (5.4.19, Service Record, ADM196/50, Part 1, p.26).

23. See Leslie Gardiner's *The Royal Oak Courts-Martial.*

24. Kenneth's credentials for membership are reasonably good, judging by his entertaining book *The Navy from Within*, and by Gardiner's mini-biography in *The Royal Oak Courts-Martial*. He was also a friend of Richmond. Alfred penned a strange booklet entitled *The Significance of Naval History*, in which he alleged that public men "love the cucumbers of peace". No doubt he had a weighty point in mind.

25. Roskill, p.332.

26. Letter to Evan-Thomas, 22.2.27, ROSK 3/3.

27. Roskill, p.338.

28. Keyes and Chatfield to Beatty, 14.8.22, quoted in Roskill, p.334.

29. Letter of 18.7.22 to Jellicoe, quoted by Jellicoe in his account of the 'Narrative' story (in ROSK 3/3). Jellicoe (writing several years later) seems to associate Corbett's words with the *Admiralty Narrative*, but they must related to the preceding Staff Appreciation.

30. Not to be confused with the cursory *Narrative of the Action with the German High Seas Fleet off Jutland* (CB 01256), produced in October 1916 by the C-in-C Grand Fleet.

31. 25.3.22, Frewen papers. Add.MSS.

32. Reginald Bacon, *Earl Jellicoe*, p.519.

33. Jellicoe to Evan-Thomas, 3.6.22, from Government House, Auckland.

34. *Dictionary of National Biography*.

35. Jellicoe to Admiralty, 27.11.22.

36. 6.11.22, Frewen papers, Add.MSS.

37. Jellicoe to Admiralty, 27.11.22.

38. My doctoral research into inter-war procurement organization exposed the skill with which Long rescued the Admiralty's supply faculties from the seemingly irresistible threat of unification.

39. 12.7.23, Frewen papers, Add.MSS.

40. See Donald Schurman, *Julian S. Corbett, 1854–1922*, Ch. 10 'The Historian and the Censor'.

41. Llwynmadoc papers.

42. *Naval and Military Record*, September 1928.

43. Geoffrey Barnard, notes on Admiral Sir Hugh Evan-Thomas, ROSK 3/3; also Add. MSS 52506.

44. 19.4.23, Add.MSS 52504.

45. Watson to Evan-Thomas, 19.7.23.

46. Hope to Evan-Thomas, 22.7.23.

47. Jellicoe to Evan-Thomas, 8 & 29.10.23.

48. Family testimony.

49. Evan-Thomas to his sister-in-law, 'Bertha' Barnard, from a nursing home in Harrogate, 10.7.26.

50. In *The Beatty Papers*, Vol.II (p.473), Bryan Ranft chooses a much milder version of the incident, from an Evan-Thomas letter of 30.6.26 to Jellicoe. The two accounts referred to here were written by Sir Hugh only ten days apart ($3\frac{1}{2}$ years afterwards), and however we may think up reasons for their difference, we can never know for sure which is the truer.

51. Letter to 'Bertha' Barnard, 10.7.26.

52. RA GV PS 40045.

53. *The Times*, 1.7.24. His (formal) command of The Nore ran its course; his early retirement was from the Active List.

54. Jellicoe to Evan-Thomas, 10.2.24.

55. RA GV PS 40045, 6.3.24, Hodges to Stamfordham (sentences transposed).

56. 3.6.24.

57. Letter to Oswald Frewen of 19.2.27.

58. 8.8.24.

59. *Morning Post*, 4.5.25.

60. He had been exempted from normal retirement criteria for non-employed admirals, by order in council in 1905 (ADM196/42).

61. 2.2.24, *Beatty Papers*, Vol.II, p.270.

62. Letter to Bertha, 10.7.26.

63. Francis Parkman, *The Tale of the 'Ripe Scholar'*.

64. p.112.

65. *Truth*, 23.2.27.

66. p.122ff.

67. p.133.

68. Geoffrey Barnard.

69. 22.2.27.

70. *The Times*, 16.2.27.

71. 17.2.27.

72. Evan-Thomas to Frewen, 19.2.27.

73. 23.2.27.

74. 9.3.27.

75. 23.2.27.

76. 4.3.27.

77. 1.4.27.

78. Evan-Thomas's obituary, 4.9.28.

79. There is a potentially incriminating nuance to Geoffrey Barnard's stout testimony that "my uncle to the end of his life was quite certain that NO executive signal was received by *Barham* at this time, and that no 'informative signal' giving any clue to the battle-cruisers' movements was ever reported to him on the bridge" (his underlining, ROSK 3/3).

80. Barnard, *ibid.*

81. *Evening News*, 4.9.28.

82. Alluded to in Roskill, p.337.

83. Llwynmadoc papers.

84. Add.MSS 52506.

85. *Dictionary of National Biography*.

86. Roskill, p.366.

87. *Ibid.*, p.369.

88. RA GV PS 40045.

Chapter 25: *Perspective*

1. Arthur Marder's *Dreadnought to Scapa Flow*, Vol.III, Chapters 5 & 6, is recommended. Most of the non-official 'Jutland-controversy' publications contain trenchant and stimulating material.

2. N. J. M. Campbell's *Jutland, an Analysis of the Fighting*, Chapter 18, is recommended.

3. The most ardent British breast-beater is probably Correlli Barnett, in *The Sword Bearers*, Part 2.

4. Milford Haven Papers (IWM).

5. Carlyon Bellairs, *The Battle of Jutland*, p.83.

6. MRK/49.

7. Leslie Gardiner, *The British Admiralty*, pp.120–1.

8. Marder, *Dreadnought*, Vol.IV, p.223.

9. Letter to Henry Jackson, 16.6.15, *Jellicoe Papers*, Vol.I, p.167.

10. Peter Kemp, *Oxford Companion to Ships and the Sea*.

11. Winston Churchill, *World Crisis, 1916–18*, Vol.I, p.136.

12. Sir Angus Cunninghame-Graham, Acc.4198 (NLS).

13. Churchill, *World Crisis*, Vol. 1, p.169.

14. My thanks to Nicholas Lambert.

15. Cunninghame-Graham.

16. See, for example, 'Notes on Tactical Exercises, 1909–1911' (Eb.012 NLMoD).

17. Jellicoe, *Grand Fleet*, p.48.

18. 'Principles involved in the war between Japan and Russia' (1904), in *Naval Administration and Warfare: Some General Principles and other Essays* (1908).

19. Evan-Thomas, letter to *The Times*, 16.2.27.

20. *Admiralty Narrative*, p.107n3.

21. Mark Kerr, *Daily Mail*, 9.3.27.

22. Roger Keyes, *Naval Memoirs*, Vol.I, p.40.

23. Harper's rejoinder to Churchill's version of events, *Argus*, 5.9.28.

24. Beatty's BCFOs.

25. Harper, *The Truth about Jutland*, p.5.

26. Beatty's BCFOs.

27. Bacon, *The Jutland Scandal*, p.59.

28. Bacon, *A Naval Scrap Book*, p.187.

29. *The Fundamentals of British Maritime Doctrine* (BR 1806), p.135.

30. *Ibid.*, p.136.

31. Carlyon Bellairs, *The Battle of Jutland: the Sowing and the Reaping*, p.264.

32. *Naval Review*, Vol.1, p.15.

33. 'The Best Laid Plans . . . The Development of British Battle Fleet Tactics, 1919–1942', *International History Review*, November 1992.

34. 'Handbook of Action Information Organization and Plotting 1945', Section 1: Development and Functions of Action Information Organization (CB 4357, Dec. 45).

35. *Ibid.*

36. See W. T. T. Pakenham, *Naval Command and Control*.

37. Sumida, 'The Best Laid Plans', *op. cit*. See also Sumida's *In Defence of Naval Supremacy*.

38. Sumida, *ibid.*

39. Correlli Barnett, *Engage the Enemy More Closely*, p.44.

40. Andrew Gordon, 'The British Navy 1918–45', Symposium on Navies and Global Defence, Royal Military College of Canada (March 1994). The Earl of Stanhope's paper is in Board Memoranda for June 1939 (ADM167/104).

41. Roskill, p.82.

42. Oliver Warner, *Cunningham of Hyndhope*, p.218.

43. Jellicoe (1916–17), Beatty (1919–27), Madden (1927–30), Field (1930–3), Chatfield (1933–8), Backhouse (1938–9), Pound (1939–43) and McGrigor (1951–5).

44. Within a few days of Jutland, Mountbatten joined *Lion* and John Cunningham briefly joined *Barham*.

45. ADM239/261.

46. Had the 1982 Falklands recovery operation failed, 'decline school' pundits would have scrambled to appear on television to say that of course disaster could have been predicted from (a) *Prince of Wales* and *Repulse* in 1941, (b) the Russian Fleet in 1904–5, (c) The Spanish Armada in 1588, etc.

47. Pakenham, *Naval Command and Control*, p.94. Pakenham cites in support of this statement the fact that, in action, COs are to be found in the ops room, wearing headphones and studying radar displays, and not on the bridge. Yet, at Jutland, while many (probably most) COs remained on the bridge, some commanded from down in the

armoured conning-tower provided for the purpose; and a Great War captain, beamed into a modern frigate or destroyer, would very quickly grasp the command dynamics.

48. As a perusal of the 1913–14 editions of the *Naval Review* will demonstrate.

49. K. G. B. Dewar, *The Navy from Within*, p.25.

50. Whether this obligingly fits the elaborate categories of doctrine discerned by this or that doctrine authority is no concern of mine.

51. In the MOD(N)'s largely presentational analysis (*The Fundamentals of British Maritime Doctrine* (BR 1806)), doctrine "covers grand strategic, military strategic, operational and tactical levels of military planning, both in conflict and in the peacetime application of military power" (cf. *Hamlet*, II.ii.424–30).

52. Captain Wayne P. Hughes USN, 'The Power in Doctrine', *Naval War College Review*, Summer 1995, Vol.XLVIII, No.3, p.14.

53. Christopher Craig, *Call for Fire*, p.149.

54. *Earl Beatty*, p.191.

55. If the genesis of the *Naval Review* owed itself to any one current of feeling, it was the proposition that the technocrats should not be running the show.

56. Sandy Woodward, *One Hundred Days*, pp.264, 286.

57. At shipboard level, and for shipboard purposes, the RN has this about right: non-technical COs are sufficiently well-informed to interrogate their heads of departments.

58. ADM1/7811.

59. *Command in War*, p.259.

60. Barrie Kent, *Signal!*, p.212.

61. Only once since the days of Howe and Kempenfelt has the trend of capacity expansion been reversed. That was in the 1880s when, as mentioned in Chapter 9, the thinning-out of masts and yards prompted signallers to diversify into semaphore and flashing-lamps.

62. Kent, p.213.

63. "It is recommended that the British adopt in peace the basic principles of organization used by the US Navy, so that, should complete tactical cooperation be required again, it can be done more quickly and with less effort" (Sir Bruce Fraser's despatches, 23.11.45, ADM199/1457).

64. Quoted by Kent, p.175.

65. Pakenham, p.93.

66. Report on Manoeuvres quoted by Kent, p.29.

67. 'Naval Manoeuvres of 1913', in ADM116/3381.

68. Kent, p.215.

69. Woodward, pp.83, 120, 310.

70. Craig, p.230.

71. Pakenham, p.93.

72. 'Clausewitz, Intelligence, Uncertainty and the Art of Command in Military Operations', *Intelligence and National Security*, Vol.10, January 1995, No. 1 (especially pp.49–50).

73. Eric Grove, *From Vanguard to Trident*, p.168ff.

74. Sandy Woodward, *One Hundred Days*, p.155.

75. Peter Laurie, *Beneath the City Streets*, p.175.

76. *Sailor's Odyssey*, p.452.

77. From S. W. C. Pack, *Cunningham the Commander*, p.210.

78. James Tritten, *Doctrine and Fleet Tactics in the Royal Navy* (US Naval Doctrine Command), p.17.

79. Pakenham, p.69.

80. *Ibid.*, p.91.

81. *Ibid.*, p.34.

82. Peter Emmett, 'Information Mania – a New Manifestation of Gulf War Syndrome?', *RUSI Journal*, February 1996, p.22.

83. *Ibid.*

84. Pakenham, p.136.

85. Emmett, p.20.

86. As *Alacrity* did to her unidentified target in Falkland Sound in May 1982: Craig, p.80.

87. Letter to mother, 2.2.15; *Life and Letters of Ralph Seymour*, p.70.

88. *Command in War*, p.260.

89. Emmett, p.19.

90. I. F. Stone, *The Listener*, 1963.

91. Pakenham, p.71.

92. Emmett, p.25.

93. For example, a view is gaining ground that computers in schools are "just the latest in a long line of faddish obstacles to real learning" (Stephan Shakespeare, 'Switch Off and Bring Back Teaching', *Evening Standard*, 16.1.96).

94. Emmett, pp.23, 19.

95. Letter to Phipps Hornby quoted in full in Chapter 10.

96. I was accused, after my book on inter-war procurement, of depicting the Admiralty as uniquely clever. Which it was.

97. Like the *Camperdown–Victoria* collision, the 'Tragedy at Honda' raised the issue of the responsibility for the safe navigation of ships in formation; although, in mitigation, the 'Honda' captains were obeying only a *latently* (as opposed to a *patently*) dangerous order, and were doing so in the context of slack navigational habits which had become institutionally acceptable.

98. Extracts from confidential papers, 'Mediterranean Fleet, 1899–1902', FISR 8/1 (CCC). I have not traced these words to Mahan. Fisher may have invented them. But they sound Mahanish, and related sentiments appear on pp.70–2 of *Types of Naval Officers*.

99. Hans & Michael Eysenck, *Mindwatching*, p.39.

100. As Fisher almost said (see Fisher to Rosebery, 22.5.01, Ruddock Mackay, *Lord Fisher of Kilverstone*, p.248).

101. Quoted by Arthur Marder, *Portrait of an Admiral*, p.237.

102. Sir Angus Cunninghame-Graham, *Random Naval Recollections*, pp.27–8.

103. Nevil Shute, *Slide Rule*, pp.147–8.

104. Captain William Outerson USN (Rtd), 'Peacetime Admirals, Wartime Admirals', USNI *Proceedings*, April 1981.

105. Craig, p.33.

106. 'Peacetime Admirals, Wartime Admirals', USNI *Proceedings*, April 1981.

107. Outerson.

108. For further debate, see James Tritten, *Navy Combat Leadership for Tomorrow: where will we get such men and women?* (US Naval Doctrine Command, 1995).

109. Rear-Admiral Penrose Lucas Albright, letter in USNI *Proceedings*, June 1981.

110. *British Seapower and Procurement Between the Wars*, p.291.

111. Extract from item (tense changed) entitled *Power of Incompetence*, by Holly Budd, in the *Spectator*, 29 October 1994. The 'Bett' review of armed forces' manpower recommended that two-star officers and above should serve for four years in each post, to "give them both the responsibility and the opportunity to bring about desirable change" (*Independent Review of the Armed Forces' Manpower, Career and Remuneration Structures* (Chairman Michael Bett) (1995), para. 2.21). The worst offenders are below that level.

112. Robert Townsend, *Up the Organisation!*, p.123.

113. Woodward, p.317.

114. Captain William Boyle, 'Individual Preparation for War', *Naval Review*, 1913, p.80.

115. The documentary, *Return to Jutland*, by Video Works, was shown on Channel Four on Remembrance Sunday, 1991.

Bibliography and List of Books Cited

Admiralty Manual of Navigation (HMSO, various editions and volumes)
Admiralty Manual of Seamanship (HMSO, various editions and volumes)
Robert Arbuthnot, *A Commander's Order Book for a Mediterranean Battleship* (Griffin, 1900)
——*Details and Station Bill for a Battleship* (Griffin, 1901)
Memoirs of the Arbuthnots of Kincardineshire and Aberdeenshire (Allen & Unwin, 1920)
George Aston, *Memoirs of a Marine* (John Murray, 1919)
Reginald Bacon, *The Life of Lord Fisher of Kilverstone* (Hodder & Stoughton, 1929)
——*A Naval Scrap Book, 1877–1900* (Hutchinson, 1924)
——*Life of John Rushworth Earl Jellicoe* (Cassell, 1936)
——*The Jutland Scandal* (Hutchinson, 1925)
Correlli Barnett, *Engage the Enemy More Closely* (Norton, 1991)
——*The Sword Bearers* (Eyre & Spottiswoode, 1969)
'Bartimeus', *The Navy Eternal* (Hodder & Stoughton, 1918)
Georgina Battiscombe, *Queen Alexandra* (Constable, 1969)
T. H. Baughman, *Before the Heroes Came* (University of Nebraska Press, 1994)
Lewis Bayly, *Pull Together* (Harrap, 1939)
Patrick Beesly, *Room 40* (Hamilton, 1982)
Carlyon Bellairs, *The Battle of Jutland, the Sowing and the Reaping* (Hodder & Stoughton, 1920)
Geoffrey Bennett, *The Battle of Jutland* (David & Charles, 1964)
——*Charlie B* (Dawnay, 1968)
——*The Naval Battles of the First World War* (Pan, 1974)
Lord Charles Beresford, *Memoirs of Admiral Lord Charles Beresford* (Methuen, 1914)
Michael Bett (Chairman), *Independent Review of the Armed Forces' Manpower* (HMSO, 1995)
Stanley Bonnett, *The Price of Admiralty* (Hale, 1968)
Nathaniel Bowden-Smith, *Naval Recollections, 1852–1914* (Army & Navy Co-operative Society, 1914)
Edward Bradford, *Life of Admiral of the Fleet Sir Arthur Knyvet Wilson* (John Murray, 1923)
Jan S. Breemer, *The Burden of Trafalgar* (Naval War College, Newport, 1993).
British Naval Documents, 1204–1960 (Scolar Press/Navy Records Society, 1993)
Bernard Brodie, *A Guide to Naval Strategy* (Princeton, 1942)
D. K. Brown, *Before the Ironclad* (Conway Maritime, 1990)
Malcolm Brown & Patricia Meehan, *Scapa Flow* (Allen Lane, 1968)
Ian Cameron, *To the Farthest Ends of the Earth* (Macdonald & Jane's, 1980)
N. J. M. Campbell, *Jutland, An Analysis of the Fighting* (Conway, 1968)

Dudley de Chair, *The Sea is Strong* (Harrap, 1961)

W. S. Chalmers, *Life and Letters of David, Earl Beatty* (Hodder & Stoughton, 1951)

Bertram Chambers, *Salt Junk* (Constable, 1927)

Lord Chatfield, *The Navy and Defence* (Heinemann, 1942)

W. S. Churchill, *My Early Life* (Butterworth, 1930)

——*World Crisis* (Thornton, Butterworth, 1923, 1927)

Shadwell Clerke, *History of the Royal Alpha Lodge No. 16* (1930)

William Laird Clowes, *The Royal Navy, a History* (Sampson Low, 7 volumes, 1897–1903)

Philip Colomb, *Naval Warfare, its Ruling Principles and Practices* etc. (W. H. Allen, 1891)

——*Slave Catching in the Indian Ocean* (Longmans, 1873)

Gary Cooper, *The Man who Sank the Titanic?* (Witan Books, 1992)

Julian Corbett, *Fighting Instructions, 1530–1815* (Conway Maritime Press, 1909, 1971)

——*Naval Operations* (Longmans, first 3 volumes of Official History, 1920ff.)

——*Signals and Instructions, 1776–1794* (Navy Records Society, 1908)

Lord Cork & Orrery, *My Naval Life* (Hutchinson, 1943)

Court-Martial, Officers of the Royal Navy Tried by, 1880–1903 (HMSO, 1905)

Christopher Cradock, *Whispers from the Fleet* (Griffin, 1907)

Christopher Craig, *Call for Fire* (John Murray, 1995)

Martin Van Creveld, *Command in War* (Harvard University Press, 1985)

Duncan Crow, *Edwardian Women* (Allen & Unwin, 1978)

Lord Cunningham of Hyndhope, *A Sailor's Odyssey* (Hutchinson, 1951)

Angus Cunninghame-Graham, *Random Naval Recollections* (1979)

Charles Benedict Davenport, *Naval Officers, their Heredity and Development* (Carnegie Institute, 1919)

Lionel Dawson, *Gone for a Sailor* (Rich & Cowan, 1936)

——*The Sound of the Guns* (biography of Walter Cowan) (Pen in Hand, 1949)

Kenneth Dewar, *The Navy from Within* (Victor Gollancz, 1939)

Norman Dixon, *On the Psychology of Military Incompetence* (Jonathan Cape, 1976; Fontana, 1979)

Barry Domvile, *From Admiral to Cabin Boy* (Boswell, 1947)

Frederick Dreyer, *Sea Heritage* (Museum Press, 1955)

John Duncan & John Walton, *Heroes for Victoria* (Spellmount, 1991)

Mary Egerton, *Admiral of the Fleet, Sir Geoffrey Phipps Hornby GCB* (Blackwood, 1896)

Hans & Michael Eysenck, *Mindwatching* (Joseph, 1981)

Melvyn Fairclough, *The Ripper and the Royals* (Duckworth, 1991)

A. E. Fanning, *Steady As She Goes* (HMSO, 1986)

Harold Fawcett & Geoffrey Hooper, *The Fighting at Jutland* (Macmillan, 1921)

Frederick William Fisher, *Naval Reminiscences* (Frederick Muller, 1938)

(J.A.) Lord Fisher of Kilverstone, *Memories* (Hodder & Stoughton, 1919)

C. C. Penrose Fitzgerald, *From Sail to Steam* (Edward Arnold, 1916)

——*Sir George Tryon KCB* (Blackwood, 1897)

——*Hints on Boat Sailing and Racing* (Griffin, 1882)

——*Some Remarks on Modern Naval Tactics* (Offices of Engineering, 1896)

Seymour Fortescue, *Looking Back* (Longmans, 1920)

Edward Fraser, *Sailors Whom Nelson Led* (Methuen, 1913)

Freemasonry – The Greatest Bluff of the Age (Coldwell, 1932)

Representative British Freemasons (Dod's Peerage, 1915)

Ludwig Freiwald, *The Last Days of the German Fleet* (Constable, 1932)

Sydney Fremantle, *My Naval Career, 1880–1928* (Hutchinson, 1949)

Dennis Friedman, *Inheritance* (Sidgwick & Jackson, 1993)

Alfred Friendly, *Beaufort of the Admiralty* (Random House, 1977)

J. F. C. Fuller, *The Army in My Time* (Rich & Cowan, 1932)

Fundamentals of British Maritime Doctrine (BR 1806) (HMSO, 1995)

Leslie Gardiner, *The Royal Oak Courts-Martial* (Blackwood, 1965)

——*The British Admiralty* (Blackwood, 1968)

Tony Gibbons, *The Complete Encyclopedia of Battleships and Battlecruisers* (Salamander, 1983)

Langhorne Gibson & John Harper, *The Riddle of Jutland* (Cassell, 1934)

Harold Gillies, *Plastic Surgery of the Face* (Hodder & Stoughton, 1920)

Mark Girouard, *Return to Camelot* (Yale, 1981)

Harry Golding (ed.), *The Wonder Book of the Navy for Boys and Girls* (Ward, Lock & Co., 1919)

James Goldrick, *The King's Ships were at Sea* (Naval Institute, 1984)

James Goldrick & John Hattendorf (eds.), *Mahan is not Enough* (Naval War College Press, 1993)

William Goodenough, *Rough Record* (Hutchinson, 1943)

G. A. H. Gordon, *British Seapower and Procurement Between the Wars* (Macmillan Press, Naval Institute Press, 1988)

Otto Groos, *Der Krieg in der Nordsee* (Mittler, 1920)

Eric Grove, *From Vanguard to Trident* (Bodley Head, 1987)

(Montagu Hainsselin), *In the Northern Mists* (Hodder & Stoughton, 1916)

——*Naval Intelligence* (Hodder & Stoughton, 1918)

Paul G. Halpern, *A Naval History of World War I* (UCL Press, 1994)

Richard Vesey Hamilton, *Naval Administration* (Royal Navy Handbooks, 1896)

Lord Hankey, *The Supreme Command* (Allen & Unwin, 1961)

Hansard (various)

John Harper (ed.), *The Record of the Battle of Jutland* (Cmd.2870) (HMSO, 1927)

John Harper, *The Truth about Jutland* (John Murray, 1927)

Michael Harrison, *Clarence* (W.H. Allen, 1972)

Basil Liddell Hart *et al.*, *Churchill Revisited* (Allen Lane, 1969)

Georg von Hase, *Kiel and Jutland* (Skeffington, 1921)

Victor Hayward, *HMS Tiger at Bay* (Kimber, 1977)

Holger Herwig, '*Luxury Fleet': The Imperial German Navy, 1888–1918* (Allen & Unwin, 1980)

——*The German Naval Officer Corps* (Christians, 1977)

Arthur Hezlet, *The Electron and Sea Power* (Peter Davies, 1975)

Christopher Hibbert (ed.), *Queen Victoria in her Letters and Journals* (John Murray, 1984)

John Horsfield, *The Art of Leadership in War* (Greenwood Press, 1980)

Richard Hough, *Admirals in Collision* (Hamish Hamilton, 1959; White Lion, 1973)

——*The Big Battleship* (Michael Joseph, 1966)

——*The Great War at Sea* (Oxford University Press, 1983)

Raymond Howell, *The Royal Navy and the Slave Trade* (Croom Helm, 1987)

Francis T. Hunter, *Beatty, Jellicoe, Sims and Rodman* (Doubleday, 1919)

William James, *The Eyes of the Navy* (biography of Blinker Hall) (Methuen, 1955)

Morris Janowitz, *The Professional Soldier* (Free Press, 1960)

Viscount Jellicoe, *The Grand Fleet, 1914–1916* (Cassell, 1919)

The Jutland Battle, by two who took part in it (Burrup, Mathieson & Spague, 1916)

(C-inC's) *Narrative of the Action with the German High Seas Fleet off Jutland* (CB 01256, 1916)

(Admiralty) *Narrative of the Battle of Jutland* (HMSO, 1924)

Battle of Jutland, Official Despatches (HMSO, 1920)

Peter Kemp (ed.), *The Oxford Companion to Ships and the Sea* (Oxford University Press, 1976)

Barrie Kent, *Signal!* (Hyden House, 1993)

Mark Kerr, *Land, Sea and Air* (Longmans, 1927)

——*The Navy in My Time* (Rich & Cowan, 1933)

——*Prince Louis of Battenberg* (Longmans, 1934)

Roger Keyes, *Naval Memoirs* (Thornton Butterworth, 1934)

Louise King-Hall (ed.), *Sea Saga* (Victor Gollancz, 1935)

Stephen King-Hall ('Etienne'), *A Naval Lieutenant 1914–1918* (Methuen, 1919)

Charles Kingsley, *Alton Locke* (1841)

Rudyard Kipling, *A Fleet in Being* (Macmillan, 1898)

Stephen Knight, *The Brotherhood* (Grafton, 1985)

Andrew Lambert, *Battleships in Transition* (Conway Maritime Press, 1984)

Peter Laurie, *Beneath the City Streets* (Allen Lane, 1970)

David Lloyd-George, *War Memoirs* (Odhams, Vol.2 1936)

Shane Leslie, *The Film of Memory* (Michael Joseph, 1938)

Geoffrey Lowis, *Fabulous Admirals* (Putnam, 1957)

Donald Macintyre, *Jutland* (Evans Bros, 1957; Pan, 1960)

Ruddock Mackay, *Lord Fisher of Kilverstone* (Clarendon Press, 1973)

John MacKenzie (ed.), *Imperialism and Popular Culture* (Manchester University Press, 1986)

Redmond McLaughlin, *The Escape of the Goeben* (Seely Service, 1974)

Robert Macoy, *A Dictionary of Freemasonry* (Masonic Publishing Co., 1869)

Alfred Mahan, *The Influence of Sea Power upon History* (Sampson Low, 1890)

——*The Influence of Sea Power upon the French Revolution* (Sampson Low, 1892)

——*Naval Administration and Warfare* (Sampson Low, 1908)

——*Types of Naval Officers* (Books for Libraries Press, 1901)

William Manchester, *The Last Lion* (Little, Brown, 1988)

Arthur Marder, *British Naval Policy, 1880–1905* (Putnam & Co., 1941)

——*Fear God and Dread Nought* (Jonathan Cape, 3 volumes, 1952–9)

——*From the Dreadnought to Scapa Flow* (Oxford University Press, 5 volumes, 1961–70 (& Vol.III 2nd edition 1976)

——*Portrait of an Admiral* (Jonathan Cape, 1952)

M. E. & F. A. Markham, *The Life of Sir Albert Hastings Markham* (Cambridge University Press, 1927)

Alastair Mars, *Court Martial* (Frederick Muller, 1954)

Robert Massie, *Dreadnought: Britain, Germany and the Coming of the Great War* (Jonathan Cape, 1992)

William May, *The Life of a Sailor* (privately printed (Wm Clowes & Sons))

Marjorie Moore, *Adventures in the Royal Navy* (biography of Arthur Moore) (privately printed, 1964)

James Morris, *Pax Britannica* (Faber & Faber, 1968)

Jan Morris, *Fisher's Face* (Penguin, 1995)

Malcolm Murfitt (ed.), *The First Sea Lords* (Praeger, 1995)

Dictionary of National Biography

Henry Newbolt, *Naval Operations* (Longmans, Green & Co., Vol.4 1928)

Harold Nicolson, *King George V* (Constable, 1952)

Richard Ollard, *Fisher and Cunningham* (Constable, 1991)

S. W. C. Pack, *Cunningham the Commander* (Batsford, 1974)

Peter Padfield, *The Battleship Era* (Military Book Society, 1972)

William T. T. Pakenham, *Naval Command and Control* (Brassey's, 1989)

Oscar Parkes, *British Battleships* (Seeley Service, 1970)

Temple Patterson (ed.), *The Jellicoe Papers* (Scolar Press/Navy Records Society, Vol.1 1966, Vol.2 1968)

Temple Patterson, *Tyrwhitt of the Harwich Force* (Military Book Society, 1973)

Geoffrey Penn, *Up Funnel, Down Screw* (Hollis, 1955)

Tobias Philbin, *Admiral von Hipper* (Grüner, 1982)

Ben Pimlott, *Hugh Dalton* (Macmillan, 1985)

E. N. Poland, *The Torpedomen: The Story of Vernon* (1993)

Anthony Pollen, *The Great Gunnery Scandal* (Collins, 1980)

Dudley Pope, *Life in Nelson's Navy* (Allen & Unwin, 1981)

James Pope-Hennessy, *Queen Mary* (Allen & Unwin, 1959)

Hugh Popham, *A Damned Cunning Fellow* (Old Ferry Press, 1991)

Reginald Pound, *Scott of the Antarctic* (World Books, 1966)

Bryan Ranft (ed.), *The Beatty Papers* (Scolar Press/Navy Records Society, Vol.1 1989, Vol.2 1992)

'A Ranker', *Life in the Royal Navy* (Chamberlain, 1891)

Eugene L. Rasor, *The Battle of Jutland, a Bibliography* (Greenwood Press, 1992)

——*Reform in the Royal Navy* (Hamden, 1976)

Nigel Rees, *The Bloomsbury Dictionary of Phrase and Allusion* (Bloomsbury, 1991)

Nicholas Rodger, *The Admiralty* (Terence Dalton, 1979)

Ernest Rodway, *Churchill: Your Questions Answered* (booklet)

Stephen Roskill, *Churchill and the Admirals* (Collins, 1977)

——*Earl Beatty* (Collins, 1981)

——*HMS Warspite* (Collins, 1957)

A. B. Sainsbury, *The Royal Navy Day by Day* (Centaur Press, 2nd edition 1992)

Gustav von Schoultz, *With the British Battlefleet* (Hutchinson, 1925)

Donald Schurman, *The Education of a Navy* (Cassell, 1965)

——*Julian S. Corbett, 1854–1922* (Royal Historical Society, 1981)

Political Diaries of C. P. Scott (Part 1 of C. P. Scott Papers, Adam Matthew)

Percy Scott, *Fifty Years in the Royal Navy* (John Murray, 1919)

Diary and Letters of Alexander Scrimgeour RN (privately printed)

Lady Seymour, *Life and Letters of Commander Ralph Seymour RN* (privately printed, 1926)

William Seymour, *Battles in Britain* (Sidgwick & Jackson, 1979)

Martin Short, *Inside the Brotherhood* (Grafton Books, 1989)

Nevil Shute, *Slide Rule* (Heinemann, 1954)

William Sims, *The Victory at Sea* (John Murray, 1920)

Humphrey Hugh Smith, *A Yellow Admiral Remembers* (E. Arnold & Co., 1932)

Mary Soames, *Clementine Churchill* (Cassell, 1979)

James L. Stokesbury, *Navy and Empire* (Wm Morrow, 1983)

Anthony Storr – see under Hart, *Churchill Revisited*

Jon Tetsuro Sumida, *In Defence of Naval Supremacy* (Unwin Hyman, 1989)

Lord Sydenham of Combe, *My Working Life* (John Murray, 1927)

'Taffrail' (Henry Tapprel Dorling), *Carry On!* (C. A. Pearson, 1916)

Tales of the Sea from Blackwood (Blackwood, 1970)

V. E. Tarrant, *Jutland, The German Perspective* (Arms & Armour, 1995)

David Thomas, *Royal Admirals* (André Deutsch, 1982)

Joseph J. Thomson, *Recollections and Reflections* (G. Bell & Sons, 1936)

Robert Townsend, *Up the Organisation!* (Coronet, 1971)

Tracts Relating to Naval Affairs (1872)

Brian Tunstall (ed. Nicolas Tracy), *Naval Warfare in the Age of Sail* (Conway Maritime, 1990)

E. S. Turner, *Gallant Gentlemen* (Michael Joseph, 1956)

The Universal Book of Craft Masonry (Toye, Kenning & Spencer, 7th edition 1968)

James Vincent, *HRH The Duke of Clarence* (John Murray, 1893)

Antony Wallace, *The Influence of Jutland on Plastic Surgery*

Claude Wallace, *From Jungle to Jutland* (Nisbet & Co., 1932)

Oliver Warner, *Cunningham of Hyndhope* (John Murray, 1967)

Victoria Baroness Wester Wemyss, *Life and Letters of Lord Wester Wemyss* (Eyre & Spottiswoode, 1935)

John Wheeler-Bennett, *King George VI* (Macmillan, 1958)

Henry Spenser Wilkinson, *The Brain of the Navy* (Constable, 1895)

John Winton, *Captains and Kings* (Bluejacket, 1981)

——*The Death of the Scharnhorst* (Bird, 1983)

Sandy Woodward, *One Hundred Days* (Fontana, 1992)

Desmond Young, *Rutland of Jutland* (Cassell, 1963)

(A.B.) Filson Young, *With the Battle-Cruisers* (Cassell, 1921)

Index

As a rule, ranks and titles have been omitted. Ships of same-names are accompanied by contextual dates (or 'WWI'). The end-notes, and details in Appendix IV, are not covered by this index.